California State Con
License Exam Stud

Law and Business
Examination

Practice Exams for the California State Contractor's License Exam

QuickPass Study Tools

Builder's Book, Inc.
Bookstore • Publisher
8001 Canoga Avenue Canoga Park, CA 91304
1-800-275-2665 / BuildersBook.com

Below is the access code to use your interactive study tool. The interactive study guide works across all platforms including Windows, MacOS; Android and iOS (iPhone). You will need a computer, phone, or tablet, and a connection to the Internet. Open your Web browser (such as Edge, Safari, Internet Explorer, or Chrome) and go to this site:

www.buildersbook.com

You'll need to create an account, then click the "Access QuickPass Study Tool Dashboard" button which will redirect you to "buildersbook.com/quickpassstudytools" where you will select the blue "Access your Dashboard" box and enter the license number below:

Kx8vgZXt

For technical support, visit www.BuildersBook.com or call 1-800-275-2665, Business hours are M-F 8:30AM - 4:30PM and Saturday 9AM - 1PM (Pacific).

California State Contractor's License Exam Study Guide Law & Business

Practice Exams for the California State Contractor's License Exam

QuickPass® Study Tools

NOTICE TO THE READER

This book and CD-ROM are designed to provide study material for the purpose of preparation for the California State Contractor's License Exam. This book and CD-ROM shall not be used for any other purpose. For code related needs see the appropriate codes. The publisher has made every effort to provide complete and accurate information, but does not guarantee the accuracy or completeness of any information published herein, nor shall the publisher have any liability or responsibility to any person or entity for any errors, omissions, or damages arising out of the use of this information. This book is provided with the understanding that the publisher is not attempting to render legal, business or any other advice or professional service. If such services are required, the assistance of an appropriate professional should be sought.

For future updates, errata, amendments and other changes, please contact Builder's Book, Inc.,

1-800-273-7375.

The information in this book is subject to change without notice.

California State Contractor's License Exam Study Guide Law & Business

Practice Exams for the
California State Contractor's License Exam
QuickPass® Study Tools

TABLE OF CONTENTS

EXAM 1: Law & Business Exam Part I 1

EXAM 2: Law & Business Exam Part II 20

EXAM 3: Law & Business Exam Part III 39

EXAM 4: Law & Business Exam Part IV 59

EXAM 5: Law & Business Exam Part V 78

EXAM 6: Law & Business Exam Part VI 94

EXAM 7: Law & Business Supplemental 104

EXAM 8: Safety Part I 186

EXAM 9: Safety Part II 202

EXAM 10: Blueprint Reading Part I 213

EXAM 11: Blueprint Reading Part II 231

EXAM 12: Math 249

Now includes both the Public Works Manual 2018 Edition

& (Circular E), Employer's Tax Guide 2023!

EXAM 1

Law & Business Exam Part I

1. You must be at least _____ to apply for a California contractor license?
   - A: 16
   - B: 18
   - C: 21
   - D: Any of the above

2. A qualifying individual must have had at least _____ years of experience before he/she can file an application to qualify for a California contractor license?
   - A: 1
   - B: 2
   - C: 4
   - D: 5

3. True or False: You don't have to meet any education requirements to apply for a contractor license.
   - A: True
   - B: False

4. If you receive credit for _____ it may be used to substitute a portion of the 4 years of required experience.
   - A: technical training
   - B: apprenticeship training
   - C: education
   - D: All of the above

5. Who are licenses issued to?
   - A: individuals
   - B: corporations
   - C: joint ventures
   - D: All of the above

6. If the total cost (labor and materials) of one or more contracts on any given project of improvement is _____ or more, you must be licensed.
   - A: $100.00
   - B: $200.00
   - C: $500.00
   - D: $1,000.00

7. True or False: You don't have to be licensed to submit bids?
   - A: True
   - B: False

8. Who of the following is exempt from the requirement of having a contractor's license?
   - A: Public personnel working on public projects
   - B: Individuals who install satellite antennas
   - C: Owners who themselves build or improve structures on the own property
   - D: All of the above

9. True or False: California recognizes contractor licenses from other states but not other countries.
   - A: True
   - B: False

10. California has a reciprocal agreement with which of the following states?
    - A: Utah
    - B: Nevada
    - C: Arizona
    - D: All of the above

EXAM 1

11. You don't need a contractor license so long as you don't _____.

    A: perform work over$500

    B: advertise yourself as a licensed contractor

    C: Both A and B

    D: Neither A nor B

12. Contracting without a license is most commonly classified as a _____ in the legal system.

    A: misdemeanor

    B: infraction

    C: felony

    D: None of the above

13. True or False: It is a misdemeanor for any person to engage in the occupation of salesman of home improvement goods or services within this state without having a registration issued by the Registrar.

    A: True

    B: False

14. A qualifying party (QP) can qualify for up to _____ licenses within a one year period.

    A: 2

    B: 3

    C: 5

    D: 8

15. Active licenses must be renewed every _____ years.

    A: 2

    B: 4

    C: 5

    D: 7

16. Which of the following changes in license structure would prevent you from renewing your current license?

    A: a change in business entity

    B: a change in the corporate registration number

    C: a change in ownership

    D: All of the above

17. True or False: If you do not renew your license before the expiration date, your license will be considered inactive.

    A: True

    B: False

18. An expired license can be renewed within _____ years of its expiration.

    A: 2

    B: 4

    C: 5

    D: 7

19. In additional to sending an "Application to Inactivate Contractor's License," the contractor must also send _____ to the CSLB Headquarters Office.

    A: current pocket card

    B: inactivation fee

    C: Both A and B

    D: Neither A nor B

Law & Business Exam Part I

20. True or False: Since a co-partnership involves more than one individual, when a co-partnership is dissolved the license can be transferred to the remaining partner.

    A: True   B: False

21. True or False: If the qualifying individual of a license entity wishes to terminate any responsibility with the licensee, he/she must submit a written notification of disassociation to the Contractor's State License Board.

    A: True   B: False

22. Once the notice of disassociation has been received by the Contractor's Board the licensee has 90 days to find a responsible managing officer or responsible managing employee to replace the one that left, failure to replace the qualifier will result in the suspension of the license.

    A: True   B: False

23. A/An _____ is a beginner receiving training in a trade who is not yet proficient enough to perform the work alone.

    A: apprentice   C: foreman

    B: journeyman   D: None of the above

24. A _____ is an individual who has completed an apprenticeship program or is an experienced worker, not a trainee and is fully qualified and able to perform the trade without supervision.

    A: journeyman   C: owner-builder

    B: foreman   D: All of the above

25. A _____ is an individual who has the knowledge and skills of a journeyman and directly supervised physical construction.

    A: journeyman   C: owner-builder

    B: foreman   D: All of the above

26. A foreman/supervisor is required to conduct safety meetings every _____ working days.

    A: 10   C: 60

    B: 30   D: 90

27. A contractor's license is valid for _____ years.

    A: 2   C: 4

    B: 3   D: 5

28. Which of the following is a reason why contractors are required to maintain a surety bond?

    A: for the protection and benefit of   C: Both A and B
       consumers

    B: for the protection and benefit of   D: Neither A nor B
       employees

Law & Business Exam Part I

29. In the construction industry, what does the acronym RME stand for?

    A: Responsible Managing Employee   C: Resource Management Essential

    B: Regional Management Employee   D: Any of the above

30. The contractor or the R.M.O/R.M.E is expected to visit he site at least _____.

    A: once a week   C: once a day

    B: twice a week   D: once an hour

31. Which of the following actions can result in both disciplinary action and legal action against a contractor?

    A: abandonment of project   C: misleading advertisement

    B: diversion of funds   D: All of the above

32. True or False: If a contractor license had been revoked because of failure to complete a job, the license could be reinstated provided you present documented evidence that demonstrates that all loss which resulted in the revocation has been fully satisfied and that all terms and conditions imposed by the decision of revocation have been fully complied with.

    A: True   B: False

33. True or False: A joint venture license is a license issued to two or more qualifying parties (QP) whose contracting licenses are current and active.

    A: True   B: False

34. A joint venture license expires _____ year(s) after it is issued.

    A: 1   C: 4

    B: 2   D: 6

35. If a QP leaves a joint venture, the remaining party can apply for _____.

    A: protraction   C: continuance

    B: permanence   D: None of the above

36. If a QP leaves a joint venture, the remaining qualifying party must report it within _____ days.

    A: 30   C: 90

    B: 60   D: 120

37. A contractor has to pay a subcontractor _____ days after receipt of each progress payment.

    A: 5   C: 10

    B: 7   D: 13

EXAM 1

38. Failure to pay a subcontractor results in having to pay the amount due plus an additional _____ percent of the amount due per month for every month that payment is not due.

    A: 1   C: 5

    B: 2   D: 10

39. The owner or public entity involved in a project must record a "Notice of Completion" within _____ days after the actual date of the project's completion.

    A: 5   C: 15

    B: 10   D: 20

40. True or False: Acceptance by the owner of a private work of improvement constitutes completion.

    A: True   B: False

41. Who must sign the Notice of Extension of Credit?

    A: the contractor   C: Both A and B

    B: the owner   D: Neither A nor B

42. True or False: The "Notice of Extension of Credit" must be filed before the recording of the mechanics lien.

    A: True   B: False

43. For a project performed for a public utility the contractor has _____ days to pay a subcontractor after a progress payment is received.

    A: 8   C: 15

    B: 7   D: 21

44. The monetary figure that must be paid to the public entity at the time of giving the Stop Payment Notice is _____.

    A: $1   C: $5

    B: $2   D: $10

45. What is the term/name given to a person who provides material or supplies to be used on a work of improvement?

    A: materialman   C: supply provider

    B: material supplier   D: Any of the above

46. True or False: A licensed Landscape Architect is considered a design professional.

    A: True   B: False

EXAM 1

47. What is the proper term/name given to any contractor who has a direct contractual relationship with the owner?

    A: original contractor

    B: direct contractor

    C: prime contractor

    D: All of the above

48. What is the proper term/name given to an agreement between an owner and any direct contractor providing for the work of improvement or any part thereof?

    A: direct contract

    B: prime contract

    C: original contract

    D: All of the above

49. True or False: A home improvement contract is not permitted between a tenant and a contractor.

    A: True

    B: False

50. What is the term/name given to the written notice given by a claimant within 20 days of first furnishing labor/materials, meant to notify the owner(s), lender(s) or contractor(s) of their right to enforce a mechanics lien or stop payment notice?

    A: Preliminary Notice

    B: Preliminary 20-Day Notice

    C: Stop Notice

    D: Mechanics Lien

51. What is the term/name given to the lien on funds to secure payment for a work of improvement?

    A: Retention

    B: Mechanics Lien

    C: Notice of Time to Enforce Payment

    D: Stop Payment Notice

52. Retention laws limit retention between the public entity and original contractor to _____ percent.

    A: 1

    B: 3

    C: 5

    D: 10

53. A contractor purposefully misclassifying an employee as an "independent contractor" can result in the contractor having to pay _____ per violation for a first offense.

    A: $5,000

    B: $10,000

    C: $15,000

    D: Any of the above

54. How many days after the Home Improvement contract is signed does the owner have to cancel the contract?

    A: One business day

    B: Three business days

    C: Seven Business days

    D: Fifteen Business days

55. Which of the following must a contractor provide the homeowner who contracts him for a home improvement project?

   A: Notice to Owner   C: copies of previous, similar jobs

   B: copy of all insurance documents   D: None of the above

56. Which of the following must change orders include?

   A: contractor's name   C: contractor's license number

   B: contractor's address   D: all of the above

57. True or False: When extra work is performed by the contractor because he feels it is necessary to accomplish the job the contractor can charge for the extra without prior consent of the owner.

   A: True   B: False

58. It is necessary for the contractor to secure _____ when a contractor and owner agree to add another bathroom to the house after the original contract is enforced.

   A: more money   C: a change order

   B: extra time   D: more square footage to complete the job

59. A home improvement contractor should specifically explain the plans and specifications to the homeowner _____.

   A: before he/she signs the contract, or   C: after signing the contract, and before
      agrees to the price   starting the job

   B: before he/she agrees to a price, but after   D: after signing the contract, but before the
      starting the job   first pay draw

60. The owner is responsible for reviewing all plans and specifications with the _____ before he/she signs the home improvement contract.

   A: engineer   C: architect

   B: designer   D: contractor

61. The "Three Day Right to Cancel" states that payments made by the buyer must be returned within _____ days after a contract is cancelled.

   A: 3   C: 10

   B: 5   D: 30

62. The "Three Day Right to Cancel" states that the buyer must make any goods that were delivered under the contract or sale available for the contractor for pickup for up to _____ days after contract cancellation.

   A: 5   C: 10

   B: 7   D: 20

Law & Business Exam Part I

63. Unless there is a lawful excuse, failure to substantially commence work within _____days from the stated starting date specified in the contract.

    A: 5   C: 20

    B: 10   D: 30

64. True or False: The California Preliminary Notice is a lien.

    A: True   B: False

65. Anyone who helps improve the property, either by providing labor or materials, and wants to file a Preliminary Notice to ensure payment must do so within _____ days of the contract being signed.

    A: 5   C: 20

    B: 10   .   D: 60

66. Who has a right to a lien?

    A: Direct Contractor   C: Material Supplier

    B: Subcontractor   D: All of the above

67. True or False: A lien is filed in the county where the property that was enforced a lien is located.

    A: True   B: False

68. True or False: If the owner paid the direct contractor but the direct contractor failed to pay the subcontractors, the subcontractors may file a claim of lien anytime after the job is completed.

    A: True   B: False

69. True or False: Any number of persons claiming liens on the same property may join in the same action to foreclose their liens and when separate actions are commenced the court may consolidate them.

    A: True   B: False

70. How many "Waiver and Release" forms are available?

    A: 2   C: 8

    B: 4   D: 12

71. Which "Waiver and Release" form if you have completed a phase of the work but have not been paid in full for that phase yet?

    A: Conditional Waiver and Release On   C: Conditional Waiver and Release On Final
       Progress Payment   Payment

    B: Unconditional Waiver and Release On   D: Unconditional Waiver and Release On
       Progress Payment   Final Payment

Law & Business Exam Part I

72. If a direct contractor wants to file a claim of lien, he/she must file the claim within _____ after recordation of a Notice of Completion.

    A: 20 days   C: 60 days

    B: 30 days   D: 90 days

73. If a subcontractor wants to file a claim of lien, he/she must file the claim within _____ after recordation of a Notice of Completion.

    A: 20 days   C: 60 days

    B: 30 days   D: 90 days

74. Consider the following statement: A stop payment notice is a lien on funds.

    A: True   B: False

75. Consider the following statement: When a Mechanics Lien is filed it binds up the property for a period of 90 days.

    A: True   B: False

76. What is a Stop Payment Notice

    A: a hold on property   C: Both A and B

    B: a hold on funds   D: Neither A nor B

77. A downpayment on a Home Improvement Contract must be _____ percent of the total cost of the contract or$1,000.00, whichever is less.

    A: 5   C: 20

    B: 10   D: 25

78. A contractor must provide _____ to the owner, when entering a Home Improvement Contract.

    A: Three Day Right to Cancel   C: Mechanics Lien Warning

    B: Statutory Notices   D: All of the above

79. As a business manager (contractor manager) you must have _____.

    A: managerial competence   C: technical competence

    B: people competence   D: All of the above

80. Which of the following is a functional area of management?

    A: Planning   C: Standardization

    B: Decision Making/Delegation   D: All of the above

Law & Business Exam Part I

81. Which of the following is a legal form of business?

    A: Sole Ownership
    C: Corporation

    B: General Partnership
    D: All of the above

82. _____ are expenses that are separate from the field such as administrative costs.

    A: Direct costs
    C: Overhead costs

    B: Indirect costs
    D: None of the above

83. Direct costs are costs directly associated with the specific project at hand, an example of a direct cost would be _____.

    A: insurance
    C: equipment

    B: fuel
    D: labor

84. It would be best to _____ to determine labor costs within your job record.

    A: use time cards
    C: divide the year-end costs by labor costs

    B: ask the supervisor to find out who worked on what jobs
    D: look at you last projects job cost records

85. A/An_____ is the task of preparing a detailed cost estimate for a work/project.

    A: bid
    C: insurance

    B: continuance
    D: None of the above

86. True or False: The estimate becomes a budget for the project.

    A: True
    B: False

87. True or False: In a company, money you still owe to suppliers, subcontractors, vendors, etc. is classified under "accounts receivable."

    A: True
    B: False

88. _____ shows the condition of a business financial standing at a certain point in time.

    A: Chart of Accounts
    C: Balance Sheet

    B: Journal
    D: Payroll

89. _____ is money owed to the owners of a company.

    A: Liability
    C: Equity

    B: Revenue
    D: All of the above

Law & Business Exam Part I

90. Which of the following terms describes an account entry with negative value for assets and positive value for liability and equity?

    A: Credit   C: Revenue

    B: Debit   D: Payroll

91. _____ is an account entry with positive value for assets and negative value for liability and equity.

    A: Credit   C: Revenue

    B: Debit   D: Payroll

92. Which of the following is the equity equation?

    A: Equity = Liabilities - Assets   C: Equity = Assets +Liabilities

    B: Equity = Assets - Liabilities   D: None of the above

93. Which of the following is the equation for assets?

    A: Assets = Liabilities - Equity   C: Assets = Liability+ Equity

    B: Assets = Equity - Liabilities   D: None of the above

94. Which of the following is an example of capital non-current asset?

    A: Construction Equipment   C: Office Equipment

    B: Real Estate   D: All of the above

95. True or False: Materials is an example of variable costs.

    A: True   B: False

96. A _____ is used for all projects that are currently in progress.

    A: Job Flow Budget   C: Cash Basis Accounting

    B: Consolidated Job Flow Budget   D: None of the above

97. Where is the best place to look for bidding advise?

    A: legal center   C: owner price suggestion

    B: other contractors bids   D: your job history

98. Which of the following procedures best ensures error-free bids?

    A: working with an attorney   C: having another person draft the bid

    B: discussing the details of the bid with the   D: rechecking the bid before submitting it to
       supplier   the client

Law & Business Exam Part I

99.   Consider the following scenario: A contractor submitting a bid for a project has asked a few subcontractors to bid a portion of the week. One of the subcontractors bids is substantially lower than the other. Whether or not you suspect a mistake _____.

   A: you should accept the low price and hold the subcontractor to it because he/she should have better estimating practices.

   C: it is ethical and good practice to call and mention the possible mistake, and give the subcontractor an opportunity to re-submit the bid

   B: you should set the bid aside

   D: None of the above

100.   Which of the following is a helpful tip to follow to successfully manage a job?

   A: invoice regularly

   C: do a final walk through at the end

   B: walk the job using punch lists

   D: All of the above

EXAM 1

1. **Answer B.** 18

   You must be at least 18 years old to be able to qualify for a California contractor license.\n\nOther requirements include:\n- valid Social Security Number (SSN) issued by the Federal Social Security Administration and\n\n- have the experience and skills required by the California State License Board (CSLB)\n\n- full set of fingerprints to provide a criminal background check

2. **Answer C.** 4

   A qualifying individual must have had at least 4 years of experience before he/she can file an application to qualify for a California contractor license.\n\nThe experience must be within the 10 years before filing the application. \nThe full 4 years must be verifiable. You must certify the accuracy of the experience information on a form provided by the CSLB titled "Certification of Work Experience Form" The person verifying your experience must \n\nhave firsthand knowledge of your experience during the time period covered. He/She must sign, under penalty of perjury, that he/she witnessed the work you did and complete.\n\nBe prepared to provide documentation of any experience you're claiming upon request. Failure to provide documentation will result in rejection of your application or denial of your license.\n\nThe 4 years of experience must be experience as a journeyman, foreman, supervising employee, or as a contractor in the filed you're testing for.

3. **Answer A.** True

   You don't have to meet any education requirements to apply for a contractor license.\n\nHowever, you may substitute a portion of the required 4 years of practical experience by receiving credit for technical training, apprenticeship training or education.

4. **Answer D.** All of the above

   You may substitute a portion of the required 4 years of practical experience by receiving credit for technical training, apprenticeship training or education. \n\nThe portion substituted may range from 1-½ years to 3 years of experience depending on which of the substitutes you present. \n\nHowever, note that you must still have a minimum of 1 year of practical experience.\n\nPresent copies of apprenticeship certificates and/or college transcripts.

5. **Answer D.** All of the above

   Licenses may be issued to all of the following:\n- individuals\n- partnerships\n- corporations\n- joint ventures \n- limited liability companies

6. **Answer C.** $500.00

   If the total cost (labor and materials) of one or more contracts on any given project of improvement is$500 or more, you must be licensed.\n\nProjects of improvements include: construction or alteration (or the offer to do so) of any building, highway, road, parking facility, railroad, excavation or any other structure in California.

7. **Answer B.** False

   You must have a license before you are able to submit bids. This is applicable to contractors, subcontractors, specialty contractors and any one involved in a business of home improvement.\n\nException: Joint ventures and projects involving federal funding.

8. **Answer D.** All of the above

   Those exempt from the requirement of having a contractor's license are the following: \n\n- project (labor and materials) is less that$500\n- Employee who is paid in wages and who does not usually work in an independently established business. \n- Public personnel working on public projects\n- Owners who themselves build or improve structures on the own property – this exception is only valid of a structure is not intended for sale within one year of completion. \n- officers of a court acting within the scope of t heir office\n- Public utilities working on specific conditions\n- Oil and gas operation performed by an owner or lessee\n- seller of installed carpet\n- security alarm company operators\n\tException: fire alarm company operators must be licensed\n- Individuals who install satellite antennas \n- individuals who sell or install products that do not become a fixed part of the structure

9. **Answer B.** False

   California does not recognize contractor licenses from other states or countries. Even when a reciprocal agreement exists between states, qualifying individuals must still take and pass the Law and Business CSLB California Exam.

10. **Answer D.** All of the above

    California has reciprocal agreements with all of the following states: Utah, Nevada and Arizona. \n\nReciprocal agreements are established between states that have comparable experience qualifications and license requirements as California. If there is a reciprocal agreement the Registrar may waive the trade portion of the examination.\n\nHowever, applicants must still pass the Law and Business CSLB California Exam.

11. **Answer C.** Both A and B

    You don't need a contractor license so long as you don't advertise yourself as a licensed contractor or perform work over$500.

12. **Answer A.** misdemeanor

    Contracting without a license is most commonly classified as a misdemeanor in the legal system.\n\nFirst offense for contracting without a license carries a sentence of up to 6 months in jail (city or country) and/or a$5,000 fine as well as potential administrative fines of$200 to$15,000\n\nContracting without a license for any project that is covered by the state of emergency or disaster proclaimed by the Governor or the President of the United States may result in a felony.

13. **Answer A.** True

    Among other things, the job of a home improvement salesman is to submit applications to solicit, sell, negotiate or furnish home improvement goods for a licensed contractor.\n\nWhen a person seeks to become a home improvement salesman, he/she must request an application from the Registrar's office. The individual seeking to become a salesperson must be registered as one.\n\nIt is a misdemeanor for any person to engage in the occupation of salesman of home improvement goods or services without having a registration issued by the Registrar.\n\nViolations by a home improvement salesman would likewise cause disciplinary action against the contractor.

14. **Answer B.** 3

    A qualifying party (QP) can qualify for up to 3 licenses within a one year period. The QP must have at least 20 percent interest in each entity.

EXAM 1

15. **Answer A.** 2

Active licenses must be renewed every 2 years. You must submit a renewal application along with the required renewal fee ($360.00 as of July 2012). If the payment is not submitted on or before the expiration date you will have to pay a delinquent fee. Current amount to renew an active delinquent license is$540.00 (as of July 2012).

16. **Answer D.** All of the above

All of the following changes in license structure will prevent you from being able to renew your current license:\n\nChange in Business Entity – if the business entity changes from sole ownership to corporation, sole ownership to partnership, partnership to corporation etc. \n\nChange In Corporate Registration Number – if there is a change in the corporate registration number assigned by the Secretary of State Office\n\nChange in Ownership – If there has been a change in Owner in a Sole Owner license or a change in Partners in a Partnership License.

17. **Answer B.** False

If you do not renew your license before the expiration date, your license will be considered expired and the following will occur:\n\n- the card will be considered delinquent and you will have to pay a delinquent fee to renew it \n- you will be required to pay the delinquent renewal fee\n- there will be a break in licensing time\n- the license will only be renewed from the date an acceptable renewal application is received through the remainder of the current renewal period\n\nNote: Any work performed while the license is expired is considered to be unlicensed (and therefore illegal) and disciplinary action can be taken against you.\n\nIf you want to make your license inactive you must file the proper inactivation form.If you do nothing, it won't be rendered inactive, it will just be considered expired and delinquent.

18. **Answer C.** 5

An expired license can be renewed within 5 years of its expiration. If license is not renewed within this allotted time, the license holder must reapply for the license.

19. **Answer A.** current pocket card

In additional to sending an "Application to Inactivate Contractor's License," the contractor must also send his/her current pocket card to the CSLB Headquarters Office. \n\nNote: If your current pocket card is lost, you must pay$11 to replace the card. Attach the money order, personal, business, certified or cashier's check.

20. **Answer B.** False

A partnership license must be canceled upon the disassociation of a general partner or upon the dissolution of the partnership.\n\nThe disassociating partner or the remaining partner or partners must notify the registrar, in writing, within 90 days of the disassociation of a general partner or dissolution of the partnership. \n\nFailure to notify the registrar of the disassociation or dissolution within 90 days will cause the license to be canceled effectively the date the written notification is received at the board's headquarters office, as well as, result is disciplinary action by the board. \n\nThe remaining general partner or partners may request a continuance of the license to complete projects contracted for or in progress prior to the date of disassociation or dissolution for a reasonable length of time to be determined by rules of the board.\n\nThe remaining general partner or partners must apply for and obtain a new license to undertake new work and to continue contracting after the continuance expires.

21. **Answer A.** True

If the qualifying individual of a license entity wishes to terminate any responsibility with the licensee, he/she must submit a written notification of disassociation to the Contractor's State License Board. Failure of the licensee or the qualifier to notify the registrar of the qualifier's disassociation within 90 days of the disassociation is grounds for disciplinary action.

22. **Answer A.** True

Once the notice of disassociation has been received by the Contractor's Board the licensee has 90 days to find a responsible managing officer or responsible managing employee to replace the one that left, failure to replace the qualifier in 90 days will result in the suspension of the license.\n \nTo replace a responsible managing officer or responsible managing employee, the licensee must file an application as prescribed by the registrar, accompanied by the fee fixed by this chapter, designating an individual to qualify as required by this chapter.

23. **Answer A.** apprentice

An apprentice is a beginner receiving training in a trade who is not yet proficient enough to perform the work alone.\n\nA journeyman is a worker who is qualified to perform work without supervision \n\nA foreman/supervisor is responsible for training and evaluating workers at or below journeyman level.

24. **Answer A.** journeyman

A journeyman is an individual who has completed an apprenticeship program or is an experienced worker, not a trainee and is fully qualified and able to perform the trade without supervision.

25. **Answer B.** foreman

A foreman is an individual who has the knowledge and skills of a journeyman and directly supervised physical construction.

26. **Answer A.** 10

A foreman/supervisor is required to conduct safety meetings ("tail-gate" meetings) every 10 working days.

27. **Answer A.** 2

A contractor's license is valid for 2 years. It expires 2 years from the last day of the month in which it was issued.\n\nLicenses must be renewed every two years. \n\nException: Inactive licenses are renewed every 4 years

EXAM 1

28. Answer C.   Both A and B

Surety bonds protect and benefit consumers by protecting them if any damage that might arise of defective construction and additional law-violations. \n\nSurety bonds protect and benefit employees by ensuring they get paid when payment is due to them.

29. Answer A.   Responsible Managing Employee

In the construction industry RME stands for Responsible Managing Employee. An RME is considered a qualifying individual.\n\nThe acronym RMO is also used in the construction industry and it stands for Responsible Managing Officer.

30. Answer C.   once a day

The contractor or the R.M.O/R.M.E is expected to visit he site at least once a day.

31. Answer D.   All of the above

Abandoning a project, diversion of funds and misleading advertisement are all actions that carry disciplinary and legal repercussions for any contractor that engages in any and all.\n\nAbandoning a project without a legal excuse is cause for disciplinary action and can result in Federal prosecution. \n\nDiversion of funds or failure to substantially account for application or uses of such funds on a construction project or operation for which such funds were received is cause for disciplinary action. In addition, diversion of funds falls under larceny with punishments ranging from a misdemeanor to a felony.\n\nMisleading advertisement is cause for disciplinary action and it is legally considered a misdemeanor.

32. Answer A.   True

In order to reinstate your license, you must file an Application for Original Contractors License. If your license was revoked, suspended, or has been expired over 5 years you must file and take and pass the law and trades portion of the written examination.\n\nYou must provide documented evidence demonstrating that all loss which resulted in the revocation or suspension of your license has been fully satisfied and that all terms and conditions imposed by the decision of revocation have been complied with. When any loss has been reduced to a monetary obligation or debt, the satisfaction of the monetary obligation or debt as a prerequisite for the issuance, re-issuance, or reinstatement of a license will not be required if the monetary obligation or debt was discharged in a bankruptcy proceeding. However, any non-monetary condition not discharged in a bankruptcy proceeding must be complied with prior to reinstatement of the license. If any other party has incurred an injury as a result of your contracting activity you will be notified during the application process. You will be required to resolve all injuries prior to your license being issued. (www.cslb.ca.gov)

33. Answer A.   True

A joint venture license is a license issued to two or more qualifying parties (QP) whose contracting licenses are current and active. A joint venture is often sought out by qualifying individuals who seek to combine their licenses and expertise for a specific project.

34. Answer B.   2

A joint venture license expires 2 years after it is issued. However, QPs may always apply for a joint venture license for future joint projects, so long as they meet the "qualified party" criteria.

35. Answer C.   continuance

If a QP leaves a joint venture, the remaining party can apply for continuance. A continuance of 1 year is granted in order for the remaining party to complete the project.\n\nNote: a continuance can be extended if additional time is necessary to complete the project.

36. Answer C.   90

If a QP leaves a joint venture, the remaining qualifying party must report it within 90 days. Note: This applies to all parties involved in the project at the time of the occurrence.

37. Answer B.   7

A contractor has to pay a subcontractor 7 days after receipt of each progress payment.\n\nNote: Same applies to subcontractors paying other subcontractors.

38. Answer B.   2

Failure to pay a subcontractor results in having to pay the amount due plus an additional 2 percent of the amount due per month for every month that payment is not due.

39. Answer C.   15

As of July 1, 2012 the owner or public entity involved in a project must record a "Notice of Completion" within 15 days after the actual date of the project's completion. The filing of a Notice of Completion constitutes acceptance of the work of improvement by the owner.

40. Answer B.   False

Acceptance by the owner of a private work of improvement used to constitute completion. However, as of July 1, 2012 acceptance by the owner of a private work of improvement no longer constitute completion.

41. Answer C.   Both A and B

Both the Contractor and the Owner must sign the Notice of Extension of Credit. This law was implemented July 1, 2012

42. Answer B.   False

As of July 1, 2012 the "Notice of Extension of Credit" may be filed within 90 days of the recording of the original "Mechanics Lien" (when that lien would expire).\n\nIf the "Notice of Extension of Credit" is recorded later than that time, it must be recorded before any purchaser or encumbrancer for value acquires rights (i.e. the property is transferred or sold).

43. Answer C.   15

For a project performed for a public utility the contractor has 15 days to pay a subcontractor after a progress payment is received.\n\nThe contractor must pay the sub contractor within 21 days after of a progress payment from a public utility.

44. Answer D. $10

The monetary figure that must be paid to the public entity at the time of giving the Stop Payment Notice is$10

45. Answer B.   material supplier

As of July 1, 2012 the name/term given to a person who provides material or supplies to be used on a work of improvement is material supplier.

EXAM 1

46. **Answer A.** True

   As of July 1, 2012 a license Landscape Architect is considered a design professional.

47. **Answer B.** direct contractor

   While all of the names given were at some point synonymous to each other, as of July 1, 2012 the term direct contractor must be used to refer to any contractor who has a direct contractual relationship with the owner.

48. **Answer A.** direct contract

   While all of the names given were at some point synonymous to each other, as of July 1, 2012 the term direct contract must be used to refer to any agreement between an owner and any direct contractor providing for the work of improvement or any part thereof.

49. **Answer B.** False

   "Home improvement contract" can be between a direct contractor and an owner or between a direct contractor and a tenant, regardless of the number of residence or dwelling units contained in the building in which the tenant resides. (www.clrc.ca.gov)

50. **Answer A.** Preliminary Notice

   As of July 1, 2012 the formerly known "Preliminary 20-Day Notice" will be called "Preliminary Notice"\n\nThe "Preliminary Notice" is a form given by a claimant within 20 days of first furnishing labor/materials. The form is meant to meant to notify the owner(s), lender(s) or contractor(s) of their right to enforce a mechanics lien or stop payment notice if they fail to pay them.

51. **Answer D.** Stop Payment Notice

   Stop Payment Notice is a form given to place a lien on funds to secure payment for a work of improvement.

52. **Answer C.** 5

   Retention laws limit retention between the public entity and original contractor to 5 percent.

53. **Answer D.** Any of the above

   A contractor purposefully misclassifying an employee as an "independent contractor" can result in the contractor having to pay$5,000 to$15,000 per violation for a first offense.\n\nAn Employer who engages in a pattern of these offenses can end up paying:$10,000 to$25,000 per violation.\n\nAdditionally, employer will be barred from bidding projects and a disciplinary action would be put into motion.

54. **Answer B.** Three business days

   The owner has up until midnight of the 3rd day to can to cancel the "Home Improvement" contract.

55. **Answer A.** Notice to Owner

   A contractor must provide the homeowner who contracts him for a home improvement project with a Notice to Owner form. The notice to owner contains valuable information that the homeowner needs.

56. **Answer D.** all of the above

   Change orders must include: the contractor's name, the contractor's address and the contractor's license number.

57. **Answer B.** False

   In order to receive compensation for any work, there must always be prior consent from all the parties involved before. Get any changes, additions in writing! For changes to the original contract you should use the "Change Order Form" for extra necessary work you should use the "Extra Work Order" form. Remember, all forms must be signed by the direct contractor and the owner/person who requested the home improvement.

58. **Answer C.** a change order

   It is necessary for the contractor to secure a change order when a contractor and owner agree to add another bathroom to the house after the original contract is enforced.

59. **Answer A.** before he/she signs the contract, or agrees to the price

   A home improvement contractor should specifically explain the plans and specifications to the homeowner before he/she signs the contract, or agrees to the price.

60. **Answer D.** contractor

   The owner is responsible for reviewing all plans and specifications with the contractor before he/she signs the home improvement contract.

61. **Answer C.** 10

   Payments made by the buyer must be returned within 10 days after a contract is cancelled.

62. **Answer D.** 20

   The "Three Day Right to Cancel" states that the buyer must make any goods that were delivered under the contract or sale available for the contractor for pickup for up to 20 days after contract cancellation. If the buyer fails to make the goods available to the contractor or if the contractor agrees to return the goods to the contractor but fails to do so, then the buyer remains liable for performance of all obligation under the contract.

63. **Answer C.** 20

   If the contractor fails to begin work within 20 days of the declared start date without lawful excuse he/she is in violation of the contract and subject to disciplinary action.

64. **Answer B.** False

   The California Preliminary Notice is not a lien. This form is simply meant to inform all interested parties that the person giving this Preliminary Notice has the right to file a mechanics lien if he/she is not paid for work performed or materials supplied.

65. **Answer C.** 20

   Anyone who helps improve the property, either by providing labor or materials, and wants to file a Preliminary Notice to ensure payment must do so within 20 days of the contract being signed. If a Preliminary Notice is not filed within these 20 days, the individual cannot file a mechanics lien in the event that he/she does not receive payment.\n\nIf a claimant fails to file a Preliminary Notice in the required time, he/she forfeits his/her rights to a mechanics lien.

EXAM 1

66. Answer D. All of the above

Direct contractor, subcontractor, material supplier, equipment lessor, laborer, design professional, builders... etc. who helped improve the property and who filed a Preliminary Notice within 20 days of entering the contract has a right to file a mechanics lien if he/she is not paid for work performed or materials supplied.

67. Answer A. True

A lien is filed in the Office of the County Recorder in the county where the property that was enforced a lien is located. (www.cab.ca.gov)

68. Answer A. True

If the subcontractors have given a Preliminary Notice within 20 of the signing of the contract, they are entitled to file a lien against the owner's property if he/she refuses to pay them. To ensure this does not occur the owner should: obtain a list of all those contributing to the home improvement job (subcontractors, laborers etc.), pay with joint checks and keep careful record of progress payments.

69. Answer A. True

Any number of persons claiming liens on the same property may join in the same action to foreclose their liens and when separate actions are commenced the court may consolidate them. (California Civil Code 3149)

70. Answer B. 4

"Waiver and Release" forms are given upon completion and payment of work. "Waiver and Release" forms are given by the direct contractor to the owner, but works to ensure protection to both because it documents payments made. \nThere are 4 different types of "Waiver and Release" forms: \n\n- Conditional Waiver and Release On Progress Payment\n\n- Unconditional Waiver and Release On Progress Payment \n\n- Conditional Waiver and Release On Final Payment\n\n- Unconditional Waiver and Release On Final Payment

71. Answer A. Conditional Waiver and Release On Progress Payment

The following is a description of when to use which release form:\n\nConditional Waiver and Release On Progress Payment – use if you have completed a phase of the work but have not been paid in full for that phase yet. \n\nUnconditional Waiver and Release On Progress Payment – use only if phase is complete and if you have been paid in full for that phase.\n\nConditional Waiver and Release On Final Payment – use only if you have completed the work in its entirety but have not been paid in full yet. "Conditional" means you still have a condition to be met, such as getting your payment. Use this form if you do not have the money in hand or if you were told that you'd get paid when you supply a Waiver and Release form.\n\nUnconditional Waiver and Release On Final Payment – Use only if you have completed the work in its entirety and you have been paid in full. "unconditional" means there are no more conditions to be met.

72. Answer C. 60 days

A direct contractor who has not been paid may file a mechanics lien if he/she submitted a Preliminary Notice within 20 days of entering the contract. \n\nThe direct contractor has 60 days to file a lien if the owner of the property files a Notice of Completion within 15 days of the date of completion. If the owner of the property does not file a Notice of Completion within 15 days of the date of completion, the direct contractor has 90 days to file a Mechanics Lien.\n\nIn California, the lien law is applicable to all private works of improvement. \n\nThe California Mechanics Lien Laws are covered in California Constitution's Article XIV Section 3.

73. Answer B. 30 days

A subcontractor who has not been paid may file a mechanics lien if he/she submitted a Preliminary Notice within 20 days of entering the contract. \n\nThe subcontractor has 30 days to file a lien if the owner of the property files a Notice of Completion within 15 days of the date of completion. If the owner of the property does not file a Notice of Completion within 15 days of the date of completion, the subcontractor has 60 days to file a Mechanics Lien.

74. Answer A. True

A stop payment notice is a lien on funds. A mechanics lien is a liens on property. You may use one or the other, or both. \n \n However, it should be noted that in public works, you cannot file a mechanics lien; and, therefore, your only remedy would be a stop payment notice.

75. Answer A. True

(a) No lien provided for in this chapter binds any property for a longer period of time than 90 days after the recording of the claim of lien, unless within that time an action to foreclose the lien is commenced in a proper court, except that, if credit is given and notice of the fact and terms of such credit is recorded in the office of the county recorder subsequent to the recording of such claim of lien and prior to the expiration of such 90-day period, then such lien continues in force until 90 days after the expiration of such credit, but in no case longer than one year from the time of completion of the work of improvement.\n\n (b) If the claimant fails to commence an action to foreclose the lien within the time limitation provided in this section, the lien automatically shall be null and void and of no further force and effect.(California Civil Code 3144)

76. Answer B. a hold on funds

A Stop Payment Notice is a hold on funds. It is similar to the mechanics lien in that it ensures payment for your services when the owner fails to pay you.

77. Answer B. 10

A downpayment on a Home Improvement Contract must be 10 percent of the total cost of the contract or $1,000.00 whichever is less.

78. Answer D. All of the above

A contractor must provide all of the following contractual notices to the owner, when entering a Home Improvement Contract:\n\n- Three Day Right to Cancel\n- Statutory Notices\n- Mechanics Lien Warning\n- Arbitration Disputes

EXAM 1

79. **Answer D.** All of the above

As a business manager (contractor manager) you must have managerial competence, people competence and technical competence. \n\nManagerial Competence: ability to plan, manage and control business affairs; plan and direct the major activities of the business\n\nPeople Competence: on-the-job supervisory experience and ability to manage employees; coordinate employee work and materials and train, direct and advice employees in supervisory and non-supervisory positions.\n\nTechnical Competence: knowledge of business practices

80. **Answer D.** All of the above

Functional Areas of Management include the following: Planning, Decision Making/Delegation, Standardization and Controls.\n\nBehavioral Aspects of Management include: Human Relations, Cooperation, Responsibility, Communication and Executive Ability.

81. **Answer D.** All of the above

All of the following are legal forms of business: Sole Ownership, General Partnership, Limited Partnership, Corporation and "S" Chapter Corporation.\n\nThe legal form of business will determine all of the following: available sources of financing, extent of personal liability, the extent of control and tax liabilities.\n\nKeep in mind that the legal form of your business may change as it grows. As the legal form of business changes, the financing requirements change as a result, the business should be reviewed.

82. **Answer C.** Overhead costs

Overhead costs are expenses that are separate from the field such as administrative and managerial costs; office space rent and advertisement are examples of overhead costs. \n\nIndirect Costs are costs that are still in the field, but are not directly related to any one specific project; tools and equipment are examples of indirect costs.

83. **Answer D.** labor

Labor is a direct cost because labor varies with each job/project. Other direct costs include: materials, permits, loan fees and subcontractors.

84. **Answer A.** use time cards

It would be best to use time cards to determine labor costs within your job record.

85. **Answer A.** bid

A bid is the task of preparing a detailed cost estimate for a work/project. This process includes determining all the material and labor costs (take-offs), overhead costs and mark-up (determining profit).

86. **Answer A.** True

The estimate, which is the basis for the bid, becomes a budget for the project, which if properly executed by following your established mark-up, should pay for the materials, work, subs, labor, equipment rental, etc. and you should be left with profit.

87. **Answer B.** False

In a company, money you still owe to suppliers, subcontractors, vendors, etc. is classified under accounts payable. Accounts receivables deals with money due to you (your company) for work performed.

88. **Answer C.** Balance Sheet

A balance sheet shows the condition of a business financial standing at a certain point in time; it is a summary of the company's financial status including assets, liabilities and equity.

89. **Answer C.** Equity

Equity is money owed to the owners of a company; it's also known as owner's equity.\n\nShareholder Equity differs from Equity (Owner's Equity) in that it is the capital and retained earnings in an entity attributed to shareholders.

90. **Answer A.** Credit

Credit is an account with negative value for assets and positive value for liability and equity.

91. **Answer B.** Debit

Debit is an account entry with positive value for assets and negative value for liability and equity.

92. **Answer B.** Equity = Assets - Liabilities

The equation for equity is the following:\nEquity = Assets – Liabilities

93. **Answer C.** Assets = Liability+ Equity

The equation for assets is the following:\nAssets = Liability+ Equity

94. **Answer D.** All of the above

Examples of capital non-current assets include: construction equipment, real estate and office equipment.

95. **Answer A.** True

Variable Cost are expenses that vary from month to month, such as materials. \n\nFixed costs are different in that they are costs or expenses that remain the same each month, such as office rent or truck payment.

96. **Answer A.** Job Flow Budget

A Job Flow Budget is used for all projects that are currently in progress and anticipated projects. It is essential for attaining control of cash movement within your company.\n\nA Consolidated Job Flow Budget is the compilation of all the individual job flow budgets, anticipated expenses, capital expenditures and changes in debt position.

97. **Answer D.** your job history

The best place to look for bidding advice is your job history. Similar jobs will reveal similar things to take into consideration. Your job history is helpful in estimating costs, time and profits.\n\nNote: It is a common pitfall to bid against the competition and not the job.

98. **Answer D.** rechecking the bid before submitting it to the client

Re-checking the bid before submitting it to the client is the best procedure to follow to ensure error-free bids.

Answers: Law & Business Exam Part I

99. **Answer C.** it is ethical and good practice to call and mention the possible mistake, and give the subcontractor an opportunity to re-submit the bid

Whether or not you suspect a mistake, it is ethical and good practice to call and mention the possible mistake, and give the subcontractor an opportunity to re-submit the bid.

100. **Answer D.** All of the above

All of the following are helpful tips to apply to successfully manage a job: invoice regularly – this means bringing attention to unpaid bills, walk the job using punch lists and so a final walk through (with your customer) at the end.",

EXAM 2

Law & Business Exam Part II

1. True or False: Contractors operate under conditions of relative uncertainty; a means of reducing a company's expense to risk is by having insurance.

    A: True   B: False

2. True or False: A liability represents the obligation to pay money for a business debt such as loans and accounts payable.

    A: True   B: False

3. True or False: Current Liabilities are debts which will mature within five years from the date of the balanced sheet.

    A: True   B: False

4. True or False: Liabilities are debt.

    A: True   B: False

5. A property with cash value owned by your business is an example of a/an _____

    A: asset   C: equity

    B: liability   D: None of the above

6. True or False: Net fixed assets are the investment in fixed assets remaining after deducting accumulated appreciation.

    A: True   B: False

7. True or False: Proprietorship is the excess of assets over total liability.

    A: True   B: False

8. True or False: Depreciation only refers to the decrease in value of a fixed asset, as a result of the passage of time.

    A: True   B: False

9. Cash plus good receivables should be equal to current liabilities in order for the financial position of the company to be sound.

    A: True   B: False

10. True or False: Labor is the largest figure on the Income Expense Statement.

    A: True   B: False

11. True or False: For working capital, commercial banks favor long-term self-liquidating loans.

    A: True   B: False

12. True or False: Equity is the ownership, especially when considered as the right to share in future profits or appreciation in value.

    A: True   B: False

13. True or False: An asset is anything of value that is owned.

    A: True   B: False

EXAM 2

14. True or False: All contractors who have employees are required to have Worker's Compensation Insurance Coverage.

    A: True   B: False

15. The contractor must provide proof of Workers Compensation Insurance coverage to the CSLB Headquarters Office within _____ days of hiring anyone.

    A: 30   C: 90

    B: 60   D: 120

16. What is a contractor's responsibility before hiring a subcontractor?

    A: making sure the subcontractor is licensed   C: Both A and B

    B: making sure the subcontractor and his   D: Neither A nor B
       workers have insurance

17. True or False: Workers Compensation is a "No-Fault" insurance purchased by the employer and supervised by the state.

    A: True   B: False

18. Who is exempt from purchasing Worker's Compensation?

    A: contractors without employees   C: contractors with expired licenses

    B: contractors with inactive licenses   D: All of the above

19. _____ is insurance that covers problems with the client or their property done by poor workmanship.

    A: Property Insurance   C: Liability Insurance

    B: Life Insurance   D: Worker's Compensation Insurance

20. A _____ is a bond that assures the owner that no liens for labor will be filed against his/her property.

    A: Payment Bond   C: Contract Bond

    B: Performance Bond   D: Contractor License Bonds

21. A _____ is a bond that guarantees the completion of the work as it is specified in the projects building plans and specifications.

    A: Payment Bond   C: Contract Bond

    B: Contractor License Bonds   D: Performance Bond

22. A _____ is a bond that guarantees both the job completion and the payment of all labor and materials.

    A: Contractor License Bonds   C: Payment Bond

    B: Contract Bond   D: Performance Bond

EXAM 2

23. A _____ requires each licensed contractor to carry a contractor bond.

    A: Contractor License Bonds

    B: Contract Bond

    C: Payment Bond

    D: Performance Bond

24. It is essential to know your company's _____ estimates to ensure a profitable business.

    A: gross income

    B: overhead expenses

    C: net profit percentage

    D: All of the above

25. True or False: Effective communication is an important part of any sound organization.

    A: True

    B: False

26. What do you need to determine your business mark-up?

    A: gross income

    B: overhead expenses

    C: net profit percentage

    D: All of the above

27. True or False: You mark-up should remain the same for all the jobs that you sell, regardless of size.

    A: True

    B: False

28. A _____ is a relatively simple bid scheduling method.

    A: Bar Chart Method

    B: Critical Path Method

    C: Pie Chart Method

    D: None of the above

29. A _____ is a complex bid scheduling method.

    A: Bar Chart Method

    B: Critical Path Method

    C: Pie Chart Method

    D: None of the above

30. True or False: According to the CPM diagram, non-critical operations may be started later without having a detrimental effect on the overall completion time.

    A: True

    B: False

31. Which of the following practices can diminish your chances of a dispute with a client/customer?

    A: invoicing regularly

    B: documenting all agreements in writing

    C: communicate clearly

    D: All of the above

32. What should be your first option to settle a dispute?

    A: work it out

    B: small claims court

    C: arbitration

    D: mechanics lien

EXAM 2

33. Which of the following is a goal of cash management?

   A: maximize the level of cash within the business

   B: maximize the return earned from investments of cash

   C: minimize the amount of time in which cash sits idly

   D: All of the above

34. Which of the following is a basic cash management principle?

   A: Accelerations of cash receipts from customers

   B: Cash Budgeting

   C: Deceleration of cash disbursement to creditors

   D: All of the above

35. _____ is a cash inflow source.

   A: Account receivables

   B: Investment by owners

   C: Sale of fixed assets

   D: All of the above

36. _____ is a cash outflow source.

   A: Accounts payable

   B: Payroll

   C: Operating expenses

   D: All of the above

37. _____ are set for all projects that are currently in progress.

   A: Job Flow Budgets

   B: Consolidated Cash Flow Budgets

   C: Both A and B

   D: Neither A nor B

38. True or False: Cash Budgeting is all about timing.

   A: True

   B: False

39. True or False: A balance sheet is considered to be a statement of your company's financial standing as of the date the balance sheet is done.

   A: True

   B: False

40. What is the first step in a basic accounting cycle?

   A: posting transactions on the ledger account

   B: recording the transaction in the general journal

   C: gathering all transactions

   D: creating a balance sheet

41. True or False: The accrual basis of accounting enables a more current and more simple method of accounting than cash basis accounting.

   A: True

   B: False

Law & Business Exam Part II

42. True or False: The cash basis of accounting is generally used by individuals for personal and family records and is also widely used by small businesses.

    A: True   B: False

43. The IRS requires contractors to keep records of employment taxes for a minimum of _____ years.

    A: 2   C: 6

    B: 4   D: 10

44. True or False: You must obtain an Employer Identification Number (EIN) before you can begin to hire employees.

    A: True   B: False

45. The _____ is a form that shows a summary of wages and taxes paid annually; it shows total income and social security taxes withheld in a calendar year.

    A: I-9   C: W-2

    B: 1099-MISC   D: W-4

46. Every employee must provide an employer a signed _____ on or before the date of employment.

    A: W-2   C: 1099-MISC

    B: W-4   D: I-9

47. Which of the following forms confirms the employees citizenship and/or their eligibility to work in the U.S.?

    A: W-2   C: 1099-MISC

    B: W-4   D: I-9

48. What constitutes as working part time?

    A: 35 or fewer hours in a week   C: 41 or more hours in a week

    B: 36-40 hours in a week   D: None of the above

49. If an employee works for$ 12.00/hr. and has recorded 60 hours this week how much did the employee earn?

    A: $480.00   C: $750.00

    B: $595.00   D: $840.00

50. Legally you are not allowed to work more than _____ out of 7 days.

    A: 4   C: 6

    B: 5   D: None of the above

Law & Business Exam Part II

51. The _____ is information required on a time card.

   A: employee's name   C: hours worked

   B: pay period   D: all of the above

52. True or False: Employees must be paid at least twice a month or every two weeks, unless a special employment contract exists.

   A: True   B: False

53. The personal responsibility and Work Opportunity Reconciliation Act of 1996 requires all employers to report newly hired and rehired employees to a state directory within _____ days of their hire/rehired date.

   A: 5   C: 20

   B: 7   D: 60

54. Which tax provides funds to train employees in targeted industries to improve the competitiveness of California businesses?

   A: SDI   C: PIT

   B: ETT   D: FIT

55. Which tax provides temporary payments to workers who are unable to perform their usual work because of pregnancy or a non-occupational illness or injury?

   A: SDI   C: PIT

   B: FUTA   D: FIT

56. Which of the following is the tax that consists of both Social Security and Medicare taxes?

   A: FUTA   C: FIT

   B: FICA   D: SIT

57. Which of the following is a tax that provides for payments of unemployment compensation to workers who have lost their jobs?

   A: FUTA   C: FIT

   B: FICA   D: SIT

58. True or False: The FIT and SIT taxes are the federal and state income taxes.

   A: True   B: False

59. When must unemployment Insurance tax returns be filed?

   A: monthly   C: quarterly

   B: bi-monthly   D: annually

Law & Business Exam Part II

60. In order to qualify for unemployment insurance benefits claimants must meet which of the following requirements?

    A: be available for work

    B: be totally or partially unemployed and registered for work

    C: be actively seeking work on their own

    D: all of the above

61. When a contractor performs work in a city other than his own city of business:

    A: a tax is due in the form of a license fee in the city where the work is performed.

    B: a tax is not charged, since the contractor already pays a license fee to his city of business address

    C: as long as the city where the work is performed is within the same county as the business address is established, no additional fee required

    D: license fees (tax) are paid in another city if the work performed exceeds 90 days

62. Considering that California is divided into several tax districts, if your job site is in one of these districts you _____.

    A: must pay the district tax on sales made at the job site

    B: must pay the district tax on purchase of materials used at the site

    C: Both A and B

    D: Neither A nor B

63. True or False: The prevailing wage rate for public works is the basic hourly rate.

    A: True

    B: False

64. Which of the following laws ensures that public works bids are not based on paying lower wage rates?

    A: UI laws

    B: HEFA laws

    C: Wage laws

    D: None of the above

65. Contractors that get a public works contract for more than _____ are required to get a payment bond.

    A: $5,000

    B: $10,000

    C: $15,000

    D: $25,000

66. True or False: To maintain your right to file a Stop Payment Notice if payment is not received, you must file a Preliminary Notice for Public Works.

    A: True

    B: False

67. What does Minimum Scope Insurance, a basic insurance coverage for public works, include?

    A: Commercial General Liability Insurance

    B: Commercial Automobile Liability Insurance

    C: Worker's Compensation Insurance

    D: All of the above

EXAM 2

68. No direct contractor whose bid is accepted for public works shall _____.

    A: substitute a subcontractor without approval

    B: permit any subcontractor to be transferred

    C: sublet or subcontract any portion of the work in excess of one-half of 1 percent of the prime contractor's total bid as to which his original bid did not designate a subcontractor

    D: all of the above

69. If a contract has all the basic necessities of a construction contract but some of the wording is ambiguous _____.

    A: the contract null and void

    B: this is a standard format and if complete, then it is acceptable

    C: construction contracts are often ambiguous because of the variety interpretations that may exist

    D: it is very important in the construction industry to exclude ambiguous wording and spell everything out in as much detail as possible

70. Every "Home Improvement" contact must have _____.

    A: the name, address, and license number of the contractor and registration of the salesman

    B: date when the work will begin and be completed

    C: description of the work, materials and equipment

    D: All of the above

71. Which of the following best describes "home improvement" as it is understood by contractors?

    A: the repairing, remodeling, altering, converting, or modernizing of, or adding to residential property

    B: construction, erection, replacement, or improvement of driveways, terraces, patios, landscaping, fences, porches, garages, fallouts shelters, basements, and other improvement of structures of land adjacent to a dwelling

    C: home improvement goods or services bought in connection with the improvement of real property

    D: All of the above

72. A home improvement contract means an agreement between _____.

    A: an owner and contractor

    B: a home improvement salesman and an owner

    C: a contractor and a tenant

    D: all of the above

Law & Business Exam Part II

73. Consent to home improvement contract is required to be given by _____.

    A: the property owner

    B: either spouse

    C: parties involved in the contract

    D: both the contractor and an attorney

74. Prior to signing the contract, both parties (the homeowner and the contractor) should critically review the _____ to ensure a clear understanding of the contractual party's commitments.

    A: suppliers list

    B: building permits

    C: request for variance

    D: plans and specifications

75. After the contractor reviews the plans and specifications the _____ is needed in order to proceed.

    A: title insurance

    B: property owner's signed approval

    C: joint control company's approval

    D: city building inspector's signature

76. Consider the following scenario: A contractor purchases another contracting business which has a 3 year collective bargaining agreement with a labor organization. The buyer (successor) wants to renegotiate the agreement, which of the following is applicable?

    A: the successor is required to wait at least a year or until the agreement expires, whichever occurs first

    B: the employees of the successor must approve the agreement to continue enforcement

    C: no agreement shall be binding on the successor for more than three years from the effective date between the contractor and the labor organization.

    D: the successor (contractor) can re-negotiate a new agreement with the labor organization after close of sale.

77. How many years does the consumer have to file a lawsuit for latent defects against a home builder/developer?

    A: 2 years

    B: 4 years

    C: 5 years

    D: 10 years

78. When does a joint control addendum take precedence?

    A: over the original contract payment

    B: when the payments exceed 110 percent

    C: when there is a labor dispute

    D: over a preliminary lien notice

79. Banks usually limit long term borrowing to _____ percent of the capitalization (debt ratio).

    A: 30

    B: 40

    C: 50

    D: 60

80. An evaluation will be made on the contractor's _____, when being evaluated for a loan.

    A: character

    B: capacity

    C: certainty

    D: all of the above

Law & Business Exam Part II

81. A _____ loan is negotiated, if a firm has a good credit with its bank.

    A: term

    B: fixed

    C: mortgage

    D: collateral

82. An employer reserves the right to require that an applicant for employment _____.

    A: take a polygraph or lie detector test

    B: disclose information concerning an arrest that did not result in conviction

    C: pay for his/her physical examination

    D: None of the above

83. The best time to explain to the client how to handle change orders is _____.

    A: after the contract has been signed

    B: during the pre-construction meeting, before signing the contract

    C: you don't have to explain, the owner should know the procedure

    D: you do not have to explain your procedures, just handle them like you normally do

84. How can a contractor ensure that change order does not cause the him/her a loss?

    A: charge an extra fee for the change order that is a percentage of the entire project

    B: specify the costs for the change order and add an administrative fee to cover the overhead

    C: the overhead cost is a cost of doing and cannot be collected beyond the change order price

    D: Losses are unavoidable. There is nothing that the contractor can do to avoid losses.

85. It is important for the contractor to keep change order in the job file because _____.

    A: it is required for tax purposes

    B: it is required by the city

    C: all records should be kept together

    D: they are not required to be kept in the job file

86. The contractor should _____ prior to an investigator visiting the site.

    A: stop work in progress

    B: have the supervisor clean the site

    C: inspect the work himself

    D: be familiar with all related codes

87. The _____ starts the process of scheduling inspections on the project.

    A: architect

    B: contractor

    C: office where inspector works

    D: owner

Law & Business Exam Part II

88. A contractor should respond to the owner's complaints _____.

    A: when a change order is filed

    B: when he/she finds the time to deal with the owner

    C: once a job-site meeting is scheduled

    D: as soon as he/she contacts the contractor

89. If a project is completed as stated in the signed contract and the owner wants additional work done, the contractor should _____.

    A: do the work free of charge because he is expected to do additional work

    B: do the work for free to ensure a good relationship with the owner

    C: have a change order prepared for the work

    D: set up another separate contract and follow through with it

90. You should look at the _____ for information about the work schedule.

    A: general provisions of the contract

    B: plans and specifications

    C: critical path schedule

    D: none of the above

91. Consider the following scenario: It takes 2 days to prepare a site. The first phase takes 10 days, the second phase takes 7 days. Clean up takes 1 day. Considering that Phase 1 and phase two of a project can be done simultaneously, how long would the project entire project from site set-up to clean-up take?

    A: 7 days

    B: 10 days

    C: 13 days

    D: 20 days

92. Using the phase "second payment due when job is 60 percent complete" as a specification for payment schedule _____.

    A: is acceptable and very typical

    B: is a bad phrase because its vague and can be interpreted in several ways

    C: can only be made upon substantial completion of the work

    D: does not include performing a "punch-list"

93. Consider the following scenario: The owner visits the site during a critical phase and has some corrections for the contractor to do. In which of the following ways should the contractor best handle this?

    A: stop everything and make the corrections

    B: hire and additional crew to make the corrections right away

    C: note the corrections and at the end of the critical phase have them completed

    D: tell him that you're in a critical phase and simply have him contact you at some other time

Law & Business Exam Part II

94. How do you obtain information about materials that are to be used in a project?

    A: call the supervisor

    B: check with the schedule

    C: check the plans and specification

    D: check the contract

95. Substitute provisions are allowed for _____ construction contracts, if the job is financed by a third party lender.

    A: roofing job

    B: landscaping job

    C: swimming pool job

    D: heating and air condition job

96. In which of the following should every licensed contractor be required to include his license number?

    A: all construction contracts

    B: subcontracts

    C: bids

    D: all of the above

97. If a salesperson seeks to renew his registration he/she must _____ before the registration he/she holds expires.

    A: renew the registration within 30 days of receiving same

    B: apply for renewal on a form prescribed by the Registrar

    C: pay the prescribed fee, the renewal is automatic

    D: None of the above

98. If a salesperson _____ it shall be cause for legal disciplinary action.

    A: fails to account for or remits any payment

    B: withholds the name of the contractor he/she is employed by

    C: accepts any compensation from any person other than the contractor he/she represents

    D: all of the above

99. Which of the following should a mobile-home contractor include?

    A: the manufacture of a mobile home when the manufacture is engaged in an on-site construction, alteration or repair or any work other than compliance under warranty

    B: any person engaged in the business of the construction, installation, alterations, repair or preparation for moving a mobile home upon a site for the purpose of occupancy as a dwelling

    C: Both A and B

    D: Neither A and B

Law & Business Exam Part II

100. Which of the following follows if a homeowner files a complaint against you which leads to a judgment against your bond or cash deposit.

    A: all legal fees will be charged against you bond or cash deposit

    B: this constitutes grounds for disciplinary action against you

    C: your bond or cash deposit requirements are doubled

    D: all of the above

EXAM 2

1. **Answer A.** True

   Contractors operate under conditions of relative uncertainty. A means of reducing a company's expense to risk is by having a comprehensive insurance package. Example of insurance that contractors must have include: General Liability Insurance, Vehicle Liability Insurance, Workers Compensation Insurance",

2. **Answer A.** True

   A liability represents the obligation to pay money for a business debt such as loans and accounts payable. Liabilities can be categorized as current or long term. Current liabilities are debts that become due in one year. Long term liabilities are due beyond one year and it includes things such as mortgages.

3. **Answer B.** False

   Current liabilities are debts, which mature within one year from the date of the balance sheet, current liabilities include: notes payable, accounts payable, accrued wages and accrued taxes.\n\n Fixed liabilities are debts which will not mature for a long period of time. Examples of fixed liabilities include: mortgages payable and long-term contracts.

4. **Answer A.** True

   Liabilities are debt. They are obligations to pay money or other assets, either now or in the future. Examples of common liabilities are accounts payable, notes payable, interest payable, mortgages payable and contract payable.

5. **Answer A.** asset

   A property with cash value owned by your business is an example of an asset. \n\nAssets can be identified as either current or fixed. Current assets can be converted into cash; they are also referred to as liquid assets. Fixed assets, such as your office building, are not intended to be sold.

6. **Answer A.** True

   Net fixed assets are the investment in fixed assets remaining after deducting accumulated appreciation.

7. **Answer A.** True

   Proprietorship is the excess of assets over total liability.

8. **Answer B.** False

   Depreciation refers to the decrease in value of a fixed asset, as a result of the passage of time, wear and tear or obsolescence. Depreciation is recorded to value the asset at any current date and distribute the cost of that asset over its useful life. Depreciation is usually shown on the balance sheet as a direct deduction from a fixed asset and becomes an expense item on the income and expense statement.

9. **Answer B.** False

   In order for the financial position of a company to be sound the amount of cash plus good receivables should be greater than the amount of the current liabilities.

10. **Answer B.** False

    Cost of materials is typically the largest figure on the Income Expense Statement.

11. **Answer B.** False

    For working capital, commercial banks favor short-term self-liquidating loans.

12. **Answer A.** True

    Equity is the ownership, especially when considered as the right to share in future profits or appreciation in value.\n\t\nEquity Funds (the stockholders equity) represents a claim of ownership of the assets of the business, basically the original investments of the owners.

13. **Answer A.** True

    Definition of asset is a single item of ownership that has exchange value; anything of value that is owned.

14. **Answer A.** True

    All contractors who have employees are required to have Worker's Compensation Insurance Coverage. If the contractor has no employees, he/she does not have to have Worker's Compensation Insurance Coverage. \n\nException: Contractors who hold a C-39 License Roofing, are required to have a Certificate of Worker's Compensation Insurance or a certificate of Self-Insurance on file with CSLB.

15. **Answer C.** 90

    The contractor must provide proof of Workers Compensation Insurance to the CSLB Headquarters Office within 90 days of hiring anyone. Failure to provide such proof will result in suspension of your license and disciplinary action.

16. **Answer C.** Both A and B

    It is the direct contractor's responsibility to ensure that the subcontractors they hire are licensed, carry insurance for themselves and their respective workers and understand the job.

17. **Answer A.** True

    Workers Compensation is a "No-Fault" insurance purchased by the employer and supervised by the state. This insurance is designed to limit the liability of the employer by reducing costly lawsuits and by providing prompt rehabilitation for job related injuries.

18. **Answer D.** All of the above

    Contractors without employees or with inactive or expired licenses are not required to have Worker's Compensation \n\nAll contractors with employees MUST have Worker's Comp. even if it is one employee working part-time.\n\nNote: You must file an exemption form if you want to be exempt and meet all the criteria to be exempt from Worker's Comp. \nSimilarly, you must file a certificate of Worker's Compensation after obtaining a policy.

19. **Answer C.** Liability Insurance

    Liability Insurance covers problems with the client or their property done by poor workmanship. It is important to understand that liability insurance does not pay for your poor workmanship it only pays for the damages that poor workmanship causes. Consider the following example: If a shelf is set wrong and it falls and chips the tile floor, liability insurance covers damage to the tile but not damage to the shelf.

EXAM 2

20. **Answer A.** Payment Bond

A Payment Bond is a bond that assures the owner that no liens for labor will be filed against his/her property.\n\nBonding is generally mandatory for large jobs financed by institutional lenders. However, many owners and lenders may impose bonding requirements to ensure payment.\n\nA bond is essentially a loan from a lender. Bonds can be attained from a bonding company for a percentage of the contract price, usually in 1 percent to 2 percent range.

21. **Answer D.** Performance Bond

A Performance Bond is a bond that guarantees the completion of the work as it is specified in the projects building plans and specifications.\n\nPerformance bonds are in case the job is abandoned or the work performed/executed proves to be unacceptable. In either case the bonding company insures the work by hiring another contractor to complete the work or by settling for damages.

22. **Answer B.** Contract Bond

A Contract Bond is a bond that guarantees both the job completion and the payment of all labor and materials.

23. **Answer A.** Contractor License Bonds

A Contractor License Bonds requires each licensed contractor to carry a contractor bond. \n\nUnlike payment performance and contract bonds, which are usually written to cover specific projects, a contractor license bond is written to cover any project the contractor agrees to perform.

24. **Answer D.** All of the above

It is essential to know your company's gross income, overhead expenses and net profitable percentage to ensure a profitable business.\n\nGross income is your estimate for your gross income for a year, in other words it is what you expect to sell, produce and get paid for during the year. \n\nOverhead Expenses: as previously defined these expenses are separate from the field and include administrative and managerial cost such as: advertising, sales, office expenses, job expenses and general expenses. \n\nNet Profit Percentage: this is answering the question "What would you like your net profit to be?" Industry statistics report 6 percent to be the average net profit for contractors (2010 Industry Statistics). So if you would like a 6 percent net profit have that clear, if you want an 8 percent net profit have that clear. Either way, decide your net profit!

25. **Answer A.** True

Effective communication is an important part of any sound organization. All personnel are entitled to be advised upon any subject, which concerns them individually. In addition, good communication improves morale and productivity, which are key to the success of a business.

26. **Answer D.** All of the above

You need to know your estimates for Gross Income, Overhead Expenses and Net Profit Percentage to determine your business Mark-Up.\n\nDetermining Your Mark-up – 3 Step Formula\n\nFirst: Add overhead expenses estimate (OE) and net profit estimate (NP)\n   Overhead Expenses estimate + Net Profit estimate = Answer 1\n\nSecond: Subtract Answer 1 (A1) from the Gross Income (GI)\n   Gross Income - Answer 1 = Job Costs\n\nThird: Divide the Gross Income (GI) by the job costs (JC) this will give you YOUR mark-up!\n   Gross Income ÷ Job Costs = Mark-Up

27. **Answer A.** True

You mark-up should remain the same for all the jobs that you sell, regardless of size.

28. **Answer A.** Bar Chart Method

A Bar Chart Method is a relatively simple bid scheduling method that shows the start and stop dates for various phases of the work. It shows the sequence of a list of activities with the start and finish of each activity displayed as a bar plotted to a time scale. Its disadvantage is that it tends to overlook some interrelated tasks.

29. **Answer B.** Critical Path Method

A Critical Path Method is a complex bid scheduling method that is typically used for larger projects. This method helps identify the critical path in which the order of events should take place. This method interrelates jobs better than the Bar Chart Method.

30. **Answer A.** True

According to the CPM diagram, non-critical operations may be started later without having a detrimental effect on the overall completion time.

31. **Answer D.** All of the above

All of the following practices can help diminish your chances of a dispute with a client/customer:\n\nCommunication – communicate with your customer on a consistent basis; use punch lists to show them the things that need to be done; listen to them.\n\nInvoice regularly – don't allow unpaid bills to accumulate; keep track of payments \n\nDocument ALL agreements in writing – agreements include any change to the contract\n\nMeet problems head on, don't dodge

32. **Answer A.** work it out

If there is a dispute with your customer your first option should always be to work it out. Lawsuits can be expensive and time consuming. Other option include:\n\nSmall Claims Court: project must be less than$5,000; no attorneys allowed; you cannot foreclose a mechanics lien in a small claims court; decisions are appealable.\n\nArbitration: Both parties must agree to arbitration, going to court is not necessary, decisions made by arbitrators are non-appealable.\n\nMechanics Lien: file a mechanics lien to receive unpaid payments; file a stop notice for public works

33. **Answer D.** All of the above

Cash management is about having financial control over your construction business. Its goals are to: \n- maximize the level of cash within the business \n- maximize the return earned from investments of cash \n- minimize the amount of time in which cash sits idly not producing income

EXAM 2

Answers: Law & Business Exam Part II

34. Answer D. All of the above

There are five essential cash management principles that should be applied to a business regardless of size, they are the following:\n   \n1. Cash Budgeting\n2. Accelerations of cash receipts from customers\n3. Deceleration of cash disbursement to creditors\n4. Raising cash when needed\n5. Short term investment to preserve the value of working capital and maximize earnings

35. Answer D. All of the above

All of the following are predictable cash inflow sources:\n- Account receivables\n- Investment by owners\n- Sale of fixed assets

36. Answer D. All of the above

All of the following are predictable cash outflow sources:\n- Accounts payable\n- Payroll\n- Operating expenses

37. Answer A. Job Flow Budgets

Job Flow Budgets are set for all projects that are currently in progress.\n\nConsolidated Cash Flow Budgets are for your entire business. This budget should combine the net cash flows from all individual projects with the operating expenses of the firm, as well as anticipated expenses, capital expenditures and changes in debt position. This budget is generally prepared for a one year period and updated ech month with new information.

38. Answer A. True

Cash budgeting is determining the time in which cash flows out of your business. Cash budgeting is all about timing. \n\nFor Job Flow Budgets, Bar Chart scheduling method and Critical Path scheduling method are extremely helpful in determining when cash flows out and for what. Remember that specific terms arranged with your subcontractors and suppliers affect the timing of disbursements.

39. Answer A. True

A balance sheet is considered to be a statement of your company's financial standing as of the date the balance sheet is done.\n\nThe most common classifications in a balance data sheet are the following: assets, liabilities and equity.

40. Answer C. gathering all transactions

The basic accounting cycle is the following:\n   \t\n1. gather all transactions\n2. record the transactions in the general journal\n3. post the transactions on the ledger account\n4. create a balance sheet\n5. create an income statement for the month

41. Answer B. False

While the accrual basis of accounting enables a more current method of accounting than cash basis accounting, it is more complex than cash basis accounting. When accrual basis is used, income is recorded for the period in which it is earned, whether it is received during that period or not. Expenses incurred in earning the income are recorded as expenses, whether or not payment has been made for them during that period.

42. Answer A. True

The cash basis of accounting is generally used by individuals for personal and family records and is also widely used by small businesses. \n\nWhen true cash basis of accounting is used, income is recorded only when cash is received and expenses are recognized only when cash is paid out. This means that in the records there must be both: accounts receivable and accounts payable.

43. Answer B. 4

The IRS requires contractors to keep records of employment taxes for a minimum of 4 years.

44. Answer A. True

You must first obtain an Employer Identification Number (EIN), referred to as an Employer Tax ID Number, before you can hire employees. In order to obtain an EIN you must file an SS-4 form. An EIN is necessary to:\n   \n- report taxes and other documents to the IRS\n\n- information about employees to state agencies

45. Answer C. W-2

The W-2 is a form that shows a summary of wages and taxes paid annually; it shows total income and social security taxes withheld in a calendar year.

46. Answer B. W-4

Every employee must provide an employer a signed W-4 on or before the date of employment. A W-4 is a withholding exemption certificate that the employer must submit to the IRS.

47. Answer D. I-9

Form I-9 is the Employee Eligibility Verification form. It is used to confirm that the employee is eligible to work in the U.S. either by citizenship or work permit. This form must be completed by new employees within 3 business days of being hired. This form requires the employer to examine acceptable forms of documentation supplied by the employee to confirm citizenship or work eligibility in the U.S.

48. Answer A. 35 or fewer hours in a week

Working 35 or fewer hours a week is considered part-time.\n\nFull time is working 36 to 40 hours a week\n\nOvertime is working 41 or more hours a week.

49. Answer D. $840.00

$12.00/hr. x 40 hrs. =$480.00\n\nOvertime:\n$12.00 +$6.00 =$18.00\n$18.00 x 20 hrs. =$360.00\n\n$480.00 +$360.00 = $840.00

50. Answer C. 6

Legally you are not allowed to work more than 6 out of 7 days. Every person employed in any occupation of labor is entitled to one days' rest there from in seven. No employer shall cause his employees to work more than six days in seven. (California Labor Code 551)

51. Answer D. all of the above

Information required on a time card includes the employee's name, the pay period and the hours worked.

52. Answer A. True

Employees must be paid at least twice a month or every two weeks, unless a special employment contract exists.

EXAM 2

53. **Answer C.** 20

The personal responsibility and Work Opportunity Reconciliation Act of 1996 requires all employers to report newly hired and rehired employees to a state directory within 20 days of their hire/rehired date.

54. **Answer B.** ETT

The Employment Training Tax (ETT) provides funds to train employees in targeted industries to improve the competitiveness of California businesses.\n\nEmployers pay this tax on a quarterly basis.

55. **Answer A.** SDI

State Disability Insurance (SDI) tax, provides temporary payments to workers who are unable to perform their usual work because of pregnancy or a non-occupational illness or injury. Note: work related disabilities are covered by worker's compensation insurance.\n\nThe employees pay this tax. It is deducted (withheld) from employees' wages.

56. **Answer B.** FICA

The Federal Insurance Contributions Act (FICA) consists of both Social Security and Medicare taxes. \nIt is paid by employers and employees alike on a quarterly basis.

57. **Answer A.** FUTA

The Federal Unemployment Tax Act (FUTA), along with state unemployment systems, provides for payments of unemployment compensation to workers who have lost their jobs.\n\nFUTA taxes are paid by employers on a quarterly basis.

58. **Answer A.** True

The FIT and SIT taxes are the federal and state income taxes. FIT and SIT are paid by employees on a quarterly basis.

59. **Answer C.** quarterly

Unemployment Insurance tax returns must filed quarterly.

60. **Answer D.** all of the above

Claimants must meet all of the following requirements in order to qualify for unemployment insurance benefits:\n \t\n1. be totally or partially unemployed and registered for work\n2. received a minimum amount of wages during the base period\n3. be physically able to work in their usual occupation, or in other work for which they are reasonably fitted\n4. be available for work\n5. be actively seeking work on their own.

61. **Answer A.** a tax is due in the form of a license fee in the city where the work is performed.

When a contractor performs work in a city other than his own city of business a tax is due in the form of a license fee in the city where the work is performed.

62. **Answer C.** Both A and B

Considering that California is divided into several tax districts, if your job site is in one of these districts you must pay the district tax on sales made at the job site and you must pay the district tax on purchase of materials used at the site.

63. **Answer A.** True

The prevailing wage rate for public works is the basic hourly rate. Check the hourly rate for changes on a periodic basis.

64. **Answer C.** Wage laws

Wage laws protect employees by ensuring that contractors are not paying them a lower wage rate to produce and pitch a better bid. Wage laws ensure that contractors are bidding ethically and nor at the cost of their employees.

65. **Answer D.** $25,000

Contractors that get a public works contract for more than$25,000 are required to get a payment bond.\n\nThe bond for public works must be filed before beginning any work on the public works project.\n\nThe bond must be in the amount of not less than 100 percent of the total amount payable.

66. **Answer A.** True

To maintain your right to file a Stop Payment Notice if payment is not received, you must file a Preliminary Notice for Public Works. If a Preliminary Notice is not filed, you forfeit your right to file a Stop Payment Notice.

67. **Answer D.** All of the above

Minimum Scope Insurance, a basic insurance coverage for public works, includes all of the following: \n   \t\n   \t - Commercial General Liability Insurance \n   - Commercial Automobile Liability Insurance \n   - Worker's Compensation Insurance \n - Employers Liability Insurance

68. **Answer A.** substitute a subcontractor without approval

Direct contractor whose bid is accepted for public works shall substitute a subcontractor without approval.

69. **Answer D.** it is very important in the construction industry to exclude ambiguous wording and spell everything out in as much detail as possible

It is very important in the construction industry to exclude ambiguous wording and spell everything out in as much detail as possible.

70. **Answer D.** All of the above

Every home improvement contract must have the following: the name, address, and license number of the contractor and registration of the salesman, date when the work will begin and be completed and description of the work, materials and equipment.

71. **Answer D.** All of the above

Home improvement means:\n   \t\n1. the repairing, remodeling, altering, converting, or modernizing of, or adding to residential property\n\n2. construction, erection, replacement, or improvement of driveways, terraces, patios, landscaping, fences, porches, garages, fallouts shelters, basements, and other improvement of structures of land adjacent to a dwelling\n\n3. home improvement goods or services bought in connection with the improvement of real property

EXAM 2

72. **Answer D.** all of the above

A home improvement contract can mean an agreement between a contractor and an owner, a contractor and a tenant or an agreement between an improvement salesperson and an owner.

73. **Answer C.** parties involved in the contract

Consent to home improvement contract is given by the parties involved in the contract, which usually includes the homeowner and the contractor.

74. **Answer D.** plans and specifications

Prior to signing the contract, both parties (the homeowner and the contractor) should critically review the plans and specifications to ensure a clear understanding of the contractual party's commitments.

75. **Answer B.** property owner's signed approval

After the contractor reviews the plans and specifications the property owner's signed approval is needed in order to proceed.

76. **Answer C.** no agreement shall be binding on the successor for more than three years from the effective date between the contractor and the labor organization.

A contractor purchases another contracting business which has a 3 year collective bargaining agreement with a labor organization. If the buyer (successor) wants to renegotiate the agreement the following is applicable: no agreement shall be binding on the successor for more than three years from the effective date between the contractor and the labor organization.

77. **Answer D.** 10 years

California law states that all homeowners have 10 years in which to file a lawsuit for latent defects against a home builder/developer. However, that 10 year period may actually be shorter if you discover the defect and don't do anything about it (i.e. other statutes of limitation may take effect). It all depends upon what type of defect exists. So, while the 10 year period is the absolute limit, it is best to speak with a qualified attorney as soon as you discover the defect to make sure that you protect your potential claim. (www.real-estate-law.com)

78. **Answer A.** over the original contract payment

A joint control addendum takes precedence over the original contract payment.

79. **Answer C.** 50

Banks usually limit long term borrowing to 50 percent of the capitalization (debt ratio).

80. **Answer D.** all of the above

An evaluation will be made on the contractor's character, capacity and certainty when being evaluated for a loan.

81. **Answer A.** term

If a firm has a good credit with its bank, it would negotiate a term loan.

82. **Answer D.** None of the above

An employer may not ask a prospective employee to: take a polygraph lie detector test or disclose information concerning an arrest that did not result in conviction, or require the prospective employer to pay for his/her physical examination.

83. **Answer B.** during the pre-construction meeting, before signing the contract

The best time to explain to the client how to handle change orders is during the pre-construction meeting, before signing the contract.

84. **Answer B.** specify the costs for the change order and add an administrative fee to cover the overhead

Change orders have a reputation of creating profit for the contractor, however that is not the case, they actually add to the overhead. The contractor should specify the costs for the change order and add an administrative fee to cover the overcharge in order to prevent loss.

85. **Answer C.** all records should be kept together

It is important for the contractor to keep change order in the job file because it is important to keep all records together. Keeping the change orders in the job file will ensure that the contractor remembers to add the costs to the total job costs.

86. **Answer C.** inspect the work himself

Prior to an inspector visiting the site, the contractor should inspect the work himself, ensuring that it is indeed ready for inspection.

87. **Answer B.** contractor

The contractor starts the process of scheduling inspections on the project.

88. **Answer D.** as soon as he/she contacts the contractor

A contractor should respond to the owner's complaints as soon as he/she contacts him.

89. **Answer D.** set up another separate contract and follow through with it

If a project is completed and the owner wants additional work done, the contractor should set up another separate contract and follow through with it.

90. **Answer C.** critical path schedule

You should look at the critical path schedule for information about the work schedule.

91. **Answer C.** 13 days

2 days(for preparing site)\n10 days (for phase 1 and phase 2)\n1 day (for clean-up)\n\n= 13 days

EXAM 2

92. **Answer B.** is a bad phrase because its vague and can be interpreted in several ways

Using the phase "second payment due when job is 60 percent complete" as a specification for payment schedule is a bad phase because it is vague and can be interpreted in several ways. Payment schedules should be clearly stated, defined and included in the specifications.

93. **Answer C.** note the corrections and at the end of the critical phase have them completed

If an owner visits the site during a critical phase to inform the contractor of corrections to be made, the contractor should note the correction and have them completed at the end of the critical phase.

94. **Answer C.** check the plans and specification

To obtain information about the material to be used in a project to be started within a few weeks, the contractor should check the plans and specifications.

95. **Answer C.** swimming pool job

Substitute provisions are allowed for swimming pool job construction contracts, if the job is financed by a third party lender.

96. **Answer D.** all of the above

Every licensed contractor is required to include his/her license number in all forms of advertising, as well as, all construction contracts, subcontracts and bids.

97. **Answer B.** apply for renewal on a form prescribed by the Registrar

If a salesperson seeks to renew his registration he/she must apply for renewal on a form prescribed by the Registrar before the registration he/she holds expires.

98. **Answer D.** all of the above

If a salesperson: fails to account for or remits any payment, withholds the name of the contractor he/she is employed by, or accepts any compensation from any person other than the contractor he/she represents he/she will be subject to legal disciplinary action. If any of the listed is committed the salesperson will be charged with a misdemeanor.

99. **Answer C.** Both A and B

A mobile-home contractor includes: the manufacture of a mobile home when the manufacture is engaged in an on-site construction, alteration or repair or any work other than compliance under warranty and any person engaged in the business of the construction, installation, alterations, repair or preparation for moving a mobile home upon a site for the purpose of occupancy as a dwelling.

100. **Answer C.** your bond or cash deposit requirements are doubled

If a homeowner files a complaint against you which leads to a judgment against your bond or cash deposit your bond or cash deposit requirements are doubled.",

EXAM 3

Law & Business Exam Part III

1. Consider the following scenario: Assume that your terms of sale with the supplier state 2 percent, 10, net 15 what so these numbers mean?

   A: the net price of the bill is due on the 10th of the month following the date of purchase and a 2 percent penalty will be added if not paid by the 15th

   B: the net price of the bill is due on the 15th of the month following the date of purchase so the 2 percent cash discount will be given if the bill is paid on or before the tenth

   C: 2 percent of the net price of the bill is due on or about the 10th of the month following the date of purchase which remains on the 15th

   D: a 2 percent discount will be on the price of the bill if it is is paid between the 10th and the 15th of the month following the date of billing

2. Which of the following billing practices is NOT recommended?

   A: bill promptly for everything you do that's easily listed on the billing statement

   B: insist on cash upon completion of project

   C: consult an attorney on collection problems

   D: encourage time payment from customers having accepted your bid

3. California workers compensation laws require you to obtain insurance protection through which of the following manners?

   A: through a standard policy from a registrar of the contractors or through any approved form of self insurance

   B: through a standard policy from the director of industrial relations or with their approval, self insurance

   C: through a policy from a licensed carrier or through self insurance after obtaining a permit from the director of industrial relations

   D: either through a policy from the registrar of contractors or any other licensed carrier

4. If a subcontractor gets injured while working for you and the subcontractor does not have insurance _____.

   A: this is the subcontractor responsibility and you (the contractor) shouldn't worry about it

   B: whether responsibility lies with you (the contractor) or with the subcontractor is something that must be determined in court

   C: the owner has to pay

   D: you (the contractor) are liable for the injuries under your workmen's compensation

Law & Business Exam Part III

5. Consider the following statement: You decide to hire employees. In an effort to diffuse any potential problem you decide to ask all applicants if they have ever been arrested and base your hiring decision on their response. Which of the following statements considering this scenario is correct?

    A: Both private and public employers are entitled to ask about the matter

    B: Private agencies can ask about an applicant's record but not public agencies

    C: As a private employer you cannot ask applicants about their arrest record although a public agency can do so

    D: Neither a public or private agency can ask an applicant about their arrest record if the arrest was not followed by a conviction.

6. Consider the following scenario: A contractor has been served with a citation. The citation is in regards to a complaint filed against the contractor for violation of the license law. The citation will be deemed a final order unless it is appealed within _____.

    A: 30 days

    B: 15 working days

    C: 30 days after the receipt of the citation

    D: 60 days after the receipt of the citation

7. Failure for the contractor to conform with the terms of a citation after its been made final can result in _____.

    A: suspension or revocation of the contractor's license

    B: the case to be turned over to the district attorney

    C: a penalty of one hundred dollars ($100.00) a day until terms have been met

    D: all of the above

8. Which of the following must appear in the Registrar's citation?

    A: A description explaining the nature of the violation

    B: reference to the specific division of the license law that has been violated",

    C: an order of correction fixing a reasonable time for correction

    D: All of the above

9. _____ states regulations for the accommodation of the disabled and requirements regarding accessibility to building for the handicapped.

    A: The Department of Rehabilitation

    B: Title 24, California Administrative Code

    C: The Uniform Building Code

    D: The Office of the State Architect

10. Which of the following is the license that a person must have to replace carpets and have the walls repainted?

    A: a general engineering contractors license

    B: a general building contractors license

    C: a specialty contractor's license for painting and flooring

    D: a remodeling license for painting and flooring

Law & Business Exam Part III

11.   _____ should sign construction contracts.

   A: Only the owner   C: Both the owner and contractor

   B: Only the contractor   D: The owner, the contractor and the Notary
                                       Public.

12.   To best ensure that disputes do not arise, the contractor must _____.

   A: make sure everything is done to code   C: have the attorney read the contract

   B: go over the plans and specifications with   D: make sure the owner is happy with the
      the owner and discuss every aspect of the   price
      work

13.   If an owner asks a contractor to submit a bid package, but the owner decides that the price is too
       high, the contractor should _____.

   A: cut the bid to time and materials   C: take whatever amount you can get

   B: stand firm on price   D: discuss the price and suggest lessening
                                                  the scope of the project

14.   If the contractor finds that the owner's desires conflict with the current codes, the contractor should
       _____.

   A: walk away from the deal   C: agree, but built it to code anyway

   B: built it; the customer is always right D: insist that it be built to code even if you
                                                  loose the job

15.   After the architect's approval, the contractor should follow which of the following steps?

   A: check if the owner wants to add anything   C: go over them personally
      else

   B: check if any other additional codes apply D: order materials and begin the project

16.   You should update the "as-built" drawings _____.

   A: everyday   C: at the end of the project

   B: when you substantially deviate from the   D: after the "punch-list"
      original plans

Law & Business Exam Part III

17.   Unless _____, no contract for public works involving an estimated expenditure in excess of twenty five thousand dollars ($25,000) for the excavation of any trench 5 feet or more in depth shall be awarded.

   A: the subcontractor fully understand the scope of the work

   B: a contract contains a clause requiring the contractor to submit detailed plans showing the design of the shoring, bracing, or sloping to provide protection from caving ground

   C: a civil engineer notes that the work can take place

   D: the contractor holds a license in the classification of general shoring and trenching

18.   The best strategy to obtain short-term working capital is to _____.

   A: sell equipment not often used

   B: avoid paying suppliers until payments are due

   C: bill customers early

   D: begin a line of credit

19.   What is a simple but adequate way to add the overhead costs to your estimate?

   A: use an average industry percentage

   B: mark up labor only

   C: mark up materials only

   D: allocate direct and indirect cost between all jobs with extreme accuracy

20.   In order to determine whether something is an "extra" when it comes to major distribution disputes be able to____.

   A: interpret the original agreement

   B: determine whether you are being asked to do something different

   C: assess if the agreement is well defined

   D: All of the above

21.   Who of the following is authorized to propose and adopt standards and other regulations as necessary to buildings, structures, sidewalks, curbs and related facilities accessible to and useable by persons with physical disabilities?

   A: local building department

   B: State Architect

   C: Department of Housing and Community Development

   D: None of the above

22.   The division of the State Architect must review and approve plans and specifications on any projects for schools and colleges, using which of the following?

   A: State Funds

   B: Municipalities and political subdivision funds

   C: County funds

   D: Any of the above

Law & Business Exam Part III

23. Every employer must adopt a written code of safe practices which must include _____.

    A: language equivalent to statement of Plate A-3 of the Construction Safety Orders, Title 8

    B: safety guidelines that fit his or her operations more exactly

    C: the code posted at each site office or be provided to each supervisory employee

    D: All of the above

24. The _____, if you change the form of your business, such as from a sole ownership to a partnership or to a corporation, and one or more of the owners of the previous business remains as an owner of the successor business.

    A: employment tax should not be reported

    B: employment tax should continue but under the registration of the new management

    C: employment tax report should be filed as though there was one business for the entire year

    D: employment tax should be changed from the existing account number to a newly assigned number

25. If two or more corporations are combined into one, the continuing corporations are required to _____.

    A: file another return

    B: file a return for both corporations until the terms of the displaced corporation filing period has expired

    C: continue to file a separate return

    D: none of the above

26. If you discontinue your business or permanently cease to pay wages, you should mark your quarterly return "final return" and file it within _____ days of quitting business.

    A: 5

    B: 10

    C: 15

    D: 20

27. The homeowner is entitled to request and receive _____ when he/she makes a payment in full on a progressive draw arrangement.

    A: an unconditional lien release for labor and materials performed up to date

    B: a conditional lien release for work completed up to date

    C: a preliminary lien notice

    D: any of the above

28. The contractor should _____ if after starting a home improvement project the contractor discovers that the details and specifications do not correctly show the existing construction.

    A: stop and work on a correction

    B: stop the job and inform the owner or his agent

    C: continue the work if variations are only minor

    D: stop the job and inform the Building Department

EXAM 3

29. The _____ may require the contractor to obtain a performance and payment bond.

    A: lender

    B: homeowner

    C: subcontractor

    D: Contractor State License Board

30. The State Board of Equalization can require a deposit of the estimated sales tax for _____.

    A: the first quarter

    B: the first 6 months

    C: the first year

    D: the first month

31. Unless _____, the contractor must collect the required sales taxes from the customer.

    A: the customer agrees to take care of it

    B: the tax on materials was already paid at the time of purchase

    C: the contractor has a Seller's Permit

    D: The tax is deducted from the Contractors tax deposit

32. _____ is an insurance that protects the insured contractor from liability to members of the public for bodily injury, property, damage, or personal injury.

    A: Worker's PMs Compensation

    B: Unemployment Insurance

    C: Commercial General Liability (CGL)

    D: Umbrella Coverage

33. The _____ administer the California Workers Compensation Insurance Laws.

    A: State Contractors Board

    B: State Department of Industrial Relations

    C: Office of the Insurance Commissioner

    D: CAL/OSHA

34. The California Worker's Compensation Law establishes a no-fault insurance plan purchased by the contractor in order to _____.

    A: avoid costly law suits for services

    B: guarantee that an employee receives weekly wages for time lost due to an injury

    C: guarantee that an injured worker receives prompt and complete medical treatment and specific benefits

    D: All of the above

35. At which of the following times must every contractor, subject to the provisions of the Worker's Compensation Laws, give written notice to his/her employees of the employee's right to receive worker's compensation benefits?

    A: before hiring

    B: at the time the employee is fired

    C: at the end of the first pay period

    D: B and C

Law & Business Exam Part III

36. Which of the following must an employer-contractor subject to the provisions of the Worker's Compensation Laws do?

A: Post in a conspicuous place a Notice to Employees poster

B: Post information regarding protection

C: Give written notice that an employee is eligible for worker's compensation

D: All of the above

37. Which of the following benefits is a worker entitled to?

A: Medical treatment

B: Supplemental job displacement (re-training)

C: Temporary disability payments

D: All of the above

38. Which of the following becomes applicable if the contractor willfully fails to provide compensation insurance on an employee, and an injury occurs?

A: The contractor must pay a fine and the attorneys fees

B: The contractor must pay the disability compensation plus 10 percent and the attorney fees

C: The contractor has 10 days to secure the coverage of compensation insurance but he/she will still have to pay the cost of the attorney fees

D: The contractor may be subject to a fine of$10,000 and six months in jail

39. Each bidder shall comply with which of the following codes?

A: The chapter of Public Contract Code

B: California's Standard Procedures

C: California's Architects Standards

D: None of the above

40. Which of the following must the bidder set forth in the bid?

A: The name and location of the place of business of each subcontractor who will perform the work

B: A subcontractor who specially fabricates and installs a portion of the work according to plans, in an amount in excess of one- half of 1 percent of the prime contractors bid

C: In the case of construction of streets, or highways, including bridges, in excess of one-half of 1 percent of the direct contractors total bid or ten-thousand dollars$ 10,000 which ever is greater

D: Any of the above

41. Public Code section _____ states that no contractor whose bid is accepted must substitute any person as a subcontractor in place of the subcontractor listed in the original bid.

A: 4100

B: 4110

C: 4113

D: 4107

Law & Business Exam Part III

42. _____, before the work of any subcontractor is started.

   A: The contractor shall review and approve the work to be performed

   B: The contractor must submit to the engineer a description of the work, the value, along with the name and business of each subcontractor

   C: When the amount of the subcontractor's contract is 1-½ percent or less it must be reported

   D: All of the above

43. The use of labor classification which would increase the extra work cost is _____.

   A: not permitted

   B: permitted

   C: assessed

   D: negotiated

44. Which of the following applies to the cost of materials reported?

   A: are in the invoice

   B: are lowest current price available

   C: include cost and delivery

   D: All of the above

45. When it comes to equipment rental, no payment will be made for the use of tools which have a replacement value of ____ or less.

   A: 100

   B: 200

   C: 300

   D: 400

46. Other than _____, a working day is any day within the period between the start of the contract and the date provided for completion.

   A: Saturday or Sunday

   B: Any day the contractor is prevented from working

   C: Designated holidays

   D: All of the above

47. In terms of a working day, to which of the following must a contractor adhere?

   A: the 8 hour day

   B: the 40-hour week

   C: Overtime, Saturday, Sunday and Holiday

   D: All of the above

48. Which of the following statements is true according to the labor code?

   A: The contractor shall provide a schedule of prevailing wage rates.

   B: The board has no file and will publish wage rates for the type of work to be performed.

   C: The agency (awarding authority) will publish the wage rates for the types of work to be performed.

   D: All of the above

EXAM 3

49. True or False: In the Department of Consumer Affairs, there is a Contractors State License Board with members appointed by the Governor.

    A: True   B: False

50. True or False: It is the Registrar's responsibility and duty to carry out all the administrating procedures, since he is the Executive Officer and Secretary of the Contractors State License Board.

    A: True   B: False

51. True or False: Any person who advertises with any sign or card or other device, which indicates to the public that he/she is a contractor, is subject to the provision of the Contractors License Law.

    A: True   B: False

52. True or False: It is a federal crime for any person to advertise as a contractor without that person having a valid contractors' license.

    A: True   B: False

53. True or False: To uphold the Contractors' License Law, the Registrar may act through the Attorney General.

    A: True   B: False

54. True or False: No person engaged in the business of acting in the capacity of a contractor may bring or maintain any action in any court of this state for the collection of compensation for the performance of any act or contract if he/she presents no proof of license.

    A: True   B: False

55. True or False: The Contractors License Law applies to the installation of any finished products, materials or articles of merchandise, which do not become a fixed part of the structure.

    A: True   B: False

56. True or False: The Contractors License Law does not apply to persons who only furnish materials or supply the contractor.

    A: True   B: False

57. True or False: The Contractors License Law does not apply to any work or operation that costs less than five-hundred dollars($500)

    A: True   B: False

58. True or False: A person may advertise as a contractor provided that he or she states in the advertisement that he or she is not licensed

    A: True   B: False

59. True or False: A contractor whose principal contracting business is in connection with any structure built, being built, or to be built, for the support, shelter, and enclosure of persons, animals, chattels, is a general building contractor.

    A: True   B: False

EXAM 3

60. True or False: A specialty contractor may take a contract involving the use of two or more crafts or trades if the performance of the work in the crafts or trades other than in which he is licensed is incidental or supplemental in the work.

    A: True   B: False

61. True or False: All licensees must notify the registrar in writing, within 90 days, of any change to information recorded under this chapter.

    A: True   B: False

62. True or False: A complaint against a licensee alleging commission of any patent acts or omissions that may be grounds for legal action must be filed in writing with the registrar within 6 years after the act or omission alleged as the ground for the disciplinary action.

    A: True   B: False

63. True or False: If a license is suspended or revoked following a hearing and was issued through the experience of a qualifying individual, any additional licenses qualified by the same individual may not be suspended by the Registrar without further notice.

    A: True   B: False

64. True or False: If the licensee voluntarily surrenders his license all disciplinary action or proceedings against him/her are dropped.

    A: True   B: False

65. True or False: A licensees must make and keep records showing all contracts, documents and receipts of disbursements for period of ten (10) years after completion of any construction project or operation to which the records refer to.

    A: True   B: False

66. True or False: Entering into a contract with an unlicensed contractor is acceptable and thus not a cause for disciplinary action.

    A: True   B: False

67. True or False: Any licensee who violates requirements or omits information in order to comply with any (or all) of the provisions of the Workmen's Compensation Insurance Report and the provisions of the Contractors License Law is guilty of a federal offence.

    A: True   B: False

68. True or False: A responsible managing employee shall be responsible for exercising direct supervision and control of his employers' construction operations to secure full compliance with the rules and regulations relating to such construction operation.

    A: True   B: False

69. True or False: Any person, or agent or officer thereof, who refused admission to the Labor Commissioner or his/her deputy or agent, is guilty of a felony, punishable by law.

    A: True   B: False

Law & Business Exam Part III

70. True or False: If an employer discharges an employee, the wages earned and unpaid at the time of discharge must be paid within 72 hours.

    A: True   B: False

71. True or False: If an employee not having a written contract for a definite period quits his employment, his wages must be payable not later than 72 hours thereafter.

    A: True   B: False

72. True or False: If an employer willfully fails to pay any wages of an employee who is discharged or who quits, the employee will continue at the same rate, as if still working, until paid or until an action is commenced.

    A: True   B: False

73. True or False: Employees, who are paid weekly, must be paid no later than 7 days after their regular work week.

    A: True   B: False

74. True or False: In a dispute over wages between employer and an employee, the employer is not required to pay any amount until instructed to do so by the Labor Commissioner.

    A: True   B: False

75. True or False: In the event of any strike, the unpaid wages earned by striking employees are due and payable on the next regular pay day.

    A: True   B: False

76. True or False: 8 hours of labor constitute a days' work.

    A: True   B: False

77. True or False: An employer may require for an employee to work seven or more consecutive days.

    A: True   B: False

78. True or False: The state of California allows jurisdictional strikes.

    A: True   B: False

79. True or False: All wages earned in any continuous employment are due and payable twice during each calendar month.

    A: True   B: False

80. True or False: When a member of the family is employed by the licensee, the licensee is not required to provide the family member workers compensation insurance coverage.

    A: True   B: False

81. True or False: It is unlawful for an employer to withhold or divert any portion of an employee's wages under all circumstances.

    A: True   B: False

EXAM 3

82. If a bond or photograph of an employee is required by the employer, the employee must pay for it.

    A: True   B: False

83. True or False: If the employee either expressly or impliedly assumed the risk of the hazard complained of, he/she cannot recover damages for the personal injury.

    A: True   B: False

84. True or False: If the employee was guilty of contributory negligence that resulted in the injuries he/she is filing complaint for, the employer must be excused from paying compensation.

    A: True   B: False

85. True or False: A report must be filed within ten (10) stating the injury or illness to the Division of Labor Statistics and Research or the workers' compensation insurance carrier.

    A: True   B: False

86. "Employee" is a person in the service of an employer and that is lawfully employed.

    A: True   B: False

87. True or False: Every employer must secure the payment of compensation by being self insured.

    A: True   B: False

88. True or False: If any employer fails to secure the payment of compensation, any injured employee or his dependents may bring an action at law against such employer for damages.

    A: True   B: False

89. True or False: If the employee brings a compensation dispute into court action, the injured employee or his dependents may not attach the property of the employer.

    A: True   B: False

90. If an injury on the job causes death, with or without disability, the employer shall be liable and must provide benefits set forth by this division, including to pay up to$2000 for the employee's burial expenses.

    A: True   B: False

91. True or False: All employees must inform their employers of injury or illness with 60 days of injury or illness.

    A: True   B: False

92. True or False: The date of injury, except in cases of occupational disease or cumulative injury, is that date during the employment on which occurred the alleged incident or exposure, for the consequences of which compensation is claimed.

    A: True   B: False

93. True or False: The burden of proof is always on the employee.

    A: True   B: False

EXAM 3

94. True or False: It is required for the employer to post a notice stating the name of the current compensation insurance carrier of the employer, in a place clearly and easily visible by the employees.

    A: True   B: False

95. True or False: Injuries and death are only reported to the dependents of the employee and to the worker's compensation provider.

    A: True   B: False

96. An injured employee may not select his own physician.

    A: True   B: False

97. True or False: Workers' Compensation Insurance premiums are based upon: specification of work duties and the rate assigned to each employee classification.

    A: True   B: False

98. True or False: If a claim of workers' compensation has been paid by all due process of law, but an aggravation arises from the old injury, the employee may not open a claim.

    A: True   B: False

99. True or False: If a work of improvement consists in the construction of two or more separate residential units, each such unit must be considered a separate "work of improvement," and the time for filing claims of lien against each such residential unit must commence to run upon the completion of each such residential unit.

    A: True   B: False

100. True or False: Labor is usually the easiest item to estimate.

    A: True   B: False

EXAM 3

1. **Answer D.** a 2 percent discount will be on the price of the bill if it is is paid between the 10th and the 15th of the month following the date of billing

   If the terms of sale with the supplier state 2 percent, 10, net 15 this translates to the following: 2 percent discount will be on the price of the bill, the bill is paid between the 10th and the 15th of the month of the following date of billing.",

2. **Answer B.** insist on cash upon completion of project

   Insisting on cash upon completion of a project (even on service calls) is not advisable.

3. **Answer B.** through a standard policy from the director of industrial relations or with their approval, self insurance

   California workers compensation laws require you to obtain insurance protection through a standard policy from the director of industrial relations or with their approval, self insurance.

4. **Answer D.** you (the contractor) are liable for the injuries under your workmen's compensation

   If a subcontractor gets injured while working for you and the subcontractor does not have insurance you (the contractor) are liable for the injuries under your workers compensation.

5. **Answer D.** Neither a public or private agency can ask an applicant about their arrest record if the arrest was not followed by a conviction.

   (a) No employer, whether a public agency or private individual or corporation, shall ask an applicant for employment to disclose, through any written form or verbally, information concerning an arrest or detention that did not result in conviction, or information concerning a referral to, and participation in, any pretrial or posttrial diversion program, nor shall any employer seek from any source whatsoever, or utilize, as a factor in determining any condition of employment including hiring, promotion, termination, or any apprenticeship training program or any other training program leading to employment, any record of arrest or detention that did not result in conviction, or any record regarding a referral to, and participation in, any pretrial or posttrial diversion program. As used in this section, a conviction shall include a plea, verdict, or finding of guilt regardless of whether sentence is imposed by the court. Nothing in this section shall prevent an employer from asking an employee or applicant for employment about an arrest for which the employee or applicant is out on bail or on his or her own recognizance pending trial. (California Labor Code 432.7)

6. **Answer B.** 15 working days

   A contractor has been served with a citation. The citation is in regards to a complaint filed against the contractor for violation of the license law. The citation will be deemed a final order unless it is appealed within 15 working days.

7. **Answer A.** suspension or revocation of the contractor's license

   Failure for the contractor to conform with the terms of a citation after its been made final can result in suspension or revocation of the contractor's license.

8. **Answer D.** All of the above

   In situations where the Registrar can issue a citation, the citation must include: a description explaining the nature of the violation, reference to the specific division of the license law that was violated and an order of correction fixing a reasonable time for correction.

9. **Answer B.** Title 24, California Administrative Code

   Title 24, California Administrative Code states regulations for the accommodation of the disabled and requirements regarding accessibility to building for the handicapped.

10. **Answer C.** a specialty contractor's license for painting and flooring

    At a minimum, the person who is to do a project that requires carpets to be changes and walls to be repainted should have a specialty contractor's license for painting and flooring.

11. **Answer C.** Both the owner and contractor

    The construction contract must be signed by both he owner and the contractor.

12. **Answer B.** go over the plans and specifications with the owner and discuss every aspect of the work

    To best ensure that disputes do not arise, the contractor should go over the plans and specifications with the owner and discuss every aspect of the work.

13. **Answer D.** discuss the price and suggest lessening the scope of the project

    If an owner asks a contractor to submit a bid package, but the owner decides that the price is too high, the contractor should discuss the price and suggest lessening the scope of the project.

14. **Answer D.** insist that it be built to code even if you loose the job

    If the contractor finds that the owner's desires conflict with the current codes, the contractor should insist that it be built to code even if it means losing the job.

15. **Answer D.** order materials and begin the project

    After the architect gives the O.K. the contractor should order materials and begin the job.

16. **Answer B.** when you substantially deviate from the original plans

    The "as-built" drawings should be updated when you substantially deviate from the original plans.

EXAM 3

Answers: Law & Business Exam Part III

17. **Answer B.** a contract contains a clause requiring the contractor to submit detailed plans showing the design of the shoring, bracing, or sloping to provide protection from caving ground

Unless a contract contains a clause requiring the contractor to submit detailed plans showing the design of the shoring, bracing, or sloping to provide protection from caving ground, no contract for public works involving an estimated expenditure in excess of twenty five thousand dollars ($25,000) for the excavation of any trench 5 feet or more in depth shall be awarded.

18. **Answer D.** begin a line of credit

The best strategy to obtain short-term working capital is to begin a line of credit.

19. **Answer B.** mark up labor only

Marking up labor only is a simple but adequate way to add the overhead costs to your estimate.

20. **Answer D.** All of the above

In order to determine whether something is an "extra" when it comes to major distribution disputes you must be able to interpret the original agreement, you must be sure the agreement is well defined, and determine whether you are being asked to do something different.

21. **Answer B.** State Architect

The State Architects are authorized to propose and adopt standards and other regulations as necessary for making buildings, structures, sidewalks, curbs and related facilities accessible to and useable by persons with physical disabilities.

22. **Answer D.** Any of the above

The division of the State Architect must review and approve plans and specifications on any projects for schools and colleges, using State funds, county funds, municipalities and political subdivision funds.

23. **Answer D.** All of the above

Every employer must adopt a written code of safe practices which must include: language equivalent to statement of Plate A-3 OF THE Construction Safety Orders, title 8, safety guidelines that fit his or her operations more exactly, the code posted at each site office or be provided to each supervisory employee.

24. **Answer C.** employment tax report should be filed as though there was one business for the entire year

If you change the form of your business, such as from a sole ownership to a partnership or to a corporation, and one or more of the owners of the previous business remains as an owner of the successor business the employment tax report should be filed as though there was one business for the entire year.

25. **Answer A.** file another return

If two or more corporations are combined into one, the continuing corporations are required to file another return.

26. **Answer B.** 10

If you discontinue your business or permanently cease to pay wages, you should mark your quarterly return "final return" and file it within 10 days of quitting business.

27. **Answer A.** an unconditional lien release for labor and materials performed up to date

When a homeowner makes a payment in full on a progressive draw arrangement, the homeowner is entitle to request and receive an unconditional lien release for labor and materials performed up to date.

28. **Answer B.** stop the job and inform the owner or his agent

The contractor should stop the job and inform the owner or his agent if after starting a home improvement project the contractor discovers that the details and specifications do not correctly show the existing construction.

29. **Answer B.** homeowner

The homeowner may require the contractor to obtain a performance and payment bond.

30. **Answer B.** the first 6 months

The State Board of Equalization can require a deposit of the estimated sales tax for the first 6 months.

31. **Answer B.** the tax on materials was already paid at the time of purchase

The contractor must collect the required sales tax from the customer unless the tax on materials was already paid at the time of purchase.

32. **Answer C.** Commercial General Liability (CGL)

Commercial General Liability (CGL) is an insurance that protects the insured contractor from liability to members of the public for bodily injury, property, damage, or personal injury. This insurance provider, provides a claim handling service, pays claims for covered damages and depends on the contractor.

33. **Answer B.** State Department of Industrial Relations

The California Workers Compensation Insurance Laws are administered by the State Department of Industrial Relations.

34. **Answer C.** guarantee that an injured worker receives prompt and complete medical treatment and specific benefits

The California Worker's Compensation Law establishes a no-fault insurance plan purchased by the contractor in order to guarantee that an injured worker receives prompt and complete medical treatment and specific benefits.

EXAM 3

35. **Answer D.** B and C

    Every contractor subject to the provisions of the Worker's Compensation Laws must give written notice to his/her employees of the employee's right to receive worker's compensation benefits at the end of the first pay period and at the time the employee is fired.

36. **Answer D.** All of the above

    Every employer-contractor subject to the provisions of the Worker's Compensation Laws must: post a Notice to Employees poster in a conspicuous place, post information regarding protection and Give written notice than an employee is eligible for worker's compensation.

37. **Answer D.** All of the above

    A worker is entitled to all of the following benefits:\n \t\n1. Medical treatment\n2. Supplemental job displacement (re-training)\n3. Rehabilitation\n4. Temporary disability payments\n5. Permanent disability payments\n6. Dependants to receive death benefits\n7. Compensation for serious and willful misconduct of employer

38. **Answer B.** The contractor must pay the disability compensation plus 10 percent and the attorney fees

    If a contractor willfully fails to provide compensation insurance on an employee, and an injury occurs, the contractor must pay the disability compensation plus 10 percent and the attorney fees.

39. **Answer A.** The chapter of Public Contract Code

    Each bidder must comply with the chapter of Public Contract Code.

40. **Answer D.** Any of the above

    The bidder shall set forth in the bid: \n \t\n1. The name and location of the place of business of each subcontractor who will perform the work.\n\n2. A subcontractor who specially fabricates and installs a portion of the work according to plans, in an amount in excess of one- half of 1 percent of the prime contractors bid.\n\ n3. In the case of construction of streets, or highways, including bridges, in excess of one-half of 1 percent of the prime contractors total bid or ten-thousand dollars$ 10,000 which ever is greater.

41. **Answer D.** 4107

    Public Code section 4107 states that no contractor whose bid is accepted must substitute any person as a subcontractor in place of the subcontractor listed in the original bid.

42. **Answer B.** The contractor must submit to the engineer a description of the work, the value, along with the name and business of each subcontractor

    The contractor must submit to the engineer a description of the work, the value, along with the name and business of each subcontractor, before the work of any subcontractor is started.

43. **Answer A.** not permitted

    The use of labor classification which would increase the extra work cost is not permitted.

44. **Answer D.** All of the above

    The cost of materials reported shall be in an invoice, be the lowest current price available and include cost and delivery.

45. **Answer B.** 200

    When it comes to equipment rental, no payment will be made for the use of tools which have a replacement value of$200 or less.

46. **Answer D.** All of the above

    A working day is any day within the period between the start of the contract and the date provided for completion. Working days shall exclude Saturdays, Sundays, designated Holidays or any days the contractor is prevented from working.

47. **Answer D.** All of the above

    In terms of a working day, a contractor shall adhere to: the 8-hour working day, 40 hours working week, overtime requirements for work during the weekend or holiday.

48. **Answer B.** The board has no file and will publish wage rates for the type of work to be performed.

    According to the labor code: The board has no file and will publish wage rates for the type of work to be performed.

49. **Answer A.** True

    In the Department of Consumer Affairs, there is a Contractors State License Board with members appointed by the Governor.

50. **Answer A.** True

    The Registrar shall be Executive Officer and Secretary of the Contractors State License Board and it is his duty to carry out all the administrating procedures.

51. **Answer A.** True

    Any person who advertises with any sign or card or other device, which would indicate to the public that he/she is a contractor, is subject to the provision of the Contractors License Law regardless whether operations as a builder would be otherwise exempted.

52. **Answer B.** False

    It is a misdemeanor for any person to advertise as a contractor unless such person holds a valid contractors' license. It is unlawful for any person to engage in the business or act in the capacity of a contractor within this state without having a license, this may result in the individual being guilty of a misdemeanor, fined or imprisoned in the county jail or both.

53. **Answer A.** True

    The Registrar may act through the Attorney General to uphold the Contractors' License Law. The Registrar may act through the District Attorney of the county in which the act practice or transaction is alleged to have been committed to in order to uphold the Contractors' License Law.

EXAM 3

54. **Answer A.** True

No person engaged in the business of acting in the capacity of a contractor may bring or maintain any action in any court of this state for the collection of compensation for the performance of any act or contract for which a license is required by this chapter without alleging and proving that he/she was truly a licensed contractor at all times during the performance of such act or contract.

55. **Answer B.** False

The contractor's License Law does not apply to the installation of any finished products, materials or articles of merchandise, which do not become a fixed part of the structure, nor shall it apply to a material supplier or manufacturer furnishing finished products, materials, or articles of merchandise who does not install or contract for the installation of those items.(CBPC 7045)

56. **Answer A.** True

The Contractors License Law does not apply to persons who only furnish materials or supply them, without fabricating them into, installing or using them in the performance of the work of the contractor.(CBPC 7052)

57. **Answer A.** True

The Contractors License Law does not apply to any work or operation on one undertaking or project by one or more contracts, the aggregate contract price which for labor, materials, and all other items, is less than five hundred dollars ($500), that work or operations being considered of casual, minor, or inconsequential nature.\n\nThis exemption does not apply in any case wherein the work of construction is only a part of a larger or major operation, whether undertaken by the same or a different contractor, or in which a division of the operation is made in contracts of amounts less than five hundred dollars ($500) for the purpose of evasion of this chapter or otherwise.\n\nThis exemption does not apply to a person who advertises or puts out any sign or card or other device which might indicate to the public that he or she is a contractor or that he or she is qualified to engage in the business of a contractor. (CBPC 7048)

58. **Answer B.** False

Any person may advertise for construction work or work of improvement but NOT under the title of contractor if they are not licensed. If they are not licensed they may advertise but they must state in the advertisement that they are not licensed.

59. **Answer A.** True

A general building contractor is a contractor whose principal contracting business is in connection with any structure built, being built, or to be built for the support, shelter, and enclosure of persons, animals, chattels, or movable property of any kind, requiring in its construction the use of at least two unrelated building trades or crafts, or to do or superintend the whole or any part thereof.

60. **Answer A.** True

A specialty contractor may take a contract involving the use of two or more crafts or trades if the performance of the work in the crafts or trades other than in which he is licensed is incidental or supplemental to the performance of the work in the craft for which the specialty contractor is licensed.

61. **Answer A.** True

All licensees must notify the registrar, on a form prescribed by the registrar, in writing within 90 days of any change to information recorded under this chapter. Failure to notify the registrar of the changes within the 90 days is grounds for disciplinary action.

62. **Answer B.** False

A complaint against a licensee alleging commission of any patent acts or omissions that may be grounds for legal action must be filed in writing with the registrar within 4 years after the act or omission alleged as the ground for the disciplinary action.

63. **Answer B.** False

When any license has been suspended by a decision of the registrar pursuant to an accusation or pursuant to subdivision any additional license issued under this chapter in the name of the licensee or for which the licensee furnished qualifying experience and appearance under the provisions of Section 7068, may be suspended by the registrar without further notice.

64. **Answer B.** False

The performance by any individual, partnership, corporation, firm, or association of any act or omission constituting a cause for disciplinary action, likewise constitutes a cause for disciplinary action against any licensee who at the time such act or omission occurred was the responsible managing employee, qualifying partner, responsible managing officer, or qualifying member of such individual, partnership, corporation, firm, or association, whether or not he had knowledge of or participated in the prohibited act or omission.

65. **Answer B.** False

A license must make and keep records showing all contracts, documents and receipts of disbursements for period of five (5) years after completion of any construction project or operation to which the records refer.\n\nFailure to make and keep records showing all contracts, documents, records, receipts, and disbursements by a licensee of all of his or her transactions as a contractor, and failure to have those records available for inspection by the registrar or his or her duly authorized representative for a period of not less than five years after completion of any construction project or operation to which the records refer, or refusal by a licensee to comply with a written request of the registrar to make the records available for inspection constitutes a cause for disciplinary action.

66. **Answer B.** False

Knowingly entering into a contract with an unlicensed contractor is a cause for disciplinary action by the Registrar of Contractors'.

67. **Answer B.** False

Any licensee or agent or officer thereof, who violates the requirements or omits information to comply with any (or all)of the provisions of the Contractors License Law, which includes the provisions of the Workmen's Compensation Insurance Report, is guilty of a misdemeanor.

68. **Answer A.** True

A responsible managing employee shall be responsible for exercising direct supervision and control of his employers' construction operations to secure full compliance with the rules and regulations relating to such construction operation.

EXAM 3

69. Answer B. False

Any person, or agent or officer thereof, who refused admission to the Labor Commissioner or his/her deputy or agent, is guilty of a misdemeanor, punishable by a fine.

70. Answer B. False

If an employer discharges an employee, the wages earned and unpaid at the time of discharge are due and payable immediately. (California Labor Code Section 201)

71. Answer A. True

If an employee not having a written contract for a definite period quits his employment, his wages shall become due and payable not later than 72 hours thereafter, unless the employee has given 72 hours previous notice of his intention to quit, in which case the employee is entitled to his wages at the time of quitting.

72. Answer A. True

If an employer willfully fails to pay any wages of an employee who is discharged or who quits, as a penalty the wages of such employee must continue (for a maximum of 30 days) at the same rate until paid or until an action is commenced.

73. Answer A. True

Employees, who are paid weekly, must be paid no later than 7 days after their regular work week.

74. Answer B. False

In case of a dispute over wages, the employer must pay, without condition and within the time set by the California Labor Code, all wages, or parts thereof, conceded by him to be due, leaving to the employee all remedies he might otherwise be entitled to as to any balance claimed.\n\nIf, after an investigation and hearing, the Labor Commissioner has determined the validity of any employee's claim for wages, the claim is due and payable within 10 days after receipt of notice is given to the employer that such wages are due. \n\nAny employer having the ability to pay who willfully fails to pay such wages within 10 days shall, in addition to any other applicable penalty, pay triple the amount of any damages occurring to the employee as a direct and foreseeable consequence of the failure of the employer to pay. (California Labor Code 206)

75. Answer A. True

In the event of any strike, the unpaid wages earned by striking employees are due and payable on the next regular pay day, and the payment or settlement thereof must include all amounts due the striking employees without abatement or reduction. The employer must return to each striking employee any deposit, money, or other guaranty required by him from the employee for the faithful performance of the duties of the employment. (California Labor Code 209)

76. Answer A. True

Eight hours of labor constitutes a day's work. However, a workday's hours can be extended, as long as the employer abides by the rules of overtime and the such. \n\nAny work in excess of 8 hours in one workday and any work in excess of 40 hours in any one workweek and the first eight hours worked on the seventh day of work in any one workweek must be compensated at the rate of no less than one and one-half times the regular rate of pay for an employee. \n\nAny work in excess of 12 hours in one day must be compensated at the rate of no less than twice the regular rate of pay for an employee. \n\nIn addition, any work in excess of eight hours on any seventh day of a workweek must be compensated at the rate of no less than twice the regular rate of pay of an employee. (California Labor Code 510)

77. Answer A. True

An employer may require for an employee to work seven or more consecutive days, as long as the employee receives during the calendar month the equivalent rests days as one day's rest in seven. (California Labor Code 554)

78. Answer B. False

A jurisdictional strike is against the public policy of the State of California and is hereby and therefore declared unlawful. (California Labor Code 1115)

79. Answer A. True

All wages earned by any person in any employment are due and payable twice during each calendar month, on days designated in advance by the employer as the regular paydays. \n\nLabor performed between the 1st and 15th days, inclusive, of any calendar month must be paid for between the 16th and the 26th day of the month during which the labor was performed, and labor performed between the 16th and the last day, inclusive, of any calendar month, shall be paid for between the 1st and 10th day of the following month.

80. Answer B. False

When a member of the family is employed by the licensee, the licensee is required to provide the family member with workers compensation insurance coverage, just as he is required to provide workers compensation to any other of his hired workers.

81. Answer B. False

Under the following circumstances, it is not unlawful for the employer to withhold or divert wages from the employee:\n\n1. When the employer is required or empowered so to do by state or federal law. \n\n2. When a deduction is expressly authorized in writing by the employee to cover insurance premiums, hospital or medical dues, or other deductions not amounting to a rebate or deduction from the standard wage arrived at by collective bargaining or pursuant to wage agreement or statute. \n\n3. When a deduction to cover health and welfare or pension plan contributions is expressly authorized by a collective bargaining or wage agreement. \n\n(California Labor Code 224)

82. Answer B. False

If a bond or photograph of an employee or applicant is required by any employer, the cost thereof must be paid by the employer. (California Labor Code 401)

EXAM 3

83. **Answer B.** False

It must be presumed that the employee was not guilty of contributory negligence. \n\nThe following cannot be used as defense:\n\n   1. The employee either expressly or impliedly assumed the risk of the hazard complained of.\n\n   2. The injury or death was caused in whole or in part by the want of ordinary or reasonable care of a fellow servant.\n\nNote: No contract, or regulation, exempts the employer from any provisions of this section. (California Labor Code 2801)

84. **Answer B.** False

It is not a defense to the employer that the employee was guilty of contributory negligence, or assumed the risk of the hazard complained of, or that the injury was caused by the negligence of a fellow servant. No contract or regulation shall restore to the employer any of the foregoing defenses. (California Labor Code 3708)

85. **Answer B.** False

An employer must file a report with the Division of Labor Statistics and Research or the workers' compensation insurance carrier for every occupational injury or illness that results in loss-time beyond the date of injury or illness, or that requires medical treatment beyond first aid. This report must be filed within five (5) days after the employer learns of the injury or illness. A death or serious injury or illness (requiring hospitalization for more than 24 hours other than for purpose of observation) must be reported to the Division of Occupational Safety and Health by telephone or telegraph within 24 hours after the employer knows or should have known of the death or illness. (Title 8, California Code of Regulations, 342)

86. **Answer B.** False

"Employee" means every person in the service of an employer under any appointment or contract of hire or apprenticeship, express or implied, oral or written, whether lawfully or unlawfully employed, and includes:\n\n   (a) Aliens and minors.\n\n   (b) All elected and appointed paid public officers.\n\n (California Labor Code 3351)

87. **Answer A.** True

Every employer, except the state, must secure the payment of compensation in one or more of the following ways: \n\n(a) By being insured against liability to pay compensation by one or more insurers duly authorized to write compensation insurance in this state.\n\n(b) By securing from the Director of Industrial Relations a certificate of consent to self-insure either as an individual employer, or as one employer in a group of employers, which may be given upon furnishing proof satisfactory to the Director of Industrial Relations of ability to self-insure and to pay any compensation that may become due to his or her employees.\n\n(c) by securing from the Director of Industrial Relations a certificate of consent to self-insure against workers' compensation claims. which certificate may be given upon furnishing proof satisfactory to the director of ability to administer workers' compensation claims properly, and to pay workers' compensation claims that may become due to its employees.\n(California Labor Code 3700)

88. **Answer A.** True

If any employer fails to secure the payment of compensation, any injured employee or his dependents may bring an action at law against such employer for damages, as if this division did not apply. (California Labor Code 3706)

89. **Answer B.** False

The injured employee or his dependents may in such action attach the property of the employer, at any time upon or after the institution of such action, in an amount fixed by the court, to secure the payment of any judgment which is ultimately obtained. The provisions of the Code of Civil Procedure, not inconsistent with this division, must govern the issuance of, and proceedings upon such attachment.

90. **Answer B.** False

When an injury causes death, either with or without disability, the employer shall be liable, in addition to any other benefits provided by this division, for all of the following:\n\n   (a) Reasonable expenses of the employee's burial, not exceeding two thousand dollars ($2,000) and for injuries occurring on and after January 1, 1991, not exceeding five thousand dollars ($5,000).\n\n   (b) A death benefit, to be allowed to the dependents when the employee leaves any person dependent upon him or her for support. (California Labor Code 4701)

91. **Answer B.** False

An employee who suffers a work-related injury or illness that requires medical treatment beyond first aid must notify his or her employer in writing within 30 days of the injury or illness. (Labor Code 5400) An employer must provide a claim form to an employee within 24 hours of the reported work-related injury or illness. (Labor Code 5401) \n\nAdditionally, all employers, except the state, are required to have workers' compensation insurance cover injuries or illnesses sustained on the job. (Labor Code 3700, et seq.) \n\nNote: Contact the Division of Workers Compensation for more information regarding workers' compensation claims and benefits or visit their website for information at (www.dir.ca.gov/dwc.)

92. **Answer A.** True

The date of injury, except in cases of occupational disease or cumulative injury, is that date during the employment on which occurred the alleged incident or exposure, for the consequences of which compensation is claimed. (California Labor Code 5411)

EXAM 3

93. Answer B. False

The burden of proof falls on either the employee or employer, it depends on the situation.\n\nAll parties and lien claimants must meet the evidentiary burden of proof on all issues by a preponderance of the evidence in order that all parties are considered equal before the law. "Preponderance of the evidence" means that evidence that, when weighed with that opposed to it, has more convincing force and the greater probability of truth. When weighing the evidence, the test is not the relative number of witnesses, but the relative convincing force of the evidence. (California Labor Code 3202.5)\n\nWhere the employee's injury is aggravated by the employer's fraudulent concealment of the existence of the injury and its connection with the employment, in which case the employer's liability must be limited to those damages proximately caused by the aggravation. The burden of proof respecting apportionment of damages between the injury and any subsequent aggravation thereof is upon the employer. (California Labor Code 3600)

94. Answer A. True

(a) Every employer subject to the compensation provisions of this division must post and keep posted in a conspicuous location frequented by employees, and where the notice may be easily read by employees during the hours of the workday, a notice that states the name of the current compensation insurance carrier of the employer, or when such is the fact, that the employer is self-insured, and who is responsible for claims adjustment.\n \n(b) Failure to keep any notice required by this section conspicuously posted constitutes as a misdemeanor and must be prima facie (the apparent nature of something upon initial observation) evidence of non-insurance.

95. Answer B. False

(a) Every employer must file a complete report of every occupational injury or occupational illness, as defined in subdivision (b) of Section 6409, to each employee which results in lost time beyond the date of the injury or illness, or which requires medical treatment beyond first aid. An insured employer shall file the report with the insurer on a form prescribed by the Administrative Director of the Division of Workers' Compensation\n\nEach report of occupational injury or occupational illness must indicate the social security number of the injured employee. In the event an employer has filed a report of injury or illness pursuant to this subdivision and the employee subsequently dies as a result of the reported injury or illness, the employer must file an amended report indicating the death with the Department of Industrial Relations, through its Division of Workers' Compensation or, if an insured employer, with the insurer, within five days after the employer is notified or learns of the death.\n\n(b) In every case involving a serious injury or illness, or death, in addition to the report required by subdivision (a), a report must be made immediately by the employer to the Division of Occupational Safety and Health by telephone or telegraph. (California Labor Code 6409.1)

96. Answer B. False

Health care services required by this article to be provided to injured employees, those employees who are subject to the contract shall receive medical services in the manner prescribed in the contract, providing that the employee may choose to be treated by a personal physician, personal chiropractor, or personal acupuncturist that he or she has designated prior to the injury, in which case the employee must not be treated by the health care organization. Every employee must be given an affirmative choice at the time of employment and at least annually thereafter to designate or change the designation of a health care organization or a personal physician, personal chiropractor, or personal acupuncturist. The choice must be memorialized in writing and maintained in the employee's personnel records. The employee who has designated a personal physician, personal chiropractor, or personal acupuncturist may change their designated caregiver at any time prior to the injury. Any employee who fails to designate a personal physician, personal chiropractor, or personal acupuncturist shall be treated by the health care organization selected by the employer. If the health care organization offered by the employer is the workers' compensation insurer that covers the employee or is an entity that controls or is controlled by that insurer, as defined by Section 1215 of the Insurance Code, this information must be included in the notice of contract with a health care organization.(California Labor Code 4600.3)

97. Answer A. True

Workers' compensation premium calculation is based upon how employees are classified according to their specific work duties and the rate assigned to each corresponding employee classification. Classifications are developed and assigned by the workers' compensation Insurance Rating Bureau (WCIRB) in most cases.(California Insurance Code)

98. Answer B. False

Even if the original claim has been settled, if an aggravation arises from the old injury the employee may file another claim.

99. Answer A. True

If a work of improvement consists in the construction of two or more separate residential units, each such unit is considered a separate "work of improvement," and the time for filing claims of lien against each such residential unit must commence to run upon the completion of each such residential unit. A separate residential unit means one residential structure, including a residential structure containing multiple condominium units, together with any common area, or any garage or other improvements appurtenant thereto.(California Civil Code 3131)

100. Answer B. False

Labor is usually the most difficult item to estimate. \n\nAccuracy in estimating labor can be improved greatly by establishing an experience record through job costing which will assist in estimating similar types of jobs in the future. Labor should also be estimated at cost. It is important to remember to add the direct labor burden to cost of labor.",

---

EXAM 4

Law & Business Exam Part IV

1.   True or False: The person filing a claim for several buildings owned by one person must at the same time designate the amount due to him on each of such works of improvement; otherwise the lien of such claim is postponed to other liens.

     A: True   B: False

2.   Within the Department of Industrial relations, DOSH is given the authority to implement and enforce the _____ program.

     A: EPA   C: DOSH

     B: CAL/OSHA   D: Safety

3.   What is the DOSH program's objective?

     A: To make sure that amends or repeals can be adopted   C: To ensure safe and healthful working conditions for employees

     B: To make sure that free on-site consultation services are provided   D: All of the above

4.   Which of the following is part of the IIPP program guidelines?

     A: including a system for communicating with employees   C: every employer must ensure the availability of emergency medical services for his/her employees

     B: including a system for identifying, evaluation and controlling existing or potential workplace hazards   D: All of the above

5.   Any injury which requires inpatient hospitalization for a period in exceeding _____ hours is classified as a serious injury or illness.

     A: 8   C: 24

     B: 12   D: 48

6.   Every occupational injury that results in absence from work for a full day or shift beyond the date of the injury, requires the employer to file a complete report about it.

     A: full day   C: minimum of 24 hours

     B: minimum of 4 hours   D: None of the above

7.   Except for employers who had no more than _____ employees, employers must keep records when injuries or illness occurs on a CAL/OSHA 300 form.

     A: 2   C: 10

     B: 5   D: 20

8. Before and employer undertakes _____, must he/she obtain a permit from the DOSH Enforcement Unit?

   A: Constructing building, false-work, scaffolding more than three stories high (36') in height

   B: Trenches 5 feet or more deep for persons

   C: Demolition of structures, false-work, scaffolding more than the three stories high

   D: Any of the above

9. If an employer demonstrates that an equivalent method will provide better safety for employees he/she may apply for a permanent variance from the established safety standard from which he is varying from to the _____.

   A: DOSH

   B: CAL/OSHA

   C: Standard Board

   D: Any of the above

10. Any one who plans _____ must contact a Regional Notification Center.

    A: to dig

    B: to drill

    C: on boring

    D: All of the above

11. The Regional Notification Centers for underground services alert, will issue an identification number that will be valid for _____ days.

    A: 12

    B: 14

    C: 28

    D: 30

12. _____ using the operator's markings, an excavator must determine the exact location of underground facilities.

    A: By researching the maps recorded within the county where the work is to be performed

    B: By contact all utility companies operating within the boundaries of the property

    C: With hand tools before any power equipment may be used

    D: All of the above

13. In every case involving a serious injury of illness or death the employer must immediately report the incident by _____.

    A: telephone

    B: telegraph

    C: e-mail

    D: fax

Law & Business Exam Part IV

14. Consider the following scenario: Assume that you allow CAL/OSHA investigators to check out questionable equipment and that they find one of these to be in dangerous condition. As a result CAL/OSHA can issue a notice that _____.

   A: prohibits use of this equipment until it is made safe

   B: prohibits any further work on the project

   C: advises all the employees that the equipment isn't safe and extreme care should be taken when it is used

   D: States you will refund a thousand ($1,000.00) for each day that this equipment is used before being repaired

15. Consider the scenario in the previous question. Suppose you decide to go ahead and use the equipment (in the previous question) for only 2 more days in order to meet a deadline. To do so you temporarily remove the notice off of the equipment. What can be the consequences of this action?

   A: you will have to pay a one thousand dollars penalty

   B: your contractors' license can be automatically suspended and you may be fined one thousand dollars ($1,000.00)

   C: you will be charged with a misdemeanor punishable by a fine of up to one thousand dollars (1,000.00) a day or a year in the city jail

   D: you will be charged with a felony punishable by a fine of one thousand dollars ($1,000.00) a day it is used or a one (1) year prison sentence

16. There is a complaint filed with D.O.S.H. by an anonymous employee about an unsafe condition within the construction project. As a result the contractor wants to fire the employee who filed the complaint, the contractor _____.

   A: may request the name of the employee who filed the complaint and can fire the person if he wants

   B: cannot request the name of the employees who filed the complaint but has a right to investigate who it was and fire the person

   C: may request the name of the employee who filed the complaint, but does not have a right to fire the person

   D: the contractor cannot request the name of the employee who filed the complaint and cannot fire the employee

17. _____ is responsible for providing safety equipment and supplies.

   A: D.O.S.H

   B: The contractor

   C: The owner

   D: The foreman/supervisor

18. Which of the following are not required by Construction Safety Orders?

   A: keeping a copy of the standards on the job

   B: following and making sure the employees follow the requirements of these standards at all times

   C: knowing which of the standards apply to the work that you do

   D: reviewing these standards every week

Law & Business Exam Part IV

19. Scaffolding requires a safety railing to be present on the equipment above the height of _____.

    A: 5 feet

    B: 6 feet, 6 inches

    C: 7 feet

    D: 7 feet, 6 inches

20. Each employer is required to post the CAL/OSHA notice Safety and Health Protection on the Job along with the Code of Safe Practices _____.

    A: in the supervisors office

    B: at the job site

    C: quarterly with the employees paycheck

    D: at each location where employees report to work each day or where they operate activities

21. If old Indian Artifact remains are found on the project you are working on, you should _____.

    A: notify the owner and let the owner decide what to do

    B: stop all work within 3 feet of the artifact

    C: remove them and bury them away from the site

    D: stop working in the area and any other area also expected to also have ruins

22. According to _____ every employer has a legal obligation to provide and maintain a safe and healthful work place for employees.

    A: The National Safety Counsel

    B: The Workers Compensation Fund

    C: CAL/OSHA

    D: All of the above

23. CAL/OSHA provides all of the following model injury and prevention programs, except:

    A: disabled workers

    B: high hazard employers

    C: non-high hazard employers

    D: intermittent workers

24. The California Code of Regulations (CCR) requires every California employer to have effective injury and illness prevention program in writing in accordance with _____.

    A: Sec. 6507

    B: T8 CCR Sec. 7060

    C: CAL/OSH

    D: T8 CCR Sec. 3203

25. When remodeling an older home, when should a contractor inform the homeowner about the possible presence of hazardous material?

    A: during their first meeting

    B: after the finalizing the plans

    C: when the contract is signed

    D: when the hazardous materials is discovered

EXAM 4

26. Any work related fatality or serious injury must be reported to the nearest DOSH district office within which of the following lapses of time?

    A: immediately   C: 48 hrs.

    B: 24 hrs.   D: 72 hrs.

27. Before an employer undertakes construction of trenches or excavations into which a person is required to descend, he/she must obtain a permit from the DOSH Enforcement Unit if the trenches or excavations are _____ feet or more deep.

    A: 4   C: 6

    B: 5   D: 7

28. The Division of Occupational Safety and Health (DOSH) _____.

    A: must obtain and present a warrant to inspect a place of business   C: may inspect an employer's place of business without notice

    B: may inspect a place of business if there is a reasonable cause without a warrant   D: does not do inspections

29. If an occupational injury or illness results in _____ employers must file a complete report.

    A: an employee reporting in sick   C: absence from work for a full day

    B: employee treatment with first aid on the job   D: the hospitalization of an employee

30. The _____ administers CAL/OSHA.

    A: Department of Human Resources   C: Divisions of Industrial Safety

    B: Department of Industrial Relations   D: Divisions of Labor Statistics

31. A DOSH permit is required for construction type excavations.

    A: True   B: False

32. How many days in advance should a person planning to dig, contact the Dig-Alert Notification Center for information?

    A: not less than 2 working days, nor more than 7 days prior to the start of the work   C: not less than 3 working days, nor more than 14 days prior to the start of the work

    B: not less than 2 working days, nor more than 14 days prior to the start of the work   D: not less than 5 working days, nor more than 21 days prior to the start of the work

33. When marking excavation and underground facilities, the proposed excavation site must be marked in _____.

    A: orange   C: blue

    B: white   D: purple

EXAM 4

34. Electric power lines, cables, conduit and lighting cables are _____ in excavation and underground facilities.

    A: yellow   C: green

    B: red   D: blue

35. In excavation and underground facilities, communication lines, alarm lines, signal lines, cables or conduit are _____.

    A: orange   C: blue

    B: pink   D: purple

36. In excavation and underground facilities, reclaimed water, irrigation and slurry lines are _____.

    A: orange   C: purple

    B: pink   D: blue

37. Temporary survey markings are _____ at excavation and underground facility sites.

    A: orange   C: blue

    B: pink   D: purple

38. Gas, bit, steam, petroleum or gaseous materials are marked in _____ at excavation and underground facility sites.

    A: blue   C: white

    B: red   D: yellow

39. Potable water is color coded in _____ at excavation and underground facility sites.

    A: blue   C: white

    B: red   D: yellow

40. Sewer and drain lines are color coded _____ at excavation and underground facility sites.

    A: purple   C: white

    B: orange   D: green

41. A ladder extended above a trench must be a minimum of _____ above the landing surface it is serving.

    A: 1 foot   C: 3 feet

    B: 2 feet   D: 4 feet

EXAM 4

42. The contractor or employer must first ask the owner whether asbestos is present in any building or structure built before the year _____.

    A: 1960   C: 1978

    B: 1970   D: 1980

43. True or False: The minimum dimension of the base of any free standing tower or rolling scaffold must not be less than 1/3 the height of the scaffold.

    A: True   B: False

44. What must be done with ladders that have broken or missing rungs or steps?

    A: red tagged for warning   C: immediately withdrawn from service

    B: repaired immediately   D: inspected for further use

45. Single cleat ladders must not exceed _____ in length.

    A: 10 feet   C: 30 feet

    B: 20 feet   D: 40 feet

46. Where is every employee required to post Material Safety Data Sheets (MSDS)?

    A: at the main office of the business   C: on the job site

    B: on the board with the construction permit   D: All the above

47. Which reference material/codes must the contractor have knowledge of to review reports to identify materials, lead, and asbestos?

    A: UBC   C: DOSH

    B: Contractors License Law   D: CAL/OSHA Construction Safety Orders

48. True or False: The Injury and Illness Prevention Program and Asbestos (IIPP) became effective July 1, 1991.

    A: True   B: False

49. True or False: Employers that have less than 10 employees are permitted to communicate with and instruct employees orally in general safety work.

    A: True   B: False

50. Records of scheduled and periodic inspections required to identify unsafe conditions and work practices, with action taken to correct the unsafe conditions, must be written and recorded and then kept for _____ years.

    A: 1   C: 3

    B: 2   D: 4

EXAM 4

51. Every employer of _____ or more people must keep records and make reports as outlined under California Occupational Safety and Health (COSH).

    A: 10   C: 50

    B: 25   D: 100

52. Which of the following organization must every employer immediately report (by phone) to regarding any work related accidents or illness causing serious injury or death of an employee?

    A: Contractors State License Board (CSLB)   C: Division of Safety Orders (DSO)

    B: Division of Occupational Safety and   D: California Code of Regulations (CCR)
       Health (DOSH)

53. The employer must report to DOSH, any anticipated operations or processes involving asbestos containing more the 1 percent asbestos if the asbestos is to be _____.

    A: sanded   C: cut

    B: sawed   D: All of the above

54. If a worker is exposed to asbestos, where must the incident be reported to?

    A: DOSH (Department of Occupational   C: EPA (Environmental Protection Agency)
       Safety and Health)

    B: AHERA (Asbestos Hazard Emergency   D: All of the above
       Response Act)

55. When a contractor is doing asbestos-abatement work in schools he or she must obtain accreditation _____.

    A: by passing a State Contractors Board   C: by passing an AHERA approved training
       training course   course

    B: by passing an EPA approved training   D: from the EPA/OSHA
       course

56. A contractor who engages in asbestos abatement work in a facility (such as a school) and violates the national emissions standards for hazardous air pollutants (NESHAP) is subject to _____.

    A: fines and penalties of$25,000 per day   C: Both A and B

    B: penalties leading to criminal charges and/ D: Neither A nor B
       or imprisonment.

57. Asbestos can be harmful when it is _____.

    A: wet   C: friable

    B: dry   D: All of the above

Law & Business Exam Part IV

58. When is asbestos most dangerous?

   A: when it is wet

   B: when it is dry

   C: when it is friable

   D: when it is encapsulated

59. According to _____ the contractor must ask the owner whether asbestos is present in the building before work begins on a job.

   A: AB 1060

   B: AB 2040

   C: CSLB

   D: DOSH

60. When is special certification for asbestos related work required?

   A: For any asbestos related work involving 50 square feet or more of contaminated material.

   B: for any asbestos related work involving 100 square feet or more of contaminated material.

   C: for any asbestos related work involving 150 square feet or more of contaminated material.

   D: for any asbestos related work involving 200 square feet or more of contaminated material.

61. During removal, asbestos must be wetted down to keep airborne fibers under control, after removal asbestos must _____.

   A: be placed in leak-tight containers with labels

   B: be kept wet

   C: be transported to a state approved waste disposal

   D: All of the above

62. How can the hazard of asbestos be reduced or eliminated?

   A: by removing it

   B: by enclosing it

   C: by encapsulating it

   D: All of the above

63. What should you do if you discover asbestos in the middle of a project?

   A: You must stop working in that area immediately.

   B: You must contact an industrial hygienist.

   C: You must contact your nearest DOSH office.

   D: All of the above

64. Employers or contractors engaged in asbestos-related work must _____.

   A: register with OSHA

   B: be covered with health and work compensation

   C: be certified with CSLB

   D: All of the above

EXAM 4

Law & Business Exam Part IV

65. If more than 50 lbs. of asbestos is removed, it must be transported by a _____.

    A: specialty abatement contractor

    B: contractor certified for asbestos abatement work

    C: registered hazardous waste hauler

    D: All of the above

66. Consider the following scenario: You are involved in a demolition project: tearing down a house. You suspect the presence of asbestos, what should you do before starting the work?

    A: contact OSHA

    B: contact DOSH

    C: contact the EPA

    D: All of the above

67. When is asbestos the most dangerous?

    A: when it is in its original form

    B: when it is encapsulated

    C: when it is sprayed

    D: when it is wet

68. Harmful chemicals take the form of _____.

    A: dust

    B: gases and fumes

    C: mist and vapors

    D: All of the above

69. Why is an LPG leak dangerous?

    A: because it is odorless

    B: because it is colorless

    C: because it is tasteless

    D: All of the above

70. True or False: Gas piping must not be installed under any building or structure. Exposed piping must be kept at least 6 inches above grade and structure.

    A: True

    B: False

71. The best way to fix a gas leak is by _____.

    A: using tape

    B: soldering the pipe

    C: clamping the pipe

    D: replacing the pipe

72. When extended to the limit, extension ladders must not exceed _____ feet in length.

    A: 34

    B: 44

    C: 54

    D: 64

73. _____ can be considered a physical hazard.

    A: Noise

    B: Vibration and temperature extremes

    C: Radiation

    D: All of the above

Law & Business Exam Part IV

74. If a contractor engages in asbestos abatement work of 100 sq. ft. or more without certification and registration, the contractor is subject to a fine of _____.

    A: not less than$2,000 dollar

    B: not less than$5,000 dollars

    C: not less than$10,000 dollars

    D: not less than$25,000 dollars

75. According to the labor code, beginning asbestos-related work without first determining if asbestos containing material is present could lead to a fine of _____.

    A: $5,000 and/or 6 months jail time for negligence.

    B: $10,000 and/or 1 year jail time.

    C: A civil penalty of no more than$2,000 for each violation.

    D: Any of the above

76. Which of the following organization does a contractor have to notify if performing a demolition job on a commercial building?

    A: The Department of Occupational Safety and Health

    B: The Federal Environmental Protection Agency

    C: The Contractors State License Board

    D: The Department of Consumer Affairs

77. Which of the following is not another name for asbestos?

    A: chrysoltile

    B: themolite

    C: clayrite

    D: amosite

78. Special drums often containing strong acids will be lined with a PVC lining or _____.

    A: polyethylene

    B: stainless steel

    C: aluminum

    D: nickel

79. If respirators are worn while working with acids they must have the joint seal of approval of _____.

    A: health administration

    B: mine safety

    C: NIOSH

    D: All the above

80. Safety meetings are required to be held every _____ at the job site.

    A: 5 days

    B: 10 days

    C: month

    D: year

81. Which of the following actions requires the use of gloves?

    A: Striking

    B: Cutting

    C: Drilling

    D: Fastening

EXAM 4

82. Poisons can be _____.

    A: inhaled   C: injected

    B: eaten   D: All of the above

83. Which of the following actions should be taken to help a person that has suffered electric shock?

    A: immediately cool down on the outside   C: use a dry stick to move the person away

    B: give water if conscious   D: All of the above

84. If a neck or spine injury occurs or is suspected as a result of electric shock, you should _____.

    A: lay victim flat   C: raise the back and head slightly

    B: raise the legs and feet 6 to 12 inches   D: try to get the victim to sit to verify if there is an injury

85. If a head injury occurs as a result of electric shock, you should _____.

    A: lay victim flat   C: raise the legs and feet 6 to 12 inches

    B: raise the back and head slightly   D: A or B

86. If a leg or abdomen injury occurs as a result of electric shock, you should _____.

    A: lay victim flat   C: raise the back and head slightly

    B: raise the legs and feet 6 to 12 inches   D: try to get the victim to sit to verify if there is an injury

87. Heat stroke is characterized by _____.

    A: red, hot, dry skin   C: rapid shallow breathing

    B: changes in consciousness   D: All of the above

88. If a person has suffered heat stroke _____.

    A: get the victim out of the heat   C: apply cool, wet cloths

    B: loosen clothing   D: All of the above

89. Consider the following statement: When trying to stop bleeding from a bleeding wound, always use a sanitary napkin, never use your bare hands.

    A: True   B: False

90. If there is bleeding from the leg, hand or arm, what additional procedure (besides the ones listed already) should you follow?

    A: lay the limb flat on the ground   C: elevate the limb so that it is higher than the victim's heart

    B: elevate the limb so that it is at level with the heart but not above it   D: All of the above

EXAM 4

91. What is one of the causes of shock?

    A: a breakdown of the circulation of blood

    B: the lack of enough blood to fill the body's volume needs

    C: an obstruction in the blood flow

    D: All of the above

92. Which of the following is a sign that a person has suffered shock?

    A: cool, clammy, moist skin

    B: bluish or gray skin color at fingernail beds and inside the mouth

    C: vomiting

    D: All of the above

93. Burns are classified as which of the following degrees?

    A: light, moderate or serious

    B: first, second or third degree

    C: 1 through 10

    D: fourth, fifth or sixth

94. If a fellow worker is lying unconscious on a high voltage conductor and you are within reach what should you do?

    A: grab the worker by the arm

    B: grab the worker by the ankles

    C: grab the worker by the shoes

    D: disconnect the power supply

95. Consider the following scenario: A man's forearm is cut and bleeding severely. Which of the following actions should you take in order to stop the bleeding?

    A: place a band below the cut

    B: tie a band around the cut

    C: press hard over the opened wound

    D: apply a tourniquet above the wound

96. If respirators are worn while working with acids they must have the _____ joint seal of approval.

    A: mine safety

    B: health administration

    C: NIOSH

    D: All of the above

97. A contractor who engages in asbestos abatement work in a facility under NESHAP jurisdiction is in violation of practices and subject to which of the following fines and penalties?

    A: $25,000 per day

    B: Penalties leading to criminal charges

    C: Imprisonment

    D: All of the above

98. During asbestos removal, asbestos may not be _____.

    A: set and left on the floor

    B: placed in leak-tight container with labels

    C: kept wet

    D: be transported to a state approved disposal

EXAM 4

99.   Gas piping may not be installed _____.

    A: through interior walls

    B: through exterior walls

    C: through concrete

    D: on the roof of a building

100.   Where should all solvent wastes, oily rags and flammable liquids be kept until removed from site?

    A: a storage room

    B: an unventilated room

    C: fire, resistant covered containers

    D: All of the above

EXAM 4

1. **Answer A.** True

   In every case in which one claim is filed against two or more buildings or other works of improvement owned or reputed to be owned by the same person or on which the claimant has been employed by the same person to do his work or furnish his materials, whether such works of improvement are owned by one or more owners, the person filing such claim must at the same time designate the amount due to him on each of such works of improvement; otherwise the lien of such claim is postponed to other liens. If such claimant has been employed to furnish labor or materials under a contract providing for a lump sum to be paid to him for his work or materials on such works of improvement as a whole, and such contract does not segregate the amount due for the work done and materials furnished on such works of improvement separately, then such claimant, for the purposes of this section, may estimate an equitable distribution of the sum due him over all of such works of improvement based upon the proportionate amount of work done or materials furnished upon such respective works of improvement. The lien of such claimant does not extend beyond the amount designated as against other creditors having liens, by judgment, mortgage, or otherwise, upon either such works of improvement or upon the land upon

   which the same are situated.(California Civil Code 3130)

2. **Answer B.** CAL/OSHA

   Within the Department of Industrial relations, DOSH is given the authority to implement and enforce the CAL/OSHA program.

3. **Answer C.** To ensure safe and healthful working conditions for employees

   DOSH works to ensure safe and healthful working conditions for employees.

4. **Answer D.** All of the above

   The Injury and Illness Prevention Program (IIPP) provides the following guidelines: \n\n1.\tmanagement commitment to safety and health\n2.\tidentify the person or person with authority and responsibility for implementing the program\n3.\tinclude a system for communicating with employees\n4.\tinclude a system for identifying, evaluation and controlling existing or potential workplace hazards\n5.\tevery employer must develop, maintain and document training programs for both supervisors and employees\n6.\tevery employer must ensure the availability of emergency medical services for his or her employees.

5. **Answer C.** 24

   Serious injury or illness is defined by any employment related injury which requires inpatient hospitalization for a period exceeding 24 hours.

6. **Answer A.** full day

   Employers must file a complete report of every occupational injury that results in absence from work for a full day or shift beyond the date of the injury.\n\nA report must be made within 5 days of the incident using Form 5020.

7. **Answer C.** 10

   Except for employers who had no more than 10 employees, employers must keep records when injuries or illness occurs on a CAL/OSHA 300 form.

8. **Answer D.** Any of the above

   Before an employer undertakes any of the following kinds of work, he/she must first obtain a permit form the DOSH Enforcement Unit:\n\nTrenches 5 feet or more deep for persons\n\nConstructing building, false-work, scaffolding more than three stories high (36') in height\n\nDemolition of structures, false-work, scaffolding more than the three stories high.

9. **Answer C.** Standard Board

   An employer may apply to the Standard Board for a permanent variance from a safety standard if the employer demonstrates that an equivalent method will provide better safety for employees.

10. **Answer D.** All of the above

    Any one who plans to dig, drill or plans on boring must contact a Regional Notification Center.

11. **Answer C.** 28

    The Regional Notification Centers for underground services alert, will issue an identification number that will be valid for 28 days. The ticket can be revalidated before expiration date.

12. **Answer C.** With hand tools before any power equipment may be used

    Using the operator's markings, an excavator must determine the exact location of underground facilities with hand tools before any power equipment may be used.

13. **Answer A.** telephone

    In every case involving a serious injury of illness or death the employer must immediately report the incident by telephone. It must be reported to the nearest DOSH district office.

14. **Answer A.** prohibits use of this equipment until it is made safe

    Assuming that you allow CAL/OSHA investigators to check out questionable equipment and that they find one of these to be in dangerous condition, CAL/OSHA can issue a notice that prohibits the use of this equipment until it is made safe.

15. **Answer D.** you will be charged with a felony punishable by a fine of one thousand dollars ($1,000.00) a day it is used or a one (1) year prison sentence

    If you remove the notice off of the equipment, such action is considered a felony punishable by a fine of$1000.00 a day or 1 year in prison.

16. **Answer D.** the contractor cannot request the name of the employee who filed the complaint and cannot fire the employee

    There is a complaint filed with D.O.S.H. by an anonymous employee about an unsafe condition within the construction project. As a result the contractor wants to fire the employee who filed the complaint, the contractor cannot request the name of the employee who filed the complaint and cannot fire the employee.

EXAM 4

Answers: Law & Business Exam Part IV

17. **Answer B.** The contractor

The contractor is responsible for providing safety equipment and supplies.

18. **Answer D.** reviewing these standards every week

Construction Safety Orders require: keeping a copy of the standards on the job, following and making sure the employees follow the requirements of these standards and knowing which of the standards apply to the work that you do.

19. **Answer D.** 7 feet, 6 inches

Scaffolding requires a safety railing to be present on the equipment above the height of 7 feet, 6 inches.

20. **Answer D.** at each location where employees report to work each day or where they operate activities

Each employer is required to post the CAL/OSHA notice Safety and Health Protection on the Job along with the Code of Safe Practices at each location where employees report to work each day or where they operate activities.

21. **Answer D.** stop working in the area and any other area also expected to also have ruins

If old Indian Artifact remains are found on the project you are working on, you should stop working in the area and any other area also expected to have ruins.

22. **Answer C.** CAL/OSHA

According to the California Occupational Safety and Health Act (CAL/OSHA) every employer has a legal obligation to provide and maintain a safe and healthful work place for employees.

23. **Answer A.** disabled workers

CAL/OSHA provides high hazard employers, non-high hazard employers and intermittent workers model injury and prevention programs.

24. **Answer D.** T8 CCR Sec. 3203

The California Code of Regulations (CCR) requires every California employer to have effective injury and illness prevention program in writing in accordance with T8 CCR Sec. 3203.

25. **Answer A.** during their first meeting

When remodeling an older home, a contractor should inform the homeowner about the possible presence of hazardous material during their fist meeting.

26. **Answer A.** immediately

Any work related fatality or serious injury must be reported to the nearest DOSH district office immediately.

27. **Answer B.** 5

Before an employer undertakes construction of trenches or excavations into which a person is required to descend, he/she must obtain a permit from the DOSH Enforcement Unit if the trenches or excavations are 5 feet or more deep.

28. **Answer C.** may inspect an employer's place of business without notice

The Division of Occupational Safety and Health (DOSH)may inspect an employer's place of business without notice.

29. **Answer C.** absence from work for a full day

If an occupational injury or illness results in absence from work for a full day, employers must file a complete report.

30. **Answer B.** Department of Industrial Relations

CAL/OSHA is administered by the Department of Industrial Relations.

31. **Answer A.** True

A DOSH permit is required for construction type excavations.

32. **Answer B.** not less than 2 working days, nor more than 14 days prior to the start of the work

Anyone wishing to dig is required by law to contact a Dig-Alert Notification Center for information not less than 2 working days and no more than 14 days prior to the start of the work.

33. **Answer B.** white

When marking excavation and underground facilities, the proposed excavation site must be marked in white.

34. **Answer B.** red

In excavation and underground facilities, electric power lines, cables, conduit and lighting cables are red.

35. **Answer A.** orange

In excavation and underground facilities, communication lines, alarm lines, signal lines, cables or conduit are orange.

36. **Answer C.** purple

In excavation and underground facilities, reclaimed water, irrigation and slurry lines are purple.

37. **Answer B.** pink

Temporary survey markings are pink at excavation and underground facility sites.

38. **Answer D.** yellow

Gas, bit, steam, petroleum or gaseous materials are marked in yellow at excavation and underground facility sites.

39. **Answer A.** blue

At excavation and underground facility sites, potable water is color coded in blue.

40. **Answer D.** green

Sewer and drain lines are color coded green at excavation and underground facility sites.

41. **Answer C.** 3 feet

A ladder extended above a trench must be 3 feet above the landing surface it is serving.

EXAM 4

42. Answer D. 1980

The contractor or employer must first ask the owner whether asbestos is present in any building or structure built before the year 1980.

43. Answer A. True

The minimum dimension of the base of any free standing tower or rolling scaffold must not be less than ⅓ the height of the scaffold.

44. Answer C. immediately withdrawn from service

Ladders that have broken or missing rungs or steps must be immediately withdrawn from service.

45. Answer C. 30 feet

Single cleat ladders must not exceed 30 feet in length.\n\nDouble cleat ladders must not exceed 24 feet in length.

46. Answer C. on the job site

Every employee is required to post Material Safety Data Sheets (MSDS) on the job site.

47. Answer D. CAL/OSHA Construction Safety Orders

The contractor must have knowledge of CAL/OSHA Construction Safety Orders to review reports to identify materials, lead, and asbestos.

48. Answer A. True

The Injury and Illness Prevention Program (IIPP) was implemented in 1991 after the 1989 Senate Bill 198 which required every employer to develop and implement a written injury and illness prevention plan. The IIPP must be applied to all businesses, regardless of if they have only one employee or are operated in a low-hazard industry. The IIPP must be written; employers having fewer than 10 employees are allowed to communicate the IIPP orally to each employee.

49. Answer A. True

Employers that have less than 10 employees are permitted to communicate with and instruct employees orally in general safety work.

50. Answer C. 3

Records of scheduled and periodic inspections required to identify unsafe conditions and work practices, with action taken to correct the unsafe conditions, must be written and recorded and then kept for 3 years.

51. Answer B. 25

Every employer of 25 or more people must keep records and make reports as outlined under California Occupational Safety and Health (COSH).

52. Answer B. Division of Occupational Safety and Health (DOSH)

Every employer must immediately report (by phone) to the Division of Occupational Safety and Health (DOSH) district office regarding any work related accidents or illness causing serious injury or death of an employee.

53. Answer D. All of the above

The employer must report to DOSH, any anticipated operations or processes involving asbestos containing more the 1 percent asbestos if the asbestos is to be: sanded, sawed, cut, ground blasted, shoveled or handled in any way in which it might produce dust.

54. Answer A. DOSH (Department of Occupational Safety and Health)

If a worker is exposed to asbestos, you must report the incident to the Department of Occupational Safety and Health (DOSH).

55. Answer D. from the EPA/OSHA

When a contractor is doing asbestos-abatement work in schools he or she must obtain accreditation from the EPA/OSHA.

56. Answer C. Both A and B

A contractor who engages in asbestos abatement work in a facility (such as a school) and violates the national emissions standards for hazardous air pollutants (NESHAP) is subject to fines and penalties of$25,000 per day and or penalties leading to criminal charges and or imprisonment.

57. Answer D. All of the above

Asbestos can be present in many form. It is still a danger regardless of the state (wet, dry, friable) it is in.

58. Answer C. when it is friable

Asbestos is most dangerous when it is friable.

59. Answer B. AB 2040

According to AB 2040 the contractor must ask the owner whether asbestos is present in the building before he or she begins work on a job.

60. Answer B. for any asbestos related work involving 100 square feet or more of contaminated material.

Special certification for asbestos related work is required for any asbestos related work involving 100 square feet or more of contaminated material.

61. Answer D. All of the above

During removal, asbestos must be wetted down to keep airborne fibers under control, after removal asbestos must be kept wet, placed in leak-tight containers with labels and transported to a state approved waste disposal.

62. Answer D. All of the above

The hazard of asbestos can be reduced or eliminated by: removing it, enclosing it or encapsulating it.

63. Answer D. All of the above

If you discover asbestos in the middle of a project you must do all of the following: stop working in that area immediately, contact an industrial hygienist and contact your nearest DOSH office and the EPA for assistance.

64. Answer D. All of the above

Employers or contractors engaged in asbestos-related work must: register with OSHA, be certified with CSLB and be covered with health and work compensation.

EXAM 4

65. **Answer C.** registered hazardous waste hauler

If more than 50 lbs. of asbestos is removed, it must be transported by a registered hazardous waste hauler.

66. **Answer C.** contact the EPA

If you are involved in a demolition project, like tearing down a house, and you suspect the presence of asbestos, you must contact the EPA before starting the work.

67. **Answer C.** when it is sprayed

Asbestos is the most dangerous when it is sprayed.\n\nAsbestos that is found in sprayed-on insulation is the most hazardous because it is friable; and thus is easily released into the air.

68. **Answer D.** All of the above

Harmful chemical take the form of dust, gases and fumes, mist and vapors.

69. **Answer D.** All of the above

An LPG leak is dangerous because it is: odorless, colorless and tasteless.

70. **Answer A.** True

Gas piping must not be installed under any building or structure. Exposed piping must be kept at least 6 inches above grade and structure.

71. **Answer D.** replacing the pipe

The best way to fix a gas leak is by replacing the pipe.\n\nAll pipes used for alteration or repair of any gas piping must be standard weight wrought iron or steel, or treated copper of iron pipe size, or approved PVC or PE in exterior buried piping systems.

72. **Answer B.** 44

When extended to the limit extension ladders must not exceed 44 feet in length.\n\nExtension ladders must not be fully extended but must have the following minimum laps: \n3 feet for 2 section ladders up to 33' \n4 feet for 2 section ladders up to 44' or\n4 feet for each 3 section ladder

73. **Answer D.** All of the above

Noise, vibration, temperature extremes and radiation are all considered physical hazards.

74. **Answer D.** not less than$25,000 dollars

If a contractor engages in asbestos abatement work of 100 sq. ft. or more without certification and registration, the contractor is subject to a fine of$25,000 dollars for a first offense.

75. **Answer D.** Any of the above

According to the labor code, beginning asbestos-related work without first determining if asbestos containing material is present could lead to a any of the following fines depending on the scenario: \n\n$5,000 and/or 6 months jail time for negligence.\n\n$10,000 and/or 1 year jail time, or \n\nA civil penalty of no more than$2,000 for each violation. \n\nIn addition, undertaking work without checking if asbestos is present can cause serious injury or even death.

76. **Answer B.** The Federal Environmental Protection Agency

A contractor must notify the Federal Environmental Protection Agency if he/she is planning to perform a demolition job on a commercial building.

77. **Answer C.** clayrite

All of the following are different names for asbestos: chrysoltile, themolite and amosite.

78. **Answer A.** polyethylene

Special drums often containing strong acids will be lined with a PVC lining or polyethylene plastic.

79. **Answer D.** All the above

If respirators are worn while working with acids they must have the joint seal of approval of the health administration, mine safety and NIOSH.

80. **Answer B.** 10 days

Safety meetings are required to be held every 10 days at the job site.

81. **Answer B.** Cutting

Cutting and sawing require the use of gloves.

82. **Answer D.** All of the above

Poisons can be inhaled, eaten, injected or absorbed through the skin.\n\nThe following things can be poisonous: \n\n-aspirin, alcohol, cosmetics, medications and detergents\n-paint, gasoline and other petroleum products\n-plants and common insects

83. **Answer D.** All of the above

If a person has suffered electric shock, you should:\n\n1. make sure the victim is not still in contact with electric current\n\n2. if the victim is still in contact with electric current, use a dry stick to move the person away\n\n3. insulate yourself from all "grounds" before attempting to move any "live" wires.\n\n4. cool the person down on the outside immediately\n\n5. give the victim water if the victim is conscious

84. **Answer A.** lay victim flat

If a neck or spine injury occurs (or is suspected) as a result of electric shock you should lay the victim flat.

85. **Answer D.** A or B

If a head injury occurs as a result of electric shock, you should lay victim flat and/or raise the back and the head slightly.

86. **Answer B.** raise the legs and feet 6 to 12 inches

If a leg or abdomen injury occurs as a result of electric shock, you should raise the legs and feet 6 to 12 inches.

87. **Answer D.** All of the above

Heat stroke is characterized by red, hot, dry skin, changes in consciousness, rapid weak pulse and rapid shallow breathing.

EXAM 4

88. Answer D. All of the above

If a person has suffered heat stroke you should do the following:\n\n1. get the victim out of the heat\n2. loosen clothing\n3. apply cool, wet cloths\n4. give the victim cool water: the victim should drink slowly (a glass of water every 15 minutes)

89. Answer B. False

Although a sanitary napkin is preferred, bare hands can be used if there are no sanitary napkins, pads of gauze or clean handkerchiefs around. The object is to stop the bleeding.\n\nPlace either of the above over the bleeding wound. Use direct pressure over the site of the wound. Apply firm, steady and direct pressure for 5 to 15 minutes. Leave the original dressing in place, otherwise you will remove the clotting and being the process again (that is why a sanitary napkin, pad of gauze or clean handkerchief is preferred).\n\nNote: Take special care if there is scalp bleeding and there is a possibility of a skull fracture. Do not press too hard. If there is bleeding from the ear, it may indicate a skull fracture. Do not attempt to stop fluid leakage if it is clear or pink.

90. Answer C. elevate the limb so that it is higher than the victim's heart

If there is bleeding from the leg, hand or arm elevate the limb so that it is higher than the victim's heart.

91. Answer D. All of the above

Shock has 4 Causes, they are the following:\n\n1. not enough blood to fill the body's volume needs\n2. a breakdown of the circulation of blood\n3. a breakdown in large body systems due to infection or fear\n4. obstruction in the flow of blood

92. Answer D. All of the above

Shock can be identified by:\n\n1. cool, clammy, moist skin\n2. bluish or gray skin color at fingernail beds and inside the mouth\n3. thirst\n4. vomiting\n5. disorientation\n6. unconsciousness\n\nNote: pinch the fingernail to white, if fingernail does not come back to red in two seconds, shock is indicated.

93. Answer B. first, second or third degree

Burns are classified as first, second or third degree burns.\n\nFirst degree burns: these burns involve only the epidermal layer of the skin; they are usually limited to redness, a white plaque and minor pain at the site of injury.\n\nSecond degree burns: these burns involve the superficial papillary dermis and may also involve the deep reticular dermis layer. This is shown by superficial blistering of the skin, and can involve more or less pain depending on the level of nerve involvement. Deep reticular dermis layer may require about 3 weeks to heal.\n\nThird degree burns: these occur when the epidermis is lost with damage to the subcutaneous tissue. These burns result in scarring and victims will also exhibit the loss of hair shafts and keratin.

94. Answer D. disconnect the power supply

If a fellow worker is lying unconscious on a high voltage conductor and you are within reach you should disconnect the power supply.

95. Answer C. press hard over the opened wound

If a man's forearm is cut and bleeding severely you should press hard over the open wound to stop the bleeding.

96. Answer D. All of the above

If respirators are worn while working with acids they must have the mine safety, health administration and NIOSH's seal of approval.

97. Answer D. All of the above

A contractor who engages in asbestos abatement work in a facility under NESHAP jurisdiction is in violation of practices and is subject to the following fines and penalties:\n\n$25,000 per day\n\nPenalties leading to criminal charges\n\nImprisonment

98. Answer A. set and left on the floor

During asbestos removal asbestos may not be set and left on the floor.

99. Answer C. through concrete

Gas piping may not be installed through concrete.\n\nGas piping cannot be installed under any building or structure. Exposed piping must be kept at least 6 inches above grade or structure.

100. Answer C. fire, resistant covered containers

Solvent wastes, oily rags and flammable liquids must be kept in fire, resistant covered containers until removed from site.\n\nAcids must be stored in a container that resists corrosion.",

EXAM 5

Law & Business Exam Part V

1. A home improvement contract means an agreement, whether oral or written, _____.

    A: contained in one or more documents

    B: between a contractor and an owner

    C: between a contractor and a tenant

    D: Any of the above

2. Any printed form must be readable; the text must be at least _____.

    A: 8-point typeface

    B: 9-point typeface

    C: 10-point typeface

    D: 12-point typeface

3. Before any work is started, the contractor must give the buyer a copy of the contract _____.

    A: signed by the contractor

    B: signed and dated by both the contractor and the buyer

    C: signed by the contractor and the buyer

    D: Any of the above

4. The buyer must be informed by the contractor that the owner may cancel the contract by returning a _____.

    A: Notice of Default

    B: Stop Payment Notice

    C: Notice of Cancellation

    D: All of the above

5. The contractor, before each payment is being made for work performed, must furnish to the person contracting for home improvements a/an _____.

    A: copy of materials purchased for the job

    B: schedule of the work to be performed

    C: unconditional mechanics lien release

    D: All of the above

6. A change order form for changes or extra work must be _____.

    A: approved by the Contractors Board

    B: incorporated into the contract

    C: completed after the work is finished

    D: None of the above

7. The contractor must inform the owner or tenant that they have a right to require the contractor to provide a _____.

    A: performance bond

    B: payment bond

    C: Both A and B

    D: Neither A nor B

8. If a contract provides for a contractor to furnish joint control, then _____.

    A: the contractor must not have any financial interest in the control

    B: the contractor must have a financial interest in the control

    C: a joint control is not permitted

    D: the Contractors Board must approve the agreement

EXAM 5

9. If a finance charge is part of the contract, _____.

   A: there must be a heading that reads: Finance Charge

   B: a statement of the dollars an cents must be printed

   C: the finance charge should be set out separately from the contract amount

   D: All of the above

10. In any form, the heading "Down Payment" must be at least _____ 12-point boldface type.

    A: 8-point typeface

    B: 9-point typeface

    C: 10-point typeface

    D: 12-point typeface

11. True or False: The down payment may not exceed$1,000.00 or 10% of the contract whichever is less.

    A: True

    B: False

12. A contractor furnishing a _____ is exempt from the minimum down payment.

    A: performance and payment bond

    B: lien and completion bond

    C: joint control approved by the Registrar

    D: Any of the above

13. It is against the law for a contractor to _____.

    A: collect payment for materials not yet delivered

    B:collect payments for work not completed

    C: employ workers without Worker's Compensation Insurance

    D: All the above

14. Extra Work or Change Order is not enforceable against a buyer unless the change order states the _____.

    A: scope of work encompassed by the order

    B: amount to be added or subtracted from the contract

    C: completion date

    D: All of the above

15. Which of the following notices must be provided to the owner as part of the contract form?

    A: Mechanics Lien Warning

    B: Worker's Compensation Insurance Information

    C: Three Day Right to Cancel

    D: All of the above

16. One way a homeowner can protect his/herself for the work performed by the contractor, his suppliers and sub contractors is by paying with a _____.

    A: cashier's check

    B: voucher

    C: joint check

    D: Any of the above

Law & Business Exam Part V

17. If a home improvement for goods or services is _____ or less, the property can not be used as security for payment.

   A: $1,000.00   C: $5,000.00

   B: $2,000.00   D: $10,000.00

18. A violation of a down payment as described in a Home Improvement contract is punishable by a min. fine of _____.

   A: $10.00   C: $500.00

   B: $100.00   D: $1000.00

19. The work in Service and Repair Contracts must not exceed _____.

   A: $100.00   C: $750.00

   B: $500.00   D: $1000.00

20. True or False: Corporations are more complex to form and operate but reduce personal liability of the owners.

   A: True   B: False

21. To form a corporation it is necessary to comply with the _____.

   A: city of residence   C: state law

   B: country of location   D: federal law

22. An incorporation provides your business with a _____.

   A: legal existence   C: fictitious name

   B: personal ownership   D: All of the above

23. A _____ is a corporation that has a limited number of investors.

   A: S corp   C: LLC

   B: C corp   D: All of the above

24. Which corporation can avoid double taxation (corporate and shareholder taxes)?

   A: S corp   C: LLC

   B: C corp   D: All of the above

25. The _____ corporation passes its items of income, loss deductions and credits through to its shareholders to be included on their separate tax returns.

   A: S corp   C: LLC

   B: C corp   D: All of the above

EXAM 5

26. A _____ is a form of company where the ownership is invested in membership rather than shares of stock.

    A: S corp
    B: C corp

    C: LLC
    D: All of the above

27. When a corporation operates exclusively in the state where it is formed, it is referred to as _____.

    A: foreign
    B: local

    C: domestic
    D: restricted

28. When operating a sole proprietorship the owner has _____.

    A: unlimited liability
    B: limited liability

    C: deferred liability
    D: shared liability

29. General partnerships have _____ liability.

    A: unlimited
    B: limited

    C: deferred
    D: shared

30. Limited partners of a partnership generally have _____.

    A: unlimited liability
    B: limited liability

    C: shared liability
    D: no personal liability

31. A series of events that is repeated each reporting period is referred to as a/an _____.

    A: trial balance
    B: post transaction

    C: financial statement
    D: accounting cycle

32. A transaction is an event that either increases or decreases an account balance; the _____ document is proof that a transaction took place.

    A: source
    B: chart

    C: journal
    D: balance

33. Daily transactions are recorded in a set of books called _____.

    A: accounts
    B: ledgers

    C: journals
    D: postings

34. Posting is the process of transferring the transaction recorded in the journals to the appropriate accounts (to register value), most companies have five basic types of accounts, which of the following is not recognized?

    A: asset
    B: equity

    C: income
    D: statement

35. A numbering system that organizes the 5 basic accounts is referred to as a _____.

    A: chart of accounts   C: ledger

    B: journal   D: balance chart

36. When you post transactions, you are transferring them from the _____ to the ledger.

    A: chart of accounts   C: adjusted trial balance

    B: journal   D: balance chart

37. When you tally the accounts you prepare a _____.

    A: chart of accounts   C: trial balance

    B: journal   D: balance chart

38. True or False: Every entry in a general ledger contains both a debit and a credit which must equal each other.

    A: True   B: False

39. There are three basic types of financial statements that companies use, which of the following is not recognized?

    A: adjusted balance   C: income statement

    B: balance sheet   D: statement of cash flow

40. _____ is when you report income in the year that you receive it and deduct expenses in the same year that you paid them.

    A: Method accounting   C: Cash method

    B: Contract accounting   D: Accrual method

41. _____ is when you recognizing income when services occur, not when you collect the money.

    A: Method accounting   C: Cash method

    B: Contract accounting   D: Accrual method

42. _____ are partial payments made to the contractor after specified phases of construction are complete.

    A: Prompt payments   C: Lump Sum payments

    B: Progress payments   D: Unit Price payments

43. _____ are payments for contracts that are calculated for the percentage of work completed.

    A: Lump sum payments   C: Unit price payments

    B: Cost plus payments   D: Final payments

EXAM 5

44. _____ are payments based on actual work units completed.

    A: Lump sum payments   C: Unit price payments

    B: Cost plus payments   D: Final payments

45. _____ are payments based on actual cost rather than a percentage of work completed.

    A: Lump sum payments   C: Unit price payments

    B: Cost plus payments   D: Final payments

46. _____ is a process of devaluing a fixed asset as a result of aging, wear and tear.

    A: Appreciation   C: Acceleration

    B: Depreciation   D: Maintenance

47. _____ is an insurance policy that typically covers your business and personal property when damage, theft or loss occurs.

    A: Equipment floater Insurance   C: Property Insurance

    B: Liability Insurance   D: Umbrella Insurance

48. _____ is an insurance that covers property owners and builders for buildings under construction.

    A: All-risk Insurance   C: Equipment floater Insurance

    B: Named Peril Insurance   D: Liability Insurance

49. _____ is an insurance that specifies which perils are covered by the insurance.

    A: Umbrella Insurance   C: Liability Insurance

    B: Named Peril Insurance   D: Business Owner Insurance

50. _____ is an insurance that can be purchased for your tools and equipment.

    A: Cargo Insurance   C: Inland Marine Insurance

    B: Commercial Insurance   D: Umbrella Insurance

51. _____ is an insurance for direct physical loss to equipment, designed to cover mobile equipment while it is stored on premises or in transit.

    A: Inland Marine Insurance   C: Transportation Floater Insurance

    B: Equipment Floater Insurance   D: Automobile Insurance

52. _____ is a policy that protects the transporter against damage that occurs to freight during transport.

    A: Transportation Floater Insurance   C: Both A and B

    B: Motor Truck Cargo Insurance   D: Neither A nor B

EXAM 5

53.   _____ is an insurance that protects against third-party claims that arise from alleged negligence resulting in bodily injury or property damage.

  A: Umbrella Insurance   C: Liability Insurance

  B: Named Peril Insurance   D: Business Owner Insurance

54.   Commercial General Liability (CGL) covers 4 types of injuries, which of the following is one of them?

  A: Advertising injury, including charges of   C: Bodily injury from physical damage or loss
     negligence that results from promotion of   for individuals who are not employees.
     goods or services.

  B: Personal injury, including slander or   D: All of the above
     damage to reputation.

55.   A policy that provides additional coverage in the areas that are not covered in the CGL policy may be supplemental with _____.

  A: Business Owners Insurance   C: Umbrella Liability Insurance

  B: Directors and Officers' Liability Insurance D: Key Man Life Insurance

56.   _____ is an insurance that provides insurance for employees who are injured on the job.

  A: Unemployment Insurance   C: Workers' Compensation Insurance

  B: Disability Insurance   D: Social Security Insurance

57.   _____ is an insurance that provides unemployment benefits to eligible workers who become unemployed.

  A: Disability Insurance   C: Social Security Insurance

  B: Unemployment Insurance   D: FICA

58.   True or False: When hiring subcontractors, provided the direct contractor has insurance, it is not necessary to verify that the subcontractor is adequately insured.

  A: True   B: False

59.   A _____ is a bond that guarantees that the contractor, if awarded the job, will do work at the submitted bid price.

  A: performance bond   C: payment bond

  B: completion bond   D: bid bond

60.   A _____ is a bond guaranteeing that the contractor will complete a contract within its time frame and conditions.

  A: performance bond   C: payment bond

  B: completion bond   D: fidelity bond

EXAM 5

61.   A _____ is a bond that guarantees subcontractors and suppliers that they will be paid.

    A: performance bond   C: payment bond

    B: completion bond   D: fidelity bond

62.   A _____ is a bond that guarantees that for a stated period, usually one year, no defective work or material will appear in the completed project.

    A: labor bond   C: payment bond

    B: maintenance bond   D: fidelity bond

63.   A _____ is a bond that provides assurance to the financial backers of a construction project that it will be completed on time.

    A: labor bond   C: payment bond

    B: completion bond   D: fidelity bond

64.   A _____ is a bond that covers business owners for losses due to dishonest acts by their employees.

    A: labor bond   C: payment bond

    B: completion bond   D: fidelity bond

65.   The _____ is a current law (act) requiring performance and payment bonds on all federal construction projects valued at greater than$100,000.

    A: Heard Act   C: Miller Act

    B: Davis Act   D: James ACT

66.   Before you become an employer and hire employees, you need a/an _____.

    A: EIN number   C: MISC Return

    B: Form W-2   D: None of the above

67.   Which of the following require an EIN number?

    A: partnerships   C: joint venture

    B: corporations   D: All of the above

68.   Which of the following is a Federal tax that you may be responsible for?

    A: Income tax   C: Employment tax

    B: Self employment tax   D: All of the above

69.   True or False: All businesses except partnerships must file an annual income tax return.

    A: True   B: False

EXAM 5

70. Partnerships file a/an _____.

    A: information form   C: annual return form

    B: excise tax form   D: Schedule C

71. _____ generally have to make estimated tax payments.

    A: Sole proprietors   C: S corporations

    B: Partners   D: None of the above

72. Other than the S corporation, corporations have to make estimated tax payments if the expected tax is _____ or more.

    A: $500   C: $2,500

    B: $1,000   D: $5,000

73. For individuals who work for themselves the self-employment tax (SE tax) includes _____.

    A: Disability and Unemployment   C: Liability and Unemployment

    B: Social Security and Worker's Compensation   D: Social Security and Medicare

74. As defined by the IRS, to be deductible, a business expense must be _____.

    A: for personal value   C: listed on the tax return

    B: ordinary and necessary   D: All of the above

75. Employers are required to withhold, deposit, report and pay _____.

    A: Social Security   C: Federal Unemployment

    B: Federal income tax   D: All of the above

76. The form used to withhold Federal income tax from an employee's wages is _____.

    A: W-2   C: 1040

    B: W-4   D: 1099

77. A statement that summarizes the employee's previous year's wages and withholding amount is _____.

    A: W-2   C: 1040

    B: W-4   D: 1099

78. Which of the following is a payroll deposit schedule?

    A: monthly   C: daily

    B: semi-weekly   D: All of the above

EXAM 5

79. To avoid penalties, be sure to make accurate and prompt deposits, the penalties can range from _____ percent.

    A: 10 to 20   C: 2 to 100

    B: 20 to 50   D: 1 to 100

80. Payments made during the year to persons not treated as employees are reported on Form _____.

    A: W-2   C: 1040

    B: W-4   D: 1099

81. Which of the following questions are you not permitted to ask when interviewing an applicant for employment?

    A: How old are you?   C: What is your sexual orientation

    B: Are you married?   D: All of the above

82. When school is in session, a minor 14 or 15 years of age may not begin work before _____.

    A: 7:00 a.m.   C: 9:00 a.m.

    B: 8:00 a.m.   D: 10:00 a.m.

83. A minor 14 or 15 years of age during school session may not work more than _____ hour(s) a day.

    A: 1   C: 3

    B: 2   D: 4

84. When school is not in session a minor 14 or 15 may not work more than _____ hours a day.

    A: 4   C: 8

    B: 6   D: 10

85. Federal restrictions on working hours or number of hours do not exist for minors _____ years of age.

    A: 14 to 15   C: 16 to 17

    B: 15 to 16   D: 17 to 18

86. All minors are prohibited from employment in occupations considered hazardous. Minors ages 14 or 15 years of age may work in _____.

    A: offices   C: sales job

    B: clerical   D: All of the above

87. The United State Customs and Immigration Service requires a _____ form to show that a worker has legal immigration status in the USA.

    A: I-9   C: W-4

    B: 409   D: W-5

Law & Business Exam Part V

88. The Federal minimum wage effective 2009 is _____.

    A: $7.25   C: $10.50

    B: $9.50   D: $12.00

89. Employers must pay overtime compensation of _____ the regular rate after 40 hours of work in a work week.

    A: ¼ times   C: 1-½ times

    B: 1 times   D: twice

90. True or False: A work week is a period of 168 hours during seven consecutive 24-hour periods.

    A: True   B: False

91. I-9 Forms must be kept on file for at least _____ years after the date of hire or fore at one year after date employment ends.

    A: 2   C: 4

    B: 3   D: 5

92. I-9 Forms must be completed within _____ days of hire.

    A: 3   C: 15

    B: 7   D: 30

93. Which of the following documents can employees provide to establishes their identity as well as employment eligibility?

    A: U.S. Passport   C: Permanent resident card

    B: Certificate of U.S. Citizenship   D: All of the above

94. Which of the following is a documents that establish employment eligibility?

    A: U.S. Social Security card   C: Certified birth certificate

    B: U.S. ID card   D: All of the above

95. This law prohibits discrimination against persons with disabilities and applies to employers with _____ or more employees.

    A: 1   C: 10

    B: 5   D: 15

96. Requires payment of prevailing wage rates and firings benefits on federally financed or assisted construction _____.

    A: Walsh-Healey Public Contracts Act   C: Service Contract Act

    B: Davis Baron Act   D: Civil Rights Act

Law & Business Exam Part V

97. Requires payment of minimum wage rates and overtime pay on contracts that provide goods to federal government _____.

    A: Walsh-Healey Public Contracts Act

    B: Davis Baron Act

    C: Service Contract Act

    D: Civil Rights Act

98. Sets overtime standard for service and construction contracts on federal projects _____.

    A: Wage Law

    B: The Contracts Work Hours and Safety Standards

    C: Garnishment Law

    D: Consumer Protection Act

99. Prohibits employers from paying different wages to men and women who perform essentially the same work under similar working conditions _____.

    A: Equal Pay Act

    B: Uniformed Services Employment and Reemployment Rights Act

    C: Right-to-work

    D: Retraining Notifications Act

100. Age Discrimination in Employment Act (ADEA) prohibits discrimination against individuals who are age 40 or older; it applies to employers with _____ or more employees.

    A: 10

    B: 15

    C: 20

    D: 25

EXAM 5

1. **Answer D.** Any of the above

   A home improvement contract means an agreement, whether oral or written: contained in one or more documents, between a contractor and an owner, a contractor and a tenant or a salesperson and an owner or tenant.",

2. **Answer C.** 10-point typeface

   Any printed form must be readable; the text must be at least 10-point typeface.

3. **Answer B.** signed and dated by both the contractor and the buyer

   Before any work is started, the contractor must give the buyer a copy of the contract signed and dated by both the contractor and the buyer.

4. **Answer C.** Notice of Cancellation

   The buyer must be informed by the contractor that the owner may cancel the contract by returning a Notice of Cancellation.

5. **Answer C.** unconditional mechanics lien release

   The contractor, before each payment is being made for work performed, must furnish to the person contracting for home improvements an unconditional mechanics lien release.

6. **Answer B.** incorporated into the contract

   A change order form for changes or extra work must be incorporated into the contract and must be signed by the parties agreeing to the change or extra work prior to commencement of any additional work.

7. **Answer C.** Both A and B

   The contractor must inform the owner or tenant that they have a right to require the contractor to provide a performance and payment bond.

8. **Answer A.** the contractor must not have any financial interest in the control

   If a contract provides for a contractor to furnish joint control, then the contractor must not have any financial interest in the control. \n\nJoint control is a third party controlling the progress of work and payments.

9. **Answer D.** All of the above

   If a finance charge is part of the contract, there must be a heading that reads: Finance Charge, a statement of the dollars an cents must be printed and the finance charge should be set out separately from the contract amount.

10. **Answer D.** 12-point typeface

    In any form, the heading "Down Payment" must be at least 12-point boldface type.

11. **Answer A.** True

    The down payment may not exceed$1,000.00 or 10% of the contract whichever is less.

12. **Answer D.** Any of the above

    A contractor furnishing a performance and payment bond, lien and completion bond and joint control approved by the Registrar is exempt from the minimum down payment.

13. **Answer D.** All the above

    It is against the law for a contractor to: collect payments for work not completed, collect payment for materials not yet delivered, employ workers without Worker's Compensation Insurance.

14. **Answer D.** All of the above

    Extra Work or Change Order is not enforceable against a buyer unless the change order states: scope of work encompassed by the order, amount to be added or subtracted from the contract and completion date.

15. **Answer D.** All of the above

    The following notices must be provided to the owner as part of the contract form: Mechanics Lien Warning, Three Day Right to Cancel and Worker's Compensation Insurance Information.

16. **Answer C.** joint check

17. **Answer C.** $5,000.00

    If a home improvement for goods or services is$5,000.00 or less, the property can not be used as security for payment.

18. **Answer B.** $100.00

    A violation of a down payment as described in a Home Improvement contract is punishable by a min. fine of$100.00. The max. fine for such violation is$5,000.00

19. **Answer C.** $750.00

    The work in Service and Repair Contracts must not exceed$750.00.

20. **Answer A.** True

    Corporations are more complex to form and operate but reduce personal liability of the owners.

21. **Answer C.** state law

    To form a corporation it is necessary to comply with the state law

22. **Answer A.** legal existence

    An incorporation provides your business with a legal existence. The corporation owns the money and assets.

23. **Answer A.** S corp

    A S corp is a corporation that has a limited number of investors.\nAn S corp is limited to 75 shareholders.

24. **Answer A.** S corp

    The S corporation can avoid double taxation (corporate and shareholder taxes).

25. **Answer A.** S corp

    The S corp corporation passes its items of income, loss deductions and credits through to its shareholders to be included on their separate tax returns.

26. **Answer C.** LLC

    A LLC is a form of company where the ownership is invested in membership rather than shares of stock. An LLC must consist of at least one owner.

EXAM 5

27. **Answer C.** domestic

When a corporation operates exclusively in the state where it is formed, it is referred to as domestic. \n\nNote: To operate the same corporation in an additional state the corporation must file foreign articles.

28. **Answer A.** unlimited liability

When operating a sole proprietorship the owner has unlimited liability.

29. **Answer A.** unlimited

General partnerships have unlimited liability.

30. **Answer D.** no personal liability

Limited partners of a partnership generally have no personal liability.

31. **Answer D.** accounting cycle

A series of events that is repeated each reporting period is referred to as an accounting cycle. An accounting cycle begins with a transaction and ends with closing the books.

32. **Answer A.** source

A transaction is an event that either increases or decreases an account balance; the source document is proof that a transaction took place.\n\nExamples of source documents include: cash, card receipts, invoices and purchase orders.

33. **Answer C.** journals

Daily transactions are recorded in a set of books called journals.

34. **Answer D.** statement

Posting is the process of transferring the transaction recorded in the journals to the appropriate accounts (to register value), most companies have five basic types of accounts, they are the following: asset, liability, equity, income and expense.

35. **Answer A.** chart of accounts

A numbering system that organizes the 5 basic accounts is referred to as a chart of accounts.

36. **Answer B.** journal

When you post transactions, you are transferring them from the journal to the ledger.

37. **Answer C.** trial balance

When you tally the accounts you prepare a trial balance.

38. **Answer A.** True

Every entry in a general ledger contains both a debit and a credit which must equal each other.

39. **Answer A.** adjusted balance

40. **Answer C.** Cash method

Cash Method is when you report income in the year that you receive it and deduct expenses in the same year that you paid them.

41. **Answer D.** Accrual method

Accrual method is when you recognizing income when services occur, not when you collect the money.

42. **Answer B.** Progress payments

Progress payments are partial payments made to the contractor after specified phases of construction are complete.

43. **Answer A.** Lump sum payments

Lump sum payments are payments for contracts that are calculated for the percentage of work completed.

44. **Answer C.** Unit price payments

Unit price payments are payments based on actual work units completed.

45. **Answer B.** Cost plus payments

Cost plus payments are payments based on actual cost rather than a percentage of work completed.

46. **Answer B.** Depreciation

Depreciation is a process of devaluing a fixed asset as a result of aging, wear and tear.\n\nNote: Land cannot be depreciated.

47. **Answer C.** Property Insurance

Property Insurance is an insurance policy that typically covers your business and personal property when damage, theft or loss occurs.\n\nProperty insurance covers building, furniture, inventory, trucks, etc.

48. **Answer A.** All-risk Insurance

All-risk Insurance is an insurance that covers property owners and builders for buildings under construction.

49. **Answer B.** Named Peril Insurance

Named Peril Insurance is an insurance that specifies which perils are covered by the insurance. Examples of Named Peril Insurance include: Water Damage Insurance, Earthquake Insurance, Fire Insurance, Lightning Insurance and Explosion Insurance.

50. **Answer C.** Inland Marine Insurance

Inland Marine Insurance is an insurance that can be purchased for your tools and equipment. This insurance covers goods in transit and projects under construction.

51. **Answer B.** Equipment Floater Insurance

Equipment Floater Insurance is an insurance for direct physical loss to equipment, designed to cover mobile equipment while it is stored on premises or in transit.\n\nNote: Equipment Floater Insurance is a type of Inland Marine Insurance.

52. **Answer C.** Both A and B

Transportation Floater Insurance and Motor Truck Cargo Insurance is a policy that protects the transporter against damage that occurs to freight during transport.

53. **Answer C.** Liability Insurance

Liability Insurance is an insurance that protects against third-party claims that arise from alleged negligence resulting in bodily injury or property damage.

EXAM 5

54. **Answer D.** All of the above

    Commercial General Liability (CGL) covers 4 types of injuries, they are the following: \n\n• Bodily injury from physical damage or loss for individuals who are not employees.\n\n• Damage or loss to property not belonging to the business.\n\n• Personal injury, including slander or damage to reputation.\n\n• Advertising injury, including charges of negligence that results from promotion of goods or services.

55. **Answer C.** Umbrella Liability Insurance

    A policy that provides additional coverage in the areas that are not covered in the CGL policy may be supplemental with Umbrella Liability Insurance.

56. **Answer C.** Workers' Compensation Insurance

    Workers' Compensation Insurance is an insurance that provides insurance for employees who are injured on the job.

57. **Answer B.** Unemployment Insurance

    Unemployment Insurance is an insurance that provides unemployment benefits to eligible workers who become unemployed.

58. **Answer B.** False

    It is always necessary to verify that the subcontractors of the direct contractor are adequately insured.

59. **Answer D.** bid bond

    A bid bond is a bond that guarantees that the contractor, if awarded the job, will do work at the submitted bid price.

60. **Answer A.** performance bond

    A performance is a bond guaranteeing that the contractor will complete a contract within its time frame and conditions.

61. **Answer C.** payment bond

    A payment bond is a bond that guarantees subcontractors and suppliers that they will be paid.

62. **Answer B.** maintenance bond

    A maintenance bond is a bond that guarantees that for a stated period, usually one year, no defective work or material will appear in the completed project.

63. **Answer B.** completion bond

    A completion is a bond that provides assurance to the financial backers of a construction project that it will be completed on time.

64. **Answer D.** fidelity bond

    A fidelity bond is a bond that covers business owners for losses due to dishonest acts by their employees.

65. **Answer C.** Miller Act

    The Miller Act is a current law (act) requiring performance and payment bonds on all federal construction projects valued at greater than $100,000.

66. **Answer A.** EIN number

    Before you become an employer and hire employees, you need an EIN number. EIN number stands for Employer Identification Number.

67. **Answer D.** All of the above

    All of the following require an EIN number: Partnerships, Corporations, Joint Venues, Sole Ownerships.\n\nException: Sole ownerships with no employees don't require an EIN number.

68. **Answer D.** All of the above

    There are three Federal types of business taxes that you may be responsible for, they are the following: Income tax, Self-Employment tax and Employment tax.

69. **Answer A.** True

    All businesses except partnerships must file an annual income tax return.

70. **Answer A.** information form

    Partnerships file an information form.

71. **Answer A.** Sole proprietors

    %Sole proprietors generally have to make estimated tax payments. Note: for$1,000.00 or more use form 1040 ES."

72. **Answer D.** $5,000

    Other than the S corporation, corporations have to make estimated tax payments if the expected tax is$5,000 or more.\n\nNote: Use Form 1120-W.

73. **Answer D.** Social Security and Medicare

    For individuals who work for themselves the self-employment tax (SE tax) includes Social Security and Medicare.\n\nUse a 1040 form at$400.00 or more in earnings.

74. **Answer B.** ordinary and necessary

    As defined by the IRS, to be deductible, a business expense must be ordinary and necessary.

75. **Answer D.** All of the above

    Employers are required to withhold, deposit, report and pay: Social Security, Medicare, Federal Income Tax and Federal Unemployment Tax.\n\nEmployers must keep records for at least four years.

76. **Answer B.** W-4

    The form used to withhold Federal income tax from an employee's wages is W-4.

77. **Answer A.** W-2

    A statement that summarizes the employee's previous year's wages and withholding amount is W-2.\n\nIt must be furnished to the employee by January 31 for the previous year.

78. **Answer D.** All of the above

    There are three payroll deposit schedules, they are the following: monthly, semi-weekly and daily.\n\nFor four quarters,$50,000.00 or less – monthly. \nFor four quarters, over$50,000.00 – semiweekly. \nFor any one day,$100,000.00 or more – daily.

79. **Answer C.** 2 to 100

    To avoid penalties, be sure to make accurate and prompt deposits, the penalties can range from 2 to 100 percent.

EXAM 5

80. **Answer D.**   1099

Payments made during the year to persons not treated as employees are reported on Form 1099.\n\nFor payments of$600.00 or more, file by January 31 for prior year.

81. **Answer D.**   All of the above

When interviewing an applicant for employment you are not permitted to ask any of the following questions:\n\n• How old are you?\n\n• Do you have any disabilities?\n\n• Are you pregnant?\n\n• Are you married?\n\n• Do you have children?\n\n• What is your religion?\n\n• What is your sexual orientation?\n\n• What is your ethnic background?

82. **Answer A.**   7:00 a.m.

When school is in session, a minor 14 or 15 years of age may not begin work before 7:00am.\n\nAdditionally, they may not work later than 7:00 p.m. or 9:00 p.m. between June 1 and Labor day

83. **Answer C.**   3

A minor 14 or 15 years of age during school session may not work more than 3 hour(s) a day.\n\nA minor can not work more than 18 hours a week.\n\nImportant Note: a minor can NOT work during school hours.

84. **Answer C.**   8

When school is not in session a minor 14 or 15 may not work more than 8 hours a day or 40 hours a week.

85. **Answer C.**   16 to 17

Federal restrictions on working hours or number of hours do not exist for minors 16 to 17 years of age.

86. **Answer D.**   All of the above

All minors are prohibited from employment in occupations considered hazardous. Minors ages 14 or 15 years of age may work in: offices, clerical or sales jobs.

87. **Answer A.**   I-9

The United State Customs and Immigration Service requires a I-9 form to show that a worker has legal immigration status in the USA.

88. **Answer A.** $7.25

The Federal minimum wage effective 2009 is$7.25

89. **Answer C.**   1-½ times

Employers must pay overtime compensation of 1-½ times the regular rate after 40 hours of work in a work week.

90. **Answer A.**   True

A work week is a period of 168 hours during seven consecutive 24-hour periods.

91. **Answer B.**   3

I-9 Forms must be kept on file for at least 3 years after the date of hire or fore at one year after date employment ends.

92. **Answer A.**   3

I-9 Forms must be completed within 3 days of hire.

93. **Answer D.**   All of the above

Employees can provide any of the following documents to establish their identity as well as their employment eligibility:\n\n• U.S. Passport\n\n• Certificate of U.S. Citizenship\n\n• Certificate of U.S. naturalization\n\n• Unexpired foreign passport with I-551 stamp or attached I-94 form indicating current employment authorization\n\n• Permanent resident card or alien registration receipt with photograph\n\nNote: Employees also have the option of providing two documents – one to establish identity and the other to establish employment eligibility. Documents that establish identity include: state-issued driver's license with photo, ID card with photo issued by federal, state or local government agencies, voter's registration card and U.S. military card

94. **Answer D.**   All of the above

All of the following documents can be used to establish employment eligibility: U.S. Social Security card, Certified birth certificate, U.S. ID card, Resident ID card or Native American tribal document.

95. **Answer D.**   15

This law prohibits discrimination against persons with disabilities and applies to employers with 15 or more employees.

96. **Answer B.**   Davis Baron Act

Requires payment of prevailing wage rates and firings benefits on federally financed or assisted construction Davis Baron Act.

97. **Answer A.**   Walsh-Healey Public Contracts Act

Requires payment of minimum wage rates and overtime pay on contracts that provide goods to federal government Walsh-Healey Public Contracts Act.

98. **Answer B.**   The Contracts Work Hours and Safety Standards

Sets overtime standard for service and construction contracts on federal projects The Contracts Work Hours and Safety Standards.

99. **Answer A.**   Equal Pay Act

Prohibits employers from paying different wages to men and women who perform essentially the same work under similar working conditions Equal Pay Act.

100. **Answer C.**   20

Age Discrimination in Employment Act (ADEA) prohibits discrimination against individuals who are age 40 or older; it applies to employers with 20 or more employees.",

EXAM 6

Law & Business Exam Part VI

1. Every employer covered by OSHA who has more than 10 employers must maintain three types of OSHA-specified records of job related injuries and illnesses, which of the following is one of them?

   A: Form 300

   B: Form 300A   C: From 301

                                D: All of the above

2. The OSHA Form _____ is an injury/illness log.

   A: 300   C: 301

   B: 300A   D: 300B

3. The OSHA Form _____ is an individual incident report.

   A: 300   C: 301

   B: 300A   D: 300B

4. Employers with _____ or fewer employees are exempt from maintaining the OSHA records stated above.

   A: 5   C: 15

   B: 10   D: 20

5. OSHA records must be kept by the employer for _____ years following the year for which they pertain.

   A: 3   C: 5

   B: 4   D: 10

6. Exposure records and medical records due to toxic substances must be maintained for _____ years.

   A: 10   C: 20

   B: 15   D: 30

7. When a work related fatality requires hospitalization of _____ employees you must report to OSHA within eight hours.

   A: two or more   C: four or more

   B: three or more   D: five or more

8. MSDS refers to _____.

   A: Medical Safety Data Sheet   C: Manufacture Safety Data Sheet

   B: Minor Safety Data Sheet   D: Material Safety Data Sheet

EXAM 6

9. Underground Utility Safety protects the contractor from unnecessary fines and repair cost. It is recommended to use a locater for underground utilities such as _____.

    A: Common Ground Alliance (CGS) C: Dig Alert (DA)

    B: Utilities Locater (UL) D: Under Ground Utilities (UGU)

10. Employees have rights to _____ to/with OSHA.

    A: complain C: participate

    B: contest D: All of the above

11. Contractors need to be aware of environmental considerations during construction; this includes the _____.

    A: pre-bid phase C: construction phase

    B: pre-construction phase D: All of the above

12. The _____ is responsible for researching and setting national standards for a variety of environmental programs.

    A: OSHA C: ASTM

    B: EPA D: CAA

13. Before beginning any demolition or renovation activities on existing buildings, you should evaluate the potential for releasing _____.

    A: gas C: asbestos

    B: dust D: lead

14. The Clean Water Act includes _____.

    A: pollutant discharge elimination C: storm water discharge

    B: storm water discharge and construction site runoff D: All the above

15. An examples of hazardous waste is _____.

    A: lead-based paint C: batteries (mercury)

    B: used oil D: All of the above

16. An underground storage tank (UST) is defined as a tank and any underground piping connected to the tank that has at least _____ percent of its combined volume underground.

    A: 10 C: 25

    B: 15 D: 30

EXAM 6

17. Lead is considered a toxic, engineering controls are recommended to reduce worker exposure, these include _____.

    A: exhaust ventilation

    B: encapsulation

    C: substituting lead

    D: Any of the above

18. A federal regulation involving contractors performing renovation in residential housing containing lead paint in known as _____.

    A: Lead abatement (La)

    B: Lead (HEPA)

    C: Lead PRE

    D: None of the above

19. Only certified contractors can perform renovation, repair and painting projects that disturb lead-based paint in homes, child care facilities, and schools built before _____.

    A: 1978

    B: 1980

    C: 1987

    D: 1990

20. Under Lead PRE, federal law requires that contractors provide lead information to residents before renovating _____.

    A: pre-1978 housing

    B: pre-1980 housing

    C: pre-1987 housing

    D: pre-1990 housing

21. Renovations under Lead PRE are modifications of all or part of any existing structure that disturbs a painted surface; which of the following is exempt?

    A: Minor repair and maintenance that disturbs two square feet or less of paint per component.

    B: Removal/modification of painted surfaces.

    C: Surface preparation activities: sanding, scraping

    D: Window replacement.

22. Which of the following factors dictates construction projects?

    A: budget

    B: scope

    C: schedule

    D: All of the above

23. What is the first step in a traditional project?

    A: bid

    B: design

    C: build

    D: None of the above

24. What is the title given to the person who plans, directs, budgets and manages a construction project?

    A: Construction Manager

    B: Construction Director

    C: Managing Officer

    D: Managing Employee

EXAM 6

25. True or False: The Engineering and Design Specification Team establishes the design and construction specifications for the various portions of a project.

   A: True   B: False

26. What is the final step in managing a project development process?

   A: Customer satisfaction   C: Design

   B: Formally documenting the authorization of   D: Bidding
      a project

27. PRD documents the _____.

   A: scope of work   C: project authorization

   B: details of the project   D: All of the above

28. True or False: Scope of Work describes the overall project purpose and gives a holistic view of the magnitude of the project.

   A: True   B: False

29. The _____ establishes the systems and processes necessary to ensure that the contractor complies with the terms and conditions during the performance of the contract.

   A: Plans and Specifications   C: Scope of Work

   B: Contract Management Plan   D: Blueprints

30. Which of the following words is used to describe the measure of experience, skill level and ability to perform?

   A: Capability   C: Both A and B

   B: Capacity   D: Neither A nor B

31. The NEPA stands for _____.

   A: National Environmental Policy Act   C: National Electric Policy Association

   B: National Electric Protection Association   D: National Energy Production Act

32. True or False: Value Engineering ensures that an organization receives full value of every dollar invested.

   A: True   B: False

33. What defines a quality assurance process for new construction and installations?

   A: Capacity   C: Commissioning

   B: Compromising   D: Capability

Law & Business Exam Part VI

34. Request for Expressions of Interest is used to gather information on _____.

    A: subcontractor capabilities and qualifications

    B: supplier capabilities and qualifications

    C: worker capabilities and qualifications

    D: customers capability to pay

35. This method involves the building owner contracting a single entity to provide both the design and the construction of a building.

    A: Draw-Build

    B: Draw-Buy

    C: Design-Bid

    D: Design-Build

36. This method involves working with an architect until the final design.

    A: Design-Build

    B: Design-Bid-Build

    C: Draw-Build

    D: Draw-Bid-Build

37. What is referred to as a combination of the DB and the DBB method?

    A: bridging

    B: comprising

    C: DBDBB

    D: None of the above

38. This type of corporation can be seen as a "pass through" entity, since all profits and losses pass through the business to the owners.

    A: S-Corporation

    B: C-Corporation

    C: Limited Liability Corporation

    D: Limited Corporation

39. True or False: LLC owners members can not vote with free transferability of ownership interest.

    A: True

    B: False

40. How many individual shareholders can an S-corporation have?

    A: 25

    B: 50

    C: 75

    D: 100

41. True or False: When a corporation makes a Subchapter S Election, the corporation is not taxed at a corporate level.

    A: True

    B: False

42. In accounting, this principle requires that accounts be prepared using the same method each period.

    A: Consistency

    B: Amortization

    C: Credit

    D: Debit

EXAM 6

Law & Business Exam Part VI

43. True or False: Risk Appetite defines the amount of risk a company is prepared to accept/be exposed to.

    A: True   B: False

44. _____ Analysis is a useful, strategic planning tool for evaluating strengths, weaknesses, opportunities and threats.

    A: MBE   C: SWOT

    B: ISC   D: DBB

45. _____ is a style of managing in which attention in paid primarily to items that are exceptional.

    A: Contract Management Plan   C: Management by Exceptions

    B: Contract Exceptions Plan   D: Management Exception Strategy

46. A _____ is the term often used to define a stipulated sum contract.

    A: Fixed Price Contract   C: Stipulated Sum Contract

    B: Lump Sum Contract   D: Total Price Contract

47. A _____ is used between a direct contractor and a subcontractor for maintenance and repair agreements.

    A: Fixed Price Contract   C: Unit Price Contract

    B: Lump Sum Contract   D: Hour Price Contract

48. In this type of arrangement the owner pays the construction manager the actual cost of the construction and the reimbursable expenses involved.

    A: Fixed Price Contract   C: Fixed Price Agreement

    B: Unit Price Agreement   D: Cost Plus Fee arrangement

49. True or False: A Request for Proposal serves as an invitation for buyers to submit a proposal on a specified type of product and/or service.

    A: True   B: False

50. True or False: "Time is of the essence" is a phrase that refers to a clause that can support a breach of contract action when a contract is not completed within the specified time.

    A: True   B: False

51. True or False: A Liquidated Damages Clause can be applied when it is difficult to calculate the total of damages.

    A: True   B: False

52. True or False: Under no circumstance can a lender be held liable for negligence claims on construction projects.

    A: True   B: False

EXAM 6

53. The _____ applies to contractors and subcontractors working on federally funded contracts exceeding$2000

    A: Davis-Bacon Act

    B: Related Acts

    C: Both A and B

    D: Neither A nor B

54. The Contract Work Hours and Safety Standards Act applies to contractors with federally funded construction contracts exceeding _____.

    A: $2,000

    B: $20,000

    C: $50,000

    D: $100,000

55. The Worker Adjustment and Retraining Notification Act requires an employer to provide advance notification of mass layoffs and/or closure of business. Notification must be given _____ calendar days prior to mass layoffs or closure of business.

    A: 15

    B: 30

    C: 60

    D: 120

56. _____ establishes Employer responsibilities and Employee Rights.

    A: The California Labor Code

    B: Title 8

    C: Both A and B

    D: Neither A nor B

EXAM 6

1. **Answer D.** All of the above

   Every employer covered by OSHA who has more than 10 employers must maintain three types of OSHA-specified records of job related injuries and illnesses, they are the following: Form 300, Form 300A and Form 301.

2. **Answer A.** 300

   The OSHA Form 300 is an injury/illness log.

3. **Answer C.** 301

   The OSHA Form 301 is an individual incident report.

4. **Answer B.** 10

5. **Answer C.** 5

   OSHA records must be kept by the employer for 5 years following the year for which they pertain.

6. **Answer D.** 30

   Exposure records and medical records due to toxic substances must be maintained for 30 years.

7. **Answer B.** three or more

   When a work related fatality requires hospitalization of 3 or more employees you must report to OSHA within eight hours.\n\nNote: If death occurs within 30 days of the incident, employers must report it within eight hours.

8. **Answer D.** Material Safety Data Sheet

   MSDS refers to Material Safety Data Sheet.\nThe MSDS Recognizes the hazards of materials.

9. **Answer A.** Common Ground Alliance (CGS)

   Underground Utility Safety protects the contractor from unnecessary fines and repair cost. It is recommended to use a locater for underground utilities such as Common Ground Alliance (CGS).

10. **Answer D.** All of the above

    Employees have rights to: complain, contest and participate to/with OSHA.

11. **Answer D.** All of the above

    Contractors need to be aware of environmental considerations during construction; this includes the: pre-bid phase, pre-construction phase and construction phase.

12. **Answer B.** EPA

    The EPA is responsible for researching and setting national standards for a variety of environmental programs, such as the Clean Water Act, the Clean Air Act, the Endangered Species Act and the National Historic Preservation Act.

13. **Answer C.** asbestos

    Before beginning any demolition or renovation activities on existing buildings, you should evaluate the potential for releasing asbestos.

14. **Answer D.** All the above

    The Clean Water Act includes: storm water discharge and construction site runoff, pollutant discharge elimination and storm water discharge.

15. **Answer D.** All of the above

    Examples of hazardous waste are:\n\n• lead-based paint\n\n• used oil\n\n• hydraulic fluid\n\n• gypsum\n\n• batteries (mercury)\n\n• thermostats (mercury)

16. **Answer A.** 10

    An underground storage tank (UST) is defined as a tank and any underground piping connected to the tank that has at least 10 percent of its combined volume underground.

17. **Answer D.** Any of the above

    Lead is considered a toxic, engineering controls are recommended to reduce worker exposure, these include all of the following: exhaust ventilation, encapsulation, substituting lead, replacing or isolating.

18. **Answer C.** Lead PRE

    A federal regulation involving contractors performing renovation in residential housing containing lead paint in known as Lead PRE.

19. **Answer A.** 1978

    Only certified contractors can perform renovation, repair and painting projects that disturb lead-based paint in homes, child care facilities, and schools built before 1978.\n\nTo qualify an 8-hour training course from an accredited EPA training provider is required.

20. **Answer A.** pre-1978 housing

    Under Lead PRE, federal law requires that contractors provide lead information to residents before renovating pre-1978 housing.

21. **Answer A.** Minor repair and maintenance that disturbs two square feet or less of paint per component.

    Renovations under Lead PRE are modifications of all or part of any existing structure that disturbs a painted surface. The following is exempt: Minor repair and maintenance that disturbs two square feet or less of paint per component.

22. **Answer D.** All of the above

    Construction projects are determined by the following factors: budget, scope and schedule.

23. **Answer B.** design

    Design is the first step in a traditional project. The structure of a traditional project is design, bib, build.

24. **Answer A.** Construction Manager

    A construction manager plans, directs, budgets and manages a construction project. Since he/she has the full authority to manage, organize and mobilize the necessary resources to complete the project, the responsibility of the success or failure of project completion heavily falls on him/her.

25. **Answer A.** True

    The Engineering and Design Specification Team establishes the design and construction specifications for the various portions of a project.

EXAM 6

26. **Answer B.** Formally documenting the authorization of a project

    The final step in managing a project development process is to formally document the authorization of a project.

27. **Answer D.** All of the above

    A Project Requirements Definition (PRD) documents the relevant scope of work, details of the project and project authorization.

28. **Answer A.** True

    The scope of work (SOW) describes the overall project purpose and gives a holistic view of the magnitude of the project. An SOW should be specific, measurable, accountable, reasonable and time-based; think of the work SMART to remember all of the component of a good SOW.

29. **Answer B.** Contract Management Plan

    The Contract Management Plan (CMP) establishes the systems and processes necessary to ensure that the contractor complies with the terms and conditions during the performance of the contract. It contains all the key information about how a contract will be managed. Additionally the CMP can be used to ensure the plan is accurate and to create a graphical display for task control management.

30. **Answer A.** Capability

    Capability describes the measure of experience, skill level and ability to perform. \n\nCapacity refers to the measure of the quantity specified resources.

31. **Answer A.** National Environmental Policy Act

    NEPA stands for the National Environmental Policy Act. The NEPA describes the process for coordinating compliance with many different laws in the United States.

32. **Answer A.** True

    Value Engineering assures that an organization receives full value of every dollar invested. It teaches techniques to improve productivity in organization, including practices, processes and procedures.

33. **Answer C.** Commissioning

    Commissioning defines a quality assurance process for new construction and installations.

34. **Answer B.** supplier capabilities and qualifications

    Request for Expressions of Interest is used to gather information on supplier capabilities and qualifications.

35. **Answer D.** Design-Build

    The Design-Build (DB) method involves the building owner contracting a single entity to provide both the design and the construction of a building. This type of building procedure is also referred to as the EPC (engineer, procure and construct) or turnkey construction.

36. **Answer B.** Design-Bid-Build

    The Design-Bid-Build (DBB) method involves working with an architect until the final design. Once the final design is reached then a contractor is hired and the design is executed.

37. **Answer A.** bridging

    Bridging is a combination of the DB and the DBB method.

38. **Answer C.** Limited Liability Corporation

    Limited Liability Corporation can be seen as a "pass through" entity, since all profits and losses pass through the business to the owners. In this type of corporation the owners must report their profits and losses as their personal taxes and thus the LLC does not have to pay federal taxes itself. Earnings of most members of an LLC may be subject to self-employment taxes.

39. **Answer B.** False

    LLC owners are members who can vote with free transferability of ownership interest.

40. **Answer C.** 75

    An S-corporation can have a maximum of 75 individual shareholders.

41. **Answer A.** True

    When a corporation makes a Subchapter S Election, the corporation is not taxed at a corporate level. Instead, profits and losses are passed through the corporation to the individual shareholders. Because of this transfer of taxes, an S-corporation is often referred as a Subchapter S corporation.

42. **Answer A.** Consistency

    In accounting the consistency principle requires that accounts be prepared using the same method each period.

43. **Answer A.** True

    Risk Appetite defines the amount of risk a company is prepared to accept/be exposed to.

44. **Answer C.** SWOT

    SWOT Analysis is a useful, strategic planning tool for evaluating strengths, weaknesses, opportunities and threats.

45. **Answer C.** Management by Exceptions

    Management by Exceptions is a style of managing in which attention in paid primarily to items that are exceptional. Exceptions are can be defined as the breaching of predefined assumption of an operational process.

46. **Answer B.** Lump Sum Contract

    A lump sum contract is a stipulated sum contract. In this type of contract a fixed amount of money is agreed to be paid upon completion of the work/project. Lump sum bids must be determined by estimating the cost of labor and materials, standard amount of overhead and profit.

47. **Answer C.** Unit Price Contract

    A unit price contract is used between a direct contractor and a subcontractor for maintenance and repair agreements. This type of contract breaks up the work into various parts – usually by construction trade.\n\nUnit price is often used for items with indefinite quantities. On the other hand, a fixed price is established for each unit of work.

EXAM 6

48. Answer D. Cost Plus Fee arrangement

In the cost plus fee arrangement the owner pays the construction manager the actual cost of the construction and the reimbursable expenses involved. In this arrangement there is a fixed fee charged for the services provided.

49. Answer B. False

A Request for Proposal serves as an invitation for suppliers to submit a proposal on a specified type of product and/or service. It compiles information and prices.

50. Answer A. True

The "time is of the essence" phrase refers to a clause that can support a breach of contract action where a contract is not completed within the specified time.

51. Answer A. True

A Liquidated Damages Clause can be applied when it is difficult to calculate the total of damages.

52. Answer B. False

Generally, lenders are not held liable for negligence claims on construction projects. However, if a lender assumes title of the project or presents him/herself as something more than a lender, then he/she becomes liable.

53. Answer C. Both A and B

Davis-Bacon and Related Acts apply to contractors and subcontractors working on federally funded contracts for the construction, alteration or repair of public buildings. These Acts apply to contracts exceeding $2000.

54. Answer D. $100,000

The Contract Work Hours and Safety Standards Act applies to contractors and subcontractors with federal service contracts, federally funded and assisted construction contracts exceeding $100,000.

55. Answer C. 60

The Worker Adjustment and Retraining Notification Act requires an employer to provide advance notification of mass layoffs and/or closure of business. Notification must be given 60 calendar days prior to mass layoffs or closure of business.

56. Answer C. Both A and B

The California Labor Code and Title 8 of the California Code of Regulations establishes Employer responsibilities and Employee Rights.",

EXAM 7

Law & Business Supplemental

General Information

1. What does public works mean?

Under the Labor Code, public works in general refers to:

- Construction, alteration, demolition, installation, maintenance, or repair work,
- Done under contract, and
- Paid for in whole or in part out of public funds

It can include preconstruction and post-construction activities related to a public works project.

2. What are prevailing wages, and who must receive them?

All workers employed on public works projects must be paid the prevailing wage determined by the Director of the DIR according to the type of work and location of the project. The prevailing wage rates are usually, but not always, based on rates specified in collective bargaining agreements.

Contractors and Contractor Registration

1. Who is a public works contractor?

A public works contractor is anyone who bids on or enters into a contract to perform work that requires the payment of prevailing wages. It includes subcontractors who have entered into a contract with another contractor to perform a portion of the work on a public works project. It includes sole proprietors and brokers who are responsible for performing work on a public works project, even if they do not have employees or will not use their own employees to perform the work.

2. Who needs to register as a public works contractor?

Anyone who fits within the definition of public works contractor (above) is required to register with the DIR.

3. Is a contractor who only does Davis-Bacon work under federal contracts required to register?

Registration is required only to bid or work on public works projects that are subject to the prevailing wage requirements of the State of California. Registration is not required for projects that are awarded by and under the complete control of the federal government. However, federally funded or assisted projects that are controlled or carried out by awarding bodies in California are subject to the state's prevailing wage laws and therefore require registration.

4. Are there any exceptions to the registration requirement?

Law & Business Supplemental

The contractor registration requirement does not apply to contractors working solely on public works projects awarded prior to April 1, 2015. Some exceptions allow contractors to bid on federally funded projects or submit joint venture bids without first being registered, as long as the contractors that are parties to the joint venture and the joint venture are registered at the time the contract is awarded.

Contractors who work exclusively on small public works projects are not required to register as a public works contractor or file electronic certified payroll reports for those projects. Contractors are still required to maintain certified payroll records on a continuous basis, and provide them to the Labor Commissioner's Office upon request. Additionally, awarding agencies are not required to submit the notice of contract award through DIR's PWC-100 system on projects that fall within the small project exemption. The small project exemption applies for all public works projects that do not exceed:

- o $25,000 for new construction, alteration, installation, demolition or repair
- o $15,000 for maintenance

5. Who is eligible to register?

Contractors must meet the following requirements to register:

- o Have workers' compensation coverage for any employees and only use subcontractors who are registered public works contractors.
- o Have a Contractors State License Board license if applicable to trade.
- o Have no delinquent unpaid wage or penalty assessments owed to any employee or enforcement agency.
- o Not be under federal or state debarment.
- o Not be in prior violation of this registration requirement once it becomes effective. However, for the first violation in a 12-month period, a contractor may still qualify for registration by paying an additional penalty.

6. How much does registration cost, and how long does it last?

Registration costs $400 and covers one fiscal year (July 1–June 30), regardless of the date on which a contractor registers. Registration is renewable annually.

7. What if I don't register (i.e., what are the consequences of noncompliance)?

Contractors who are required to register but fail to do so are ineligible to bid or work on a public works contract and can be removed from any public works project on which they currently are working. For a single violation in a 12-month period, a contractor who is otherwise eligible may still register by paying a $2,000 penalty in addition to the $400 registration fee. Registered contractors who inadvertently fail to renew by June 30, but continue to work on public works after that date, have a 90-day grace period to renew retroactively by paying a $400 penalty in addition to the registration renewal fee.

Law & Business Supplemental

8. How long does it take for DIR to process contractor registrations, verify submitted information, and post contractor information in the registration list that is accessible online?

This process can take less than 24 hours if registration fees (including penalties, if applicable) are paid by credit card. Verification of payment by other means can take up to eight weeks.

9. How can a list of all registered contractors be obtained?

The name and registration number of any contractor who has registered with the DIR can be found using the public works contractor search tool. An up-to-date list of all registered contractors can be obtained by entering the percentage symbol, %, in the "Contractor Legal Name" field.

10. I forgot to print out the contractor coupon, can I still mail in the check or do I have to start over? If I can still mail in the check, where should I mail it to?

You do not need to start over. You may mail the check to: State of California, Department of Industrial Relations, Public Works Contractor Registration Unit, P.O. Box 511215, Los Angeles, California 90051-3013. Please include the contractor registration number.

Awarding Bodies

1. What is an awarding body?

An awarding body is the entity that awards a contract for public works and is sometimes known as the project owner. The awarding body can be any kind of public agency (state, county, city, school board, water district, etc.) or a private entity using public funds (Labor Code, section 1722).

2. Do all trades need to be identified on the PWC-100 at the time projects are registered?

Awarding bodies should list information for all trades identified when they register projects (using the PWC-100 form). Awarding bodies are not required to provide information that is not available at the time of project registration.

3. What happens if an awarding body does not register a project within five days of awarding the contract for a public works project?

Failure to provide timely notice can jeopardize an awarding body's ability to obtain state funding for a project. It can also compromise important objectives of the public works laws. An official who intentionally ignores this requirement may be subject to criminal prosecution.

4. If an awarding body has an annual open purchase order for over $1,000 for a registered contractor, does it need to report that contract only once a year?

Law & Business Supplemental

Yes, an awarding body can report the master agreement to comply with the PWC-100 notice requirements. Individual task orders do not need to be reported.

5. **What if an awarding body has a single small job for $250 or a series of jobs with the same contractor/vendor that total over $1,000?**

Prevailing wage requirements apply to public works projects over $1,000. The law does not permit jobs to be parceled in order to avoid the $1,000 threshold. If the awarding body knows that total yearly project costs or projects awarded to the same vendor will exceed $1,000, that vendor must be registered with the DIR as a public works contractor, and the contract for those projects should be registered using the PWC-100 form.

6. **If an agency is subject to the California Uniform Public Construction Cost Accounting Act (Public Contract Code, section 22002), which excludes "maintenance work" from its definition of "public project," do contractors hired for maintenance work still need to register? Are public agencies required to report projects that do not go through the competitive bidding process, such as emergency work and maintenance projects?**

Public agencies are not required to report maintenance projects and emergency work. Contractors on maintenance projects that are part of public works projects are required to continue paying prevailing wages, but are not required to register with the DIR.

7. **What is the process for projects funded through Proposition 84? Is the contracting agency required to register (i.e., fill out the PWC-100 form), and will the contractors and subcontractors be required to submit/upload certified payroll records to the Labor Commissioner?**

Awarding bodies must provide project information to DIR using the PWC-100 form on all public works projects regardless of the funding source, including projects funded by Proposition 84. Certified payroll records are required for Proposition 84 projects, and awarding bodies are still required to have a DIR-approved Labor Compliance Program (LCP) for those projects. Contractors on these Proposition 84 projects must submit certified payroll records to both the DIR and the LCP.

8. **If an awarding body is awarded a contract directly by a federal agency, must it comply with California public works law?**

The awarding body must pay careful attention to whether the project is administered and controlled by the federal agency or the federal agency is only providing financial support or assistance to a project under the direction and control of a state or local agency. California's prevailing wage requirements do not apply to projects awarded by and under the complete control of the federal government. However, federally funded or assisted projects that are controlled or carried out by awarding bodies in California, including most highway construction projects, are subject to the state's prevailing wage laws. Those projects must comply with state requirements, including contractor and project registration, reporting certified payroll records, and payment of California's prevailing wage rates, if they exceed corresponding Davis-Bacon rates.

9. Are awarding bodies required to use registered contractors or submit a PWC-100 for any of the following?

   o Professional service contracts

   o Mechanics who service vehicles at the local dealership or auto shop

   o Engineering firms or construction managers hired to manage public works projects

   o Design consultants, architects, and engineers performing professional design services

   o Material or product suppliers

   o BIM (Building Information Modeling) or CAD (Computer-Aided Design) consultants

   o Consultants providing Division of State Architect inspection services;

   o Trucking companies and truck drivers

   o Furniture dealers who deliver and install furniture

   o Community Conservation Corps certified by the California Conservation Corps

Awarding bodies are required to use registered contractors and register the project for any work subject to prevailing wage requirements. California's public works prevailing wage requirements extend broadly to workers employed "in the execution of the public works contract" (Labor Code, section 1774). Coverage is not necessarily limited to work performed at the construction site by those in traditional construction trades. Awarding bodies and other interested parties can ask DIR's Director to make a formal determination on whether a particular work or project is subject to public works requirements. public works coverage determinations issued by the Director since 2002 are available online.

Apprenticeship

1. Do I have to employ apprentices on all public works projects?

   Contractors working on a public works project valued at $30,000 or more have an obligation to hire apprentices. With few exceptions, this duty applies to all contractors and subcontractors on a project, even if their part of the project is valued at less than $30,000. These exceptions include:

   o General contractors whose contract is worth under $30,000.

   o When the craft or trade is not appropriate for apprentices.

   o When the contractor holds a sole proprietor license and personally performs all the work from start to finish, unassisted.

Law & Business Supplemental

---

       o In the case of a federal project when funding does not include any city, county, or state monies and that is not administered, controlled, or carried out by awarding bodies in California.

    Division of Apprenticeship Standards Public Works Requirements

Labor Compliance Programs

1. What is a Labor Compliance Program?

Labor Compliance Programs (LCPs) are entities that are approved by the DIR to monitor and enforce compliance with state prevailing wage laws on public works projects as described in Labor Code section 1771.5 (b). As of 2016, LCPs were only required for public works projects funded in whole or in part by Proposition 84 (Safe Drinking Water, etc., Bond Act of 2006) as well as for certain older projects under a handful of other statutes. The DIR also continues to oversee four "legacy" LCPs that were approved prior to 2000. For more information go to:

    o Labor Compliance Programs: Office of the Director home page
    o FAQs about LCPs, including when and how to go about adopting a DIR-approved LCP for a project funded by Proposition 84

Certified Payroll Reporting

1. Who must submit certified payroll records?

All contractors and subcontractors working on public works projects (except for those listed below) must submit electronic certified payroll records to the Labor Commissioner. The Labor Commissioner has exempted the following projects from the requirement:

(a) Projects monitored by the following legacy Labor Compliance Programs:

    o California Department of Transportation (Caltrans)
    o City of Los Angeles
    o Los Angeles Unified School District
    o County of Sacramento

(b) Projects covered by a qualifying project labor agreement.

(c) Projects covered by the small project exemption. The small project exemption applies for all public works projects that do not exceed:

    o $25,000 for new construction, alteration, installation, demolition or repair
    o $15,000 for maintenance

2. Is the electronic certified payroll reporting system the only way to submit certified payroll records to the Labor Commissioner?

Law & Business Supplemental

Yes. All contractors must submit their certified payroll records to the Labor Commissioner using the DIR's online system. It offers two options for submitting certified payroll records: entering the information directly using the online form or uploading xml files.

3. Is every company responsible for submitting its own payroll for each project on which it is working?

Yes. Each contractor and subcontractor must submit certified payroll records directly to the Labor Commissioner using DIR's online system

4. When/how frequently must the certified payroll records be submitted?

Certified payroll records must be submitted at least monthly (within a month after the end of the payroll period) or more frequently if more frequent submission is required by the contract with the awarding body. The best practice is to submit the records weekly or at the conclusion of each payroll period.

5. If the awarding body has not registered the project with the DIR, how can I submit my certified payroll records?

Projects must be registered with the DIR using the PWC-100 form in order for contractors and subcontractors to submit certified payroll records for those projects. You should contact the awarding body to confirm that the project was registered. If the awarding body has not registered the project, you should ask it to complete the registration as soon as possible. If you have made this request, but the awarding body still has not registered the project, please contact the DIR for further assistance at publicworks@dir.ca.gov.

6. If I am required to submit certified payroll records to a union, to the prime contractor, or to the awarding body or a Labor Compliance Program, do I still have to submit certified payroll records to the DIR?

Yes. Submitting certified payroll records to other agencies does not fulfill the requirement to submit certified payroll records to the Labor Commissioner/DIR.

7. How do I identify the public works project that I am working on (or will be working on) on the reports?

Public works projects have a unique DIR Project ID, often referred to as the "PWC-100" number. Any registered project can be located in the DIR's searchable database of public works projects. Entering just a few pieces of information in the search tool should yield a list that includes your project.

8. I am an owner/operator, sole proprietor, or business owner, and I do not receive payroll checks or pay myself an hourly salary. How do I handle certified payroll reporting for my own work, and how do I determine how much I am being paid for that work?

Even if you are paid by salary, draw, or contract payments, you still should be able to provide the following information for any work you perform on public works projects: (a) your name, address, and SSN (or FEIN, if you have no SSN);

(b) the work classification for your prevailing wage work; (c) the hourly rate for that classification; (d) the number of hours that you performed that work; and (e) the estimated amount paid to you for your labor for that work. To calculate how much you were paid for your own labor, subtract all your other expenses (including materials, pro rata share of business overhead, and payments to other workers or subcontractors) from the gross contract price. The net amount should be your labor cost, and it should be equal to or higher than the compensation required for your work classification (determined by multiplying your work hours by the applicable rates) in order to comply with prevailing wage requirements.

9. **Can I review the payroll record before I submit it?**

   At any time before you sign the record, you can use the navigation tools to review and modify it. After the record is signed, you will no longer be able to access or change it.

10. **Can I view and print out all certified payroll records associated with a project?**

    All electronic certified payroll records submitted to the DIR can be viewed and printed in fully redacted form after locating them with the certified payroll records search tool. If you would like to save or print an unreacted (complete) version of your own payroll record, you must click on the PDF icon that appears on the confirmation page. After you close that page, the unreacted version will no longer be available.

11. **Which information is redacted (omitted) from electronic certified payroll records that are available to the public?**

    Full redaction removes all personal, identifiable employee information (name, address, phone number, and SSN) as well as the contractor's federal ID (FEIN) or SSN and email address.

12. **Can I change the date or make corrections to payroll records after I submit them? If not, can I delete the record?**

    You cannot change or delete records that have already been submitted. However, you may correct errors by submitting a new record for the same pay period. The new or "amended" record for an employee will take precedence over the original record submitted. However, if you are only correcting the payroll of one or more employee/s, you do not need to re-submit the information for any employees whose information was entered correctly. And if you are adding payroll for one or more employee/s not in the original record, you do not need to resubmit payroll for all the other employees (unless there are errors in them that need correction). The original record will remain on file and will be visible along with all associated amendments when users viewing submitted payroll records select "Show Amendment." The payroll number will be modified to indicate the amendment (e.g.: original record # 15-0; amended record # 15-1).

13. **What happens if I mistakenly submitted payroll for a period in which no work was performed?**

Law & Business Supplemental

If payroll was submitted for a period in which no work was performed, you may submit a Statement of Non-Performance for the same period. That Statement of Non-Performance will take precedence over the record submitted in error.

Concrete Delivery Requirements (AB 219)

1. **The bill says it does not apply to public works contracts that were advertised for bid or awarded prior to July 1, 2016. What about contracts that are still in process?**

   If a public works contract was advertised for bid or awarded prior to July 1, 2016, the delivery of concrete to that public work is not subject to AB 219. If the contract was advertised for bid before July 1, 2016, but awarded after that date, AB 219 does not apply.

2. **How will ready-mix suppliers know if an order is for public works? Who will be held responsible if they are not informed?**

   If the worksite owner is a public entity (e.g. school, library), it is likely a public work. The entities engaging the ready-mix services should know if the project is subject to the public works statutes, and it should be noted as part of the written agreement required by AB 219.

3. **What if it is discovered that an order is for public works after the fact? How will a ready-mix supplier know if a project is public works but under the minimum threshold for applying prevailing wages?**

   The companies engaging the ready-mix services should also know if a project is exempt. There are potential legal consequences for misleading contractors and subcontractors about whether a project is exempt, including joint liability for back wage and penalty assessments.

4. **Do apprenticeship requirements apply to this law?**

   Yes, if the prevailing wage rate is based on a qualifying craft (i.e. a craft for which there is an approved apprenticeship program). Qualifying crafts are usually indicated with a pound or hashtag sign (#) by the applicable prevailing wage rate.

5. **Ready-mix companies often donate concrete to schools, parks, and charitable organizations. Are these donations subject to prevailing wages?**

   It depends. If the project owner is a public entity, then it is probably a public works project. However, this is something the ready-mix company can and should clarify with whoever is receiving the donated concrete.

6. **How does this law apply to deliveries from out-of-state? For instance, material might be delivered from Reno for a highway project in California.**

   AB 219's requirements apply to deliveries that originate out of state. If the Director

Law & Business Supplemental

has not specified a prevailing wage for the geographic area in which the factory or batching plant is located, the contractor should use a rate from the nearest geographic area.

7. **Which prevailing wage rate applies? Do different rates apply to different parts of the delivery work?**

   The applicable prevailing wage rate is for the classification of "Driver - Mixer Trucks." This rate applies to all parts of the mixer - truck driver's work.

8. **What portion of the driver's work is covered? What if the driver is not on a round trip?**

   For delivery to a public works project, prevailing wage rates apply from the time the driver receives concrete at the batch plant to the time the driver returns to the batch plant. If a truck hauling concrete to a prevailing wage job does not return to the same batch plant, the post-delivery drive to a different batch plant should be counted as the return. There will always be a return trip as the trucks will not be left indefinitely at the job site.

9. **What if the driver is delivering to some prevailing wage projects and some non-prevailing wage projects?**

   The statute does not allow any exceptions from payment of prevailing wages for time spent making intermediate stops at other potentially non-public works locations. The entire delivery process and the return trip are covered and must be paid at the applicable prevailing wage rate.

10. **How would the round-trip wage be calculated if a driver goes from plant #1 (in DIR prevailing wage region X), unloads concrete at public works project A, then goes to plant #2 (in DIR prevailing wage region Y), then delivers a load of concrete to commercial project B, then goes to plant #3 (in DIR wage region Z), then delivers to public works project C, and then returns to plant #1?**

    From the time the driver begins receiving the concrete at plant #1 until the time the driver reaches plant #2, the rate will be the prevailing wage rate for region X. From that time until the driver begins receiving the concrete at plant #3, the driver may be paid a non-prevailing wage rate. From the time the driver begins receiving the concrete at plant #3 until he or she returns to plant #1, the driver is entitled to the prevailing wage rate for region Z.

11. **If a mixer driver spends two hours at a plant, four hours delivering to public works projects, and four hours delivering to commercial projects, which wage order applies? Will it be Wage Order #1 for manufacturing, Wage Order #16 for construction, or both, depending on where the driver is at any one time?**

    The Labor Commissioner made the following determination in a 2001 opinion letter: Ready-mix drivers engaged in the delivery of cement from a cement plant to a construction job-site, if employed by the business that manufactures the cement, are covered by IWC Order 1-2001 [Wage Order #1].

Law & Business Supplemental

12. How frequently will wage rates be updated?

Existing rates in every county covered by AB 219 are under the classification of *Driver - Mixer Trucks*. Some rates are based on survey data and others are based on local collective bargaining agreements. Those based on survey data begin with C-MT-830; those based on collective bargaining agreements begin with C-MT-261.

Rates based on survey data cannot be updated without a new wage survey, usually done in response to a specific request and supporting petition under Labor Code section 1773 and Title 8, California Code of Regulations, sections 16200 and 16302. However, wage rates that are based on collective bargaining agreements are regularly adjusted as the agreements are revised.

13. **Which rate applies if a company has a union rate of $60 an hour, but the prevailing wage is $18 an hour?**

State law would require that the driver be paid at least $18 an hour. However, the employer may be bound to pay the higher rate because of its contractual obligation to the workers under the collective bargaining agreement.

14. **Do ready-mix hauling and delivery companies need to submit electronic payrolls to DIR in addition to submitting payrolls to the general contractor and subcontractor who engaged them?**

Yes, payroll records have to be submitted electronically to DIR in addition to being submitted to the party who engaged the ready-mixed concrete delivery. Payroll records must be submitted to DIR on a monthly basis or as otherwise specified by the awarding body. Please note that the requirement to submit payroll records electronically is currently on hold pending system upgrades. The upgrades will allow simplified online reporting on multiple projects. The requirement to prepare and keep certified payroll records has not changed.

15. **What is the penalty for failure to submit payroll records within five days?**

There is no penalty in the statute for not submitting payroll records to the general contractor and party who engaged the ready-mixed concrete services within five days. However, the consequences of not meeting this deadline may be covered in their contract or agreement.

16. **How will submission of payroll records under this law differ from how they are submitted by other subcontractors?**

The new law requires ready-mix companies to submit copies of their certified payroll records (CPRs) to the party that engaged them and to the general contractor (which may be the same entity). Because public works contractors are jointly and separately liable for prevailing wage violations with the subcontractors working under them, many will include this requirement to provide CPRs as part of the purchase agreement or subcontract. However, AB 219 also makes this a legal requirement and further specifies when the CPRs must be furnished, as well as the need for the

Law & Business Supplemental

CPRs to be accompanied by time records certified by the drivers.

The law does not specify whether the CPRs and other records must be on paper or electronic format. It is up to the parties to determine that in their agreement. Once DIR's electronic Certified Payroll Reporting system is fully deployed with identity management features, contractors will have access to their subcontractors' CPRs through DIR's system at the same time that DIR does. However, that will not necessarily meet the deadline specified in AB 219 nor will it include the certified driver time records.

The law does not specify what happens if the five-day submission deadline or driver certification requirements are not met. These are not requirements that would fall within the Labor Commissioner's enforcement responsibilities, but they would affect the rights and responsibilities of contractors and subcontractor suppliers in relationship to each other.

17. The law says payroll records should be accompanied by a written time record that shall be certified by each driver for the performance of job duties. Can the time records be certified electronically by the driver?

Electronic certifications are allowed, as there is no particular format that is required as long as there is a way to tie the certification to the person who provides it. It depends on how the driver's time is recorded for purposes of determining the hours worked and compensation due for prevailing wage jobs.

18. How should certified payrolls be organized? Are they per driver, per plant, or per project?

They should be organized by project, which is how prevailing wages are traditionally reported and how they will need to be reported on DIR's electronic Certified Payroll Reporting (CPR) system.

19. What constitutes a "written subcontract agreement"? What does it mean to be a subcontractor "only for the purpose of this [prevailing wage] chapter"? For example, will mechanics lien laws still apply?

"Written subcontract agreement" refers to the contract or other agreement between the public agency, company, or person who wants to obtain ready-mixed concrete and the ready-mixed concrete supplier. There must be some type of agreement, in writing, between the two.

"Only for purposes of this chapter" means that a ready-mixed concrete supplier will have the status of a subcontractor under the public works chapter of the Labor Code (sections 1720 – 1861) and will have all the responsibilities of a subcontractor under that chapter when providing ready-mixed concrete to a public works project, including but not necessarily limited to being registered with the Department of Industrial Relations and paying prevailing wages to workers who deliver the ready-mixed concrete to the project. However, this does not make the company a subcontractor under the mechanics lien laws found in the Civil Code or under any

Law & Business Supplemental

other set of laws outside of the public works chapter of the Labor Code. The rights and responsibilities of a ready-mixed concrete supplier under any other set of laws depend on their status under those laws.

20. **Will DIR specify minimum requirements for what must be included in a contract? Can DIR provide a template?**

DIR suggests that an invoice or purchase order that includes the required statutory language may be sufficient. However, the party who engages the ready-mix company may require more. DIR does not provide templates for contracts between private parties or between a private party and any public entity as these contracts may involve additional requirements and considerations with which DIR is not familiar.

21. **Will a different section of the Uniform Commercial Code now apply to ready-mix suppliers for public works?**

No, the requirements of AB 219 are limited to the public works chapter of the Labor Code and not intended to change the status of ready-mix suppliers under any other set of laws outside of the public works chapter of the Labor Code.

22. **Will ready-mix suppliers now be listed under the Subletting and Subcontracting Fair Practices Act, like other subcontractors?**

AB 219 does not define ready-mix suppliers as subcontractors for purposes of the Subletting and Subcontracting Fair Practices Act or any other laws outside of the public works chapter of the Labor Code.

EXAM 7

Law & Business Supplemental

SUMMARY CHART ON CHILD LABOR LAWS

	Ages 16 & 17 Must have completed 7th grade to work while school in session.	Ages 14 & 15 Must have completed 7th grade to work while school in session.	Ages 12 & 13
School in Session	4 hours per day on any school day. 8 hours on any non-school day. 48 hours per week. WEE* students & personal attendants may work more than 4 hours on a school day but never more than 8.	3 hours per school day outside of school hours. 8 hours on any non-school day. 18 hours per week. WEE students may work during school hours & up to 23 hours per week.	May be employed only during school holidays and vacations (usually construed to include weekends). May never be employed on any school day, either before or after school. Daily and weekly work hour maximums while school is in session are not specified in statute, but may not exceed the maximum allowed when school is not in session or the maximum stated on permit. Not eligible for WEE programs.
School not in Session	8 hours per day. 48 hours per week.	8 hours per day. 40 hours per week.	8 hours per day. 40 hours per week.
Spread of Hours	5 a.m. – 10 p.m. However, until 12:30 a.m. on any evening preceding a non-school day. WEE students, with permission, until 12:30 a.m. on any day. Messengers: 6 a.m. – 9 p.m.	7 a.m. – 7 p.m. except that from June 1 through Labor Day, until 9 p.m.	7 a.m. – 7 p.m. except that from June 1 through Labor Day, until 9 p.m.

* WEE – Work Experience Education

EXAM 7

Law & Business Supplemental

ABOUT QUICK-PREP FLASHCARDS STUDY GUIDE

"QUICK-PREP FLASHCARDS" is a unique supplemental study guide that cuts right to the core of your exam. It contains easy to read Subject Reviews that cover all the essential information you need to know to pass your exam! No unnecessary fillers! It is written in a clear and straightforward manner to help maximize your learning capability. It contains helpful interactive Flashcard sections at the end of each Subject Review section to help you retain information through the proven interactive learning method.

No matter what material(s) you are currently using to study for your exam, <u>this guide</u> is a valuable asset that you shouldn't do without!

STUDY TIPS-HOW TO EFFECTIVELY USE QUICK-PREP FLASHCARDS STUDY GUIDE

INTERACTIVE METHOD

The key to testing is memory, and the key to memory is interaction. This guide will help you put this method in practice.

SET ASIDE TIME

Research shows you retain more information studying in small sessions. Study about 1 to 2 hours per session in a quiet, well lit area. Take breaks in between the study sessions. Have a snack. Your mind will actively review what you have studied on its own.

LEARN TROUBLING SUBJECTS

If you're having trouble with a subject, stop and learn it right then and there - study the topic until you understand it. Do not skip or wait to learn it later. <u>Learn it while there</u>, that way it won't be something that's pending in the back of your mind. There is no need for unnecessary stress! Having something weighing on your mind will interfere with your studying all together.

FOCUS ON THE SUBJECT

Studying questions word-for-word does not work because the State has the same question written in different formats. So, instead: <u>LEARN THE SUBJECT</u> that way you will know the answer of the question regardless of how the question is worded.

HIGHLIGHT THE ANSWERS

As you review any material, highlight the right answers. Highlighting does two important things:

1. It helps you focus on the subject - the right answer

2. It makes you interact with the material. Interacting with information helps you retain it.

WRITE TO REMEMBER

You'll be surprised to see how much more information you retain by simply writing it down!

Make notes or write bullet point lists of what you learn as you go. Highlight, circle key words, draw pictures, manually check your math, etc.

Writing helps you retain the subject because you're interacting with it!

INTERACT WITH THE FLASHCARDS

Once you're familiar with the subject, use the flashcards. They're designed to make you review the key words you have just learned. So go ahead, interact!

Quiz yourself or have someone quiz you, either way you'll be using a highly efficient study technique – <u>interaction</u>.

* Each flashcard only takes <u>a few minutes</u> to review!

EXAM 7

Law & Business Supplemental

ABOUT YOUR LAW & BUSINESS EXAM

WHAT TO EXPECT

- The Law & Business test is given first.

- It is a closed book exam, which means... no outside material allowed.

- It consists of 120 questions in random order

- It's a 4-part multiple choice exam

- You are given 3-1/2 hours to take the test

- You need approximately 70% to pass

- You can find out if you passed on the spot

WHAT TO BRING TO EXAM

The night before your test gather the following:

- "Notice to appear for Exam" (sent by the state)

- Picture I.D. (current valid Driver's License, Department of Motor Vehicles Identification Card or Military Identification Card)

* Everything else that you will need for the exam will be provided at the test center, including: pencils, scratch paper, calculators and scaled rulers.

* All personal items must be placed in a common storage area at own risk. The test center staff does not watch the storage area. You are advised to leave articles of value at home or locked in your vehicle.

OTHER IMPORTANT TIPS

- Map out the test site

- Get a good night rest before the exam

- Set your alarm

- Have a back-up alarm just in case!

- Eat a healthy breakfast – you will need it to stay awake, alert and focused during the exam.

- Be early!

- Go to the bathroom before walking into the exam room. You don't want to waste anytime worrying about your bodily needs during the exam!

NEW COMPUTER TESTING

Tests are now given on computers. However, no computer experience is required. It is easy to use. You'll first be given an 8 question practice test to show you how to take your test.

You'll be using the **UP, DOWN, LEFT** and **RIGHT** arrow keys and the **SPACE BAR.**

TYPES OF QUESTIONS TO BE AWARE OF

Be aware of these different types of questions that might lead you to misinterpretation!

"ONE IS WRONG" QUESTIONS: For these types of questions remember that you are asked to look for the wrong answer. Look for words like "WHICH IS WRONG" "LEAST" and "EXCEPT".

"STATE" QUESTIONS: These questions have to do with the State – they reflect the interest of the consumer and the state, not you! Look for LEGAL and OFFICIAL LANGUAGE as well as the answer that favors the consumer.

"CHOOSE THE BEST ANSWER" QUESTIONS: These types of questions provide answers that are all acceptable, find the best answer suited for what is being asked. Look carefully at what the question is asking.

"OPINION" QUESTIONS: These questions are based on "good business practices." Look for the answer that is the ethical response a.k.a. What is the right thing to do?

EXAM 7

Law & Business Supplemental

TEST TIPS - POINTERS ON HOW TO TAKE YOUR EXAM!

TIME PER QUESTION

You have 3-1/2 hours to answer 120 questions, that is over a minute and a half per question.

SKIM THE TEST

Skim through the entire test first. This will give you an idea of what you're dealing with. It will also warm up your memory. Remember, you know this stuff so seeing words you are familiar with will help you recall what you studied.

FIRST DO THE EASY ONES!

Skim through the exam and answer the questions you know. Doing this:

- Helps you remember the material you studied and the information you know.

- Gives you a confidence boost, eliminating a lot of the stress that comes along with taking an exam.

- Gives you more time to answer difficult questions because you won't spend a long time answering what you know!

* Think about it, you can be done with half of the test in just 30 minutes! Leaving you 3 hours for the other, more difficult, questions!

DON'T GET STUCK ON A QUESTION

If you are taking too long on a question, skip it and return to it later (write the # of the qt. and return to it later). Other questions might tip you off to the right answer or you might remember something you thought you didn't know as you move along the test.

USE YOUR SCRATCH PAPER

The State gives you scratch paper, so use it! Don't do math in your head, use the paper to work the math problem out. Use the scratch paper to write formulas, draw pictures, make sketches etc. Use it for anything that will help you visualize and select the correct answer.

READ QUESTIONS CAREFULLY

Make sure you understand what the question is asking, especially for those questions that contain words like LEAST, MOST, BEST, EXCEPT and WRONG. Pay close attention to other words too, such as NEW, COMPLETED and PHASE.

Paying close attention to the wording of questions that can be misleading will allow you to know what the question is <u>really</u> asking.

DON'T RUSH

Your score depends on accuracy not speed! Take the time to fully read the questions to avoid careless mistakes. If you finish the test and there is time remaining, review your answers.

ANSWER EVERY QUESTION

Don't leave any questions unanswered. There is no penalty for guessing so if you're running out of time... guess!

GUESSING STRATEGIES

- Process of elimination – eliminate all the answers you know for sure are wrong and then guess! Doing so will maximize the chances of you answering right.

- Go with your first hunch.
  Don't second guess yourself!

- When the choice "All of the above" is given, the answer is more often than not...
  "All of the above"

- Look for the answer that is fair, legal and makes sense according to the interest of the consumer, especially when it comes to "State" questions.

NOW TAKE A DEEP BREATH. RELAX.
Remember your goal is to pass! With a little studying and only 70% required to pass... you'll do just fine!

EXAM 7

Law & Business Supplemental

CONTRACTORS STATE LICENSE BOARD (C.S.L.B.)

The C.S.L.B. is part of the Department of Consumer Affairs. It consists of a 15-member board whose mission is to protect consumers by regulating the construction industry through policies that promote the health, safety and general welfare of the public in matters of construction.

The C.S.L.B. accomplishes this by:

- Ensuring that construction is performed in a safe, competent and professional manner
- Licensing contractors and enforcing licensing laws
- Requiring licensure for any person practicing or offering to practice construction contracting
- Enforcing the laws, regulations and standards governing construction contracting in a fair and uniform manner
- Providing resolution to disputes that arise from construction activities
- Educating consumers so they make informed choices

WHAT YOU NEED TO QUALIFY

- 18 years of age (min.)

- 4 years of experience (min.)
  Experience must be out of the last 10 years
* Credit for experience is given only for experience at a journeyman level or foreman, supervising employee, contractor or owner-builder.

TYPES OF LICENSES

Licenses are issued per entity either as a/an

- Individual License
- Partnership License
- Corporation License

* Joint Venture License is made up of 2 individual active licenses for a specific purpose

LICENSE CLASSIFICATIONS

- A-General Engineering License
- B-General Building License
- C-Specialty Classes License (for full list see Appendix A in back of the book).
* you can qualify for up to 3 licenses within a 1 year period – provided that you have at least 20% interest in each entity.

LICENSE STATUSES

Active License: renew every 2 years; renewal fee $360.00

Inactive License: renew every 4 years; renewal fee $180.00

Expired License: can be renewed within 5 years of it being expired; renewal fee is $540.00
  * if license is not renewed within 5 years of its expiration, the license holder must reapply for the license.

Cancelled License: cancellation occurs by written request, by disassociation of partner or by death of the qualifier (license holder).

Suspended License: licensee is not entitled to operate during the period of suspension. Depending on the action taken to suspend the license, a disciplinary bond may be required before the license can be reinstated or reused.

Revoked License: revocation of your license means that your license is taken away. License will not be reissued or reinstated for 1 to 5 years of the effective date of the decision.

CONTINUANCE

If absence of the qualifier occurs: remaining personnel can continue work-in-progress for 90 days or request up to 1 year to finish the work.

Law & Business Supplemental

| LICENSE LAW (CONTINUED) | 11% OF YOUR TEST |

Qualifier: A qualifier is the person listed on the CSLB records who meets the experience and examination requirements for the license. A qualifier is required for every classification on each license issued by the CSLB. Every active license must have a designated qualifier.

Sole Ownership: A license issued to an individual; name often given to a qualifying individual possessing a sole owner license

Q.P.: Stands for Qualifying Partner; is a licensed qualifier that has entered a partnership (whether general or limited) with another licensed qualifier. Title of the qualifying individual on a partnership license.

R.M.E.: Stands for Responsible Managing Employee, it is the title of an employee who serves as the qualifying individual on a sole owner, partnership or corporate license.

R.M.O.: Stands for Responsible Managing Officer. It is a title of an officer who serves as the qualifying individual on a corporate license.

License Type	**INDIVIDUAL**	**PARTNERSHIP**	**CORPORATION**
Qualifier Type	OWNER	Q.P.	R.M.O.
	or	or	or
Alternative	R.M.E.	R.M.E.	R.M.E.

INCIDENTAL AND SUPPLEMENTAL TRADE WORK

A contractor is NOT prohibited from taking and executing a contract involving the use of two or more crafts or trades, if the performance of the work is "incidental and supplemental" to the primary job.

Work outside the "incidental and supplemental" must be performed by a licensed subcontractor.

THINGS YOU <u>CAN'T</u> AND SHOULDN'T DO!

- **Can't Abandon a Contract!** Abandoning a contract without legal excuse constitutes a cause for disciplinary action. It is classified as a "Breach of Contract."

- **Can't Use False or Misleading Advertisement!** It is illegal to misrepresent information – this includes using false, misleading or deceptive advertisements as an inducement to enter into a contract for a work of improvement. It is considered a misdemeanor.

- **Can't Remove Asbestos Without Proper Certification!** You must pass an asbestos certification examination developed and administered by the CSLB, obtain certification and register with the DOSH to be allowed to remove asbestos totaling 100 sq. ft. or more.

- **Can't Knowingly Sub Work to Unlicensed Contractors!** Entering into a contract with an unlicensed contractor is cause for disciplinary action.

- **Can't Lend Your License to Others!** licenses are not transferable! You cannot lend your license or license number to another individual! Lending your license is a crime categorized under "Aiding and Abetting" criminal laws.

- **Can't Take Funds From One Project and Use Them for Another!** The misuse of funds, including diversion of funds, is prohibited. Diversion/Misuse of funds is illegal, it is categorized under the crime of "Larceny" with punishment ranging from a misdemeanor to a felony.

EXAM 7

Law & Business Supplemental

1. **Who must be licensed as a contractor?** .... **All who construct or alter**
   All businesses and individuals who construct or alter either residential or commercial works that cost $500 (labor + materials) or more must be licensed by the C.S.L.B.

2. **How old do you have to be to obtain a contractor license?** .... **18 years old**
   You must be a minimum of 18 years of age to qualify to apply for a C.S.L.B. license.

3. **How many years of experience are required?** .... **4 years**
   4 full years of experience at a journeyman level or as a foreman, supervising employee, contractor or owner-builder is required. These 4 years must be within the last 10 years. The applicant must fill and submit the Certification of Work Experience form.

4. **Is anyone exempt from the requirements to be licensed?** .... **Yes**
   For list of all who are exempt from having a contractor's license see C.S.L.B website.

5. **Licenses are issued** .... **per entity**
   Individual license, Partnership License, Joint Venture License etc. each count as an entity.

6. **Does California recognize contractor licenses issued by other states or countries?** .... **No**
   Although California does not recognize contractor licenses issued by other states or countries, it does have reciprocal agreements with some states that recognize the experience qualification.

7. **What happens if you contract without a license?** .... **Misdemeanor charge**
   Unlicensed contractors face potential sentences of up to six months in jail and/or a $500 fine, and potential administrative fines of $200 to $15,000 because it is illegal to contract without a contractor's license.

8. **Are there educational requirements to obtain a contractor license?** .... **No**
   However, many community colleges and private schools offer instruction in vocational education.

9. **Can technical training substitute the required experience?** .... **Yes**
   Education in the trade or technical training and apprenticeship training can substitute the 4 years of experience required, so long as the applicant has a min. of 1 year of practical experience.

10. **Are there special requirements for contractors who work with asbestos?** .... **Yes**
    Certification, registration, reporting, and safety requirements are required by the DOSH, OSHA and C.S.L.B for anyone who is planning to work with asbestos. Special knowledge and training is needed.

11. **Are all applicants submitted to a criminal background check?** .... **Yes**
    All applicants must submit a full set of fingerprints for the purpose of providing a criminal background check. This requirement comes with additional fees including a live-scan fee.

12. **How do I apply for a contractor license?** .... **Fill Application for Original Contractor's License**
    Obtain application by visiting www.cslb.ca.gov or calling 1(800) 321-CSLB(2752) or visiting our-store Builder's Book Bookstore for a free copy. You must fill and mail this application to the C.S.L.B.

13. **Is there an application processing fee?**.. **Yes - $300**
    Yes, there is a nonrefundable application processing fee of $300 + $75 for each additional classification.

14. **What is the total amount of fees I must pay to obtain a contractor license?** **$480**
    This amount includes the nonrefundable processing fee of $300 and the two-year initial license fee of $180. Fees are subject to change. Current fees are printed on the application forms and notices.

EXAM 7

Law & Business Supplemental

> ### FLASH CARD - RENEWING & MAINTAINING A LICENSE   11%
> **Read. Write. Interact!** A powerfully effective way to retain information! Read questions, write down each question in the form of a statement. Quiz yourself or have someone else quiz you.

1. How often must I renew my active license? .... **every 2 years**
Licenses must be renewed every two years. There is a fee for renewing your license.

2. Will I receive notice before my active license expires? .... **Yes, 60-days**
Approximately 60 days before your license expires the CSLB will send you a renewal application. Remember, it is <u>your</u> responsibility to make sure your license is renewed. Do not rely on the C.S.L.B. for reminders, it is your license and your business and it is therefore your responsibility to renew.

3. What is the active license renewal fee? **$360.00**
Renewal fee for an active license is $360.00 You are required to renew your license every 2 years.

4. What is the renewal fee for an active license that is not renewed in time? **$540.00**
This includes the renewal fee charge $360.00 + the delinquent late fee of $180.00 (active license)

5. What is the inactive license renewal fee? **$180.00**
Renewal fee for an inactive license is $180.00. Inactive licenses must be renewed every 4 years.

6. What is the renewal fee for an inactive license that is not renewed in time? **$270.00**
This includes the renewal fee of $180.00 + the delinquent late fee of $90.00 (inactive license)

7. What is the min. operating capital that you must have to qualify to be a contractor? **$2,500.00**
Operating capital is defined as your current assets minus your current liabilities. C.A. - C.L. = O.C.

8. You must notify the state of any changes within how many days? .... **90 days**
These include changes in business name or address, as well as changes in personnel and business type.

9. Can I renew my current license if there have been changes in license structure? .... **No**
If there are changes in License structure you cannot renew your license, you have to apply for a new one. Changes in license structure include: change in business entity, corporate registration number and owner.

10. Can your license be re-issued? .... **Yes**
If your license has been expired between 3 to 5 years it can be re-issued.

11. What is another term for the qualifier? .... **Test taker**
The qualifier is the test-taker a.k.a. the person to whom the license is going to be issued.

12. What is the qualifier called if he/she is an individual? .... **Owner**
When a license is issued to an individual, the name often given to that qualifying individual is "owner."

13. What is the qualifier called if he/she is a partner? .... **Qualifying Partner**
Qualifying Partner (Q.P.) is the title given to the qualifying individual in a partnership license.

14. What is the qualifier called if he/she is a officer? .... **RMO**
If the qualifier is an officer, the title given to the individual is RMO (Responsible Managing Officer).

15. What is a qualifier called if he/she is a employee? .... **RME**
If the qualifier is an employee, the title given to the individual is RME (Responsible Managing Employee)

16. How many hours is an RME required to work? .... **32 hrs./80% min.**
A Responsible Managing Employee (RME) is required to work a minimum of 32 hours or 80%

17. How many licenses can an RME qualify for at a time? **1**
A Responsible Managing Employee (RME) can only qualify for one license at a time.

18. Other qualifiers, (besides RMOs and RMEs) can qualify for how many licenses at a time? **3**
Qualifiers (besides RMEs and RMOs) can qualify for up to 3 licenses at a time.

EXAM 7

Law & Business Supplemental

Read. Write. Interact! A powerfully effective way to retain information! Read questions, write down each question in the form of a statement. Quiz yourself or have someone else quiz you.

1. **Can you lend someone your license?** .... **No**
   The license must only be used by the person to whom it is assigned to. Using someone else's license or license # or letting someone use your license or license # is illegal and punishable by law.

2. **Can you abandon a project without legal excuse?** .... **No**
   Abandonment of any construction project or operation engaged in or undertaken without legal excuse is cause for disciplinary action, including legal action that can result in Federal prosecution.

3. **Can you use funds from one project to finish another?** .... **No**
   Diversion of funds or failure to substantially account for the application or uses of such funds on a construction project or operation for which such funds were received is cause for disciplinary action. It is qualified as larceny with punishment ranging from a misdemeanor to a felony.

4. **Can you use misleading advertisement?** .... **No**
   It is a misdemeanor to use false, misleading, or deceptive advertising as an inducement to enter into any contract for a work of improvement. The FTC investigates and prosecutes acts or practices that are deceptive.

5. **What is a joint venture license?** .... **Combination of 2 licenses**
   A Joint Venture Contractor License is a license issued to two or more licensees together (sole owners, partnerships, corporations, or other joint ventures) whose licenses are current and active. It is sought by qualifying individuals who seek to combine their licenses and expertise for a specific project.

6. **When does a joint venture expire?** .... **2 years after first given**
   Since a joint-venture license is made up of 2 individual active licenses for a specific purpose it has a short active life of 2 years. However, you may always apply for a joint-venture license for other, future joint-projects, so long as the individuals that are applying for a joint venture license are qualifiers.

7. **If a QP leaves, what can the remaining party file to get more time?** .... **Continuance**
   A continuance of up to 1 year is granted in order for the remaining party to complete the project.

8. **Can a continuance be extended?** .... **Yes**
   The Registrar may approve an extension to the one year provision if additional time is necessary to complete projects contracted for or commenced before the disassociation with a qualifier or his/her death.

9. **If a QP leaves, the remaining party must report it within how many days?** .... **90 days**
   If a QP leaves a project, the remaining party must report it within 90 days of this occurrence. This applies to all parties involved in the project at the time of the occurrence.

10. **What must qualifiers do every day?** .... **Visit the site**
    Qualifiers are required to visit the construction site at least once a day, every day.

11. **When must subcontractors be paid?** .... **7 days after each progress payment**
    Subcontractors must be paid no later than 7 days after each progress payment is given by the owner to the Direct Contractor. The only exception to this requirement exists only if the direct contractor and subcontractor entered a written agreement that states otherwise before the start of the project.

12. **Who must pay the subcontractors?** .... **Direct Contractor**
    The Direct Contractor is responsible for paying the subcontractors, however it is the responsibility of the owner to make sure that the Direct Contractor is paying his/her subs.

13. **Failure to pay subs result in having to pay what % for every month payment is not paid?** **2%**
    A Direct Contractor or subcontractor that fails to pay his/her subcontractors is subject to a penalty. The direct contractor will be accountable for paying the amount due, plus 2% of the amount due per month for every month that payment is not made. So for your sake... make sure you pay your subs. on time!

Law & Business Supplemental   **125**

EXAM 7

CONTRACT REQUIREMENTS & EXECUTION: BIDDING *15% OF YOUR TEST*

DEFINITION

Bidding is the task of preparing a detailed cost estimate for the work. It includes determining all the material and labor costs (take-offs) and overhead costs, as well as determining profit which is referred to as the mark-up.

Direct costs: are any costs directly associated with the project. Direct costs include costs for:

- materials
- labor
- permits
- loan fees
- subs
- etc ...

Overhead costs: are identified as expenses that are separate from the field such as administrative and managerial costs. Overhead costs include costs for:

- office space rent
- office supplies
- advertising
- staff
- insurance
- utility bills

Indirect costs: are costs that are still in the field, but are not directly related to any one specific project. Indirect costs include costs for:

- equipment maintenance
- truck maintenance
- lubrication
- tools
- fuel
- equipment

CONSTRUCTION BIDS

Construction Bids are written offers from contractors to undertake a construction job in return of a certain sum of money.
Bids can be either:
- Negotiated Bid
- Limited competition or selective Bid
- Open competition Bid

BIDDING ADVICE

Things you <u>SHOULD DO</u> to ensure effective Bidding
- Walk the Job
- Review Plans and Specifications...thoroughly!
- Look at past similar jobs
- Plan out the entire process
- Decide a financial method
- Check if there is a need for subs
- Recheck your bid estimate before you submit it
- Eliminate – errors take your time and be critical!

COMMON PITFALLS TO AVOID WHEN BIDDING:

- Bidding against the competition and not the job
- Bidding on plans and specifications that you don't really understand
- Insufficient planning
- Overextending your financial resources
- Including cash discounts in your bid – unless you are certain that sufficient financial resources will be available to have accounts payable be repaid during the discount period...discounts should not be included!

PROBLEMS YOU MIGHT RUN INTO AND HOW TO HANDLE THEM!

- Owner decides the price is too high
- suggest lessening the scope of the work
- Owner asks you/tells you that he/she is okay with you building against the code
- Insist to build to code, even if you lose the job!

EXAM 7

Law & Business Supplemental

BIDDING	15% OF YOUR TEST

GROSS INCOME, OVERHEAD EXPENSES AND NET PROFIT ESTIMATES

Let's define these terms and why it is important for you to incorporate them to your business!

Gross Income: is your estimate for your gross income for a year, in other words it is <u>what you expect to sell, produce and get paid for during the year.</u> This takes time and research but it is an <u>essential</u> estimate for any business, especially a construction business. So take your time, do the research, produce your estimate for the year...believe me, your company will be better for it!

Overhead Expenses: as previously defined these expenses are separate from the field and include administrative and managerial cost such as: advertising, sales, office expenses, job expenses and general expenses. <u>You need to have a clear estimate of your overhead expenses</u> that too, is essential for running a profitable business!

Net Profit Percentage: Determine your net profit!
That is answering the question <u>"What would you like your net profit to be?"</u>

Industry statistics report 6% to be the average net profit for contractors.

So if you would like a 6% net profit have <u>that </u>clear, if you want an 8% net profit have <u>that</u> clear. Either way, decide your net profit!

You **need** to know your estimates for **Gross Income, Overhead Expenses** and **Net Profit %** to determine your business **Mark-Up!**

DETERMINING YOUR MARK-UP! 3-STEP FORMULA

Here's how to determine the mark up for your business!
First: <u>Add</u> overhead expenses estimate (OE) and net profit estimate (NP)
Overhead Expenses estimate + Net Profit estimate = Answer 1
Second: <u>Subtract</u> Answer 1 (A1) from the Gross Income (GI)
Gross Income - Answer 1 = Job Costs
Third: <u>Divide</u> the Gross Income (GI) by the job costs estimate (JC), this will give you YOUR mark-up!
Gross Income ÷ Job Costs = Mark-Up

DETERMINING YOUR "MARK-UP": THEORETICAL EXAMPLE

So you took your time and did your research to reach the 3 essential estimates (gross income, overhead costs and net profit) and the following are your estimates:
GI = $ 100,000
OE = $ 25,000
NP (6%) = $ 6,000

Now that you know your estimates you can apply the 3-step formula to find your mark-up:

First: OE + NP = A1	**Second:** GI - A1 = JC	**Third:** GI ÷ JC = Mark-up
$25,000 + $6,000 = $31,000	$100,000 - $31,000 = $69,000	$100,000 ÷ $69,000 = 1.449
		= 1.45

So your mark-up for all your projects will be <u>1.45</u>
*This mark-up should remain the same for **ALL** the jobs that you sell, regardless of size!

Law & Business Supplemental   **127**

EXAM 7

Law & Business Supplemental

BIDDING	*15% OF YOUR TEST*

GROSS INCOME, OVERHEAD EXPENSES AND NET PROFIT ESTIMATES

Since you have determined your mark-up, all you have to do now is take the total job costs (of any job you land) and multiply it by the mark-up to give you the price you should quote to your customers (a.k.a. your bid). It's that simple!

NOW LET'S SEE THIS IN ACTION!

Example 1: Tom and Susan hire you for a small remodeling job which you estimate will cost $1,560.00

Total Job Costs:	$1,560.00
Mark-Up:	x 1.45
Your Sales Quote:	$2,262.00

You should charge Tom and Susan $2,262.00 for the remodeling job.

Example 2: Billy hires you for a remodeling job that you estimate will cost $8,728.00

Total Job Costs:	$8,728.00
Mark-Up:	x 1.45
Your Sales Quote:	$12,655.60

You should charge Billy $12,655.60 for the remodeling job.

Example 3: Linda hires you for a remodeling job which you estimate will cost $800.00

Total Job Costs:	$800.00
Mark-Up:	x 1.45
Your Sales Quote:	$1,160.00

You should charge Linda $1,160.00

Example 4: Charles hires you for a remodeling job which you estimate will cost $525.00

Total Job Costs:	$525.00
Mark-Up:	x 1.45
Your Sales Quote:	$761.25

You should charge Charles $761.25

REMEMBER THE 3's

REMEMBER THESE 3 IMPORTANT ESTIMATES:

1. Gross Income Estimate

2. Overhead Expenses Estimate

3. Profit %

USE THE 3-STEP FORMULA TO FIND YOUR MARK-UP

1. OE + NP = A1

2. GI - A1 = JC

3. GI ÷ JC = Mark up!

Remember to keep your mark-up the same to determine your selling price for every job you sell! Consistency with your mark-up is <u>key</u>! Doing so will ensure you stick to the net profit you have set for yourself which will ensure you get profit! All these things ensure you run a profitable business.

EXAM 7

Law & Business Supplemental

SCHEDULING METHODS

Scheduling: Schedule is a plan for carrying out a job. It is used to determine how many workers and what equipment is going to be needed for the job. A schedule should plan out the sequence of the trades on the job and the sequence of the work done by each trade.

A schedule should show:
• when each operation should begin and
• when each operation should end
These expected dates will help you determine when to set delivery times for materials; determine when each trade has to be performed and help you determine the arrival time of each subcontractor.

Bar Chart Method: A relatively simple technique showing start & stop dates for various phases of the work. This scheduling approach is simple but overlooks some interrelates tasks. A bar chart shows the sequence of a list of activities with the start duration and finish of each activity displayed as a bar plotted to a time scale. This method is the easiest and most widely used scheduling method in construction.

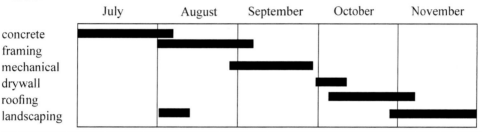

Critical Path Method: A more complex approach typically <u>used for larger projects</u>. This method helps identify the critical path in which the order of events should take place. This method interrelates the jobs better. The object of a critical path method is to combine all information relevant to the planning and scheduling of functions related to a project.

This method is intended to:

• coordinate all work required to finish the project
• show how all work will be coordinated
• point out which efforts are critical to timely completion of the project
• create the most efficient use of equipment and manpower

This method takes into consideration both planning and scheduling.
Planning: Planning consists of analyzing the project in order to be able to form a working model of the project. Planning breaks the job into work elements. These are then arranged into the arrow diagram, see below.
Scheduling: After the project has been planned on an arrow diagram, the next step is to schedule it. Scheduling consists of adding timelines to the elements mapped out. Here is where you map out the "when" of the project: when each job must be performed, when deliveries must take place and when to expect completion of the whole project.

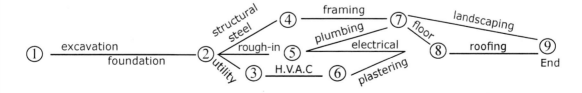

EXAM 7

Law & Business Supplemental

FLASH CARD - BIDDING   **15%**

Read. Write. Interact! A powerfully effective way to retain information! Read questions, write down each question in the form of a statement. Quiz yourself or have someone else quiz you.

1. **What is a bid?**.. **a detailed cost estimate**
   Bidding is the task of preparing a detailed cost estimate for the work at hand.
2. **What are material and labor costs known as?**... **Take-offs**
   Determining take-off costs is the first step to take when determining the bid of a project.
3. **What are permits, subcontractors and loan fees costs examples of?**............. **Direct Costs**
   Direct costs – are any costs directly associated with a project, such as materials, labor and permit fees.
4. **Tools, equipment & truck maintenance are examples of what kind of costs?**........... **Indirect Costs**
   Indirect costs – are costs that are still in the field, but not directly related to any one specific project.
5. **What are office space rent, office supplies, staff and insurance examples of?**........... **Overhead Costs**
   Overhead costs – are identified as expenses that are separate from the field, ex. administrative and managerial.
6. **The contractor will seriously jeopardize his business if he/she omits** .... **Profit**
   Insufficient profits threaten both capitalization (losses reduce retained earnings) and cash flows (payments to vendors may exceed receipts) to the extent that bankruptcy and/or dissolution of business may be the result.
7. **Which 3 estimates must you know?**........................... **Gross Income, Overhead Expenses, Net Profit%**
   It is essential for you to estimate: Gross Income and Overhead Expenses and Net Profit Percentage, knowing these will help determine your mark-up. Remember that these estimates are annual estimates.
8. **What is Gross Income Estimate?**.. **estimate for gross income for the year**
   This is your estimate for your gross profit for the year. It is what you expect to sell, produce and get paid for.
9. **What is an overhead estimate?**...................................... **estimate of your annual overhead expenses**
   The overhead estimate is your estimate for your overhead expenses for the year. It is an estimate of "what" you expect to spend. These expenses are separate from the field and include things such as rent.
10. **What is net profit percentage estimate?**... **% of what you want to profit**
    A net profit percentage estimate is what you determine that you want your profit percentage to be.
11. **What is the industry net profit?** .... **6% (2010 Industry Statistics)**
    The Industry Standards report that 6% is the average net profit for contractor businesses. However, keep in mind that YOU determine what you want your net profit % to be. Net profit will help you determine mark-up.
12. **What do you need to determine your mark-up percentage?**..................................... **the 3 estimates**
    You need to know your gross income estimate, overhead estimate and net profit % estimate to be able to determine your business mark-up! Determining a mark-up and staying consistent with the mark-up is crucial. Keeping your mark-up consistent, regardless of size of project (big or small) makes sure you produce profit!
13. **What is used to determine the mark-up percentage?**... **3-Step Formula**
    Use the "3-Step Formula" provided in this chapter to determine the mark-up percentage.
14. **What is a relatively simple bid scheduling method?** .... **Bar Chart Method**
    The Bar chart scheduling method is a relatively simple method showing start and stop dates for various phases of the work. It shows the sequence of a list of activities with the start and finish of each activity displayed as a bar plotted to a time scale. Its disadvantage is that it tends to overlook some interrelated tasks.
15. **What is a more complex bid scheduling method?**.. **Critical Path Method**
    The critical Path Scheduling method is a more complex approach typically used for larger projects. This method helps identify the critical path of when the order of events should take place. This method interrelates jobs better.

EXAM 7

Law & Business Supplemental

FLASH CARD - BIDDING POINTERS   15%

Read. Write. Interact! A powerfully effective way to retain information! Read questions, write down each question in the form of a statement. Quiz yourself or have someone else quiz you.

1. Where is the best place to look for bidding advice?............................ **Your job history**
Similar jobs will reveal similar things to take into consideration. Your job history is helpful in estimating costs, time and profits of a particular type of job by comparing it to a similar job done in the past.

2. What should you use to aid you in job costs for present and future references?..... **Time cards**
Much like your job history, time cards can greatly help you in estimating time and labor expenses.

3. Is it a good idea to walk the job before bidding?.. **Yes**
A careful review of the job requires on-site inspection. Walk the job to get a clear view of what is being requested and a clear idea of what is required and of what will be needed.

4. Should cash discounts be included in your bid estimate?.. **No**
Unless you are certain that sufficient financial resources will be available so that accounts payable may be repaid during the discount period, cash discounts should not be included in the bid.

5. Do sales tax costs need to be included in your bid estimate?.................................... **Yes**
Anything that you have to pay for (for a particular job) must be accounted for. This includes: sales tax and material deliveries. It is important for you to include all these expenses in your bid estimate.

6. Where should you look for information about materials?........... **Plans and Specifications**
Information about materials needed for a job can be found in "Plans and Specifications."

7. Where should you look for information about the work schedule?........... **Work Schedule**
Information about the work schedule of a particular job can be found in the work schedule.

8. Should identification of equipment be considered in the bidding estimate?............... **Yes**
Identification of equipment required and the financing method (purchase, lease, rental) used to obtain it, must be included in your bidding estimate. Like labor and materials, equipment is an expense that must be accounted for and is therefore important for you to include it in your bid.

9. If the customer thinks the cost is too high, what should you do?... **lessen the scope of the work**
You should propose lessening the scope of the work, if the customer finds the bid for the job too high.

10. If the sub's bid is too low should you bring it to his/her attention?....................................... **Yes**
It is ethical and good practice to call the sub and inform him/her when the bid he/she placed is too low.

11. Should you build against code if the customer insists?... **No!**
Even if the customer/owner asks you to build against code (because it will be less expensive for both of you) you must insist on building to code! It is illegal to build against code. Remember, no job is worth breaking the law! Even if it saves you money, in the end, not following the code will cost you a lot more.

12. Is bidding against competition good practice?... **No**
It is a common pitfall to bid against the competition and not the job. Bidding against the competition will cause you to sell the job for less than what it's worth. Bidding against the competition as opposed to the job will result in a loss of profit and make you have trouble paying subs, material and equipment needed.

13. Is taking your time and being critical with a bid estimate a pitfall?....................................... **No!**
Take your time and be critical! Double check everything! Ensure you understand all aspects of the plans and specifications, plan thoroughly, walk the job and double check the bid estimate!

Law & Business Supplemental

CONTRACTS   15% OF YOUR TEST

CONTRACTS

Contract: an agreement with specific terms between two or more persons or entities. Since we are dealing with contractor laws, a contract is a mutual agreement between two or more people for performance and compensation (payment) for that performance.

NUMBERS TO REMEMBER

2 Signatures – A contract is not enforceable unless it has been signed and dated by both parties involved.

10% or $1,000 whichever is less – is the required down payment

3rd business day (midnight) – time given to the customer to cancel the contract.

10 days – time given to the contractor to return all money given by the customer back to him/her. This time begins the day the customer cancels the contract.

20 days – are given to the customer to make all materials left on the property available for pick-up.

20 days late – if the contractor fails to begin work within 20 days of the declared start date without lawful excuse he/she is in violation of the contract and subject to disciplinary action.

Builder's Book Inc. sells ALL the forms needed for your contracting business, including:

• Home Improvement Contract

• Preliminary Notice

• Mechanics Lien and many more!

Call: 1.818.887.7828

Visit: www.buildersbook.com

Stop By: 8001 Canoga Ave. Canoga Park, CA 91304

HOME IMPROVEMENT CONTRACT

All Home Improvement Contracts <u>must</u> contain the following:

• <u>Contractor's Information</u>: contractor's name, contractor's license number, address, telephone and fax

• <u>Owner's Information</u>: name, home address and business address

• <u>Construction Lender Information</u>: name and address of Construction Fund Holder

• <u>Description of the Project</u> and Description of the Significant Materials to be used and Equipment to be Installed.

• Approximate Start Date

• Approximate Completion Date

• Contract Price

• Downpayment information

• Schedule of Progress Payments

• Salesman information: name and registration number

• Three-Day Right to Cancel

• Commercial General Liability Insurance (CGL)

• Workers Compensation Insurance

• Notice of Cancellation

• Statutory Notices

• Information about the California State License Board (CSLB)

• Mechanics Liens Warning

• Preliminary Notices Information

• Arbitration of Disputes - Voluntary

• Any other matters that the customer and contractor agree upon must be attached to the contract and listed under "Lists of Documents to be Incorporated into the contract."

• Signature and date of signing of both the direct contractor and the owner

EXAM 7

Law & Business Supplemental

- **Additional Description Form:** to be used with Home Improvement Contract to add additional description of work that did not fit in the space provided on the form.

- **Contract Change Order:** to be used if there is any change regarding the project. This form modifies and amends the contract and protects both the owner and the contractor in case of a dispute by setting changes in writing and having both parties sign & date the change.

- **Preliminary Notice:** Notifies the Owner that a Mechanics Lien can be filed against them if they fail to pay. This must be filed by the contractor if he/she wants to maintain his/her right to file a Mechanics Lien.

- **Conditional Waiver and Release On Progress Payment:** It is to be used by a party who applies for a progress payment. It is to be used when the progress payment check has not yet cleared the bank. Thus, this release only becomes effective when the check, properly endorsed has cleared the bank.

- **Unconditional Waiver and Release On Progress Payment:** is like the Conditional Waiver and Release On Progress Payment form, except that it releases the owner unconditionally. It is to be used to release claims, acknowledging that a progress payment has actually been received by the releasing party.

- **Conditional Waiver and Release On Final Payment:** this release covers the final payment to the undersigned for all labor, services, equipment or material furnished on the job. The release is not effective until the check that constitutes final payment has been properly endorsed and has cleared the bank.

- **Unconditional Waiver and Release On Final Payment:** Like the Conditional Waiver and Release On Final Payment form, except that it releases the owner unconditionally. With this form the claimant asserts that he/she has been paid the final payment and frees the owner from the possibility of Mechanics Lien.

- **Mechanics Lien:** Form filed by contractor when payment for labor and materials for improvements on the property of the owner is not paid. This is a foreclosure action in which the contractor will seek a sale of the property of the owner to obtain money for unpaid labor, materials or improvements provided on the owner's property.

---

* You can find ALL forms needed for all your construction needs as well as codes, study guides, helplful publications, videos, software and more at Builders Book Bookstore.
Call 818.887.7828 • visit www.buildersbook.com, or stop by our store
8001 Canoga Ave. Canoga Park, CA. 91304

HOME IMPROVEMENT CONTRACT

HOME IMPROVEMENT CONTRACT
NOT APPLICABLE TO SWIMMING POOLS OF SPAS
(Complies with Section 7159 of California Business and Professions Code, and Civil Code Section 8170 as amended)
AGREEMENT BETWEEN DIRECT CONTRACTOR AND PROPERTY OWNER
The Notice of Cancellation may be mailed to the address of the direct contractor as shown below:

THREE-DAY RIGHT TO CANCEL

COMMERCIAL GENERAL LIABILITY INSURANCE (CGL)

WORKERS' COMPENSATION INSURANCE

NOTICE OF CANCELLATION

NOTICE OF CANCELLATION

ARBITRATION OF DISPUTES

ARBITRATION OF DISPUTES

CUSTOMER ACKNOWLEDGMENT

STATUTORY NOTICES
Information about the Contractors' State License Board (CSLB)

MECHANICS LIEN WARNING

EXAM 7

Law & Business Supplemental

Read. Write. Interact! A powerfully effective way to retain information! Read questions, write down each question in the form of a statement. Quiz yourself or have someone else quiz you.

1. **What is the "standard" contract used by customers and contractors?.... Home Improvement Contract**
   The Home Improvement Contract is the standard contract used by contractors. It establishes an agreement between customer and contractor for performance and compensation for a Home Improvement job.

2. **How many signatures do contracts require?... 2**
   A contract requires the signatures of those entering the contract; usually 2 signatures (the customer's and the contractor's). The contract is not valid without these two signatures.

3. **If more work is requested while a job is already in progress?.............. File a Contract Change Order**
   If more work is requested while a job is already in progress use a "Change Order" to amend the contract. The Change Order document is an organized procedure for documenting changes in the construction contract, it is for when work is added, deleted or altered from how it's stated in the original contract.

4. **What should you do if you complete a job and there is a request placed for more work?..... New Contract**
   If you complete a job (as according to contract) and the owner requests more work, fill a new contract.

5. **Should all change orders be in writing?.. Yes**
   ALL changes must be set in writing! This will protect both parties: the customer and contractor.

6. **What is the downpayment a contractor can request?......................... $ 1,000 or 10% of the project cost**
   A contractor can charge up to $1000.00 or 10% of the total project cost, whichever is less, as a downpayment

7. **Should you spell everything out in detail?.. Yes**
   Everything in a contract must be written in a clear, explanatory way. Wording should be very specific, especially in regards to the job request, job descriptions, specifics of a job etc. Avoid being general or vague.

8. **How much time does the customer have to cancel?... 3 business days**
   The customer can cancel the transaction (the contract agreement), without penalty or obligation, within three (3) business days from the date the Notice of Right to Cancel form is given (within 3 days of signing the contract).

9. **How long does the contractor have to return the customer any money taken? .... 10 days**
   If the customer cancels, any property traded, any payments made under the contract or sale and any negotiable instruments executed must be returned to the customer within 10 days following the receipt of the cancellation order.

10. **You must start the work within how many days of the specified Approximate Start Date?.............. 20 days**
    If work is not begun within 20 days of specified commencement date, you (the contractor) will be in violation of the Contractor's License Law. Violations result in disciplinary action by the C.S.L.B. Board.

11. **How many days does the customer have to make the materials available for pickup?..................... 20 days**
    After cancelling a contract, the customer has 20 days to make the materials available to the seller for pick-up. If the customer does not do so, or if you (the contractor) agree to return the goods to the seller but fail to do so, then you (the contractor) remain liable for performance of all obligations under the contract.

12. **Contracts should always be in writing but they MUST be in writing when the job cost is .... $500 or more**
    The contractor is _required_ to record (in writing) any agreement he/she enters with a customer for a work of home improvement if the amount of the project exceeds $500.00 Setting the agreement in writing will prevent disputes

13. **Does the customer have the right to request a performance or payment bond?..................................Yes**
    For details on Bonds, including: performance bonds or payment bonds look at corresponding section in this book.

14. **What is the Notice to the Owner about?... Contractor's right to a Mechanics Lien**
    The "Notice to the Owner" is a form that informs the owner of the contractor's right to a Mechanics Lien.

15. **Am I required to put my contractor license # on all contracts?.. Yes**
    Your License number must go on all contracts that you enter with anyone. It must go on everything!

Law & Business Supplemental

LIENS AND NOTICES	*13% OF YOUR TEST*

CALIFORNIA PRELIMINARY NOTICE

This form is a pre-lien that informs all interested parties that a claimant is providing labor and/or materials and will have rights to a construction lien, Stop Payment Notice and bond claim if the claimant is not paid for his/her work.

The pre-lien is a pre-requisite for filing a construction lien, Stop Payment Notice or making a claim against a bond to obtain payment.

You must serve the notice within 20 days after first furnishing labor, service, equipment or materials to the job site.

This notice is required for both private construction jobs and Public Works of improvement for California's state or local government agencies.

IMPORTANT

• Without giving a Preliminary Notice, a Direct Contractor, a subcontractor and a supplier cannot file a valid mechanic's lien on the property for which they supplied labor or materials.

• Without a proper and timely Preliminary Notice, a supplier or subcontractor will find his/herself without any legal right whatsoever to file a mechanics lien to obtain any payment from the owner.

*The best way to avoid these problems is to serve a Preliminary Notice <u>as soon as the contract is signed.</u> It is legally acceptable to serve the Notice before the materials are delivered and before work is performed, as long as the contract has been made, agreed on and signed.

MECHANICS LIEN

A mechanics lien is a lien that places <u>a "hold" against the owner's property</u>.

This lien is filed if the owner fails to pay the contractor, subcontractor or supplier.

If what is owed remains unpaid, the mechanics lien allows a foreclosure action, forcing the sale of the owner's property to pay the amount that is owed to the person who files the lien.

STOP PAYMENT NOTICE

A Stop Payment Notice is a lien that places a <u>"hold" on funds</u>.

Since the Stop Payment Notice is a lien on funds, it may be preferable to a mechanics lien in some instances, but you can file a mechanics lien, a stop notice or both.

In Public Works, you cannot file a mechanics lien so your solution for unpaid labor and materials is a Stop Payment Notice.

WHO HAS THE RIGHT TO A LIEN?

Anyone who helps improve the property and that has filed a Preliminary Notice within 20 days of entering a contract, but who is not paid for the performed work or supplied materials, may record a lien against that property. This includes but is not limited to the following:

• Direct Contractor   • Sub-contractors   • Material suppliers

WHERE AND HOW TO RECORD A LIEN

The unpaid contractor, subcontractor or supplier must file the complaint in the proper court to foreclose on the mechanics lien. He/She must then record in the office of the county recorder (of the county where the property is situated) a notice of the pendency of the proceedings on or before 20 days after the filing of the mechanics lien foreclosure action. The owner of the property affected must be notified, in a constructive manner, of the pendency of the action, after the notice is recorded.

EXAM 7

Law & Business Supplemental

THINGS YOU CAN DO TO DIMINISH YOUR CHANCES OF A DISPUTE:
- Communicate with the customer, use punch-lists to let them see the things that need to be done!
- Invoice regularly - don't allow bills to accumulate!
- Document ALL agreements, changes etc. in writing!
- Negotiate changes as they occur and record all changes in writing!
- Meet problems head on, don't dodge resolutions!
- On that same note, don't hide, if there's a problem, face it!

OPTIONS FOR SETTLING A DISPUTE
- <u>Work it out</u>! Lawsuits take time and money, so if possible work it out.
- <u>Small Claims Court</u>: if the project is less than $5,000 and working it out with the owner was not possible take it to small claims court, it is fast and inexpensive. Judgments are binding, but the defendant has the right to appeal. Things to know: NO attorneys allowed and CANNOT foreclose a Mechanics Lien in a small claims court.
- <u>Arbitration</u>: Both parties must agree to it. No going to court needed. The arbitrators review the case and make a decision. Decisions made by the arbitrators are non-appealable.
- <u>File a Mechanics Lien</u>: if you are not paid, you have the right to lien the property.
- <u>Stop Payment Notice</u>: if you are not paid, you have the right to lien construction funds.
- <u>Civil Suit</u>: in addition you can file a Civil Lawsuit for breach of contract.

NOTICE OF COMPLETION
What is a Notice of Completion? A Notice of Completion is a written notice that notifies everyone who worked on a project that the project has been completed. The Notice of Completion must be signed and verified by the owner or his/her agent and must be recorded in the County Recorder's Office in the county where the property is located.

Who must record it? The owner of the property that is being improved (or his/her agent); the person that you've entered into the contract with must record the notice.

When must the Notice of Completion be recorded? The Notice of Completion must be recorded within 15 days of the project being completed.

Who must be notified? All individuals who served and filed a Preliminary Notice must be notified about the recording of a Notice of Completion by the County Recorder's Office.

What happens if the Notice of Completion is not recorded within the given time? If the Notice of Completion is not recorded within 15 days of the project being completed then the time allowed to record a Mechanics Lien is extended.

NOTICE OF CESSATION
What is a Notice of Cessation? A Notice of Cessation is a written notice that states that work has ceased (stopped) for a continuous period of 30 days.

Who must record it? The owner of the property that is being improved (or his/her agent); the person that you've entered into contract with must record the notice.

When must the Notice of Cessation be recorded? The Notice of Cessation must be recorded when there has been a continuous cessation of labor for at least 30 days.

Where must the Notice of Cessation be recorded? The Notice of Cessation must be recorded in the County Recorder's Office in the County where the property is located.

Who must be notified? All individuals who served a Preliminary Notice must be notified about the recording of a Notice of Cessation by the County Recorder's Office.

What happens if the Notice of Cessation is not recorded within the given time? If the Notice of Cessation is not recorded within the required time, the time allowed to record a Mechanics Lien is extended.

NOTICE OF NON-RESPONSIBILITY
What is a Notice of Non-Responsibility? A Notice of Non-Responsibility is a written notice that notifies the contractors involved in the work of improvement that you don't want to be held responsible for payments and you don't want your property to be subject to liens. It is used in Owner-Tenant rental relationships.

EXAM 7

Law & Business Supplemental

MECHANICS LIEN AND STOP PAYMENT NOTICE FLOW CHART 13% OF YOUR TEST

CHECKLIST BEFORE FILING
1. Legal address of the property **2.** Owner's Name **3.** Name of the person who requested the work

DIRECT CONTRACTOR
Contractor who has a direct contractual relationship with the owner

SUBCONTRACTORS
(Subcontractors, Equipment Lessors and Material Suppliers,... anyone who contributes to the work of improvement)

- - - - - - - - - - *START OF PROJECT INVOLVEMENT* - - - - - - - - - -

PRELIMINARY NOTICE
Serve a Preliminary Notice within 20 days of first furnishing work, labor, equipment or materials. Serve the Preliminary Notice to the property owner, direct contractor and construction lender (if any). File the Preliminary Notice in the County Recorder's Office of the county where the property is located.

- - - - - - - - - - *WORK COMPLETED* - - - - - - - - - -

90 DAYS IF NOTICE OF COMPLETION IS NOT RECORDED
If the owner does NOT record a Notice of completion within 15 days of the completion of the project... you have **90 days** to file the lien.

60 DAYS IF NOTICE OF COMPLETION IS NOT RECORDED
If the owner does NOT record a Notice of completion within 15 days of the completion of the project... you have **60 days** to file the lien.

60 DAYS IF NOTICE OF COMPLETION IS RECORDED
If the owner records a Notice of completion within 15 days of the completion of the project... you have **60 days** to file the lien.

30 DAYS IF NOTICE OF COMPLETION IS RECORDED
If the owner records a Notice of completion within 15 days of the completion of the project ... you have **30 days** to file the lien.

90 DAYS TO FORECLOSE
You must file a lawsuit to foreclose a lien within 90 days of recording the mechanics lien. If a lawsuit is not filed within the allotted time, the mechanics lien will expire and be ineffective.

SCHEDULE OF NOTICES – Private Works

FORM NAME	WHO SERVES/FILES/RECORDS?	TIME TO FILE/SERVE/RECORD	EFFECT	BBI FORM
Preliminary Notice	Subcontractors Equipment Lessors & Material Suppliers	Serve within 20 days of first furnishing work, labor, equipment or materials to the project; remember to file it in the County Recorder's Office in the county where the property is located.	Secures your right to file Mechanics Lien if you are not paid. Notifies Owner, Direct Contractor and Construction Lender (if any) of your lien rights	209
Notice of Completion	Owner or the Agent of the owner	Record within 15 days of the project being completed	Shortens the time to file a lien for Direct Contractors from 90 days to 60 days and for Subcontractors and Material Suppliers, etc. from 60 days to 30 days	213
Notice of Cessation	Owner or the Agent representing the owner	Record after 30 days of continuous cessation of labor	Shortens the time to file a lien for Direct Contractors from 90 days to 60 days and for Subcontractors and Material Suppliers, etc. from 60 days to 30 days	225
Notice of Non-Responsibility	Owner or the Agent representing the owner	Within 10 days of learning work is being done to the property	Protects owner from liens where a lessor, renter or tenant hires a contractor for work of improvement.	212
Conditional Waiver & Release On Progress Payment	Requested by the owner recorded by the direct contractor	Upon receipt of incomplete progress payment	Use only if you have completed a phase of the work but have not been paid in full for that phase or check has not cleared	207
Unconditional Waiver & Release On Progress Payment	Requested by the owner but recorded by the direct contractor	Upon receipt of progress payment	Use only if you have completed a phase of the work and have been paid in full for that phase and the check has cleared.	207A
Conditional Waiver & Release On Final Payment	Requested by the owner but recorded by the direct contractor	Upon receipt of incomplete payment	Use only if you have completed the work in its entirety but you have not been paid in full for the work performed, or the check has not cleared.	208
Unconditional Waiver & Release On Final Payment	Requested by the owner but recorded by the direct contractor	Upon receipt of complete final payment	Use only if you have completed the work in its entirety, you have been paid in full, and the check has cleared	208A
California Mechanics Lien	Direct Contractors, Subcontractors, Equipment Lessors, Material Suppliers and anyone entitled to the Lien	Direct Contractors: within 60 days (if Notice of Completion is recorded within 15 days) within 90 days (if Notice of Completion is not recorded within 15 days) Subcontractors, Material Suppliers, Etc. within 30 days (if Notice of Completion is recorded within 15 days) within 60 days (if Notice is not recorded within 15 days)	A mechanics lien is a "hold" against property to secure payment for unpaid labor and materials. The mechanics lien allows a foreclosure action, forcing the sale of the owner's property to provide payment.	205
Stop Payment Notice	Direct Contractors, Subcontractors, Equipment Lessors, Material Suppliers and anyone entitled to the Lien	Direct Contractors: within 60 days (if Notice of Completion is recorded within 15 days) within 90 days (if Notice of Completion is not recorded within 15 days) Subcontractors, Material Suppliers, Etc. within 30 days (if Notice of Completion is recorded within 15 days) within 60 days (if Notice of Completion is not recorded within 15 days)	A Stop Payment is a "hold" against funds, to secure payment for unpaid labor and materials.	211
California Mechanics Lien Release	Direct Contractors, Subcontractors, Material Suppliers and anyone who has recorded a Mechanics Lien	Upon receipt of unpaid payment or agreement about said payment with owner	This form releases the property from the Mechanics Lien recorded against it	210

EXAM 7

WAIVERS & RELEASES
13% OF YOUR TEST

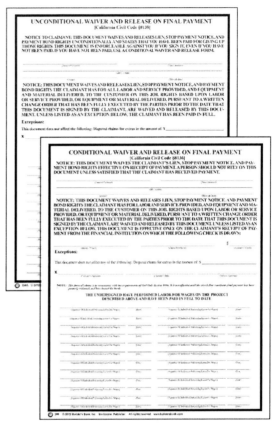

WAIVER AND RELEASES - 4 DIFFERENT TYPES

- **Conditional Waiver and Release On Progress Payment:** Use only if you have completed a phase of the work but you have not been paid in full for that phase yet or if the check has not cleared the bank.

- **Unconditional Waiver and Release On Progress Payment:** Use only if phase is complete and if you have been paid in full for that phase and the check has cleared the bank.

- **Conditional Waiver and Release On Final Payment:** Use only if you have completed the work in its entirety but you have not been paid in full yet or if the check has not cleared the bank. "Conditional" means you still have a condition to be met - such as getting your payment.
  *If you do not have the money in hand or were told that you'd get paid after you supply a Waiver and Release form then use this form.

- **Unconditional Waiver and Release On Final Payment:** Use only if you have completed the work in its entirety and you have been paid in full and the check has cleared the bank. "Unconditional" means there are no more conditions to be met.

EXAM 7

Law & Business Supplemental

FLASH CARD - LIENS   **13%**

Read. Write. Interact! A powerfully effective way to retain information! Read questions, write down each question in the form of a statement. Quiz yourself or have someone else quiz you.

1. **What is a Mechanics Lien?** .... **A lien on property**
   It is a lien placed upon the property that received construction. This lien is filed when you (the contractor) do not receive payment for your work. It is an action to foreclose the property that you worked on, in order to get the payment for your services.

2. **What is a Stop Payment Notice?** .... **A lien on construction funds**
   This is similar to a Mechanics Lien except that with a Stop Payment Notice the lien is placed upon the funds and not the property. It is used to get payment for your services when the owner fails to pay.

3. **Can you record both a Mechanics Lien and a Stop Payment Notice on private work?... Yes**
   You can record both a Mechanics Lien and a Stop Payment Notice for Private Works.

4. **Can you record both a Mechanics Lien and a Stop Payment Notice on public work? ..... No**
   To get payment for unpaid work and unpaid supplies in Public Works, you must file a Stop Payment Notice. Remember that a Mechanics Lien is limited to Private Works.

5. **What must you file to keep the right to a Mechanics Lien?................. Preliminary Notice Form**
   In order to keep your right to file a Mechanics Lien, you (the contractor) must file a "Preliminary Notice" within 20 days of signing the contract. Subcontractors, suppliers and anyone who is going to participate in the job in question must also file a Preliminary Notice" if they want to keep their right.

6. **Who must file the "Notice of Completion"?** .... **the owner**
   The owner must file the "Notice of Completion" when the work on his/her property is completed.

7. **How many days does the owner have to file a "Notice of Completion".......................... 15 days**
   The "Notice of Completion" must be filed within 15 days of when the work is completed.

8. **How many days does the contractor have to file a Mechanics Lien?............................ 90 days**
   If the owner does not file a "Notice of Completion" within 15 days, the contractor has 90 days. If the owner does file the "Notice of Completion" within 15 days, the contractor only has 60 days to file a Mechanics Lien.

9. **How many days does the subcontractor have to file a Mechanics Lien?..................... 60 days**
   If the owner <u>does not</u> file a "Notice of Completion" within 15 days, the sub has 60 days. If the owner <u>does</u> file the "Notice of Completion" within 15 days, the sub only has 30 days to file a Mechanics Lien. These deadlines apply for subs, material suppliers, etc. anyone (but not the contractor) involved in the project.

10. **Can you file a Mechanics Lien if you don't file a "Preliminary Notice"** .... **No**
    If you fail to file a "Preliminary Notice" you forfeit your right to file a Mechanics Lien and Stop Payment Notice.

11. **Small claims courts can only handle cases that are less than what amount?** **$7,500**
    An individual or a business owned by an individual can file up to two cases of $7,500 per year. All other businesses or corporations can file up to two cases of $5,000 per year.

12. **Can you appeal a decision made in a small claim court?** .... **Yes**
    Decisions made in small claims courts can be appealed; deadline for appealing is 10 to 30 days.

13. **Can you appeal a decision made in arbitration?** .... **No**
    Decisions made through the process of arbitration cannot be appealed. Here all decisions are final.

14. **Can you file a Civil Suit?** .... **Yes**
    In addition to filing a Mechanics Lien and/or Stop Payment Notice, you may also file a Civil Suit for breach of contract. A civil suit is an option to consider if you've missed the lien deadlines.

15. **What is the name of the form that notifies people that there is a pending lawsuit? .. Lis Pendens**
    "Lis Pendens" is the name of the form that notifies people that there is a pending lawsuit on their property.

16. **If you record a lien but then get paid,** .... **file a Lien Release Form**
    If you file and record a Lien but then get paid, you must file a Lien Release form. This form releases the party you were suing.

EXAM 7

Law & Business Supplemental

JOB MANAGEMENT – CUSTOMERS

CUSTOMERS

Being able to successfully communicate with customers is essential to your contracting business. Here are a few tips to help avoid disputes with customers, as well as to help you develop loyal clientele and a good reputation as a contractor.

BEFORE SIGNING A CONTRACT...

• Thoroughly review all plans and specifications with the customer and answer any and all questions your customer has!

• Do not rush the process just to get the contract signed.

• Take your time explaining and clarifying.

• Explain to your customer how you handle change orders, schedules, work hours, material deliveries and other concerns.

Why? Because if your rush them and don't allow them to ask their questions and if you don't inform them of the way you handle things, a number of issues might arise, for example:

• They will notice they are not being given their place as valued customers which will most likely cause them not to hire you again or worse cause you to loose that very job.

• Not being willing to clarify and explain creates a bad reputation for you as a contractor.

• Not explaining and answering questions often results in disputes over the interpretation of the plans that were not discussed.

• Not telling them how you handle changes,

OTHER TIPS HELPFUL TIPS!

• Invoice regularly – bring the customer's attention to unpaid bills
• Walk the job using punch lists
• Do a final walk-through at the end

BEFORE STARTING ANY WORK...

• Recheck everything before starting any work.
• Check with the owner more than once for any changes – do they still want what was discussed in the plans?
• If changes have arisen, check to see if additional codes apply.
• Recheck the plans and specifications for any errors.
• Re-discuss the responsibilities of the sub-contractors with the subcontractors.
• Recheck the plans! Even if the architect OK'ed the plans – never start working without rechecking!
Why? Double-checking:
• prevents errors that can be prevented
• saves time and money – once already done, an error can result costly on both your time and money.

ENCOURAGE COMMUNICATION!

• Communicate with your customer whenever possible. Keep them informed on how things are going, where you are on schedule, etc.
• Encourage customers to communicate with you! Make yourself accessible to their inquiries.
• Respond to customers' complaints as soon as you can!
• If you are in a critical phase, note the complaints and address them at the end of the critical phase.
Why? Encouraging communication can significantly diminish disputes.
• Consistent communication throughout the project causes both sides to address problems as they arise, preventing a snowball effect and avalanche in the end.
• Allows both sides to speak up and make suggestions if something is not working.

EXAM 7

FLASH CARD - JOB MANAGEMENT: CUSTOMERS   12%

Read. Write. Interact! A powerfully effective way to retain information! Read questions, write down each question in the form of a statement. Quiz yourself or have someone else quiz you.

1. What should you do before signing the contract?................ walk the job, ask questions
Walk the job and ask questions to make sure you understand what the customer wants and expects.

2. Should you re-check what you need to do even if you already checked it? .... Yes
Check the plans for errors, even if the architect OK'ed them! Never start working without rechecking!

3. Should you explain everything to your customer before the contract is signed? .... Yes
Explain to your customer what the job is going to require as well as the way you handle change orders schedules, work hours, material deliveries and other concerns to avoid frustrations and disputes.

4. What is the one thing that you should encourage? .... Communication
Communication with customers is the key to any successful business, especially a construction business.

5. How can you encourage communication?..................................... Make yourself accessible!
Encourage communication by making yourself accessible. Be open to questions, don't reply in a hasty manner, don't be rude. This will help you prevent disputes that could arise out of misunderstandings.

6. How often should you communicate with your customer?.............................whenever possible
Communicate with your customer whenever possible – keep them informed of how things are going, where you are on the schedule, if they have any concerns or questions regarding the project etc.

7. Why is communication important?.. helps prevent disputes
Communication is important for several reasons: helps prevent disputes over misinterpretations, builds you a good reputation as a contractor (friendly, approachable, accessible are words you want to attach to your reputation), makes the project flow more smoothly for both you and your customer.

8. When should you respond to customer complaints? .... As soon as possible
Complaints should be addressed as soon as they are placed. If you are in a critical phase, write the complaint down and address it as soon as you are out of the critical phase. Explain the situation to the owner and why you are not addressing the complaint immediately so they don't feel dismissed or ignored.

9. Which changes should be placed in writing? .... All changes
All changes should be set in writing to avoid disputes. Use a "Contract Change Order" form to amend the contract.

10. When should you check in with the customer to ensure plans have not changed?...Periodically
Check with the owner more than once for any changes, example: do they still want what they originally requested? Are things going according to how they envisioned them? Check with them on a periodic basis!

11. If changes are made, what should you do? .... Check for new applicable codes
If changes are made, check to see if additional codes apply and then proceed accordingly. Remember to file a "Contract Change Order" to record the changes requested in writing. Always record in writing!

12. Should you re-discuss the responsibilities with your subcontractors before the job begins? ...... Yes
Even if you have already discussed how the responsibilities are going to be split and who is going to do what, you should always re-discuss responsibilities with the subcontractors before the job begins.

13. Why is it important to double-check? .... It saves time and money!
Double-checking prevents errors that can be prevented and thus saves time, money and stress level.

EXAM 7

JOB MANAGEMENT: CONTRACTOR, SUBS & OTHER WORKERS 12%

CONTRACTOR'S ON & OFF SITE RESPONSIBILITIES

The direct contractor is the overall responsible party for work contracted.

His/Her duties include but are not limited to:

- scheduling
- inspections
- contacting the dig alert notification center
- updating "as-built" drawings
- ensuring subs are licensed and insured
- ensuring codes are followed
- making sure all payments are made
- accounting for supplies on site
- making sure there is a min. of 1 bathroom for every 20 employees
- making sure there is drinking water on site
- making sure there is a first aid kit on site
- making sure that the employees of the subs are qualified
- dealing with changes
- dealing with disputes
- establishing & maintaining safety code according to Cal/OSHA, DOSH and IIPP

OTHER WORKERS – DEFINITIONS

Apprentice: a beginner receiving training in a trade, but who is not yet proficient enough to perform the work alone.

Journeyman: A worker qualified to perform work without supervision.

Foreman / Supervisor: Responsible for training and evaluating worker at or below journeyman level. They are required to conduct safety meeting every 10 working days.

WORKING WITH SUBS

Direct Contractors are responsible for the subcontractors they hire.

- ensure subcontractor is licensed
- obtain proof of sub's insurance and workers' compensation
- Review all plans and specifications with them
- Answer all their questions before they begin assigned work
- accurately specify the work and write it as detailed as possible
- pay subs within 7 days of receiving a progress payment
- it is good practice and ethical to call out a subs bidding mistake

CONTRACTOR – FINAL WALK-THROUGH

A final walk-through with your customer will ensure the owner approves of the work and that everything is OK.

- Note any people present that are witnesses to the owner's approval
- Don't delay the walk through
- Once the work is approved, attempt to get an agreement at that time

PAYMENT MUST NOT EXCEED WORK PERFORMED

Progress payments cannot exceed the value of the work performed at any given time. In other words,... you CAN'T get paid beyond the work you perform.

EXAM 7

FLASH CARD – JOB MANAGEMENT: CONTRACTORS, SUBS & OTHER WORKERS   12%

Read. Write. Interact! A powerfully effective way to retain information! Read questions, write down each question in the form of a statement. Quiz yourself or have someone else quiz you.

1. **Who is the overall responsible party for work contracted? .... Direct Contractor**
   The Direct Contractor is the one responsible for the work contracted. His responsibilities include on and off-site duties. See appropriate section in this chapter for details.

2. **Who has to ensure that the subcontractors are licensed and insured?.. Direct Contractor**
   It is the Direct Contractor's responsibility to make sure that all subs are licensed and insured.

3. **How many bathrooms must be provided for every 20 employees? .... 1 (min.)**
   Bathrooms must be provided on the job site. The requirement is a minimum of 1 per 20 employees.

4. **Are workers required to bring their own water to work? .... No**
   The work site is required to provide clean and accessible drinking water to employees.

5. **Does there need to be an emergency kit on site? .... Yes**
   There must be a minimum of one emergency kit on job site at all times. Employees must be informed of the location of the emergency kit as well as how to properly use its components.

6. **Should the contractor review the plan and specifications with his subs? .... Yes**
   Thoroughly review plans and specifications with subs and answer all the questions the subs might have.

7. **Should a contractor write everything down in detail for the sub? .... Yes**
   Besides explaining what the sub is to do, the contractor should accurately specify the work and write it as detailed as possible. Writing down instructions will help prevent misunderstandings.

8. **Can a contractor receive payment for work that has not been completed? .... No**
   Progress payments cannot exceed the value of the work performed at any given time. In other words... you can't get paid for work that you haven't yet done. This rule protects both the consumer and the contractor.

9. **When must you pay the subs? .... within 7 days of receiving progress payment**
   The Direct Contractor must pay his/her subs within 7 days of receiving a progress payment from the owner.

10. **Should you call out a sub if he/she makes a bidding mistake? .... Yes**
    If the sub makes a bidding mistake, it is ethical and good practice to bring it to his/her attention to it.

11. **What is the term given to a "worker in training"? .... Apprentice**
    An apprentice is a worker who is not yet able and/or allowed to perform work unsupervised; a "worker in training".

12. **What is the term given to a worker who is able to perform trade work unsupervised? .... Journeyman**
    A journeyman is a worker who has been trained and is thus able and allowed to perform work unsupervised.

13. **Who is responsible for training employees?.. Foreman/Supervisor**
    The person responsible for training employees is the Foreman or Supervisor.

14. **What is a foreman required to do every 10 days? .... conduct a safety meeting**
    The supervisor and/or foreman is required to conduct safety meetings (a.k.a "tail-gate" meetings) every 10 days.

15. **What must you do if you substantially change the existing structure? .... Update "as-built" drawings**
    You must update "as-built" drawings if your work of improvement substantially changes the structure.

16. **When walking the job with the customer what should you carry? .... Punch list, clip board.**
    Note comments and important information as you walk the job. If there are people standing around when the customer is giving the approval write them down as witnesses, this helps support your completion of the job.

17. **Should you delay the final walk through with the customer? .... No**
    Have the walk through with your customer as soon as you finish the job to get the "okay."

EXAM 7

Law & Business Supplemental

INSURANCE & BONDS -INSURANCE   *13% OF YOUR TEST*

BUSINESSES & RISK MANAGEMENT

Insurance is a means of reducing the company's exposure to risk, unexpected damage and casual damage.

TIP: To minimize insurance expenses, shop around to compare the costs and coverage of various insurance providers.

OTHER TYPES OF INSURANCE

Property Insurance: Covers your property tools and office against fire, storm, theft, etc. Note: It does not cover your employees' tools

Vehicle Insurance: Covers your vehicles, trucks, equipment or trailers while you or your employees are driving them.

Builder's Risk Insurance: Covers you and your property at the site against fire, storm, theft, vandalism, etc. during entire period of work.

"Key Person" Insurance: covers the loss of a "key-person," a person that performs a crucial role in the business by compensating the owner.

Business Interruption Insurance: also known as Business Insurance, it covers interruptions such as lawsuits, absents of owner, severe weather, etc.

Health Insurance: Covers healthcare and other related health issues.

Life Insurance: covers the death of a person by compensating the survivors, such as a family member.

Umbrella Policy: this policy goes above and beyond standard insurances and is therefore more expensive.

Note: If you are just starting your business, the umbrella policy is the least convenient insurance for you. This insurance is usually for larger, more established companies that can afford the extra coverage.

WORKER'S COMPENSATION INSURANCE

Is a NO-FAULT insurance purchased by the employer and supervised by the state. It is designed to limit the liability of the employer by reducing costly lawsuits and by providing prompt rehabilitation for job related injuries.

CSLB requirements for Worker's Comp.

- If the contractor does not have any employees, workers' compensation is not required. If this is the case, the contractor must file an exemption form available online at www.cslb.ca.gov.

- A Worker's Compensation policy is NOT required for inactive or expired licenses.

- If you have one (1) employee, even for part-time, a policy must be obtained and filed.

- File a certificate of Worker's Compensation

LIABILITY INSURANCE

Liability Insurance: Covers problems with the client or their property such as bodily injury and property damage. Liability insurance can be a little tricky to understand, for example: It covers the damage done by poor workmanship, it does not cover the work itself.

Consider the following example: If a shelf is set wrong and it falls and chips the tile floor, the damage to the tile would be covered but not the damage to the shelf.

So liability insurance does not pay for your poor workmanship, it only pays for the damages that poor workmanship causes.

There are two different types of Liabilities available:

- **Claims Made:** covers claims made only while the policy was enforced.

- **Occurrences:** covers claims made during or after having insurance, regardless of policy period.

EXAM 7

Law & Business Supplemental

BONDS

BONDS

Bonding is generally mandatory for large jobs financed by institutional lenders, such as savings and loans, insurance companies, or commercial banks.

*However, many owners and lenders, as well as other contractors, impose bonding requirements.

- Bonds can be obtained from bonding companies for a percentage of the contract price, usually in the 1% to 2% range.

- This requirement is a cost of doing business that should be recognized when the bid is submitted.

- Bonds may be classified as: performance bonds, payment bonds, contract bonds and contractor license bonds.

PERFORMANCE BONDS

Performance Bonds guarantee the completion of the work as it is specified in the project's building plans and specifications.

Performance bonds are in case:

- the job is abandoned or

- the work proves to be unacceptable

In either of the scenarios the bonding company insures the work by hiring another contractor to complete the work or by settling for damages – either way the completion of the work is insured.

PAYMENT BONDS

Payment bonds assure the owner that no liens for labor and materials will be filed against the property.

CONTRACT BONDS

Contract bonds: guarantee both job completion and payment of all labor and materials.

In general, unless the bonding company has taken on responsibility for completing the project, the bonding company will not have to pay more than the face amount of the bond.

The new contractor should be aware that bonding requirements may exclude the new business from bidding on desired jobs.

Bonding companies will not take risks without verifying the technical and resource capabilities of the bonded contractor.

* It is essential to practice sound business management techniques if you hope to be able to qualify for bonding in the future.

CONTRACTOR LICENSE BONDS

Contractor license bonds require each licensed contractor to carry a contractor bond.

Unlike payment, performance and contract bonds, which are usually written to cover specific projects, a contractor license bond is written to cover any project the contractor agrees to perform. The penal sum of the contractor license bond is $12,500.

EXAM 7

Law & Business Supplemental

INSURANCE vs. BONDS	13% OF YOUR TEST

SUMMARY OF INSURANCE

Property Insurance: Covers your property tools and office against fire, storm, theft, etc.

Vehicle Insurance: Covers your vehicles, trucks, equipment or trailers while you or your employees drive.

Liability Insurance: Covers customer's property damage or bodily injury

Builder's Risk Insurance: Covers you and your property

Business Insurance: Covers interruptions to your business

"Key Person" Insurance: Covers the loss of a "key-person" that performs a crucial role in your business.

Business Interruption Insurance: also known as Business Insurance, it covers interruptions such as lawsuits, absents of owner, severe weather, etc.

Health Insurance: Covers healthcare and other related health issues.

Life Insurance: covers the death of a person by compensating the survivors, such as a family member.

Workers Compensation Insurance: No-fault insurance for prompt rehabilitation for job related injuries.

SUMMARY OF BONDS

Payment Bond - ensures payments to 3rd parties

Performance Bond - ensures job completion

Contract Bond - ensures both 3rd party payments and job completion

INSURANCE VS. BONDS

Insurance and Bonds are both forms of indemnity (payment for losses), however they have several key differences.

• Insurance typically protects you, while bonds protects everyone but you

• Bonds have to be reimbursed after a claim is paid

• Bonds are usually harder to get, but cost less than insurance

• Insurance covers a period of time and is an overhead expense, while bonds are usually per project and are considered a direct cost.

INSURANCE vs. BONDS

	Insurance	Bonds
Covers	You	Everyone except you
Reimbursement	None	Yes
Premium	Monthly, Quarterly, Yearly, etc	% of the job (usually 1% to 2%)
Term	Yearly	Per project
Type of Cost	Overhead	Direct Cost

EXAM 7

Law & Business Supplemental

FLASHCARD – INSURANCE & BONDS   **13%**

Read. Write. Interact! A powerfully effective way to retain information! Read questions, write down each question in the form of a statement. Quiz yourself or have someone else quiz you.

1. **Which insurance covers your property?** .... **Property Insurance**
   Property insurance covers your property, tools and office against fire, storm, theft, etc.
2. **Which insurance covers your customer's property?** .... **Liability Insurance**
   Liability insurance covers customer's property damage or bodily injury.
3. **Which insurance covers theft and vandalism at the site?** .... **Builder's Risk Insurance**
   Builder's risk insurance is insurance that covers you (the contractor) and your property.
4. **Which insurance covers the loss of a "key-person"?** .... **"Key Person" Insurance**
   "Key Person" insurance covers the loss of a "key-person," a person that performs a crucial role in the business. The insurance compensates the owner if he/she loses his/her "key person."
5. **Which insurance covers the death of a person?** .... **Life Insurance**
   Life Insurance covers the death of a person by compensating the survivors, such as a family member.
6. **Which insurance covers your company truck and vehicles?** .... **Vehicle insurance**
   Vehicle Insurance covers your vehicles, trucks, equipments or trailers while you or your employees drive
7. **Insurance that covers your company from interruptions?** .... **Business Interruption Insurance**
   Business Interruption Insurance, also known as Business Insurance, covers interruptions such as lawsuits, absence of owner, severe weather, etc... anything that interrupts (puts a project on hold) a project.
8. **What type of policy goes above and beyond any other policy?** .... **Umbrella Policy**
   This insurance is usually for larger, more established companies that can afford the extra coverage.
9. **Which policy are new businesses advised NOT to get?** .... **Umbrella policy**
   If you are just starting your business it is the least convenient insurance for you because it is too expensive.
10. **Is worker's compensation insurance required if you only have 1 employee?** .... **Yes**
    Worker's compensation must be obtained and filed even if you have only 1 part-time employee.
11. **If you have no employees, do you need Worker's Compensation?** .... **No**
    Worker's comp is not required for contractors that do not have employees. If this is the case, you (the contractor) must file an exemption form. Remember, you can't have employees without providing them with worker's comp.
12. **If your license is inactive, do you need a worker's compensation policy?** .... **No**
    Having an inactive license is another exception to having Worker's Comp. Insurance. However, remember that you cannot provide contracting services if your contractors license is inactive.
13. **What should be considered when selecting insurance?** .... **Cost and coverage**
    When selecting insurance the two things you should look at is cost and coverage. Be realistic. What can you afford to spend on insurance? What must absolutely be covered? Shop for insurance accordingly.
14. **Bond that assures the owner that no liens for labor will be filed against property** ...... **Payment Bonds**
    Payment bonds assure the owner that liens for labor and materials cannot be filed against his/her home.
15. **Which bond covers the completion of contract?**.. **Performance Bond**
    Performance bonds are in case the job is abandoned or the work proves to be unacceptable.
16. **Which bond covers both payments and completion of contract?** .... **Contract Bond**
    A contract bond is a bond that incorporates performance bonds with payment bonds.

EXAM 7

Law & Business Supplemental

INTRODUCTION TO CASH MANAGEMENT

Cash management is one of the most important concepts to understand in order to carry out an effective business. However, it is lengthy and involved (so much so that it can be a book of its own!)... So in this section we will cover all the basics you need to know about Cash Management.

Cash management is about having financial control over your construction business. Its goals are to:

- maximize the level of cash within the business

- maximize the return earned from the investment of cash and

- minimize the amount of time in which cash sits idly not producing income

5 BASIC CASH MANAGEMENT PRINCIPLES

These principles apply to small and large businesses:

1. Cash budgeting (which is related to planning the business' cash needs)

2. Acceleration of cash receipts from customers

3. Deceleration of cash disbursements to creditors

4. Raising cash when needed

5. Short term investment to preserve the value of working capital and maximize earnings

PUTTING CASH TO WORK!

Successful cash management for the contractor requires that cash be viewed just like any other income-producing asset. Cash should not sit idle! If it is sitting there, it can't increase.

Cash should be acquired as best as possible.

4 PRIMARY REASONS FOR PROPER LEVEL OF CASH MAINTENANCE

The proper level of cash must be maintained for 4 primary reasons:

1. Transactions

2. Compensating Balance Requirements

3. Precautionary Reasons

4. Investment/Speculations

The contractor's cash management system should be geared to minimize the use of cash for transactions, compensating balance requirements and precautionary reasons because these 3 are non-income producing.

Cash should be available for investment that way cash is maximized, producing the highest return.

CASH INFLOW & CASH OUTFLOW

Any number of special circumstances may cause big fluctuations in the supply and demand of business' cash. However, there are a few predictable and certain inflow and outflow sources:

Cash Inflows
- Accounts receivable collection
- Investment by owners
- Sale of Fixed Assets
- Debt

Cash Outflows
- Accounts Payable Payments
- Payroll
- Indirect Job Costs
- Operating Expenses
- Debt Repayment

- Fixed Asset Acquisition
- Dividends to Owners

EXAM 7

Law & Business Supplemental

CASH INFLOW AND CASH OUTFLOW FLOW CHART   *18% OF YOUR TEST*

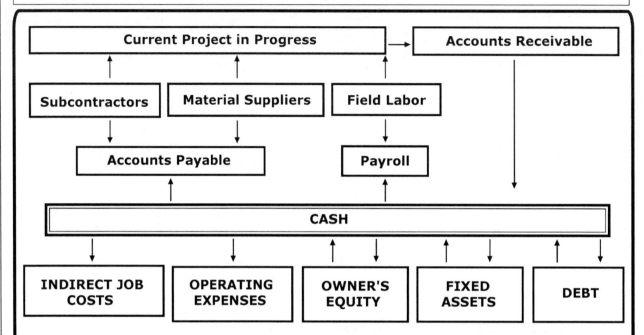

*The arrows directed <u>into</u> the "CASH" box indicate the cash going into the business (sources of cash).
*The arrows moving <u>away</u> from the "CASH" box indicate expenses (cash usage) of the business.

BUDGET & PLANNING

CASH BUDGETING

Cash budgeting is determining the time in which cash flows out of your business. When dealing with cash outflow, timing IS everything!

It is important to know the movement of funds throughout your business. Two ways to help you get control of this is to develop:

Specific movement of funds within the business – needs for cash within the business use:

• job flow budgets - for all projects that are currently in-progress and other anticipated projects.

• a consolidated cash flow budget - for your entire business. This budget should combine the net cash flows from all individual projects with the operating expenses of the firm.

JOB FLOW BUDGET

• Estimate of the timing of cash disbursements for each specific project. Bar Chart Scheduling Method as well as Critical Path Method are extremely helpful in determining WHEN cash should be spent and for WHAT.

Note: Remember that specific terms arranged with your subcontractors and suppliers affect the timing of disbursements.

CONSOLIDATED CASH FLOW BUDGET

This is the compilation of all the individual job cash flow budgets, as well as anticipated expenses, capital expenditures and changes in debt position.

This budget is generally prepared for a one year period and updated each month with the new information.

EXAM 7

Law & Business Supplemental

ACCOUNTING
18% OF YOUR TEST

ACCOUNTING TERMS

Accounting: process of identifying, measuring and reporting financial information of an entity.

Accounting Equation: assets = liabilities + equity.

Accounts Payable: money you owe to suppliers and subcontractors for work performed as well as money owed to vendors and lending companies.

Accounts Receivable: money due to you for work performed by you.

Accrual Accounting: method in which entries are made regardless of when cash changes hands.

Amortization: gradual reduction of amounts in an account over time, either assets or liabilities.

Asset: property with a cash value that is owned by a business or individual. Assets can be identified as either current or fixed. Current assets can be converted into cash within one year. Fixed assets, such as your office building or land, are not intended to be sold.

Audit Trail: a record of every transaction, includes: when it was done, by whom and where. It is used by auditors when validating the financial statement.

Balance Sheet: Shows the condition of a business at a certain point in time; it is a summary of a company's financial status, including: assets, liabilities and equity.

Bookkeeping: recording financial information. Financial statements are the basic tools used to plan, coordinate, control & manage a company.

Budget: A company plan or goal that helps guide job costs and job control.

Budgeting: the process of assigning forecasted income and expenses to accounts, which amounts will be compared to actual income and expense for analysis of variances.

ACCOUNTING TERMS

Calendar Year: The standard annual accounting period starting January 1st and ending December 31st.

Chart of Accounts: a listing of a company's accounts and their corresponding numbers.

Cash-Basis Accounting: a method in which income and expenses are recorded when they are paid. Involves making entries only when cash changes hands.

Cash Discounts: Contractors usually receive discounts for paying for materials early; this discount is usually 1% to 2%

Cash Flow: a summary of cash received and disbursed showing the beginning and ending amounts.

Change in Form Business: If you change from a sole ownership to a partnership or corporation and one or more of the previous owners remains, the employment taxes should be filed as though one business for the entire year.

Closing the Books/Year End Closing: the process of reversing the income and expense for a fiscal or calendar year and netting the amount into "retained earnings."

Corporate Merger: If two or more corporations are combined, the continued corporation is required to file one return as if the two companies are now one entity.

Cost Accounting: a type of accounting that focuses on recording, defining and reporting costs associated with specific operating functions.

Credit: an account entry with a negative value for assets, and positive value for liabilities and equity.

Debit: an account entry with a positive value for assets, and negative value for liabilities and equity.

Double-Entry Bookkeeping: system of accounting in which every transaction has a corresponding positive and negative entry (debits and credits).

Law & Business Supplemental
151

EXAM 7

Law & Business Supplemental

ACCOUNTING TERMS

Equity: money owed to the owner or owners of a company, also known as "owner's equity"

Financial Accounting: accounting focused on reporting an entity's activities to an external party; example: shareholders

Financial Statement: a record containing the balance sheet and the income statement

Fixed Asset: long-term tangible property; building, land, computers, etc.

Fixed Cost: costs or expenses that remain the same each month, such as office rent or a truck payment

General Ledger: a record of all financial transactions within an entity

Income Statement: Summarizes the operations of a business for a period of time. An income statement shows the income expenses - resulting profit and loss. It is a summary of income and expenses

Inventory: a company's assets in inventory such as materials, labor, direct and indirect and overhead on jobs currently in progress.

Invoice: the original billing from the seller to the buyer, outlining what was purchased and the terms of sale, payment, etc.

Job Costing: system of tracking costs associated with a job or project (labor, equipment, etc.) and comparing with forecasted costs

Journal - a record where transactions are recorded, also known as an "account"

Liability: Represents the obligation to pay money for a business debt such as loans, accounts payable etc. Liabilities can be categorized as either current or long term. Current liabilities are debts which become due in one year. Long term liabilities are due beyond one year and it includes things such as mortgages or a bank loan.

ACCOUNTING TERMS

Liquid Asset: cash or other property that can be easily converted to cash.

Loan: money borrowed from a lender and usually repaid with interest.

Net Income: money remaining after all expenses and taxes have been paid.

Non-Cash Expense: recognizing the decrease in the value of an asset; example: depreciation and amortization.

Non-operating Income: income generated from non-recurring transactions; example sale of an old building.

Note: a written agreement to repay borrowed money; sometimes used in place of a "loan"

Operating Income: income generated from regular business operations

Owner's Equity: Represents the net worth or equity of the owner's interest in a business.

Payroll: a list of employees and their wages

Posting: the process of entering then permanently saving or "archiving" accounting data.

Revenue: total income before expenses.

Shareholder Equity: the capital and retained earnings in an entity attributed to the shareholders

Single-Entry Bookkeeping: system of accounting in which transactions are entered into one account.

Statement of Account: a summary of amounts owed to a vendor, lender, etc.

Variable Cost: Expenses that vary or change each month, such as materials.

EXAM 7

Law & Business Supplemental

BALANCE SHEET

The balance sheet is an expanded version of the following accounting equation.

Assets = Liabilities + Equity   **Equity = Assets - Liability**

The balance sheet is considered to be a statement of your company's financial standing as of the date the balance sheet is done.

The most common classifications in a balance data sheet are the following:

- Assets
- Liabilities
- Equity (Stockholder's Equity)

ASSETS	**CAPITAL (NON-CURRENT) ASSETS**	**LIABILITIES**	**EQUITY**
Current Assets	• Construction Equipment	**Current Liabilities**	• Capital Stock
• Cash and Equivalents	• Trucks and Autos	• Payables	• Paid-In-Capital
• Receivables	• Office Equipment	• Accrued Liabilities	• Retained Earnings
• Inventories	• Real Estate	• Payroll Withholdings	
• Prepaid Expenses	**Deferred Items**	• Income Taxes Payable	
	• Taxes	**Long Term Liabilities**	
	• Other Charges	• Notes Payable	
		• Deferred Taxes	

SUMMARY OF ACCOUNTING CYCLE

BASIC ACCOUNTING CYCLE:

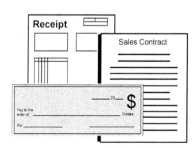

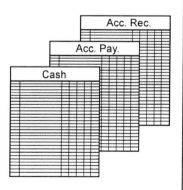

1. GATHER ALL TRANSACTIONS   **2. RECORD THE TRANSACTIONS IN THE GENERAL JOURNAL**   **3. POST TRANSACTIONS ON THE LEDGER ACCOUNT**

EXAM 7

ACCOUNTING & BALANCE SHEET	*18% OF YOUR TEST*

4. CREATE A BALANCE SHEET – FOR A SPECIFIC PERIOD OF TIME

BALANCE SHEET

COMPANY NAME:		DATE: _____ through _____	
ASSETS	**AMOUNT**	**LIABILITIES**	**AMOUNT**
CURRENT ASSETS	**AMOUNT**	**CURRENT LIABILITIES**	**AMOUNT**
Cash/Equivalents	$0.00	Accrued Liabilities	$0.00
Accounts Recievables	$0.00	Accounts Payable	$0.00
Inventory	$0.00	Income Taxes Payable	$0.00
Prepaid Expenses	$0.00	Payroll Withholdings	$0.00
CAPITAL (NON-CURRENT ASSETS)	**AMOUNT**		**AMOUNT**
Real Estate	$0.00	Notes Payable	$0.00
Office Equipment	$0.00	Deferred Taxes	$0.00
Construction Equipment	$0.00	Other Long-Term Liabilities	$0.00
Trucks and Autos	$0.00		$0.00
SHAREHOLDER'S EQUITY			
SHAREHOLDER'S EQUITY			**AMOUNT**
Capital stock			$0.00
Retained Earnings			$0.00
Paid-In-Capital			$0.00

5. CREATE AN INCOME STATEMENT FOR THE MONTH

INCOME STATEMENT

COMPANY NAME: DATE: _____ through _____		
	INCOME	**EXPENSES**
Revenues	$20,000.00	
Operating Expenses		$3,000.00
Administration Expenses		$4,500.00
Income Tax		$3,300.00
Net Profit		$9,200.00

EXAM 7

Law & Business Supplemental

Read. Write. Interact! A powerfully effective way to retain information! Read questions, write down each question in the form of a statement. Quiz yourself or have someone else quiz you.

1. **What is cash management about?** .... **financial control**
Cash management is about having financial control over your business and managing cash.

2. **How many goals does cash management have according to this chapter?** .... **3 goals**
The 3 goals are the following: 1. maximize the level of cash within the business, 2. maximize the return earned from the investment of cash and 3. minimize the amount of time in which cash sits idly.

3. **How many essential cash management principles are outlined in this chapter?** ...... **5 principles**
These 5 principles are: 1. cash budgeting, 2. acceleration of cash receipts from customers, 3. deceleration of cash disbursements to creditors, 4. Raising cash when needed and 5. Short term investments.

4. **Why is it not advisable to let cash sit, undisturbed?** .... **it can't increase**
If cash sits idly it can't increase in value. It is advisable to take cash and make wise investments with it.

5. **Primary reasons for proper level of cash management outlined in this chapter?** **4**
The 4 primary reasons for proper level management that are outlined in this chapter are the following: transactions, compensating balance requirements, precautionary reasons and investment/speculation purposes.

6. **What is a non-income producing cash use?** .... **Cash transactions**
Non-income producing cash uses: cash transactions, compensating balance requirements & money saved for precautionary reasons are non-income producing applications of cash because they don't produce income.

7. **What is an income-producing cash use?** .... **Investments**
Investments, as well as, speculations for money use are both income producing money moves.

8. **How does cash produce the highest return?** .... **by investing it**
Cash produces the highest return when it's invested. Investments can help your money grow.

9. **Are there predictable cash inflow sources in a business?** .... **Yes**
For a business there are always predictable cash inflow sources. Predictable cash inflow sources include: accounts receivables collection, investment by owners, sale of fixed assets, debt.

10. **Are there predictable cash outflow sources in a business?** .... **Yes**
Predictable cash outflow sources include: accounts payable payments, payroll, indirect job costs, operating expenses, debt repayment, fixed asset acquisition and dividends to owners.

11. **"Determining the time in which cash flows out of your business" is** .... **Cash Budgeting**
Cash Budgeting is defined as "determining the time in which cash flows out of your business." In cash outflow...timing is everything! The success of your business largely depends on when to send payments.

12. **Controlling cash movement within your company relies on** .... **Job Flow Budget**
A Job Flow Budget and a Consolidated Cash Flow Budget are essential in attaining control of cash movement within your company. A job flow budget is used for all projects that are currently in progress and other anticipated projects. A consolidated cash flow budget is the compilation of all the individual job cash flow budgets, anticipated expenses, capital expenditures and changes in debt position. Having and keeping these two types of budgets is crucial to keeping control of your cash by controlling its inflow and outflow.

EXAM 7

Law & Business Supplemental

Read. Write. Interact! A powerfully effective way to retain information! Read questions, write down each question in the form of a statement. Quiz yourself or have someone else quiz you.

1. **A consolidated cash flow budget is generally prepared for what period of time?** .... **1 year**
   This budget is generally prepared for a 1 year period and is updated each month with the new information.

2. **What helps you determine WHEN cash should be spent and for what?** .... **Job Scheduling**
   Job scheduling methods, such as bar chart scheduling or critical path scheduling methods are very useful, they help you determine when cash should be spent and for what. Use a scheduling method for every job.

3. **Terms arranged with your subcontractors and suppliers affect?** .... **cash outflow**
   Specific terms arranged with your subcontractors and suppliers affect the timing of disbursements of cash.

4. **Process of identifying, measuring & reporting of financial information** .... **Accounting**
   Accounting is the process of identifying, measuring and reporting financial information of an entity.

   Assets = Liability + Equity   Equity = Assets - Liabilities

5. **Where would you list amounts you still owe?** .... **Accounts Payable**
   Accounts payable is money you owe to suppliers and subcontractors for work performed as well as money owed to vendors and lending companies. Accounts payable is part of your cash outflow.

6. **Where would you list amounts due to you?** .... **Accounts Receivables**
   Accounts receivable is money owed to you for work performed. It is part of your inflow of money.

7. **Name given to an annual accounting period starting January 1st** .... **Calendar Year**
   A calendar year is the name given to an annual accounting period that starts on January 1st

8. **What is an annual accounting period starting when a company chooses?** .... **Fiscal Year**
   A fiscal year is the name given to an annual accounting period that begins when the company chooses.

9. **Accounting form that makes entries ONLY when cash changes hands?** .... **Cash-Basis**
   Cash-Basis Accounting is a method in which income and expenses are recorded ONLY when they are paid. It involves making changes in recording only when cash changes hands.

10. **Accounting form that makes entries regardless of when cash changes hands** .... **Accrual**
    Accrual accounting makes entries regardless of whether or not money has actually changed hands.

11. **Focuses on recording, and reporting costs of operating functions?** .... **Cost Accounting**
    Cost accounting focuses on recording, defining and reporting costs associated with operating functions.

12. **Is accounting and bookkeeping the same thing?** .... **No**
    Bookkeeping is the recording of financial information. Financial statements are the basic tools used.

13. **What are examples of variable costs?** .... **Utilities, office supplies, materials**
    Variable costs are expenses whose amount changes each month, such as: utility bills, office supplies and materials. There are always going to be changes in variable costs.

EXAM 7

Law & Business Supplemental

1. **Cash discounts from suppliers are usually what %?** .... **1% to 2%**
   Cash discounts given to you by material suppliers and others should not be passed down to customers.

2. **If you change your business form, you should file employment taxes as** .... **1 business**
   If you change from a sole ownership to a partnership or a corporation and one or more of the previous owners remains, the employment taxes should be filed as one business for that entire year.

3. **What is the best strategy for getting short term capital?** .... **Open a line of credit**
   The best way to get a short term capital is to open a line of credit. Line of credit should be opened with a bank.

4. **What shows income and expenses?** .... **An Income Statement**
   An income statement shows income and expenses over a period of time.

5. **What shows total assets and total liabilities?** .... **A Balance Sheet**
   A balance sheet shows total assets and total liabilities on a specific date.

6. **What is the equity equation?** .... **Equity = Assets - Liabilities**
   Equity is money that is owed to the owner or owners of the company.

7. **What is one of the classifications in a data sheet?** .... **Assets**
   The following are the three most common classifications that are (and must be) included in a data sheet: Assets, Liabilities and Equity (stockholder's equity).

8. **An example of a current asset is** .... **accounts receivables**
   Current assets are cash and the equivalent, receivables, inventories and prepaid expenses.

9. **What is an example of a non-current asset?** .... **Real Estate**
   Non-Current Assets are also known as Capital Assets. Examples of Non-Current Assets include things like: construction equipment, trucks and autos, office equipment and real estate.

10. **What is an example of a current liability?** .... **Income taxes payments**
    Liability represents the obligation to pay money for a business debt such as loans. Liabilities can be categorized as either current or long term liabilities. The following are examples of current liabilities: payables, accrued liabilities, payroll withholdings and income taxes – payable.

11. **What is an example of a long term liability?** .... **Deferred taxes**
    Notes payable and deferred taxes are both examples of long term liabilities.

12. **What is an example of equity?** .... **Capital stock**
    The following are examples of equity: capital stock, paid-in-capital and retained earnings.

13. **When accounting what is the first thing you should do?** .... **Gather all transactions**
    There is an accounting cycle that you should follow in order to be successful in estimating your net gross and gross expenses. The first step in this cycle is to gather all transactions.

14. **Last step in this model accounting cycle is** .... **Income Statement**
    Here are the five steps in this accounting cycle: 1. gather all transactions, 2. record the transactions in the general journal, 3. Post transactions on the ledger account, 4. create a balance sheet, 5. create an income statement for the month. Follow these steps to successfully estimate.

EXAM 7

EMPLOYMENT REGULATIONS - HIRING EMPLOYEES *15% OF YOUR TEST*

WHO IS AN EMPLOYER?

An employer is a person or legal entity who hires one or more persons to work for a wage or salary.

Employers include sole proprietors, partnerships (including co-ownerships), corporations, S corporations...etc.

REGISTERING WITH THE EDD

The Employment Development Department (EDD) requires all employers who have paid over $100 in total wages to one or more employees in a calendar quarter to register.

1st Quarter: January, February, March

2nd Quarter: April, May, June

3rd Quarter: July, August, September

4th Quarter: October, November, December

RECORDS OF EMPLOYMENT TAXES

The IRS requires for you to keep records of employment taxes for at least 4 years

In addition, keeping good records helps you:

• monitor the progress of your business,

• prepare your financial statements,

• identify source of receipts,

• keep track of deductible expenses,

• prepare your tax returns, and

• support items reported on tax returns

HIRING EMPLOYEES & EIN

• Before you can begin to hire employees you must first obtain your Employer Identification Number (EIN), referred to as an Employer Tax ID Number.

• You must fill and file an SS-4 Form

Why is it necessary?

• The EIN is necessary for reporting taxes and other documents to the IRS.

• The EIN is necessary when reporting information about your employees to state agencies.

• It is required and enforced by the U.S. Internal Revenue Service (IRS)

* for more information contact the IRS online or over the phone:

U.S. Internal Revenue Service
Phone: 1-800-829-4933

INDEPENDENT CONTRACTORS

Hiring an independent contractor instead of an employee makes the employer NOT responsible for withholding taxes, Workers Comp. etc.

In this case, employers use a 1099-MISC Form at the end of the year as receipt.

The IRS pays close attention of who you declare as an employee and who you declare as an independent contractor... so play by the rules!

EXAM 7

3 TYPES OF WITHHOLDING TAXES   15% OF YOUR TEST

1. FEDERAL INCOME TAX WITHHOLDING (FORM W-4)

Every employee must provide an employer with a signed withholding exemption certificate (Form W-4) on or before the date of employment. The employer must then submit Form W-4 to the IRS. For specific information on employer responsibilities regarding withholding of federal taxes, read the IRS' Employer's Tax Guide.

2. FEDERAL WAGE AND TAX STATEMENT (FORM W-2)

- On an annual basis, employers must report to the federal government the wages paid and taxes withheld for each employee.

- This report is filed using Form W-2 Wage and Tax Statement.

- Employers must complete a W-2 Form for each employee to whom they pay a salary, wage or other compensation.

- Employers must send Copy A of Form W-2 to the Social Security Administration (SSA) by the last day of February (or last day of March if you file electronically) to report the wages and taxes of their employees for the previous calendar year.

    NOTE: In addition, employers should send copies of Form W-2 to their employees by Jan. 31 of the year following the reporting period.

3. EMPLOYEE ELIGIBILITY VERIFICATION (FORM I-9)

- Federal law requires employers to verify an employee's eligibility to work in the United States.

- Within 3 days of hire, employers must complete an Employment Eligibility Verification Form (I-9 form). This requires you to examine acceptable forms of documentation supplied by the employee to confirm the employee's citizenship or eligibility to work in the U.S.

- Employers can only request documentation specified on the I-9 form. Employers who ask for other types of documentation not listed on the I-9 form may be subject to discrimination lawsuits.

- Employers do not file the I-9 with the federal government. Rather, an employer is required to keep an I-9 form on file for three years after the date of hire or one year after the date of the employee's employment termination, whichever is later.

    The U.S. Immigration and Customs Enforcement (ICE) agency conducts routine workplace audits to ensure that employers are properly completing and retaining I-9 forms, and that employee information on I-9 forms matches government records.

STATE TAXES

Depending on the state where your employees are located, you may be required to withhold state income taxes, in addition to the federal taxes. For CA taxes, see appropriate section in this book.

EXAM 7

Law & Business Supplemental

SUMMARY OF TAX-RELATED FORMS	
FORM	**DESCRIPTION**
W-2	**Federal Wage and Tax Statement (Form W-2)** is a summary of wages and taxes paid annually. Shows total income and Social Security taxes withheld in a calendar year. Employers must send Copy A of Form W-2 to the Social Security Administration (SSA) <u>by the last day of February</u> <u>(or last day of March if you file electronically)</u> to report the wages and taxes of your employees for the previous calendar year. Employers must send copies of Form W-2 to their employees by Jan. 31 of the year following the reporting period.
W-4	**Federal Income Tax Withholding (Form W-4)** Every employee must provide an employer with a signed withholding exemption certificate (Form W-4) <u>on or before</u> the date of employment. The employer must then submit Form W-4 to the IRS. For specific information on employer responsibilities regarding withholding of federal taxes, read the IRS' <u>Employer's Tax Guide</u>.
I-9	**Employee Eligibility Verification (Form I-9)** Completed by new employees within 3 business days of hire. This form requires the employer to examine acceptable forms of documentation supplied by the employee to confirm the employee's citizenship or eligibility to work in the U.S.
1099-MISC	**Miscellaneous Income (Form 1099)** must be filed for each person whom you have paid. • At least $10 in royalties or broker payments in lieu of dividends or tax-exempt interest; • At least $600 in rents, services (including parts and materials), prizes and awards, other income payments, medical and health care payments, crop insurance proceeds, cash payments for fish (or other aquatic life) you purchase from anyone engaged in the trade or business of catching fish, or, generally, the cash paid from a notional principal contract to an individual, partnership, or estate; • Any fishing boat proceeds; or • Gross proceeds of $600 or more paid to an attorney during the year In addition, use Form 1099-MISC to report that you made direct sales of at least $5,000 of consumer products to a buyer for resale anywhere other than a permanent retail establishment. You must also file Form 1099-MISC for each person from whom you have withheld any federal income tax under the backup withholding rules regardless of the amount of the payment.
EIN (SS-4)	**Application for Employer Identification Number (EIN) (SS-4 Form)** Use Form SS-4 to apply for an EIN. An EIN is a nine-digit number (for example, 12-3456789) assigned to sole proprietors, corporations, partnerships, estates, trusts, and other entities for tax filing and reporting purposes. The information you provide on this form will establish your business tax account.

EXAM 7

Law & Business Supplemental

WAGES, HOURS & MANAGING EMPLOYEES   15% OF YOUR TEST

UNLICENSED SUBCONTRACTORS STATUTORY EMPLOYEES

If a licensed or unlicensed Direct Contractor subs with a contractor who does not hold a valid license in the appropriate classification, the subcontractor (and all of his/her employees) are considered to be statutory employees of the Direct Contractor.

If this is the case the Direct Contractor (you) can be held liable for FICA, FUTA, UI, ETT & Workers Comp. taxes. So make sure ALL subs you hire are licensed and that their employees are all legal!

HOURS & WAGES

Work Hours
Can't work more than 6 days in 7 days

Part-time, Full-time and Over-time

0 to 35 hours   = Part-time

36 to 40 hours = Full-Time

41 hours or more = Overtime

*number of hours - based on hours worked in a week

EVALUATING EMPLOYEES

Training and evaluating employees at or below journeyman level is responsibility of the foreman or supervisor.
*Remember though, before an employee's performance can be evaluated, you must make sure that the employee understands what his job is. You must clearly define their job task.

FIRING EMPLOYEES

In case this unfortunate event has to occur, be sure to document habits of each worker, for example: tardiness, mistakes, etc. This will be your line of defense as an employer.
If an employee is terminated the employer must pay all current unpaid wages immediately.

MINIMUM WAGE

- $8.00 per/hr. in California
- Overtime is paid as time and a half – in this case $12 per/hour

PAYING EMPLOYERS

- Employees must be paid at least twice a month or every 2 weeks, unless a special employment contract exists.
- Employers must keep all employee records for a min. of 4 years.

FEDERAL REGULATIONS ON EMPLOYMENT RELATIONSHIPS

TITLE VII
Prohibits employers from discriminating in the hiring process based on race, color, religion, sex, or national origin.

FAIR LABOR STANDARDS ACT
Provides regulation as to the duration of work days, and breaks an employer must provide; governs applicable salary and overtime.

FAMILY AND MEDICAL LEAVE ACT
Preserves qualified employees' job position for the duration of the leave. Their leave must be medical or family related.

AMERICANS WITH DISABILITIES ACT (ADA)
Prohibits discrimination against a person with a qualified disability if he/she can perform essential functions with or without reasonable accommodations.

AGE DISCRIMINATION IN EMPLOYMENT ACT
Prevents employers from giving preferential treatment to younger workers to the detriment of older workers.

EXAM 7

Law & Business Supplemental

POINTERS & EMPLOYEE RIGHTS   *15% OF YOUR TEST*

INFORMATION & ORGANIZATION
- Get organized and keep yourself informed
- Maintain a healthy and fair workplace
- Provide benefits
- Keep employees informed about your company's policies

SET UP RECORDKEEPING
Set up and maintain a sound and organized system to record all personnel records.

ADOPT WORKPLACE SAFETY PRACTICES
- The Occupational Safety and Health Administration's (OSHA) Quick Start tool provides a clear, step-by-step guide that helps you identify many of the major OSHA requirements and informational materials that may apply to your workplace.
- Understand Employee Benefit Plans!
  If you will be providing benefits to your employees, you should become familiar with the uniform minimum standards required by federal law to ensure that employee benefit plans are established and maintained in a fair and financially sound manner.

LEARN MANAGEMENT BEST PRACTICES
While you aren't legally required to be a good manager, it sure helps when trying to recruit and retain good employees. Learning management practices will greatly help you.

APPLY STANDARDS THAT PROTECT EMPLOYEE RIGHTS
Complying with standards for employee rights in regards to equal opportunity and fair labor standards is a requirement. Following statutes and regulations for minimum wage, overtime, and child labor will help you avoid errors and legal trouble, such as a lawsuit.

WORKPLACE RIGHTS

Depending upon where you live, the kind of job you have and the size of your employer, the rights of workers where you are employed may include:

- The right to a safe work environment, free from undue dangers

- The right to a degree of privacy in your personal matters - applies to the employee's personal possessions, including handbags or briefcases, storage lockers etc.

- An employer may not conduct a credit or background check of an employee or prospective employee unless the employer notifies the individual in writing and receives the employee's permission to do so.

- The right not to be discriminated against on grounds of your age, race, national origin, gender, ethnicity, pregnancy, religion, disability or on the basis of marital status, gender identity, sexual orientation etc.

- The right to fair pay, meaning at least a minimum wage, plus overtime for any overtime hours worked.

- The right to a workplace environment with no harassment.

- The right to take time from work to tend to your own, or a family member's, illness, or birth of a child.

EXAM 7

Law & Business Supplemental

FLASHCARD – EMPLOYMENT REGULATIONS 15%

Read. Write. Interact! A powerfully effective way to retain information! Read questions, write down each question in the form of a statement. Quiz yourself or have someone else quiz you.

1. **What must you obtain before you can begin to hire employees?** .... **EIN**
   The Employer Identification Number (EIN) is referred to as an Employment Tax ID. If you plan to have employees, you must apply for an EIN. You cannot legally hire employees without it.

2. **Who requires and enforces the EIN?** .... **The IRS**
   The U.S. Internal Revenue Service (IRS) requires and enforces EIN requirements.

3. **You must keep records of employment taxes for how many years** .... **4 years**
   The IRS requires all employers to keep records of employment taxes for a minimum of 4 years.

4. **Who must you register with when you have employees?** .... **The EDD**
   The Employment Development Department (EDD) requires for all employers who have paid $100 in total wages to one or more employees in a calendar quarter to register.

5. **How many types of withholding taxes are covered in this chapter** .... **3 types**
   There are 3 types of withholding taxes, they are: Federal Income Tax Withholding (Form W-4), Federal Wage and Tax Statement (Form W-2) and Employee Eligibility Verification (Form I-9).

6. **Is it true that you may be required to withhold state income taxes?** .... **Yes**
   California employers are required to pay certain taxes required by the state, including Disability Insurance, taxes, unemployment taxes and employment training taxes.

7. **What is the maximum amount of days that an employee is allowed to work?** .... **6 days**
   Employees can't work more than 6 consecutive days out of 7 consecutive days.

8. **How many hours is "part-time"?** .... **35 hours or fewer**
   "Part-time" is when a worker works 35 hours or fewer in a working week (in 6 out of 7 days).

9. **How many hours is "full-time"?** .... **36 to 40 hours**
   "Full-time" is when a worker works 36 to 40 hours in a working week (in 6 out of 7 days).

10. **What is over-time?** .... **41 hours or more**
    Overtime is when a worker works 41 hours or more in a working week (in 6 out of 7 days).

11. **What is the minimum wage in California?** .... **$8.00 per/hour**
    Minimum wage varies according to state. California has a higher minimum wage than the one implemented by the Federal government. Minimum wage in California is $8.00 per/hour.

12. **How often must employees be paid?** .... **every 2 weeks**
    Unless a special employment contract exists between the employer and employees, the employer is required (by law) to pay the employees at least twice a month or every 2 weeks.

13. **Who is responsible for training employees?** .... **Foreman or Supervisor**
    The foreman or supervisor is responsible for training and evaluating employees.

14. **When must an employee be evaluated?** .... **After job has been defined**
    Only after job has been clearly defined may the employee be held for an evaluation.

15. **If you fire an employee, when must you pay his/her unpaid wages?** .... **Immediately**
    If an employee is fired, the employer must pay all current unpaid wages immediately.

16. **What are unlicensed subcontractors considered?** .... **Statutory employees**
    Unlicensed subcontractors (and all of his/her employees) are considered "Statutory Employees." If you have statutory employees, you can be held accountable for federal and state taxes that must be paid. So, make sure all your subs are licensed and that all of his/her workers are qualified to work. Remember, if they are not you will be held accountable for paying all the state and federal taxes required by law.

EXAM 7

TAXES & FINANCIAL REPORTING   18% OF YOUR TEST

THINGS YOU MUST DO WHEN YOU HIRE AN EMPLOYEE

In addition to the requirements in the previous page, the following is a list of things you must do when you hire an employee:

Register with Your State's New Hire Reporting Program
The Personal Responsibility and Work Opportunity Reconciliation Act of 1996 requires all employers to report newly hired and rehired employees to a state directory within 20 days of their hire or rehire date.

Obtain Workers' Compensation Insurance
Businesses with employees are required to carry Workers' Compensation Insurance coverage through a commercial carrier, on a self-insured basis or through the State Workers' Compensation Insurance program.

Unemployment Insurance Tax Registration
Businesses with employees are required to pay unemployment insurance taxes under certain conditions. If your business is required to pay these taxes, you must register your business with your State's workforce agency.

Obtain Disability Insurance (Required in California)
Employers must provide partial wage replacement insurance coverage to their eligible employees for non-work related sickness or injury.

Post Required Notices
Employers are required by State and Federal laws to prominently display certain posters in the workplace that inform employees of their rights and employer responsibilities under labor laws. These posters are available for free from federal and state labor agencies.

ADVICE FOR NEW EMPLOYERS - FILE YOUR TAXES

If you are a new employer, there are new Federal and State tax filing requirements that you should know:

• Each quarter, employers who pay wages subject to income tax withholding, Social Security and Medicare taxes must file IRS Form 941, Employer's Quarterly Federal Tax Return.

• Small businesses with an annual income tax liability of $1,000 or less may file IRS Form 944, Employer's Annual Federal Tax Return instead of Form 941.

• You must also file IRS Form 940, Employer's Annual Federal Unemployment (FUTA) Tax Return, if you paid wages of $1,500 or more in any calendar quarter, or if you had one or more employees work for you in any 20 or more different weeks of the year.

Note: New and existing employers should consult the IRS Employer's Tax Guide to understand all their Federal tax filing requirements.

EXAM 7

Law & Business Supplemental

CALIFORNIA PAYROLL TAXES & WHO PAYS THEM

ETT TAXES

What are they?
The Employment Training Tax (ETT) provides funds to train employees in targeted industries to improve the competitiveness of California businesses. ETT funds promote a healthy labor market and helps California businesses invest in a skilled and productive workforce and develop the skills of workers who directly produce or deliver goods and services.

Who Pays?
• Employer
• Paid Quarterly

SDI TAXES

SDI Taxes
What are they?
State Disability Insurance (SDI) provides temporary payments to workers who are unable to perform their usual work because of pregnancy or a non-occupational illness or injury.

Note: work-related disabilities are covered by workers' compensation.

Also includes Paid Family Leave (PFL), which provides benefits to workers who need to care for a seriously ill family member or to bond with a newborn child.

Who pays for them?
• Employees
• It is deducted (withheld) from employees' wages.

PIT TAXES

What are they?
California Personal Income Tax (PIT) is an elective coverage that is offered to specific types of individuals and classes of employees who are excluded from UI and/or SDI. These can include: self-employed individuals; sole proprietors, husband/wife co-ownerships etc.

Who pays for them?
• Employees
• It is withheld from their wages.

FICA TAXES

What are they?
The Federal Insurance Contributions Act (FICA) consists of both Social Security and Medicare taxes.

Who Pays?
• Employers
• Employees
• they each pay half
• Paid quarterly

FUTA TAXES

What are they?
Federal Unemployment Tax Act (FUTA), is a tax that along with state unemployment systems, provides for payments of unemployment compensation to workers who have lost their jobs.

Who Pays?
• Employers
• Paid quarterly

UI TAXES

What are they?
Unemployment Insurance (UI) tax provides temporary payments to individuals who are unemployed through no fault of their own.

Who pays for them?
• Employers

FIT & SIT TAXES

What are they?
Federal Income Taxes (FIT) taxes that go to the IRS.
State Income Taxes (SIT) taxes that go to the State.

Who pays for them?
• Employees
• These taxes are withheld from the taxable wages of employees and are collected along with the UI and SDI.

EXAM 7

Law & Business Supplemental

SUMMARY OF EMPLOYMENT TAXES

WHO PAYS WHAT?

EMPLOYEE

(BOTH)

EMPLOYER

FICA
(paid by employer AND employee)
What: Federal Insurance Contributions Act
When: Quarterly
Where: IRS
Why: Social Security & Medicare

FIT & SIT
What: Federal & State Income Tax
When: Quarterly
Where: Fed = IRS, State = EDD
Why: Government Spending

FUTA
What: Federal Unemployment Tax Act
When: Yearly, Due Next January 31st
Where: IRS
Why: Unemployment Compensation

SDI
What: State Disability Insurance
When: Quarterly
Where: EDD
Why: Unemployed & Unable to Work

UI
What: State Unemployment Insurance
When: Quarterly
Where: EDD
Why: Unemployed & Able to Work

PIT
What: California Personal Income Tax
Where: EDD
Why: For those who do not qualify for UI and/or SDI

ETT
What: Employment Training Tax
When: Quarterly
Where: EDD
Why: Job Training Programs

EXAM 7

Law & Business Supplemental

FLASHCARD – TAXES & FINANCIAL REPORTING	18%

Read. Write. Interact! A powerfully effective way to retain information! Read questions, write down each question in the form of a statement. Quiz yourself or have someone else quiz you.

1. Where must employers report all newly hired employees? .... New Hire Reporting Program
All employers must report newly hired employees to their state directory within 20 days of the day they were hired. The same 20 day requirement applies for rehired employees.

2. Who is responsible for obtaining Worker's Compensation Insurance? ....The Employer
Businesses with employees are required to carry Worker's Compensation Insurance coverage.

3. What is the most valuable advice given to new employers? .... File your taxes!
It is incredibly important for employers (especially new employers) to remember and to file both their Federal and State taxes.

4. Two important components to establish and manage a business are .... Info. and Org.
Staying informed of all the current policies, laws and changes is important for making sure you are complying with the law. Staying organized allows you to keep records you need to keep, make payments you need to make and run a business smoothly and successfully. So stay informed and organized!

5. Is maintaining a healthy and fair work place required?...Yes
Maintaining a healthy and fair workplace is required by law. Follow safety and employment standards.

6. Federal law prohibits employers from discriminating against race or sex .... Title VII
Title VII prohibits employers from discriminating based on race, color, religion, sex or national origin in the hiring process. It is a law to ensure everyone gets an equal employment opportunity.

7. Federal law that prohibits employers from discriminating against disabilities .... ADA
The Americans with Disabilities Act (ADA) prohibits employers from discriminating against a person with a qualified disability if he/she can perform essential functions with or without reasonable accommodation.

8. Law that prevents age discrimination .... The Age Discrimination Employment Act
The Age Discrimination in Employment Act prevents employers from discriminating employees based on age. For example, it prevents giving preferential treatment to younger workers to the detriment of older workers.

9. Federal law that provides regulations on workdays .... Fair Labor Standards Act
The Fair Labor Standards Act provides regulation on workdays; these regulations include duration of work days, breaks an employer must provide, applicable salary and overtime.

10. Federal law that preserves a qualified employees' position .... Family and Medical Leave Act
The Family and Medical Leave Act preserves qualified employees' positions for the duration of the family and/or medical leave. This covers both times you are ill and times you have to take leave to care for an ill family member. It also includes maternity leave and time to care for your newborn.

11. What tax consists of both Social Security and Medicare taxes? .... FICA
FICA stands for the Federal Insurance Contributions Act. The FICA tax consists of both Social Security and Medicare taxes. Both the employer and employees are required to pay this tax - they split the required %.

Law & Business Supplemental   167

EXAM 7

Law & Business Supplemental

FLASHCARD – TAXES   **18%**

Read. Write. Interact! A powerfully effective way to retain information! Read questions, write down each question in the form of a statement. Quiz yourself or have someone else quiz you.

1. What tax provides for payments of unemployment compensation? .... FUTA
The Federal Unemployment Tax Act (FUTA) along with state unemployment systems provide for unemployment compensation to qualified individuals who have lost their jobs.

2. Who pays the FUTA taxes? .... Employers and Employees
Both employers and employees pay for federal and state unemployment taxes. These taxes allow qualified workers who have lost their jobs to receive unemployment payments while they find a new job.

3. What tax is provided so that employees receive training by the EDD? .... ETT
The Employment Training Tax (ETT) pays for employee training that is provided by the Employment Development Department (EDD). ETT funds helps CA businesses invest in a skilled workforce.

4. Who pays SIT and FIT taxes? .... Employees
State Income Tax (SIT) and Federal Income Tax (FIT) are both taxes that are paid by the employees.

5. Where do SIT taxes go? .... State general fund
State Income Taxes (SIT) are taken from the employee. These taxes go to the State's general fund and are then allocated to where the State legislature deems them necessary. These taxes help run the state.

6. Where do FIT taxes go?.. The IRS
Federal Income Taxes (FIT) are taken from the employee. These taxes go to the IRS.

7. What is UI tax?.. Unemployment Insurance Tax
Unemployment Insurance (UI) provides temporary payments to individuals who are unemployed through no fault of their own. These taxes are paid by the employer. It is paid quarterly to the EDD.

8. What is SDI tax? .... State Disability Insurance
State Disability Insurance (SDI) provides temporary payments to workers who are unable to perform their usual work because of a pregnancy or a non-occupational related illness or injury.

9. Who pays for SDI taxes? .... Employees
Employees pay for State Disability Taxes (SDI) taxes. SDI is deducted from their wages.

10. PIT taxes are paid by those who do not qualify for what? .... UI or SDI
California Personal Income Tax (PIT) is an elective coverage that is offered to specific types of individuals and classes of employees who are excluded from UI and/or SDI insurance.

11. Who pays for PIT?.. Employees
Like SIT and FIT taxes, California Personal Income Tax (PIT) is paid by the employee.

12. What are the taxes that need to be paid by the Employer? .... FICA, FUTA, UI and ETT
The employer is required and held responsible for paying all of the following taxes: FICA (Federal Insurance Contribution Act), FUTA (Federal Unemployment Tax), UI (State Unemployment Insurance) and ETT (Employment Training Tax). Look through this chapter for details on each tax.

13. What are the taxes that need to be paid by the Employee?.......... FICA, FIT, SIT and SDI
The employee is required and held responsible for paying all of the following taxes: FICA (Federal Insurance Contribution Act), FIT (Federal Income Tax), SIT (State Income Tax) and SDI (State Disability Insurance). Look through this chapter for details on each tax.

EXAM 7

Law & Business Supplemental

PREVAILING WAGE REQUIREMENTS

The prevailing wage rate is the basic hourly rate paid on public work projects to a majority of workers engaged in a particular craft, classification or type of work.

- Contractors and his/her Subcontractors hired for Public Works projects are required to pay the specified, general prevailing wage rates to ALL workers employed for the construction and completion of the project.
- The contractor is responsible for attaining information of what the current prevailing wage rate is, as well as, stay informed to see if there is any change in the minimum wage requirement during the project.

The purpose of wage laws are to ensure that Public Works contracts are not based on paying lower wage rates to your employees, in order to have a better bid than your competition.

ALL bidders are required to use the same wage when bidding on a Public Works project.

BONDING REQUIREMENTS

Every contractor that gets a Public Works contract must get a payment bond.
- This is for Public Works that exceed $25,000.
- This bond must be filed before beginning any work on any Public Works project.
- The bond must be in the amount of no less than 100% of the total amount payable by the terms of the contract.
- The bond provides payment in case the original contractor or a subcontractor fails to pay.
- Except for an original contractor: trade workers, laborers and suppliers furnishing right to a provisions, provender, or other supplies, may serve a Stop Payment Notice.
* Make sure to file the Preliminary Notice to preserve your right to a Stop Payment Notice.

INSURANCE REQUIREMENTS

- The contractor must obtain and maintain insurance.
- This insurance must include insurance against claims for injuries or damages of property that may arise from, or be in connection with, the performance of the services provided.

The insurance must provide:

Minimum Scope Insurance
- Commercial general liability coverage
- Automobile Liability for all owned and non-owned and hired automobiles
- Workers' Compensation as required by the Labor of the State of California and Employers Liability Insurance

Minimum Limits of Insurance
- Commercial General Liability: $1,000 per occurrence for bodily injury, personal injury and property damage.
- Automobile Liability: $1,000 per occurrence for bodily injury, personal injury and property damage.
- Workers' Compensation and Employers Liability Insurance: Workers' Compensation limits as required by the State of California. Employers Liability limits of $1,000,000 per accident.

Deductibles and Self-Insured Retentions
- Any deductibles or self-insured retentions must be declared to, and approved by, the City.

Other Insurance Provisions
- See the requirements of the city in which your project is located.
* Insurance must be acceptable and coverage must undergo verification.

Law & Business Supplemental   **169**

EXAM 7

Law & Business Supplemental

Read. Write. Interact! A powerfully effective way to retain information! Read questions, write down each question in the form of a statement. Quiz yourself or have someone else quiz you.

1. What is the prevailing wage rate?.. **Basic hourly rate**

The prevailing wage rate is the basic hourly rate paid on public work projects to a majority of workers engaged in a particular craft, classification or type of work. Check the hourly rate for changes on a periodic basis.

2. Laws that ensure that Public Works bids are not based on paying lower wage rates ...... Wage laws

Wage Laws protect employees by ensuring that contractors are not paying them a lower wage rate to produce and pitch a better bid. Wage Laws help ensure that contractors are bidding ethically and not at the cost of their employees.

3. Whose responsibility is it to stay informed on what the minimum wage is? .... The contractor

The contractor is responsible for attaining information of what the current prevailing wage rate is, as well as, staying informed of any change in the minimum wage requirement during the project.

4. Does every contractor that gets a Public Works contract have to get a payment bond? ....
No

Contractors that get Public Works contracts that exceed $25,000 are required to get a payment bond.

5. When must the bond for Public Works be filed? .... Before beginning any work

A Public Works bond must be filed before beginning any work on the Public Works project.

6. Bond must be in the amount of no less than what % of the total amount payable?..... 100%

The bond must be in the amount of no less than 100% of the total amount payable.

7. What is the required bond for? .... Payment Insurance

The bond provides payment in case the original contractor or a subcontractor fails to pay.

8. To serve a "Stop Payment Notice" you need to file a .... Preliminary Notice

Trade workers, laborers and suppliers furnishing provisions (or other supplies), and any other qualifying party may serve a Stop Payment Notice, so long as they file a Preliminary Notice form within 20 days of starting work. This notice preserves their right to file a Stop Payment Notice in case payment is not made.

9. Must the contractor provide insurance in Public Works?... Yes

The contractor must obtain and maintain insurance in all contracting, this includes Public Works. This insurance must include: insurance against claims for injuries or damages of property that may arise from, or is in connection with the performance of the services provided.

10. What is Minimum Scope Insurance? .... basic insurance coverage

Minimum Scope Insurance provides the basic insurance coverage that you must have, it includes:

EXAM 7

Law & Business Supplemental

CAL/OSHA
California Occupational Safety and Health Act, 1970

The Cal/OSHA Program is responsible for enforcing California laws and regulations pertaining to workplace safety and health and for providing assistance to employers and workers about workplace safety and health issues. It was established to provide safe & healthful conditions in the work place. It enforces standards, addresses complaints, performs routine inspections and it investigates injuries and illnesses in the workplace.

DOSH
State of California Division of Occupational Safety and Health

Sometimes referred to as Cal/OSHA, it protects workers and the public from safety hazards. It ensures safe and healthful conditions in the work place. DOSH deals with asbestos related work, such as helping contractors obtain asbestos certification. DOSH also issues excavation permits and permits for building or demolition for structures 3 stories or higher.

IIPP

Every employer must establish, implement and maintain an effective Injury and Illness Prevention Program (IIPP). The Program must be in writing and, must, at a minimum:

- Identify the person or persons with authority and responsible for implementing the Program.
- Include a system for ensuring that employees comply with safe and healthy work practices.
- Include a system for communicating with employees in a form readily understandable by all affected employees on matters relating to occupational safety and health, including provisions designed to encourage employees to inform the employer of hazards at the worksite without fear of reprisal.
    Exception: Employers having fewer than 10 employees are permitted to communicate to and instruct employees orally.
- Include procedures for identifying and evaluating work place hazards including scheduled periodic inspections to identify unsafe conditions and work practices. Inspections must be made to identify and evaluate hazards.
- Whenever new substances, processes, procedures, or equipment are introduced to the workplace that represent a new occupational safety and health hazard; and whenever the employer is made aware of a new or previously unrecognized hazard he/she must post this information.
- Include a procedure to investigate occupational injuries or occupational illnesses.
- Include methods and/or procedures for correcting unsafe or unhealthy conditions, work practices and work procedures in a timely manner based on the severity of the hazard.

Provide training and instruction:
- To all new employees;
- To all employees given new job assignments for which training has not previously been received;
- Whenever new substances, processes, procedures or equipment are introduced to the workplace and represent a new hazard;
* For more information visit http://www.dir.ca.gov/serp.html and select the Cal/OSHA tab.

EXAM 7

Law & Business Supplemental

SAFETY PROGRAMS - REQUIREMENTS   *11% OF YOUR TEST*

REPORTING INJURIES & FATALITIES

Basic requirement: Within 8 hours after the death of any employee from a work-related incident or the in-patient hospitalization of three or more employees as a result of a work-related incident, you must orally report the fatality/multiple hospitalization by telephone or in person to the area office of the Occupational Safety and Health Administration (OSHA), U.S. Department of Labor, that is nearest to the site of the incident.

CAL/OSHA CONSTRUCTION SAFETY ORDER

Cal/OSHA safety manual is based on the California Code of Regulations (Title 8, Subchapter 4 – Construction Safety). In essence, it is a manual for all things regarding construction and the potential risk each implies, including the use of miscellaneous construction tools and equipment.

CAL/OSHA "SAFETY & HEALTH PROTECTION ON THE JOB" POSTER

This poster explains the basic requirements and procedures for compliance with the state's job safety and health laws and regulations. The law requires that this poster be displayed.

* Failure to do so could result in a penalty of up to $7,000

CAL/OSHA SUMMARY OF OCCUPATIONAL INJURY AND ILLNESS

The employer must record information about every work-related injury or illness that results in:
• death
• loss of consciousness
• restriction of work activity
• a job transfer
• days away from work
• medical treatment beyond first aid or
• a physician or licensed health care professional diagnosis

CAL/OSHA CODE OF SAFE PRACTICES

Cal/OSHA Code of Safe Practices is a written code of safe practices that the employer must adopt.

• Every employer must establish, implement and maintain an effective Injury and Illness Prevention Program.

• Cal/OSHA Code of Safe Practices must be posted in a conspicuous location at each job site office or be provided to each supervisory employee who must always have it readily available.

• Periodic meetings of supervisory employees must be held under the direction of management for the discussion of safety problems and accidents that have occurred.

• Supervisory employees must conduct "tool box" or "tailgate" safety meetings, or the equivalent, with their crews at least every 10 working days to emphasize safety.

VARIANCES FROM STANDARD SAFETY REGULATIONS

Temporary Variance: Employers may apply for a temporary variance from DOSH if they can't comply with a new standard by its effective date, or need more time to correct violations in a newly purchased plant.

Permanent Variance: Employers may apply for a "permanent variance" from Cal/OSHA standards if they have an alternative method that provides equal or better safety.

EXAM 7

Law & Business Supplemental

MSDS AND ASBESTOS   *11% OF YOUR TEST*

MSDS (MATERIAL SAFETY DATA SHEET)

MSDS provides information on each hazardous chemical. The information provided for each hazardous chemical includes:

- health hazards
- special chemical and physical characteristics
- use of each chemical

- protective measures
- precautions for safe handling
- storage of each chemical

Employers can use the information contained in MSDS to educate employees on hazards associated with chemicals found in their workplace.

Employers must review the MSDS and ensure that employees are provided with the most current version.

Employers must make sure that employees have ready access to MSDS and are trained to understand the information in it.

SAFETY STANDARDS – ASBESTOS

ASBESTOS

Asbestos became increasingly popular among manufacturers and builders in the late 19th century because of its sound absorption, average tensile strength, and its resistance to fire, heat, electrical and chemical damage.

It was used in such applications as electrical insulation for hotplate wiring and in building insulation.

BAN ON ASBESTOS

In 1976, Congress passed a law to regulate toxic substances (known as the Toxic Substances Control Act) but a total ban was not suggested.

In 1989, EPA issued a final rule banning most asbestos-containing products.

In 1991, this regulation was overturned by the Fifth Circuit Court of Appeals in New Orleans.

CURRENT REGULATION

As a result of the Court's decision, the following specific asbestos-containing products remain banned: flooring felt, rollboard, and corrugated, commercial, or specialty paper. In addition, the regulation continues to ban the use of asbestos in products that have not historically contained asbestos, otherwise referred to as "new uses" of asbestos.

The contractor or employee must ALWAYS ask the owner if asbestos is present in the building. You need special training and special protective equipment to work with asbestos.

VIOLATION FINES

First offence penalty ranges from $1,200 to $4,800 depending on the asbestos violation. Second offence penalty ranges from $2,400 to $9,600 depending on the asbestos violation.

Law & Business Supplemental

ASBESTOS   *11% OF YOUR TEST*

ASBESTOS RELATED ILLNESSES
3 Major Health Effects Associated With Asbestos Exposure:

Asbestosis –a serious, progressive, long-term non-cancer disease of the lungs. It is caused by inhaling asbestos fibers that irritate lung tissues and cause the tissues to scar. The scarring makes it hard for oxygen to get into the blood.

Lung Cancer – malignant lung tumors. People who work in the mining, milling, manufacturing of asbestos, and those who use asbestos and its products are more likely to develop lung cancer than the general population.

Mesothelioma – a rare form of cancer that is found in the thin lining (membrane) of the lung, chest, abdomen, and heart. Almost all cases of mesothelioma are linked to exposure to asbestos.

WORKING WITH ASBESTOS

Working with asbestos requires for contractors to pass the C.S.L.B. Asbestos Certification Test. In addition, contractors must have appropriate health insurance and worker's comp insurance, and the necessary equipment and training to work with asbestos.

- If less than 100 sq. ft. – must contact and inform the DOSH

- If more than 100 sq. ft. – must contact, inform and register with the DOSH

- If more than 200 sq. ft. – must contact, inform and register with the DOSH and contact NESHAP under the EPA (Environmental Protection Agency)

HANDLING ASBESTOS

It is best to handle it when it is wet.

It is most dangerous when it is in a "friable state" because it can become airborne.

<u>Air monitoring</u>
If action level of 0.1 fibers per cubic centimeter is reached during initial air monitoring you must establish a regulated work area.

REGISTERED HAZARDOUS WASTE HAULER

Required when moving 50 lbs. or more of asbestos.

DEMOLITION OF A STRUCTURE

- Notify the EPA.
- Remove the asbestos before demolishing structure to prevent emission of asbestos
- Use state approved waste disposal site.

MONITORING EMPLOYEES AFTER
ASBESTOS EXPOSURE

Employers must keep records of all employee exposure monitoring for at least 30 years, including the following information:

- Date of measurement
- Operation involving asbestos exposure that you monitored
- Methods of sampling and analysis that you used and evidence of their accuracy
- Number, duration, and results of samples taken
- Type of protective devices worn
- Names, social security numbers, and exposures of ALL the employees involved.

EXAM 7

SAFETY STANDARDS - FIRST AID   *11% OF YOUR TEST*

ELECTRIC SHOCK

If a person has suffered electric shock, you should:

1. make sure the victim is not still in contact with electric current

2. if the victim is still in contact with electric current, use a dry stick to move the person away

3. insulate yourself from all "grounds" before attempting to move any "live" wires.

4. cool the person down on the outside immediately

5. give the victim water if the victim is conscious

ELECTRIC SHOCK INJURIES

• If a neck or spine injury occurs (or is suspected) as a result of electric shock you should lay the victim flat.

• If a head injury occurs as a result of electric shock, you should lay victim <u>flat and/or raise</u> the back and the head slightly.

• If a leg or abdomen injury occurs as a result of electric shock, you should raise the legs and feet 6" to 12"

POISONS

• Poisons can be inhaled, eaten, injected or absorbed through the skin.

The following things can be poisonous:

• aspirin, alcohol, cosmetics, medications and detergents

• paint, gasoline and other petroleum products

• plants and common insects

HEAT STROKE

Heat stroke is characterized by red, hot, dry skin, changes in consciousness, rapid weak pulse and rapid shallow breathing.

If a person has suffered heat stroke you should do the following:

1. get the victim out of the heat
2. loosen clothing
3. apply cool, wet cloths
4. give the victim cool water: the victim should drink slowly (a glass of water every 15 minutes)

BURNS

Burns are classified as first, second or third degree burns.

• <u>First degree burns</u>: these burns involve only the epidermal layer of the skin; they are usually limited to redness, a white plaque and minor pain at the site of injury.

• <u>Second degree burns</u>: these burns involve the superficial papillary dermis and may also involve the deep reticular dermis layer. This is shown by superficial blistering of the skin,

and can involve more or less pain depending on the level of nerve involvement. Deep reticular dermis layer may require about 3 weeks to heal.

• <u>Third degree burns</u>: these occur when the epidermis is lost with damage to the subcutaneous tissue. These burns result in scarring and victims will also exhibit the loss of hair shafts and keratin.

EXAM 7

Law & Business Supplemental

BLEEDING - GENERAL FIRST AID

• Stop the bleeding!

• Although a sanitary napkin is preferred, bare hands can be used if there are no sanitary napkins, pads of gauze or clean handkerchiefs around. The object is to stop the bleeding.

• Place either of the above over the bleeding wound.

• Use direct pressure over the site of the wound. Apply firm, steady and direct pressure for 5 to 15 minutes.

• Leave the original dressing in place, otherwise you will remove the clotting and begin the process again (that is why a sanitary napkin, pad of gauze or clean handkerchief is preferred).

• Contact 911 immediately.

SCALP BLEEDING

• Take special care if there is scalp bleeding because that means there is a possibility of a skull fracture.

• Do not press too hard

• If there is bleeding from the ear, it may indicate a skull fracture.

• Do not attempt to stop fluid leakage if it is clear or pink.

• Contact 911 immediately

LEG, HAND OR ARM BLEEDING

• If there is bleeding from the leg, hand or arm elevate the limb so that it is higher than the victim's heart.

• Contact 911 immediately

SHOCK

Shock has <u>4 causes</u>, they are the following:

1. not enough blood to fill the body's volume needs

2. a breakdown of the circulation of blood

3. a breakdown in large body systems due to infection or fear

4. obstruction in the flow of blood

Shock can be identified by:

• cool, clammy, moist skin

• bluish or gray skin color at fingernail beds and inside the mouth

• thirst

• vomiting

• disorientation

• unconsciousness

*Note: pinch the fingernail to white, if fingernail does not come back to red in two seconds, shock is indicated.

SOLVENTS, ACIDS & VOLITILE SUBSTANCES

• Solvent wastes, oily rags and flammable liquids must be kept in fire-resistant covered containers until removed from site.

• Acids must be stored in a container that resists corrosion.

• When using carbon tetrachloride, avoid inhaling the fumes. Exposure to high concentrations of carbon tetrachloride (including vapor) can affect the central nervous system and degenerate the liver and kidneys. Prolonged exposure may result in coma and even death.

EXAM 7

Law & Business Supplemental

---

1. Program responsible for enforcing CA laws and regulations for workplace safety?..... Cal/OSHA
Cal/OSHA is the program responsible for enforcing California laws and regulations for workplace safety. Cal/OSHA enforces standards, addresses complaints and performs routine inspections to make sure employers are complying with safety and health requirements and investigates injuries and illnesses in the workplace.

2. What is the program that protects workers and the public from safety hazards? .... DOSH
The State of California Division of Occupational Safety and Health (DOSH) ensures safe and healthy conditions in the work place. The DOSH is sometimes referred to as Cal/OSHA.

3. What must employers establish, implement and maintain in the work place?................... IIPP
Employers are required, by law, to provide a healthy and safe work environment by implementing and maintaining an Injury and Illness Prevention Program (IIPP) that provides a system that ensures safe and healthy work practices to prevent accidents and to keep employees safe. The IIPP must be in writing.

4. Where is it required for you to call to report a work-related injury or fatality? .... OSHA
Work-related injuries resulting in loss of consciousness, hospitalization or death must be reported to the DOSH within 8 hours of the happening. These reports must also be made orally to the OSHA closest to the job site and to your local DOSH office. These oral reports must be made immediately/as soon as possible.

5. "Toolbox" or "tailgate" safety meetings must be conducted .... every 10 working days
Supervisory employees must conduct "toolbox" or "tailgate" safety meetings, or the equivalent, in order to emphasize safety practices with their crews. These meetings must be held every 10 working days (min.)

6. Name of the poster that is required to be displayed .... "Safety & Health Protection on the Job"
The "Safety & Health Protection on the Job" poster explains the basic requirements and procedures for compliance with the State's job safety and health laws and regulations. The poster must be placed in a conspicuous place.

7. What is the fine for not displaying the "Safety & Health Protection on the Job" poster? $7,000
The law requires that this poster be displayed, failure to do so could result in a fine of up to $7,000

8. Must a work-related injury that restricts work activity be recorded? .... Yes
The employer must record information about every work-related injury or illness that results in: death, loss of consciousness, restriction of work activity, a job transfer, days away from work, medical treatment beyond first aid and injuries and illnesses that require a diagnosis of a physician or licensed health care professional.

9. What provides information on every hazardous chemical?.. MSDS
Material Safety Data Sheet (MSDS) provides information on every hazardous chemical, including: health hazards, protective measures, storage requirements and usage of each chemical. MSDS must be made accessible to employees.

10. Can employers apply to have an alternative method of safety standards? .... Yes
Employers may apply for a "permanent variance" from Cal/OSHA standards if they have an alternative method that provides equal or better safety than the Injury and Illness Prevention Program (IIPP).

EXAM 7

Law & Business Supplemental

Read. Write. Interact! A powerfully effective way to retain information! Read questions, write down each question in the form of a statement. Quiz yourself or have someone else quiz you.

1. **Popular material among manufacturers and builders in the late 19th century?........... Asbestos**
   Asbestos was a popular material among manufacturers and builders in the late 19th century because of its sound absorption, average tensile strength, fire resistance and electrical and chemical damage resistance.

2. **Where was asbestos used? .... Insulation**
   Asbestos was used in such applications as electrical insulation for hotplate wiring and in building insulation.

3. **In what year did the EPA ban asbestos containing products? 1989**
   In 1989, the Environmental Protection Agency (EPA) issued a final rule banning most asbestos-containing products. Regulation continues to ban the use of asbestos in products that have not historically contained asbestos. In other words, regulation continues to ban uses in "new-applications" of asbestos.

4. **Who must ALWAYS ask the owner if asbestos is present in the building? .... The Contractor**
   The contractor must ALWAYS ask the owner if asbestos is present in the building. You must take an exam to work with asbestos. You also need special training and special protection equipment to work with asbestos.

5. **How many major health effects are associated with asbestos exposure?.............................. 3**
   The 3 major health effects associated with asbestos exposure are: asbestosis, lung cancer and mesothelioma.

6. **If you are going to work with 100 sq. ft or less of asbestos contact .... The DOSH**
   Whenever you come across a project that requires you to work with asbestos, you must report it. You (the contractor) must contact and inform the DOSH if you are planning to work in a site containing 100 sq. ft or less of asbestos. You must contact, inform and register with the DOSH if you are planning to work in a site containing more than 100 sq. ft of asbestos. Special knowledge and training is required.

7. **To work with asbestos contractors must pass .... C.S.L.B. Asbestos Certification Test**
   Working with asbestos requires for contractors to pass the C.S.L.B. Asbestos Certification Test. In addition, contractors must have appropriate health insurance and worker's compensation insurance; attain the necessary equipment and obtain proper training to work with asbestos.

8. **When is asbestos most dangerous?... Friable state**
   Asbestos is most dangerous when it is in a "friable state" because it can become airborne.

9. **Before beginning to work in an area containing asbestos, what must you monitor?............. The Air**
   Monitor the air before you begin work in an area that contains asbestos, if action level of 0.1 fibers per cubic centimeter is reached, you are required to establish a regulated work area.

10. **If you plan to demolish a building that contains asbestos, who must you notify?.......... The EPA**
    You MUST notify the EPA if you are planning to demolish a building that contains asbestos.

11. **To prevent emission of asbestos into the air in demolitions .... Remove asbestos**
    When demolishing a building containing asbestos, the EPA requires you (the contractor) to remove the asbestos before demolishing the structure that contains asbestos. This helps prevent emissions of asbestos into the air.

12. **If you are moving 50 lbs. (or more) of asbestos us .... a hazardous waste hauler**
    A hazardous waste hauler is required when moving 50 lbs. or more pounds of asbestos.

EXAM 7

Law & Business Supplemental

Read. Write. Interact! A powerfully effective way to retain information! Read questions, write down each question in the form of a statement. Quiz yourself or have someone else quiz you.

1. **What hazard can be inhaled, eaten, injected or absorbed through the skin?** .... **Poisons**
   All of the following products can be poisonous: aspirin, alcohol, cosmetics, medications, detergents, paint, gasoline plants and common insects. Poisons can be inhaled, eaten, injected and/or absorbed through the skin.

2. **What should you use to remove a person in contact with electric current** .... **A dry stick**
   If the victim is still in contact with electric current, use a dry stick to move the person away. Do NOT attempt to move them using your body, remember you are a conductor! If you use your body, the current will pass on to you and you will be electrocuted as well. So use a dry stick - it is not a conductor.

3. **What should you do to help an electric shock victim not in contact with a current?**... **Cool the person down**
   Once the electric shock victim is not in contact with the electrical current, cool person down (on the outside) immediately. If the victim is conscious, give them water. Cooling them down is best way to help.

4. **What is characterized by hot, dry skin and changes in consciousness,** .... **Heat Stroke**
   Heat stroke is characterized by red, hot, dry skin, changes in consciousness, rapid weak pulse and rapid shallow breathing. The first thing to do to aid a heat stroke victim is to get them out of the sun. Once out of the sun, loosen clothing, and apply cool, wet cloths.

5. **Should you give water to a heat stroke victim?** .... **Yes**
   Give the victim cool water. The victim should drink slowly (a glass of water every 15 minutes).

6. **What should you do to help a person that has a bleeding wound?** .... **Stop the bleeding**
   Follow the helpful steps outlined in this chapter to successfully aid a person with a bleeding wound.

7. **What does bleeding from the ear usually indicate?** .... **Skull fracture**
   If there is bleeding from the ear, it may indicate a skull fracture. Do not attempt to stop fluid leakage if it is clear or pink. Either way contact 911 for assistance and the ambulance immediately.

8. **If there is bleeding from a limb, what should you do?** .... **elevate the limb**
   If there is bleeding from the leg, hand or arm elevate the limb so that it is higher than the victim's heart.

9. **Cool, clammy, and bluish or gray skin inside the mouth indicate?** .... **Shock**
   Characteristics of shock symptoms include: cool, clammy, moist skin, bluish gray skin inside mouth and at fingernail beds, thirst, vomiting, disorientation and unconsciousness.

10. **How many causes does shock have?** .... **4 causes**
    Shock has 4 causes. This chapter outlines all 4 causes. See appropriate section for details.

11. **How are burn injuries classified?** .... **First, Second or Third degree burns**
    Burns are classified as first, second or third degree burns. These degrees are distinguished by the damage done to the different layers of the skin. See this chapter for details on each.

12. **Where must acids be stored?** .... **Corrosion resistant container**
    Acids must be stored in a container that resists corrosion. Acid is dangerous; it can cause burns & death.

13. **Inhaling what chemical can affect the central nervous system?**.......................... **Tetrachloride**
    Exposure to high concentrations of carbon tetrachloride (including vapor) can affect the central nervous system and degenerate the liver and kidneys. Prolonged exposure may result in coma and even death.

EXAM 7

Law & Business Supplemental

---

1. What three factors dictate construction projects? .... **budget, scope and schedule**
Construction projects are determined by the following factors: budget, scope and schedule.

2. What is the first step in a traditional project? .... **design**
Design is the first step in a traditional project. The structure of a traditional project is design, bib, build.

3. Who manages a construction project? .... **Construction Manager**
A construction manager plans, directs, budgets and manages a construction project. Since he/she has the full authority to manage, organize and mobilize the necessary resources to complete the project, the responsibility of the success or failure of the project heavily falls on him/her.

4. Establishes the design and construction specifications .... **Engineering & Design Specification Team**
The Engineering and Design Specification Team establishes the design and construction specifications for the various portions of a project.

5. The final step in the project development process is .... **documenting the authorization**
The final step in managing the project development process is to formally document the authorization of the project.

6. What is PRD? .... **Project Requirements Definition**
PRD stands for Project Requirements Definition. A Project Requirements Definition (PRD) documents the relevant scope of work, details of the project and project authorization.

7. What gives a holistic view of the magnitude of the project? .... **Scope of Work**
The scope of work (SOW) describes the overall project purpose and gives a holistic view of the magnitude of the project. An SOW should be specific, measurable, accountable, reasonable and time-based; think of the acronym SMART to remember all of the components of a good SOW.

8. What does CMP stand for? .... **Contract Management Plan**
CMP stands for Contract Management Plan. The CMP establishes the systems and processes necessary to ensure that the contractor complies with the terms and conditions during the performance of the contract. It contains all the key information about how a contract will be managed. Additionally, the CMP can be used to ensure the plan is accurate and to create a graphical display for task control management.

9. A document that outlines how a project is to be managed .... **Project Management Plan**
The Project Management Plan is a document that outlines how a project is to be managed, executed, controlled and closed through its phases.

10. What word describes the measure of experience and skill level .... **Capability**
Capability describes the measure of experience, skill level and ability to perform.

11. What word refers to the measure of the quantity of specified resources? .... **Capacity**
Capacity refers to the measure of the quantity of specified resources.

12. What does NEPA stand for? .... **National Environmental Policy Act**
NEPA stands for National Environmental Policy Act. The NEPA describes the process for coordinating compliance with many different laws in the United States.

EXAM 7

Law & Business Supplemental

FLASHCARD - LAW AND BUSINESS OVERVIEW - MUST READ!

Read. Write. Interact! A powerfully effective way to retain information! Read questions, write down each question in the form of a statement. Quiz yourself or have someone else quiz you.

13. Value Engineering teaches techniques to improve .... productivity

Value Engineering teaches techniques to improve productivity in organization, practices, processes and procedures. Value Engineering ensures that an organization receives full value of every dollar invested.

14. What defines a quality assurance process for new construction .... Commissioning

Commissioning defines a quality assurance process for new construction and installations.

15. What does RFEI stand for?...................................... Request for Expressions of Interest

RFEI stands for Request for Expressions of Interest. An RFEI is used to gather information on supplier capabilities and qualifications.

16. What does the DB method stand for?.. Design Build

DB method stands for Design Build. The design build method involves the building owner contracting a single entity to provide both the design and the construction of a building. This type of building procedure is also referred to as the EPC (engineer, procure and construct) or turnkey construction.

17. What does the DBB method stand for?... Design, Bid, Build

The DBB method stands for Design, Bid, Build. The DBB method involves working with an architect until the final design. Once the final design is reached then a contractor is hired and the design is executed.

18. What is referred to as a combination of the DB and the DBB method? .... bridging

Bridging is a combination of the Design-Build (DB) and the Design-Bid-Build (DBB) method.

19. What does LLC stand for?.. Limited Liability Corporation

LLC stands for Limited Liability Corporation. This type of corporation can be seen as a "pass through" entity, since all profits and losses pass through from the business to the owners. In this type of corporation the owners must report their profits and losses as their personal taxes and thus the LLC does not have to pay federal taxes itself. Earnings of most members of an LLC may be subject to self-employment taxes.

20. Are LLC owners members who can vote with free transferability of ownership interest? ...... Yes

LLC owners are members who can vote with free transferability of ownership interest.

21. How many individual shareholders can an S-corporation have? 75

An S-corporation can have a maximum of 75 individual shareholders.

22. When a corporation makes a Subchapter S Election .... it is not taxed at a corporate level

When a corporation makes a Subchapter S Election, the corporation is not taxed at a corporate level. Instead, profits and losses are passed through the corporation to the individual shareholders. Because of this transfer of taxes, an S-corporation is often referred as a Subchapter S corporation.

23. Accounting that records revenues when they are earned .... Accrual Accounting

Accrual accounting records revenues when they are earned and not necessarily when cash changes hands.

24. Requires accounts to be prepared using the same method each period .... Consistency Principle

In accounting the consistency principle requires accounts to be prepared using the same method each period.

EXAM 7

Law & Business Supplemental

FLASHCARD - LAW AND BUSINESS OVERVIEW - MUST READ!

Read. Write. Interact! A powerfully effective way to retain information! Read questions, write down each question in the form of a statement. Quiz yourself or have someone else quiz you.

---

25. What defines the amount of risk a company is prepared to accept? .... Risk Appetite
Risk Appetite defines the amount of risk a company is prepared to accept and/or be exposed to.

26. A useful, strategic planning tool for evaluating strengths and weaknesses ... SWOT Analysis
SWOT Analysis is a useful, strategic planning tool for evaluating strengths, weaknesses, opportunities and threats.

27. What does MBE stand for?..Management by Exceptions
MBE stands for Management by Exceptions; this defines a style of managing in which attention is paid primarily to items that are exceptional. Exceptions can be defined as the breaching of predefined assumptions of an operational process.

28. What is the term often used to define a stipulated sum contract? .... Lump Sum Contract
A lump sum contract is a stipulated sum contract. In this type of contract a fixed amount of money is agreed to be paid upon completion of the work/project. Lump sum bids must be determined by estimating the cost of labor and materials, standard amount of overhead and profit.

29. Contract often used between direct contractor and subcontractor? .... Unit Price Contract
A unit price contract is used between a direct contractor and a subcontractor for maintenance and repair agreements. This type of contract breaks up the work into various parts, usually by construction trade. Unit price is often used for items with indefinite quantities.

30. In this type of arrangement the owner pays the construction manager the actual cost of the construction and the reimbursable expenses involved ...... cost plus fee arrangement
In the cost plus fee arrangement the owner pays the construction manager the actual cost of the construction expense and the reimbursable expenses involved. In this arrangement there is a fixed fee charged for the services provided.

31. Invites suppliers to submit a proposal on a product/service? .... A Request for Proposal
A Request for Proposal serves as an invitation for suppliers to submit a proposal on a specified type of product and/or service. It compiles information and prices.

32. This phrase refers to a clause that can support a breach of contract action where a contract is not completed within the specified time ...."time is of the essence"
The "time is of the essence" phrase refers to a clause that can support a breach of contract action where a contract is not completed within the specified time.

33. Applied when difficult to ascertain the value of damages ...... Liquidated Damages Clause
A Liquidated Damages Clause is applied when it is difficult to calculate the total cost of damages.

34. Pre-negotiation exchanges help you complete .... the proposal analysis
Pre-negotiation exchanges help you obtain the necessary contractor information needed to complete the proposal analysis.

35. Are lenders liable for negligence claims on construction projects? .... No
Lenders are not held liable for negligence claims on construction projects. However, if a lender assumes title of the project or presents him/herself as something more than a lender, then he/she becomes liable.

EXAM 7

Law & Business Supplemental

> ### FLASHCARD - LAW AND BUSINESS OVERVIEW - MUST READ!
> **Read. Write. Interact!** A powerfully effective way to retain information! Read questions, write down each question in the form of a statement. Quiz yourself or have someone else quiz you.

36. **These types of bonds guarantee the project's completion .... Performance Bonds**
    Performance Bonds guarantee the project's completion according to its specifications.

37. **These types of bonds assure the owner that no liens will be filed .... Payment Bonds**
    Payment Bonds assure the building owner that no liens will be filed against his/her property.

38. **Bonds that guarantee job completion and payment for labor and materials .... Contract Bonds**
    Contract Bonds guarantee job completion as well as payment for labor and materials.

39. **What is the simplest form of business organization? .... Sole Ownership**
    Sole Ownership/Sole Proprietorship is the simplest form of business organization.

40. **Business that runs by using the financial resources of multiple individuals .... Partnership**
    A general partnership is run by using the financial and personal resources of multiple individuals. In this type of business organization the multiple individuals share the ownership and operation of the business. The rights and responsibilities of partners may be governed by a partnership agreement; rights and responsibilities usually refer to management and profit-sharing.

41. **Limited partnerships allow some investors to join without taking full .... responsibility**
    A limited partnership allows some investors to join partnership without taking full responsibility.

42. **Act that applies to contractors working on federally funded contracts .. Davis-Bacon Act**
    Davis-Bacon and Related Acts apply to contractors and subcontractors working on federally funded contracts for the construction, alteration or repair of public buildings. These Acts apply to contracts exceeding $2000. A limited partnership allows some investors to join the partnership without taking full responsibility.

43. **The Contract Work Hours and Safety Standards Act applies to contractors with federally funded construction contracts exceeding $100,000**
    The Contract Work Hours and Safety Standards Act applies to contractors and subcontractors with federal service contracts and federally funded and assisted construction contracts exceeding $100,000.

44. **This act requires an employer to provide advance notification of mass layoffs and/or closure of business? .... The Worker Adjustment and Retraining Notification Act**
    The Worker Adjustment and Retraining Notification Act requires an employer to provide advance notification of mass layoffs and/or closure of business. Notification must be given 60 calendar days prior to mass layoffs or closure of business.

45. **Which organization develops safety and health standards for the workplace? .... OSHA**
    The Occupational Safety and Health Administration (OSHA) develops safety and health standards for the workplace.

46. **Which organization administers the Cal/OSHA? .... The DOSH**
    The Division of Occupational Safety and Health (DOSH) administers the Cal/OSHA. The Federal OSHA approves monitors and partially funds the Cal/OSHA. The OSHA board adopts, amends and repeals safety and health standards.

Law & Business Supplemental 183

EXAM 7

Law & Business Supplemental

47. **How many posters are required to be posted at the workplace?** **2**
    The Cal/OSHA poster and Code of Safe Practices poster are both required to be posted at each work site and at each work place.

48. **What does IIPP stand for?** .... **Injury and Illness Prevention Program**
    The Injury and Illness Prevention Program (IIPP) was implemented in 1991 after the 1989 Senate Bill 198 which required every employer to develop and implement a written injury and illness prevention plan. The IIPP must be applied to all businesses, regardless of if they have only one employee or are operated in a low-hazard industry. The IIPP must be written; employers having fewer than 10 employees are allowed to communicate the IIPP orally to each employee.

49. **The California Labor Code establishes .... Employer Responsibilities and Employee Rights**
    The California Labor Code and Title 8 of the California Code of Regulations establishes Employer Responsibilities and Employee Rights.

50. **In California, the lien law is applicable to .... all private works of improvement**
    In California, the lien law is applicable to all private works of improvement. The California Mechanics Lien Laws are covered in the California Constitution, Article XIV, Section 3.

EXAM 7

Law & Business Supplemental

C.S.L.B. LICENSES LIST

A-License: General Engineering

B-License: General Building

C-2   Insulation and Acoustical

C-4   Boiler, Hot Water Heating and Steam Fitting

C-5   Framing and Rough Carpentry

C-6   Cabinet, Millwork and Finish Carpentry

C-7   Low Voltage Systems

C-8   Concrete

C-9   Drywall

C-10 Electrical

C-11 Elevator

C-12 Earthwork and Paving

C-13 Fencing

C-15 Flooring and Floor Covering

C-16 Fire Protection

C-17 Glazing

C-20 Warm-Air Heating, Ventilating and Air-Conditioning

C-21 Building Moving and Demolition

C-23 Ornamental Metal

C-27 Landscaping

C-28 Lock and Security Equipment

C-29 Masonry

C-31 Construction Zone Traffic Control

C-32 Parking and Highway Improvement

C-33 Painting and Decorating

C-34 Pipeline

C-35 Lathing and Plastering

C-36 Plumbing

C-38 Refrigeration

C-39 Roofing

C-42 Sanitation System

C-43 Sheet Metal

C-45 Sign

C-46 Solar

C-47 General Manufactured Housing

C-50 Reinforcing Steel

C-51 Structural Steel

C-53 Swimming Pool

C-54 Ceramic and Mosaic Tile

C-55 Water Conditioning

C-57 Well Drilling

C-60 Welding

C-61 Limited Specialty (No trade exam required)

ASB Asbestos Abatement Certification

HAZ Hazardous Substances Removal Certification

EXAM 8

Safety Part I

1.   A DOSH permit is required for construction type excavations.

    A: True   B: False

2.   A ladder extended above a trench must be a minimum of _____ above the landing surface it is serving.

    A: 1 foot   C: 3 feet

    B: 2 feet   D: 4 feet

3.   The contractor or employer must first ask the owner whether asbestos is present in any building or structure built before the year _____.

    A: 1960   C: 1978

    B: 1970   D: 1980

4.   True or False: The minimum dimension of the base of any free standing tower or rolling scaffold must not be less than 1/3 the height of the scaffold.

    A: True   B: False

5.   What must be done with ladders that have broken or missing rungs or steps?

    A: red tagged for warning   C: immediately withdrawn from service

    B: repaired immediately   D: inspected for further use

6.   Single cleat ladders must not exceed _____ in length.

    A: 10 feet   C: 30 feet

    B: 20 feet   D: 40 feet

7.   Where is every employee required to post Material Safety Data Sheets (MSDS)?

    A: at the main office of the business   C: on the job site

    B: on the board with the construction permit   D: All of the above

8.   Which reference material/codes must the contractor have knowledge of to review reports to identify materials, lead, and asbestos?

    A: UBC   C: DOSH

    B: Contractors License Law   D: CAL/OSHA Construction Safety Orders

9.   True or False: The Injury and Illness Prevention Program and Asbestos (IIPP) became effective July 1, 1991.

    A: True   B: False

10.   True or False: Employers that have less than 10 employees are permitted to communicate with and instruct employees orally in general safety work.

    A: True   B: False

EXAM 8

11. Records of scheduled and periodic inspections required to identify unsafe conditions and work practices, with action taken to correct the unsafe conditions, must be written and recorded and then kept for _____ years.

   A: 1   C: 3

   B: 2   D: 4

12. Every employer of _____ or more people must keep records and make reports as outlined under California Occupational Safety and Health (COSH).

   A: 10   C: 50

   B: 25   D: 100

13. Which of the following organization must every employer immediately report (by phone) to regarding any work related accidents or illness causing serious injury or death of an employee?

   A: Contractors State License Board (CSLB)   C: Division of Safety Orders (DSO)

   B: Division of Occupational Safety and Health (DOSH)   D: California Code of Regulations (CCR)

14. The employer must report to DOSH, any anticipated operations or processes involving asbestos containing more the 1 percent asbestos if the asbestos is to be _____.

   A: sanded   C: cut

   B: sawed   D: All of the above

15. If a worker is exposed to asbestos, where must the incident be reported to?

   A: DOSH (Department of Occupational Safety and Health)   C: EPA (Environmental Protection Agency)

   B: AHERA (Asbestos Hazard Emergency Response Act)   D: All of the above

16. When a contractor is doing asbestos-abatement work in schools he or she must obtain accreditation _____.

   A: by passing a State Contractors Board training course   C: by passing an AHERA approved training course

   B: by passing an EPA approved training course   D: from the EPA/OSHA

17. A contractor who engages in asbestos abatement work in a facility (such as a school) and violates the national emissions standards for hazardous air pollutants (NESHAP) is subject to _____.

   A: fines and penalties of $25,000 per day   C: Both A and B

   B: penalties leading to criminal charges and/ or imprisonment.   D: Neither A nor B

Safety Part I

18. Asbestos can be harmful when it is _____.

    A: wet

    B: dry

    C: friable

    D: All of the above

19. When is asbestos most dangerous?

    A: when it is wet

    B: when it is dry

    C: when it is friable

    D: when it is encapsulated

20. According to _____ the contractor must ask the owner whether asbestos is present in the building before work begins on a job.

    A: AB 1060

    B: AB 2040

    C: CSLB

    D: DOSH

21. When is special certification for asbestos related work required?

    A: For any asbestos related work involving 50 square feet or more of contaminated material.

    B: for any asbestos related work involving 100 square feet or more of contaminated material.

    C: for any asbestos related work involving 150 square feet or more of contaminated material.

    D: for any asbestos related work involving 200 square feet or more of contaminated material.

22. During removal, asbestos must be wetted down to keep airborne fibers under control, after removal asbestos must _____.

    A: be placed in leak-tight containers with labels

    B: be kept wet

    C: be transported to a state approved waste disposal

    D: All of the above

23. How can the hazard of asbestos be reduced or eliminated?

    A: by removing it

    B: by enclosing it

    C: by encapsulating it

    D: All of the above

24. What should you do if you discover asbestos in the middle of a project?

    A: You must stop working in that area immediately.

    B: You must contact an industrial hygienist.

    C: You must contact your nearest DOSH office.

    D: All of the above

25. Employers or contractors engaged in asbestos-related work must _____.

    A: register with OSHA

    B: be covered with health and work compensation

    C: be certified with CSLB

    D: All of the above

EXAM 8

26. If more than 50 lbs. of asbestos is removed, it must be transported by a _____.

    A: specialty abatement contractor

    B: contractor certified for asbestos abatement work

    C: registered hazardous waste hauler

    D: All of the above

27. Consider the following scenario: You are involved in a demolition project: tearing down a house. You suspect the presence of asbestos, what should you do before starting the work?

    A: contact OSHA

    B: contact DOSH

    C: contact the EPA

    D: All of the above

28. When is asbestos the most dangerous?

    A: when it is in its original form

    B: when it is encapsulated

    C: when it is sprayed

    D: when it is wet

29. Why is an LPG leak dangerous?

    A: because it is odorless

    B: because it is colorless

    C: because it is tasteless

    D: All of the above

30. True or False: Gas piping must not be installed under any building or structure. Exposed piping must be kept at least 6 inches above grade and structure.

    A: True

    B: False

31. The best way to fix a gas leak is by _____.

    A: using tape

    B: soldering the pipe

    C: clamping the pipe

    D: replacing the pipe

32. When extended to the limit, extension ladders must not exceed _____ feet in length.

    A: 34

    B: 44

    C: 54

    D: 64

33. If a contractor engages in asbestos abatement work of 100 sq. ft. or more without certification and registration, the contractor is subject to a fine of _____.

    A: not less than $2,000 dollar

    B: not less than $5,000 dollars

    C: not less than $10,000 dollars

    D: not less than $25,000

34. According to the labor code, beginning asbestos-related work without first determining if asbestos containing material is present could lead to a fine of _____.

    A: $5,000 and/or 6 months jail time for negligence.

    B: $10,000 and/or 1 year jail time.

    C: A civil penalty of no more than $2,000 for each violation.

    D: Any of the above

Safety Part I

35. Which of the following organization does a contractor have to notify if performing a demolition job on a commercial building?

    A: The Department of Occupational Safety and Health

    B: The Federal Environmental Protection Agency

    C: The Contractors State License Board

    D: The Department of Consumer Affairs

36. Which of the following is not another name for asbestos?

    A: chrysoltile

    B: themolite

    C: clayrite

    D: amosite

37. Special drums often containing strong acids will be lined with a PVC lining or _____.

    A: polyethylene

    B: stainless steel

    C: aluminum

    D: nickel

38. If respirators are worn while working with acids they must have the joint seal of approval of _____.

    A: health administration

    B: mine safety

    C: NIOSH

    D: All the above

39. Safety meetings are required to be held every _____ at the job site.

    A: 5 days

    B: 10 days

    C: month

    D: year

40. Which of the following actions requires the use of gloves?

    A: Striking

    B: Cutting

    C: Drilling

    D: Fastening

41. Poisons can be _____.

    A: inhaled

    B: eaten

    C: injected

    D: All of the above

42. Which of the following actions should be taken to help a person that has suffered electric shock?

    A: immediately cool down on the outside

    B: give water if conscious

    C: use a dry stick to move the person away

    D: All of the above

43. If a neck or spine injury occurs or is suspected as a result of electric shock, you should _____.

    A: lay victim flat

    B: raise the legs and feet 6 to 12 inches

    C: raise the back and head slightly

    D: try to get the victim to sit to verify if there is an injury

EXAM 8

44. If a head injury occurs as a result of electric shock, you should _____.

    A: lay victim flat
    B: raise the back and head slightly

    C: raise the legs and feet 6 to 12 inches
    D: A or B

45. If a leg or abdomen injury occurs as a result of electric shock, you should _____.

    A: lay victim flat
    B: raise the legs and feet 6 to 12 inches

    C: raise the back and head slightly
    D: try to get the victim to sit to verify if there is an injury

46. Heat stroke is characterized by _____.

    A: red, hot, dry skin
    B: changes in consciousness

    C: rapid shallow breathing
    D: All of the above

47. If a person has suffered heat stroke _____.

    A: get the victim out of the heat
    B: loosen clothing

    C: apply cool, wet cloths
    D: All of the above

48. Consider the following statement: When trying to stop bleeding from a bleeding wound, always use a sanitary napkin, never use your bare hands.

    A: True

    B: False

49. If there is bleeding from the leg, hand or arm, what additional procedure (besides the ones listed already) should you follow?

    A: lay the limb flat on the ground

    B: elevate the limb so that it is at level with the heart but not above it

    C: elevate the limb so that it is higher than the victim's heart

    D: All of the above

50. What is one of the causes of shock?

    A: a breakdown of the circulation of blood

    B: the lack of enough blood to fill the body's volume needs

    C: an obstruction in the blood flow

    D: All of the above

51. Which of the following is a sign that a person has suffered shock?

    A: cool, clammy, moist skin

    B: bluish or gray skin color at fingernail beds and inside the mouth

    C: vomiting

    D: All of the above

EXAM 8

Safety Part I

52. Burns are classified as which of the following degrees?

    A: light, moderate or serious

    C: 1 through 10

    B: first, second or third degree

    D: fourth, fifth or sixth

53. If a fellow worker is lying unconscious on a high voltage conductor and you are within reach what should you do?

    A: grab the worker by the arm

    C: grab the worker by the shoes

    B: grab the worker by the ankles

    D: disconnect the power supply

54. Consider the following scenario: A man's forearm is cut and bleeding severely. Which of the following actions should you take in order to stop the bleeding?

    A: place a band below the cut

    C: press hard over the opened wound

    B: tie a band around the cut

    D: apply a tourniquet above the wound

55. If respirators are worn while working with acids they must have the _____ joint seal of approval.

    A: mine safety

    C: NIOSH

    B: health administration

    D: All of the above

56. A contractor who engages in asbestos abatement work in a facility under NESHAP jurisdiction is in violation of practices and subject to which of the following fines and penalties?

    A: $25,000 per day

    C: Imprisonment

    B: Penalties leading to criminal charges

    D: All of the above

57. During asbestos removal, asbestos may not be _____.

    A: set and left on the floor

    C: kept wet

    B: placed in leak-tight container with labels

    D: be transported to a state approved disposal

58. Gas piping may not be installed _____.

    A: through interior walls

    C: through concrete

    B: through exterior walls

    D: on the roof of a building

59. Where should all solvent wastes, oily rags and flammable liquids be kept until removed from site?

    A: a storage room

    C: fire, resistant covered containers

    B: an unventilated room

    D: All of the above

60. Which of the following is safest when you are finished with a power tool?

    A: clean the tool

    B: warn coworkers that you have just used it

Safety Part I

C: post a notice on the machine

D: wait until all motion has stopped before leaving the machine

61. What do you do with materials if you are done with them?

    A: cover them with a tarp

    B: keep them close by in case you need them again

    C: put them aside

    D: move them out of the way to keep the area clean, uncluttered and safe

62. Where should you keep the brooms and shovels on a jobsite?

    A: off the jobsite

    B: locked in the flammable materials cabinet

    C: in a place safe to get to

    D: where the customer wants them

63. A back-up warning device is required on a vehicle with a body capacity of at least:

    A: ½ cu yd

    B: 2-½ cu yd

    C: 3 cu yd

    D: 5 cu yd

64. You have finished a job and must transport a cement mixer 20 miles. Which of the following should you do after hitching the trailer to your truck?

    A: clean the mixer

    B: put gas in the mixer

    C: check the air in the tires

    D: attach the safety chains

65. When is foot protection required?

    A: when you need to walk over 800 ft

    B: when you are walking on rock

    C: when you are walking on a metal roof

    D: when there is a danger of objects falling on your feet

66. What should you do FIRST if a gas line is severed while you are doing excavation work?

    A: call 911

    B: evacuate the area

    C: call the utility company

    D: turn off equipment

67. How many rungs on a ladder must be over the edge of a roof?

    A: 2 rungs

    B: 3 rungs

    C: 4 rungs

    D: 5 rungs

68. If a piece of heavy equipment broke down, what would be the least practical way of fixing it?

    A: block the wheels

    B: put it in gear

    C: stop the motor

    D: lower the equipment

69. When does Cal/OSHA require new employees to be trained?

    A: at the time of being hired

    B: on the job

    C: prior to entering the jobsite

    D: after an accident

70. What is the minimum plank width for a ladder jack scaffold?

    A: 14"

    B: 16"

    C: 18"

    D: 20"

71. What color tag does Cal/OSHA place on a piece of equipment that is unsafe and needs repair?

    A: red

    B: orange

    C: blue

    D: purple

72. What does not have to keep Cal/OSHA records of injuries and illnesses?

    A: employers with 10 or fewer employees

    B: employers with 20 or fewer employees

    C: a family owned and operated business

    D: labor unions

73. Extension ladders must overlap at least _____ of the working length.

    A: 1%

    B: 5%

    C: 10%

    D: 20

74. Landing platforms must be provided every _____ if a worker must climb to a height of greater than 20 ft on a ladder.

    A: 10 ft

    B: 20 ft

    C: 30 ft

    D: 40 ft

75. A flagger should stand within _____ of the work area with a(n) _____ flag.

    A: 50 ft ... 12 in

    B: 50 ft ... 18 in

    C: 75 ft ... 12 in

    D: 100 ft ... 18 in

76. A tar kettle should be filled no more than _____ of its capacity.

    A: 25%

    B: 50%

    C: 75%

    D: 90

77. Whom should you call for a DOSH permit?

    A: the Registrar of Contractors

    B: the district office of the Contractor's State License Board

    C: the building inspector

    D: the district or field office of the Division of Occupational Safety and health (DOSH)

EXAM 8

Safety Part I

78. Which safety method is not approved by Cal-OSHA on a 5:12 monolithic roof 25 ft high?

    A: ropes

    B: handrails

    C: warning lines and headers

    D: eave barriers

79. Intervals (spans) between roof jacks must not be more than:

    A: 5 ft

    B: 10 ft

    C: 15 ft

    D: 20 ft

80. A roofing jobsite should have fire extinguishers placed:

    A: one on the roof and one on the ground

    B: one in the building and one on the grounds

    C: both on the ground

    D: both on the roof

81. What type of fire extinguisher must be used near a hot tar kettle in use on a roofing job?

    A: AA

    B: BC

    C: B

    D: A

82. If a worker can fall 7-1/2 ft or more, Cal/OSHA requires:

    A: railings

    B: periphery cables

    C: safety belts or nets

    D: any of the above

83. Cal/OSHA would approve of the following practice on a 4:12 roof:

    A: using mastic cans to carry hot tar

    B: carrying a bucket of hat tar up a ladder

    C: filling buckets with hot tar to the lip

    D: carrying two buckets at once on the roof

84. If cables, safety belts, or nets are not provided, a guardrail must be provided for workers on open sides or ends of work areas elevated _____ or higher.

    A: 5 ft

    B: 6 ft

    C: 7 ft

    D: 7-½ ft

85. Ladder rungs must be spaced _____ apart and be _____ long

    A: 11" ... 11"

    B: 11-½" ... 11-½"

    C: 12" ... 11-½"

    D: 12" ... 12"

86. What should you use to wash off a toxic chemical burn?

    A: water

    B: milk

    C: soda

    D: rubbing alcohol

Safety Part I

87. The proper technique for lifting heavy loads is to:

    A: bend knees and keep back straight   C: bend knees and back

    B: bend back and keep knees straight   D: stand straight at all times

88. There must be at least one toilet for every _____ employees (or portion thereof) working at a construction jobsite.

    A: 10   C: 20

    B: 15   D: 25

89. An employer must provide a first-aid kit if he or she has _____ or more employees.

    A: 1   C: 20

    B: 5   D: 25

90. Every truck with a body capacity of 2-1/2 cubic yards or more, used to haul dirt, rock, concrete or other construction material, must be equiped with a warning device that operates automatically while the vehicle is:

    A: loading   C: backing

    B: braking   D: turning

91. When an automatic backup warning device is used it must normally be audible form a distance of:

    A: 50 ft   C: 200 ft

    B: 100 ft   D: 300 ft

92. Platforms or floors of suspended (swing) scaffolds must be free from knots or fractures impairing their strength and must not be less than _____ wide.

    A: 14 in   C: 18 in

    B: 16 in   D: 20 in

93. Safe access to scaffold platform must be provided for a scaffold over _____ in height.

    A: 3 ft   C: 5 ft

    B: 4 ft   D: all platforms

94. A safety rail of wood or other equally rigid material of adequate strength is required if the working platform of any scaffolding swung or suspended from an overhead support is more than:

    A: 7-½ ft high   C: 14 ft high

    B: 12 ft high   D: 16 ft high

EXAM 8

Safety Part I

95. The maximum permitted height for a ladder-jack scaffold is:

    A: 8 ft   C: 12 ft

    B: 10 ft   D: 16 ft

96. The minimum width of platforms for light trades is:

    A: 18 in   C: 24 in

    B: 20 in   D: 36 in

97. The minimum width of platforms for heavy trades such as bricklaying, stonemasonry, stonecutting, or concrete work is:

    A: 3 ft   C: 5 ft

    B: 4 ft   D: 6 ft

98. Permanent or temporary stairways are required in a building:

    A: when there are no ladders   C: when there are no elevators

    B: when the building is two or more stories in height   D: when the building is three or more stories in height

99. Safety devices such as guardrails are required when someone is working on a platform:

    A: over 17 ft high   C: 7-½ ft or higher

    B: over 57 ft high   D: 5 ft or higher

100. A permit from DOSH is required for erection of scaffolds higher than:

    A: 12 ft   C: 36 ft

    B: 24 ft   D: 48 ft

Safety Part I

EXAM 8

1. **Answer A.** True

   A DOSH permit is required for construction type excavations.

2. **Answer C.** 3 feet

   A ladder extended above a trench must be 3 feet above the landing surface it is serving.

3. **Answer D.** 1980

   The contractor or employer must first ask the owner whether asbestos is present in any building or structure built before the year 1980.

4. **Answer A.** True

   The minimum dimension of the base of any free standing tower or rolling scaffold must not be less than ⅓ the height of the scaffold.

5. **Answer C.** immediately withdrawn from service

   Ladders that have broken or missing rungs or steps must be immediately withdrawn from service.

6. **Answer C.** 30 feet

   Single cleat ladders must not exceed 30 feet in length.

   Double cleat ladders must not exceed 24 feet in length.

7. **Answer C.** on the job site

   Every employee is required to post Material Safety Data Sheets (MSDS) on the job site.

8. **Answer D.** CAL/OSHA Construction Safety Orders

   The contractor must have knowledge of CAL/OSHA Construction Safety Orders to review reports to identify materials, lead, and asbestos.

9. **Answer A.** True

   The Injury and Illness Prevention Program (IIPP) became effective July 1, 1991.

10. **Answer A.** True

    Employers that have less than 10 employees are permitted to communicate with and instruct employees orally in general safety work.

11. **Answer C.** 3

    Records of scheduled and periodic inspections required to identify unsafe conditions and work practices, with action taken to correct the unsafe conditions, must be written and recorded and then kept for 3 years.

12. **Answer B.** 25

    Every employer of 25 or more people must keep records and make reports as outlined under California Occupational Safety and Health (COSH).

13. **Answer B.** Division of Occupational Safety and Health (DOSH)

    Every employer must immediately report (by phone) to the Division of Occupational Safety and Health (DOSH) district office regarding any work related accidents or illness causing serious injury or death of an employee.

14. **Answer D.** All of the above

    The employer must report to DOSH, any anticipated operations or processes involving asbestos containing more the 1 percent asbestos if the asbestos is to be: sanded, sawed, cut, ground blasted, shoveled or handled in any way in which it might produce dust.

15. **Answer A.** DOSH (Department of Occupational Safety and Health)

    If a worker is exposed to asbestos, you must report the incident to the Department of Occupational Safety and Health (DOSH).

16. **Answer D.** from the EPA/OSHA

    When a contractor is doing asbestos-abatement work in schools he or she must obtain accreditation from the EPA/OSHA.

17. **Answer C.** Both A and B

    A contractor who engages in asbestos abatement work in a facility (such as a school) and violates the national emissions standards for hazardous air pollutants (NESHAP) is subject to fines and penalties of $25,000 per day and or penalties leading to criminal charges and or imprisonment.

18. **Answer D.** All of the above

    Asbestos can be present in many form. It is still a danger regardless of the state (wet, dry, friable) it is in.

19. **Answer C.** when it is friable

    Asbestos is most dangerous when it is friable.

20. **Answer B.** AB 2040

    According to AB 2040 the contractor must ask the owner whether asbestos is present in the building before he or she begins work on a job.

21. **Answer B.** for any asbestos related work involving 100 square feet or more of contaminated material.

    Special certification for asbestos related work is required for any asbestos related work involving 100 square feet or more of contaminated material.

22. **Answer D.** All of the above

    During removal, asbestos must be wetted down to keep airborne fibers under control, after removal asbestos must be kept wet, placed in leak-tight containers with labels and transported to a state approved waste disposal.

23. **Answer D.** All of the above

    The hazard of asbestos can be reduced or eliminated by: removing it, enclosing it or encapsulating it.

24. **Answer D.** All of the above

    If you discover asbestos in the middle of a project you must do all of the following: stop working in that area immediately, contact an industrial hygienist and contact your nearest DOSH office and the EPA for assistance.

25. **Answer D.** All of the above

    Employers or contractors engaged in asbestos-related work must: register with OSHA, be certified with CSLB and be covered with health and work compensation.

 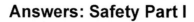

EXAM 8

26. **Answer C.** registered hazardous waste hauler

    If more than 50 lbs. of asbestos is removed, it must be transported by a registered hazardous waste hauler.

27. **Answer C.** contact the EPA

    If you are involved in a demolition project, like tearing down a house, and you suspect the presence of asbestos, you must contact the EPA before starting the work.

28. **Answer C.** when it is sprayed

    Asbestos is the most dangerous when it is sprayed.

    Asbestos that is found in sprayed-on insulation is the most hazardous because it is friable; and thus is easily released into the air.

29. **Answer D.** All of the above

    An LPG leak is dangerous because it is: odorless, colorless and tasteless.

30. **Answer A.** True

    Gas piping must not be installed under any building or structure; exposed piping must be kept at least 6 inches above grade and structure.

31. **Answer D.** replacing the pipe

    The best way to fix a gas leak is by replacing the pipe.

    All pipes used for alteration or repair of any gas piping must be standard weight wrought iron or steel, or treated copper of iron pipe size, or approved PVC or PE in exterior buried piping systems.

32. **Answer B.** 44

    When extended to the limit extension ladders must not exceed 44 feet in length.

    Extension ladders must not be fully extended but must have the following minimum laps:

    3 feet for 2 section ladders up to 33'

    4 feet for 2 section ladders up to 44' or

    4 feet for each 3 section ladder

33. **Answer D.** not less than $25,000

    If a contractor engages in asbestos abatement work of 100 sq. ft. or more without certification and registration, the contractor is subject to a fine of $25,000 for the first offense.

34. **Answer D.** Any of the above

    According to the labor code, beginning asbestos-related work without first determining if asbestos containing material is present could lead to a any of the following fines depending on the scenario:

    $5,000 and/or 6 months jail time for negligence. $10,000 and/or 1 year jail time, or A civil penalty of no more than $2,000 for each violation. In addition, undertaking work without checking if asbestos is present can cause serious injury or even death.

35. **Answer B.** The Federal Environmental Protection Agency

    A contractor must notify the Federal Environmental Protection Agency if he/she is planning to perform a demolition job on a commercial building.

36. **Answer C.** clayrite

    All of the following are different names for asbestos: chrysoltile, themolite and amosite.

37. **Answer A.** polyethylene

    Special drums often containing strong acids will be lined with a PVC lining or polyethylene plastic.

38. **Answer D.** All the above

    If respirators are worn while working with acids they must have the joint seal of approval of the health administration, mine safety and NIOSH.

39. **Answer B.** 10 days

    Safety meetings are required to be held every 10 days at the job site.

40. **Answer B.** Cutting

    Cutting and sawing require the use of gloves.

41. **Answer D.** All of the above

    Poisons can be inhaled, eaten, injected or absorbed through the skin.

    The following things can be poisonous:

    -aspirin, alcohol, cosmetics, medications and detergents

    -paint, gasoline and other petroleum products

    -plants and common insects

42. **Answer D.** All of the above

    If a person has suffered electric shock, you should:

    1. make sure the victim is not still in contact with electric current

    2. if the victim is still in contact with electric current, use a dry stick to move the person away

    3. insulate yourself from all "grounds" before attempting to move any "live" wires.

    4. cool the person down on the outside immediately

    5. give the victim water if the victim is conscious

43. **Answer A.** lay victim flat

    If a neck or spine injury occurs (or is suspected) as a result of electric shock you should lay the victim flat.

44. **Answer D.** A or B

    If a head injury occurs as a result of electric shock, you should lay victim flat and/or raise the back and the head slightly.

45. **Answer B.** raise the legs and feet 6 to 12 inches

    If a leg or abdomen injury occurs as a result of electric shock, you should raise the legs and feet 6 to 12 inches.

EXAM 8

Answers: Safety Part I

46. **Answer D.** All of the above

    Heat stroke is characterized by red, hot, dry skin, changes in consciousness, rapid weak pulse and rapid shallow breathing.

47. **Answer D.** All of the above

    If a person has suffered heat stroke you should do the following:

    1. get the victim out of the heat

    2. loosen clothing

    3. apply cool, wet cloths

    4. give the victim cool water: the victim should drink slowly (a glass of water every 15 minutes)

48. **Answer B.** False

    Although a sanitary napkin is preferred, bare hands can be used if there are no sanitary napkins, pads of gauze or clean handkerchiefs around. The object is to stop the bleeding.

    Place either of the above over the bleeding wound. Use direct pressure over the site of the wound. Apply firm, steady and direct pressure for 5 to 15 minutes. Leave the original dressing in place, otherwise you will remove the clotting and being the process again (that is why a sanitary napkin, pad of gauze or clean handkerchief is preferred).

    Note: Take special care if there is scalp bleeding and there is a possibility of a skull fracture. Do not press too hard. If there is bleeding from the ear, it may indicate a skull fracture. Do not attempt to stop fluid leakage if it is clear or pink.

49. **Answer C.** elevate the limb so that it is higher than the victim's heart

    If there is bleeding from the leg, hand or arm elevate the limb so that it is higher than the victim's heart.

50. **Answer D.** All of the above

    Shock has 4 Causes, they are the following:

    1. not enough blood to fill the body's volume needs

    2. a breakdown of the circulation of blood

    3. a breakdown in large body systems due to infection or fear

    4. obstruction in the flow of blood

51. **Answer D.** All of the above

    Shock can be identified by:

    1. cool, clammy, moist skin

    2. bluish or gray skin color at fingernail beds and inside the mouth

    3. thirst

    4. vomiting

    5. disorientation

    6. unconsciousness

    Note: pinch the fingernail to white, if fingernail does not come back to red in two seconds, shock is indicated.

52. **Answer B.** first, second or third degree

    Burns are classified as first, second or third degree burns.

    First degree burns: these burns involve only the epidermal layer of the skin; they are usually limited to redness, a white plaque and minor pain at the site of injury.

    Second degree burns: these burns involve the superficial papillary dermis and may also involve the deep reticular dermis layer. This is shown by superficial blistering of the skin, and can involve more or less pain depending on the level of nerve involvement. Deep reticular dermis layer may require about 3 weeks to heal.

    Third degree burns: these occur when the epidermis is lost with damage to the subcutaneous tissue. These burns result in scarring and victims will also exhibit the loss of hair shafts and keratin.

53. **Answer D.** disconnect the power supply

    If a fellow worker is lying unconscious on a high voltage conductor and you are within reach you should disconnect the power supply.

54. **Answer C.** press hard over the opened wound

    If a man's forearm is cut and bleeding severely you should press hard over the open wound to stop the bleeding.

55. **Answer D.** All of the above

    If respirators are worn while working with acids they must have the mine safety, health administration and NIOSH's seal of approval.

56. **Answer D.** All of the above

    A contractor who engages in asbestos abatement work in a facility under NESHAP jurisdiction is in violation of practices and is subject to the following fines and penalties:

    -$25,000 per day -Penalties leading to criminal charges -Imprisonment

57. **Answer A.** set and left on the floor

    During asbestos removal asbestos may not be set and left on the floor.

58. **Answer C.** through concrete

    Gas piping may not be installed through concrete.

    Gas piping cannot be installed under any building or structure. Exposed piping must be kept at least 6 inches above grade or structure.

59. **Answer C.** fire, resistant covered containers

    Solvent wastes, oily rags and flammable liquids must be kept in fire, resistant covered containers until removed from site.

    Acids must be stored in a container that resists corrosion.

60. **Answer D.** wait until all motion has stopped before leaving the machine

61. **Answer D.** move them out of the way to keep the area clean, uncluttered and safe

62. **Answer C.** in a place safe to get to

EXAM 8

63. **Answer B.** 2-½ cu yd

64. **Answer D.** attach the safety chains

65. **Answer D.** when there is a danger of objects falling on your feet

   Foot protection is required when there is a danger of objects falling on the worker's feet or when there is a danger of a crushing or penetrating type injury. Foot protection is also required for employees who work in abnormally wet conditions or where there are hot or corrosive substances present.

66. **Answer B.** evacuate the area

   Equipment should be left as it is, if it is running do NOT turn it off, just evacuate the area. The next thing you should do is call 911 and then call the utility company.

67. **Answer B.** 3 rungs

   Ladders must overlap the top support by at least 3 ft and the rungs on a ladder are spaced 1 ft apart.

68. **Answer D.** lower the equipment

69. **Answer A.** at the time of being hired

   The Construction Safety Orders require employers to give instructions regarding the hazards and safety precautions applicable to the type of work in question when the workers are first employed.

70. **Answer A.** 14"

71. **Answer A.** red

   A YELLOW tag may be issued by a Cal/OSHA compliance officer to completely shut down a job. If the State does not offer yellow as an answer, the choice is red.

72. **Answer A.** employers with 10 or fewer employees

73. **Answer C.** 10

74. **Answer B.** 20 ft

75. **Answer D.** 100 ft ... 18 in

76. **Answer C.** 75

77. **Answer D.** the district or field office of the Division of Occupational Safety and health (DOSH)

78. **Answer C.** warning lines and headers

   Warning lines are allowed for 4:12 roof, but they are not safe enough for a steeper 5:12.

79. **Answer B.** 10 ft

80. **Answer A.** one on the roof and one on the ground

81. **Answer B.** BC

82. **Answer D.** any of the above

   The most common protection is a guard-rail system.

83. **Answer D.** carrying two buckets at once on the roof

84. **Answer D.** 7-½ ft

85. **Answer C.** 12" ... 11-½"

86. **Answer A.** water

   Cool water is the safest, especially since you may not know the nature of the chemical.

87. **Answer A.** bend knees and keep back straight

88. **Answer C.** 20

89. **Answer A.** 1

   First-aid kits must be provided at a job site even if there is only one employee.

90. **Answer C.** backing

91. **Answer C.** 200 ft

92. **Answer A.** 14 in

93. **Answer D.** all platforms

94. **Answer A.** 7-½ ft high

95. **Answer D.** 16 ft

96. **Answer B.** 20 in

97. **Answer B.** 4 ft

98. **Answer B.** when the building is two or more stories in height

99. **Answer C.** 7-½ ft or higher

100. **Answer C.** 36 ft

   Equivalent to three stories.

EXAM 9

Safety Part II

1. On a three-story building, what type of device would you use to get to the top?

    A: stairway

    B: ladder

    C: elevator

    D: scaffolding

2. Unless suitable handholds are provided, the side rails of all ladders used to serve a platform must extend at least _____ above the upper landing.

    A: 30 in

    B: 32 in

    C: 34 in

    D: 36 in

3. In a 5-ft deep trench, you must space ladders no more than _____ apart to enable workers to get out in an emergency.

    A: 50 ft

    B: 100 ft

    C: 150 ft

    D: 200 ft

4. The operator of a powder-actuated tool must:

    A: wear eye protection

    B: unload the tool when it is left unattended

    C: have a valid operator's card

    D: all of the above

5. "Tailgate" safety regulations require:

    A: a safety check every 10 days

    B: a meeting with the foremen every 30 days

    C: posting of safety rules

    D: all of the above

6. Which of the following must be provided by the employer?

    A: sanitary facilities

    B: safety devices

    C: medical (first-aid) attention

    D: all of the above

7. On a one-story building, the employer must provide safety railings if the building is _____ or more high.

    A: 7-½ ft

    B: 12 ft

    C: 15 ft

    D: 17 ft

8. In general, what kind of extension cord should you use?

    A: two-wire

    B: any standard commercial cord such as one carried in hardware stores

    C: three-prong wire

    D: multiconductor "S" type cord or equivalent

Safety Part II

9. The posts, ledgers, ribbons, and bracing for tube and coupler scaffolds must be constructed from _____ steel tubing.

   A: 1" ID

   B: 2" OD

   C: 3" ID

   D: 3" OD

10. What is the longest ladder that Cal/OSHA allows?

    A: 34 ft

    B: 44 ft

    C: 48 ft

    D: 50 ft

11. In general, what is the maximum safe depth that you may cut a trench without shoring?

    A: 3 ft

    B: 5 ft

    C: 7 ft

    D: 15 ft

12. Which of the following fire extinguishers is allowed in California?

    A: carbon tetrachloride

    B: chlorobromomethane

    C: methyl bromide

    D: all are prohibited due to toxicity

13. In a work place, travel distance to a fire extinguisher must not be more than:

    A: 25 ft

    B: 50 ft

    C: 75 ft

    D: 100 ft

14. How often should a fire extinguisher be serviced (tested)?

    A: every 6 months

    B: every year

    C: every 18 months

    D: every 2 years

15. The safety valve on a portable air compressor should be popped at least:

    A: daily

    B: weekly

    C: biweekly

    D: monthly

16. The safest way to handle asbestos is when it is:

    A: cold

    B: warm

    C: wet

    D: dry

17. Medical and monitoring records regarding asbestos exposure at a work place must be kept for at least _____ years.

    A: 3

    B: 5

    C: 7

    D: 30

Safety Part II

18. When operating a forklift, carry the forks:

    A: as high as possible   C: tilted away from operator

    B: as low as possible   D: mid-level

19. All guardrails must be able to withstand a load of _____ pounds per lineal foot.

    A: 6   C: 12

    B: 8   D: 13

20. How often should the boom-angle indicator on a crane be inspected by the operator?

    A: every day   C: every month

    B: every week   D: every year

21. Mobile cranes with booms over 200 feet or with a capacity greater than _____ require a load-indicating device.

    A: 10 tons   C: 40 tons

    B: 25 tons   D: 50 tons

22. Cranes with a boom longer than 60 feet or with a rating greater than _____ require a boom-angle-indicator

    A: 5 tons   C: 15 tons

    B: 10 tons   D: 20 tons

23. Every crane, derrick, or cableway exceeding 3 tons capacity must be certified every _____ by a qualified person.

    A: month   C: six months

    B: 3 months   D: year

24. If a material contains more than _____ asbestos and is sanded, ground, blasted, sawed, cut, shoveled, removed, or handled so as to produce dust during construction, it must be reported to Cal/OSHA authorities.

    A: 0.1%   C: 5.0

    B: 0.5%   D: 10.0

25. Over an 8-hour period, an employee must not be exposed to more than _____ asbestos fibers/cc air, as determined by membrane filter method for testing concentrations.

    A: 0.1   C: 1.5

    B: 0.2   D: 5.0

Safety Part II

26. An employer must test the air at a work place for asbestos concentration if it exceeds _____ fibers/cc air over an 8-hour period.

    A: 0.1   C: 1.5

    B: 1.0   D: 2.0

27. When placing a ladder, the distance from the wall to the foot of the ladder should be equal to _____ of the distance from the ground to the top support.

    A: ¹⁄₁₀   C: ¼

    B: ⅕   D: ⅓

28. A second guide for ladder placement is to locate the ladder at a _____ angle from the floor to the ladder.

    A: 60°   C: 70°

    B: 65°   D: 75.5°

29. It is unsafe to use a step ladder taller than:

    A: 10 ft   C: 20 ft

    B: 15 ft   D: 25 ft

30. Do not stand on the top _____ rung(s) of a ladder without a safety belt.

    A: 4   C: 2

    B: 3   D: 1

31. When a ladder is not in use, it should be stored:

    A: vertically   C: on the ground

    B: horizontally   D: inclined

32. The vertical length of the extended part of a trestle ladder must not be greater than _____ of the height of the base ladder.

    A: ⅔   C: ⅓

    B: ½   D: ¼

33. Ladder rungs must be at least _____ long.

    A: 10 in   C: 12 in

    B: 11-½ in   D: 13-½ in

34. Ladder rungs must be spaced at _____ intervals.

    A: 8 in   C: 11-½ in

    B: 10 in   D: 12 in

EXAM 9

35. which of the following will require a skirted plug?

    A: 110-volt spray gun   C: 440-volt welding machine

    B: 220-volt drill   D: any service in a wet environment

36. The safe-distance requirement from overhead electrical lines energized between 600 to 50,000 volts is _____ for people and boom-type equipment in transit.

    A: 3 ft   C: 6 ft

    B: 4 ft   D: 8 ft

37. A rolling stage requires locking wheels at _____ in height

    A: 4 ft   C: 10 ft

    B: 6 ft   D: always

38. You must use safety lines on spiders and swing stages:

    A: over 10 ft   C: only when using safety belts

    B: over 30 ft   D: always

39. The minimum clearance required from overhead high-voltage (600V to 50,000V) conductors for boom-type lifting or hoisting equipment while being operated is:

    A: 4 ft   C: 7-½ ft

    B: 6 ft   D: 10 ft

40. The minimum allowable oxygen concentration at a work site is:

    A: 50%   C: 25

    B: 35%   D: 19.5%

41. A flammable gas, vapor, or combustible particle creates a dangerous air contamination if the concentration is greater than _____ of its lower explosive (flammable) limit or concentration.

    A: 50%   C: 25

    B: 35%   D: 20%

42. The operator should inspect an industrial truck, forklift, and industrial tow tractor at least:

    A: at the start of the shift   C: once a week

    B: once a day   D: every two weeks

43. You must obtain a DOSH permit for:

    A: construction of trenches or excavations   C: construction of any structure more than
        deeper than 3 ft   three stories

    B: demolition of any building over one story   D: all of the above

---

Safety Part II

44. Lumber piles must be no higher than _____ if handled with equipment.

    A: 12 ft   C: 20 ft

    B: 16 ft   D: 24 ft

45. All blasting accidents affecting worker safety must be reported to DOSH:

    A: immediately   C: within 48 hours

    B: within 24 hours   D: no later than 3 days after the accident occurred

46. Explosives must be kept clear of electrical circuits by at least:

    A: 15 ft   C: 50 ft

    B: 25 ft   D: 100 ft

47. Which of the following tools require a constant-contact on/off switch?

    A: circular saws   C: rock drills

    B: powered tampers   D: all of the above

48. If the wall facing electrical equipment (rated at 600V or less with energized and exposed parts) is well insulated, the minimum clearance required is:

    A: 2 ft   C: 3-½ ft

    B: 3 ft   D: 4 ft

49. What is the minimum distance a worker must remain from an overhead high-voltage line?

    A: 4 ft   C: 7-½ ft

    B: 6 ft   D: 10 ft

50. What color shirt must a street or highway worker wear?

    A: orange   C: red

    B: white   D: black

51. How many workers are allowed on a suspended scaffold at any one time?

    A: 1   C: 3

    B: 2   D: 4

52. If a worker is exposed to a fall of more than _____, a safety belt and lifeline must be provided.

    A: 15 ft   C: 50 ft

    B: 25 ft   D: 75 ft

53. When working on a suspended scaffold, each worker must be provided a safety belt and lifeline at:

    A: one story

    B: two stories

    C: three stories

    D: always

54. ROPS stands for:

    A: roll-over protective structure

    B: railing on protective structure

    C: rope on public scaffold

    D: roof offset personnel scaffold

55. Which of the following wires is hot?

    A: white

    B: black

    C: green

    D: none of the above

56. Service conductors must have a clearance of not less than _____ from windows.

    A: 3 ft

    B: 4 ft

    C: 8 ft

    D: 10 ft

57. For optimal safety when deenergizing a circuit:

    A: take out fuses

    B: turn circuit breaker off and put a tape on it

    C: lock circuit breaker in open position and tag it

    D: wear a hard hat

58. Which of the following is a Class-I hazardous location?

    A: combustible vapors or gases

    B: combustible dust

    C: combustible fibers or flyings

    D: all of the above

59. What is the minimum size lumber that can be used to build scaffolding?

    A: 2" x 4"

    B: 2" x 6"

    C: 4" x 4"

    D: only metal should be used to build scaffolding

60. There are acceptable safety precautions when investigating an active circuit. Which one don't you do?

    A: verify voltage

    B: wear a hard hat

    C: make sure overcurrent device is off

    D: permit yourself to become grounded

61. If a co-worker falls down and suffers a deep, bleeding gash to the head, you should:

    A: apply direct pressure to the wound

    B: apply a tourniquet

    C: find and depress the main supply artery

    D: administer CPR

EXAM 9

62. The symptoms of shock are:

    A: pale and sweaty skin, slow and weak pulse

    B: pale and sweaty skin, fast and strong pulse

    C: pale and sweaty skin, rapid and weak pulse

    D: flushed (reddened) skin

63. Service drops over public streets, sidewalks, and commercial areas subject to truck traffic must have a minimum clearance of _____ from final grade.

    A: 10 ft

    B: 12 ft

    C: 15 ft

    D: 18 ft

64. Where the voltage is limited to 300 volts to ground, service drops over residential property and driveways must have a minimum clearance of:

    A: 10 ft

    B: 12 ft

    C: 15 ft

    D: 18 ft

65. In order to be classified as "high voltage", voltage must be greater than:

    A: 240 volts

    B: 300 volts

    C: 600 volts

    D: 700 volts

66. After a major accident, Cal/OSHA must investigate within _____ days.

    A: 3

    B: 5

    C: 7

    D: 10

67. The safe-distance requirement from overhead electrical lines energized between 600V and 50,000V is _____ for boom-type lifting and hoisting equipment when not in use.

    A: 4 ft

    B: 6 ft

    C: 7-½ ft

    D: 10 ft

68. Cal/OSHA requires handrails for scaffolds over _____ in height.

    A: 5 ft

    B: 7-½ ft

    C: 17 ft

    D: 36 ft

69. What is the minimum distance a worker must be from an overhead high-voltage line?

    A: 4 ft

    B: 7-½ ft

    C: 6 ft

    D: 10 ft

Safety Part II

70. Equipment of _____ must be located either in a locked room or in such a location as to be under the supervision of authorized personnel only.

    A: 100 volts   C: 400 volts

    B: 200 volts   D: 600 volts

71. Utility-owned overhead coaxial lines are permitted at a height of not less than _____ above swimming pools or towers.

    A: 6 ft   C: 15 ft

    B: 10 ft   D: 18 ft

72. What is the maximum width of a trench before a bridge is required?

    A: 24"   C: 36"

    B: 30"   D: 40"

73. What is the required height for guardrails around a trench?

    A: 34" - 38"   C: 42" - 45"

    B: 36" - 40"   D: 43" - 48"

EXAM 9

Answers: Safety Part II

1. **Answer A.** stairway
   Stairways are required on 3-story buildings but elevators are not.
2. **Answer D.** 36 in
3. **Answer A.** 50 ft
   Ladders are required in trenches 4 ft or deeper within 25 ft of workers: i.e., every 50 ft.
4. **Answer D.** all of the above
5. **Answer D.** all of the above
6. **Answer D.** all of the above
7. **Answer A.** 7-½ ft
8. **Answer C.** three-prong wire
   "S" cord is heavily insulated but not necessarily grounded
9. **Answer B.** 2" OD
10. **Answer B.** 44 ft
    The longest ladder permitted is an extension ladder, which is limited to 44 ft.
11. **Answer B.** 5 ft
12. **Answer D.** all are prohibited due to toxicity
13. **Answer C.** 75 ft
14. **Answer B.** every year
    A fire extinguisher should be tested once every year, but should be inspected monthly.
15. **Answer B.** weekly
16. **Answer C.** wet
17. **Answer B.** 5
18. **Answer B.** as low as possible
19. **Answer D.** 13
20. **Answer B.** every week
21. **Answer D.** 50 tons
22. **Answer C.** 15 tons
23. **Answer D.** year
24. **Answer A.** 0.1
25. **Answer A.** 0.1
26. **Answer B.** 1.0
27. **Answer C.** ¼
28. **Answer D.** 75.5°
29. **Answer C.** 20 ft
30. **Answer B.** 3
31. **Answer B.** horizontally
32. **Answer B.** ½
33. **Answer B.** 11-½ in

34. **Answer D.** 12 in
35. **Answer C.** 440-volt welding machine
36. **Answer C.** 6 ft
37. **Answer D.** always
38. **Answer D.** always
39. **Answer D.** 10 ft
40. **Answer D.** 19.5
41. **Answer D.** 20
42. **Answer A.** at the start of the shift
43. **Answer C.** construction of any structure more than three stories
    DOSH permits are required for construction of trenches or excavations 5 ft or deeper that workers must enter, and for construction or demolition of any building over three stories.
44. **Answer C.** 20 ft
45. **Answer B.** within 24 hours
46. **Answer B.** 25 ft
47. **Answer A.** circular saws
48. **Answer B.** 3 ft
49. **Answer B.** 6 ft
50. **Answer A.** orange
51. **Answer B.** 2
52. **Answer A.** 15 ft
53. **Answer D.** always
54. **Answer A.** roll-over protective structure
55. **Answer B.** black
    White is neutral; green is ground.
56. **Answer A.** 3 ft
57. **Answer C.** lock circuit breaker in open position and tag it
58. **Answer A.** combustible vapors or gases
59. **Answer A.** 2" x 4"
    The minimum size lumber that can be used to build scaffolding for light-trades is 2" x 4". Light-trades are carpenters, sheet metal workers, painters, and other trades not using heavy tools or storing heavy materials. The minimum size lumber that can be used to build scaffolding for heavy-trades is 4" x 4". Heavy-trades are masons, concrete workers, and other trades that require heavy tools or materials.
60. **Answer D.** permit yourself to become grounded
    Read the question carefully. The question asks for what you DON'T do.

Answers: Safety Part II

61. **Answer A.** apply direct pressure to the wound

62. **Answer C.** pale and sweaty skin, rapid and weak pulse

63. **Answer D.** 18 ft

64. **Answer B.** 12 ft

65. **Answer C.** 600 volts

66. **Answer A.** 3

67. **Answer B.** 6 ft

68. **Answer B.** 7-½ ft

69. **Answer C.** 6 ft

70. **Answer D.** 600 volts

71. **Answer B.** 10 ft

72. **Answer B.** 30"

A bridge is required when a trench is at least 6' deep and wider than 30".

73. **Answer C.** 42" - 45"

Guardrails for fall protection must be between 42" and 45" high. Handrails for ramps and stairs must be between 34" and 38" high.

EXAM 10

Blueprint Reading Part I

1.   Prior to signing a contract, the contractor must thoroughly review all _____.
     A: plans   C: estimates
     B: specifications   D: A and B.

2.   The purpose of contract specifications is to _____.
     A: complete the contract   C: aid in estimating labor and materials
     B: help prevent disputes   D: All the above.

3.   Contained within the contract specifications are contractual allocations of _____ that will be
     assumed by the contractor and owner during construction.
     A: risk   C: safety
     B: performance   D: None of the above.

4.   Most specifications for large projects follow the _____ format.
     A: Brief Form Specifications   C: Construction Specifications Institute
     B: Federal Housing Administration
        Description of Materials

5.   Basic CSI information categories include _____.
     A: Contract Forms   C: Bid Lists
     B: Site Plans

6.   Articles addressed in the Contract General Conditions include _____.
     A: special provisions and site conditions   C: funding and exposure to risk
     B: contractor and payments   D: materials and time

7.   When there is a discrepancy between various parts of the contract documents, legal precedence
     establishes the _____ as the governing document.
     A: specifications   C: plan Drawings
     B: agreement   D: addenda

8.   Bid bonds, Performance bonds and Labor and Materials Payment bonds are included in the _____
     section of the contract specifications.
     A: Bid Analysis   C: Insurance Forms
     B: Contract Forms   D: General Conditions

9.   The Technical Specifications section includes _____.
     A: actual products   C: execution of individual trades
     B: divisions of segments of work   D: All the above.

Blueprint Reading Part I

10. _____ are changes to contract documents made during the bidding process period.

    A: Alternatives   C: Allowances

    B: Addenda   D: All the above.

11. A _____ is made ready to be issued, for certain items not ready for inclusion in the contract.

    A: cash alternative   C: cash allowance

    B: provision

12. The only means of determining how long the project will last and what the time-sensitive expenses will be is the _____.

    A: project schedule   C: project closeout

    B: project meeting   D: project submittal

13. The simplest scheduling method, commonly used for many years is a _____ Chart.

    A: Line   C: Bar

    B: Pie   D: Timeline

14. A scheduling method used for large complex projects, which is the most effective planning tool, is the _____.

    A: critical path   C: Timeline

    B: S-curve chart   D: None of the above.

15. Down payments or deposits before work begins cannot exceed _____, whichever is less.

    A: 20 percent or $2000   C: 10 percent or $10,000

    B: 10 percent or $1000   D: 15 percent or $1000

16. _____ are amendments to the existing contract for work added, deleted or changed.

    A: Plan Changes   C: Change Orders

    B: Requests for Change   D: Plan Revisions

17. Plans submitted for simple residential building permits must include _____.

    A: a site plan   C: acoustics plan

    B: an interior decor plan   D: All the above

18. A typical set of house plans includes a _____.

    A: contractor list   C: landscape planting list

    B: plot plan   D: timeline

EXAM 10

19. Basic plumbing plans for a multi-family dwelling should include _____.

    A: decks and joints

    B: sanitary waste and risers

    C: occupancy and gas piping

    D: hot water and cold water

20. Mechanical plans and specifications are usually required for buildings having an area of _____ sq. ft. or more.

    A: 1,500

    B: 15,000

    C: 350,000

    D: 35,000

21. Initial drawings used to show the basics of "How a building will work" are _____ drawings.

    A: detail

    B: working

    C: preliminary

    D: schematic

22. Drawings that incorporate all adjustments, changes, and refinements are _____ drawings.

    A: detail

    B: preliminary

    C: working

    D: final

23. A _____ is used as the accepted ratio between full size, and what is seen on the drawing.

    A: plan

    B: scale

    C: dimension

    D: None of the above.

24. Construction details are scaled on plan drawings at _____.

    A: ⅜" = 1'-0"

    B: ½" = 1'-0"

    C: ¾" = 1'-0"

    D: All the above.

25. A revision (marker) is shown on the completed set of working drawings by a _____.

    A: scalloped enclosure

    B: revision number

    C: triangle indicating the revision

    D: All the above.

26. _____ lines are the most important since they define the outline of the structure or object.

    A: Hidden

    B: Center

    C: Main

    D: Extension

27. _____ lines indicate an entire length in a small space.

    A: Break

    B: Center

    C: Extension

    D: None of the above.

EXAM 10

Blueprint Reading Part I

28. The most common type of architect's plan view is the _____.

    A: detail view   C: exterior elevation

    B: floor plan   D: site plan

29. Exterior _____ show a view of exterior walls, windows, doors, and type of facade.

    A: elevations   C: views

    B: sections   D: assemblies

30. A _____ is any cut-away view which indicates to the contractor what components and arrangement must be constructed.

    A: wall section   C: detail

    B: building section   D: All the above.

31. When drawing or reading a blueprint or plans, the north arrow on the plans should always point _____.

    A: right   C: up

    B: direction varies according to how the   D: left
       structure is located on the site plan

32. Dimensions representing increments of one primary dimension are called _____ dimensions.

    A: section   C: incremental

    B: chain   D: None of the above.

33. The simplest drawing to make of an orthographic projection is the _____ drawing.

    A: straight line   C: proportion

    B: isometric   D: None of the above.

34. Feet multiplied by feet is expressed in _____.

    A: feet   C: square feet

    B: feet squared   D: None of the above.

35. When rounding a decimal fraction, the digit following the desired number of decimal places is increased by 1, if the digit directly following it is _____ or more.

    A: 9   C: 6

    B: 5   D: None of the above.

36. _____ is 0.145, expressed as a common fraction.

    A: 14.5/1000   C: 145/1000$

    B: 145/10   D: 1.45/10

216   **Blueprint Reading Part I**

37. _____ is used to calculate the length of an unknown leg of a triangular shape.

   A: A = L x W   C: Right Triangle Law

   B: Pythagorean Theorem   D: B and C

38. The _____ of a circle is a line from the center point within a circle to a point on the circumference.

   A: arc   C: radius

   B: diameter   D: chord

39. The circumference (distance around a circle) is _____.

   A: 3.14 x diameter   C: 360

   B: 12   D: Any of the above.

40. Volume for footings or pilecaps is calculated using a _____ formula.

   A: prism   C: cone

   B: cylinder   D: Combination of A and C.

41. A 6:3 slope means _____.

   A: a 3-foot rise or drop for every 6 feet of   C: the first number always designates
      horizontal distance   horizontal distance; the second number
                                                          the vertical distance

   B: a 6-foot rise or drop for every 3 feet of   D: A and C.
      horizontal distance

42. A contractor receives _____ of his profit, (after costs and overhead are paid) if he receives $1560.00 on a $7800.00 job

   A: 20 percent   C: 30 percent

   B: 25 percent   D: 40 percent

43. A contractor is given $460.00, which is 40 percent of his contract price of _____.

   A: $11,500.00   C: $1,840.00

   B: $1,150.00   D: $8,700.00

44. Five gallons of water weighs _____.

   A: ½ lb.   C: 41-½ lbs.

   B: 3-¼ lbs.   D: 2-½ lbs.

45. The amount of sq. yds. of stucco or plaster needed to cover 1248 sq. ft. is _____.

   A: 104   C: 139

   B: 208   D: 748

46. A footing is _____ CF, if its dimensions are: 6" at the top, 1'-8" at the bottom, and 1'-6" high, and 78' long.

    A: 130   C: 127.68

    B: 128.36   D: 126.36

47. _____ drawings give the contractor limits of the excavation for the foundation.

    A: Mechanical   C: Structural

    B: Drainage   D: Utilities

48. _____ drawings provide the contractor with information needed for removal or relocation of existing site features which extend below grade, such as trees and benches.

    A: Mechanical   C: Grading plan

    B: Drainage   D: Utilities

49. _____ drawings are often overlooked. They must be reviewed for existing, or required, installations of features under the slab-on-grade.

    A: Mechanical   C: Grading plan

    B: Electrical   D: A and B only.

50. Prior to construction, _____ made of geotextile fabric tied to metal posts may be used around a building site in an effort to prevent ground water and contaminants from seeping into and impacting sensitive environmental areas or eroding the site and adjacent properties.

    A: silt fences   C: check dams

    B: cofferdams   D: None of the above.

51. Stripping topsoil during the clearing and grubbing project phase is calculated and expressed as _____ in the take-off.

    A: cubic yards   C: tons

    B: cubic feet   D: Any of these.

52. Take-off considerations when dealing with demolition work includes _____.

    A: linear foot   C: lump sum

    B: square foot   D: All the above.

53. Excavation is taken off as a calculation of length, width and depth of the area to be excavated expressed in _____.

    A: cubic yards   C: cubic feet

    B: cubic meters   D: Any of the above.

Blueprint Reading Part I

54. Earthwork cuts that are in excess of _____ ft., and fill over _____ ft. in vertical depth at the deepest point, require a Grading Permit.

    A: 4, 3   C: 6, 4

    B: 5, 3   D: 5, 7

55. Bulk excavation is tabulated using the _____ method involving cuts and fills.

    A: cut-fill   C: contour

    B: cross-section   D: bulk excavation

56. Earthwork material over _____ cu. yds. excavated and hauled out, or hauled in as fill, requires a permit.

    A: 50   C: 100

    B: 75   D: None of the above.

57. A typical drainage trench should be at least _____ wide, and at least _____ below the bottom of the pipe.

    A: 24", 14"   C: 12", 12"

    B: 18", 12"   D: 18", 14"

58. _____ cubic yards of material will be excavated from a trench 6 ft. deep x 3 ft. wide x 100 ft. long.

    A: 65.67   C: 76.77

    B: 66.67   D: 76.57

59. The _____ is a trench side slope measured from the horizontal plane at the bottom of the excavation to the top of grade, to prevent soil materials from sliding back into an excavated trench.

    A: slope grade angle   C: angle of repose

    B: stabilizing force   D: None of the above.

60. Shoring is calculated by multiplying the _____ by the _____ of shoring, expressed in _____.

    A: perimeter of the shored area, depth, SY   C: perimeter of the shored area, width, SF

    B: perimeter of the shored area, height, SF   D: perimeter of the shored area, length, SY

61. Simple slope excavations, which are 12 ft. or less in depth shall have a maximum allowable slope of _____.

    A: 5:8   C: 1:1

    B: ¾:1   D: ½:1

Blueprint Reading Part I

62. When cutting a ditch section, for preliminary roadway/ditch work, you must calculate the distance from the centerline of a roadway to the bottom of the ditch for a cut section, if the slope into the ditch is 4:1, the finished depth of the ditch is 3 ft. and the finished shoulder distance is 20 ft, what is the distance from the centerline of the roadway to the bottom of the ditch for the cut section?

   A: 30   C: 32

   B: 35   D: 36

63. Grading is taken-off by the _____.

   A: square foot   C: acre

   B: square yard   D: All the above.

64. _____ becomes necessary, for support, when excavation goes below foundations of existing structures.

   A: Shoring   C: Stabilizing

   B: Underpinning   D: None of the above.

65. During initial excavation, if ground water is encountered, one of the best methods of correcting it before proceeding is to _____.

   A: install a French drain   C: place fabric

   B: over-excavate the area   D: All the above.

66. Perforated pipe, or bell and spigot pipe, is a subterranean pipe used _____.

   A: as an overflow drain pipe   C: to discharge collected silt and ground water

   B: around exterior basement walls

                                      D: beside a roof drain to dissipate rain runoff

67. Pumping and dewatering takeoff is quantified as _____.

   A: lump sum   C: time

   B: time and equipment   D: None of the above.

68. Drilling or blasting rock is taken-off by it's _____ CY quantity.

   A: delivered   C: in-ground

   B: excavated   D: Any of the above.

69. Concrete is taken-off by the _____.

   A: cubic foot   C: cubic yard

   B: cubic inch   D: cubic foot converted to cubic yard

Blueprint Reading Part I

70. Prior to placement operations, the _____ and _____ should be examined and reviewed.

    A: forms, joints

    B: class of concrete, slump

    C: batching plant, scheduled rounds

    D: All the above.

71. Factors affecting concrete work, and concrete work estimations, include _____.

    A: compressive strength per square inch

    B: additives

    C: air entrainment

    D: All the above.

72. Type III - _____ concrete is used when quick-curing concrete.

    A: High Heat

    B: Low Sulfate

    C: High Early

    D: High Sulfate Resistant

73. The ratio between water and cement is indicated by the number of gallons of water per sacks of cement. A _____ ratio indicates high-strength cement, and a _____ ratio indicates low-strength cement.

    A: 8:5, 4:1

    B: 4:1, 6:3

    C: 4:1, 8:5

    D: 4:1, 1:4

74. When mixing concrete, what is the equivalent water weight of 17.2 lbs./gallon, if 8.6 lbs/gal equals 62.4 lbs/CF?

    A: 134.6

    B: 124.8

    C: 129.4

    D: None of these.

75. When pouring in cold weather, concrete is kept a minimum of 70 degrees for 3 days or _____.

    A: a minimum of 60 degrees for two weeks

    B: a minimum of 50 degrees for five days

    C: a minimum of 50 degrees for one month

    D: a minimum of 50 degrees for one month

76. When pouring concrete, place it evenly in horizontal layers, ___ to ___ inches in depth.

    A: 12, 24

    B: 6, 12

    C: 6, 8

    D: 6, 24

77. Concrete pumps can only be used for _____.

    A: standard mixes only

    B: low slump mixes only

    C: standard and low slump mixes only

    D: a variety of mixes

78. The take-off for _____ is based on the actual area that comes in contact with the concrete, listed as the SFCA, or square foot of contact area.

    A: foundation

    B: formwork

    C: pilings

    D: decks

Blueprint Reading Part I

79. Strip footings are taken-off by _____.

    A: each foot

    B: linear feet

    C: square foot

    D: None of the above.

80. A _____ foundation is used where there is too much ground water.

    A: slab-on-grade

    B: basement

    C: crawl-space

    D: All the above.

81. The type of foundation having shallow footings, which transfer loads to the soil through these footings at the bottom of a foundation wall or column is a _____.

    A: pile foundation

    B: spread foundation

    C: caisson pile foundation

    D: None of the above.

82. A widely used shallow foundation used in warm climates where the soil provides the necessary bearing capacity is called _____.

    A: slab on grade foundation

    B: mat foundation

    C: grade beam foundation

    D: steel grillage footings

83. Pile foundations using long wood piles that reach rock or other load-bearing strata when driven, and transmit the load through the end are _____.

    A: friction piles

    B: timber piles

    C: end-bearing piles

    D: None of the above.

84. The _____ form is the simplest type of form commonly used to contain shallow pours such as for slab-on-grade or walks.

    A: edge

    B: beam

    C: slab

    D: None of the above.

85. Concrete formwork includes distinct operations such as _____ and _____ which helps ensure it is designed and built properly to achieve stability.

    A: fabrication, alignment

    B: erection, nailing

    C: bracing, hanging

    D: bracing, covering

86. Concrete flatwork, or slab, pouring is estimated and taken-off by the _____.

    A: square yard

    B: square foot

    C: cubic yard

    D: cubic foot

EXAM 10

Blueprint Reading Part I

87. Expansion joints and control joints, provided by a combination of methods, are taken-off by _____.

    A: each foot   C: linear foot

    B: lump sum   D: None of the above.

88. Total linear footage for rebar placement in walls or footings is calculated according to _____.

    A: spacing   C: weight

    B: horizontal or vertical placements   D: length

89. To calculate the quantity per each of rebar in slabs, the length and width of the slab are respectively divided by the longitudinal and transverse _____.

    A: spacing   C: weight

    B: size   D: length

90. Typical considerations made when taking-off masonry includes _____.

    A: installation method   C: weather conditions

    B: materials   D: All the above.

91. Mortar quantities are directly related to the _____, calculated in cubic feet, converted to cubic yards.

    A: number of bricks   C: Both A and B.

    B: size of joints   D: amount of water added

92. For a contractor to effectively interpret plans and make accurate brick take-off estimations, he/she must be familiar with brick _____.

    A: nomenclature   C: classification

    B: characteristics   D: All the above.

93. The popular sized modular brick is based on the modular measure of ___ inches.

    A: 3-⅜   C: 4

    B: 3   D: 3-⅝

94. Since brickwork is modular, to determine take-off, the contractor must determine the _____ of brick for each application, and list the work separately by the _____ of wall.

    A: wythe   C: length

    B: width   D: both A and B

95. The maximum deviation of a masonry wall or column from plumb, or from vertical plans, should be less than ____ in 10 feet.

    A: ¼"   C: ³⁄₁₆"

    B: ½"   D: ¾"

Blueprint Reading Part I

96. _____ are primarily used for walls and partitions intended to support a structural load.

    A: CMUs

    B: Concrete unit masonry

    C: Both A and B.

    D: Brick veneers

97. The procedure for calculating take-off for hollow-core concrete block is the same as _____.

    A: for concrete brick

    B: for modular units

    C: slump block

    D: All the above.

98. Low-lift grout is placed within the cells of a hollow-core concrete block wall erected at a maximum of _____.

    A: 5'-0"

    B: 4'-0"

    C: 3'-0"

    D: 3'-6"

99. Stone veneer used in wall and fireplace applications is calculated by _____.

    A: square feet

    B: square feet converted to tons

    C: square feet converted to square yards

    D: cubic feet converted to cubic yards

100. A general rule for calculating waste allowances for regular-shaped stone is between _____ and _____.

    A: 4 percent, 10 percent

    B: 3 percent, 5 percent

    C: 5 percent, 7 percent

    D: 7 percent, 9 percent

EXAM 10

Answers: Blueprint Reading Part I

1. **Answer D.** A and B.

   Before signing the contract: everything must be clearly explained and understood and all questions must be answered. Payment schedules,how change orders will be handled, work hours, delivery of materials, and other concerns must be made clear, before the contract is signed.

2. **Answer D.** All the above.

   Specifications provide qualitative information, complete the contract and provide a legal document with directions for bidding, insurance, bond forms and owner-contractor agreements. They help prevent owner-contractor or contractor-designer/architect disputes. Materials and labor are detailed, and together, with working drawings, they complete the contract. Specifications explain required quality and type of materials, color, finishes, and workmanship.

3. **Answer A.** risk

   Various types of risk and allocation of responsibility are contained in contract clauses. An exculpatory clause should be inserted as well, intended to shift the responsibility, for example, from the designer's errors and omissions to the contractor. Allocations of risk denote who is lawfully responsible and liable for violations under the law in connection to the work. Responsibilities are usually the contractor's, however some may be shared with the owner, such as acts of God and weather extremes, etc.

4. **Answer C.** Construction Specifications Institute

   On smaller projects, a brief form may be used. On construction projects intended to be financed by a FHA loan, the Federal Housing Administration Description of Materials is generally used. The typical specifications format for large projects is established by the Construction Specification Institute (CSI format). The CSI format is intended to make finding information within a large project easier.

5. **Answer A.** Contract Forms

   Requirements, Contract Forms, General Conditions and Specifications. These sections are further subdivided into 16 divisions.

6. **Answer B.** contractor and payments

   General conditions are rules and regulations on which the contract is based. The content addresses 14 basic articles found in AIA201: General Provisions, Owner, Contractor, Administration of the Contract, Subcontractors, Construction by Owner/Separate Contractors; Changes in Work, Time, Payments and Completion: Protections of Persons and Property, Insurance and Bonds, Uncovering and Correction of Work, Miscellaneous Provisions, and Terminations or Suspension of Contract.

7. **Answer B.** agreement

   General Conditions within the contract cite the specific order so a dispute may be settled without the need for interpretation or arbitration. However, the legal precedent dictates that the Contract Agreement has priority, followed by the Specifications and Plan Drawings.

8. **Answer B.** Contract Forms

   Public and private bid forms must address the specific project and be in accordance with the Contract Documents. All information applicable to the bidder's company must be included, such as subcontractors, cost breakdowns and any special authorized forms and bond information.

9. **Answer D.** All the above.

   Technical Specifications are divided into three parts: scope or project and work limits, intended products to be used, and the methods, techniques and quality of workmanship. Addenda, Alternates, Allowances, Unit Prices, and the Summary of all qualitative requirements of the contract are also included.

10. **Answer B.** Addenda

    Modifications, revisions or additional clarifications for any reason, added to the contract during the bidding period, after the drawings are issued, are addenda. They can only be issued by the designer, must be in writing, and become part of the contract document.

11. **Answer C.** cash allowance

    As an alternative to leaving the contract item or estimated price out, a fixed lump sum allowance, or unit price, is to be included in contract documents, ready to be issued, for the purchase, delivery and installation of items not yet finalized and not yet ready for inclusion in the contract.

12. **Answer A.** project schedule

    Drafting a schedule is necessary to determine project progress, and tentative task and project completions.

13. **Answer C.** Bar

    Gantt Charts are the basis for bar charts, which were originally used for production scheduling, but increasingly are used for planning construction and recording it's progress. It's primary advantage is it's simplicity and ability to be understood by all levels of management. Even though it is not the most efficient, it is the choice of most contractors in the residential/light commercial market.

14. **Answer A.** critical path

    The critical path method, used on larger more complex projects, helps identify the order and interdependence of events. The basic concept of the Critical Path Method (CPM) is to show the start of each given activity and it's dependence upon the completion of proceeding activities and how it's completion also restricts following activities.

15. **Answer B.** 10 percent or $1000

    Except for pool contracts, which cannot require a down payment or deposit more than 2 percent or $2000, whichever is less, contract deposits must not exceed the lesser of 10 percent or $10,000.

16. **Answer C.** Change Orders

    Change Orders must always be in writing and contain the name and address of the contractor, the contractor's license, the signatures of both parties, the approximate starting and ending dates, the project address or location, and "Notice to Owner."

Answers: Blueprint Reading Part I

17. Answer A. a site plan

Simple residential building plans require a plot or site plan indicating the proposed building vicinity, lot and building dimensions, existing and proposed buildings, etc. Other plans included in the building plans are the floor plan, exterior elevations, cut-away plan, construction details, materials lists and specifications, and specialty items.

18. Answer B. plot plan

Included in the set of house plans are: the plot plan, floor plan, foundation or basement plan, elevation drawings showing front, rear and side views of the building, electrical, plumbing, heating, and AC layouts.

19. Answer D. hot water and cold water

Plumbing plans also include sanitary waste and gas piping in the forms of schematic riser and isometric diagram, as well as the plumbing details, notes and specifications.

20. Answer B. 15,000

Buildings which require mechanical plans and specifications have an area of 15,000 sq. ft. or more, which includes the basement. Buildings with environmental heating or absorption cooling systems with a BTU input capacity greater than 350,000 also require mechanical plans and specifications.

21. Answer D. schematic

The schematic drawings are conceptual and are the first representation of the owner's needs, spatial requirements and how the building will ultimately function.

22. Answer C. working

Working drawings must comply with all regulatory agency requirements and include all of the detail that the contractor will need to prepare an estimate.

23. Answer B. scale

Two major types of scales are the architect's scale, and the engineer's scale. The architect's scale used on floor plans is ¼ scale where ¼" = 1' or ⅛ scale where ⅛" = 1'. The engineer's scale is in increments of 10, 20, 30, 40 and 50, where, for example, the 10 scale represents 10 feet per inch, the 20 scale represents 20 feet per inch, and so on.

24. Answer D. All the above.

Construction details on plan drawings may also be scaled at 1" =1'-0". Elevation plans are scaled at ¼" = 1'-0". Plot plans are scaled at either ¹⁄₁₆" = 1'0" or

⅛" = 1'-0". Site plans are scaled at ¹⁄₃₂" = 1'-0".

25. Answer D. All the above.

Major changes may require re-drafting, but smaller changes are shown as a noted revision, clearly recognized by a "cloud," or scallop, encircling the revised area. A triangle enclosing the number of the revision is attached to the "cloud" and noted in the Revision area in the title block, or close to it, by revision number and date.

26. Answer C. Main

Main lines are heavy, unbroken lines that show the main outlines of the wall, floor, elevation, detail, or section. Hidden or invisible lines are light, dashed lines that indicate the outlines of an object hidden or obstructed from immediate view.

27. Answer A. Break

Dimension lines are not broken when break lines are used. Center lines are alternating long and short lines indicating the center of an object. Extension or dimension lines indicate dimensions, extending from one main object line to the other with arrowheads on either end.

28. Answer B. floor plan

The function of the architect's floor plan is to show the use of space, identify room locations, means of egress/ingress and major features such as doors, window and built-ins.

29. Answer A. elevations

Elevations show the height and location of items. They do not show interior views or details. Items such as windows and doors are indicated with letters in circles, which correspond to information schedules.

30. Answer B. building section

A building section, commonly called a "section," is any vertical slice or cut through a particular part of the building. Different sections incorporated into the drawings may include cross-sections, taken from a plan view, longitudinal or wall sections, taken from an elevation. Sections are often a different scale than the plan or elevation view they are taken from. Details offer greater, enlarged clarification of certain areas of a floor plan, elevation, or particular part of the drawing.

31. Answer C. up

The property site plan, vicinity map and structures should be situated so North is towards the top of the plan sheet regardless of what direction the rest of the structures face.

32. Answer B. chain

It is often necessary to show location dimensions of several construction features in a straight line. The total chain of dimensions should equal the overall total dimension if one is given.

33. Answer B. isometric

By including dimensions, the contractor can construct a simple single sketch drawing with instructions for workers to use. The intent is to show shapes, locations, and dimensions of construction details.

34. Answer C. square feet

It is important to use correct units of measure when calculating area and volume. Feet multiplied by feet equals square feet. Yards multiplied by yards equals square yards. Feet multiplied by feet, multiplied by feet equals cubic feet. Yards multiplied by yards, multiplied by yards equals cubic yards. Multiplying a dimension in feet by a dimension in inches is erroneous and one of the dimensions must be converted before the calculation can be correctly made. Example: Calculate the area of a space 12'-6" x 20'-4" : 12'-6" = 12.50' ; 20'-3" = 23.33' ; 12.50' x 23.33' = 291.63 sq. ft.

EXAM 10

35. Answer B.   5

Round 0.62871 to three decimal places: 0.629; Round 0.47201 to three decimal places: 0.472

36. Answer C.   145/1000

To express a decimal fraction as a common fraction, the number after the decimal point is written as the numerator of the common fraction, and the denominator is written as a 1 followed by as many zeros as there are digits to the right of the decimal point.

37. Answer D.   B and C

The Pythagorean Theorem, and Right Triangle Law, or 3-4-5 Triangle Rule, allows framers and contractors to square up work in the field. Basically, the sum of the squares of two sides (A(2) + B(2)) is equal to the square of the hypotenuse (C(2)). Contractors doing roofing, rafter or truss work, or measuring and cutting stringers or winders for stairways readily use this formula.

38. Answer C.   radius

All radii of the same circle are equal in length. By definition, a radius is one-half of the diameter. The diameter is a chord through the center of the circle. Contractors are often required to calculate more complex, irregular shapes such as polygons, hexagons, octagons, etc. It is best to divide the area into more common shapes and add or subtract the pieces to arrive at the total.

39. Answer A.   3.14 x diameter

The circumference of a circle is pi (3.14) x the circle's diameter.

40. Answer A.   prism

For shapes whose ends and opposites are parallel, V= A x h (Volume = area x height). Concrete needed to fill a sonotube can be calculated using the cylinder formula, V = pi x R(2) x h (Volume = 3.1416 x radius squared x height)

41. Answer D.   A and C.

A slope grade is specified by its pitch, or ratio of horizontal run (distance) to rise or fall (height). A slope of 6:3 indicates there is a 3-foot rise, or 3- foot drop, for every 6 feet of horizontal distance.

42. Answer A.   20 percent

$1560.00/$7800.00 = 20 percent

43. Answer B. $1,150.00

Divide the amount received by 40 percent (convert 40 percent to decimal form) $460.0%.40 = $1,150.00

44. Answer C.   41-½ lbs.

One gallon of water = 8.3 lbs. 8.3 x 5 = 41.5 = 41-½ lbs.

45. Answer C.   139

The conversion factor to change sq. ft. to sq. yds. is "9". 124⁸⁄₉ = 138.6 = 139 sq. yds.

46. Answer D.   126.36

Convert inches to decimals of feet: T + B/2 x H x L = CF ; 0.5 + 1.6⅝ x 1.5 x 78 = CF ; 2.1½ x 117 = 1.08 x 117 = 126.36 CF

47. Answer C.   Structural

Specifically, architects' foundation plans and details give the site contractor the limits of the excavation for the foundation, as well as show interior details such as footings or depressed areas in the slab, which require excavation, backfill, or compaction.

48. Answer B.   Drainage

Information needed to take off the drainage work, as well as the limits of excavation and backfill, and general site improvements such as paving and curbs, is provided in the drainage plans. Utilities drawings are used to take off trench excavation and backfill for various utilities, which service the building, as well as piping and related work, such as manholes.

49. Answer D.   A and B only.

Mechanical and electrical drawings must be reviewed for pipe trenching or conduits that are in the basement or under slab-on-grade. This work is often overlooked since it is not shown in civil drawings. Most site work is shown on the civil drawings, which the contractor uses to determine the cut and fill quantities to bring the site to the new grade.

50. Answer A.   silt fences

Federal and State agencies require protection to endangered species and environmentally sensitive areas around construction and building sites. Silt fences may be taken-off as LF, or fabric and metal stakes separately at SY, respectively. Take-off should reflect estimated installation cost.

51. Answer A.   cubic yards

Stripped topsoil is listed in the take-off as an area multiplied by the depth, expressed as cubic yards. The area of topsoil to be removed should be enlarged to accommodate any clearance needed and removal of stumps, as well as trucking and fees for disposal.

52. Answer D.   All the above.

Demolition work is the dismantling and removal of unwanted existing work. Demolition tasks are difficult to label and can be quantified by linear foot, square foot, cubic foot, or cubic yard. Demolition tasks containing more than one operation are classified as lump sum. Demolition work requiring erection of barriers, ramps, etc. must include these costs for protection of the demolition site as well as hauling and disposal costs and fees.

53. Answer C.   cubic feet

Excavation is taken off as the calculation of length, width and depth of area to be excavated in CF, and converted to CY, where 1 CY = 27 CF.

54. Answer B.   5, 3

The grading permit application must describe the amount of earth to be moved, removed, or added, as shown on attached topographic plans indicating existing and proposed contour lines and drainage devices.

Answers: Blueprint Reading Part I

55. **Answer B.** cross-section

Bulk excavation includes moving large amounts of material to establish new grades for buildings, roads, parking lots, etc. The cross-section method divides the specified area for excavation and/or grading into grid sections. Cut and fill information is plotted and connected forming contours. An efficient procedure is to place the new contour over the existing contour, or grading plan. Elevations of the intersection of horizontal and vertical lines are used to interpolate calculations of necessary cut and fill quantities.

56. **Answer A.** 50

Material imported or hauled away from a building site in excess of 50 cu. yd. loads, must be "permitted" to be sure of proper supplier provisions as well as the availability of proper disposal sites and/or methods of disposal of sometimes contaminated materials.

57. **Answer B.** 18", 12"

A typical drainage trench is a min. of 18 in. wide, and accurately fits the grade of pipe. The trench must extend a min. of 12 in. below the bottom of the drainage pipe. Crushed rock is used in the bottom 12 inches of the trench below the pipe. A min. of 2 in. crushed rock cover and geotech fabric or paper is placed over the pipe. Backfill with a min. 12 in. layer of compacted native material to finish grade. Backfill material should be free of rocks and sharp objects. Take-offs include trench excavation at the LF, and crushed rock and backfill by the CY.

58. **Answer B.** 66.67

$6 \times 3 \times 10\frac{1}{2}/_{27} = 66.67$ cu. yd.

59. **Answer C.** angle of repose

Soil stability determines the angle of repose. The more cohesive the soil, the steeper the angle of repose. Non-cohesive soils such as sand and gravel, require more shallow slopes and may further require shoring, or a trench box, to mitigate a potential cave-in. OSHA has specific requirements for trenches and slope ratios based on soil stability type, trench depth and duration of openness.

60. **Answer B.** perimeter of the shored area, height, SF

Units are calculated by multiplying the perimeter of the area to be shored by the height of the shoring from the bottom of the trench to the top of the excavation. The take-off for shoring must remain separate from the work it is meant to protect. The take-off must include materials, labor and equipment to install and remove the shoring.

61. **Answer B.** ¾:1

The exception to this is the short-term trench, open 24 hours or less, which is 12 ft. or less in depth, and of stable Type A soil material. The short-term trench may be laid back at a max. slope of ½:1.

62. **Answer C.** 32

$(4 \times 3) + 20 = 32$

63. **Answer D.** All the above.

Hand grading is taken-off by the SF or SY. Machine grading is taken-off by the SF and converted to a larger unit such as SY or acres.

64. **Answer B.** Underpinning

It is the contractor's responsibility for safety and for any damage that might occur to adjacent structures during construction. Underpinning requires the existing foundation support to be brought to the depth of the proposed structure. This is generally a costly procedure and should be paid for by lump sum, item unit prices, or on force account for labor, equipment and materials with applicable markups.

65. **Answer D.** All the above.

Methods to contain, block or remove water at the onset of excavation is essential in stabilizing the building site. Installing a French drain will channel water away from the site. Over-excavating the area may result in achieving a depth below the swale or water table. Placing construction or geotextile fabric over the wet area backfilling and compacting may also be a means of stabilizing the area. After the water is contained or removed, clean fill must be placed and compacted to ensure stability.

66. **Answer B.** around exterior basement walls

Perforated pipe is used to dewater it is usually found around exterior basement walls and at the bottom of foundations, approx. 2 ft. out from the foundation wall. As with all pipe installation, take-off is by LF for pipe. Excavation and backfill are paid for by the CY.

67. **Answer C.** time

It is advised that the contractor secure an independent contractor for the work. However, dewatering is quantified according to the time the pumping operation takes; by the day, week, or month.

68. **Answer C.** in-ground

Blasted or drilled rock must be listed separately from other excavation. For estimation purposes, rock may exceed in-ground volume by as much as 60 percent which should be accounted for. Rock type, proximity to existing structures, or drilling depth required, special permits and the quantity of rock to be blasted or drilled all affect the contractor's estimation. It is advised that a rock blaster or drilling specialist be hired to perform this operation.

69. **Answer D.** cubic foot converted to cubic yard

Concrete is taken off by the CF, converted to CY. For estimating and purchasing purposes, 1 CY = 27 CF.

70. **Answer D.** All the above.

Prior to placement, forms should be clean and all forms, falsework, reinforcing steel and embedded items must have been completed (and inspected). Construction joints and dowels should be sandblasted and treated to remove laitance. Batch plant and hauling should be approved and scheduled to ensure quality and the correct mix upon delivery.

71. **Answer D.** All the above.

Additional considerations include chemicals added to the mix (drying agents) and type and size of aggregate used, as well as lightweight aggregates used to reduce weight per CY. Hot water requirement, ready-mixed concrete, and stiffness (ease of pour) also affect cost estimation.

EXAM 10

72. **Answer C.** High Early

Types of concrete range from Type I - Normal (contains no special properties), Type II - Modified (when cement will be exposed to acids or salts), Type III - High Early (when quick curing is desired or necessary), Type IV - Low Heat (used on massive concrete pours such as dams where the concrete will generate a lot of heat as it cures) and Type V - High Sulfate Resistant (for structures coming in direct contact with the sea).

73. **Answer C.** 4:1, 8:5

The amount of water in concrete determines its strength. The total amount of water in the mix includes free water in the aggregate and admixture, as well as the added water. When mixing concrete, no more water than is absolutely necessary to make the concrete workable should be used. The lower the water content, the stronger the concrete will be.

74. **Answer B.** 124.8

If water weighs 62.4 lbs/CF or 8.6 lbs./gal., then 2 x 8.6 lbs/gal = 124.8 lbs/CF

75. **Answer B.** a minimum of 50 degrees for five days

When pouring concrete in cold weather, it is important to keep the concrete above freezing for the first few days, and is usually covered with plastic to contain heat and moisture from the mixture in order to encourage curing.

76. **Answer D.** 6, 24

Concrete should be placed and vibrated within the forms, and the next layer placed before the initial set takes place.

77. **Answer D.** a variety of mixes

Concrete pumps are economical and expedient and can handle economically, structural mixes, standard mixes, low slump mixes, mixes with 2"-min. size aggregate and light weight concrete.

78. **Answer B.** formwork

Other methods for take-off of formwork for walls are by the LF where contact area is less critical than the size of the form panels used. LF are most often used by contractors. Formwork varies in size and composition but is often constructed from a wood facing applied over a steel or wood frame. Quantities of formwork must include the erection and bracing of forms until concrete is hardened, and stripping and cleaning of forms when work is completed. These tasks should be priced separately.

79. **Answer B.** linear feet

Productivity is reduced for stepped footings so they must be listed separately, but still per LF. Spread footings are generally isolated square masses of concrete

with varying thicknesses. Typically they are taken-off per each item. If templates for anchor bolts to support columns become necessary, they will also be taken-off separately.

80. **Answer C.** crawl-space

Where the frost line is near the surface, and when there is not enough space for a full basement, crawl space foundations are constructed to provide access to plumbing and wiring.

81. **Answer B.** spread foundation

Spread foundations utilize spread footings to distribute building loads over large enough soil areas to provide bearing capacity. Pile foundations use long wood, concrete or steel piles driving into earth and get their load carrying ability by friction on the sides of the pile or from the end resting on load-bearing strain. Caisson pile foundations are formed by drilling holes in the earth and filling them with concrete. They get their load-carrying ability the same as pile foundations.

82. **Answer A.** slab on grade foundation

The slab can be thickened within the building to support interior load-bearing partitions. It is quick and cost effective. Mat foundations are reinforced slabs several feet thick which spread the weight of the building over the entire area below the building and reduces the load per sq. ft. on the soil. Grade beam foundations are reinforced beams supported on a series of piles or piers creating a foundation wall.

83. **Answer C.** end-bearing piles

Timber piles are stripped tree trunks driven with the small end down into soft soils. Friction piles get their load-bearing capacity from friction between the sides of the pile and the earth.

84. **Answer A.** edge

Edge forms are constructed from typical rough-grade 2' x 4', 2' x 6' or 1' 6' lumber, held together with metal or wood stakes. Edge forms are taken-off by LF.

85. **Answer A.** fabrication, alignment

The entire formwork system must be stable, watertight, and resistant to pressure of wet concrete. Operations to help ensure that this is included are designing, fabrication, erection, alignment, and bracing.

86. **Answer B.** square foot

Concrete flatwork, or slab, pouring is estimated and taken-off by the square foot.

87. **Answer C.** linear foot

Expansion joints are taken-off by LF, but should be listed separately by size and thickness. Control joints, provided by tooling, saw cutting, and forming, involves take-off quantities by LF.

88. **Answer B.** horizontal or vertical placements

Horizontal bars are taken-off by total length multiplied by the number of bars shown. Vertical bars are taken-off by dividing the total length of wall or footing by the spacing, and multiplying by their height or length.

89. **Answer A.** spacing

After the quantity is calculated, it is multiplied by the length of each, and the total linear footage is computed. Example: For a #4 bar in a 20' x 30' slab, bars spaced at 12" O.C. EW (each way) Longitudinal length = 30'/12" O.C. = 30' pcs x 20' = 600 LF Transverse width = 20'/12" O.C. = 20' pcs x 30' = 600 LF Total #4 bar - 1200 LF

Answers: Blueprint Reading Part I

90. **Answer D.** All the above.

Typical considerations made when taking-off masonry include: installation method, materials, weather conditions, the need for a scaffolding, reinforcement requirements, miscellaneous items and allowance for waste.

91. **Answer C.** Both A and B.

The general rule for estimating quantities of mortar for setting stone is: 4-5 CF of mortar for 100 CF of stone. Quantities of mortar for stone vary with the varying sizes of stone and joint.

92. **Answer D.** All the above.

Bricks come in numerous types and sizes. Sizes are nominal, not actual. The difference between actual and nominal is made up by the thickness of the mortar. Most are modular in design, and generally a multiple of 4".

93. **Answer C.** 4

Modular bricks are 3-⅜" high x 3" wide x 11-⅜" long. When the mortar joint is added the brick unit becomes 4" x 12". This allows combinations of these sized bricks to be used to make up a wall based on the 4-inch modular.

94. **Answer D.** both A and B

Brick masonry units are taken-off by SF of wall in the case of single-wythe walls such as veneers. Multiple-wythe walls are taken off in CF. In each case, the contractor must calculate the final conversion of the number of brick per SF to brick per CF based on the size of the brick, size of the mortar joint, and brick bond (pattern).

95. **Answer A.** ¼"

Tolerances for a story height is ¾", or ½" in 40 feet or more. Wall thickness tolerance must be within ¼" plus or minus ½" of the dimensions shown on the plans.

96. **Answer C.** Both A and B.

Concrete unit masonry are commonly referred to as CMU. CMU is widely used in commercial and industrial building applications. It is also used in residential construction as foundation material.

97. **Answer D.** All the above.

The quantity for take-off is the computation of the SF area. A standard waste factor of 3-5 percent should be added.

98. **Answer B.** 4'-0"

Low-lift grout ensures cells are filled solid down to the previously poured lift. However, additional costs are incurred due to the delay created in erecting the wall. High-lift grout is placed in cells upon completion of the top course of masonry work. High-lift grouting is a continuous process unlike low-lift grouting. The vertical reinforcing is placed after the wall is completed. Weep holes must be made at the base of the wall.

99. **Answer B.** square feet converted to tons

Stone veneer is half-face requiring square footage conversion. Stone used in landscaping walls is calculated by CF volume, converted to tons, based on the stone's volume per ton. Each stone varies according to size, shape and density.

100. **Answer A.** 4 percent, 10 percent

Calculating waste for irregular-shaped stone such as rubble or fieldstone is higher than 10 percent depending on the amount of "unusable" stone in the delivered batch. Lower-grade stone waste factors may be as high as 20 percent.

EXAM 11

Blueprint Reading Part II

1. To find the number of anchors or ties, taken-off per each, the area of the wall must be calculated per _____ and divided by the specified _____.

    A: CF, spacing

    B: SF, spacing

    C: SF, wythe

    D: None of the above.

2. _____ joints are required for masonry walls of considerable length, taken off by the _____.

    A: Horizontal control, LF

    B: Vertical control, LF

    C: Horizontal control, HLF

    D: Vertical control, VLF

3. When converting the SF of surface area of masonry to the actual number of scaffolding and planks needed, the take-off conversion is based on _____.

    A: scaffold planking size

    B: actual size of the staging units available

    C: brackets needed per SF of scaffolding

    D: None of the above.

4. When taking-off structural steel, _____ should be considered.

    A: erection

    B: field welding

    C: shop drawings

    D: All the above.

5. Structural steel work is shown in structural drawings in _____ views.

    A: elevation

    B: detail

    C: plan

    D: None of the above.

6. Proper sizing and gauging of steel stud for steel stud wall assemblies depends upon location and loading condition _____.

    A: bending stress

    B: axial stress

    C: Both A and B.

    D: Neither A nor B.

7. Primary flexural reinforcement should not be spaced farther apart than _____ in walls and slabs.

    A: 3 times the wall or slab thickness or 18 inches

    B: 2 times the wall or slab thickness or 48 inches

    C: 3 times the wall or slab thickness or 36 inches

    D: 3 times the wall or slab thickness or 48 inches

8. Structural steel is taken-off by the _____ of the piece, then converted to weight in _____.

    A: length, pounds

    B: length, tons

    C: length, metric tons

    D: None of the above.

Blueprint Reading Part II

9. Steel reinforcing bar numbers indicate the _____ of the bar.

    A: grade

    B: diameter

    C: manufacturer

    D: strength

10. Standard mill lengths of reinforcing bars are _____ feet.

    A: 60

    B: 20

    C: 40

    D: All the above.

11. Grade 60 is the _____ grade of rebar which has a yield strength of 60,000 psi.

    A: lower strength

    B: standard

    C: premium

    D: high-strength

12. The letter and numbers classification for structural steel pieces represent it's _____ respectively.

    A: depth and weight

    B: shape, depth, and weight

    C: fabricator, shape, and weight

    D: shape and weight

13. Proper sizing and gauging of steel stud for steel stud wall assemblies depend upon location and loading condition _____.

    A: bending stress

    B: axial stress

    C: Both A and B.

    D: Neither A nor B.

14. Metal decking for installation of roofing materials, or for concrete floor slab forms, must be calculated with allowances for _____.

    A: overlap

    B: varying lengths

    C: finishes

    D: different gauges

15. Taking-off metal studs and track, used as wall system components, may include _____.

    A: taking-off studs and track separately

    B: calculating the SF area of the entire wall system

    C: taking-off the wall by LF

    D: Any of the above.

16. Priming fabricated steel components are taken-off according to the _____ of steel to be primed.

    A: type

    B: amount

    C: length

    D: complexity

17. _____ show the skeleton of the structure and illustrate the structural wood members used.

    A: Structural plans

    B: Elevations

    C: Framing plans

    D: All the above.

Blueprint Reading Part II

18. Building _____ provide essential information for taking-off wall framing and sheathing.

    A: cross-sections

    B: plans

    C: wall sections

    D: A and B only.

19. The total board feet of 62 pieces of lumber T 3/4" x W 10" x L 18'-0" is _____ board feet.

    A: 930

    B: 940

    C: 945

    D: 950

20. When cutting stock lumber, material should be cut _____ in. wider than needed.

    A: $\frac{1}{16}$

    B: $\frac{1}{8}$

    C: $\frac{1}{4}$

    D: $\frac{1}{2}$

21. Wood framing take-offs begin with the _____ framing.

    A: wall

    B: roof

    C: floor

    D: Any of the above.

22. Take-offs for determining floor joists consist of the _____ of the floor frame, divided by the _____ plus one joist at the end.

    A: length, spacing

    B: length, width of joist

    C: area, number of joists

    D: None of the above.

23. Subfloor sheathing is typically manufactured in _____ sheets.

    A: 4' x 6'

    B: 3'-6" x 6'

    C: 4' x 8'

    D: 4'-6" x 8'-6"

24. Plywood panels are grade-stamped, Grade _____ representing face veneer with a solid face, tight knots and repairs allowed.

    A: "A"

    B: "B"

    C: "C"

    D: "D"

25. For a wall 260 ft. long, that has 14 corners, 12 intersections and 22 openings, placed 16" O.C., _____ studs will be needed.

    A: 292

    B: 290

    C: 289

    D: 291

26. One of three generally accepted rules for calculating the rise-run or riser-tread ratio is _____.

    A: riser + riser + tread = 25" - 26"

    B: riser height x tread width = 68" - 74"

    C: riser + tread = 19"

    D: None of the above.

Blueprint Reading Part II

27. When working drawings that do not specify tread or riser information, the number of risers may be calculated by first _____.

    A: dividing the total tread by 7
    B: dividing the total rise by 7
    C: dividing the stinger length by 7-½
    D: dividing the total tread by 7-¾

28. Building code residential building requirements limit openings between balustrades to less than ____ in.

    A: 4
    B: 5-½
    C: 4-¼
    D: 4-½

29. Most pre-fabricated truss rafters are made of ____ or ____ lumber connected by gang-nail plates in ceiling spans from ____ feet to ____ feet.

    A: 2 x 4, 2 x 6, 18, 46
    B: 2 x 6, 2 x 12, 16, 46
    C: 2 x 4, 2 x 6, 16, 48
    D: 2 x 4, 2 x 6, 16, 46

30. The number of trusses is determined by dividing the length of the _____ by the _____.

    A: trussed area, spacing
    B: truss, span area
    C: truss, spacing
    D: None of the above.

31. Cabinetry is taken-off by _____ and plastic laminate countertops are taken-off by _____.

    A: each item, each item
    B: linear foot, linear foot
    C: each item, linear foot
    D: linear foot, each item

32. Cabinet shelves should be laid out accurately and level, and be supported every _____ or closer.

    A: 36"
    B: 42"
    C: 43"
    D: 45"

33. Methods for supporting shelves include _____.

    A: wood screws
    B: glue
    C: nails
    D: None of the above.

34. _____ sections and details indicate surfaces to be waterproofed and dampproofed above and below grade.

    A: Wall
    B: Foundation
    C: Framing
    D: A and B only.

35. Take-off units used for metallic and membrane waterproofing include _____.

    A: each item
    B: square foot
    C: linear foot
    D: All the above.

Blueprint Reading Part II

36. The primary function of dampproofing is to prevent _____ the foundation wall in below-grade applications.

    A: ground water penetration through

    B: water pressure

    C: penetration of moisture through

    D: All the above.

37. Insulation requirements are found on _____ of the exterior envelope plans.

    A: wall sections

    B: cross-sections

    C: details

    D: All the above.

38. The amount of insulation needed for exterior walls for a 152 SF perimeter room with 8 ft. ceiling, and a 12 x 8 window wall equals _____ packages of fiberglass batts, if each package contains 50 sq. ft. of 6" batt.

    A: 22

    B: 24

    C: 25

    D: 23

39. When interior insulation is unfaced, having no water-resistant paper covering on its blankets or batts, _____ is used to form a vapor barrier.

    A: plastic sheeting

    B: a layer of rigid batting

    C: gypsum spray

    D: All the above.

40. Before siding is installed, the sheathing is covered with _____.

    A: a water-protective film coating

    B: asphalt-impregnated builder's paper

    C: asphalt-impregnated builder's paper

    D: acetate wrapping

41. When estimating wood siding take-offs, allowances for _____ should be included.

    A: overlapping

    B: waste

    C: joining

    D: mitering

42. Take-offs for roof systems depend on the _____.

    A: materials used

    B: surfacing

    C: type

    D: All the above.

43. Stucco specifications denote mixing proportions of water, Portland cement, lime and sand and the type and location of trim pieces, and is taken-off _____.

    A: by cubic foot

    B: by cubic yard

    C: by square foot

    D: according to individual components

Blueprint Reading Part II

44. The rough opening size required for an interior door measuring 2'-6" x 6'-8" is _____.

    A: 2'-8" x 7'-0"   C: 2'-8-½" x 6'-11"

    B: 2'-6" x 6'-8"   D: 2'-8" x 6'-10 ½"

45. The standard interior door size is _____ high.

    A: 7'-0"   C: 6'-8"

    B: 6'-10"   D: 7'-2"

46. When purchasing or ordering casing lengths for interior doors, how many lengths would be needed to trim both sides, plus the width, of a 6'-8" door?

    A: two 7'-0" lengths, one 6'-0" length   C: two 7'-0" lengths, one 8'-0" length

    B: three 8'-0" lengths   D: Any of the above.

47. When ordering base, crown, cove, panel, or shoe moldings a _____ percent waste factor is typically calculated.

    A: 5-10   C: 10-15

    B: 7-10   D: 10-20

48. A _____ is used to quickly mark the height of the window head, which is generally _____ above the floor.

    A: tape measure, 7'-0"   C: story pole, 6'-8"

    B: tape measure, 6'-10"   D: window guard, 6'-8"

49. Drywall take-off is by the _____.

    A: square foot   C: individual components

    B: whole system   D: All the above.

50. Minimum ceiling drywall single-nail spacing is _____, and screwed every _____.

    A: 4", 12"   C: 7", 12"

    B: 5", 12"   D: None of the above.

51. The number of wall sheathing sheets needed for a net calculated area of 2060 SF, if the fiberboard sheets are 4' x 9', are _____.

    A: 59   C: 58

    B: 60   D: 57

52. Before plastering or applying wall finish, joints between the gypsum wall panels are _____.

    A: filled with a joint compound   C: filled with a joint compound and taped

    B: covered with tape   D: All the above.

Blueprint Reading Part II

53. Ceramic tiles of various types, except for special tiles such as logos, designs, etc., are taken-off by _____.

    A: square foot   C: linear foot

    B: each item   D: None of the above.

54. Setting materials and grout are calculated and converted according to the manufacturer's _____.

    A: specifications   C: calculations

    B: coverage per product   D: None of the above.

55. For a 150 SF area, to estimate the number of cartons of 6" x 6" tile needed, one must _____.

    A: check the manufacturer's supply chart   C: add 15 percent to the sq. ft. area for a 12.5 sq. ft. per carton order

    B: add 10 percent to the sq. ft. area and check the manufacturer's supply chart for sq. ft. per carton size   D: None of the above.

56. When take-off for acoustical ceiling tile is calculated according to individual components, tiles are taken-off by _____ and converted to _____.

    A: square inches, square foot   C: square foot, each

    B: square inches, each   D: square foot, linear foot

57. The _____ and required nailing pattern determine nail quantities for face or blind nailing wood flooring.

    A: area   C: number of planks or wood pieces

    B: square feet   D: A and B only.

58. Wood flooring installed with adhesives is _____.

    A: hardwood plank   C: standard

    B: parquet   D: All the above.

59. Estimate the number of bundles of board feet of strip flooring 3/4" x 2-1/4'" needed for a 900 SF straight-across room, if there are 24 boards per bundle. (Given: side-matching allowance + 5 percent end matching = 38-1/3 percent).

    A: 50   C: 52

    B: 49   D: 53

60. _____ resilient flooring offers the maximum wear potential.

    A: Rubber   C: Asphalt

    B: PVC   D: Clay tile

Blueprint Reading Part II

61. With the exception of carpet tiles, all carpeting, regardless of backing or underlayment, is taken-off at _____.

    A: square feet

    B: square feet converted to square yards

    C: square yards

    D: Any of the above.

62. Take-offs for exterior painting must take into account reduction in _____ as a result of periodic staging changes.

    A: quality

    B: time

    C: productivity

    D: pricing

63. _____ are limited to no more than 420 g/l, or 3.5 lb./gal., and are used to protect surfaces against chemical corrosion, high temps, abrasion, immersion in water and solvents.

    A: Architectural coatings

    B: Industrial maintenance primers and topcoats

    C: Clear coatings

    D: None of the above.

64. Coating specifications which designate the MWF thickness, are referring to _____.

    A: the maximum water vapor factor tolerance thickness for the coating application

    B: the minimum wet film thickness for the paint application

    C: the maximum wet vapor factor for epoxy coatings

    D: the maximum wet film thickness for clear coatings

65. Interior wall painting is calculated by multiplying the perimeter of the room by the wall height, and deducting openings larger than _____.

    A: 4 SF

    B: 5 SF

    C: 4'-6"

    D: 5'

66. The cheapest cabinetry/wood finish sealer is _____.

    A: shellac

    B: sanding sealer

    C: lacquer

    D: None of the above.

67. The most desirable stains to use on cabinets when they will be exposed to continuous sunlight are _____ stains.

    A: oil

    B: water

    C: spirit

    D: pigment oil

68. Main components of a fire protection system include _____.

    A: suppression

    B: detection

    C: alarm

    D: All the above.

Blueprint Reading Part II

69. When a manual fire suppression system in a multi-story building does not have enough water pressure to supply all fire hose stations, _____ are added to the system.

   A: sprinklers

   B: standpipes

   C: more hose stations in order to redistribute existing water supplies

   D: All the above.

70. Riser and distribution piping for standpipe and automatic sprinkler systems are taken-off by LF, and are listed by pipe type, size and _____.

   A: function

   B: main application

   C: method of connection

   D: None of the above.

71. There are three common types of fires: A, B and C. Another type of fire is Type D, which involves _____.

   A: live electrical equipment

   B: lubricants

   C: metals that burn

   D: liquids

72. The best fire extinguisher to have at the worksite is Class _____.

   A: A

   B: B

   C: C

   D: ABC

73. Fixture and Equipment _____ aid the contractor in determining piping quantities, types of plumbing fixtures and equipment to be furnished or installed.

   A: Details

   B: Lists

   C: Schedules

   D: Specifications

74. The size of any required water supply pipe depends on _____.

   A: available pressure

   B: friction in the pipe

   C: number of fittings

   D: All the above.

75. Every fixture has a _____ that keeps water in the trap of the fixture and eliminates the chance of it being siphoned out when another fixture is used.

   A: vent stack

   B: vent pipe

   C: vent fixture

   D: air vent

76. Drainage and vent piping for waste lines and sewers may be of _____.

   A: cast-iron

   B: copper

   C: ABS

   D: All the above.

Blueprint Reading Part II

239

Blueprint Reading Part II

77. Plumbing fixtures and equipment are taken-off by _____ and may involve work by those in other trades.

    A: lump sum   C: labor hours

    B: each   D: None of the above.

78. For waterlines where water containing corrosive elements flows through, red brass pipe or _____ pipe is used.

    A: welded steel   C: copper

    B: galvanized steel   D: All the above.

79. Take-off for special drainage fittings such as valves, bends and tees are _____.

    A: listed separately per each item C: included in the lump sum pipe take-off

    B: incidental to the pipe take-off by LF   D: None of the above.

80. Valves most practical for controlling water flows under pressure are _____ and _____.

    A: saddle valves, water hammer arrestors   C: float valves, T and P valves

    B: pressure regulators, strainers   D: pressure regulators, saddle valves

81. Pipe _____ are taken-off by dividing the total linear foot of water piping in each category by the specified intervals.

    A: hangers   C: fittings

    B: supports   D: A and B only.

82. Thermoplastic piping should be supported at intervals, roughly ___, normally required for steel pipe.

    A: ½ to ¾   C: ½

    B: ¾   D: ½ to ¼

83. A family of 4 live in a single-family residence with 2 full bathrooms, a dishwasher, and a washing machine. At the two-hour peak load between 7 pm and 9 pm, the demand for hot water is _____ gallons, with a recovery rate of _____ gal/hr., determining the water heater size needed.

    A: 100, 50   C: 84, 42

    B: 90, 45   D: 102, 51

84. _____ square feet equals five acres.

    A: 215,800   C: 207,800

    B: 217,800   D: 218,700

EXAM 11

85. A _____ engineer is required to design HVAC plans.

    A: Fluids

    B: Hydraulics

    C: Water

    D: A and B.

86. Energy sources used for HVAC include electricity and _____.

    A: solar

    B: geothermal

    C: ground heat

    D: All the above.

87. In HVAC units, _____ valves provide zone control for hydronic heating and cooling systems.

    A: flow control

    B: shut-off

    C: regulator

    D: None of the above.

88. The most common forced air heating and air conditioning package systems used for residential buildings include _____.

    A: water-cooled draw-through units$

    B: all-electric systems with electric duct coils and cooling towers

    C: all-electric systems with chillers and duct heaters

    D: variable air volume systems

89. HVAC packages commonly used in commercial and industrial buildings include _____.

    A: rooftop multi-zone units with combination heating/cooling

    B: all-electric systems with electric duct coils and cooling towers

    C: all-electric systems with chillers and duct heaters

    D: All the above.

90. Ductwork and flexible ducts for short runs to diffusers are taken off by _____.

    A: each according to the number of sections installed

    B: linear foot for the entire run

    C: square feet according to the surface area spanned

    D: None of the above.

91. _____ support, sometimes enclose, and protect electrical wires.

    A: Raceways

    B: Hangers

    C: Cable trays

    D: All the above.

92. Take-offs of conduit are categorized into _____.

    A: branch lighting

    B: distribution power

    C: branch power

    D: A and C only.

93. Electric current flows along conductors made of _____.
    A: aluminum
    B: copper
    C: Both A and B.
    D: brass

94. Service entrance cable is classified as _____.
    A: UF
    B: USE
    C: SE
    D: B and C.

95. When extending a circuit and installing new outlet boxes, and estimating the amount of cable needed for the job, the amount of recommended cable slack for each box is approximately _____ inches.
    A: 12
    B: 8
    C: 6
    D: 4

96. Ground wires and hot wires are color-coded _____ and _____ respectively.
    A: green, gray
    B: white, black
    C: green, red
    D: gray, white

97. Permits and fees for tie-ins are taken-off per _____ and may be listed as a lump sum.
    A: occurrence
    B: project
    C: contract
    D: All the above.

Answers: Blueprint Reading Part II

1. **Answer B.** SF, spacing

   Example: For a 1000 SF masonry wall, ties spaced 2'-0" O.C. each way; 1 tie is required every 4 SF of wall; 1000 SF = 250 ties; 4 SF per tie

2. **Answer D.** Vertical control, VLF

   Vertical control joints are provided for expansion and contraction support for the wall. They require compressible pre-molded joint filler. Control joints vary by thickness and are taken-off by the vertical linear foot (VLF).

3. **Answer B.** actual size of the staging units available

   This take-off consists of frame sections, cross braces, outriggers and planks. All of these comprise the actual size of the staging unit. Many contractors have some scaffolding available. If more scaffolding is needed, the contractor may need to include rental costs as well as the erecting, dismantling and moving around of the scaffold during construction, and lost productivity.

4. **Answer D.** All the above.

   Structural steel items are capable of supporting large loads, and are available in a variety of sizes and shapes. Steel is an ideal flexural material and provides an economical solution to many engineering problems. Shop and field priming, items installed by others and open-web bar joists and metal decking are additional considerations in calculating take-off.

5. **Answer C.** plan

   Plan views in structural drawings show steel work. Details, elevations and sections are included for clarification. Details provide connections necessary for individual pieces. Schedules are used to list columns or lintels and save time calculating take-offs.

6. **Answer C.** Both A and B.

   Bending stress is an important consideration for exterior walls exposed to wind. Axial stress is considered for loadbearing walls. For non-bearing walls, 18 gauge studs, 16" O.C. (3-⅝" or 4") may be used for interior walls up to 10 feet high bracing, 12 feet with bracing; for exterior walls with 20 psf wind loads, 3-⅝" studs may be used up to 9 ft. high; 4" studs up to 10 ft. high and 6" studs up to 14" high.

7. **Answer A.** 3 times the wall or slab thickness or 18 inches

   Primary flexural reinforcement should not be spaced any farther apart than 3 times the wall or slab thickness, or 18 in., except in concrete joists

   construction.

8. **Answer A.** length, pounds

   The take-off is from the steel piece's length, converted to weight in pounds, and finally converted into tons. Individual component pieces should be separated and listed according to designation, then by application, for the purpose of estimating the cost of erection rather than solely the materials.

9. **Answer B.** diameter

   The bar number indicates the diameter in eighths of an inch, and range between No. 3 and No. 18. (No. 5 bar has a diameter of ⅝ in.) Metric sizes are available as well.

10. **Answer D.** All the above.

    Mill lengths of reinforcing bar, stocked by suppliers, come in 20, 40 and 60-foot lengths. Non-standard lengths are by special order and specially fabricated.

11. **Answer B.** standard

    Lower strength, Grade 40 rebar, has a yield strength of 40,000 psi. Premium grade, Grade 75, is usually not stocked by suppliers, and has a yield strength of 75,000 psi. When more tension than its yield strength is put on the Grade 75 bar, it will become permanently deformed.

12. **Answer B.** shape, depth, and weight

    The letter classification, for a structural steel piece, refers to its shape, except for angle shapes, in which case, the first 2 of 3 numbers represents the length of the angle legs in inches. The first of the two numbers of the piece designation refers to the actual or nominal depth in inches of the section. The second number refers to the weight per linear foot of the section in lbs/SF.

13. **Answer C.** Both A and B.

    Bending stress is an important consideration for exterior walls exposed to wind. Axial stress is considered for loadbearing walls. For non-bearing walls, 18 gauge studs, 16" O.C. (3-⅝" or 4") may be used for interior walls up to 10 feet high without bracing, 12 feet with bracing; for exterior walls with 20 psf wind loads, 3-⅝" studs may be used up to 9 ft. high, 4" studs up to 10 ft. high, 6" studs up to 14" high.

14. **Answer A.** overlap

    The manufacturer specifies overlap requirements for the sides and ends of the individual sheets. Metal decking is taken-off by the SF of area to be covered and extended to the square (SQ) where SQ = 100 SF.

15. **Answer D.** Any of the above.

    Studs are used as the vertical components of the metal wall system, and the steel track is the horizontal component. Regardless of the take-off method used, the contractor must separate walls of different stud widths, gauges, height, on-center spacing, etc.

16. **Answer B.** amount

    The amount of steel, in tons, determines the cost of shop priming. Field touch-ups are based on labor hours, and must be listed as a separate item.

17. **Answer C.** Framing plans

    Framing plans are modified structural drawings. For residential construction, plan, elevation, section, and detail drawings show most wood framing and finish carpentry work.

18. **Answer D.** A and B only.

    Roof framing and sheathing and ceiling system take-offs are also derived from cross-sections. The most common of framing methods among residential and light commercial contractors is platform framing, where the load-bearing walls begin at the top of the subfloor sheathing and continue to the underside of the platform above. Cross-sections showing this provide adequate take-off information.

Answers: Blueprint Reading Part II **243**

EXAM 11

19. **Answer A.** 930

Board feet is the equivalent of a piece of wood measuring 1-foot wide, 1-foot long, and 1-inch thick. For calculation purposes, lumber measuring less than 1" thick, is counted as the full inch. The board's width in inches, must be converted to feet. Board feet = (T x W x L) n = (1 ft. x 1⁹⁄₁₂ ft. x 18 ft.) 62 = 930; Where: T = nominal thickness; W = nominal width; L = length in feet of the individual piece; n = number of pieces

20. **Answer B.** ⅛

Stock material should be cut ⅛"-½ " longer than needed. An extra piece or a few extra feet of each piece should also be cut. In case one of the required pieces is destroyed (cut short), the spare will be available.

21. **Answer C.** floor

Floor framing includes the girder, sill plates, sill sealer, joists, band or box joist and subfloor sheathing. The girder is at a specific midpoint in width intended to reduce the overall span of the joist. Sills or sill plates are typically 2" x 6" or 2" x 8". Sills are doubled-up on some plans. Anchor bolts secure sills to the top of the foundation. The sill sealer acts as an insect and air infiltration barrier. Joists provide floor support and are spaced typically at 12", 16" or 24" O.C. Box or band joists run perpendicular to the joists at their ends. Subflooring is laid perpendicular to the joists and is typically plywood. Take-offs for girders, sills and sill sealer are by the LF. Built-up girders and sills must be multiplied by the number of members or pieces.

22. **Answer A.** length, spacing

The take-off must list the quantity of each length of joist separately and extend total LF for that length.; Length = span of joist + required bearing at each end. Example: Length of the floor frame = 32'-0"; 32' 0" = 24 joists + 1 end joist = 25 joists, 16" O.C., 1.33

23. **Answer C.** 4' x 8'

Subfloor sheathing is taken-off by the SF. Quantity of sheets required is calculated by dividing the total SF area by the area of an individual sheet. Example: Room area = 24' x 30' = 720 SF = 22.5 sheets; 23 sheets, 32 SF per sheet

24. **Answer B.** "B"

The grade of face veneer depends on the number and size of knots, loose and plugged holes, splits and other defects. "A" has no defects; "B" is a solid face with tight knots and repairs allowed; "C" is a plugged veneer with splits limited to ⅛" wide and holes from ¼ " to ½" in size; D is the lowest grade with open spaces and no repair allowed.

25. **Answer D.** 291

(Length x ¾) + 2 studs for each corner, intersection and opening.; (260 x ¾) + 2(14 + 12 + 22); 195 + 96 = 291 studs

26. **Answer D.** None of the above.

There are three generally accepted rules for calculating the rise-run or riser-tread ratio: 1) riser + riser + tread = 24" - 25"; 2) riser + tread = 17" - 18"; 3) riser height x tread width = 70" - 75"

27. **Answer B.** dividing the total rise by 7

Total rise/riser height = number of risers; 110 in./7 in. = 15.71; The total number of risers generally comes out to an uneven number. It is suggested in this case to try the whole numbers above and below the fractional number to see what rise they would require. Total rise/number of risers = riser height; 110 in./15 = 7-⅓ in.; 110 in./16 = 7-⅞ in. Code specification dictates a riser to be no less than 4", and no greater than 7-½".

28. **Answer A.** 4

Residential building code requirements limit balustrades openings to less than 4 inches to prevent a child's head from getting caught in-between.

29. **Answer D.** 2 x 4, 2 x 6, 16, 46

Pre-fabricated trusses, or gang-nailed trusses, are commonly used for ceiling assemblies spanning 16 ft. to 46 ft. Roof trusses are made with flat parallel chords in lengths of 50 ft. to 150 ft. Truss rafters are sized depending on the shape and span of the roof framing.

30. **Answer A.** trussed area, spacing

Trusses must be listed separately according to length, span, pitch, type and if they are special trusses intended for end conditions, such as gable-end trusses. Bracing from trusses is taken-off and listed by LF.

31. **Answer C.** each item, linear foot

Cabinetry and casework, as well as hardware, are taken-off by each. Plastic laminate countertops are taken-off by the LF, done by measuring the countertop at the abutting wall. Alternatively, countertop surface, laminate sheets for field fabrications, are taken-off by SF.

32. **Answer B.** 42"

Standard ¾" shelving should be supported every 42" even for heavy loads. The front edge of the plywood shelving should be overlaid with a strip of matching wood material as the cabinet. Stock or thin strips may be glued to the plywood edge.

33. **Answer D.** None of the above.

Methods for supporting shelves include the use of brackets carried in notches, brackets held with wood screws, wood pins and metal or plastic shelf pins. When plywood shelving is used, it should be faced with solid stock.

34. **Answer D.** A and B only.

Waterproofing and dampproofing include the application of coatings to prevent migration of moisture through the structure above and below grade. Insulation reduces loss of heat through the exterior envelope. Roofing materials such as metal flashing provide watertightness for the uppermost surfaces. Siding provides protection from the elements on the vertical surfaces. Details and cross-sections of roof systems, wall systems and foundation sections indicate application locations, and corresponding specifications denote materials to be used and application procedures.

EXAM 11

35. **Answer B.** square foot

    The SF unit can be extended to the square (100 SF). The area to be protected is determined by the amount of surface area below grade. For foundations, the perimeter of the foundation is multiplied by the distance from finish grade at the exterior to the bottom of the footing.

36. **Answer C.** penetration of moisture through

    Dampproofing is applied to the foundation area below grade and is not intended to resist water pressure. Common methods of dampproofing include applying bituminous-based, tar-like, coatings on the protected areas, and plastering a cement-based mixture (parging) over the surface area to be protected. Quantities for bituminous applications should be separated according to method of application. Parging is taken-off by the thickness (generally ¼" - 1") and number of coats.

37. **Answer D.** All the above.

    Batt or roll insulation, rigid insulation, loose fill insulation, and polyethylene vapor barriers are taken-off by SF.

38. **Answer D.** 23

    152 x 8 = 1216; Window wall = 12 x 8 = 96; Net Area = 1216 - 96 = 1120 sq. ft.; 112%₅₀ = 22.40 = 23 pkgs.

39. **Answer A.** plastic sheeting

    Insulation blankets and batts with protective water-resistant paper coverings are installed with the paper facing the interior of the building to keep dampness and moisture away from the wallboard and batting. Plastic sheeting forms a vapor barrier in place of the insulation paper. When unfaced blankets are used, the entire wall must be covered with plastic sheets.

40. **Answer C.** asphalt-impregnated builder's paper

    Before siding is installed the sheathing is usually covered with asphalt-impregnated builder's paper in a water-tight vapor-permeable plastic sheet. This permits water vapor in wall cavities to pass through to the outside, preventing moisture damage.

41. **Answer B.** waste

    The species and grade of wood and type of application must be considered during estimation of wood siding. The final quantity of siding materials must include deductions for all openings greater than 4 SF, such as doors and windows. The species and grade of wood and type of application must be considered during estimation of wood siding. The final quantity of siding materials must include deductions for all openings greater than 4 SF, such as doors and windows. The species and grade of wood and type of application must be considered during estimation of wood siding. The final quantity of siding materials must include deductions for all openings greater than 4 SF, such as doors and windows.

42. **Answer C.** type

    Basic types of roof systems include built-up, single-ply, metal and shingles and tile. Individual components of a built-up and single-ply systems are taken-off separately. Metal roofs are taken-off by the SF, with trim pieces taken-off by LF. For shingle and tile roof systems, underlayments are taken-off by the SF, and can be extended to the square. Special hip and ridge tiles or cap shingles are taken off by the LF, or in cases of clay tiles, by each. Drip edges and ridge vents are taken-off by the LF and can be converted to each.

43. **Answer C.** by square foot

    Stucco is taken-off by measuring the length and width of the various surfaces to be covered. For pricing, the SF may be converted to SY. Metal lath quantities are taken-off at SF of area to be covered. Trim are taken-off by the LF.

44. **Answer C.** 2'-8-½" x 6'-11"

    Interior doors and door frames are usually roughed in approximately 3" higher than the door height and approximately 2-½" more than the door width to provide for jambs and leveling within the opening. Most common types of doors are paneled and flush. Rough opening width = 2'-6" + 0'-2-½" = 2'-8-½"; Rough opening height = 6'-8" + 0'-3" = 6'-11"; Total rough opening = 2'-8-½" x 6'-11"

45. **Answer C.** 6'-8"

    A standard interior door is 6'-8" high, 2'-0" to 3'-0" wide and typically 1-⅜" thick, with 1-¾" thick, softwood frames.

46. **Answer D.** Any of the above.

    The molding for the door sides must be 6'-11" to allow for mitering. Two side casings can be made from one 14' - 0" stock piece, or one can be made from an 8'-0" piece. Head casing moldings must allow for mitering and are 3'-2" wide. Two head casings can be made from one 8'-0" piece, or three can be made from one 10'-0" piece.

47. **Answer C.** 10-15

    When figuring the amount of length of molding, the length of the perimeter of the room, minus openings, is measured. The 10-15 percent waste factor is added. Suppliers generally send slightly more since they send the length on hand that adds up close to the amount ordered.

48. **Answer C.** story pole, 6'-8"

    A story pole is a straight piece of wood with the desired height marked on that is used to mark the trimmer stud at each window with the required height. In most cases, designers desire that the window heads be lined up with the door head jamb, which is usually 6'-8" (2.03 m) above the floor.

49. **Answer D.** All the above.

    When drywall is taken-off by the whole system, all components are included and quantified as SF. When individual drywall components are taken off, drywall is taken-off by the SF of surface area to be covered, with quantities separated according to the type and thickness, and may be extended to the number of specific size sheets required. Multiple layers of fire-rated assemblies should be listed in the take-off according to their position in the assembly. Taping, finishing, joint compound and texturing are taken-off by the SF of coverage. Reinforcing tape and trim are taken-off by LF.

EXAM 11

50. **Answer C.** 7", 12"

Generally ceiling panels are installed first and may be single or double nailed. Single-nailed ceilings are usually spaced approx. 7 in. O.C. Screws are spaced 12" on the ceiling.

51. **Answer C.** 58

Net area = perimeter x height - wall openings = 2060; Sheet area = 4 x 9 = 36; Number of sheets = 2060⁄36 = 57.22 = 58

52. **Answer C.** filled with a joint compound and taped

The long edges are made with a taper allowing the compound and tape to fill it flush with the surface. The joint is covered with a thin layer of compound and the tape is pressed in with a finishing knife. A thin coat of compound is applied over the tape and allowed to dry before applying plaster finish.

53. **Answer A.** square foot

Field tile for ceramic and quarry tile applications are taken-off by SF. Special tiles are taken-off by each. Ceramic and quarry trim pieces are taken-off by LF.

54. **Answer B.** coverage per product

Setting materials, thin-set or adhesive, are calculated by the SF of the tile to be set and converted to sales units based on the manufacturer's recommended coverage for the particular product. The manufacturer specifies the ratio of liquid to dry material for bonding additives. Tile joint grout is calculated the same as setting materials.

55. **Answer B.** add 10 percent to the sq. ft. area and check the manufacturer's supply chart for sq. ft. per carton size

To determine quantities of tile needed, measure the square footage, add 10 percent to compensate for breakage, cuts and extras for future repairs, and then consult the manufacturer's supply chart for quantity per 12.5 sq. ft. per carton, and for 11.5 sq. ft. per carton.

56. **Answer C.** square foot, each

Quantities must be separated according to type, color, size, shape, etc. Suspension systems may be converted from SF (of tile areas) to LF of wall angle and main runner. Individual components are taken-off per each item.

57. **Answer D.** A and B only.

Wood flooring is taken-off by SF according to type, species of wood, grade, finishing and method of application. Adhesives, such as those used for parquet, are taken-off by SF and converted to gallons, based on the manufacturer's recommended coverage. Underlayment is also taken-off by SF but converted to rolls with allowances for side an end laps.

58. **Answer D.** All the above.

Standard (wood strip) flooring is manufactured in various thicknesses and is nailed or installed with adhesives according to the manufacturer's recommendations. Parquet is generally installed with adhesives. Hardwood plank that is impregnated with acrylic and pre-finished laminate and hardwood veneer are installed with adhesives as well.

59. **Answer C.** 52

900 + (900 x .3833); 900 + 345; 1245⁄24 = 51.88 = 52 bundles

60. **Answer B.** PVC

PVC refers to polyvinyl chloride material, or vinyl floor covering. Solid vinyl floor covering offers the maximum wear potential, particularly where a heat welded surface is required. Rubber flooring provides walking comfort and resists damage from solvents, oils, acids, alkalis and other chemicals. Asphalt resilient flooring is available in four grades based on color and grades, and are proved to be fire resistant, durable, and are bonded to wood or concrete subfloors with mastic. Take-off is SF of area covered. Accessories are by LF or by each item.

61. **Answer B.** square feet converted to square yards

Estimating carpeting is divided into three categories: carpet installed with separate pad, pre-backed carpet glued directly to the substrate and carpet tiles. Padding materials are taken-off at SF and converted to SY. Carpet strip fasteners are taken-off by LF.

62. **Answer C.** productivity

Frequent moves of ladders or scaffolding, or staging, reduces the accuracy of labor pricing. Installed wood moldings and trim which must be painted also reduce productivity due to time needed for "cutting in."

63. **Answer B.** Industrial maintenance primers and topcoats

Industrial maintenance primers and topcoats are used to protect against more severe environment conditions where architectural coatings protect against more mild environments.

64. **Answer B.** the minimum wet film thickness for the paint application

Coating specifications may include wet film thickness or dry film thickness, or the MWF, which states the applied rate of xx mils per coat minimum wet film thickness. A mil is a unit of measure equal to 0.025 mm, or 0.01 in.

65. **Answer A.** 4 SF

Openings smaller than 4 SF are negligible. Ceilings are calculated by multiplying the length by width of the area to be covered. Walls and ceilings should be listed separately.

66. **Answer A.** shellac

Shellac can be diluted depending on how porous the wood is, and the amount of control desired. Shellac is diluted with denatured alcohol in order to perform as a sealer. Lacquer is a good sealer when the top dressing will be lacquer. Sanding sealer is a relatively new product and can be purchased in clear or color stains.

Answers: Blueprint Reading Part II

67. Answer B.   water

Water stain is the most penetrating of all stains, especially when used on base wood. Water-soluble powder is made from aniline dyes. Best results are obtained when the powder is added to very warm water and dissolved completely. Spirit stains are also aniline dyes, but are mixed with alcohol and are difficult to use since they dry quickly and possibly unevenly. Pigment oil stains are powders and are soluble in naphtha or turpentine. Pigments are made from various oxides and silicates mixtures.

68. Answer D.   All the above.

Standpipe systems, automatic sprinkler systems or the combination of the two, accomplishes fire suppression. It is the contractor's responsibility to study plans for sprinkler head locations, piping sizes and materials and location of valves, fittings and appurtenances. Riser diagrams may indicate compressors for dry systems, backflow preventers and alarm bells.

69. Answer B.   standpipes

Standpipes are pipes or tanks on roofs of buildings, which store a supply of water and provide an extra supply when normal water pressures fall.

70. Answer C.   method of connection

Piping connections may be grooved joint or threaded. Fittings are taken-off by each, and classified by type (elbow, tee, reducer, etc.), and method of connection and material composition (steel, PVC, iron, etc.). Valves and special appurtenances (gauges, flanges, etc.) are take-off by each, and listed according to type, manufacturer, model, size and application. Sprinkler heads and discharge nozzles are taken-off by each, and listed according to type (pendent, sidewall, etc.), temperature range, manufacturer and model.

71. Answer C.   metals that burn

Type A fires involve burning wood, paper, cloth and trash. Type B fires involve flammable liquids such as gas, oil and paint. Type C fires occur with live electrical equipment. Type D fires involve exotic kinds of metals that can catch fire and burn.

72. Answer D.   ABC

Class ABC fire extinguishers are multipurpose dry chemical extinguishers, which cover the possibility of the three basic types of fires.

73. Answer C.   Schedules

Plumbing drawings with plan views and riser diagrams are also used to determine piping quantities. Special equipment plans must also be studied for equipment that is furnished by others and installed under the plumbing contract.

74. Answer D.   All the above.

Determining pipe size requires pressure, head, elbows and demand to be calculated using EPA flow pressures and flow rates for fixtures.

75. Answer B.   vent pipe

Fixtures are vented to keep water in the trap under atmospheric pressure. Each vent pipe is connected to a vent stack running through the roof, which vents gases generated by wastes.

76. Answer D.   All the above.

Waste system pipes which provide adequate flow of wastes, protect against cross-connection and keep noxious fumes from escaping may be cast iron, copper, brass, galvanized steel, or in buildings up to 3 stories in height, ABS or PVC-DWV plastic pipe.

77. Answer B.   each

Power wiring of water heaters, draft inducers and special flues, and penetrations through roofing systems, and flashing of roof vents, may be required work done by other trades.

78. Answer C.   copper

Copper is considered an excellent hot and cold water distribution material. It is resistant to corrosion and does not rust. Hot and cold water piping is referred to as domestic water piping and excludes piping for fire protection systems. Standard piping materials are types L and K copper tubing. Water piping is taken-off by LF and fittings are taken-off individually.

79. Answer A.   listed separately per each item

All pipe is taken-off by the LF. Cost for cutting to specific lengths in the must be included. Quantities for cutting larger-diameter pipe are taken-off by each item. Special pipe fittings are listed separately by each item. Structures such as manholes, catch basins, tanks, etc. are listed separately per each item.

80. Answer D.   pressure regulators, saddle valves

Pressure regulator valves limit water pressure preventing damage. Saddle valves are also installed on pipes, which have water under pressure. Water hammer arrestors absorb shock waves produced by sudden changes in water flow, float valves control water levels and capacity in tanks, globe valves control flows of hot and cold water, oil and gas, T and P valves are safety relief valves that sense temperature buildups and open to release excess pressure thus preventing explosions, and strainers collect dirt and debris in a 20 mm mesh screen. Take-offs for each valve is listed according to type, manufacturer, model, size and application.

81. Answer D.   A and B only.

The specified intervals are as noted in the contract specifications or code. Materials used for joining copper water pipe are solder, flux and gas, which are difficult to estimate. Using industry standard charts estimating "pounds of soft solder required to make 100 joints," the contractor may arrive at a fairly accurate amount for each.

82. Answer D.   ½ to ¼

Plastic pipe support is very important but receives little attention with adverse results. Support spacing depends upon pipe size, operating temp, wall thickness and mechanical properties of the specific pipe material. Specific support spacings are available from the pipe manufacturers.

83. Answer B.   90, 45

2 persons at 20 gal./person, 40 gal.; 2 persons at 5 gal/person, 10 gal,; Second full bath 10 gal.; Dishwasher 10 gal.; Washer 20 gal.; Total 90 gal.; 9½ = 45 gal./hr recovery rate

84. Answer B.   217,800

43,560 sq. ft. = 1 acre; 43,560 x 5 = 217,800

EXAM 11

85. **Answer D.** A and B.

HVAC designs require knowledge and understanding of thermodynamics, fluid mechanics, and weather conditions. Heating equipment is designed by size according to its heating capacity. Air flow in ducts produce static pressure and velocity pressure.

86. **Answer D.** All the above.

The type, and occupancy, of the building is a primary consideration in determining what is the most effective and efficient energy source to operate an HVAC system.

87. **Answer A.** flow control

HVAC equipment can develop hazardous pressures or temperatures when the water level in a steam boiler drops below a predetermined level. Relief valves protect the system against excessive line pressure.

88. **Answer A.** water-cooled draw-through units

The most common forced air heating and air conditioning package systems used for residential buildings also include ¾ to 2 ton heat pumps, electric furnaces with top mounted evaporators and remote air-cooled electrically-operated condensing units (2-10 tons). Chilled water systems are commonly used in multi-story residential buildings. Take-offs for equipment are by each item. Components such as flues for the furnace, thermostat wiring controls, filters, etc. may be listed separately, but taken-off either as individual items or collectively priced by lump sum.

89. **Answer D.** All the above.

Most HVAC manufacturers make these modular units, which may be assembled vertically or horizontally. Commercial ducts are regulated and classified in one of 2 groups determined by flamespread and smoke developed or spread.

90. **Answer B.** linear foot for the entire run

Vertical risers and drips are also necessary for air distribution between floors in addition to the horizontal mains. Ductwork is taken-off by LF and fittings and devices installed in the finished space are taken-off by each. After the contractor calculates the ductwork, and fittings, the quantity of insulation must be calculated. To do this, the total surface area of all ductwork and fittings must be determined. The sound lining (insulation) in the interior of the duct is taken-off and listed separately by SF.

91. **Answer A.** Raceways

Raceways enclose and protect bare wires, while cable trays provide support for electric wires that have adequate insulation and do not require the added protection. Open raceways only support the wires and are open to inspection and modifications. Conduits, underfloor ducts, wireways and surface metal raceways support insulated electric wire and provide protection. They may be metal, non-metallic, PVC or PE. Raceways are taken-off per LF. Fittings required to make turns and extensions are taken-off per each item.

92. **Answer D.** A and C only.

Power distribution includes installation of the main conductors that supply power to panels. Branch power and branch lighting refer to branching the panels to provide power and lighting to various project locations. Quantities may be determined according to system. Raceway installation exceeding 15' in height should be noted separately since it requires more equipment and labor, reducing productivity.

93. **Answer C.** Both A and B.

Copper is a better conductor of current than aluminum. Larger diameter wire is required in order for aluminum to obtain equal conductivity as that of copper.

94. **Answer D.** B and C.

SE and USE cable are moisture-resistant, fire-resistant insulated cable that has a braid of armor providing protection against atmospheric corrosion. USE has a lead covering permitting it to be used underground. SE is used for service entrance wiring or general interior use.

95. **Answer B.** 8

Recommended slack at each outlet is 8". However when estimating a wire-run, an additional 20 percent should be added to the length to account for wire not running in a straight line. All wires and conductors are taken-off per LF. All fittings, devices and boxes are taken-off per each item.

96. **Answer B.** white, black

Ground wires are white or gray. Hot wires may be black or other colors, but never white or gray.

97. **Answer D.** All the above.

Fees for electrical permits are typically assessed per job. Utility companies typically assess a hook-up charge to tie in a service or transformer per occurrence.

EXAM 12

Math

1. The supply department forgot to put the total on a recent invoice. If the cost of each of the three items was $12.56, $141.08, and $76.33, how much should the total bill be?

   A: $228.97
   B: $229.87
   C: $229.97
   D: $230.87

2. Which of the following represents 11% as a decimal?

   A: .011
   B: .11
   C: 1.1
   D: 11

3. There is a rectangular pool that is 35 m × 80 m. A 2.5 m wide pebble walkway is going to be made around the pool. What is the area of the pebble walkway?

   A: 600 m²
   B: 900 m²
   C: 2,800 m²
   D: 3,400 m²

4. A house is going to be constructed. The scale of the drawing is 2 in:5 ft. If the house on the drawing is 10.2" tall, how tall will the actual house be?

   A: 22.9 ft.
   B: 25.5 ft.
   C: 26.8 ft.
   D: 29.4 ft.

5. At the start of the day, inventory reports showed that there were 37 drills in stock at the store. After a sale, the receipts showed that nine drills were sold. How many drills were left in stock?

   A: 25
   B: 26
   C: 28
   D: 46

6. A clerk accidentally scanned in an item twice, which cost $7.80. If the total bill with the mistake was $37.24, what should the correct bill be?

   A: $28.44
   B: $29.44
   C: $45.04
   D: $45.06

7. A certain telephone customer has two long distance plans from which to choose. Option 1 costs $7/month for 200 minutes and 5 cents for each minute over the allotted 200 minutes. Option 2 costs $.07 cents/min with no monthly charge. Which is a better deal for a customer who only talks 140-155 minutes per month?

   A: Option 1
   B: Option 2
   C: They would both cost the same.
   D: Not enough information.

8. Lacey can clean a renovated room in 14 minutes alone and Maria can clean a room in 19 minutes. If Lacey and Maria work together, how many complete rooms can they clean in one hour?

   A: 6 rooms
   B: 7 rooms
   C: 8 rooms
   D: 9 rooms

Math

9. On a recent paycheck, Martha was paid $376.80 for a total of 18 hours of work. About how much does Martha earn per hour?

   A: $15.24

   B: $17.16

   C: $20.93

   D: $22.81

10. Each month $68.50 is taken out of Claire's paycheck for taxes, social security, and other government deductions. How much money per year is being sent to the government?

    A: $685.00

    B: $753.50

    C: $787.75

    D: $822.00

11. The ratio of 6 : 3 : 1 represents the inventory of 6-foot, 8-foot, and 12-foot pieces of wood. If the total number of pieces is 1,400. How many 8-foot pieces are there?

    A: 140

    B: 280

    C: 420

    D: 840

12. A water heater will be marked up 15% before the 25% off sale. How much will the water heater cost if the original price was $1,850 and there is a sales tax of 6.5%?

    A: $1,543.89

    B: $1,605.41

    C: $1,699.35

    D: $1,785.25

13. Matt purchased 100 faucets from the distributor at $29 each. From the store data, he is guaranteed to sell at least 80 faucets in the next three months. How much should he price the faucets for if he wants to make at least $3,870 profit from selling them?

    A: $78.45

    B: $81.95

    C: $82.15

    D: $84.65

14. A plumber purchased 18 new fittings that cost $48 each. How much was the bill before tax?

    A: $754

    B: $834

    C: $864

    D: $944

15. In order to pay for a $16.54 bill, a customer hands the cashier a $50 bill. How much change is due back to the customer?

    A: $33.56

    B: $33.46

    C: $34.46

    D: $34.56

16. A square piece of sheet metal with a length of 16 inches must be cut and formed into an open box. If a 3 inch square is cut from each corner, the box can be formed. What is the volume that this new box can hold?

    A: 300 in3

    B: 442 in3

    C: 507 in3

    D: 768 in3

Math

17. How many pounds of aggregate that cost $5.25/lb. should be added to a 5 lb. mixed rock mixture that currently costs $3.25/lb. to end up with a mixture that costs $4.50/lb.?

    A: 5 lbs   C: 8.33 lbs

    B: 6.2 lbs   D: 9.02 lbs

18. Baseboards are sold in 16 foot sections. How many baseboards are necessary to complete a room with 322 linear feet of wall space?

    A: 18 boards   C: 20 boards

    B: 19 boards   D: 21 boards

19. A gas tanker started the day with 310 gallons in it's tank, which was already 2/5 empty. The first stop depleted the supply by 2/9 and the second stop took 1/3 of the remaining gas. At a fill up, how much will the tanker take?

    A: 264.1 gallons   C: 426.6 gallons

    B: 356 gallons   D: 470.8 gallons

20. A painter has a service charge of $35 per hour plus the cost of the paint. How much is the total bill for a project if she spent $32 on paint and worked for six hours?

    A: $67   C: $227

    B: $192   D: $242

21. A landscaper is hired to plant a row of orange trees along the edge of a client's land which measures 60 yards in length. Each tree needs to be at least 20 feet apart, and each tree must be 20 feet from both edges of the land. What is the maximum number of trees that he can plant?

    A: 2   C: 8

    B: 4   D: 10

22. A carpenter has been hired to install a shelf in a bedroom. The bedroom wall is 12 feet wide and the shelf is 5.6 feet. In order for the shelf to be exactly centered on the wall, how much space should she leave on each side?

    A: 0.4 feet   C: 3.2 feet

    B: 2.3 feet   D: 6.4 feet

23. A landscaper has six trees to trim. Each tree takes 20 minutes for set-up, two hours for trimming, and 40 minutes for clean up. He only has two days to complete this project and would like to work the same amount of time each day. How many hours will he need to work each day in order to complete his project on time?

    A: 6 hrs   C: 9 hrs

    B: 8 hrs   D: 12 hrs

Math

24. An electrician needs to calculate how many centimeters of electrical tape he needs for a job. If there are 100 centimeters in 1 meter, how many centimeters of electrical tape will he need if he needs 10 meters of tape?

   A: 110 centimeters   C: 10,000 centimeters

   B: 1,000 centimeters   D: 1,100 centimeters

25. Lee is constructing a frame for a poster. The poster is 24 inches wide by 32 inches long and he wants the frame to expand beyond the poster 2 inches on every side. What will the perimeter of the frame be?

   A: 112 in   C: 120 in

   B: 116 in   D: 128 in

26. A cube-shaped piece of metal must be coated with a special Teflon covering. If the cube has a side of 15 cm, what is the total surface area that needs to be coated?

   A: 600 sq. cm   C: 1350 sq. cm

   B: 900 sq. cm   D: 3375 sq. cm

27. A contractor has 80 feet of fencing to enclose a Jacuzzi area. There should be a walkway around the Jacuzzi that is 3 feet wide. What shape of Jacuzzi should be built in order to have the largest amount of area with the given perimeter?

   A: a square   C: a rectangle

   B: a cross   D: a circle

28. A mason worker has been hired to tile a rectangular area of a patio that measures 2 yds × 4 yds. He has been instructed to tile the entire area with no space left in between the tiles. Each tile is square and measures 3 in × 3 in. How many tiles will he need in order to cover the area of the patio?

   A: 96 tiles   C: 1,152

   B: 864   D: 3,456

29. F = 25A is the formula to find the number of pounds of fertilizer needed to cover a lawn. A is the area of the lawn in square feet. How many pounds of fertilizer (F) are needed to cover a lawn with an area (A) of 500 square feet?

   A: 12,500 pounds   C: 525 pounds

   B: 2,000 pounds   D: 100 pounds

30. To calculate his weekly earnings (E), a salesperson uses the formula E= 0.22s + 150, where s is his total sales. What did he earn last week if his sales were $2,200?

   A: $590   C: $980

   B: $634   D: $2,350

EXAM 12

Math

31. Ohm's Law states I = E/R where I is the current in amperes, E is the electromotive force in volts, and R is the resistance in ohms. Solve Ohm's Law for E.

   A: E = IR
   B: E = I/R
   C: E = I + R
   D: E = ERI

32. A bag of concrete mix makes 15 cubic feet of concrete. How many bags of concrete mix need to be purchased to fill a walkway that is 50 cubic feet?

   A: 3
   B: 4
   C: 5
   D: 6

33. The perimeter of a rectangular garden is 50 feet. Find the width of the garden if the length is 15 feet.

   A: 10 feet
   B: 5 feet
   C: 20 feet
   D: 7 feet

34. A farmer has 24 feet of fencing. She wants to create the animal pen with the greatest possible area using exactly 24 feet of fencing. Which of the following dimensions would create the pen with the greatest area and use exactly 24 feet of fencing?

   A: 6 feet by 6 feet
   B: 8 feet by 4 feet
   C: 2 feet by 10 feet
   D: 10 feet by 14 feet

35. The purchaser for the power tools department of a major retailer can purchase 120 grinders at a cost of $900. What is the cost per sweater?

   A: $1,020.00
   B: $13.00
   C: $7.50
   D: $8.00

36. Two pipes are being used to fill a pool. One fills the pool at the rate of five gallons per minute. The other works at the rate of six gallons per minute. How long will the pipes take to fill a 6,000 gallon pool if they are used together? Round your answer to the nearest minute.

   A: 500 minutes
   B: 545 minutes
   C: 1,000 minutes
   D: 1,200 minutes

37. A worker has run out of window cleaning fluid and wishes to purchase more. At the store, she finds that a 44-ounce bottle of cleaner costs $2.75, while a 55-ounce bottle of a different brand costs $3.70. Which is the better buy?

   A: the 44-ounce bottle
   B: the 55-ounce bottle
   C: The costs are the same per unit.
   D: The answer cannot be determined from the information provided.

EXAM 12

Math

38. You are trying to keep your employees from working overtime, which is anything over 40 hours in a week. If there is an employee who already has worked 9 hours on Monday, 6.5 hours on Tuesday, 8 hours on Thursday, and 10.5 hours on Friday, how many hours can you schedule that employee to work on Saturday?

    A: 5 hours   C: 6 hours

    B: 5.5 hours   D: 4.5 hours

39. You have 62.7 feet of rope. If 1 meter = 3.28 feet, approximately how many meters of rope do you have?

    A: 5.2 meters   C: 20.9 meters

    B: 19.1 meters   D: 33.5 meters

40. There are 65 applicants for four job openings. Approximately how many people are applying per job?

    A: 15   C: 17

    B: 16   D: 18

41. A cleaning service charges $75 for a job and pays the cleaner $42. How much profit does the cleaning service receive?

    A: $1.8   C: $75

    B: $33   D: $117

42. A Realtor made 3.5% commission on the sale of a house. If the purchase price of the house was $224,500, how much money did the Realtor make?

    A: $6,735.50   C: $78,575.00

    B: $7,857.50   D: $785,750.00

43. A tanker is 1/10 empty, What percentage of the capacity is available?

    A: 10%   C: 90%

    B: 50%   D: 100%

44. A delivery truck company damaged 12 bricks out of a total shipment of 145 bricks. What percentage of the bricks was not damaged?

    A: 8.3%   C: 85.1%

    B: 13.3%   D: 91.7%

45. To mail an invoice, postage costs 37 cents for one ounce and 23 cents for each additional ounce or fraction of an ounce. How much will it cost to send an invoice that weighs 4.2 oz?

    A: $1.06   C: $1.52

    B: $1.29   D: $1.85

Math

46. For an electric job, 22 new recessed can lights will be installed. The cans come in boxes of five and the baffles (rims) come in sets of eight. How many of each should you purchase in order to have the least amount of materials left over?

    A: 4 boxes of cans and 4 boxes of baffles   C: 6 boxes of cans and 3 boxes of baffles

    B: 5 boxes of cans and 3 boxes of baffles   D: 8 boxes of cans and 5 boxes of baffles

47. The sales tax in a certain state is 6.2%. In the state, what is the total cost for a purchase that costs $30 before tax?

    A: $3.86   C: $36.29

    B: $31.86   D: $48.60

48. Today, 175 new electric chain saws were supposed to be delivered. Unfortunately, 50 chainsaws were not delivered. Of those 50 late chainsaws, 32 will be rush delivered the following day. What percentage of the 50 missing chainsaws will still be missing the following day?

    A: 10%   C: 36%

    B: 18%   D: 42%

49. A commercial box of nails weighs 34 lbs. If each nail weighs approximately 1 oz, how many nails are in the box? (1 lb = 16 oz. The weight of the box is negligible.)

    A: 34   C: 2,176

    B: 544   D: 4,352

50. Two thirds of the remaining "last year" model tractors will be discounted at the end of the day. Each tractor will be discounted around $1,500 and there are still 291 last year models available. What is the total dollar value discount that this price reduction will bring for all of the tractors combined?

    A: $145,500   C: $436,000

    B: $291,000   D: $654,750

51. Guests in a hotel have been charged $168.50 for their stay. When the guests review their bill, they notice that there is an overcharge of $13.20. When the mistake is corrected, what will the new bill be?

    A: $142.10   C: $168.50

    B: $155.30   D: $181.70

52. A tanker truck is 4/5 full, what is this fraction represented as a percent?

    A: 40%   C: 75%

    B: 45%   D: 80%

Math

53. You have 274.8 inches of electrical wiring. How many feet of wiring do you have?

    A: 19.6 feet   C: 23.4 feet

    B: 22.9 feet   D: 27.48 feet

54. A cleaning service pays an employee $90 for a particular job. If the employee earns $15 per hour, how many hours did she work?

    A: 5 hours   C: 6 hours

    B: 5.5 hours   D: 10 hours

55. The state sales tax is 7.15%. What is the total cost for a purchase that costs $20 pre-tax?

    A: $1.43   C: $22.53

    B: $21.43   D: 26.33

56. A stock-person just received a shipment of 126 cans of paint that need to be displayed. If each shelf holds 9 cans, how many shelves will he need to display all of the paint?

    A: 9 shelves   C: 16 shelves

    B: 14 shelves   D: 32 shelves

57. A plumbing service representative wants to know the average number of phone calls that she receives. At work that day, she records that she received 104 phone calls between the hours of 9:00 a.m. to 5:00 p. m. What is the average number of phone calls she received per hour?

    A: 13 calls/hr   C: 20 calls/hr

    B: 15 calls/hr   D: 8 calls/hr

58. A telemarketer figures that 1 in every 16 calls results in a sale of her company's product. She needs 12 sales to make her bonus. If her next shift is 8 hours straight, how many phone calls per hour will she need to make in order to reach her bonus goal?

    A: 16   C: 12

    B: 24   D: 48

59. A store is currently having a sale where every faucet is 30% off the original price. A customer wants to purchase a faucet that was originally priced at $24.90. What is the new sale price?

    A: $7.47   C: $16.60

    B: $8.30   D: $17.43

60. A customer buys two hand saws for $37.50 each. Sales tax is 8%. If the customer pays with a hundred dollar bill, how much change should the customer get?

    A: $19.00   C: $81.00

    B: $25.00   D: $54.00

EXAM 12

Math

61. Teresa is following the directions for mixing cement. According to the directions, she needs 13 gallons of water for the amount of cement mix she is using. She has a container that measures liters only. If 1 gallon = 3.8 liters, how many liters will she need?

    A: 3.4 L   C: 39.0 L

    B: 494 L   D: 49.4 L

62. Edmund is doing repairs on a house and needs to cut a square in the wall for an intercom. Each side of the square needs to be 18 cm. If 1 inch = 2.54 centimeters, how many inches is each side? (Round to the nearest tenths place)

    A: 7.1 in   C: 7.8 in

    B: 9.0 in   D: 45.7 in

63. Mishka took a water measurement that read 174 milliliters. All of his records need to be in liters. Based on the 174 milliliters reading, how many liters should he record?

    A: 174 L   C: 1.74 L

    B: 0.174 L   D: 0.0174 L

64. Tess works at a hardware store and is helping a customer who wants to buy two yards of rope. If the price of the rope is $0.75 per foot, what is the total cost to the customer?

    A: $1.50   C: $4.30

    B: $3.00   D: $4.50

65. Horatio is asked by his supervisor to consolidate three bins of sand into one. The first bin has 5 lbs 6 oz of sand, the second has 7 lbs 12 oz, and the third has 14 lbs 4 oz. After he puts all the sand into one bin, what is the total weight of the sand? (1 pound = 16 ounces)

    A: 26 lbs 6 oz   C: 28 lbs 2 oz

    B: 27 lbs 6 oz   D: 27 lbs 12 oz

66. To calculate her fee, an electrician uses the expression $30n where n is the number of hours worked. What is her fee if she works 3 hours?

    A: $33   C: $60

    B: $90   D: $27

67. To calculate profit, P, a retailer uses the formula P = I - E. If the income, I, is $3,500 and the expenses, E, are $1,700, what is the profit?

    A: $5,200   C: $800

    B: $1,800   D: $2,200

Math

68. A wholesale retailer is having a store-wide sale. Every item is 10% off its original price. If p = the original price, which expression below represents the sale price of each item?

    A: p - 0.10p

    B: p + 0.10p

    C: 0.10p

    D: p + 0.10

69. A post is needed for every four feet of fencing. Which expression can be used to calculate the number of posts needed to fence a rectangular area if f is the number of feet of fencing?

    A: f + 4

    B: f - 4

    C: f × 4

    D: f/4

70. Joon is in charge of ordering bulk fertilizer for landscaping. He purchases fertilizer on a weekly basis but recently switched vendors and needs to recalculate his order for the upcoming week. He estimates that they use 8 lbs of fertilizer each day (they are operating 6 days a week). The new vendor only sells fertilizer in 20 lb containers. According to his estimate, what is the minimum number of containers Joon must order in order to guarantee he has enough fertilizer for the week?

    A: 3 containers

    B: 4 containers

    C: 5 containers

    D: 6 containers

71. A supply company charges 15% of the total bill for delivery. Which expression represents the delivery charge on a total bill, t?

    A: 15 + t

    B: 0.15 + t

    C: 0.15t

    D: 15t

72. Long distance phone calls cost ten cents for the first minute plus four cents for each additional minute. Which expression below represents the cost of a phone call in cents? Let m equal the total number of minutes.

    A: m + 40

    B: 10 + 4(m - 1)

    C: 10m + 4m

    D: (10 + m)(4 + m)

73. Rick works at a paint supply store and has been instructed to set up a sale display with canned paint. Each can weighs 4/5 lb. A sign on the shelf warns that each shelf cannot support more than 30 lbs of weight. What is the maximum number of cans that Rick can place on a shelf without exceeding the weight limit?

    A: 37 cans

    B: 38 cans

    C: 30 cans

    D: 25 cans

Math

74. A shipping company charges $2.95 for the first 2 pounds and then $0.30 for every ounce over 2 pounds. The cost for shipping a package is found using the formula $C = $2.95 + $0.30w, where w is the number of ounces over 2 pounds. What is the cost to ship a package that weighs 2 pounds 14 ounces?

    A: $3.09   C: $7.15

    B: $2.14   D: $4.55

75. A painter must paint the walls of a room that measures 12 feet by 15 feet. The ceiling of the room is 8 feet high. Each gallon of paint costs $25.50 and covers 300 square feet of wall. How much will the paint cost him assuming that the painter will paint only one coat on each wall?

    A: $105.50   C: $65.00

    B: $75.50   D: $51.00

76. Joe needs to deliver a washing machine across town. The company truck can travel 65 mph on the highway, which comprises 13 miles of his trip. For the remaining 12 miles, Joe will average 24 mph. Assuming he does not hit traffic, at what time must Joe leave the warehouse in order to arrive at his destination by 1:30 p.m.

    A: 1:00 p.m   C: 12:50 p.m.

    B: 12:55 p.m.   D: 12:48 p.m.

77. Whiz-Bang Construction can construct a 1,400 ft2 home for $20,000. Smitheo Building can construct a 2,200 ft2 home for $28,000. DJK Builders can construct a 2,500 ft2 home for $35,000. If a contractor is looking for a construction company to construct 2,800 ft2 homes in a new subdivision, and uses the most economical of the three construction companies, approximately how much will the construction of each home in the subdivision cost? Round your answer to the nearest thousand dollars.

    A: $36,000   C: $40,000

    B: $35,000   D: $39,000

78. How many drills, costing $58 each, can be purchased with $854?

    A: 13   C: 15

    B: 14   D: 16

79. At a nursery there are baby palm trees on sale for $135 each. How much will it cost to purchase six baby palm trees?

    A: $675   C: $840

    B: $810   D: $945

80. If a parking lot is 3/4 full, what is the fraction represented as a percent?

    A: .75%   C: 25%

    B: 3.4%   D: 75%

Math

81. Decorative light switches are sold individually for $1.45 each, or sold in packages of 20 for $26.50. If 36 new switches are needed, what is the best combination to purchase?

    A: 2 packages of 20   C: 36 individual switches

    B: 1 package of 20 and 16 individual   D: 20 individual switches and 1 package of
       switches   20

82. Mark completed 1/6 of his weekly hours of work on Saturday and then 2/5 of his hours on Sunday. What fraction of his hours has he finished?

    A: $3/11$ C: $2/30$

    B: $1\,7/30$ D: $1\,7/11$

83. A cleaning company charges a flat fee of $25/house. There is an additional cost of $4.50 per room, with the first room included in the flat fee. What is the total charge for cleaning two houses that have seven rooms each?

    A: $52   C: $113

    B: $104   D: $175

84. A equipment rental company is offering a 20% discount for customers during the week. If the weekday price quote was $35, what is the weekend price?

    A: $42.00   C: $55.00

    B: $43.75   D: $57.14

85. A cylindrical tank is 10 ft tall with a diameter of 4 ft. What is the potential volume of the tank?

    A: 40 cu. ft.   C: 62.8 cu. ft.

    B: 54.5 cu. ft.   D: 125.6 cu. ft.

86. Jeff is paid double rate for hours worked over his required 50 hours/week. What is his regular hourly wage if he made a total of $1,244.25 for a 64.5 hour work week?

    A: $15.75/hour   C: $16.85/hour

    B: $16.45/hour   D: $19.29/hour

87. A small business owner has saved up a substantial amount of money to invest. He has $15,000 and would like to invest 40% of the money into a fund that returns 12% annually and the rest of the money in bonds that return 7% annually. How much money has he earned at the end of a year?

    A: $1,350   C: $1,500

    B: $1,425   D: $16,350

Math

88. Mike, Steve, and DJ are contractors with a total of 440 clients between them. Steve has 3/8 the number of clients Mike has, and DJ has three times the number Steve has. How many clients does DJ have?

   A: 176

   B: 183

   C: 198

   D: Not enough information.

89. A staircase with stairs is being constructed in a new house. Each stair case has a ratio of 3:7 for the height and depth respectively. If each stair is 15 inches deep, what is the height of the entire staircase?

   A: 7.5 feet

   B: 9.3 feet

   C: 17.5 feet

   D: 90 feet

90. An equipment rental company charges $45/week and an additional 5 cents/mi. Which equation would calculate the weekly rental cost? (C = cost, m = miles)

   A: C = 75 + 5m

   B: C = .05m + 45

   C: C= 45m + .05

   D: C = 5(m + 45)

EXAM 12

Answers: Math

1. **Answer C.** $229.97

   To find the total bill, add up the cost of the items for a total of $229.97, $12.56 + $141.08 + $76.33 = $229.97

2. **Answer B.** .11

   To switch from percentages to decimals, divide the percentage by 100, $11\frac{1}{100}$ = .11. You can also move the decimal point two places to the left.

3. **Answer A.** 600 m2

   Note: m^2 = sq. meter. The pebble walkway is acting like a border around the pool. There is now a larger rectangle around the pool with an additional 5 m on each side, 2.5 + 2.5 = 5. If you find the area of the larger rectangle and subtract away the area inside, you are left with the area of the border. It is almost like cutting out the middle of the big rectangle.

   The area of the large rectangle is:

   3,400 m^2, l × w = A, 85 × 40 = 3,400.

   The area of the pool is only 2,800 m^2, 80 × 35 = 2,800.

   Subtract the two areas to find that the walkway is

   600 m^2, 3,400 - 2,800 = 600.

4. **Answer B.** 25.5 ft.

   This is a problem disguised with confusing information. The 2:5 ratio must be held in a proportion similar to this, where × represents the real height of the house:

   $\frac{2}{5}$ = 10.2/x; 2x = 51;x = 25.5

5. **Answer C.** 28

   To find out how many are left, subtract the original amount by the amount that was sold: 37 - 9 = 28.

6. **Answer B.** $29.44

   The customer has been overcharged by $7.80, so subtract this mistake from the total bill:

   $37.24 - $7.80 = $29.44.

7. **Answer A.** Option 1

   For a customer who only talks 140-155 minutes, Option 1 would only cost $7 per month. Option 2 would cost the same customer between $9.80 and $10.85:

   $.07 × 140 = $9.80 and .$07 × 155 = $10.85.

   For someone who talks between 140-155 minutes per month, Option 1 is a better deal.

8. **Answer B.** 7 rooms

   Find out how many rooms Lacey can clean in one hour and add it together with how many rooms Maria can clean in one hour. The total time to clean is 1 hour = 60 minutes.

   Lacey can clean 4.29 rooms, 6⁰⁄₁₄ = 4.29.

   Maria can clean 3.16 rooms, 6⁰⁄₁₉ = 3.16.

   When you add their efforts together they can clean 7.45 rooms, but because it asks for complete rooms, you must round down to 7 rooms.

9. **Answer C.** $20.93

   To find out how much Martha Earns in an hour, divide the total money by the hours to find out "money per hour":

   $376.8⁰⁄₁₈ = $20.93.

10. **Answer D.** $822.00

    There are 12 months in a year and $68.50 is held each month for the government. To find the total for the year, multiply the cost each month by 12 to represent an entire year:

    12 × $68.50 = $822.

11. **Answer C.** 420

    The total number of pieces can be represented,

    6x + 3x +x = 1,400 because of the ratio that is held.

    6x represents the number of 6-foot pieces, 3x represents the number of 6-foot pieces, and × represents the number of 12-foot pieces. Combine like terms to get,

    10x = 1,400, sox = 140.

    Therefore, there are 3(140) = 420 eight-foot pieces.

12. **Answer C.** $1,699.35

    The water heater is marked up 15% from

    $1,850, $1,850 × 1.15 = $2,127.50,

    and then discounted 25%,

    $2,127.50 × .75 = $1,595.63.

    The last piece is to add the tax,

    $1,159.63 × .065 = $103.72,

    To the total price, $1,595.63 + $103.72 = $1,699.35.

13. **Answer D.** $84.65

    Matt needs a profit of $3,870 and he has purchasing costs of :

    $2,900, 100 × $29 = $2,900

    For a total of $6,770 that he needs to collect from sales. He is guaranteed to sell at least 80 faucets, so the money should be distributed among the 80 faucets by dividing $6,770/80 = $84,625, and rounding up to the nearest penny. Even though the exact value is not on the list, choose the price that is close and a little above to guarantee the profit.

14. **Answer C.** $864

    When multiple items are purchased for the same price, simply use multiplication, $48 × 18 = $864.

15. **Answer B.** $33.46

    Calculating change requires subtraction. Take the money the customer gives and subtract the total bill, $50 - $16.54 = $33.46.

16. **Answer A.** 300 in3

    Volume is calculated by multiplying the length, height, and width together. The new length is 10", 16 - 3 - 3 = 10. The height is determined by the squares that are removed, 3". The volume is 300 in3, 3 × 10 × 10 = 300.

EXAM 12

17. Answer C. 8.33 lbs

When mixing products together to end up with a new product, you must take into account the contribution of the parts. Aggregate cost $5.25/lb, but we do not know how many pounds, x, are being mixed, so aggregate can be represented by 5.25x The pre-made mixture costs $3.25/lb and there are 5 lbs of it, so the mixture can be represented by 3.25(5). These first two parts are being added together to make a new mixture worth $4.50/lb, and there will be a total of 5 + x lbs in the end (pre-made mixture + aggregate). So (5 + x) 4.50 = 5.25x + 3.25 (5). Solving for x, x = 8.33.

18. Answer D. 21 boards

Take the total distance and divide it by the length of the board, $32^2/_{16}$ = 20.125, and then you will need to round up to 21. Twenty boards is not enough because it only covers, 20 × 16 = 320, 320 linear feet.

19. Answer B. 356 gallons

The tank was $^2/_5$ empty, which means it was $^3/_5$ full,

$1 - ^2/_5 = ^5/_5 - ^2/_5 = ^3/_5$.

$^3/_5$ of the total capacity is equal to 310 gallons so the capacity of the tanker is 516.7 gallons

$(^3/_5)x = 310$

$x = 310 × ^5/_3, x = 516.7$.

The first stop took $^2/_9$ of the original 310 which means 241.1 gallons remain,

$^2/_9 × 310 = 68.9$,

$310 - 68.9 = 241.1$.

The next stop took $^1/_3$ of the remaining 241.1 gallons, resulting in 160.7 gallons left over,

$^1/_3 × 241.1 = 80.4 = 160.7$.

For the fill up at the end, the truck will need **356 gallons**,

$516.7 - 160.7 = 356$.

20. Answer D. $242

To figure out the painter's total service charge, multiply her hourly rate, $35/hr and the number of hours she worked, 6 hours;

$35/hr × 6 hours = $210.

Take this total and add the cost of the paint $32;

$210 + $32 = $242.

21. Answer C. 8

The length of the plot is 60 yards. Convert this to feet by multiplying by 3. The length of the plot is 180 feet. Break this up into 20 foot sections, since each tree must be 20 feet apart; $18^0/_{20}$ = 9 sections. Make a picture of the plot of land with the trees drawn in to determine the maximum number of trees. There can be a maximum of 8 trees, since each tree must be 20 feet from the edge.

22. Answer C. 3.2 feet

Subtract the length of the shelf, 5.6 ft, from the total length of the wall, 12 ft, in order to find out how much extra wall space there is; 12 ft - 5.6 ft = 6.4 ft. Since the shelf has to be centered, the extra 6.4 ft. must be distributed evenly on either side; 6.4 ft/2 = 3.2 ft must be left on each side of the shelf.

23. Answer C. 9 hrs

Add up the various stages in order to figure out the total amount of time he must spend per tree;

20 min + 120 min + 40 min = 180 min or 3 hrs.

It takes him 3 hours per tree and he has 6 trees to trim;

6 trees × 3 hrs/tree = 18 hrs total.

He has 2 days to accomplish 18 hrs of work;

18 hrs/2 days = 9 hrs/day.

24. Answer B. 1,000 centimeters

If there are 100 centimeters in 1 meter, than to find how many centimeters are in 10 meters, multiply 100 by 10;

100 cm/m × 10 m = 100 centimeters.

25. Answer D. 128 in

To calculate the perimeter, add up all four sides of the rectangle. The length of the frame will be the length of the poster, 32 in, plus two more inches on each side;

32 in + 2 in + 2 in = 36 in.

The width of the frame is the width of the poster, 24 in, plus two inches on each side;

24 in + 2 in + 2 in = 28 in.

To find the perimeter add the two widths and two lengths together;

28 in + 28 in + 36 in + 36 in = 128 in.

26. Answer C. 1350 sq. cm

The total surface area is 1,350 sq. cm. Find the surface area of one side and then multiply by six because a cube has six equal faces. The surface area of one side is 225,

15(2) = 15 × 15 = 225, for a total of 1,350, 6 × 225 = 1,350.

27. Answer D. a circle

A circle will provide the largest area. In order to find the area of the circle, you must find the radius using the circumference (perimeter), which is 12.73 ft,

C = 3.14 × 2 × r, 80 = 3.14 × 2 × r;

r = 12.

73. The area of a circle is calculated by A = 3.14r(2), giving a total of 509.8 sq. ft. If a square shape were built, the sides would be 20 × 20 (8%/4 = 20) giving an area of only 400 sq. ft., 20 × 20 = 400. Playing around with numbers for a rectangle will show that the area would not be able to exceed the circle.

EXAM 12

Answers: Math

28. Answer C. 1,152

Convert the values to a single unit. There are 3 ft in a yd, so 2 yds × 3 ft/yd = 6 feet, and 4 yds × 3 ft/yd = 12 feet. Now, convert feet to inches. There are 12 inches per 1 foot, so 6 feet × 12 in/ft = 72 in, and 12 feet × 12 in/ft = 144 in. Therefore, the patio is 72 inches by 144 inches. To figure out the area of the patio, multiply the length times the width;

72 in × 144 in = 10,368 sq.

in. The surface area of each tile is 3" × 3" = 9 sq. in. Divide the total surface area of the patio by the surface area of an individual tile to figure out how many tiles are needed. Thus, 10,368 sq. in./9 sq. in. = 1,152 tiles.

29. Answer A. 12,500 pounds

Multiply 25 by the area of the lawn, 500 square feet;

25 × 500 = 12,500; 12,500 pounds are needed.

30. Answer B. $634

Replace s with $2,200. The equation becomes

E = 0.22 × 2,200 + 150.

The rules for order of operations state that multiplication is always done before addition, Therefore, complete the multiplication,

0.22 × 2,200 = 484,

first, then add 150 to the result;

484 + 150 = $634.

31. Answer A. E = IR

To solve I = E/R for E, multiply both sides of the equation by R. The Rs cancel each other out on the right side of the equation, so the equation becomes IR = E. The equation can be flipped around to become E = IR, which is Answer A..

32. Answer B. 4

Divide the size of the walkway, 50 cubic feet, by the amount that each bag makes, 15 cubic feet;

5%₁₅ = 3.3.

A little over 3 bags are needed to fill the walkway.

Therefore, 4 bags need to be purchased.

33. Answer A. 10 feet

The formula for the perimeter of a rectangle is P = l + l + w + w. Since the two lengths add up to 30, the two widths must add up to 20 to make the perimeter of 50. Since the two widths are the same they must each be 10 feet.

34. Answer A. 6 feet by 6 feet

Answer D. can be eliminated because the dimensions do not make a perimeter of 24 feet, 10 + 10 + 14 + 14 = 48. The other choices do make a perimeter of 24 feet. Determine which dimensions create the greatest area by multiplying the length by the width;

6 × 6 = 36, 8 × 4 = 32, and 2 × 10 = 20.

Therefore a 6-foot by 6-foot pen has the greatest area.

35. Answer C. $7.50

To find the cost per grinder, divide the total cost, $900, by the number of grinders, 120;

$900 ÷ 120 = $7.50.

36. Answer B. 545 minutes

With both pipes working, the pool is being filled at a rate of 11 gallons per minute, 5 gallons/minute + 6 gallons/minute = 11 gallons/minute. Now, divide the total amount of gallons in the pool, 6,000, by the rate, 11 gallons/minute;

6,000 ÷ 11 = 545.45.

Round to the nearest minute, 545 minutes.

37. Answer A. the 44-ounce bottle

The first cleaner costs $2.75 for 44 ounces. Since the cost per ounce is needed, divide $2.75 by 44 to get about $.0625 per ounce, or about $.06 per ounce. The second cleaner costs $3.70 for 55 ounces;

$3.70 ÷ 55 = $.067 per ounce,

or about $.07 per ounce. Therefore, the first cleaner is the better buy because it is cheaper per ounce.

38. Answer C. 6 hours

Take the total time allowed, 40 hours, and subtract the time already used,

9 + 6.5 + 8 + 10.5 = 34,

to find the leftover time, 40 - 34 = 6.

39. Answer B. 19.1 meters

When converting from feet to meters (smaller unit, larger unit), divide the total feet by 3.28, 62.7/3.28 = 19.1 meters.

40. Answer B. 16

To find out how many people are applying for each job, divide the total number of applicants by the total number of positions available, 6¼ = 16.25, which rounded to the nearest whole number is 16.

41. Answer B. $33

To find the profit, subtract the amount the company pays its worker, $42, from the total money charged, $75, to result in $33, $75 - $42 = $33.

42. Answer B. $7,857.50

Find out what 3.5% of 224,500 is by multiplying the two numbers, remembering to divide the percentage by 100, 224,500 × 3.5⁄100 = 7,857.50.

43. Answer C. 90%

The fraction ¹⁄₁₀ is the same as 10%, ¹⁄₁₀ × 100 = 10%. 10% is the amount that is used; so 90% is available,

100% - 10% = 90%.

44. Answer D. 91.7%

The number of undamaged bricks is 133, 145 - 12 = 133. To find the percentage available, divide the number of available bricks by the total number that were sent and multiply by 100 to get a percentage, 133/145 × 100 = 91.7%.

EXAM 12

45. **Answer B.** $1.29

The invoice weighs 4.2 oz. The first ounce is covered in the initial charge of $.37 and the rest of the 3.2 ounces must be calculated with the additional charge. For postage they round up to the next ounce so the 3.2 ounces rounds up to 4 ounces. An additional 4 ounces will cost $.92,

  4 × $.23 = $.92.

The total cost is $.37 + $.92 = $1.29.

46. **Answer B.** 5 boxes of cans and 3 boxes of baffles

Find the smallest number of boxes for each part. 22 cans are needed and are sold in sets of 5, so 5 boxes are necessary, 5 × 5 provides 25 cans. 22 baffles are also needed and they are sold in sets of 8, so only 3 boxes are necessary, 3 × 8 provides 24 baffles. It is okay to have different amounts of each, as long as there are enough supplies for the job.

47. **Answer B.** $31.86

To calculate the tax, multiply the cost, $30, by the decimal value of the tax, .062, and add that to the original item, $30 × .062 = $1.86 + $30 = $31.86. You are not just trying to find out the tax, but how much it costs altogether.

48. **Answer C.** 36%

32 chainsaws are being delivered the next day, so 18 are still unaccounted for, 50 - 32 = 18. Calculate the percentage out of 50 that these 18 chainsaws represent, 18/50 × 100 = 36%.

49. **Answer B.** 544

Use the conversion to calculate;

  if 1 lb = 16 oz, then multiply 34 by 16 to find the total number of 544 oz, 34 × 16 = 544.

If each nail weighs 1 oz, there are 544 nails in a 34 lb box.

50. **Answer B.** $291,000

First find the number of tractors that will have a discounted price, ⅔ of the 291 tractors is 194,

  ⅔ × 291 = 194.

Each car will be discounted $1,500 for a total discount of $291,000, 194 × $1,500 = $291,000.

51. **Answer B.** $155.30

The guests are refunded $13.20, which means it must be subtracted from their bill, $168.50 - $13.20 = $155.30;

  $155.

30 is the new charge.

52. **Answer D.** 80%

The first step is to find out what ⅘ is as a decimal, ⅘ = .8. A decimal can be converted to a fraction by multiplying it by 100,

  8 × 100 = 80; 80%.

53. **Answer B.** 22.9 feet

To convert inches into feet you must divide by 12 because there are 12 inches for every foot, 274.8/12 = 22.9;

  22.9 ft.

54. **Answer C.** 6 hours

In order to find out how many hours she worked, divide the total amount paid by the hourly wage, 90/15 = 6; 6 hours.

55. **Answer B.** $21.43

The tax for this purchase is calculated by multiplying the pre-tax price by the percent of tax written in decimal form;

  $20 × 0.0715 = $1.43.

Then, add the tax to the original sales amount for the total,

  $20 + $1.43 = $21.43;

  $21.43 is the total.

56. **Answer B.** 14 shelves

Since each shelf can hold 9 cans, divide 126 by 9; 126/9 = 14.

57. **Answer A.** 13 calls/hr

The first step is to figure out how many hours the representative worked. 9:00 a.m. to 5:00 p.m. is 8 hours. In order to find the average number of calls per hour, divide the total number of calls, 104, by the number of hours worked, 8 hours; 104/8 = 13 calls/hr.

58. **Answer B.** 24

Since the telemarketer has to make 16 calls in order to achieve 1 sale, multiply the number of sales she needs by 16;

  12 sales × 16 calls/sale = 192 calls.

She has 8 hours to make 192 calls. Divide 192 by 8 in order to figure out the number of calls per hour;

  192 calls/8 hours = 24 calls/hr.

She has to make an average of 24 calls per hour in order to make the bonus goal.

59. **Answer D.** $17.43

Translate _____ is 30% of $24.90 into an equation:

  y = 30 × $24.90.   Solve: y = $7.47,

which represents the 30% savings. In order to find the new price of the faucet, subtract the 30% savings, $7.47, from the original price, $24.90;

  $24.90 - $7.47 = $17.43.

60. **Answer A.** $19.00

Figure out the subtotal cost of the two hand saws;

  $37.50 × 2 = $75.

To calculate the tax, translate _____ is 8% of $75 into an equation:

  y = .08 × $75.   Solve y = $6

which represents the 8% tax. In order to find the total cost of the sweaters, add the 8% tax, $6, to the original price, $75;

  $75 + $6 = $81.

To figure out the customer's change, subtract the total, $81, from the amount of cash given, $100;

  $100 - $81 = $19 change.

EXAM 12

61. **Answer D.** 49.4 L

There are 3.8 L per 1 gallon. To figure out how many liters Teresa will need for her mix, convert gallons to liters by multiplying 13 gal × 3.8 L/gal = 49.4 L.

62. **Answer A.** 7.1 in

To calculate inches, divide 18 cm by 2.54 cm/in;

18 cm/2.54 = 7.0866 inches.

Rounding to the tenths place, 7.0866 = 7.1 inches.

63. **Answer B.** 0.174 L

There are 1,000 milliliters in 1 liter. To calculate how many liters 174 milliliters are, divide 174 by 1,000;

174 mL/1,000 mL/L= 0.174 L.

64. **Answer D.** $4.50

First convert yards to feet. Since there are 3 ft. in a yard, the customer wants to buy 6 ft of rope: 2 yds × 3 ft/yd = 6 ft. Multiply 6 ft by the cost of rope per foot to get the total price;

6 ft × $0.75/ft = $4.50.

65. **Answer B.** 27 lbs 6 oz

To find the total weight, add up the pounds and ounces seperately. The sum of the pounds is 5 lbs + 7 lbs + 14 lbs = 26 lbs. Next, add the ounces from each bin,

6 oz + 12 oz + 4 oz = 22 oz.

Since there are 16 oz in 1 lb, 22 oz is equal to 1 lb and 6 oz. Add this number to the total pounds from the first step;

26 lbs + 1 lb 6 oz = 27 lbs 6 oz.

66. **Answer B.** $90

Replace n with 3. Complete the multiplication:

$30 × 3 = $90.   Her fee is $90.

67. **Answer B.** $1,800

Replace I with $3,500 and E with $1,700 and subtract;

$3,500 - $1,700 = $1,800.

68. **Answer A.** p - 0.10p

Subtract 10% of the original price, p, from the original price. To find 10% of the original price, multiply the decimal equivalent of 10%, 0.10, by the original price, p, 0.10p. Subtract this amount from the original price, p - 0.10p.

69. **Answer D.** f/4

Since a post is needed for every four feet of fencing, divide the number of feet of fencing, f, by four to find the number of posts needed. The expression is f/4.

70. **Answer A.** 3 containers

The landscaping uses 8 lbs of fertilizer per day. They are operating 6 days a week, so to find the amount of fertilizer they use in a week, multiply 8 lbs/day × 6 days/wk = 48 lbs/wk. Since the fertilizer is sold in 20 lb containers, Joon needs to buy 3 containers to cover them for a week, even though there may be 12 lbs left over.

71. **Answer C.** 0.15t

Multiply the total bill, t, by the decimal equivalent of 15%, 0.15. This expression is 0.15t.

72. **Answer B.** 10 + 4(m - 1)

The cost of a phone call is ten cents plus four cents multiplied by one less than the total number of minutes (the first minute costs ten cents, so it is not multiplied by four cents). This translates into 10 + 4(m - 1); m - 1 is in parentheses because it must be calculated before multiplying by four cents.

73. **Answer A.** 37 cans

First, start by converting ⅘ to a decimal;

4 ÷ 5 = 0.8.

Since each can weighs 0.8 lbs and the shelf can hold 30 lbs, divide 30 by 0.8 to calculate how many cans can be placed;

30 lbs/0.8 lbs/can = 37.5 cans.

Since you can't put 0.5 of a can on the shelf, the maximum number of cans that can be set on the shelf without exceeding the 30 pound weight limit is 37 cans.

74. **Answer C.** $7.15

Replace w with 14 since the package weighs 14 ounces over 2 pounds. The formula is then $C = $2.95 + $0.30 × 14. The order of operations states that multiplication is always done before addition. Multiply $0.30 by 14;

$0.30 × 14 = $4.20, then add the result to $2.95;

$2.95 + $4.20 = $7.15.

75. **Answer D.** $51.00

Find the area of the four walls. Two of the walls are 15 feet by 8 feet. The other two walls are 12 feet by 8 feet;

15 × 8 = 120 square feet; 12 × 8 = 96 ft².

The total area of the walls in the room is 120 + 120 + 96 + 96 = 432 square feet. Next, find the number of gallons of paint that must be purchased. Each gallon covers 300 square feet, so two gallons will be needed. Last, calculate the cost of those two gallons of paint;

2 × $25.50 = $51.00.

76. **Answer D.** 12:48 p.m.

For the highway portion of the trip. Joe will average 65 mph for 13 miles. Since 13 is ⅕ of 65, this portion of the trip will take Joe ⅕ of an hour, or 12 minutes. For the remaining 12 miles of the trip, Joe will average 24 mph. Since 12 is half of 24, this portion of the trip will take half an hour or 30 minutes. The total time will be 12 minutes + 30 minutes = 42 minutes. To arrive by 1:30 p.m., Joe must leave no later than 12:48 p.m. since 1:30 p.m. - 42 minutes = 12:48 p.m. Therefore, the correct answer is 12:48 p.m.

EXAM 12

77. **Answer A.** $36,000

The 1,400 ft² home costs about $14.29 per ft²:

$20,000 ÷ 1,400 square feet = $14.29 per ft².

The 2,200 ft² home costs about $12.23 per ft²:

$28,000 ÷ 2,200 square feet = $12.73 per ft².

The 2,500 ft² home costs about $14 per ft²:

$35,000 ÷ 2,500 square feet = $14 per ft².

The cheapest price per ft² is $12.73 by Smithco. If this company is hired to construct 2,800 ft² homes, it will cost $35,644 per home:

2,800 square feet times $12.73 per ft² = $35,644.

Rounded to the nearest thousand, the answer is $36,000.

78. **Answer B.** 14

Take the total money and divide it by the cost to find out how many can be purchased, $854/$58 = 14.72. For this problem you must round down to 14 drills. If you try to purchase 15 drills the total bill will be too high, 15 × $58 = $870.

79. **Answer B.** $810

For multiple items, take the cost per item and multiply it by the number of items purchased, $135 × 6 = $810.

80. **Answer D.** 75%

To convert from a fraction to a percent, simply multiply the fraction by 100 and simplify, ¾ × 100 = 30¾ = 75%.

81. **Answer B.** 1 package of 20 and 16 individual switches

One package and 16 individual switches costs $49.70,

$26.50 + 16($1.45) = $26.50 + $23.20 = $49.70.

The first option, 2 packages, costs

$53.00, 2 × $26.50 = $53.

Purchasing 36 individual switches is not economical and costs

$52.20, 36 × $1.45 = $52.20.

The last option has too many switches and also costs more,

20 × $1.45 + $26.50 = $29 + $26.50 = $55.50.

82. **Answer B.** 1⁷⁄₃₀

Take the fractions that Mark has already worked and add them together by finding a common denominator,

⅙ + ⅖ = 1(5)/30 + 2(6)/30 = (5 + 12)/30 = 1⁷⁄₃₀.

83. **Answer B.** $104

The final calculation is for two houses, so it may be easier to find out how much it costs to clean one house and then double it at the end. One room in the house costs $25 so the additional six rooms will cost $27, 6 × $4.50 = $27, so the total for one house is $52, $25 + $27 = $52. We are trying to find the cost for two houses, so by doubling the cost for one house we find the total cost is $104, $52 × 2 = $104.

84. **Answer B.** $43.75

If a discount of 20% is offered, then the $35 quote represents 80% of the original price,

100% - 20% = 80%.

Translate the following information into an equation to solve: 80% of the original price equals $35. Use p as the original price and solve the equation;

8⁰⁄₁₀₀ × p = $35; .80p = $35; .80p/.80 = $35/.80;

p = $43.75.

85. **Answer D.** 125.6 cu. ft.

The volume of a cylinder is the area of the base, a circle, times its height. The diameter is 4 ft. so the radius is 4 ft./2 = 2 ft. The area of the base is pi times r(2), or approximately

3.14 × (2 ft) (2) = 12.56 sq. ft.

The volume = area of base × height = 12.56 sq. ft. × 10 ft = 125.6 cu. ft.

86. **Answer A.** $15.75/hour

Let Jeff's regular rate be y and his overtime rate be 2y. He worked a total of 64.5 hours, so he worked his regular 50 hours plus 14.5 hours of overtime, 64.5 hrs - 50 hrs = 14.5 hrs. The money he earned from the regular week is time × rate, which is represented by

$50y, 50 × $y = $50y.

The money he earned from overtime work is also time × rate, which is $29y,

14.5 × $2y = $29y.

His regular salary plus overtime gives the total and can be written as $50y + $29y = $1,2445.25. Solve for y: $79y = $1,2445.25;

$79y/79 = $1,244.2⁵⁄₇₉;

$y = $15.75/hour.

87. **Answer A.** $1,350

There is $15,000 to invest, 40% of which is invested at 12%;

40% of $15,000 is $6,000, .

40 × 15,000 = 6,000, so the remainder of the money is $9,000, $15,000 - $6,000 = $9,000. To find the interest made, multiply the money invested by the rate that is given. For the $6,000 the rate is 12%, so the money returned is $720, .12 × $6,000 = $720, and for the $9,000 the rate is 7%, so the money returned is

$630, .07 × $9,000 = $630.

To find the total money earned, simply add the interest earned from each, $720 + $630 = $1,350.

88. **Answer C.** 198

This problem is simplified when an equation is used. Use x to represent the number of clients Mike has, (⅜)x to represent Steve's clients, and 3(⅜)(x) to represent the clients for DJ. The total number of clients is 440, so add them up and solve for x.

EXAM 12

89. **Answer A.** 7.5 feet

There are 14 stairs with a ratio of 3:7. The total depth is 210 in, 14 × 15 = 210 and using a simple proportion will help find the height. $3/7 = x/10$;

$7x = 3(210)$; $(7x)/7 = 63\%$; $x = 90$.

90 inches is the same as 7.5 ft, $9\%_{12} = 7.5$.

90. **Answer B.** C = .05m + 45

To find the cost of renting equipment, start with the weekly rate, $45, and add that to the additional cost of the miles traveled. There is a charge of 5 cents per mile, and since we have m miles in this problem, .05m represents the additional charge. Make sure to put 5 cents into dollar form so that all the information is in the same unit, the weekly charge is already in terms of dollars so it is easier to transfer everything into dollars. The total charge is found by adding the parts together 45 +.05m.

State of California
Department of Industrial Relations

OFFICE OF THE LABOR COMMISSIONER

PUBLIC WORKS MANUAL

California Labor Commissioner Julie A. Su

May 2018

DEPARTMENT OF INDUSTRIAL RELATIONS
Headquarters Office

455 Golden Gate Avenue, 9th Floor
San Francisco, CA 94102
Tel: (415) 703-4810 Fax: (415) 703-4807

MAILING ADDRESS:
P. O. Box 420603
San Francisco, CA 94142-0603

Julie A. Su
California Labor Commissioner
Office of the Labor Commissioner

May 2018

It is with great pride that the Office of the Labor Commissioner releases this updated Public Works Manual. This Manual has been revised to reflect the most recent changes in prevailing wage laws, including:

- Enhanced penalties for violations of Public Works Contractor Registration requirements, including penalties on awarding agencies who use unregistered contractors and the power of the Labor Commissioner to issue a stop order (SB 96); and

- Additional streamlining of investigative tools and processes to effectively combat prevailing wage theft while educating the public and law-abiding contractors to create a more level playing field and promote economic justice for the middle-class.

This Manual is designed to be used by the Labor Commissioner's Office to ensure consistent, timely, and accurate enforcement of the law statewide and is also intended as an educational tool for our public works stakeholder community.

My gratitude and acknowledgement for their hard work and tremendous expertise go to the following staff, who have brought this updated Manual to fruition: Acting Assistant Chief Susan Nakagama and the Legal Unit's Tom Fredericks, Bill Snyder, Luong Chau, and Lance Grucela.

I hope you find this useful.

Julie A. Su
State Labor Commissioner

Table of Contents

1. Introduction .... - 1 -
  1.1 .... - 1 -
2. Who Does the Law Protect? .... - 2 -
  2.1 "Workers", Defined: .... - 2 -
  2.2 Statutory References To Workers "Employed" On Public Works, Explained: .... - 2 -
  2.3 Title or Status of Worker Irrelevant. .... - 3 -
  2.4 "Public Works" Defined: .... - 4 -
    2.4.1 .... - 4 -
    2.4.2 .... - 4 -
    2.4.3 .... - 5 -
    2.4.4 .... - 5 -
  2.5 "Public Funds" Defined: .... - 5 -
    2.5.1 .... - 6 -
    2.5.2 Federally Funded or Assisted Projects. .... - 6 -
  2.6 Director's Authority To Determine Coverage. .... - 6 -
  2.7 Posted Public Works Coverage Determinations. .... - 7 -
    2.7.1 Coverage Determinations are Project-Specific. .... - 8 -
  2.8 Exclusions From Prevailing Wage Requirements. .... - 8 -
    2.8.1 Volunteers. .... - 8 -
    2.8.2 Public Agency's Own Forces. .... - 9 -
    2.8.3 Janitorial Services. .... - 9 -
    2.8.4 Guards. .... - 10 -
    2.8.5 Landscape Maintenance Work At 'Sheltered Workshops.' .... - 10 -
  2.9 Chartered Cities. .... - 10 -
  2.10 University Affairs. .... - 11 -
3. What Must Public Works Contractors Do To Comply With the Law? .... - 12 -
  3.1 Contractors' Obligations To Maintain and Furnish Records: .... - 12 -
    3.1.1 Payroll Records Must be Certified: .... - 13 -
    3.1.2 Statement of "Employer Payments" .... - 13 -
    3.1.3 Payroll Records, Defined: .... - 14 -
    3.1.4 Itemized Statements. .... - 14 -
    3.1.5 Requests For Certified Payroll Records ("CPRs"). .... - 15 -
    3.1.6 Contractors' Obligation To Electronically Submit Certified Payroll Records ("eCPRs"). .... - 15 -
    3.1.7 Responses To Inspection Requests. .... - 17 -
    3.1.8 Responses To Requests For Copies. .... - 18 -
    3.1.9 Costs, Limited Reimbursement To Contractors and Public Agencies. .... - 19 -
    3.1.10 CPR Privacy Concerns. .... - 19 -
    3.1.11 Two Exceptions: .... - 19 -
    3.1.12 Full Social Security Numbers Required. .... - 20 -
    3.1.13 Retention of Payroll Records by Public Works Contractors. ... - 21 -
  3.2 Contractors' Obligations To Pay Prevailing Wage Rates: .... - 21 -
    3.2.1 "Prevailing Rate of Per Diem Wages," Defined: .... - 21 -
    3.2.2 Director's Authority to Determine Prevailing Wage Rates. ..... - 22 -
    3.2.3 Issue Date / Effective Date. .... - 22 -

3.2.4   Effective Date / Bid Advertisement Date. ....- 22 -

3.2.5   Expiration Date / Double Asterisk / Predetermined Increases. ....- 23 -

3.2.6   Expiration Date / Single Asterisk. ....- 23 -

3.2.7   Overtime. ....- 24 -

    3.2.7.1   Worker Performing Work During The Same Workday In Two Or More Different Classifications With Different Rates Of Pay..- 24 -

    3.2.7.2   Worker Performing Work On Public and Private Projects During the Same Workday With Different Rates of Pay. ....- 25 -

3.3   Contractors' Obligations To Comply With Apprenticeship Standards. ....- 26 -

3.3.1   Three Overall Categories Of Apprenticeship Violations. ....- 27 -

    3.3.1.1   Failure To Submit Contract Award Information / Violations. ....- 28 -

    3.3.1.2   Failure to Submit Contract Award Information / Penalties.................- 30 -

    3.3.1.3   Minimum Ratio Violations. ....- 31 -

    3.3.1.4   Affirmative Defense to Minimum Ratio Violations. ....- 32 -

3.3.2   Apprenticeship Violations Which Also Result In Prevailing Wage Underpayments. ....- 33 -

    3.3.2.1   Unregistered Apprentices. ....- 34 -

    3.3.2.2   Nonpayment Of Training Fund Contributions. ....- 35 -

    3.3.2.3   Maximum Ratio Violations...- 35 -

    3.3.2.4   Journeyman On Duty Violations..- 36 -

4.   The Labor Commissioner's Prevailing Wage Enforcement Process. ....- 37 -

4.1   Calculation of Wages Due. ....- 37 -

4.1.1   Travel and Subsistence Requirements. ....- 38 -

4.1.2   "Scope of Work" Provisions Published by the DIR...................................- 39 -

4.1.3   Factual Disputes Concerning the Type of Work Performed. ....- 40 -

4.1.4   Different Classifications For the Same Worker. ....- 40 -

4.1.5   Compensable Travel Time. ....- 42 -

4.1.6   Calculation of Overtime and Saturday/Sunday/Holiday Wages..................- 42 -

    4.1.6.1...- 43 -

4.1.7   Exceptions to Overtime Requirements. ....- 43 -

    4.1.7.1   Exception 1:...- 43 -

    4.1.7.2   Exception 2:...- 44 -

    4.1.7.3   Exception 3:...- 44 -

    4.1.7.4   Exception 4:...- 44 -

4.1.8   Restriction on Alternative Workweek Schedules: ....- 44 -

4.1.9   Saturday Make-Up Days:..- 45 -

4.2   Credit for Employer Payments. ....- 45 -

4.2.1   Employer Payments Are A Credit Against The Obligation To Pay The General Prevailing Wage Rate Of Per Diem Wages..- 45 -

4.2.2   No Reduction of the Basic Hourly Rate. ....- 47 -

    4.2.2.1   Example:..- 47 -

    4.2.2.2   Different for Purely Federal Projects Under Davis-Bacon Act...........- 48 -

4.2.3   Application to All Hours Worked. ....- 48 -

    4.2.3.1   Example:..- 49 -

4.2.4   Types of Employer Payments for Which An Employer May Take a Credit Against Its Prevailing Wage Obligations..- 50 -

    4.2.4.1   Types Of Benefits Which Do Not Constitute Employer Payments:......- 50 -

4.2.5. "Employer Payments" Defined: .... - 51 -

4.2.5.1 .... - 51 -

4.2.5.2 Irrevocably Made to a Trustee or Third Person Pursuant to a Plan, Fund, or Program .... - 51 -

4.2.5.2.1 Employer Payments made to these types of plans must be made regularly. - 52 -

4.2.5.2.2 Employer Payments Must Be Determined Separately For Each Worker. ... - 52 -

4.2.5.2.3 Vesting Does Not Normally Affect Right to Credit. .... - 52 -

4.2.5.3 Employer Payments That Are Reasonably Anticipated to Benefit Workers. - 53 -

4.2.5.3.1 Example. .... - 53 -

4.2.5.4 Payments to the California Apprenticeship Council. .... - 53 -

4.2.5.4.1 Includes Payments Made to An Approved Apprenticeship Program. .... - 54 -

4.2.5.4.2 Training Contributions Not Paid to the Worker. .... - 54 -

4.2.5.4.3 Exception - Non-Apprenticeable Crafts. .... - 54 -

4.2.6. Annualization. .... - 54 -

4.2.6.1 Exceptions: .... - 55 -

4.2.6.2 .... - 55 -

4.2.6.3 Annualization Calculation. .... - 56 -

4.2.6.4 Representative Period. .... - 56 -

4.2.6.4.1 Example: .... - 56 -

4.2.6.5 Payments To The California Apprenticeship Council Pursuant To Section 1777.5.. - 58 -

4.3 Calculation of Labor Code § 1775 Penalties. .... - 59 -

4.3.1.1 Limited Prime Contractor Safe Harbor. .... - 60 -

4.4 Calculation of Labor Code § 1813 Penalties. .... - 62 -

4.5 Calculation of Unpaid Training Fund Contributions. .... - 62 -

4.6 Determination of Hours Worked and Amounts Paid. .... - 62 -

4.6.1 Releases Signed By Workers As Proof Of Amounts Paid. .... - 62 -

4.7 Civil Wage and Penalty Assessments ("CWPAs"). .... - 63 -

4.7.1 Service of the CWPA / Statute of Limitations / Tolling. .... - 63 -

4.8 Administrative Review of CWPAs. .... - 64 -

4.8.1 Role of DIR / OD-Legal. .... - 64 -

4.8.2 Prevailing Wage Hearing Regulations. .... - 65 -

4.8.3 Settlement Meetings and Settlements. .... - 65 -

4.8.4 Liquidated Damages. .... - 66 -

4.9 CWPAs Which Become Final / Collection From Awarding Body / Judgments. - 67 -

4.10 Debarment. .... - 67 -

4.10.1 Debarment Investigations. .... - 68 -

4.10.2 Posting of Debarment Orders. .... - 68 -

4.11 The Labor Commissioner's Jurisdiction to Enforce California's Prevailing Wage Laws is Not Exclusive. .... - 68 -

4.11.1 Action by Joint Labor-Management Committee. .... - 70 -

4.11.2 Worker's Private Right of Action. .... - 70 -

4.11.3 Third Party Beneficiary. .... - 70 -

4.12   Industrial Welfare Commission (IWC) Wage Order 16-2001. ....- 71 -

4.12.1   Referral of Wage Order Violations to BOFE..................................- 71 -

5.   The Labor Commissioner's Role in Prevailing Wage Enforcement by Labor Compliance Programs ("LCPs"). ....- 71 -

5.1   Forfeitures Requiring Approval by the Labor Commissioner. ....- 72 -

5.2   Determination of Amount of Forfeiture by the Labor Commissioner. ....- 73 -

5.3   Director's Authority to Approve / Revoke LCPs. ....- 74 -

6   Public Works Reforms (SB854). ....- 75 -

6.1   SB96. ....- 75 -

6.1.1   Penalties Assessed Against Unregistered Contractors. ....- 76 -

6.1.2   Penalties Assessed Against Contractors That Employ Unregistered Subcontractors. ....- 76 -

6.1.3   Stop Orders Issued to Unregistered Contractors.....................................- 76 -

6.1.4   Awarding Bodies Must Ensure that the Contractors Utilized on Public Works Projects Are Registered. ....- 77 -

6.1.5   Awarding Body's Ineligibility to Receive State Funding or Financial Assistance....- 77 -

6.1.6   "Small Project Exception". ....- 78 -

ADDENDUM 1...i

ADDENDUM 2...iii

ADDENDUM 3..v

1.   **Introduction**

1.1

This Public Works Manual is designed as a training tool for the Division of Labor Standards Enforcement ("Labor Commissioner Office") staff to better understand the Labor Commissioner's functions in carrying out its responsibilities to conduct investigations and undertake enforcement actions under the Public Works Chapter of the California Labor Code (LC § 1720-1861). Those statutory provisions are collectively referred to in the Manual as the prevailing wage laws. The Manual relies in part on judicial and administrative decisions whenever case-specific resolutions of legal issues are available. It is not intended as a comprehensive summary of existing law or duly promulgated regulations, or a pronouncement of the Labor Commissioner's enforcement policies, with regard to prevailing wage compliance. Rather, the purpose of the Manual is to familiarize staff assigned to prevailing wage enforcement with processes and historical issues which have arisen, and may continue to arise, as investigations are conducted and enforcement actions are initiated, and administratively reviewed, under the statutory scheme. To the extent the Manual's text might be viewed as purporting to establish rules of general application, but fails to present interpretations as a restatement or summary of existing laws, regulations or judicial and administrative decisions, it is invalid and should not be relied upon for that purpose. The Manual's text, standing alone, is therefore not binding on the enforcement activities of the Labor Commissioner, or the Department of Industrial Relations ("DIR"), in subsequent proceedings or litigation, or on the courts when reviewing DIR proceedings under the prevailing wage laws.

2.   **Who Does the Law Protect?**

2.1   "**Workers", Defined:**

Except for public works projects of one-thousand dollars ($1,000) or less, Labor

Code § 1771 requires that "all workers employed on public works" be paid at not

less than the "general prevailing rate of per diem wages." Labor Code § 1772

provides that workers employed "by contractors or subcontractors in the

execution of any contract for public work" are deemed to be so employed. Labor

Code § 1723 defines a worker as including "a laborer, worker, or mechanic." A

standard dictionary definition of a "worker" is a "person engaged in a particular

field or activity." (Random House Dictionary of the English Language) The issue

presented in the prevailing wage context is the inclusiveness of the term

"workers." In *Lusardi Construction Co. v. Aubry* (1992) 1 Cal. 4th 976, 987, the

California Supreme Court interpreted section 1771 and found that "By its express

terms, this statutory requirement is not limited to those workers whose employers

have contractually agreed to pay the prevailing wage; it applies to 'all workers

employed on public works.'" This interpretation is consistent with the U.S.

Department of Labor's position (41 U.S. Op. Atty. Gen. 488) that any individual

who personally performs skilled or unskilled labor in construction work is

protected under the Davis-Bacon Act (40 U.S.C. § 276(a), the federal prevailing

wage law) even though he or she is not an "employee." These authorities support

the position that protected workers under Labor Code § 1771 include not only

employees, but also extends to other workers performing work covered by the

prevailing wage laws.

2.2   **Statutory References To Workers "Employed" On Public Works, Explained**:

Labor Code §§ 1771 and 1772 refer, respectively, to workers "employed" by

contractors or subcontractors "in the execution of any contract for public work" or

"employed" on public works. Courts long ago recognized that "employed" may mean several things including, for example, a person whose services are "utilized" in furtherance of the business of another, notwithstanding the technical absence of an employer-employee relationship, or a person "engaged in" a task for another under contract, or orders to do it. (*Johnston v. Farmers Mutual Exchange of Calhoun, Inc.*, 218 F. 2d 588 (5th Cir. 1955); *United States v. Morris* (1840) 39 U.S. 463, 475.) These authorities, likewise, support the position that prevailing wage requirements are not limited to employees of a contractor or subcontractor. Moreover, public works contractors may not avoid the prevailing wage requirement by "contracting out" all or a portion of the work performed to subcontractors. In *O. G. Sansone v. Department of Transportation* (1976) 55 Cal.App.3[d] 434, 463, the Court explained that the prevailing wage laws apply to "all" workers employed on public projects, and that the legislation cannot be "frustrated" because of the subcontracting of work required to be done under the terms of the prime contract.

2.3   **Title or Status of Worker Irrelevant**.

A worker's title or status with the employer is not determinative of an individual's coverage by the prevailing wage laws. What is determinative is whether the duties performed by the individual on a public works project constitute covered work. An individual who performs skilled or unskilled labor on a public works project is entitled to be paid the applicable prevailing wage rate for the time the work is performed, regardless of whether the individual holds a particular status such as partner, owner, owner-operator, independent contractor or sole proprietor, or holds a particular title with the employer such as president, vice-president, superintendent or foreman. For example, a "working" foreman or a "working" superintendant – one who performs labor on the project in connection with supervisorial responsibilities – is entitled to compensation at not less than the prevailing rate for the type of work performed. Of course, if the person holding

- 3 -

the status or titles as listed above does not actually perform covered work on a project, his or her presence alone does not trigger the prevailing wage requirement.

2.4   **"Public Works" Defined**:

Labor Code §§ 1720-1720.6 contain within their provisions all of the basic facts and conditions which must be present for a work of improvement to fall within the statutory definition of "public works." If those facts and conditions do not exist, the statutory enforcement mechanism available to the Labor Commissioner under Labor Code § 1741 cannot be used to recover unpaid wages or penalties authorized by the prevailing wage laws. It is therefore necessary for staff to determine at the earliest possible stage of assignment to an investigation whether the required facts and conditions appear to be present. The four separate statutory sections identify four somewhat different scenarios which comprise the public works model:

2.4.1

Labor Code § 1720(a) defines public works as construction and other enumerated construction-related tasks (including "maintenance," see LC § 1771) done under contract and paid for in whole, or in part, with public funds. Maintenance is defined at 8 CCR § 16000.

2.4.2

Labor Code § 1720.2 extends the public works definition to include construction work done under private contract if (1) the construction contract is between private persons, and (2) the property subject to the construction is privately owned, but more than 50 percent of the assignable square feet of the property is leased to the state or a political subdivision thereof, and either (1) the lease was entered into prior to the construction contract, or (2) the lease was entered into before completion of the construction if the work was performed according to plans or criteria furnished by the state.

2.4.3

Labor Code § 1720.3 extends the public works definition to the hauling of refuse from a public works site to an outside disposal location. The Director has opined in a web-posted Public Works Coverage Determination (see Section 2.7 of this Manual) that "refuse" is defined as "the worthless or useless part of something," and that if, for example, dirt excavated from trenches dug for a public works contract is being put to a useful purpose, such as the covering of garbage at a landfill, it would not be considered "refuse" under those circumstances. (Public Works Case No. 2001-005 (Trash/Debris Removal from Railroad Rights-of-Way and Facilities, Blue and Green Lines).)

2.4.4

Labor Code § 1720.6 extends the public works definition to private contracts to include construction, alteration, demolition, installation, or repair work done under private contract if (1) the work is performed in connection with the construction or maintenance of renewable energy generating capacity or energy efficiency improvements, and (2) is performed on the property of the state or a political subdivision thereof, and either (1) 50 percent of the energy generated is purchased by the state or political subdivision thereof, or (2) the efficiency improvements are primarily intended to reduce energy costs that would otherwise be incurred by the state or political subdivision.

2.5

"Public Funds" Defined:

Labor Code § 1720(b) defines at some length what the statutory language "paid for in whole or in part out of public funds" means. The six examples of public funds are listed specifically at Labor Code § 1720(b), subdivisions (1)-(6), and are

May 2018

not limited to the payment of money (subd. (b)(1)) by the state or a political subdivision directly to a public works contractor. The five other categories include work performed (subd. (b)(2)) by the state or political subdivision; transfer of an asset (subd. (b)(3)) for less than fair market price; fees or costs reduced, waived, or forgiven (subd. (b)(4)) by the state or political subdivision; money loaned (subd. (b)(5)) by the state or political subdivision to be repaid on a contingent basis; and credits applied (subd. (b)(6)) by the state or political subdivision against repayment obligations.

2.5.1

Public funds include state, local and/or federal monies. (8 CCR § 16000.)

2.5.2

Federally Funded or Assisted Projects.

State prevailing wage rates when higher are required whenever federally funded or assisted projects are controlled or carried out by California awarding bodies of any sort. The state prevailing wage laws cannot be applied to a project, however, which is under the complete control of the federal government. (8 CCR § 16001(b); *Southern Cal. Labor Management Committee v. Aubry* (1997) 54 Cal.App.4th 873, 886.)

2.6

Director's Authority To Determine Coverage.

The California Code of Regulations authorizes the Director of the Department of Industrial Relations to determine coverage under the prevailing wage laws regarding either (1) a specific project or (2) type of work to be performed. (8 Cal. Code of Regs § 16001(a) (1).) The Director's authority to determine coverage of projects under the prevailing wage laws is quasi-legislative, and a final determination on any appeal is subject to judicial review pursuant to California Code of Civil Procedure section 1085. (8 Cal. Code Regs § 16002.5(c).) The Director's determination in any specific inquiry brought forth under the DIR's

May 2018

regulatory coverage process (8 CCR §§ 16001-16002.5) is subject to judicial review. The Labor Commissioner is not required to file with the Director a request to determine coverage under the regulatory process before proceeding with its investigations, although it is not precluded from doing so. Under circumstances where the Labor Commissioner issues a Civil Wage and Penalty Assessment ("CWPA") before any coverage determination dealing with that same project has been requested, any affected contractor or subcontractor may timely request a review hearing to contest a CWPA under Labor Code § 1742, and a claim that either the project or the type of worked performed was not subject to the prevailing wage laws may be raised in the administrative review proceedings. (See Sections 4.7 – 4.9 for specifics on CWPAs.)

2.7   **Posted Public Works Coverage Determinations**.

The DIR posts on the DIR website, letters and decisions on administrative appeal issued by the Director in response to requests to determine coverage under the prevailing wage laws made pursuant to 8 CCR § 16000(a). The determinations are indexed by date and project, as compiled by DIR staff. The Director's Office of Policy, Research, and Legislation ("OPRL") maintains this portion of the website, and the determinations can be accessed by clicking on the topic <u>Public works coverage determinations</u>, which is listed on the OPRL homepage. The rates may also be accessed from the public works page on the Labor Commissioner's website. Investigators typically review any applicable determinations as a research tool and for general guidance when confronted with factual situations which may raise issues of whether a particular project or type of work is subject to, or excluded from, coverage under the Labor Code.

2.7.1   **Coverage Determinations are Project-Specific**.

Beginning in 2001, the Director designated certain coverage determinations as "precedential" under Government Code § 11425.60. Pursuant to § 11425.60, only those coverage determinations designated by the Director as precedential could be specifically relied upon by the DIR in making future coverage determinations. In 2007, as a result of case law developments, the Director decided to no longer rely upon § 11425.60 and ceased designating any public works coverage determinations as precedential. Thereafter, the coverage determinations are considered by the DIR to be advice letters directed to specific individuals or entities about whether a specific project or type of work is public work subject to prevailing wage requirements. According to the DIR, the coverage determination letters present the Director's interpretation of statutes, regulations and court decisions on public works and prevailing wage coverage issues, and provide advice current only as of the date each letter is issued. See Department of Industrial Relations' Important Notice to Awarding Bodies and Interested Parties Regarding The Department's Decision to Discontinue Use of Precedent Determinations at http://www.dir.ca.gov/OPRL/Notices/09-04-2007(pwcd).pdf.

2.8   **Exclusions From Prevailing Wage Requirements**.

At least five specially defined categories of work are excluded from prevailing wage requirements, either under the Labor Code itself, or duly promulgated regulations.

2.8.1   **Volunteers.**

Labor Code § 1720.4 provides that the prevailing wage laws do not apply to work performed by a "volunteer." "Volunteer" is defined as "an individual who performs work for civic, charitable, or humanitarian reasons, for a public agency or

May 2018

corporation qualified under Section 501(c)(3) of the Internal Revenue Code as a tax-exempt organization, without promise, expectation, or receipt of any compensation for work performed." (Labor Code § 1720.4(a)(1).) The exclusion does not apply to work performed by anyone other than those persons specifically falling within the definition. Pressure or coercion, direct or implied, from an employer, or any form of compensation for work performed results in the loss of volunteer status. (Labor Code § 1720.4(a)(1)(A) and (B).) Additionally, a volunteer may not be employed for compensation at any time in the construction, alteration, demolition, installation, repair, or maintenance work performed on the same project. (Labor Code § 1720.4(a)(1)(C).) However, an individual may receive reasonable meals, lodging, transportation, and incidental expenses or nominal nonmonetary awards without losing volunteer status if, in the entire context of the situation, those benefits and payments are not a substitute form of compensation for work performed. (Labor Code § 1720.4(a)(1)(B).)

2.8.2   **Public Agency's Own Forces**.

Labor Code § 1771 expressly provides that the prevailing wage requirement is "not applicable to work carried out by a public agency with its own forces." (See also *Ramirez v. Yosemite Water Co.* (1999) 20 Cal.4th 785, 794.) The California Attorney General has opined that the public agency exclusion for its own forces applied to actual "employees" of a county, and there is no published judicial decision which extends the exclusion to non-employees. (35 Op.Atty.Gen. 1.) As with all specific exemptions from a minimum wage law, exclusionary language must be narrowly construed.

2.8.3   **Janitorial Services**.

The definition of "maintenance" found at 8 CCR § 16000 requires payment of wages at the prevailing rate and includes a variety of specific examples of work related to the "preservation, protection and keeping of publicly owned or publicly operated" facilities. The prevailing wage requirement does not apply, however, to "[j]anitorial services of a routine, recurring or usual nature." (8 CCR § 16000.) This exception to the prevailing wage requirements applies to routine and recurring janitorial services, such as washing, vacuuming, litter removal, etc. at a public facility. The exclusion does not apply to non-routine clean-up which, for example, might occur during, or at the conclusion of, a public works construction project.

2.8.4   **Guards.**

The "maintenance" definition also excludes from the prevailing wage requirements "[p]rotection of the sort provided by guards, watchmen, or other security forces." (8 CCR § 16000.)

2.8.5   **Landscape Maintenance Work At 'Sheltered Workshops.'**

The "maintenance" definition also excludes this particular and unique type of work from the prevailing wage requirements. "Sheltered workshop" is defined as a nonprofit organization, licensed by the Labor Commissioner, employing mentally and/or physically disabled workers. (8 CCR § 16000.)

2.9   **Chartered Cities.**

Under Article XI, Section 5 of the California Constitution, a "chartered city" may exempt those of its public works projects which are completely within the realm of the chartered city's "municipal affairs" from the requirements of the prevailing wage laws. (*City of Pasadena v. Charleville* (1932) 215 Cal. 384.) Cities in California are classified as "general law cities" (organized under the general laws of the state) or "chartered cities" (organized under a charter). (Govt. Code §§ 34100, 34101, 34102.) There are approximately 120 California cities organized

May 2018

under a charter. The courts have identified three factors in evaluating whether a particular public works project is a "municipal affair" of a chartered city, or a matter of statewide concern. If the project would be viewed as a statewide concern, the prevailing wage requirements will apply. (*So. Cal. Roads Co. v. McGuire* (1934) 2 Cal.2d 115.) The factors to be considered are: (1) the extent, if any, of extra-municipal control over the project; (2) the source and control of the funds used to finance the project; and (3) the nature and purpose of the project. (Public Works Case No. 2006-016.) It should also be noted that the California Supreme Court has held that consideration of these judicially created factors for determining whether a project is a matter of statewide concern for prevailing wage purposes cannot be ignored merely because the Legislature expresses its own view in legislative enactments that prevailing wages constitute a matter of statewide concern. (*State Building and Construction Trades v. City of Vista* (2012) 54 Cal. 4th 574.) Although application of the factors in any particular investigation is fact driven, and interpretation of the judicially created factors has historically been the source of much litigation, the Labor Commissioner will typically review prior coverage decisions of the Director dealing with the topic in reaching a conclusion whether the exemption applies or not. A straightforward example of when the exemption was properly claimed is found on the OPRL website in Public Works Case No. 2006-016 (New Public Library, City of Lindsay.)

2.10 **University Affairs.**

This limited exemption from the prevailing wage laws is applicable only to public works of improvement awarded by the Regents of the University of California. In some respects similar to the chartered city exemption for municipal affairs (see Section 2.9 of this Manual), Article IX, section 9 of the California Constitution grants the Regents powers of government as to its internal "university affairs" and not involving statewide concern. (*San Francisco Labor Council v. Regents of*

University of California (1980) 26 Cal.3d. 785.) The exemption was not recognized in the case of *DLSE v. Ericsson Information Systems, Inc.* (1990) 221 Cal.App.3d 114), where the court concluded that the protection afforded private sector employees working on the University's public construction projects was a "matter of statewide concern." The decision reached in *Regents v. Aubry* (1996) 42 Cal.App.4th 579, however, specifically allowed the exemption when the University contracted with private companies to build subsidized married student and faculty/staff housing on university-owned land, holding that such a project was part of the University's core educational function, rather than a statewide concern. In instances in which the limited exemption is claimed to exist, the Labor Commissioner will make a determination based upon application of the case law to the specific facts in the matter. If the University's bid documents or contract for the work requires the payment of prevailing wage, the Labor Commissioner will conclude that the exemption does not exist and enforce the prevailing wage requirements.

3.   **What Must Public Works Contractors Do To Comply With the Law**?

Contractors and subcontractors which bid on and are awarded public works projects must comply with three general obligations which are enforced by the Public Works Unit of the Labor Commissioner's Office. The three categories of obligations are set forth in detail below.

3.1   **Contractors' Obligations To Maintain and Furnish Records**:

Labor Code § 1776(a) requires each public works contractor and subcontractor to keep accurate payroll records, including the name, address, social security number, work classification, straight time and overtime hours worked each day and week, and the actual wages paid to each worker. The "work classification" refers to the craft classification (or type of work performed) as fixed by the

Director and specified by title on the prevailing wage determinations published and maintained by the OPRL. (Labor Code § 1773 and 8 CCR § 16203.) Payroll records which do not identify the Director's specified title (e.g., records which only identify a worker by status, such as "journeyman" or "apprentice" or "partner," and do not refer to the Director's published classification, such as "Laborer Group 1" or "Carpenter") are inadequate. Payroll records shall be on forms provided by the Labor Commissioner or in a manner containing the same information as the forms provided by the Labor Commissioner. This form (DIR Form A-1-131) is available on the Labor Commissioner's website in the Public Works/prevailing wage section. The payroll records may consist of printouts that are maintained as computer records so long as the printouts contain the same information as the forms. The required certification language is also on the Labor Commissioner's website.

3.1.1   **Payroll Records Must be Certified**:

Labor Code § 1776(b) requires that payroll records, as defined above, shall be "certified," that is, verified by written declaration made under penalty of perjury, that the information contained in the records is true and correct. (8 CCR § 16000.) The certification language is found on the back of the form furnished by the Labor Commissioner. Payroll records furnished to Labor Commissioner which are not certified are inadequate.

3.1.2   **Statement of "Employer Payments"**.

The prevailing wage laws permit contractors employing workers on public works to pay a certain portion of the "Total Hourly Rate" reflected on the applicable prevailing wage determination published by the Director, either in cash to workers, or as contributions to specified plans or entities as "Employer Payments" Labor Code § 1773.1(b) and (c), as defined at 8 CCR § 16000 The Labor

Commissioner developed a form (see website for Form PW 26) to simplify both the preparation by contractors of the required information and the Labor Commissioner's review of that information. (See Section 4.2.5, following).

3.1.3   **Payroll Records, Defined**:

California regulations define Payroll Records to mean "[a]ll time cards, cancelled checks, cash receipts, trust fund forms, books, documents, schedules, forms, reports, receipts or other evidences which reflect job assignments, work schedules by days and hours, and the disbursement by way of cash, check, or in whatever form or manner, of funds to a person(s) by job classification and/or skill pursuant to a public works project." (8 CCR § 16000.) The Labor Commissioner may request a contractor to produce any such payroll records to assist the Labor Commissioner in determining whether the contractor paid its workers all wages due.

3.1.4   **Itemized Statements**.

Labor Code § 226, although not part of the prevailing wage laws, requires all employers to regularly furnish each of his or her employees with an accurate itemized statement, in writing, including up to nine separate categories of information. Labor Code § 226 itemized statements fall within the broad definition of "payroll records," and must be made available for inspection by the Labor Commissioner upon request. (NOTE: Employers who fail to keep or furnish itemized statements to their employees are subject to civil and criminal penalties in accordance with the provisions found at Labor Code §§ 226-226.6. Penalties available under those sections are not enforced by the issuance of a Civil Wage and Penalty Assessment, but through a citation procedure set forth in detail at sections 226.4-226.5. Investigators who encounter violations of section 226 should proceed in accordance with those sections, which are entirely distinct from the remedies available under the Public Works Chapter, which is the subject of this Manual.)

3.1.5   **Requests For Certified Payroll Records ("CPRs").**

Labor Code § 1776(b)(2) requires contractors and subcontractors to make a certified copy of all payroll records as enumerated in Labor Code § 1776(a) available for inspection or furnished to the Labor Commissioner, upon the Labor Commissioner's written request, to be provided within ten days of the contractor's receipt of that request. Failure to timely "file" (furnish) the requested records subjects the contractor, or affected subcontractor, to monetary penalties. (Labor Code § 1776(d) and (h).) The Labor Commissioner developed a form letter entitled "Request For Certified Payroll Records" (Form PW 9) which constitutes the statutorily required written request and sets forth the penalties for noncompliance. The form letter typically requests CPRs for all workers employed by a named contractor or subcontractor for the entire duration of work performed on the project identified. Blank copies of DIR Form A-1-131 and Form PW 26 are enclosed with the form letter. The request should be mailed (first class and certified mail, return receipt requested) and/or sent electronically (facsimile or e-mail). Satisfactory evidence (certified mail receipt, facsimile confirmation, or e-mail receipt) reflecting the date of receipt by the contractor will be needed to calculate monetary penalties assessed for noncompliance.

3.1.6   **Contractors' Obligation To Electronically Submit Certified Payroll Records ("eCPRs").**

Labor Code Section 1771.4 was added to the Public Works Chapter by the Legislature as part of the Public Works Reforms contained in SB854 which became effective on June 20, 2014. Labor Code Section 1771.4(a)(3) requires each contractor and subcontractor to furnish "the records specified in Section 1776 directly to the Labor Commissioner." This obligation exists independently of

May 2018

any written request from the Labor Commissioner. Rather, the legislation requires that the records shall be furnished at least "monthly or more frequently if specified in the contract with the awarding body" (Section 1771.4(a)(3)(A)), and in "a format prescribed by the Labor Commissioner" (Section 1771.4(3)(B)). The format prescribed by the Labor Commissioner is found on the Labor Commissioner's website, and specifies that contractors and subcontractors must electronically submit certain payroll information by following the specific on-line instructions. The legislation was designed to enhance the Labor Commissioner's ability to evaluate compliance with prevailing wage requirements. (Section 1771.4(a)(3)(4).) The Labor Commissioner is now able to monitor (on an ongoing basis and without the need for a written request for payroll records or a formal investigation) whether contractors and subcontractors at least appear to be in compliance with the prevailing wage laws, based solely upon the eCPRs submitted. Electronic submission of Certified Payroll Records ("eCPRs") was also designed to complement the on-line registration of public works contractors now required by SB854's Public Works Reforms. The on-line submission of eCPRs also enables contractors and subcontractors to provide this short format of payroll information with keystrokes, rather than preparing and delivering written documents. It is extremely important for contractors and subcontractors to understand that submission of certain payroll information electronically is a requirement separate and distinct from the obligation already found in Labor Code Section 1776(d) "to file a certified copy of the records with the entity that requested the records enumerated in subdivision (a) [of Section 1776] within 10 days after receipt of a written request" for such records. So there can be no confusion, all contractors must comply with both requirements. Thus, a contractor that has electronically furnished eCPRs is not excused from timely furnishing to the Labor Commissioner "a certified copy of all payroll records" within 10 days after receipt of such a written request.

May 2018

Conversely, a contractor that provides payroll records in response to a written request from the Labor Commissioner is not excused from continuing to furnish eCPRs on an ongoing basis. There are at least two reasons why this is so. First, eCPRs do not contain, and were neither intended nor designed to contain, all of the payroll information and records which may be required for a contractor to comply with written requests by the Labor Commissioner for payroll records made pursuant to Labor Code Section 1776(d). According to the provisions of the California Code of Regulations (specifically, 8 CCR 16401(b)), "the format for reporting of payroll records requested pursuant to Labor Code Section 1776" is a form identified in the regulation as the "Public Works Payroll Reporting Form" (Form A-1-131) which is available at any of the Labor Commissioner's Offices throughout the state. Additionally, the Labor Commissioner includes Form A-1-131 in all written requests for certified payroll records. The regulation also provides: "Acceptance of any other format shall be conditioned upon the requirement that the alternate format contain all of the information required pursuant to Labor Code Section 1776." As noted above, the prescribed format for eCPRs does not include all of this information. The information not available in eCPRs but which is required in Form A-1-131 submissions includes: work classifications, gross amounts earned each week, itemized deductions or contributions for federal taxes, state taxes, state disability insurance, vacation or holiday pay, health and welfare benefits, pension, union dues, if any, travel and subsistence, and savings.

3.1.7   **Responses To Inspection Requests**.

While the Labor Commissioner is authorized to inspect a certified copy of CPRs at all reasonable hours, at the principal office of the contractor or subcontractor (Labor Code § 1776(b)(2)), investigators typically do not request inspection. Rather, copies of CPRs are routinely requested to be furnished instead.

3.1.8   **Responses To Requests For Copies**.

The deadline for contractors or subcontractors to furnish the requested copies of CPRs is within ten days after receipt of a written request. (Labor Code § 1776(d).) The statutory language does not specify "calendar" or "working" days, however, 8 CCR § 16000 defines "days" as calendar days unless otherwise specified. Labor Code § 1776(c) permits contractors to use copies of payroll records or printouts of payroll data, so long as the documents furnished contain the same information as the forms provided by the Labor Commissioner, and the records are certified in the manner specified at 8 CCR § 16000. If the documentation furnished does not meet both of these requirements, the contractor or affected subcontractor is subject to monetary penalties under Labor Code § 1776(h). Computation Example: The first penalty day is the calendar date after the ten day response period has expired. The last penalty day is the calendar date upon which the tardy CPRs are received by the Labor Commissioner. The assessment is calculated by multiplying the total number of penalty days times the number of workers listed on the tardy CPRs, times $100.00. If no CPRs are produced, the last penalty day is the date a Civil Wage and Penalty Assessment assessing penalties under Labor Code § 1776 is served, and the number of workers is estimated based upon the best evidence available. In the event a contractor fails to timely comply with a request for CPRs, including any follow-up request for additional underlying payroll records listed in the definition of "payroll records" found at 8 CCR 16000 (i.e., "All time cards, cancelled checks, cash receipts, trust fund forms, books, documents, schedules, forms, reports, receipts or other evidences which reflect job assignments, work schedules by days and hours, and the disbursement by way of cash, check, or in whatever form or manner, of funds to a person(s) by job classification and/or skill pursuant to a public works project"), the penalty will continue beyond the date of

May 2018

service of the CWPA and "until strict compliance is effectuated." (See, Labor Code section 1776(h).)

3.1.9   **Costs, Limited Reimbursement To Contractors and Public Agencies**.

The Labor Commissioner has no statutory or regulatory obligation either to pay contractors or affected subcontractors for requested copies of CPRs as a precondition to compliance with a Labor Commissioner-initiated request for CPRs, or to reimburse contractors for any expenses incurred. Recovery of costs for preparing or furnishing CPRs are only available to contractors (or public entities) under 8 CCR § 16402, a regulation which applies only if the request for CPRs was made by the "public" pursuant to Labor Code § 1776(b)(3). That statutory subdivision, when read in conjunction with that regulation, sets forth with specificity the timing and amounts of costs for reproduction of CPRs available to contractors and public entities (including the Labor Commissioner).

3.1.10   **CPR Privacy Concerns**.

Labor Code § 1776(e) mandates special handling of CPRs obtained by the Labor Commissioner and two other public entities -- awarding bodies and the Division of Apprenticeship Standards ("DAS") – who are also statutorily authorized to request CPRs from public works contractors. Before making CPRs available for inspection as copies, and furnished upon request to the public or any other public agency pursuant to Labor Code § 1776(b)(3), CPRs obtained by staff must be "marked or obliterated to avoid disclosure" of workers' names, addresses and social security numbers. That same obligation is set forth at 8 CCR § 16403.

3.1.11   **Two Exceptions**:

The first exception applies to copies of CPRs furnished to a "joint labor-management committee" established pursuant to the Federal Labor Management

Cooperation Act of 1978 (29 U.S.C. § 175(a)). The redaction of personal information from copies of CPRs provided to those specially authorized joint labor-management committees is <u>limited to the workers' social security numbers only</u>. The workers' addresses are not to be obliterated. (Labor Code § 1776(e).) The second exception applies to agencies that are included in the Joint Enforcement Strike Force on the Underground Economy established pursuant to California Unemployment Insurance Code section 329, and other law enforcement agencies investigating violations of law. These particular agencies are entitled to be provided with copies of certified payroll records <u>without any redaction</u> of names, addresses, and social security numbers. However, any copies of such records received by these law enforcement agencies made available for inspection or furnished to the public by these agencies must be redacted to prevent disclosure of an individual's name, address, and social security number. (Labor Code § 1776(f)(1).)

3.1.12 **<u>Full Social Security Numbers Required</u>.**

Labor Code § 226(a), which sets forth certain record keeping requirements for employers, limits an employer's obligation to provide only the last four digits of employees' social security numbers. Labor Code § 1776(a) has not been so amended and requires the inclusion of the full social security number. For enforcement purposes, however, it should not be considered as a violation of Labor Code § 1776 warranting the issuance of a CWPA if a contractor makes available for inspection, or furnishes upon request, the full social security number for all affected employees on a separate written report, signed under penalty of perjury, to the entities identified in 1776(b)(2) within the time limits specified in Labor Code 1776. These entities include a representative of the body awarding the contract, the Labor Commissioner, and the Division of Apprenticeship Standards (DAS).

May 2018

3.1.13   **Retention of Payroll Records by Public Works Contractors**.

There is no provision in the prevailing wage laws which specifies a records retention period for CPRs or all of the types of "payroll records" as defined and listed at 8 CCR § 16000. The limitations period for legally recognized wage underpayment remedies available against public works contractors, however, vary depending upon the remedy available. Accordingly, contractors should retain CPRs for the duration of any applicable limitations period. Contractors must also separately comply with any record keeping requirements set forth in the Labor Code and applicable Industrial Welfare Commissioner wage order.

3.2   **Contractors' Obligations To Pay Prevailing Wage Rates**:

Not less than the specified prevailing rates of per diem wages must be paid to all workers employed in the execution of public works contracts. (Labor Code § 1774.) Workers employed by contractors or subcontractors in the execution of any contract for public work are deemed to be employed upon public work. (Labor Code § 1772.) Note: rates are also accessible through the Labor Commissioner's Public Works website.

3.2.1   "**Prevailing Rate of Per Diem Wages**," Defined:

Labor Code § 1773.1 specifies the components which comprise the rates published by the Director, and are available on the DIR website as "General Prevailing Wage Determinations." The specific rates applicable for each craft, classification, or type of work, and for each geographic locality throughout the state, can be located on the DIR website.

May 2018

3.2.2   **<u>Director's Authority to Determine Prevailing Wage Rates</u>**.

Labor Code § 1773 requires any body awarding a contract for public work to obtain from the Director the prevailing rates for all hours worked, including holiday and overtime rates, and provides to the Director the general methodology for making such determinations. Labor Code § 1773.9 further expands that methodology, and Labor Code § 1773.4 provides the regulated public with a process by which to request review of the Director's wage determinations. The Director is authorized by Labor Code § 1773.5 to establish rules and regulations to implement the prevailing wage laws, and the Director has done so at length with respect to the setting and publishing of the rates applicable on public works projects. 8 CCR §§ 16000-16304 The Director has the sole responsibility for establishing the prevailing wage rates for all classifications of workers.

3.2.3   **<u>Issue Date / Effective Date</u>**.

The issue date listed on each prevailing wage determination refers to the date the OPRL placed copies of the Director's new determinations in the mail to awarding bodies and other interested persons. (8 CCR § 16000.) The more important date, however, is the effective date, which is not listed on the determination. The effective date is the first date upon which the wage rates set forth in the determinations apply to work performed on a project. The effective date is ten days after the issue date. (8 CCR § 16000.) Because rates are generally issued by OPRL twice a year (February 22nd and August 22nd), those rates go into effect ten days thereafter (March 3rd in leap years and March 4th in non-leap years, and September 1st, respectively).

3.2.4   **<u>Effective Date / Bid Advertisement Date</u>**.

The Bid Advertisement Date (or Date of Notice or Call for Bids) is defined at 8 CCR § 16000. This is the date an awarding body published the "first notice inviting bids" in a newspaper (or otherwise legally promulgated notice) of a prospective public works project which results in a contract being awarded. For the Labor Commissioner's enforcement purposes, if the effective date of a determination is on or after the bid advertisement date but before the listed expiration date, the rates listed on that particular determination constitute the prevailing wage rates for work performed under that public works contract. Consistent with the Department's enforcement policy, if an awarding body does not advertise the public works project for bid, other benchmark events, including the first written memorialization of the agreement concerning the public works elements of project or the contract governing the award of public funds will be utilized instead. (See e.g., Baldwin Park Market Place, City of Baldwin Park, Public Works Case No. 2003-028, October 16, 2003.)

3.2.5   **Expiration Date / Double Asterisk / Predetermined Increases**.

Each prevailing wage determination also includes a specified expiration date. This is defined as the date upon which the determination is "subject to change." (8 CCR § 16000.) If there are "predetermined" changes (generally, increases to the wage rate), the expiration date will be followed by a double (**) asterisk. The new prevailing wage rate goes into effect on the day following the expiration date listed in the determination. Predetermined increases are published and available on the OPRL homepage, and specify the date upon which the increase(s) must be paid to workers. The predetermined increase web posting informs the investigator and public of applicable future predetermined increases to the rates listed in the original wage determination for work performed on that project.

3.2.6   **Expiration Date / Single Asterisk**.

If there are no "predetermined" changes, the expiration date on each prevailing wage determination will be followed by a single (*) asterisk. Single asterisk expiration dates mean the rates listed on that particular wage determination apply for the entire duration of the project, no matter how long work under the original public works contract continues.

3.2.7 **Overtime**.

The worker must be paid the applicable overtime rate set forth in the wage determination. This includes the requirement that any overtime performed under the public works contract must be compensated at the overtime rate required by the prevailing wage determination in effect on that project for the craft.

3.2.7.1 **Worker Performing Work During The Same Workday In Two Or More Different Classifications With Different Rates Of Pay**.

In the situation where a worker performs work during the same workday in two or more different classifications with different rates of pay, the worker must be paid the overtime rate *in effect* for the type of work he or she is performing during those overtime hours. The same requirement applies to a worker performing work on two or more public works projects during the same workday. All hours must be counted for overtime purposes, and the worker must be paid the applicable overtime rate *in effect* for the type of work performed for all overtime hours worked in the workday. *Example*: If a worker is performing work in the Inside Wireman's classification for four (4) hours and then performs work in the Painter's classification for six (6) hours, the worker would be entitled to no less than the total of four (4) hours of pay at the Inside Wireman's straight time rate of pay, four (4) hours of pay at the Painter's straight time rate of pay, and two (2) hours of pay at the Painter's overtime rate of pay for the two (2) hours worked in excess of eight (8) hours per day. As in all circumstances on public works projects where the worker is paid at two or more different rates of pay during the same workday, the employer is responsible for maintaining records showing that

May 2018

the worker was paid the appropriate rate of pay for all hours worked in each classification.

3.2.7.2   **Worker Performing Work On Public and Private Projects During the Same Workday With Different Rates of Pay**.

In the situation where a worker is paid two rates during the course of a workday and one of those rates is based upon work on a public works project and the other rate is based upon work performed on a private works project during that same workday, the regular rate for calculating the overtime rate for work performed on the public works project is based on the higher of either the weighted average or the prevailing wage rate in effect at the time that the work is performed, *which is often dependent upon when that public work was performed.*

Example: If a worker is employed in a workday for four (4) hours on a private construction job at $15.00 per hour and then, after completing the work on the private project, is employed during the same workday for eight (8) hours on a public work project at $30.00, the worker would be entitled to $15 per hour for the four (4) hours worked on the private project, $30 per hour for the first four (4) hours worked on the public works project, and the applicable overtime rate (e.g. $45 per hour) set forth in the prevailing wage determination for the final four (4) hours worked on the public works project. This is the case because the worker cannot be paid less than the applicable prevailing wage straight time or overtime rate for work performed on a public works project and since all hours worked are counted for overtime purposes, four of the worker's hours worked on the public works project were worked in excess of eight (8) hours during the workday. Conversely, if the same worker performs four (4) hours of work on a public works project and then, later in the same workday, the worker performs eight (8) hours of work on a private construction project, the worker would be entitled to $30 per hour for the first four (4) hours worked on the public works project, $15 per hour for the first four (4) hours worked on the private project, and the weighted

May 2018

average of the two rates for the final four (4) hours worked on the private works project. Investigators should refer to the Labor Commissioner's 2002 Enforcement Policies and Interpretations Manual, sections 49.2.5- 49.2.6.1, for a detailed explanation of how to establish the regular rate of pay for calculating overtime under the weighted average method. Applying that methodology here, and assuming the worker only worked one twelve (12) hour day during that workweek, the weighted average calculation results in a regular rate of $20 per hour (4 hours x $30 per hour ($120) + 8 hours x $15 per hour ($120) = $240, divided by 12 total hours worked during that workweek = $20 per hour) and the correct overtime rate for the worker would be $30 per hour (1.5 x the regular rate of $20).

3.3 **Contractors' Obligations To Comply With Apprenticeship Standards.**

Labor Code § 1777.5 identifies the obligations of contractors (including subcontractors) to employ apprentices on public works projects. The requirements to employ apprentices do not apply to "contracts of general contractors or to contracts of specialty contractors not bidding for work through a general or prime contractor when the contracts of general contractors or those specialty contractors involves less than thirty-thousand dollars ($30,000)." Labor Code § 1777.5(o).) Contractors who "knowingly violate" any of these requirements are subject to monetary penalties (up to $300.00 for each full calendar day of noncompliance) under Labor Code § 1777.7, and may also be "debarred," i.e., denied the right to bid on or be awarded a contract for public works, or perform work as a subcontractor on a public works project, for up to a period of three years. The appropriate remedy in each case will be based upon a consideration of five circumstances listed in the statute. Effective June 27,2012, the Legislature amended section 1777.7 to transfer enforcement of these

May 2018

apprenticeship obligations from the Chief of the Division of Apprenticeship Standards (DAS) to the Labor Commissioner.

3.3.1   **Three Overall Categories Of Apprenticeship Violations.**

All public works contractors must: (1) Timely submit contract award information to an authorized apprenticeship program both before commencing work on the project and after work has been concluded. (See, LC § 1777.5(e) and 8 CCR 230); (2) Employ DAS-registered apprentices, including compliance with minimum and maximum ratios of work hours performed by apprentices to journeymen. (See, LC § 1777.5(d) and (g), and (h)-(l), LC § 3077 and 8 CCR 230.1(a) and (c)); (3) Make training fund contributions to the California Apprenticeship Council ("CAC") in specified amounts. (See, LC § 1777.5(m)(1) and 8 CCR 230.2.) The statutory references and/or the regulations cited are extremely detailed and explain with particularity: (1) The procedures contractors must follow to properly submit contract award information (what, when, and where) and to request dispatch of apprentices to the project (when and from whom); (2) The calculation of minimum and maximum ratios for determining the number of hours apprentices are to be employed before the end of the contract or subcontract; (3) Optional payment of training fund contributions to approved apprenticeship programs rather than to the CAC; (4) Compliance with the "journeyman on duty" rule (when required); (5) Specified exceptions to any of these requirements. The cited regulations were written and adopted by the CAC. The Labor Commissioner enforces apprenticeship standards when apprenticeship violations are the specific subject of new complaints and will include apprenticeship compliance during the course of investigations arising from complaints alleging other violations of the prevailing wage laws, such as wage underpayments to workers.

May 2018

3.3.1.1   **Failure To Submit Contract Award Information / Violations.**

Labor Code section 1777.5(e) requires every contractor on a public works project "to submit contract award information" to an applicable DAS-approved apprenticeship program that can supply apprentices in a particular apprenticeable occupation to the public works site. The CAC regulation found at 8 CCR 230(a) explains and supplements that requirement. DAS Form 140 was created to allow contractors to fill-in-the-blanks on that form to provide all information required by either the statute or the regulation. Specifically, DAS Form 140 seeks the following: (1) The contractor's name, address, telephone number, and state license number; (2) Full name and address of the public work awarding body; (3) The exact location of the public work; (4) Date of the contract award; (5) Expected start date of the work; (6) Estimated journeymen hours; (7) Number of apprentices to be employed; and (8) Approximate dates apprentices will be employed. The form itself is available to the public on the DAS website, along with an interactive list of contact information for all of the approved apprenticeship programs in defined geographical areas throughout the state. Read together the statutory and regulatory provisions suggest three different deadlines to provide the DAS Form 140 information. The statutory deadline is "prior to commencing work" on the project, but the CAC regulation alternatively requires providing the information "to the applicable apprenticeship committee within ten days of execution" of the prime contract (or subcontract), "but in no event later than the first day" the contractor has workers employed upon the public work. For the Labor Commissioner's enforcement purposes the deadline for submission of DAS Form 140 information by each contractor (for each applicable craft) is the first day a journeyman in that craft works on the project for that contractor. Because neither the provisions of Labor Code 1777.5(e) nor the language in the

CAC regulation specify any particular method of submission, the Labor Commissioner relies upon the definition of acceptable "service" of documents found in the Director's regulations under Labor Code section 1742 (which by law apply to the review of the Labor Commissioner's penalty assessments for apprenticeship violations) as controlling. Under the Director's regulation found at 8 CCR 17210(b), DAS Form 140 information is deemed submitted to an approved apprenticeship program "at the time of personal delivery or mailing, or at the time of transmission by facsimile or other electronic means." It is the responsibility of the contractor to provide satisfactory evidence to the Labor Commissioner that DAS Form 140 information has been timely submitted / transmitted by one of these methods. It should be noted that while contractors using electronic means (fax or e-mail) to transmit a completed DAS Form 140 to an apprenticeship program will likely have easy access to documentary proof of the date of electronic transmission, no similarly reliable evidence may be available to contractors to establish the date of submission when first class mail is the only method used. In that situation, the date of mailing may be established by additional documents (such as a certified mail receipt, or a receipt for delivery of certified mail which reflects the date of mailing, or a proof of service by first class mail which accompanied the DAS Form 140) which would constitute reliable evidence that the DAS Form 140 was in fact mailed on or before the deadline. The obligation to submit DAS Form 140 information is not identical for all contractors. The CAC regulation found at 8 CCR 230(a) explains that contractors who have been approved to train apprentices "in the area of the site of the public works project" in a particular apprenticeable craft need only submit DAS Form 140 information to those programs. Contractors who are not already approved by an apprenticeship program sponsor in the area must provide DAS Form 140 information to all of the applicable apprenticeship programs whose geographic area of operation "includes the area of the public works project."

May 2018

3.3.1.2 **Failure to Submit Contract Award Information / Penalties.**

Penalties for violations of DAS Form 140 requirements are assessed in accordance with Labor Code section 1777.7(a)(1) for "each full calendar day of noncompliance." The first penalty day for failing to submit / transmit DAS Form 140 information for each apprenticeable craft is the calendar day <u>after</u> the deadline date has passed. A contractor's certified payroll records, if accurate, generally provide the most easily available evidence to establish the first penalty day. Thus, if a contractor first employed a journeyman carpenter on May 1, 2015, the <u>first penalty day</u> for failing to submit / transmit DAS Form 140 information would be May 2, 2015. The penalty <u>continues</u> to be assessed for each full calendar day thereafter until the calendar date upon which the DAS Form 140 is actually submitted / transmitted. If the DAS form 140 information is <u>never</u> submitted / transmitted, the penalty continues to be assessed for each calendar day thereafter until and including the last calendar date the contractor performed any work in <u>any</u> apprenticeable craft on the project. Investigators should include in their Penalty Review form a simple explanation of their calculation of the penalty days being assessed for DAS Form 140 violations, showing the first penalty date, the last penalty date, and the total number of penalty days. Two examples, again using May 1, 2015, as the date our contractor first employed a journeyman carpenter on the project:

Example 1: Failure to <u>timely</u> submit / transmit contract award information for craft of carpenter on or before May 1, 2015. <u>First</u> penalty day = 5/2/15; <u>Last</u> penalty day (based on the calendar date <u>before</u> submission, assuming here that 6/3/15 is the date of submission) = 6/2/15. Total number of penalty days is 32.

Example 2: Failure to ever submit / transmit contract award information for the craft of carpenter; First penalty day = 5/2/15; Last penalty day (based on the last date the same contractor performed any work in any apprenticeable craft on the project, assuming here that 7/7/15 is the last date of work) = 7/7/15. Total number of penalty days is 67.

3.3.1.3   **Minimum Ratio Violations.**

Understanding the minimum ratio requirement ("one hour of apprentice work for every five hours of journeyman work") and the mathematical calculation of penalties when violations occur lends itself to a step-by-step approach: (1) To determine whether a violation has occurred, the investigator must first count the *total number of journeyman hours* worked in a particular craft by a specific contractor "before the end of the contract or, in the case of a subcontractor, before the end of the subcontract." (See, subdivision (h) of § 1777.5.) *Assume* the contractor in question has submitted certified payroll records ("CPRs") which reflect that *journeyman carpenters* worked a total of *750 straight-time hours* over the course of the contract. (Note that hours worked by journeymen in excess of 8 per day or 40 per week are *excluded* from this calculation, also pursuant to subdivision (h) of § 1777.5.) (2) Calculate 20% of 750 journeyman hours to determine the minimum number of apprentice hours required before the end of the contract. (750 x 0.20 = *150 minimum apprentice hours*.) (3) *Assume* that this contractor's CPRs only reflect a total of *40 apprentice hours worked* in the carpenter craft during the contract. That number is *less apprentice hours than the minimum required* under the statutory formula. *Violation* of the minimum ratio requirement has therefore been established. (4) The investigator must now determine the penalty. The Legislature did *not* base the penalty upon the number of hours a contractor may have fallen short in providing apprentices with work on the project. Rather, § 1777.7(a)(1) provides that contractors who knowingly violate *any* of the apprenticeship standards found in § 1777.5 "shall forfeit as a civil penalty" an amount not exceeding $100 "for each full calendar day of noncompliance." (Note that the maximum increases to *$300 per day* when two or more violations occur within a three-year period. *Assume* that our contractor does not have a prior violation.) Because subdivision (h) of § 1777.5 informs us that *compliance with* the minimum ratio requirement applies during "any day or portion of a day when any journeyman is employed at the jobsite," *noncompliance with* the ratio should be also measured against that *same* total number of calendar days. (Note that it is therefore *irrelevant* for penalty purposes whether the contractor's apprentices and journeymen were employed in accordance with the ratio on *any single day*. This is so because our statute mandates that compliance with the ratio is not to be determined at the end *of each day*, but only by "the end of the contract.") *Assume* the CPRs in our example reflect that the total count of calendar days during which one or more journeyman carpenters were employed by this contractor was *50.* (5) The contractor is therefore subject to a *maximum penalty of $5000* ($100 x 50 days of noncompliance = $5000) for failing to employ apprentice carpenters in accordance with the minimum ratio required by § 1777.5.

3.3.1.4   **Affirmative Defense to Minimum Ratio Violations.**

A contractor which fails to accumulate a sufficient number of apprentice hours before the end of the contract or subcontract may raise an affirmative defense to avoid minimum ratio penalties under the CAC regulation found at 8 CCR 230.1(a). The regulation explains that contractors not already employing sufficient apprentices to comply with the minimum one-to-five ratio "must request dispatch of required apprentices" from DAS-approved apprenticeship committees providing training in the applicable craft or trade in the geographic area of the public work. That regulation served as the template for DAS Form 142, use of which enables contractors to be excused from the minimum ratio obligation even if the minimum ratio of apprentice hours is not actually achieved before the end of the contract or subcontract. To do so, it is the contractor's burden to establish that all of the regulation's request-to-dispatch requirements have been satisfied. The requirements may be summarized as follows: (1) Did the contractor request dispatch from each apprenticeship committee in the geographic area of the site of the public work? (2) Has the contractor provided the Labor Commissioner with a copy of each written request, with proof that it was sent by first class mail, facsimile or e-mail? (3) Did the request give the committee written notice of at least 72 hours (excluding Saturdays, Sundays and holidays) before the date on which one or more apprentices were required? (4) Was the request made in enough time to meet the above-stated ratio? (5) Did the contractor actually employ each of the apprentices dispatched? Failure of the contractor to establish that each of these requirements has been satisfied will be insufficient to establish an affirmative defense to a minimum ratio violation.

3.3.2   **Apprenticeship Violations Which Also Result In Prevailing Wage Underpayments**.

The Labor Commissioner's enforcement of the obligation of all contractors and subcontractors to pay not less than the specified prevailing rates of per diem wages may include situations where underpayments resulted from certain violations of the apprenticeship standards identified in Section 3.3.1 above. The first three apprenticeship-related examples of wage underpayments, as explained below in Sections 3.3.2.1 (Unregistered Apprentices), 3.3.2.2 (Nonpayment Of Training Fund Contributions) and 3.3.2.3 (Maximum Ratio Violations), have all been historically addressed by the Labor Commissioner as prevailing wage

May 2018

violations when discovered during the course of our prevailing wage investigations. The last example, explained below in Section 3.3.2.4 (Journeyman On Duty Violations), involves a discrete obligation applicable only to those public works contractors who have elected to employ and train apprentices under the rules and regulations of the CAC. Previously, it had been a policy decision that the Labor Commissioner would refer complaints alleging violations of this "journeyman on duty" rule (8 CCR 230.1(c)) to DAS for investigation. Because the Labor Commissioner has now replaced DAS as the state agency responsible for enforcing contractor violations of apprenticeship standards, violations of this and other duly adopted CAC regulations which may result in prevailing wage underpayments will also be enforced under LC § 1741, and therefore subject to penalties authorized by LC §§ 1775 and 1813.

3.3.2.1   **Unregistered Apprentices**.

Labor Code section 1777.5(b) and (c) authorize contractors to pay certain workers at "the prevailing rate of per diem wages for apprentices." If a prevailing rate for apprentices is included in the Director's published wage determinations for a particular craft or trade, it is always less than the journeymen rate. The lower apprentice rates serve as a monetary incentive for contractors to satisfy the required minimum ratio of apprentice hours to journeymen hours before the end of the contract. To be paid at the lower apprentice rates, a worker must be "registered" (i.e., be party to a written apprenticeship agreement confirming that the worker is "in training under apprenticeship standards that have been approved by the Chief" of the DAS). A worker's eligibility to be paid at an apprenticeship rate may be verified by referring to the online data base maintained on the DAS website for each particular craft or trade. However, investigators generally require the contractor to provide a copy of the worker's written apprenticeship agreement to establish eligibility. Regardless of the perceived level of skills (or lack thereof) that a worker in a particular craft or trade may actually possess, he or she must be enrolled in a DAS-approved apprenticeship training program at the time the work was performed. If not, hours worked in that craft or trade must be paid at the higher journeymen rate.

3.3.2.2 **Nonpayment Of Training Fund Contributions**.

Labor Code § 1777.5(m)(1) requires contractors who employ journeymen or apprentices in any "apprenticeable craft" (the Director's wage determinations include a symbol (#) next to the craft designation to indicate an apprenticeable craft) must contribute to the California Apprenticeship Council ("CAC") the amount reflected as the hourly "training" rate that appears on the Director's wage determination, for each hour worked. A contractor is also entitled to take credit for such contributions made to a DAS-approved apprenticeship program that can supply apprentices to the site of the public work. The training contribution is a distinct obligation of the contractor under Labor Code § 1777.5(m)(1) and cannot be satisfied by paying the required hourly contribution directly to the worker. The Labor Commissioner may issue a Civil Wage and Penalty Assessment against a contractor if the contractor fails to pay the required hourly training contributions to a DAS-approved apprenticeship program or the CAC.

3.3.2.3 **Maximum Ratio Violations**.

Labor Code § 1777.5(g) includes a "maximum ratio" limitation on the total number of hours of work performed by apprentices in a particular craft as measured against the total number of hours performed by journeymen in that craft under a public works contract. The applicable maximum ratio (if any) is not contained in either the Labor Code itself or duly promulgated regulations, but found only in the apprenticeship standards under which the apprenticeship program operates if the contractor agrees to be bound by those standards. If a maximum ratio violation is

May 2018

suspected, the Labor Commissioner will request a copy of the standards under which the apprenticeship program operates, including the maximum ratio requirement, as well as evidence that the contractor has agreed to be bound by those standards. Any violation of a maximum ratio requirement can be measured only by determining the total hours worked by apprentices and journeymen at "the end of" the contract or the subcontract, rather than on a daily basis. (LC § 1777.5(h).) If such a violation is found, the aggregate prevailing wage underpayment is typically calculated and remedied by raising a sufficient number of the excess hours originally paid at the apprentice rate to be paid at the journeymen rate, thereby ensuring compliance with the maximum ratio.

3.3.2.4   **Journeyman On Duty Violations**.

Labor Code § 1777.5(c)(2) allows a contractor to elect to have its apprentices employed and trained in accordance with the "rules and regulations" of the CAC to satisfy its statutory obligation to employ apprentices (and to simultaneously qualify its DAS-registered apprentices as eligible to be paid at lower apprentice wage rates). Alternatively, under LC §1777.5(c)(1,) the contractor may elect to have its apprentices employed and trained in accordance with the standards of a DAS-approved apprenticeship committee. If the contractor elects to follow the CAC rules, the applicable regulation is found at 8 CCR 230.1(c), and expressly requires that apprentices so employed "must at all times work with or under the direct supervision of journeyman/men." This is not a ratio requirement (such as the maximum ratio limitation explained above at Section 3.3.2.3) for which compliance is determined "at the end of the contract." Rather, this is a mandatory, daily obligation that is in effect whenever a worker paid as an apprentice is working on the public works project. Thus, apprentices who are not at all times working "with or under" a journeyman (for the same classification of work in which the apprentice is being trained) must be paid not less than the journeyman rate. The lower apprentice wage rate is simply not available for the worker in this situation because his or her employment and training under LC § 1777.5(c)(2) is by definition "not in accordance" with the CAC rules which the contractor has elected to follow. This is so even though the worker may be registered as an apprentice with the DAS. The regulation found at 8 CCR 230.1(c) is frequently referred to as the "journeyman on duty" rule. Violations are remedied by the Labor Commissioner's issuance of a Civil Wage and Penalty Assessment. Note that the rule would not apply if a contractor elects the alternative method to employ and train apprentices set forth at LC § 1777.5(c)(1). From a practical standpoint, investigators should routinely request that contractors provide evidence of their compliance with their obligation to submit contract award information to an authorized apprenticeship program before commencing work on the project, as required by LC § 1777.5(e). A completed DAS form entitled "Public Works Contract Award Information" (DAS 140) includes the contractor's selection of either the CAC rules or a particular apprenticeship committee's standards under which their apprentices will be employed.

4.   **The Labor Commissioner's Prevailing Wage Enforcement Process**.

The Labor Commissioner enforces California's prevailing wage requirements.

4.1   **Calculation of Wages Due**.

Labor Code § 1774 requires payment of not less than the "specified prevailing rates of wages" for all hours worked. The specified rates are the rates found in the Director's wage determinations which correspond with the type of work performed by individual workers. Contractors are required to select the applicable wage determination based on the work actually performed by a worker for each hour of work on the project. Contractors also must identify one of the Director's classifications (such as "carpenter" or "drywall finisher") for each of the

May 2018

hours worked by an individual worker.   In its investigations, the Labor Commissioner will determine the difference between the total wages required to be paid and the total wages actually paid.

4.1.1   **Travel and Subsistence Requirements**.

Labor Code § 1773.1 includes within its definition of "per diem wages" both "travel" and "subsistence" payments in the Director's determination of the applicable prevailing wages due for a particular type of work. Historically, the amounts required for either travel or subsistence are fixed daily amounts due to workers whenever the terms of a collective bargaining agreement are adopted by the Director as setting forth the prevailing wage rates in a particular locality. These fixed amounts are not specifically set forth in any of the Director's published wage determinations, but are only noted in footnotes appearing on the wage determinations. The footnote language appears in bold on each affected determination under the heading: "TRAVEL AND/OR SUBSISTENCE PAYMENT." The text below the footnote directs the reader to the DIR website to obtain the travel and subsistence requirements, and the fixed daily amounts if the requirements are met. There is little uniformity among the requirements found in the OPRL's posted collective bargaining agreement (CBA) provisions, and contractors must verify the provisions in each case to determine when and under what circumstances travel and/or subsistence payments may be required. The requirements differ among classifications, but are usually based on the distance a worker must travel from a designated location to the public work jobsite. The fixed daily amount also differs among classifications. SPECIAL NOTE: Compensable travel time is distinct from travel and/or subsistence payments. Compensable travel time is included in the calculation of hours worked. Travel and/or subsistence payments are a separate and distinct obligation of public works contractors if the conditions set forth in the CBA are adopted by the Director to apply to work on a public works project.

4.1.2   **"Scope of Work" Provisions Published by the DIR.**

The classification of work subject to a specific, Director-issued wage determination is often a primary area of dispute between Labor Commissioner and public works contractors in enforcement proceedings under the prevailing wage laws. In addition to routine factual disputes (such as workers claiming they performed certain duties while the employing contractor claims otherwise), even if the duties performed are not in dispute, the correct classification for that very type of work (and therefore the prevailing rate which applies) may be contested. The Director will make the final determination on the correct classification. (*DLSE v. Ericsson Information Services, Inc.* (1990) 221 Cal.App.3d 114.) Occasionally, the wage determination itself may include references to specific types of work subject to that determination (such as a particular "Operating Engineer" Group Number referring to a particular type of equipment). Other determinations may not include that level of specificity. When such an issue arises, the Director has typically relied on the Scope of Work provisions published by the OPRL, along with that particular wage determination. It is therefore important that investigators review those Scope of Work provisions whenever this issue arises during an investigation. It is irrelevant from the Labor Commissioner's perspective whether a worker happens to be a member of a union whose CBA provisions are posted by OPRL with the wage determination, or whether an affected contractor is signatory to that CBA. In the prevailing wage context, the Labor Commissioner does not enforce CBA provisions which may be in effect between public works contractors and one or more labor organizations. The applicable wage rate is determined by the worker's classification and is based on the work actually performed. Rather, the Labor Commissioner enforces the rates set forth in the Director's wage determinations and the Scope of Work provisions may provide guidance in interpreting the determinations. Workers may be reclassified when the duties or work tasks do not accurately reflect the work being performed.

4.1.3   **Factual Disputes Concerning the Type of Work Performed**.

Factual issues of this nature are one of the primary areas of dispute arising in investigations by the Labor Commissioner. From a practical standpoint, the best approach for investigators is to obtain as much evidence as may become available. Although it is impossible to predict the weight which might be assigned to any evidence by a trier-of-fact in the event a CWPA is contested, the following sources of evidence may be available (this listing is not meant to be all-inclusive):

     (1)   Worker complaints, statements (preferably, written) or questionnaires identifying the duties and equipment used by the worker;

     (2)   Public works contracts and subcontracts, including specifications;

     (3)   Inspection reports or logs maintained by awarding bodies, contractors or any other observers of the work performed;

     (4)   Time and pay records, prepared either by workers (such as calendars) or contractors, which may include descriptions of duties.

4.1.4   **Different Classifications For the Same Worker**.

The minimum prevailing wage for hours worked in the execution of a contract for pubic works is based upon the specified prevailing rates "for work of a similar character" (LC §§ 1771 and 1774.) Therefore, it is possible that one worker may perform more than one type of work during the course of a project. Two important considerations for staff encountering this situation during an investigation are: (1) The potentiality that even though two different classifications of work identified in the Director's wage determinations may sometimes provide the minimum rates required to be paid for the worker's separate duties, the higher minimum rate may apply for all of the hours worked. The U.S. Department of Labor analyzed this issue under similar provisions in the Davis-Bacon Act (40 U.S.C. § 276(a), the federal prevailing wage law) and determined that when a worker performs duties in a higher paying classification (such as a Pipefitter), the fact that some of the work performed by that same worker is similar to a type of work in a lower paying classification (such as Laborer Group 1), when that same work is performed by a Pipefitter (as a small or large part of his or her whole assigned task on any given job) it is the work of a Pipefitter, and must be compensated at the higher rate. (*In re Corley* (1978), Case No. 77-DB-114, 23 Wage and Hour Cases, 1071, 1075.) The *In re Corley* analysis is not intended to presumptively apply to all situations where a contractor's CPRs identify the same worker as performing work during the same day in two different classifications at two different rates of pay. Consistent with the language of Labor Code 1771, a contractor is generally not required to pay its workers at a rate higher than that specified in a particular wage determination for the type of work performed. The *In re Corley* rationale is applicable only where both types of work performed by the same worker are part of the work assigned to that worker in accomplishing the overall task performed under the higher-paying classification. Absent compelling evidence as to the type of work performed, any uncertainties will likely be resolved in the favor of worker testimony (and against the affected contractor whose failure to maintain the required records created the uncertainties) concerning the duties actually performed. (See, *Hernandez v. Mendoza* (1988), 199 Cal.App.3d 721.)

4.1.5   **Compensable Travel Time**.

Travel time related to a public works project constitutes "hours worked" on the project, which is payable at not less than the prevailing rate based on the worker's classification, unless the Director's wage determination for that classification specifically includes a lesser travel time rate. (See Director's Decision in *In the Matter of Kern Asphalt Paving & Sealing Co., Inc.* (March 28, 2008), Case No. 04-0117-PWH. (See also *Morillion v. Royal Packing Co.* (2000) 22 Cal.4th 575).) Travel time required by an employer after a worker reports to the first place at which his or her presence is required by the employer is compensable travel time, and includes travel **to a public work site**, whether from the contractor's yard, shop, another public work site, or a private job site. All such compensable travel time must be paid at the same prevailing wage rate required for the work actually performed by the worker **at the public works site.** No additional facts, such as whether tools or supplies are being delivered by the worker to the site, need be present.

4.1.6   **Calculation of Overtime and Saturday/Sunday/Holiday Wages**.

Labor Code § 1815 requires that work performed on public works projects in excess of 8 hours per day, or 40 hours per week, must be compensated at not less than time and one-half the basic rate of pay. Failure to pay the appropriate overtime rates subject the contractor to penalties pursuant to Labor Code § 1813. In addition to Labor Code § 1815, the Director's wage determinations generally designate specific premium rates for straight-time hours worked on Saturday and/or Sunday and Holiday work. The DIR website identifies the particular Holidays covered by the premium rate requirements under each wage determination. Saturday, Sunday, and Holiday premium rates apply for the hours worked on each of those days as specified in the applicable determination. If more than 8 hours per day are worked on the Saturday, Sunday and Holiday or

- 42 -

the hours worked, including Saturday, Sunday and Holiday exceeds 40 hours for the week, then overtime rates (calculated from the premium rate) also applies and the contractor is subject to penalties pursuant to Labor Code § 1813.

4.1.6.1

Note: In some cases, the wage determination for a specific classification may specify the requirement that overtime be paid for hours worked in excess of a maximum number that is less than 8 hours per day or 40 hours per week. For instance, the general prevailing wage determination may require that overtime be paid for all hours worked in excess of seven (7) hours per day or 35 hours per week. In those circumstances, overtime must be paid in accordance with the conditions set forth in the general wage determination. (*See*, 8 CCR 16200(a)(3)(F), Exception 4, discussed below at 4.1.7.4.) Contractors that fail to comply with this requirement are subject to penalties under Labor Code § 1775 in addition to the amount of any wages due.

4.1.7   **Exceptions to Overtime Requirements**.

Overtime is to be paid as indicated in the applicable wage determination. There are four limited exceptions to the overtime requirements under 8 CCR 16200(a)(3)(F). They are:

4.1.7.1   **Exception 1**:

If a workweek other than Monday through Friday is a fixed business practice or is required by the awarding body, no overtime payment is required for the first eight hours on Saturday or Sunday. The "fixed business practice" portion of this exemption is construed narrowly. It will not be permitted in circumstances where the contractor cannot establish that such a practice exists on all its projects, including public and private projects.

4.1.7.2   **Exception 2**:

If the collective bargaining agreement provides for Saturday and Sunday work at straight-time, no overtime payment is required for the first eight hours on Saturday or Sunday.

4.1.7.3   **Exception 3**:

If the awarding body determines that work cannot be performed during normal business hours, or work is necessary at off hours to avoid danger to life or property, no overtime is required for the first eight hours in any one calendar day, and 40 hours during any one calendar week.

4.1.7.4   **Exception 4**:

No overtime payment is required for less than 40 hours in a standard work week, or for less than eight hours in a calendar workday, unless specified in the collective bargaining agreement used as the basis for the prevailing wage determination.

4.1.8   **Restriction on Alternative Workweek Schedules**:

The California Labor Code requires that workers employed on public works in excess of eight hours per day receive compensation for all such hours at not less than the specified overtime rate. (Labor Code §§ 1810, 1811, and 1815.) The California Constitution also restricts the hours that may be worked on public works projects to eight hours a day, except in specified circumstances. (Article XIV, section 2). Notwithstanding Labor Code §§ 511, 514 and Wage Order 16, these restrictions apply to all workers performing work on public works projects, including workers covered under collective bargaining agreements and workers covered by an alternative workweek schedule adopted under Labor Code § 511 or Wage Order 16. Accordingly, no worker may be employed on a public works project for more than eight hours a day unless the worker receives the overtime compensation specified by the applicable prevailing wage determination.

4.1.9 **Saturday Make-Up Days**:

The determinations for some crafts permit contractors to pay straight time rates for Saturday work if certain conditions are satisfied. Any such exception from the general prevailing wage requirements is construed narrowly in accordance with its express terms. Furthermore, the exception must be included in the applicable prevailing wage determination in order to apply. The Labor Commissioner will not recognize exceptions which may exist in underlying collective bargaining agreements which rates are adopted by the Director for purposes of public works unless the Director also adopts the exception and it is included in the determination.

4.2 **Credit for Employer Payments**.

California prevailing wage law requires the payment of per diem wages, which includes two components. The first component is the Basic Hourly Rate. The second component is the Employer Payments. Taken together, these two components make up the Total Hourly Rate which must be paid to each worker for any work performed on a public works project.

4.2.1 **Employer Payments Are A Credit Against The Obligation To Pay The General Prevailing Wage Rate Of Per Diem Wages**.

Contractors obligated to pay prevailing wages may take credit for amounts up to the *aggregate* total of all benefits, such as pension, health & welfare, etc., listed as prevailing in the applicable wage determination. Contractors are not limited to the individual amounts specifically listed under the various categories of benefits specified in a wage determination in taking credit for providing Employer Payments. Rather, the contractor may take a credit for the aggregate total of permissible Employer Payments made on behalf of the affected worker. For example, the Director's statewide prevailing wage Determination (C-20-X-1-2017-1) for the Iron Worker (Ornamental, Reinforcing, Structural) classification for the craft of Iron Worker , reflects a Basic Hourly Rate of $36.00, with permissible Employer Payments of $9.55 per hour (Health and Welfare), $13.32 per hour (Pension), $4.00 per hour (Vacation/Holiday), $2.865 per hour (Other Payments), and one mandatory employer payment of $0.72 per hour (Training), which must be paid to the California Apprenticeship Council ("CAC") or an approved apprenticeship program. The Sum of all these components ($66.455) is the Total Hourly Straight-Time Rate listed on the Determination. The aggregate total of permissible Employer Payments (excluding the amount required for Training) is $29.735. The permissible Employer Payment amounts listed here typically reflect the particular hourly benefit rates found in a collective bargaining agreement which the Director determined had established the prevailing rate for this craft and classification of work in this geographic area. Absent contractual obligations which may apply to a particular contractor, the total of $29.735 per hour may be paid by an employer in full or in part to any category of permissible Employer Payments, and the employer will be entitled to credit against the total prevailing wage obligation. Thus, an employer may choose to contribute $20 of the aggregate total to a private medical insurance plan or a pension plan for its workers, and pay the remainder of $9.735 directly to the workers. The employer may take credit for the medical insurance or pension payments, and all of the payments added together ($45.735 paid to workers + $20.00 paid to medical or pension plan + $0.72 to CAC = $66.455), which would reflect compliance by this employer with the prevailing wage rate obligation. (*WSB Electric, Inc. v. Curry*

(9th Cir. 1996) 88 F.3d 788.) This credit may be taken only as to amounts which are actual payments. (8 Cal. Code of Regs. § 16200(a)(3)(I).) No credit may be taken for benefits required to be provided by other state or federal law. (Labor Code § 1773.1(c).) For instance, a contractor may not take a credit against its prevailing wage obligations for benefits such as workers' compensation, unemployment benefits, and social security and Medicare contributions.

4.2.2   **No Reduction of the Basic Hourly Rate**.

California law prohibits the use of credits for Employer Payments to reduce the obligation to pay the hourly straight time or overtime wages specified as the Basic Hourly Rate in the general prevailing wage determination. (Labor Code § 1773.1(c) and 8 Cal. Code of Regs. § 16200(a)(3)(I).) Two legislatively created exceptions to this general rule are now found at Labor Code section 1773.1(c) and section 1773.8. Both exceptions are extremely limited in scope and are only applicable to increases in employer payment contributions made pursuant to criteria set forth in a collective bargaining agreement ("CBA"), and only if the specific statutory conditions listed in the Labor Code have been met. Investigators will typically require a contractor claiming an exception under these sections to submit satisfactory evidence that the exception applies, including, but not limited to, a certified copy of the CBA upon which the exception is based, and to certify that the CBA's terms applied to the workers identified on the contractor's certified payroll records.

4.2.2.1   **Example:**

Basic Hourly Rate	$ 25.00
Employer Payments	$ 15.00

Total Hourly Rate $ 40.00

The contractor can comply with California prevailing wage laws by paying:

1. $40.00 per hour in wages;

2. $25.00 per hour in wages plus $15.00 in Employer Payments.

3. Any combination of the wages and Employer Payments so long as the Basic Hourly Rate is not less than $25.00 per hour and the Total Hourly Rate meets or exceeds $40.00 per hour.

4.2.2.2   **Different for Purely Federal Projects Under Davis-Bacon Act**.

The California law restricting the reduction of the Basic Hourly Rate is distinct from the federal prevailing wage laws under the Davis-Bacon Act. The Davis-Bacon Act does not prohibit the crediting of employer payments or benefit contributions towards fulfilling the hourly wage rate listed in the contract wage determination on federally funded projects. Contractors performing work on projects which are governed by both the federal Davis-Bacon Act and the California prevailing wage requirements must, however, continue to comply with state requirements in order to be in compliance with California law. Investigators may encounter this issue when dealing with contractors on public works projects which have mixed funding (both federal and state) or federally funded projects which are controlled or carried out by California awarding bodies of any sort. In both of these situations, the application of state prevailing wage rates when higher is required. (See 8 CCR § 16001(b).)

4.2.3   **Application to All Hours Worked**.

May 2018

Employer Payments must be paid for all hours worked, including overtime hours, unless expressly provided otherwise in the general prevailing wage determination. The general prevailing wage determinations specify the applicable daily, Saturday, Sunday, and Holiday overtime payment. Although the applicable overtime rates set forth in the determination include the Employer Payments, the overtime rate (for example, time and one half) is based upon the Basic Hourly Rate only. The Employer Payment is therefore excluded from calculating the applicable overtime premium due as overtime compensation.

4.2.3.1 **Example**:

An employee worked 12 hours in the workday as an Iron Worker on a public works project. The Basic Hourly Rate of pay in the determination is $32.00 plus $22.00 in Employer Payments. The overtime rate for the first 2 daily overtime hours is $48.00 (one and one half (1½) times the Basic Hourly Rate of $32.00, or $32.00 + $16.00). The wages due for each overtime hour is $70.00 (the overtime rate plus Employer Payments, or $48.00 + $22.00). The wages due per hour for all other overtime is $86.00 (two (2) times the Basic Hourly Rate plus Employer Payments, or $64.00 + $22.00).

The worker would be due.

8 Hours at $54.00 ($32.00 + $22.00)	$432.00
2 Hours at $70.00	$140.00
2 Hours at $86.00	$172.00
Total Wages Due	$744.00[1]

---

[1] This example is for illustration purposes. The general prevailing wage determinations specify the applicable Total Hourly Rates that must be paid to workers for straight time, overtime, Saturday and Sunday work, and there is no need for contractors to independently determine the hourly amount to be paid.

4.2.4   **Types of Employer Payments for Which An Employer May Take a Credit Against Its Prevailing Wage Obligations**.

The types of employee benefits recognized as Employer Payments under Labor Code § 1773.1 include payments for:

(1)   Health and welfare.

(2)   Pension.

(3)   Vacation.

(4)   Travel.

(5)   Subsistence.

(6)   Apprenticeship or other training programs authorized by Section 3093, so long as the cost of training is reasonably related to the amount of the contributions.

(7)   Worker protection and assistance programs or committees established under the federal Labor Management Cooperation Act of 1978 (Section 175a of Title 29 of the United States Code) to the extent that the activities of the programs or committees are directed to the monitoring and enforcement of laws related to public works.

(8)   Industry advancement and collective bargaining agreements administrative fees, provided that these payments are required under a collective bargaining agreement pertaining to the particular craft, classification, or type of work within the locality or the nearest labor market area at issue.

(9)   Other purposes similar to those specified in paragraphs (1) to (8), inclusive.

4.2.4.1   **Types Of Benefits Which Do Not Constitute Employer Payments**:

The types of benefits for which an employer may not take a credit against its prevailing wage obligations include benefits such as the use of a cell phone or company vehicle, gas reimbursement, or a Christmas bonus.

May 2018

4.2.5.   **"Employer Payments" Defined**:

Labor Code § 1773.1 defines Employer Payments to include all of the following:

(1)   The rate of contribution irrevocably made by the employer to a trustee or third person pursuant to a plan, fund, or program.

(2)   The rate of actual costs to the employer reasonably anticipated in providing benefits to workers pursuant to an enforceable commitment to carry out a financially responsible plan or program communicated in writing to the workers affected.

(3)   Payments to the California Apprenticeship Council pursuant to Section 1777.5.

4.2.5.1

It is not necessary that the Employer Payment satisfy all of these three conditions in order for the credit to be valid.   It is sufficient that the Employer Payment satisfies any one of the specified conditions in order to be considered an Employer Payment for which a contractor is entitled to take a credit against its prevailing wage obligation.

4.2.5.2   **Irrevocably Made to a Trustee or Third Person Pursuant to a Plan, Fund, or Program**.

Examples of these types of Employer Payments include contributions by a union signatory contractor to a labor-management affiliated pension, health & welfare, training, and vacation programs, contractor payments for health insurance premiums, contractor payments irrevocably made to a trustee or third party for pension benefits, and similar types of payments.

May 2018

4.2.5.2.1   **Employer Payments made to these types of plans must be made regularly.**

A contractor may take credit for Employer Payments "if the employer regularly makes the contributions, or regularly pays the costs, for the plan, fund, or program on no less than a quarterly basis." (Labor Code § 1773.1(d).)

4.2.5.2.2   **Employer Payments Must Be Determined Separately For Each Worker.**

Credit against the prevailing wage obligation may be taken only toward the prevailing wage requirement for each applicable worker. Employers may not take credit for an individual worker based upon an average payment or contribution made on behalf of a group of workers. For a specific example demonstrating the Labor Commissioner's method of converting a contractor's monthly or annual contributions to a typical benefit plan into an hourly wage equivalent to calculate the amount of credit available against the prevailing wages due to an individual worker, please refer to Section 4.2.6.4.1 of this Manual.

4.2.5.2.3   **Vesting Does Not Normally Affect Right to Credit.**

Many pension plans, particularly union-affiliated pension plans, contain "vesting" requirements which, under the plan, require that the worker complete a certain length of service before the worker has a nonforfeitable right to benefits under the plan. The existence of such vesting requirements does not affect the amount of credit an employer may take for such contributions, provided that the pension plan is a bona fide plan that meets the applicable requirements under ERISA, including the minimum vesting requirements. Under no circumstances, however, may the forfeited contributions revert to the employer.

May 2018

4.2.5.3   **Employer Payments That Are Reasonably Anticipated to Benefit Workers**.

Employer Payments that are not irrevocably made to a trustee or third person pursuant to a plan, fund, or program may still be valid as a credit against the prevailing wage obligation, provided that they meet all of the conditions set forth in Labor Code § 1773.1(b)(2). Such rate of actual costs for such plan or programs can be credited against the prevailing wage only if the plan or program:

(1)   Can be reasonably anticipated to provide benefits to workers;

(2)   Is pursuant to an enforceable commitment;

(3)   Is carried out under a financially responsible plan or program; and

(4)   Has been communicated to the workers affected.

4.2.5.3.1   **Example**.

The type of Employer Payments contemplated under § 1773.1(b)(2) may include certain vacation and holiday plans for which the employee accrues the benefit during the time worked on a public works project. Such payments must meet all the conditions set forth above. In addition, the credit may be taken only as to amounts which are "actual payments." (8 CCR § 16200(a)(3)(I).)

4.2.5.4   **Payments to the California Apprenticeship Council**.

Employer Payments for which a contractor may take a credit against its prevailing wage obligations also include payments made to the CAC pursuant to Labor Code § 1777.5(m)(1). The amount of contribution is listed on the general prevailing wage determination for those crafts which are recognized by the Director of the DIR as an apprenticeable craft. Such amounts are typically listed in the general prevailing wage determination under the heading Training or similar type heading.

4.2.5.4.1   **Includes Payments Made to An Approved Apprenticeship Program**.

A contractor may take as a credit for payments to the CAC any amounts paid by the contractor to an approved apprenticeship program that can supply apprentices to the site of the public work project. (Labor Code § 1777.5(m)(1).)

4.2.5.4.2   **Training Contributions Not Paid to the Worker**.

Although such payments constitute part of the Total Hourly Rate required to be paid by the employer, such payments are not paid to the worker. Rather, such payments are made to either the CAC or the applicable approved apprenticeship program. The contractor may add the amount of the contributions in computing his or her bid for the public works contract. (Labor Code § 1777.5(m)(1).)

4.2.5.4.3   **Exception - Non-Apprenticeable Crafts**.

For non-apprenticeable crafts, any training contributions should be paid to the worker as wages and not paid to the CAC. Some crafts are not identified on the Director's wage determinations with a symbol (#) which indicates an apprenticeable craft. If that is the case, any training contribution listed in the general prevailing wage determination should be paid to the worker, or to the applicable training program, if the contractor is contractually obligated to make such payments under its collective bargaining agreement.

4.2.6.   **Annualization**.

Annualization is a principle adopted by the federal Department of Labor in enforcing the Davis-Bacon Act for crediting contributions made to fringe benefit plans based on effective rate of contributions for all hours worked during a year by an employee on both public (Davis-Bacon) and private (non-Davis-Bacon) projects. (*Miree Construction v. Dole* (11th Cir. 1991) 930 F.2d 1536, 1539.) California law requires that the credit for employer payments must be computed on an annualized basis where the employer seeks credit for employer payments that are higher for public works projects than for private construction performed by the same employer. (Labor Code § 1773.1(e).)

4.2.6.1   **Exceptions**:

Annualization is required except where one or more of the following occur:

(1)   The employer has an enforceable obligation to make the higher rate of payments on future private construction performed by the employer.

(2)   The higher rate of payments is required by a project labor agreement.

(3)   The payments are made to the CAC pursuant to Section 1777.5.

(4)   The director determines that annualization would not serve the purposes of this chapter.

4.2.6.2

The annualization principle requires that when converting an employer's contribution to a pension or medical plan into an hourly amount, the amount of payments must be divided by the total number of hours worked in a year on all projects, public and private, not just the number of hours worked during that year on public projects. This method of calculation, the "annualization" principle, provides a means to permit an employer to take credit only for employer contributions paid to workers while employed on covered public works projects.

4.2.6.3   **Annualization Calculation**.

For enforcement purposes, the Labor Commissioner follows the federal enforcement guidelines. *See* Department of Labor Field Enforcement Handbook – 6/29/90, Section 15f11. (See http://www.dol.gov/whd/FOH/index.htm to review the handbook.) Under the federal enforcement guidelines, where a contractor makes annual payments in advance to cover the coming year and actual hours will not be determinable until the close of that year, the total hours worked by the workers performing work covered by California's prevailing wage laws, if any, for the preceding calendar year (or plan year) will be considered as representative of a normal work year for purposes of annualization. Similarly, where the contractor pays monthly health insurance premiums in advance on a lump sum basis, the total actual hours worked in the previous month, or in the same month in the previous year, may be used to determine (i.e. estimate) the hourly equivalent credit per employee during the current month. It is not considered a violation if the contractor uses the full year equivalent of 2,080 (40 hours x 52 weeks) hours in determining the applicable credit unless, of course, the affected employee worked more than 2,080 hours in that applicable year.

4.2.6.4   **Representative Period**.

Any representative period may be utilized in such cases, provided the period selected is reasonable. Employers using other methods to calculate the allowable credit have the burden of establishing that their method satisfies the annualization requirements set forth in Labor Code 1773.1(d).

4.2.6.4.1   **Example:**

An employee works as a carpenter where the basic hourly rate set forth in the wage determination for Carpenter is $30 and the total employee benefit (Employer Payment) package is $15, excluding the training contribution. Accordingly, the total hourly rate required to be paid under California's prevailing wage laws is $45.

Where the employer provides the carpenter with medical insurance in the amount of $4,800 per year, the employer would divide the total annual cost of the benefit by the total hours worked by the employee for the preceding year. The employer may also use 2,080 hours, which is the equivalent of full year employment to arrive at the allowable Employer Payment credit.

For instance, where the employer uses the equivalent of full year employment, or 2,080 hours, the applicable credit is as follows:

($400 x 12 months) divided by 2,080 hours = $2.31 per hour.

If the worker in this example receives no other employee benefits which are recognized as bona fide Employer Payments under California law, then for each hour worked on a project covered by California's prevailing wage laws, the employer is entitled to take a credit of no more than $2.31 against its obligation to pay the worker $45 per hour, up to a maximum credit of $4,800, which is the total amount paid for medical insurance. The difference between the $15.00 per hour employer payment required under the applicable wage determination and the credit allowed for the provision of medical insurance must be paid to the worker as part of his or her hourly wage for work performed on the public works project.

Basic Hourly Rate $ 30.00

May 2018

Medical Insurance Benefit	$ 2.31
Additional Wages Due	$ 12.69
Total Due Per Hour	$ 45.00

If the worker works the entire year only on projects covered by California's prevailing wage laws, or under circumstances otherwise exempt under the exceptions set forth above in Labor Code § 1773.1(e)(1)-(4), the employer would be entitled to take the full credit of $2.31 up to a maximum of $4,800.

Conversely, if the worker worked only 1,500 hours of the year on projects covered by California's prevailing wage laws and 580 hours of the year on other jobs which are not covered by California's prevailing wage laws or are otherwise not exempted under Labor Code § 1773.1(e)(1)-(4), the employer would be entitled to take a credit of only $2.31 per hour towards meeting the employer's obligation to pay the prevailing wage on the California public works projects. Therefore, although an employer may have paid $4,800 in insurance premiums for that year, the employer is entitled to take a total annual credit of only $3,465.00 (1,500 x. $2.31) against its prevailing wage obligation because the employer may take the credit only for those hours worked on a public works project.

4.2.6.5   **Payments To The California Apprenticeship Council Pursuant To Section 1777.5**.

As specified in Labor Code section 1773.1(e)(3), payments made to the CAC, or to an applicable approved apprenticeship program pursuant to Labor Code § 1777.5(m)(1), do not need to be annualized. For enforcement purposes, the Labor Commissioner takes the position that the exemption from the annualization requirements under section 1773.1(e)(3) is limited to the training contribution amounts set forth in the applicable general prevailing wage determination. An employer may not claim credit against a worker's per diem wages for training contribution amounts paid in excess of the amount set forth in the applicable general prevailing wage determination <u>unless the worker actually benefits from the payment.</u> (See Director's Decision *In the Matter of Request for Review of DBS Painting, Inc.* (December 10, 2007), Case No. 06-0168-PWH). Credit for contribution amounts which meet this requirement must be annualized unless otherwise exempt under section1773.1(e)(3).

4.3   **Calculation of Labor Code § 1775 Penalties**.

The Labor Code provides that the contractor and subcontractor, if any, under the contract shall forfeit not more than two hundred dollars ($200.00) for each calendar day, or portion thereof, for each worker paid less than the required prevailing wage rate. This dual liability is most easily described as a penalty which is combined, united, and shared by both the contractor and subcontractor. The fact that a contractor may have been totally ignorant of its subcontractor's prevailing wage underpayment is not, standing alone, a defense to liability for this penalty. Moreover, and contrary to an argument sometimes raised by prime contractors, the language of the statute does not mean that the prime contractor only becomes responsible for the penalty if the subcontractor fails to pay it first. While the Labor Commissioner may only collect the total penalty once, the contractor and subcontractor equally share full responsibility for the amount assessed. The only exception is found in the "safe harbor" provisions available to prime contractors who meet the requirements of Labor Code § 1775(b), discussed in detail below in Section 4.3.1 of this Manual. In assessing the amount of the penalty, the Labor Commissioner considers two factors. The first factor is whether the failure of the contractor or subcontractor to pay the correct rate of per diem wages was a good faith mistake and, if so, the error was promptly and voluntarily corrected when brought to the attention of the contractor or subcontractor. The second factor is whether the contractor or subcontractor

- 59 -

has a prior record of failing to meet its prevailing wage obligations. There are minimum penalties. The Labor Commissioner may assess not less than forty dollars ($40.00), unless the failure of the contractor or subcontractor to pay the correct rate of per diem wages was a good faith mistake and, if so, the error was promptly and voluntarily corrected when brought to the attention of the contractor or subcontractor. The Labor Commissioner may assess not less than eighty dollars ($80.00) if the contractor or subcontractor has been assessed penalties within the previous three years for failing to meet its prevailing wage obligations on a separate contract, unless those penalties were subsequently withdrawn or overturned. The Labor Commissioner may assess not less than one hundred twenty dollars ($120.00) if the Labor Commissioner determines that the violation was willful, as defined in subdivision (c) of Section 1777.1. The Labor Commissioner's determination of the penalty amounts is reviewable for abuse of discretion. Any outstanding wages shall be satisfied before applying that amount to the penalties.

4.3.1.1 **Limited Prime Contractor Safe Harbor**.

Section 1775(b) provides that a prime contractor may avoid liability for section 1775 penalties when workers employed by its subcontractor were paid less than the required prevailing wage.

The prime contractor of the project is not liable for any penalties under section 1775 unless (a) the prime contractor had knowledge of that failure of the subcontractor to pay the specified prevailing rate of wages to those workers or (b) the prime contractor fails to comply with all of the following requirements:

(1)   The contract executed between the contractor and the subcontractor for the performance of work on the public works

project shall include a copy of the provisions of Sections 1771, 1775, 1776, 1777.5, 1813, and 1815.

(2) The contractor shall monitor the payment of the specified general prevailing rate of per diem wages by the subcontractor to the employees by periodic review of the certified payroll records of the subcontractor.

(3) Upon becoming aware of the failure of the subcontractor to pay his or her workers the specified prevailing rate of wages, the contractor shall diligently take corrective action to halt or rectify the failure, including, but not limited to, retaining sufficient funds due the subcontractor for work performed on the public works project.

(4) Prior to making final payment to the subcontractor for work performed on the public works project, the contractor shall obtain an affidavit signed under penalty of perjury from the subcontractor that the subcontractor has paid the specified general prevailing rate of per diem wages to his or her employees on the public works project and any amounts due pursuant to Section 1813.

Important. Even if a prime contractor avoids section 1775 penalties where the evidence presented to the Labor Commissioner satisfies the conditions of Labor Code § 1775(b)(1)-(4), a prime contractor remains jointly and severally liable for all wage underpayments occasioned by its subcontractors, and penalties and liquidated damages available under Labor Code §§ 1813 and 1742.1.

4.4   **Calculation of Labor Code § 1813 Penalties**.

The dollar amount of this penalty is fixed at $25.00 for each worker for each calendar day during which the worker is required or permitted to work more than eight hours in any one calendar day or 40 hours in any one calendar week. Unlike Labor Code § 1775 penalties, the Labor Commissioner has no discretion to not assess or to reduce or modify the penalty amount under § 1813.

4.5   **Calculation of Unpaid Training Fund Contributions**.

Absent credit having been given to the contractor for payments made in satisfaction of this prevailing wage obligation, the Labor Commissioner will calculate the unpaid contributions based upon the hours worked in any particular classification, and reflect the amounts due under the "Training Fund" heading. NOTE: Not all payments for training funds are entitled to credit against the total prevailing wage obligation.

4.6   **Determination of Hours Worked and Amounts Paid**.

While CPRs furnished by public works contractors must reflect both hours worked and amounts paid, there may be frequent conflicts between the information provided by workers and contractors on these two components of the audit. The Labor Commissioner will consider other sources to determine the accuracy of the payroll records and to determine whether the workers were paid fully for all hours worked on the public works projects.

4.6.1   **Releases Signed By Workers As Proof Of Amounts Paid**.

May 2018

California law prohibits an employer from requiring an employee to release wages due unless such wages have been paid in full. (Labor Code § 206.5.) The Labor Commissioner will generally not accept "Releases" provided by contractors, standing alone, as conclusive proof that these payments have actually been paid for hours worked on the project in question. Such releases must be supported by independent proof that the payment reflected in the release has actually been made (for example, cancelled checks), and confirmation with the worker who signed the release that payment was actually received for work performed on the project in question.

4.7   **Civil Wage and Penalty Assessments ("CWPAs").**

Labor Code § 1741 describes in detail the statutory process by which the Labor Commissioner enforces its claims for unpaid wages and penalties. The Labor Commissioner's compliance with that process has been achieved by the creation and use of the form entitled "Civil Wage and Penalty Assessment" (Form PW 33) which tracks, in all respects, the statutory language. The use of this specific form by investigators is mandatory to initiate statutory enforcement actions under the prevailing wage laws.

4.7.1   **Service of the CWPA / Statute of Limitations / Tolling.**

Labor Code section 1741 provides that the CWPA shall be served not later than 18 months after the filing of a valid notice of completion in the office of the county recorder in which the public work was performed, or not later than 18 months after acceptance of the public work, whichever occurs last. Labor Code section 1741 also provides that the period for service of assessments shall be tolled for three reasons: (1) For the period of time required by the Director of Industrial Relations to determine whether a project is a public work; (2) For the period of time that a contractor or subcontractor fails to provide in a timely manner certified

- 63 -

payroll records pursuant to a request from the Labor Commissioner; (3) For the period of time that an awarding body fails to timely furnish (upon written request) the Labor Commissioner with a copy of the valid notice of completion filed in the office of the county recorder, or a document evidencing the awarding body's acceptance of the public work, until the Labor Commissioner's actual receipt of those documents.

4.8   **Administrative Review of CWPAs**.

Labor Code § 1742 provides contractors served with a CWPA an opportunity to timely request administrative review of the monetary assessment. If no hearing is requested "within 60 days after service," the CWPA becomes final (Labor Code § 1742(a)), and enables the Labor Commissioner to either obtain contract funds withheld by the awarding body or, if insufficient funds have been retained, to enter a court judgment against the contractors served, without the necessity of an administrative hearing and without filing a lawsuit. (Labor Code §§ 1742(d) and (e).) If any of the contractors served with the CWPA do timely transmit a written request for a review hearing, a hearing will be provided by the DIR before the assessment can become a final order. (Labor Code § 1742(b).) The administrative review process involves several different participants from the Labor Commissioner and DIR, and their respective roles follow.

4.8.1   **Role of DIR / OD-Legal**.

The Director, currently through the Office of the Director's Legal Unit, is responsible under Labor Code § 1742(b) to both hold an administrative review hearing in accordance with the procedures established under the Prevailing Wage Hearing Regulations found at 8 CCR §§ 17201-17270, and "issue a written decision affirming, modifying, or dismissing the assessment." The hearing process is required to be fair and impartial, and the findings in the written decision "must be supported by substantial evidence in the light of the whole record." The proceedings must provide affected contractors with the protections of due process. To guarantee due process, affected contractors are specifically provided with an opportunity to obtain court review of any written decision by filing a writ under Code of Civil Procedure 1094.5. (Labor Code § 1742(c).)

4.8.2   **Prevailing Wage Hearing Regulations**.

The regulations which are in effect during the entire period after a contractor files a request for a review hearing and until those proceedings conclude, either by dismissal of the proceedings by the Hearing Officer (generally, because of settlement) or on the date which a written decision signed by the Director affirming, modifying, or dismissing the assessment becomes final, are found at 8 CCR §§ 17201-17270. Two particular regulations which have not been previously addressed in this Manual are important to investigators: (1) No direct or indirect communication regarding any issue in the review proceeding is permitted between the investigator and the Hearing Officer without notice and the opportunity for all parties to participate in the communication. (8 CCR § 17207(a).) Investigators typically ensure compliance with this rule prohibiting "ex parte" communications by avoiding any communications with the Hearing Officer, except during the formal proceedings; (2) The required method of service of a CWPA and the required contents of a CWPA are restated at 8 CCR § 1720.

4.8.3   **Settlement Meetings and Settlements**.

Labor Code § 1742.1, in addition to providing the availability of liquidated damages (an amount equal to the wages covered by the CWPA if those wages remain unpaid 60 days after service of the CWPA), requires that the Labor Commissioner afford contractors served with a CWPA an opportunity to meet to attempt to settle any dispute regarding the assessment, if such a request is made by the contractor within 30 days following service. The CWPA form (at page 3) identifies the investigator who issued the CWPA as the person to contact to arrange a settlement meeting. The meeting may be held by phone or in person, and nothing said in the meeting is either subject to discovery, or admissible as evidence, in any administrative or civil proceeding. The investigator may handle the meeting with or without involvement by Legal, but it is always prudent to review the issues which might be discussed in the meeting with either a Senior Deputy or Legal. Either a Senior Deputy or Legal should be notified if settlement can be achieved. In the event a contractor requests that a written settlement agreement or release be signed by the Labor Commissioner, Legal must be notified and must review any such document before signing. The proposed terms of a post-CWPA settlement are to be approved by a Senior Deputy or Legal.

4.8.4   **Liquidated Damages.**

Contractors and their sureties are also subject to liquidated damages (LC § 1742.1(a)) in an amount equal to the wages, or portion thereof, that still remain unpaid for 60 days after service of a CWPA issued by the Labor Commissioner or a Notice To Withhold Contract Payments issued by a DIR-approved LCP. Liquidated damages are distributed to workers. If the assessment is overturned or modified after administrative or judicial review, liquidated damages are only available on the wages found to be due and unpaid. Additionally, the statute provides that a contractor may avoid liability for liquidated damages by depositing in escrow with the DIR the full amount of the assessment, including penalties, within 60 days following service of the CWPA or Notice. (LC § 1742.1(b).) The Labor Commissioner's CWPA form specifies that a check or money order in the full amount of the assessment is required, accompanied by a copy of the contested CWPA or Notice, and mailed to: Department of Industrial Relations, Attention Cashiering Unit, P.O. Box 420603, San Francisco, CA 94142. The DIR will release such funds (plus any interest earned) at the conclusion of all administrative and judicial review to the persons or entities who are found to be entitled to the amounts so deposited.

4.9   **CWPAs Which Become Final / Collection From Awarding Body / Judgments**.

Labor Code § 1742(a) provides that a CWPA becomes "final" if no review hearing has been requested within 60 days after service. CWPAs that have become final may be submitted to the awarding body withholding contract funds under that CWPA to obtain the amounts due. (Labor Code § 1742(f).) If funds are not available from the awarding body, Legal may request entry of judgment in the Superior Court in any county in which the affected contractors have property or a place of business. (Labor Code § 1742(d).) Legal will decide whether to proceed with either collection from the awarding body, or by pursuing entry of a court judgment against the contractors.

4.10   **Debarment**.

Labor Code section 1777.1 authorizes the Labor Commissioner to seek an order of debarment against contractors, subcontractors and specific individuals identified in Labor Code section 1777.1(a) and (d). An order of debarment prohibits the named contractors and others named in the order from either bidding on or being awarded a contract for public work, or performing work as a subcontractor on any public works project. There are four separate bases for debarment: (1) Section 1777.1(a) - Violation of the Public Works Chapter with "intent to defraud" as that term is defined at 8 CCR 16800; (2) Section 1777.1(b) - The commission of two or more separate willful (defined at Labor Code section 1777.1(e)) violations within a three-year period; (3) Section 1777.1(c) - Failure to provide a timely response to a request to produce certified payroll records within 30 days after receipt of the specified written notice from the Labor Commissioner described in Section 1777.1(c), entitled "Notice Of Intent To

Debar"; (4) Section 1777.1(d) - Knowingly committing a serious violation of any provision of Labor Code section 1777.5. The period of debarment is from one to three years, except for debarments under Labor Code section 1777.1(d), which provides for debarment for a period of <u>up to</u> one year for the first violation of Labor Code section 1777.5, and for a period of <u>up to</u> three years for a second or subsequent serious violation of that section. The procedures the Labor Commissioner must follow in initiating a debarment proceeding and obtaining an order of debarment are set forth in regulations duly promulgated by the Labor Commissioner and found at 8 CCR 16800-16802.

4.10.1 **Debarment Investigations**.

The Labor Commissioner conducts investigations to determine if a contractor, subcontractor, or individual has committed violations of the prevailing wage laws which authorize the debarment remedy. Generally, the investigations are based upon the facts and circumstances discovered in prior investigations which resulted in the issuance and service of CWPAs. However, the Labor Commissioner may also conduct debarment investigations resulting from complaints filed by any "person" as that term is defined at 8 CCR 16800.

4.10.2 **Posting of Debarment Orders**.

In accordance with Labor Code section 1777.1(f), a list of contractors, subcontractors or other entities or individuals ordered debarred by the Labor Commissioner, the periods of debarment, and the contractor's State License Board license number, are posted on the Commissioner's Internet Web site.

4.11 **The Labor Commissioner's Jurisdiction to Enforce California's Prevailing Wage Laws is Not Exclusive**.

The Labor Commissioner does not have exclusive jurisdiction to enforce California's prevailing wage laws. The California Labor Code authorizes specified

May 2018

awarding bodies to initiate and enforce a labor compliance program for public works projects, as specified, under the authority of the awarding body. (Labor Code §§ 1771.5, 1771.7, 1771.8, and 1771.9.) In addition, statutes and case law authorize other entities and individuals to enforce California's prevailing wage laws.

It should be noted that the availability of private rights of action to enforce the prevailing wage laws as specified in Sections 4.11.1, 4.11.2 and 4.11.3 below do not provide the much more favorable administrative procedures and burdens of proof which are set forth in Labor Code section 1741 - 1743, and the relevant Prevailing Wage Hearing Regulations found at 8 CCR 17221 - 17251. Thus, the likelihood of recovery in prevailing wage enforcement cases filed in state or federal courts under private rights of action should be carefully considered in comparison with the alternative approach of filing a complaint with the Labor Commissioner against contractors or subcontractors for investigation and enforcement by the Labor Commissioner on behalf of workers, as specified in Labor Code section 1741. It must also be recognized that in these private rights of action workers cannot recover liquidated damages (under Labor Code section 1742.1) otherwise available through the Labor Commissioner's enforcement. In addition, when the Labor Commissioner takes enforcement action, no portion of a workers' recovery of wages will be reduced by attorney fees or any other costs of litigation. All attorneys considering representing workers in private rights of action to seek recovery of unpaid prevailing wages are therefore encouraged to provide workers with the pros and cons of proceeding directly in court rather than simply filing a complaint with the Labor Commissioner.

4.11.1   **Action by Joint Labor-Management Committee.**

Labor Code § 1771.2 authorizes a joint labor-management committee established pursuant to the federal Labor Management Cooperation Act of 1978 (29 U.S.C. 175a) to bring a civil action against an employer that fails to pay the prevailing wage to its employees. The action must be commenced not later than 18 months after the filing of a valid Notice of Completion in the office of the County Recorder in each county in which the public work or some part thereof was performed, or not later than 18 months after acceptance of the public work, whichever last occurs.

4.11.2   **Worker's Private Right of Action.**

In a 2002 decision, the California Court of Appeal held that a union, as assignee of the worker's statutory rights, had standing to assert the employer's duty to pay prevailing wages under the California Labor Code. (*Road Sprinkler Fitters Local Union No. 669 v. G & G Fire Sprinklers, Inc.* (2002) 102 Cal.App.4th 765, 770.) In so holding, the court concluded that the workers have private statutory rights to recover unpaid prevailing wages under Labor Code §§ 1194 and 1774 as well as waiting time penalties under Labor Code § 203. (*Id.* At 809.)

4.11.3   **Third Party Beneficiary.**

The California Court of Appeal found that a worker on a public works project may maintain a private suit against the contractor to recover unpaid prevailing wages as a third party beneficiary of the public works contract if the contract provides for the payment of prevailing wages. (*Tippett v. Terich* (1995) 37 Cal.App.4th 1517, 1531-32.)

May 2018

4.12   **Industrial Welfare Commission (IWC) Wage Order 16-2001.**

Contractors employing workers on California public works projects must comply with any applicable provisions of Wage Order 16, or other applicable wage order. These obligations are in addition to any prevailing wage obligations that may apply on the public works project. These obligations include, among other things, requirements concerning record keeping, meal and rest periods, uniform and equipment, and reporting time. (See Addendum 5 for the IWC order 16.)

4.12.1   **Referral of Wage Order Violations to BOFE.**

The requirements under Wage Order 16, or any other applicable wage order that may apply to workers employed on a public works project, are not enforced by means of the administrative procedures set forth in Labor Code § 1741. However, the Public Works Unit will issue citations under other Labor Code provisions for violations it finds, such as the Labor Code 226 requirement of itemized wage statements. In appropriate circumstances, the Public Works Unit of the Labor Commissioner's Office will bring in the Bureau of Field Enforcement (BOFE) for investigation and prosecution by the Bureau of Field Enforcement. In addition, workers who believe that they may have a claim for violation of Wage Order 16, or any applicable wage order, may file an administrative claim with the Labor Commissioner under Labor Code § 98.

5.   **The Labor Commissioner's Role in Prevailing Wage Enforcement by Labor Compliance Programs ("LCPs").**

Labor Code § 1771.5 first became effective in 1990 and authorized certain awarding bodies to "initiate and enforce" a labor compliance program to assist the Labor Commissioner in handling compliance with the prevailing wage laws. To qualify as a statutory LCP, applicants must obtain approval to operate as such from the Director. (LC § 1771.5(c).) The number of approved LCPs expanded

May 2018

after 2003, when new Labor Code provisions (such as LC § 1771.7) and other new laws required that LCPs be utilized for prevailing wage compliance whenever certain public funds (such as statutorily specified bonds or other legislation-generated monies) are used to finance any part of a public works project. Regulations dealing with LCP activities were duly promulgated by the Director nearly 20 years ago, and have been amended several times since. The current LCP regulations are approximately 30 pages in length and are found at 8 CCR §§ 16421-16439. New amendments to the existing regulations were approved by the Office of Administrative Law and became effective January 21, 2009. Only a few of the existing regulations directly involve tasks to be performed by the Labor Commissioner in LCP matters. This Manual will not attempt to explain any of the LCP regulations which do not directly involve the Labor Commissioner's Office staff. This Manual will highlight certain LCP regulations which require the Labor Commissioner's participation in prevailing wage enforcement activities handled by LCPs.

5.1   **Forfeitures Requiring Approval by the Labor Commissioner**.

The regulation found at 8 CCR § 16436 defines the categories of "forfeitures" which LCPs are required to withhold from public works contractors who are subject to LCP prevailing wage compliance activities on projects for which an awarding body has a statutory duty to utilize an LCP. Under the LCP statutes, the LCP activities may be conducted by the awarding body's own DIR-approved LCP or by a third-party LCP, likewise approved by the Director. In either situation, the amount of the "forfeiture" must be submitted to and approved by the Labor Commissioner (or staff designated by the Labor Commissioner), if the forfeiture is more than $1000, before the LCP can implement the statutory enforcement mechanism. That mechanism is the issuance and service of a "Notice of Withholding Contract Payments," a document which is the mirror image of the Labor Commissioner's CWPA form. The method by which the LCP seeks the

Labor Commissioner's approval of the desired forfeiture is delivery of a written "request for approval of the forfeiture" for review by staff. Forfeitures less than $1000 are deemed approved upon service of the Labor Commissioner of copies of the Notice of Withholding, audit and a brief narrative summarizing the nature of the violation(s). (See 8 CCR § 16436.) A suggested form or format for these written requests can be found as Appendix D following § 16437. The LCP regulations specify the items which must be included with any submission. The required items are spelled out in detail at 8 CCR § 16437. Staff who typically have been assigned the responsibility of approving or denying LCP forfeiture requests has been at the Senior Deputy level or higher. The two types of forfeitures which require the Labor Commissioner's approval are: (1) Unpaid prevailing wages found by the LCP to be due under Labor Code § 1774 and (2) Penalty assessments under Labor Code §§ 1775, 1776 and 1813. (8 CCR § 16436.) Because LCPs must enforce the requirements of the prevailing wage laws "consistent with the practice of the Labor Commissioner" (8 CCR § 16434), all of the sections of this Manual which describe the Labor Commissioner's method of calculating amounts due for wages (including giving credit available to contractors for Employer Payments) and the formulas, amounts and circumstances giving rise to the listed statutory penalties apply. Staff assigned to handle LCP requests for approval of forfeitures must be familiar with all of these sections, which will not be individually referenced by the applicable Section numbers here.

5.2   **Determination of Amount of Forfeiture by the Labor Commissioner**.

The regulation found at 8 CCR § 16437, as noted above, lists all of the items required to be included in any LCP's request for approval of a defined "forfeiture." Those items are self-explanatory and will not be repeated here. The regulation also includes time deadlines for both the LCP's submission of a written request for approval (not less than 30 days before final payment is due from the awarding body to the contractor, and never less than 30 days before expiration of the statute of limitations set forth in Labor Code § 1741), and the Labor Commissioner's response to the request for approval. The deadline for Labor Commissioner's response is required within 30 days of the receipt of the proposed forfeiture. For LCPs with "extended authority" from the Director to operate, approval is automatically effective 20 days after the requested forfeitures are served on the Labor Commissioner, unless the Labor Commissioner notifies the LCP (within the 20-day period) that the proposed forfeiture is subject to further review. (8 CCR § 16437(e)(2).) In this situation, the Labor Commissioner has an additional 30 days (from the date of service of the Labor Commissioner's notice of extension to the LCP) to serve the LCP with the Labor Commissioner's approval, modification, or disapproval of the proposed forfeitures. Although the language of the regulation is couched in mandatory terms ("shall"), there is no specific mention in the regulation that the Labor Commissioner would lose the authority to respond in an untimely manner. Under longstanding Supreme Court precedent, it would therefore appear that delays by the Labor Commissioner in responding timely would have no effect on the authority to approve, modify, or disapprove the proposed forfeitures in an untimely manner. (See, *Edwards v. Steele* (1979) 25 Cal.3d 405.) Nevertheless, staff assigned to handle requests for approval of forfeitures from LCPs is expected to respond timely.

5.3   **Director's Authority to Approve / Revoke LCPs**.

Although the LCP regulations authorize only the Director to approve or revoke LCPs to operate as approved labor compliance programs (8 CCR §§ 16425-16429), the Director's Office has historically relied upon staff to make recommendations to the Director concerning an applicant's qualifications to become an approved LCP, or to assist in various ways during the course of LCP revocation proceedings. The Labor Commissioner's staff will, of course, assist the Director in whatever manner is required in performing these functions.

6   **Public Works Reforms (SB854).**

The Legislature has made several changes to the laws governing how the Department of Industrial Relations (DIR) monitors compliance with the prevailing wage requirements on public works projects. New Labor Code section 1777.1 now requires that a contractor or subcontractor shall not be qualified to bid on, be listed in a bid proposal, or engage in the performance of a contract for public work unless currently registered and qualified to perform work in the manner specified in new Labor Code section 1725.5. New Labor Code section 1773.3 now requires awarding bodies to electronically notify DIR of any public works contract within five days of the award using the online PWC-100 form. The Director of Industrial Relations is in the process of establishing rules and regulations for carrying out all of these new statutory provisions. In the interim, all public works contractors, awarding bodies and the general public should refer to two informational notices currently available online:

"Important Information for Awarding Bodies":

> www.dir.ca.gov/public-works/SB854.html

"Precautionary Legal Notice to Awarding Bodies":

> www.dir.ca.gov/DLSE/PrecautionaryLegalNoticetoAwardingBodies.html

6.1   **SB96.**

The Legislature created new enforcement mechanisms for the Labor Commissioner to enforce the Public Works Contractor Registration requirements through the passage of SB96. The bill also provided other minor changes to assist in public works enforcement generally. SB 96 creates penalties for contractors who fail to register and establishes new penalties and sanctions for awarding bodies that hire or permit unregistered contractors to work on public works projects.

6.1.1 **Penalties Assessed Against Unregistered Contractors.**

Labor Code section 1771.1(g) provides that a contractor that is required to be registered in order to work on a public works contract and fails to do is subject to penalties of $100 per day for each day the unregistered contractor performs work in violation of the registration requirements, not to exceed a total penalty of $8,000. This $8,000 limit is *in addition to* the $2,000, which the contractor will be required to pay in order to become qualified to register. (Labor Code §1771.1(g).)

6.1.2 **Penalties Assessed Against Contractors That Employ Unregistered Subcontractors.**

Labor Code section 1771.1(h) provides that a higher-tiered public works contractor or subcontractor found to have entered into a subcontract with a lower-tiered unregistered contractor is subject to penalties of $100 per day for each day the unregistered lower-tier subcontractor performs work in violation of the registration requirements, not to exceed a total penalty of $10,000. The only exception to this liability for a higher tiered contractor is where a lower tiered subcontractor's performance violates the registration requirements because its registration was revoked. Higher-tiered contractors are prohibited from requiring subcontractors to indemnify them from liability for these penalties.

6.1.3 **Stop Orders Issued to Unregistered Contractors.**

Labor Code section 1771.1(j) provides that if an unregistered contractor or subcontractor is found performing on a public works project, the Labor Commissioner shall issue a stop order prohibiting the unregistered contractor or subcontractor from performing work on all public works until the unregistered

May 2018

contractor or subcontractor become registered. A contractor or subcontractor, owner, director, officer, or managing agent of the contractor or subcontractor who fails to observe a stop order issued and served upon him or her, is guilty of a misdemeanor punishable by imprisonment in county jail not exceeding 60 days or by a fine not exceeding ten thousand dollars ($10,000), or both.

6.1.4 **Awarding Bodies Must Ensure that the Contractors Utilized on Public Works Projects Are Registered.**

Labor Code section 1773.3(c)(1) provides that an awarding agency is subject to penalties of $100 per day, up to $10,000 per project, for the following violations: (1) Failing to timely submit required notice of award pursuant to Labor Code section 1773.3(a); (2) Entering into a contract directly with an unregistered contractor; or (3) Allowing an unregistered contractor to perform work on a project it awarded. In addition, Labor Code section 1773.3(d) provides that where final payment has been made and it is later discovered that an unregistered contractor or subcontractor worked on the project, the awarding body is subject to penalties of $100 for each calendar day of noncompliance, for a period of up to 100 days, for each unregistered contractor or subcontractor.

6.1.5 **Awarding Body's Ineligibility to Receive State Funding or Financial Assistance.**

Labor Code §1773.3(f) provides that if the Labor Commissioner determines an awarding agency has committed two or more "willful violations" of public works laws within a one-year period, the awarding agency shall be ineligible to receive state funding or financial assistance for any construction project undertaken on behalf of the awarding agency for one year. These sanctions are enforced against the most problematic awarding bodies according to the same contractor debarment procedures found in Labor Code section 1777.1.

May 2018

6.1.6   **"Small Project Exception".**

SB 96 created limited exemptions to some of the requirements created by SB 854 for contractors and awarding bodies for new construction, alteration, installation, demolition or repair projects that do not exceed $25,000 or maintenance projects that do not exceed $15,000. As of July 1, 2017, contractors or subcontractors who work or bid exclusively on small public works projects will not be required to register as a public works contractor or file eCPRs for those "small" projects. (Labor Code §§1771.1(n) and 1771.4(a)(4).) However, contractors are still required to maintain accurate certified payroll records, retain them for at least three years, and provide them to the Labor Commissioner's Office upon request pursuant to Labor Code §1776. Additionally, awarding bodies are not required to submit the notice of contract award through DIR's PWC-100 system on projects that fall within the "small project" exemption. (Labor Code §1773.3(i).)

ADDENDUM 1

LIST OF COURT CASES

City of Pasadena v. Charleville (1932) 215 Cal. 384

DLSE v. Ericsson Information Systems, Inc. (1990) 221 Cal.App.3d 114

Edwards v. Steele (1979) 25 Cal.3d 405.

Hernandez v. Mendoza (1988), 199 Cal.App.3d 721

Johnston v. Farmers Mutual Exchange of Calhoun, Inc., 218 F. 2d 588 (5th Cir. 1955)

Lusardi Construction Co. v. Aubry (1992) 1 Cal. 4th 976

Miree Construction v. Dole (11th Cir. 1991) 930 F.2d 1536

Morillion v. Royal Packing Co. (2000) 22 Cal.4th 575

O. G. Sansone v. Department of Transportation (1976) 55 Cal.App.3d 434

Ramirez v. Yosemite Water Co. (1999) 20 Cal.4th 785

Regents v. Aubry (1996) 42 Cal.App.4th 579

Road Sprinkler Fitters Local Union No. 669 v. G & G Fire Sprinklers, Inc. (2002) 102 Cal.App.4th 765

San Francisco Labor Council v. Regents of University of California (1980) 26 Cal.3d. 785

Southern Cal. Labor Management Committee v. Aubry (1997) 54 Cal.App.4th 873

So. Cal. Roads Co. v. McGuire (1934) 2 Cal.2d 115

State Building and Construction Trades v. City of Vista (2012) 54 Cal.4th 547

Tippett v. Terich (1995) 37 Cal.App.4th 1517, 1531-32

United States v. Morris (1840) 39 U.S. 463

WSB Electric, Inc. v. Curry (9th Cir. 1996) 88 F.3d 788

ADDENDUM 2

<u>ABREVIATIONS USED</u>

CAC	California Apprenticeship Council
CBA	Collective Bargaining Agreement
CCR	California Code of Regulations
CMU	Compliance Monitoring Unit
CPR	Certified Payroll Records
CWPA	Civil Wage and Penalty Assessment
DAS	Division of Apprenticeship Standards
DIR	Department of Industrial Relations
DLSE	Division of Labor Standards Enforcement or Labor Commissioner's Office
LC	Labor Code
LCP	Labor Compliance Program
OD-Legal	Office of the Director's Legal Unit
OPRL	Director's Office of Policy, Research, and Legislation
PW	Public Works

ADDENDUM 3

<u>RESOURCES AND USEFUL WEB LINKS</u>

Prevailing Wage Rates and Coverage Information

- Director's General Prevailing Wage Determinations
  - http://www.dir.ca.gov/OPRL/DPreWageDetermination.htm

- Important Notices (Index 2001-1 to Present)
  - http://www.dir.ca.gov/OPRL/NoticeIndex.htm

- Public Works Coverage Determinations
  - http://www.dir.ca.gov/OPRL/pwdecision.asp

- Current Residential Prevailing Wage Determinations
  - http://www.dir.ca.gov/oprl/Residential/reslist.html

- Frequently Asked Questions – Prevailing Wage
  - http://www.dir.ca.gov/OPRL/FAQ_PrevailingWage.html

- Frequently Asked Questions – Off-Site Hauling
  - http://www.dir.ca.gov/OPRL/FAQ_Hauling.html

SB854 Requirements

- Certified Payroll Reporting
  - http://www.dir.ca.gov/Public-Works/Certified-Payroll-Reporting.html

- Public Works Contractor Registration
  - http://www.dir.ca.gov/Public-Works/Contractors.html

- Awarding Body Information
  - http://www.dir.ca.gov/dlse/dlseform-pw26.pdf

Apprenticeship

- Apprenticeship Requirements
  - http://www.dir.ca.gov/Public-Works/Apprentices.html

- Frequently Asked Questions – Apprenticeship
  - http://www.dir.ca.gov/das/publicworksfaq.html

- Apprenticeship Program Information Public Works – Search
  - http://www.dir.ca.gov/databases/das/pwaddrstart.asp

- Checking Apprenticeship Status of an Individual
  - http://www.dir.ca.gov/das/appcertpw/appcertsearch.asp

- Public Works Apprentice Wage Determinations (2004 – 2012)
  - http://www.dir.ca.gov/DAS/PWAppWage/PWAppWageStart.asp

May 2018

- Public Works Apprentice Wage Determinations (2012 – present)
  - http://www.dir.ca.gov/OPRL/pwappwage/PWAppWageStart.asp

Apprenticeship (continued)

- Public Works Contract Award Information Form (DAS Form 140 (Rev. 1/04))
  - http://www.dir.ca.gov/DAS/dasform140.pdf

- Request for Dispatch of an Apprentice Form (DAS Form 142 (Rev. 4/11))
  - http://www.dir.ca.gov/DAS/dasform142.pdf

- California Apprenticeship Council – Training Fund Contributions
  - https://www.dir.ca.gov/das/TF/CAC2.asp

- Apprenticeship Debarments
  - http://www.dir.ca.gov/DAS/debarment.htm

Enforcement

- How to File a Public Works Complaint
  - http://www.dir.ca.gov/dlse/HowToFilePWComplaint.htm

- Public Works Complaint Form – English (PW 1) (Rev. 9/12))
  - http://www.dir.ca.gov/dlse/Forms/PW/PW1_English.pdf

- Public Works Complaint Form – Spanish (PW 1) (Rev. 9/12))
  - http://www.dir.ca.gov/dlse/Forms/PW/PW1_Spanish.pdf

- Director's Prevailing Wage Enforcement Decisions (Labor Code Section 1742) (2007 to present)
  - http://www.dir.ca.gov/OPRL/PrevWageEncDecision.htm

- Debarments of Public Works Contractors
  - http://www.dir.ca.gov/dlse/debar.html

- Labor Code Section 1741(c) Judgments – Public Works
  - http://www.dir.ca.gov/dlse/DLSE-Databases.htm

- Labor Compliance Programs
  - http://www.dir.ca.gov/lcp.asp

Department of Industrial Relations (DIR) Regulations

- Payment of Prevailing Wages upon Public Works (Sections 1600-16414)
  - http://www.dir.ca.gov/t8/ch8sb3.html

- Awarding Body Labor Compliance Programs (Sections 16421-16802)
  - http://www.dir.ca.gov/t8/ch8sb4.html

- Department of Industrial Relations – Prevailing Wage Hearings (Sections 17201-17270)
  - http://www.dir.ca.gov/t8/ch8sb6.html

Department of the Treasury
Internal Revenue Service

Publication 15
Cat. No. 10000W

(Circular E), Employer's Tax Guide

For use in **2023**

Get forms and other information faster and easier at:
- *IRS.gov* (English)
- *IRS.gov/Spanish* (Español)
- *IRS.gov/Chinese* (中文)
- *IRS.gov/Korean* (한국어)
- *IRS.gov/Russian* (Русский)
- *IRS.gov/Vietnamese* (Tiếng Việt)

Dec 13, 2022

Contents

What's New 1

Reminders 2

Calendar 8

Introduction 10

1. Employer Identification Number (EIN) 11

2. Who Are Employees? 11

3. Family Employees 13

4. Employee's Social Security Number (SSN) . . . 14

5. Wages and Other Compensation 15

6. Tips 18

7. Supplemental Wages 19

8. Payroll Period 20

9. Withholding From Employees' Wages 21

10. Required Notice to Employees About the
    Earned Income Credit (EIC) 26

11. Depositing Taxes 26

12. Filing Form 941 or Form 944 32

13. Reporting Adjustments to Form 941 or
    Form 944 34

14. Federal Unemployment (FUTA) Tax 37

15. Special Rules for Various Types of
    Services and Payments 40

16. Third-Party Payer Arrangements 45

How To Get Tax Help 46

Index 49

Future Developments

For the latest information about developments related to Pub. 15, such as legislation enacted after it was published, go to *IRS.gov/Pub15*.

What's New

Social security and Medicare tax for 2023. The rate of social security tax on taxable wages, including qualified sick leave wages and qualified family leave wages paid in 2023 for leave taken after March 31, 2021, and before October 1, 2021, is 6.2% each for the employer and employee or 12.4% for both. Qualified sick leave wages and qualified family leave wages paid in 2023 for leave taken after March 31, 2020, and before April 1, 2021, aren't subject to the employer share of social security tax; therefore, the tax rate on these wages is 6.2%. The social security wage base limit is $160,200.

The Medicare tax rate is 1.45% each for the employee and employer, unchanged from 2022. There is no wage base limit for Medicare tax.

Social security and Medicare taxes apply to the wages of household workers you pay $2,600 or more in cash wages in 2023. Social security and Medicare taxes apply to election workers who are paid $2,200 or more in cash or an equivalent form of compensation in 2023.

Qualified small business payroll tax credit for increasing research activities. For tax years beginning before January 1, 2023, a qualified small business may elect to claim up to $250,000 of its credit for increasing research activities as a payroll tax credit. The Inflation Reduction Act of 2022 (the IRA) increases the election amount to $500,000 for tax years beginning after December 31, 2022. The payroll tax credit election must be made on or before the due date of the originally filed income tax return (including extensions). The portion of the credit used against payroll taxes is allowed in the first calendar quarter beginning after the date that the qualified small business filed its income tax return. The election and determination of the credit amount that will be used against the employer's payroll taxes are made on Form 6765, Credit for Increasing Research Activities. The amount from Form 6765, line 44, must then be reported on Form 8974, Qualified Small Business Payroll Tax Credit for Increasing Research Activities.

Starting in the first quarter of 2023, the payroll tax credit is first used to reduce the employer share of social security tax up to $250,000 per quarter and any remaining credit reduces the employer share of Medicare tax for the quarter. Any remaining credit, after reducing the employer share of social security tax and the employer share of Medicare tax, is then carried forward to the next quarter. Form 8974 is used to determine the amount of the credit that can be used in the current quarter. The amount from Form 8974, line 12, or, if applicable, line 17, is reported on Form 941 or Form 944. For more information about the payroll tax credit, see *IRS.gov/ResearchPayrollTC*. Also see the line 16 instructions in the Instructions for Form 941 (line 13 instructions in the Instructions for Form 944) for information on reducing your record of tax liability for this credit.

Forms 941-SS and 941-PR discontinued after 2023. Form 941-SS, Employer's QUARTERLY Federal Tax Return—American Samoa, Guam, the Commonwealth of the Northern Mariana Islands, and the U.S. Virgin Islands, and Form 941-PR, Planilla para la Declaración Federal TRIMESTRAL del Patrono, will no longer be available after the fourth quarter of 2023. Instead, employers in the U.S. territories will file Form 941, Employer's QUARTERLY Federal Tax Return, or, if you prefer your form and instructions in Spanish, you can file new Form 941 (sp), Declaración del Impuesto Federal TRIMESTRAL del Empleador.

Pubs. 51, 80, and 179 discontinued after 2023. Pub. 51, Agricultural Employer's Tax Guide; Pub. 80, Federal Tax Guide for Employers in the U.S. Virgin Islands, Guam, American Samoa, and the Commonwealth of the Northern

Mariana Islands; and Pub. 179, Guía Contributiva Federal para Patronos Puertorriqueños, will no longer be available after 2023. Instead, information specific to agricultural employers and employers in the U.S. territories will be included in Pub. 15 beginning with the Pub. 15 for use in 2024 (published December 2023). Beginning in 2024, there will be a new Pub. 15 (sp) that is a Spanish-language version of Pub. 15.

Reminders

The COVID-19 related credit for qualified sick and family leave wages is limited to leave taken after March 31, 2020, and before October 1, 2021. Generally, the credit for qualified sick and family leave wages as enacted under the Families First Coronavirus Response Act (FFCRA) and amended and extended by the COVID-related Tax Relief Act of 2020 for leave taken after March 31, 2020, and before April 1, 2021, and the credit for qualified sick and family leave wages under sections 3131, 3132, and 3133 of the Internal Revenue Code, as enacted under the American Rescue Plan Act of 2021 (the ARP), for leave taken after March 31, 2021, and before October 1, 2021, have expired. However, employers that pay qualified sick and family leave wages in 2023 for leave taken after March 31, 2020, and before October 1, 2021, are eligible to claim a credit for qualified sick and family leave wages in 2023. See the March 2023 revision of the Instructions for Form 941 or the 2023 Instructions for Form 944 for more information.

Disaster tax relief. Disaster tax relief is available for those impacted by disasters. For more information about disaster relief, go to *IRS.gov/DisasterTaxRelief*.

Payroll tax credit for certain tax-exempt organizations affected by qualified disasters. Section 303(d) of the Taxpayer Certainty and Disaster Tax Relief Act of 2020 allows for a payroll tax credit for certain tax-exempt organizations affected by certain qualified disasters **not** related to COVID-19. This credit is claimed on Form 5884-D (not on Form 941 and Form 944). Form 5884-D is filed after the Form 941 for the quarter or Form 944 for the year for which the credit is being claimed has been filed. For more information about this credit, go to *IRS.gov/Form5884D*.

2023 withholding tables. The Percentage Method and Wage Bracket Method withholding tables, the employer instructions on how to figure employee withholding, and the amount to add to a nonresident alien employee's wages for figuring income tax withholding are included in Pub. 15-T, Federal Income Tax Withholding Methods, available at *IRS.gov/Pub15T*.

Moving expense reimbursement. P.L. 115-97 suspends the exclusion for qualified moving expense reimbursements from your employee's income for tax years beginning after 2017 and before 2026. However, the exclusion is still available in the case of a member of the U.S. Armed Forces on active duty who moves because of a permanent change of station due to a military order. The exclusion applies only to reimbursement of moving expenses that the member could deduct if they had paid or incurred them without reimbursement. See *Moving Expenses* in Pub. 3, Armed Forces' Tax Guide, for the definition of what constitutes a permanent change of station and to learn which moving expenses are deductible.

Withholding on supplemental wages. P.L. 115-97 lowered the withholding rates on supplemental wages for tax years beginning after 2017 and before 2026. See section 7 for the withholding rates.

Backup withholding. P.L. 115-97 lowered the backup withholding rate to 24% for tax years beginning after 2017 and before 2026. For more information on backup withholding, see *Backup withholding*, later.

Certification program for professional employer organizations (PEOs). The Stephen Beck, Jr., Achieving a Better Life Experience Act of 2014 required the IRS to establish a voluntary certification program for PEOs. PEOs handle various payroll administration and tax reporting responsibilities for their business clients and are typically paid a fee based on payroll costs. To become and remain certified under the certification program, certified professional employer organizations (CPEOs) must meet various requirements described in sections 3511 and 7705 and related published guidance. Certification as a CPEO may affect the employment tax liabilities of both the CPEO and its customers. A CPEO is generally treated for employment tax purposes as the employer of any individual who performs services for a customer of the CPEO and is covered by a contract described in section 7705(e)(2) between the CPEO and the customer (CPEO contract), but only for wages and other compensation paid to the individual by the CPEO. To become a CPEO, the organization must apply through the IRS Online Registration System. For more information or to apply to become a CPEO, go to *IRS.gov/CPEO*. Also see Revenue Procedure 2017-14, 2017-3 I.R.B. 426, available at *IRS.gov/irb/2017-03_IRB#RP-2017-14*.

Outsourcing payroll duties. Generally, as an employer, you're responsible to ensure that tax returns are filed and deposits and payments are made, even if you contract with a third party to perform these acts. You remain responsible if the third party fails to perform any required action. Before you choose to outsource any of your payroll and related tax duties (that is, withholding, reporting, and paying over social security, Medicare, FUTA, and income taxes) to a third-party payer, such as a payroll service provider or reporting agent, go to *IRS.gov/OutsourcingPayrollDuties* for helpful information on this topic. If a CPEO pays wages and other compensation to an individual performing services for you, and the services are covered by a contract described in section 7705(e)(2) between you and the CPEO (CPEO contract), then the CPEO is generally treated as the employer, but only for wages and other compensation paid to the individual by the CPEO. However, with respect to certain employees covered by a CPEO contract, you may also be treated as an employer of the employees and, consequently, may also be liable for federal employment taxes imposed on wages and other compensation paid by the CPEO to such employees. For more information on the different types of third-party payer arrangements, see section 16.

Aggregate Form 941 filers. Approved section 3504 agents and CPEOs must complete Schedule R (Form 941), Allocation Schedule for Aggregate Form 941 Filers, when filing an aggregate Form 941. Aggregate Forms 941 are filed by agents approved by the IRS under section 3504 of the Internal Revenue Code. To request approval to act as an agent for an employer, the agent files Form 2678 with the IRS unless you're a state or local government agency acting as an agent under the special procedures provided in Revenue Procedure 2013-39, 2013-52 I.R.B. 830, available at *IRS.gov/irb/2013-52_IRB#RP-2013-39*. Aggregate Forms 941 are also filed by CPEOs approved by the IRS under section 7705. To become a CPEO, the organization must apply through the IRS Online Registration System at *IRS.gov/CPEO*. CPEOs file Form 8973, Certified Professional Employer Organization/Customer Reporting Agreement, to notify the IRS that they've started or ended a service contract with a client or customer. CPEOs must generally file Form 941 and Schedule R (Form 941) electronically. For more information about a CPEO's requirement to file electronically, see Revenue Procedure 2017-14, 2017-3 I.R.B. 426, available at *IRS.gov/irb/2017-03_IRB#RP-2017-14*.

Other third-party payers that file aggregate Forms 941, such as non-certified PEOs, must complete and file Schedule R (Form 941) if they have clients that are claiming any employment tax credit (for example, the qualified small business payroll tax credit for increasing research activities).

Aggregate Form 940 filers. Approved section 3504 agents and CPEOs must complete Schedule R (Form 940), Allocation Schedule for Aggregate Form 940 Filers, when filing an aggregate Form 940, Employer's Annual Federal Unemployment (FUTA) Tax Return. Aggregate Forms 940 can be filed by agents acting on behalf of home care service recipients who receive home care services through a program administered by a federal, state, or local government. To request approval to act as an agent on behalf of home care service recipients, the agent files Form 2678 with the IRS unless you're a state or local government agency acting as an agent under the special procedures provided in *Revenue Procedure 2013-39*. Aggregate Forms 940 are also filed by CPEOs approved by the IRS under section 7705. CPEOs file Form 8973 to notify the IRS that they've started or ended a service contract with a client or customer. CPEOs must generally file Form 940 and Schedule R (Form 940) electronically. For more information about a CPEO's requirement to file electronically, see *Revenue Procedure 2017-14*.

Work opportunity tax credit for qualified tax-exempt organizations hiring qualified veterans. Qualified tax-exempt organizations that hire eligible unemployed veterans may be able to claim the work opportunity tax credit against their payroll tax liability using Form 5884-C. For more information, go to *IRS.gov/WOTC*.

Medicaid waiver payments. Notice 2014-7 provides that certain Medicaid waiver payments are excludable from income for federal income tax purposes. See Notice 2014-7, 2014-4 I.R.B. 445, available at *IRS.gov/irb/*

2014-04_IRB#NOT-2014-7. For more information, including questions and answers related to Notice 2014-7, go to *IRS.gov/MedicaidWaiverPayments*.

No federal income tax withholding on disability payments for injuries incurred as a direct result of a terrorist attack directed against the United States. Disability payments for injuries incurred as a direct result of a terrorist attack directed against the United States (or its allies) aren't included in income. Because federal income tax withholding is only required when a payment is includible in income, no federal income tax should be withheld from these payments. See Pub. 907, Tax Highlights for Persons With Disabilities, and Pub. 3920, Tax Relief for Victims of Terrorist Attacks.

Voluntary withholding on dividends and other distributions by an Alaska Native Corporation (ANC). A shareholder of an ANC may request voluntary income tax withholding on dividends and other distributions paid by an ANC. A shareholder may request voluntary withholding by giving the ANC a completed Form W-4V. For more information, see Notice 2013-77, 2013-50 I.R.B. 632, available at *IRS.gov/irb/2013-50_IRB#NOT-2013-77*.

Definition of marriage. A marriage of two individuals is recognized for federal tax purposes if the marriage is recognized by the state, possession, or territory of the United States in which the marriage is entered into, regardless of legal residence. Two individuals who enter into a relationship that is denominated as marriage under the laws of a foreign jurisdiction are recognized as married for federal tax purposes if the relationship would be recognized as marriage under the laws of at least one state, possession, or territory of the United States, regardless of legal residence. Individuals who have entered into a registered domestic partnership, civil union, or other similar relationship that isn't denominated as a marriage under the law of the state, possession, or territory of the United States where such relationship was entered into aren't lawfully married for federal tax purposes, regardless of legal residence.

Severance payments. Severance payments are wages subject to social security and Medicare taxes, income tax withholding, and FUTA tax.

You must receive written notice from the IRS to file Form 944. If you've been filing Forms 941 (or Forms 941-SS or Formularios 941-PR), and believe your employment taxes for the calendar year will be $1,000 or less, and you would like to file Form 944 instead of Forms 941, you must contact the IRS during the first calendar quarter of the tax year to request to file Form 944. You must receive written notice from the IRS to file Form 944 instead of Forms 941 before you may file this form. For more information on requesting to file Form 944, including the methods and deadlines for making a request, see the Instructions for Form 944.

Employers can request to file Forms 941 instead of Form 944. If you received notice from the IRS to file Form 944 but would like to file Forms 941 instead, you must contact the IRS during the first calendar quarter of the tax year to request to file Forms 941. You must receive written notice from the IRS to file Forms 941 instead of Form 944 before you may file these forms. For more information on requesting to file Forms 941, including the methods and deadlines for making a request, see the Instructions for Form 944.

Correcting Form 941 or 944. If you discover an error on a previously filed Form 941, make the correction using Form 941-X. If you discover an error on a previously filed Form 944, make the correction using Form 944-X. Forms 941-X and 944-X are filed separately from Forms 941 and 944. Forms 941-X and 944-X are used by employers to claim refunds or abatements of employment taxes, rather than Form 843. See section 13 for more information.

Zero wage return. If you haven't filed a "final" Form 940 and "final" Form 941 or 944, or aren't a "seasonal" employer (Form 941 only), you must continue to file a Form 940 and Forms 941 or Form 944, even for periods during which you paid no wages. The IRS encourages you to file your "zero wage" Form 940 and Form 941 or 944 electronically. Go to *IRS.gov/EmploymentEfile* for more information on electronic filing.

Federal tax deposits must be made by electronic funds transfer (EFT). You must use EFT to make all federal tax deposits. Generally, an EFT is made using the Electronic Federal Tax Payment System (EFTPS). If you don't want to use EFTPS, you can arrange for your tax professional, financial institution, payroll service, or other trusted third party to make electronic deposits on your behalf. Also, you may arrange for your financial institution to initiate a same-day wire payment on your behalf. EFTPS is a free service provided by the Department of the Treasury. Services provided by your tax professional, financial institution, payroll service, or other third party may have a fee.

For more information on making federal tax deposits, see *How To Deposit* in section 11. To get more information about EFTPS or to enroll in EFTPS, go to *EFTPS.gov* or call 800-555-4477. To contact EFTPS using Telecommunications Relay Services (TRS) for people who are deaf, hard of hearing, or have a speech disability, dial 711 and then provide the TRS assistant the 800-555-4477 number above or 800-733-4829. Additional information about EFTPS is also available in Pub. 966.

Pub. 5146 explains employment tax examinations and appeal rights. Pub. 5146 provides employers with information on how the IRS selects employment tax returns to be examined, what happens during an exam, and what options an employer has in responding to the results of an exam, including how to appeal the results. Pub. 5146 also includes information on worker classification issues and tip exams.

Electronic Filing and Payment

Businesses can enjoy the benefits of filing and paying their federal taxes electronically. Whether you rely on a tax professional or handle your own taxes, the IRS offers you convenient programs to make filing and payment easier.

Spend less time worrying about taxes and more time running your business. Use *e-file* and EFTPS to your benefit.

- For *e-file*, go to *IRS.gov/EmploymentEfile* for additional information. A fee may be charged to file electronically.

- For EFTPS, go to *EFTPS.gov* or call EFTPS Customer Service at 800-555-4477. To contact EFTPS using TRS for people who are deaf, hard of hearing, or have a speech disability, dial 711 and then provide the TRS assistant the 800-555-4477 number above or 800-733-4829.

- For electronic filing of Forms W-2, Wage and Tax Statement, go to *SSA.gov/employer*. You may be required to file Forms W-2 electronically. For details, see the General Instructions for Forms W-2 and W-3.

 If you're filing your tax return or paying your federal taxes electronically, a valid employer identification number (EIN) is required at the time the return is filed or the payment is made. If a valid EIN isn't provided, the return or payment won't be processed. This may result in penalties. See section 1 for information about applying for an EIN.

Electronic funds withdrawal (EFW). If you file your employment tax return electronically, you can *e-file* and use EFW to pay the balance due in a single step using tax preparation software or through a tax professional. However, don't use EFW to make federal tax deposits. For more information on paying your taxes using EFW, go to *IRS.gov/EFW*.

Credit or debit card payments. You can pay the balance due shown on your employment tax return by credit or debit card. Your payment will be processed by a payment processor who will charge a processing fee. Don't use a credit or debit card to make federal tax deposits. For more information on paying your taxes with a credit or debit card, go to *IRS.gov/PayByCard*.

Online payment agreement. You may be eligible to apply for an installment agreement online if you can't pay the full amount of tax you owe when you file your employment tax return. For more information, see the instructions for your employment tax return or go to *IRS.gov/OPA*.

Forms in Spanish

You can provide Formulario W-4(SP), Certificado de Retenciones del Empleado, in place of Form W-4, Employee's Withholding Certificate, to your Spanish-speaking employees. For more information, see Pub. 17(SP), El Impuesto Federal sobre los Ingresos (Para Personas Físicas). For nonemployees, such as independent contractors, Formulario W-9(SP), Solicitud y Certificación del Número de Identificación del Contribuyente, may be used in place of Form W-9, Request for Taxpayer Identification Number and Certification.

Hiring New Employees

Eligibility for employment. You must verify that each new employee is legally eligible to work in the United States. This includes completing the U.S. Citizenship and Immigration Services (USCIS) Form I-9, Employment Eligibility Verification. You can get Form I-9 at *USCIS.gov/Forms*. For more information, go to the USCIS website at *USCIS.gov/I-9-Central*, or call 800-375-5283 or 800-767-1833 (TTY).

You may use the Social Security Number Verification Service (SSNVS) at *SSA.gov/employer/ssnv.htm* to verify that an employee name matches an SSN. A person may have a valid SSN but not be authorized to work in the United States. You may use E-Verify at *E-Verify.gov* to confirm the employment eligibility of newly hired employees.

New hire reporting. You're required to report any new employee to a designated state new hire registry. A new employee is an employee who hasn't previously been employed by you or was previously employed by you but has been separated from such prior employment for at least 60 consecutive days.

Many states accept a copy of Form W-4 with employer information added. Go to the Office of Child Support Enforcement website at *acf.hhs.gov/programs/css/employers* for more information.

W-4 request. Ask each new employee to complete the 2023 Form W-4. See section 9.

Name and social security number (SSN). Record each new employee's name and SSN from their social security card. Any employee without a social security card should apply for one. See section 4.

Information Returns

You must file Forms W-2 to report wages paid to employees. You may also be required to file information returns to report certain types of payments made during the year. For example, you must file Form 1099-NEC, Nonemployee Compensation, to report payments of $600 or more to persons not treated as employees (for example, independent contractors) for services performed for your trade or business. For details about filing Forms 1099 and for information about required electronic filing, see the General Instructions for Certain Information Returns for general information, and the separate, specific instructions for each information return you file (for example, the Instructions for Forms 1099-MISC and 1099-NEC). Generally, don't use Forms 1099 to report wages and other compensation you paid to employees; report these on Form W-2. See the General Instructions for Forms W-2 and W-3 for details about filing Form W-2 and for information about required electronic filing.

Technical Services Operation (TSO). The IRS operates the TSO to answer questions about reporting on Forms W-2, W-3, and 1099, and other information returns. If you have questions related to reporting on information returns, call 866-455-7438 (toll free) or 304-263-8700 (toll

Employer Responsibilities

The following list provides a brief summary of your basic responsibilities. Because the individual circumstances for each employer can vary greatly, responsibilities for withholding, depositing, and reporting employment taxes can differ. Each item in this list has a page reference to a more detailed discussion in this publication.

New Employees:	Page
☐ Verify work eligibility of new employees	5
☐ Record employees' names and SSNs from social security cards	5
☐ Ask employees for Form W-4	5

Each Payday:	
☐ Withhold federal income tax based on each employee's Form W-4	21
☐ Withhold employee's share of social security and Medicare taxes	24
☐ Deposit:	
• Withheld income tax	
• Withheld and employer social security taxes	
• Withheld and employer Medicare taxes	26
Note: Due date of deposit generally depends on your deposit schedule (monthly or semiweekly).	

Quarterly (By April 30, July 31, October 31, and January 31):	
☐ Deposit FUTA tax if undeposited amount is over $500	38
☐ File Form 941 (pay tax with return if not required to deposit)	32

Annually (see *Calendar* for due dates):	Page
☐ File Form 944 if required (pay tax with return if not required to deposit)	32
☐ Remind employees to submit a new Form W-4 if they need to change their withholding	21
☐ Ask for a new Form W-4 from employees claiming exemption from income tax withholding	22
☐ Reconcile Forms 941 (or Form 944) with Forms W-2 and W-3	34
☐ Furnish each employee a Form W-2	9
☐ File Copy A of Forms W-2 and the transmittal Form W-3 with the SSA	9
☐ Furnish each other payee a Form 1099 (for example, Form 1099-NEC)	9
☐ File Forms 1099 and the transmittal Form 1096	9
☐ File Form 940	9
☐ File Form 945 for any nonpayroll income tax withholding	9

call). The center can also be reached by email at *mccirp@irs.gov*. Don't include taxpayer identification numbers (TINs) or attachments in email because email isn't secure.

Federal Income Tax Withholding

Withhold federal income tax from each wage payment or supplemental unemployment compensation plan benefit payment according to the employee's Form W-4 and the correct withholding table in Pub. 15-T. If you're paying supplemental wages to an employee, see section 7. If you have nonresident alien employees, see *Withholding income taxes on the wages of nonresident alien employees* in section 9.

See section 8 of Pub. 15-A, Employer's Supplemental Tax Guide, for information about withholding on pensions (including distributions from tax-favored retirement plans), annuities, and individual retirement arrangements (IRAs).

Nonpayroll Income Tax Withholding

Nonpayroll federal income tax withholding (reported on Forms 1099 and Form W-2G, Certain Gambling Winnings) must be reported on Form 945, Annual Return of Withheld Federal Income Tax. Separate deposits are required for payroll (Form 941 or Form 944) and nonpayroll (Form 945) withholding. Nonpayroll items include the following.

- Pensions (including distributions from tax-favored retirement plans, for example, section 401(k), section 403(b), and governmental section 457(b) plans), annuities, and IRA distributions.

- Military retirement.

- Gambling winnings.

- Indian gaming profits.

- Certain government payments on which the recipient elected voluntary income tax withholding.

- Dividends and other distributions by an ANC on which the recipient elected voluntary income tax withholding.

- Payments subject to backup withholding.

For details on depositing and reporting nonpayroll income tax withholding, see the Instructions for Form 945.

Distributions from nonqualified pension plans and deferred compensation plans. Because distributions to participants from some nonqualified pension plans and deferred compensation plans (including section 457(b) plans of tax-exempt organizations) are treated as wages and are reported on Form W-2, income tax withheld must be reported on Form 941 or Form 944, not on Form 945. However, distributions from such plans to a beneficiary or estate of a deceased employee aren't wages and are reported on Forms 1099-R, Distributions From Pensions, Annuities, Retirement or Profit-Sharing Plans, IRAs, Insurance Contracts, etc.; income tax withheld must be reported on Form 945.

Backup withholding. You must generally withhold 24% of certain taxable payments if the payee fails to furnish you with their correct TIN. This withholding is referred to as "backup withholding."

Payments subject to backup withholding include interest, dividends, patronage dividends, rents, royalties, commissions, nonemployee compensation, payments made in settlement of payment card or third-party network transactions, and certain other payments you make in the course of your trade or business. In addition, transactions by brokers and barter exchanges and certain payments made by fishing boat operators are subject to backup withholding.

 Backup withholding doesn't apply to wages, pensions, annuities, IRAs (including simplified employee pension (SEP) and SIMPLE retirement plans), section 404(k) distributions from an employee stock ownership plan (ESOP), medical savings accounts (MSAs), health savings accounts (HSAs), long-term-care benefits, or real estate transactions.

You can use Form W-9 or Formulario W-9(SP) to request payees to furnish a TIN. Form W-9 or Formulario W-9(SP) must be used when payees must certify that the number furnished is correct, or when payees must certify that they're not subject to backup withholding or are exempt from backup withholding. The Instructions for the Requester of Form W-9 or Formulario W-9(SP) includes a list of types of payees who are exempt from backup withholding. For more information, see Pub. 1281, Backup Withholding for Missing and Incorrect Name/TIN(s).

Recordkeeping

Keep all records of employment taxes for at least 4 years. These should be available for IRS review. Your records should include the following information.

- Your EIN.
- Amounts and dates of all wage, annuity, and pension payments.
- Amounts of tips reported to you by your employees.
- Records of allocated tips.
- The fair market value of in-kind wages paid.
- Names, addresses, SSNs, and occupations of employees and recipients.
- Any employee copies of Forms W-2 and W-2c returned to you as undeliverable.
- Dates of employment for each employee.
- Periods for which employees and recipients were paid while absent due to sickness or injury and the amount

and weekly rate of payments you or third-party payers made to them.

- Copies of employees' and recipients' income tax withholding certificates (Forms W-4, W-4P, W-4(SP), W-4S, and W-4V).
- Dates and amounts of tax deposits you made and acknowledgment numbers for deposits made by EFTPS.
- Copies of returns filed and confirmation numbers.
- Records of fringe benefits and expense reimbursements provided to your employees, including substantiation.
- Documentation to substantiate any credits claimed. Records related to qualified sick leave wages and qualified family leave wages for leave taken after March 31, 2021, and before October 1, 2021, and records related to qualified wages for the employee retention credit paid after June 30, 2021, should be kept for at least 6 years. For more information on substantiation requirements, go to *IRS.gov/PLC* and *IRS.gov/ERC*.
- Documentation to substantiate the amount of any employer or employee share of social security tax that you deferred and paid for 2020.

Change of Business Name

Notify the IRS immediately if you change your business name. Write to the IRS office where you file your returns, using the *Without a payment* address provided in the instructions for your employment tax return, to notify the IRS of any business name change. See Pub. 1635 to see if you need to apply for a new EIN.

Change of Business Address or Responsible Party

Notify the IRS immediately if you change your business address or responsible party. Complete and mail Form 8822-B to notify the IRS of a business address or responsible party change. For a definition of "responsible party," see the Instructions for Form SS-4.

Filing Addresses

Generally, your filing address for Form 940, 941, 943, 944, 945, or CT-1 depends on the location of your residence or principal place of business and whether or not you're including a payment with your return. There are separate filing addresses for these returns if you're a tax-exempt organization or government entity. See the separate instructions for Form 940, 941, 943, 944, 945, or CT-1 for the filing addresses.

Private Delivery Services

You can use certain private delivery services (PDSs) designated by the IRS to meet the "timely mailing as timely filing" rule for tax returns. Go to *IRS.gov/PDS* for the current list of PDSs.

The PDS can tell you how to get written proof of the mailing date.

For the IRS mailing address to use if you're using a PDS, go to *IRS.gov/PDSstreetAddresses*. Select the mailing address listed on the webpage that is in the same state as the address to which you would mail returns filed without a payment, as shown in the instructions for your employment tax return.

 PDSs can't deliver items to P.O. boxes. You must use the U.S. Postal Service to mail any item to an IRS P.O. box address.

Dishonored Payments

Any form of payment that is dishonored and returned from a financial institution is subject to a penalty. The penalty is $25 or 2% of the payment, whichever is more. However, the penalty on dishonored payments of $24.99 or less is an amount equal to the payment. For example, a dishonored payment of $18 is charged a penalty of $18.

E-News for Payroll Professionals

The IRS has a subscription-based email service for payroll professionals. Subscribers will receive periodic updates from the IRS. The updates may include information regarding recent legislative changes affecting federal payroll reporting, IRS news releases and special announcements pertaining to the payroll industry, new employment tax procedures, and other information specifically affecting federal payroll tax returns. To subscribe, go to *IRS.gov/ENewsPayroll*.

Telephone Help

Tax questions. You can call the IRS Business and Specialty Tax Line with your employment tax questions at 800-829-4933.

Help for people with disabilities. You may call 800-829-4059 (TDD/TTY for persons who are deaf, hard of hearing, or have a speech disability) with any employment tax questions. You may also use this number for assistance with unresolved tax problems.

Additional information. Go to *IRS.gov/EmploymentTaxes* for additional employment tax information. For information about employer responsibilities under the Affordable Care Act, go to *IRS.gov/ACA*. For information about COVID-19 tax relief, go to *IRS.gov/Coronavirus*.

Ordering Employer Tax Forms, Instructions, and Publications

You can view, download, or print most of the forms, instructions, and publications you may need at *IRS.gov/Forms*. Otherwise, you can go to *IRS.gov/OrderForms* to place an order and have them mailed to you. The IRS will process your order as soon as possible. Don't resubmit requests you've already sent us. You can get forms, instructions, and publications faster online.

Instead of ordering paper Forms W-2 and W-3, consider filing them electronically using the SSA's free *e-file* service. Go to the SSA's Employer W-2 Filing Instructions & Information webpage at *SSA.gov/employer* to register for Business Services Online. You'll be able to create Forms W-2 online and submit them to the SSA by typing your wage information into easy-to-use fill-in fields. In addition, you can print out completed copies of Forms W-2 to file with state or local governments, distribute to your employees, and keep for your records. Form W-3 will be created for you based on your Forms W-2.

Photographs of Missing Children

The IRS is a proud partner with the *National Center for Missing & Exploited Children® (NCMEC)*. Photographs of missing children selected by the Center may appear in this publication on pages that would otherwise be blank. You can help bring these children home by looking at the photographs and calling 1-800-THE-LOST (1-800-843-5678) if you recognize a child.

Calendar

The following is a list of important dates and responsibilities. The dates listed here haven't been adjusted for Saturdays, Sundays, and legal holidays (see the *TIP* next). Pub. 509, Tax Calendars (for use in 2023), adjusts the dates for Saturdays, Sundays, and legal holidays. See section 11 for information about depositing taxes reported on Forms 941, 944, and 945. See section 14 for information about depositing FUTA tax. Due dates for forms required for health coverage reporting aren't listed here. For these dates, see Pub. 509.

 If any date shown next for filing a return, furnishing a form, or depositing taxes falls on a Saturday, Sunday, or legal holiday, the due date is the next business day. The term "legal holiday" means any legal holiday in the District of Columbia. A statewide legal holiday delays a filing due date only if the IRS office where you're required to file is located in that state. However, a

statewide legal holiday doesn't delay the due date of federal tax deposits. See <u>Deposits Due on Business Days Only</u> in section 11. For any filing due date, you'll meet the "file" or "furnish" requirement if the envelope containing the return or form is properly addressed, contains sufficient postage, and is postmarked by the U.S. Postal Service on or before the due date, or sent by an IRS-designated PDS on or before the due date. See <u>Private Delivery Services</u> under Reminders, *earlier, for more information.*

Fiscal year taxpayers. The due dates listed next apply whether you use a calendar or a fiscal year.

By January 31

File Form 941 or Form 944. File Form 941 for the fourth quarter of the previous calendar year and deposit any undeposited income, social security, and Medicare taxes. You may pay these taxes with Form 941 if your total tax liability for the quarter (Form 941, line 12) is less than $2,500. File Form 944 for the previous calendar year instead of Form 941 if the IRS has notified you in writing to file Form 944. Pay any undeposited income, social security, and Medicare taxes with your Form 944. You may pay these taxes with Form 944 if your total tax liability for the year (Form 944, line 9) is less than $2,500. For additional rules on when you can pay your taxes with your return, see *Payment with return* in section 11. If you timely deposited all taxes when due, you may file by February 10.

File Form 940. File Form 940 to report any FUTA tax. However, if you deposited all of the FUTA tax when due, you may file by February 10. See <u>section 14</u> for more information on FUTA tax.

Furnish Forms 1099 and W-2. Furnish each employee a completed 2022 Form W-2. Furnish a 2022 Form 1099-NEC to payees for nonemployee compensation. Most Forms 1099 must be furnished to payees by January 31, but some can be furnished by February 15. For more information, see the *Guide to Information Returns* chart in the General Instructions for Certain Information Returns.

File Form W-2. File with the SSA Copy A of all 2022 paper and electronic Forms W-2 with Form W-3, Transmittal of Wage and Tax Statements. For more information on reporting Form W-2 information to the SSA electronically, go to the SSA's Employer W-2 Filing Instructions & Information webpage at *SSA.gov/ employer*. If filing electronically, via the SSA's Form W-2 Online service, the SSA will generate Form W-3 data from the electronic submission of Form(s) W-2.

File Form 1099-NEC reporting nonemployee compensation. File with the IRS Copy A of all 2022 paper and electronic Forms 1099-NEC. Paper forms must be filed with Form 1096, Annual Summary and Transmittal of U.S. Information Returns. For information on filing information returns electronically with the IRS, see Pub. 1220, Specifications for Electronic Filing of Forms 1097, 1098, 1099, 3921, 3922, 5498, and W-2G.

File Form 945. File Form 945 to report any nonpayroll federal income tax withheld. If you deposited all taxes when due, you may file by February 10. See *Nonpayroll Income Tax Withholding* under *Reminders,* earlier, for more information.

By February 15

Request a new Form W-4 from exempt employees. Ask for a new Form W-4 from each employee who claimed exemption from income tax withholding last year.

On February 16

Forms W-4 claiming exemption from withholding expire. Any Form W-4 claiming exemption from withholding for the previous year has now expired. Begin withholding for any employee who previously claimed exemption from withholding but hasn't given you a new Form W-4 for the current year. If the employee doesn't give you a new Form W-4, withhold tax as if they had checked the box for Single or Married filing separately in Step 1(c) and made no entries in Step 2, Step 3, or Step 4 of the 2023 Form W-4. See <u>section 9</u> for more information. If the employee gives you a new Form W-4 claiming exemption from withholding after February 15, you may apply the exemption to future wages, but don't refund taxes withheld while the exempt status wasn't in place.

By February 28

File paper 2022 Forms 1099 and 1096. File Copy A of all paper 2022 Forms 1099, except Forms 1099-NEC, with Form 1096 with the IRS. For electronically filed returns, see *By March 31*, later.

File paper Form 8027. File paper Form 8027, Employer's Annual Information Return of Tip Income and Allocated Tips, with the IRS. See <u>section 6</u>. For electronically filed returns, see *By March 31* next.

By March 31

File electronic 2022 Forms 1099 and 8027. File electronic 2022 Forms 1099, except Forms 1099-NEC, with the IRS. Also file electronic Form 8027 with the IRS. For information on filing information returns electronically with the IRS, see Pub. 1220 and Pub. 1239, Specifications for Electronic Filing of Form 8027, Employer's Annual Information Return of Tip Income and Allocated Tips.

By April 30, July 31, October 31, and January 31

Deposit FUTA taxes. Deposit FUTA tax for the quarter (including any amount carried over from other quarters) if over $500. If $500 or less, carry it over to the next quarter. See <u>section 14</u> for more information.

File Form 941. File Form 941 and deposit any undeposited income, social security, and Medicare taxes. You may pay these taxes with Form 941 if your total tax liability for the quarter (Form 941, line 12) is less than $2,500. If you timely deposited all taxes when due, you may file by May 10, August 10, November 10, or February 10, respectively. Don't file Form 941 for these quarters if you have been notified to file Form 944 and you didn't request and receive written notice from the IRS to file quarterly Forms 941.

Before December 1

New Forms W-4. Remind employees to submit a new Form W-4 if their filing status, other income, deductions, or credits have changed or will change for the next year.

Introduction

This publication explains your tax responsibilities as an employer. It explains the requirements for withholding, depositing, reporting, paying, and correcting employment taxes. It explains the forms you must give to your employees, those your employees must give to you, and those you must send to the IRS and the SSA. References to "income tax" in this guide apply only to federal income tax. Contact your state or local tax department to determine their rules.

When you pay your employees, you don't pay them all the money they earned. As their employer, you have the added responsibility of withholding taxes from their paychecks. The federal income tax and employees' share of social security and Medicare taxes that you withhold from your employees' paychecks are part of their wages that you pay to the U.S. Treasury instead of to your employees. Your employees trust that you pay the withheld taxes to the U.S. Treasury by making federal tax deposits. This is the reason that these withheld taxes are called trust fund taxes. If federal income, social security, or Medicare taxes that must be withheld aren't withheld or aren't deposited or paid to the U.S. Treasury, the trust fund recovery penalty may apply. See section 11 for more information.

Additional employment tax information is available in Pubs. 15-A, 15-B, and 15-T. Pub. 15-A includes specialized information supplementing the basic employment tax information provided in this publication. Pub. 15-B, Employer's Tax Guide to Fringe Benefits, contains information about the employment tax treatment and valuation of various types of noncash compensation. Pub. 15-T includes the federal income tax withholding tables and instructions on how to use the tables.

Most employers must withhold (except FUTA), deposit, report, and pay the following employment taxes.

- Income tax.
- Social security tax.
- Medicare tax.
- FUTA tax.

There are exceptions to these requirements. See section 15 for guidance. Railroad retirement taxes are explained in the Instructions for Form CT-1. Employment taxes for agricultural employers are explained in Pub. 51. If you have employees in the U.S. Virgin Islands, Guam, American Samoa, or the Commonwealth of the Northern Mariana Islands, see Pub. 80.

Comments and suggestions. We welcome your comments about this publication and suggestions for future editions.

You can send us comments through *IRS.gov/FormComments*.

Or, you can write to:

Internal Revenue Service
Tax Forms and Publications
1111 Constitution Ave. NW, IR-6526
Washington, DC 20224

Although we can't respond individually to each comment received, we do appreciate your feedback and will consider your comments and suggestions as we revise our tax forms, instructions, and publications. **Don't** send tax questions, tax returns, or payments to the above address.

Getting answers to your tax questions. If you have a tax question not answered by this publication, check *IRS.gov* and *How To Get Tax Help* at the end of this publication.

Getting tax forms, instructions, and publications. Go to *IRS.gov/Forms* to download current and prior-year forms, instructions, and publications.

Ordering tax forms, instructions, and publications. Go to *IRS.gov/OrderForms* to order current forms, instructions, and publications; call 800-829-3676 to order prior-year forms and instructions. The IRS will process your order for forms and publications as soon as possible. **Don't** resubmit requests you've already sent us. You can get forms and publications faster online.

Federal government employers. The information in this publication, including the rules for making federal tax deposits, applies to federal agencies.

State and local government employers. Payments to employees for services in the employ of state and local government employers are generally subject to federal income tax withholding but not FUTA tax. Most elected and appointed public officials of state or local governments are employees under common law rules. See chapter 3 of Pub. 963, Federal-State Reference Guide. In addition, wages, with certain exceptions, are subject to social security and Medicare taxes. See section 15 for more information on the exceptions.

If an election worker is employed in another capacity with the same government entity, see Revenue Ruling 2000-6 on page 512 of Internal Revenue Bulletin 2000-6 at *IRS.gov/pub/irs-irbs/irb00-06.pdf*.

You can get information on reporting and social security coverage from your local IRS office. If you have any questions about coverage under a section 218 (Social Security Act) agreement, contact the appropriate state official. To find your State Social Security Administrator, go to the National Conference of State Social Security Administrators website at _NCSSSA.org_.

Indian tribal governments. See Pub. 4268 for employment tax information for Indian tribal governments.

Disregarded entities and qualified subchapter S subsidiaries (QSubs). Eligible single-owner disregarded entities and QSubs are treated as separate entities for employment tax purposes. Eligible single-member entities must report and pay employment taxes on wages paid to their employees using the entities' own names and EINs. See Regulations sections 1.1361-4(a)(7) and 301.7701-2(c)(2)(iv).

1. Employer Identification Number (EIN)

If you're required to report employment taxes or give tax statements to employees or annuitants, you need an EIN.

The EIN is a nine-digit number the IRS issues. The digits are arranged as follows: 00-0000000. It is used to identify the tax accounts of employers and certain others who have no employees. Use your EIN on all of the items you send to the IRS and the SSA. For more information, see Pub. 1635.

If you don't have an EIN, you may apply for one online by going to _IRS.gov/EIN_. You may also apply for an EIN by faxing or mailing Form SS-4 to the IRS. If the principal business was created or organized outside of the United States or U.S. territories, you may also apply for an EIN by calling 267-941-1099 (toll call). Don't use an SSN in place of an EIN.

You should have only one EIN. If you have more than one and aren't sure which one to use, call 800-829-4933 or 800-829-4059 (TDD/TTY for persons who are deaf, hard of hearing, or have a speech disability). Give the numbers you have, the name and address to which each was assigned, and the address of your main place of business. The IRS will tell you which number to use. For more information, see Pub. 1635.

If you took over another employer's business (see _Successor employer_ in section 9), don't use that employer's EIN. If you've applied for an EIN but don't have your EIN by the time a return is due, file a paper return and write "Applied For" and the date you applied for it in the space shown for the number.

 Always be sure the EIN on the form you file exactly matches the EIN the IRS assigned to your business. Don't use your SSN or individual taxpayer identification number (ITIN) on forms that ask for an EIN. If you used an EIN (including a prior owner's EIN) on

Form 941, or Form 944, that is different from the EIN reported on Form W-3, see Box h—Other EIN used this year _in the_ General Instructions for Forms W-2 and W-3. _The name and EIN on Form 945 must match the name and EIN on your information returns where federal income tax withholding is reported (for example, backup withholding reported on Form 1099-NEC). Filing a Form 945 with an incorrect EIN or using another business's EIN may result in penalties and delays in processing your return._

2. Who Are Employees?

Generally, employees are defined either under common law or under statutes for certain situations. See Pub. 15-A for details on statutory employees and nonemployees.

Employee status under common law. Generally, a worker who performs services for you is your employee if you have the right to control what will be done and how it will be done. This is so even when you give the employee freedom of action. What matters is that you have the right to control the details of how the services are performed. See Pub. 15-A for more information on how to determine whether an individual providing services is an independent contractor or an employee.

Generally, people in business for themselves aren't employees. For example, doctors, lawyers, veterinarians, and others in an independent trade in which they offer their services to the public are usually not employees. If the business is incorporated, corporate officers who work in the business are employees of the corporation.

If an employer-employee relationship exists, it doesn't matter what it is called. The employee may be called an agent or independent contractor. It also doesn't matter how payments are measured or paid, what they're called, or if the employee works full or part time.

Statutory employees. If someone who works for you isn't an employee under the common law rules discussed earlier, don't withhold federal income tax from their pay, unless backup withholding applies. Although the following persons may not be common law employees, they're considered employees by statute for social security and Medicare tax purposes under certain conditions.

- An agent or commission driver who delivers meat, vegetable, fruit, or bakery products; beverages (other than milk); laundry; or dry cleaning for someone else.

- A full-time life insurance salesperson who sells primarily for one company.

- A homeworker who works at home or off premises according to guidelines of the person for whom the work is done, with materials or goods furnished by and returned to that person or to someone that person designates.

- A traveling or city salesperson (other than an agent or commission driver) who works full time (except for sideline sales activities) for one firm or person getting orders from customers. The orders must be for merchandise for resale or supplies for use in the customer's business. The customers must be retailers, wholesalers, contractors, or operators of hotels, restaurants, or other businesses dealing with food or lodging.

For FUTA tax, an agent or commission driver and a traveling or city salesperson are considered statutory employees; however, a full-time life insurance salesperson and a homeworker aren't considered statutory employees.

Statutory nonemployees. Direct sellers, qualified real estate agents, and certain companion sitters are, by law, considered nonemployees. They're generally treated as self-employed for all federal tax purposes, including income and employment taxes. See Pub. 15-A for more information.

H-2A agricultural workers. On Form W-2, don't check box 13 (Statutory employee), as H-2A workers aren't statutory employees.

Treating employees as nonemployees. You'll generally be liable for social security and Medicare taxes and withheld income tax if you don't deduct and withhold these taxes because you treated an employee as a nonemployee. You may be able to figure your liability using special section 3509 rates for the employee share of social security and Medicare taxes and federal income tax withholding. The applicable rates depend on whether you filed required Forms 1099. You can't recover the employee share of social security tax, Medicare tax, or income tax withholding from the employee if the tax is paid under section 3509. You're liable for the income tax withholding regardless of whether the employee paid income tax on the wages. You continue to owe the full employer share of social security and Medicare taxes. The employee remains liable for the employee share of social security and Medicare taxes. See section 3509 for details. Also see the Instructions for Form 941-X or the Instructions for Form 944-X.

Section 3509 rates aren't available if you intentionally disregard the requirement to withhold taxes from the employee or if you withheld income taxes but not social security or Medicare taxes. Section 3509 isn't available for reclassifying statutory employees. See *Statutory employees*, earlier.

If the employer issued required information returns, the section 3509 rates are the following.

- For social security taxes: employer rate of 6.2% plus 20% of the employee rate of 6.2%, for a total rate of 7.44% of wages.

- For Medicare taxes: employer rate of 1.45% plus 20% of the employee rate of 1.45%, for a total rate of 1.74% of wages.

- For Additional Medicare Tax: 0.18% (20% of the employee rate of 0.9%) of wages subject to Additional Medicare Tax.

- For federal income tax withholding, the rate is 1.5% of wages.

If the employer didn't issue required information returns, the section 3509 rates are the following.

- For social security taxes: employer rate of 6.2% plus 40% of the employee rate of 6.2%, for a total rate of 8.68% of wages.

- For Medicare taxes: employer rate of 1.45% plus 40% of the employee rate of 1.45%, for a total rate of 2.03% of wages.

- For Additional Medicare Tax: 0.36% (40% of the employee rate of 0.9%) of wages subject to Additional Medicare Tax.

- For federal income tax withholding, the rate is 3.0% of wages.

Relief provisions. If you have a reasonable basis for not treating a worker as an employee, you may be relieved from having to pay employment taxes for that worker. To get this relief, you must file all required federal tax returns, including information returns, on a basis consistent with your treatment of the worker. You (or your predecessor) must not have treated any worker holding a substantially similar position as an employee for any periods beginning after 1977. See Pub. 1976, Do You Qualify for Relief Under Section 530.

IRS help. If you want the IRS to determine whether a worker is an employee, file Form SS-8.

Voluntary Classification Settlement Program (VCSP). Employers who are currently treating their workers (or a class or group of workers) as independent contractors or other nonemployees and want to voluntarily reclassify their workers as employees for future tax periods may be eligible to participate in the VCSP if certain requirements are met. File Form 8952 to apply for the VCSP. For more information, go to *IRS.gov/VCSP*.

Business Owned and Operated by Spouses

If you and your spouse jointly own and operate a business and share in the profits and losses, you may be partners in a partnership, whether or not you have a formal partnership agreement. See Pub. 541 for more details. The partnership is considered the employer of any employees and is liable for any employment taxes due on wages paid to its employees.

Exception—Qualified joint venture. For tax years beginning after 2006, the Small Business and Work Opportunity Tax Act of 2007 (Public Law 110-28) provides that a "qualified joint venture," whose only members are spouses filing a joint income tax return, can elect not to be treated as a partnership for federal tax purposes. A qualified joint venture conducts a trade or business where:

- The only members of the joint venture are spouses who file a joint income tax return,

- Both spouses materially participate (see *Material participation* in the instructions for Schedule C (Form

1040), line G) in the trade or business (mere joint ownership of property isn't enough),

- Both spouses elect to not be treated as a partnership, and

- The business is co-owned by both spouses and isn't held in the name of a state law entity such as a partnership or limited liability company (LLC).

To make the election, all items of income, gain, loss, deduction, and credit must be divided between the spouses, in accordance with each spouse's interest in the venture, and reported as sole proprietors on a separate Schedule C (Form 1040) or Schedule F (Form 1040). Each spouse must also file a separate Schedule SE (Form 1040) to pay self-employment taxes, as applicable.

Spouses using the qualified joint venture rules are treated as sole proprietors for federal tax purposes and generally don't need an EIN. If employment taxes are owed by the qualified joint venture, either spouse may report and pay the employment taxes due on the wages paid to the employees using the EIN of that spouse's sole proprietorship. Generally, filing as a qualified joint venture won't increase the spouses' total tax owed on the joint income tax return. However, it gives each spouse credit for social security earnings on which retirement benefits are based and for Medicare coverage without filing a partnership return.

Note. If your spouse is your employee, not your partner, see _One spouse employed by another_ in section 3.

For more information on qualified joint ventures, go to _IRS.gov/QJV_.

Exception—Community income. If you and your spouse wholly own an unincorporated business as community property under the community property laws of a state, foreign country, or U.S. possession, you can treat the business either as a sole proprietorship (of the spouse who carried on the business) or a partnership. You may still make an election to be taxed as a qualified joint venture instead of a partnership. See _Exception—Qualified joint venture_, earlier.

---

3. Family Employees

Child employed by parents. Payments for the services of a child under age 18 who works for their parent in a trade or business aren't subject to social security and Medicare taxes if the trade or business is a sole proprietorship or a partnership in which each partner is a parent of the child. If these payments are for work other than in a trade or business, such as domestic work in the parent's private home, they're not subject to social security and Medicare taxes until the child reaches age 21. However, see _Covered services of a child or spouse_, later. Payments for the services of a child under age 21 who works for their parent, whether or not in a trade or business, aren't subject to FUTA tax. Payments for the services of a child of any age who works for their parent are generally subject to income tax withholding unless the payments are for domestic work in the parent's home, or unless the

payments are for work other than in a trade or business and are less than $50 in the quarter or the child isn't regularly employed to do such work.

One spouse employed by another. The wages for the services of an individual who works for their spouse in a trade or business are subject to income tax withholding and social security and Medicare taxes, but not to FUTA tax. However, the payments for services of one spouse employed by another in other than a trade or business, such as domestic service in a private home, aren't subject to social security, Medicare, and FUTA taxes.

Covered services of a child or spouse. The wages for the services of a child or spouse are subject to income tax withholding as well as social security, Medicare, and FUTA taxes if they work for:

- A corporation, even if it is controlled by the child's parent or the individual's spouse;

- A partnership, even if the child's parent is a partner, unless each partner is a parent of the child;

- A partnership, even if the individual's spouse is a partner; or

- An estate, even if it is the estate of a deceased parent.

In these situations, the child or spouse is considered to work for the corporation, partnership, or estate, not you.

Parent employed by their child. When the employer is a child employing their parent, the following rules apply.

- Payments for the services of a parent in their child's (the employer's) trade or business are subject to income tax withholding and social security and Medicare taxes.

- Payments for the services of a parent not in their child's (the employer's) trade or business are generally not subject to social security and Medicare taxes.

 Social security and Medicare taxes do apply to payments made to a parent for domestic services if all of the following apply.

- _The parent is employed by their child (the employer)._

- _The employer has a child or stepchild (including an adopted child) living in the home._

- _The employer is a surviving spouse, divorced and not remarried, or living with a spouse who, because of a mental or physical condition, can't care for their child or stepchild for at least 4 continuous weeks in the calendar quarter in which the service is performed._

- _The child or stepchild of the employer is either under age 18 or, due to a mental or physical condition, requires the personal care of an adult for at least 4 continuous weeks in the calendar quarter in which the service is performed._

Payments made to a parent employed by their child aren't subject to FUTA tax, regardless of the type of services provided.

4. Employee's Social Security Number (SSN)

You're required to get each employee's name and SSN and to enter them on Form W-2. This requirement also applies to resident and nonresident alien employees. You should ask your employee to show you their social security card. The employee may show the card if it is available.

 Don't accept a social security card that says "Not valid for employment." An SSN issued with this legend doesn't permit employment.

You may, but aren't required to, photocopy the social security card if the employee provides it. If you don't provide the correct employee name and SSN on Form W-2, you may owe a penalty unless you have reasonable cause. See Pub. 1586, Reasonable Cause Regulations & Requirements for Missing and Incorrect Name/TINs, for information on the requirement to solicit the employee's SSN.

Applying for a social security card. Any employee who is legally eligible to work in the United States and doesn't have a social security card can get one by completing Form SS-5, Application for a Social Security Card, and submitting the necessary documentation. You can get Form SS-5 from the SSA website at *SSA.gov/forms/ss-5.pdf*, at SSA offices, or by calling 800-772-1213 or 800-325-0778 (TTY). The employee must complete and sign Form SS-5; it can't be filed by the employer. You may be asked to supply a letter to accompany Form SS-5 if the employee has exceeded their yearly or lifetime limit for the number of replacement cards allowed.

Applying for an SSN. If you file Form W-2 on paper and your employee applied for an SSN but doesn't have one when you must file Form W-2, enter "Applied For" on the form. If you're filing electronically, enter all zeros (000-00-0000 if creating forms online or 000000000 if uploading a file) in the SSN field. When the employee receives the SSN, file Copy A of Form W-2c, Corrected Wage and Tax Statement, with the SSA to show the employee's SSN. Furnish Copies B, C, and 2 of Form W-2c to the employee. Up to 25 Forms W-2c for each Form W-3c, Transmittal of Corrected Wage and Tax Statements, may be filed per session over the Internet, with no limit on the number of sessions. For more information, go to the SSA's Employer W-2 Filing Instructions & Information webpage at *SSA.gov/employer*. Advise your employee to correct the SSN on their original Form W-2.

Correctly record the employee's name and SSN. Record the name and SSN of each employee as they're shown on the employee's social security card. If the employee's name isn't correct as shown on the card (for example, because of marriage or divorce), the employee should request an updated card from the SSA. Continue to report the employee's wages under the old name until the employee shows you the updated social security card with the corrected name.

If the SSA issues the employee an updated card after a name change, or a new card with a different SSN after a change in alien work status, file a Form W-2c to correct the name/SSN reported for the most recently filed Form W-2. It isn't necessary to correct other years if the previous name and number were used for years before the most recent Form W-2.

IRS individual taxpayer identification numbers (ITINs) for aliens. Don't accept an ITIN in place of an SSN for employee identification or for work. An ITIN is only available to resident and nonresident aliens who aren't eligible for U.S. employment and need identification for other tax purposes. You can identify an ITIN because it is a nine-digit number, formatted like an SSN, that starts with the number "9" and has a range of numbers from "50–65," "70–88," "90–92," and "94–99" for the fourth and fifth digits (for example, 9NN-7N-NNNN). For more information about ITINs, see the Instructions for Form W-7 or go to *IRS.gov/ITIN*.

 An individual with an ITIN who later becomes eligible to work in the United States must obtain an SSN. If the individual is currently eligible to work in the United States, instruct the individual to apply for an SSN and follow the instructions under Applying for an SSN, earlier. Don't use an ITIN in place of an SSN on Form W-2.

Verification of SSNs. Employers and authorized reporting agents can use the Social Security Number Verification Service (SSNVS) to instantly verify that an employee name matches an SSN for up to 10 names and SSNs (per screen) at a time, or submit an electronic file of up to 250,000 names and SSNs and usually receive the results the next business day. Go to *SSA.gov/employer/ssnv.htm* for more information. A person may have a valid SSN but not be authorized to work in the United States. Employers may use E-Verify at *E-Verify.gov* to confirm the employment eligibility of newly hired employees.

Registering for SSNVS. You must register online to use SSNVS. To register, go to the SSA's website at *SSA.gov/bso* and click on the *Register* link under *Business Services Online*. Follow the registration instructions to obtain a user identification (ID) and password. You'll need to provide the following information about yourself and your company.

- Name.
- SSN.
- Date of birth.
- Type of employer.
- EIN.
- Company name, address, and telephone number.
- Email address.

When you have completed the online registration process, the SSA will mail a one-time activation code to you.

You must enter the activation code online to use SSNVS. Your employees must receive authorization from you to use SSNVS. If your employees register, the one-time activation code will be mailed to you.

5. Wages and Other Compensation

Wages subject to federal employment taxes generally include all pay you give to an employee for services performed. The pay may be in cash or in other forms. It includes salaries, vacation allowances, bonuses, commissions, and taxable fringe benefits. It doesn't matter how you measure or make the payments. Amounts an employer pays as a bonus for signing or ratifying a contract in connection with the establishment of an employer-employee relationship and an amount paid to an employee for cancellation of an employment contract and relinquishment of contract rights are wages subject to social security, Medicare, and FUTA taxes and income tax withholding. Also, compensation paid to a former employee for services performed while still employed is wages subject to employment taxes.

More information. See section 6 for a discussion of tips and section 7 for a discussion of supplemental wages. Also, see section 15 for exceptions to the general rules for wages. Pub. 15-A provides additional information on wages, including nonqualified deferred compensation, and other compensation. Pub. 15-B provides information on other forms of compensation, including:

- Accident and health benefits,
- Achievement awards,
- Adoption assistance,
- Athletic facilities,
- De minimis (minimal) benefits,
- Dependent care assistance,
- Educational assistance,
- Employee discounts,
- Employee stock options,
- Employer-provided cell phones,
- Group-term life insurance coverage,
- Health savings accounts,
- Lodging on your business premises,
- Meals,
- No-additional-cost services,
- Retirement planning services,
- Transportation (commuting) benefits,
- Tuition reduction, and
- Working condition benefits.

Employee business expense reimbursements. A reimbursement or allowance arrangement is a system by which you pay the advances, reimbursements, and charges for your employees' business expenses. How you report a reimbursement or allowance amount depends on whether you have an accountable or a nonaccountable plan. If a single payment includes both wages and an expense reimbursement, you must specify the amount of the reimbursement.

These rules apply to all allowable ordinary and necessary employee business expenses.

Accountable plan. To be an accountable plan, your reimbursement or allowance arrangement must require your employees to meet all three of the following rules.

1. They must have paid or incurred allowable expenses while performing services as your employees. The reimbursement or advance must be payment for the expenses and must not be an amount that would have otherwise been paid to the employee as wages.

2. They must substantiate these expenses to you within a reasonable period of time.

3. They must return any amounts in excess of substantiated expenses within a reasonable period of time.

Amounts paid under an accountable plan aren't wages and aren't subject to income, social security, Medicare, and FUTA taxes.

If the expenses covered by this arrangement aren't substantiated (or amounts in excess of substantiated expenses aren't returned within a reasonable period of time), the amount paid under the arrangement in excess of the substantiated expenses is treated as paid under a nonaccountable plan. This amount is subject to income, social security, Medicare, and FUTA taxes for the first payroll period following the end of the reasonable period of time.

A reasonable period of time depends on the facts and circumstances. Generally, it is considered reasonable if your employees receive their advance within 30 days of the time they pay or incur the expenses, adequately account for the expenses within 60 days after the expenses were paid or incurred, and return any amounts in excess of expenses within 120 days after the expenses were paid or incurred. Alternatively, it is considered reasonable if you give your employees a periodic statement (at least quarterly) that asks them to either return or adequately account for outstanding amounts and they do so within 120 days.

Nonaccountable plan. Payments to your employee for travel and other necessary expenses of your business under a nonaccountable plan are wages and are treated as supplemental wages and subject to income, social security, Medicare, and FUTA taxes. Your payments are treated as paid under a nonaccountable plan if:

- Your employee isn't required to or doesn't substantiate timely those expenses to you with receipts or other documentation,

- You advance an amount to your employee for business expenses and your employee isn't required to or doesn't return timely any amount they don't use for business expenses,

- You advance or pay an amount to your employee regardless of whether you reasonably expect the employee to have business expenses related to your business, or
- You pay an amount as a reimbursement you would have otherwise paid as wages.

See section 7 for more information on supplemental wages.

Per diem or other fixed allowance. You may reimburse your employees by travel days, miles, or some other fixed allowance under the applicable revenue procedure. In these cases, your employee is considered to have accounted to you if your reimbursement doesn't exceed rates established by the federal government. The standard mileage rate for auto expenses is provided in Pub. 15-B.

The government per diem rates for meals and lodging in the continental United States can be found by going to the U.S. General Services Administration website at *GSA.gov/PerDiemRates*. Other than the amount of these expenses, your employees' business expenses must be substantiated (for example, the business purpose of the travel or the number of business miles driven). For information on substantiation methods, see Pub. 463.

If the per diem or allowance paid exceeds the amounts substantiated, you must report the excess amount as wages. This excess amount is subject to income tax withholding and payment of social security, Medicare, and FUTA taxes. Show the amount equal to the substantiated amount (that is, the nontaxable portion) in box 12 of Form W-2 using code "L."

Wages not paid in money. If in the course of your trade or business you pay your employees in a medium that is neither cash nor a readily negotiable instrument, such as a check, you're said to pay them "in kind." Payments in kind may be in the form of goods, lodging, food, clothing, or services. Generally, the fair market value of such payments at the time they're provided is subject to federal income tax withholding and social security, Medicare, and FUTA taxes.

However, noncash payments for household work, agricultural labor, and service not in the employer's trade or business are exempt from social security, Medicare, and FUTA taxes. Withhold income tax on these payments only if you and the employee agree to do so. Nonetheless, noncash payments for agricultural labor, such as commodity wages, are treated as cash payments subject to employment taxes if the substance of the transaction is a cash payment.

Meals and lodging. The value of meals isn't taxable income and isn't subject to federal income tax withholding and social security, Medicare, and FUTA taxes if the meals are furnished for the employer's convenience and on the employer's premises. The value of lodging isn't subject to federal income tax withholding and social security, Medicare, and FUTA taxes if the lodging is fur-

nished for the employer's convenience, on the employer's premises, and as a condition of employment.

"For the convenience of the employer" means you have a substantial business reason for providing the meals and lodging other than to provide additional compensation to the employee. For example, meals you provide at the place of work so that an employee is available for emergencies during their lunch period are generally considered to be for your convenience. You must be able to show these emergency calls have occurred or can reasonably be expected to occur, and that the calls have resulted, or will result, in you calling on your employees to perform their jobs during their meal period.

Whether meals or lodging are provided for the convenience of the employer depends on all of the facts and circumstances. A written statement that the meals or lodging are for your convenience isn't sufficient.

50% test. If over 50% of the employees who are provided meals on an employer's business premises receive these meals for the convenience of the employer, all meals provided on the premises are treated as furnished for the convenience of the employer. If this 50% test is met, the value of the meals is excludable from income for all employees and isn't subject to federal income tax withholding or employment taxes. For more information, see Pub. 15-B.

Health insurance plans. If you pay the cost of an accident or health insurance plan for your employees, including an employee's spouse and dependents, your payments aren't wages and aren't subject to social security, Medicare, and FUTA taxes, or federal income tax withholding. Generally, this exclusion also applies to qualified long-term-care insurance contracts. However, for income tax withholding, the value of health insurance benefits must be included in the wages of S corporation employees who own more than 2% of the S corporation (2% shareholders). For social security, Medicare, and FUTA taxes, the health insurance benefits are excluded from the 2% shareholder's wages. See Announcement 92-16 for more information. You can find Announcement 92-16 on page 53 of Internal Revenue Bulletin 1992-5.

Health savings accounts (HSAs) and medical savings accounts (MSAs). Your contributions to an employee's HSA or Archer MSA aren't subject to social security, Medicare, or FUTA taxes, or federal income tax withholding if it is reasonable to believe at the time of payment of the contributions they'll be excludable from the income of the employee. To the extent it isn't reasonable to believe they'll be excludable, your contributions are subject to these taxes. Employee contributions to their HSAs or MSAs through a payroll deduction plan must be included in wages and are subject to social security, Medicare, and FUTA taxes and income tax withholding. However, HSA contributions made under a salary reduction arrangement in a section 125 cafeteria plan aren't wages and aren't subject to employment taxes or withholding. For more information, see the Instructions for Form 8889.

Medical care reimbursements. Generally, medical care reimbursements paid for an employee under an employer's self-insured medical reimbursement plan aren't wages and aren't subject to social security, Medicare, and FUTA taxes, or income tax withholding. See Pub. 15-B for a rule regarding inclusion of certain reimbursements in the gross income of highly compensated individuals.

Differential wage payments. Differential wage payments are any payments made by an employer to an individual for a period during which the individual is performing service in the uniformed services while on active duty for a period of more than 30 days and represent all or a portion of the wages the individual would have received from the employer if the individual were performing services for the employer.

Differential wage payments are wages for income tax withholding, but aren't subject to social security, Medicare, or FUTA taxes. Employers should report differential wage payments in box 1 of Form W-2. For more information about the tax treatment of differential wage payments, see Revenue Ruling 2009-11, 2009-18 I.R.B. 896, available at _IRS.gov/irb/2009-18_IRB#RR-2009-11_.

Fringe benefits. You must generally include fringe benefits in an employee's wages (but see _Nontaxable fringe benefits_ next). The benefits are subject to income tax withholding and employment taxes. Fringe benefits include cars you provide, flights on aircraft you provide, free or discounted commercial flights, vacations, discounts on property or services, memberships in country clubs or other social clubs, and tickets to entertainment or sporting events. In general, the amount you must include is the amount by which the fair market value of the benefit is more than the sum of what the employee paid for it plus any amount the law excludes. There are other special rules you and your employees may use to value certain fringe benefits. See Pub. 15-B for more information.

Nontaxable fringe benefits. Some fringe benefits aren't taxable (or are minimally taxable) if certain conditions are met. See Pub. 15-B for details. The following are some examples of nontaxable fringe benefits.

- Services provided to your employees at no additional cost to you.
- Qualified employee discounts.
- Working condition fringes that are property or services that would be allowable as a business expense or depreciation expense deduction to the employee if they had paid for them. Examples include a company car for business use and subscriptions to business magazines.
- Certain minimal value fringes (including an occasional cab ride when an employee must work overtime and meals you provide at eating places you run for your employees if the meals aren't furnished at below cost).
- Qualified transportation fringes subject to specified conditions and dollar limitations (including transportation in a commuter highway vehicle, any transit pass, and qualified parking).

- The use of on-premises athletic facilities operated by you if substantially all of the use is by employees, their spouses, and their dependent children.
- Qualified tuition reduction an educational organization provides to its employees for education. For more information, see Pub. 970.
- Employer-provided cell phones provided primarily for a noncompensatory business reason.

However, don't exclude the following fringe benefits from the wages of highly compensated employees unless the benefit is available to other employees on a nondiscriminatory basis.

- No-additional-cost services.
- Qualified employee discounts.
- Meals provided at an employer-operated eating facility.
- Reduced tuition for education.

For more information, including the definition of a highly compensated employee, see Pub. 15-B.

When taxable fringe benefits are treated as paid. You may choose to treat certain taxable noncash fringe benefits as paid by the pay period, by the quarter, or on any other basis you choose, as long as you treat the benefits as paid at least once a year. You don't have to make a formal choice of payment dates or notify the IRS of the dates you choose. You don't have to make this choice for all employees. You may change methods as often as you like, as long as you treat all benefits provided in a calendar year as paid by December 31 of the calendar year. See section 4 of Pub. 15-B for more information, including a discussion of the special accounting rule for fringe benefits provided during November and December.

Valuation of fringe benefits. Generally, you must determine the value of fringe benefits no later than January 31 of the next year. Before January 31, you may reasonably estimate the value of the fringe benefits for purposes of withholding and depositing on time.

Withholding on fringe benefits. You may add the value of fringe benefits to regular wages for a payroll period and figure withholding taxes on the total, or you may withhold federal income tax on the value of the fringe benefits at the optional flat 22% supplemental wage rate. However, see _Withholding on supplemental wages when an employee receives more than $1 million of supplemental wages during the calendar year_ in section 7.

You may choose not to withhold income tax on the value of an employee's personal use of a vehicle you provide. You must, however, withhold social security and Medicare taxes on the use of the vehicle. See Pub. 15-B for more information on this election.

Depositing taxes on fringe benefits. Once you choose when fringe benefits are paid, you must deposit taxes in the same deposit period you treat the fringe benefits as paid. To avoid a penalty, deposit the taxes following the general deposit rules for that deposit period.

If you determine by January 31 you overestimated the value of a fringe benefit at the time you withheld and deposited for it, you may claim a refund for the overpayment or have it applied to your next employment tax return. See *Valuation of fringe benefits*, earlier. If you underestimated the value and deposited too little, you may be subject to a failure-to-deposit (FTD) penalty. See section 11 for information on deposit penalties.

If you deposited the required amount of taxes but withheld a lesser amount from the employee, you can recover from the employee the social security, Medicare, or income taxes you deposited on their behalf and included in the employee's Form W-2. However, you must recover the income taxes before April 1 of the following year.

Sick pay. In general, sick pay is any amount you pay under a plan to an employee who is unable to work because of sickness or injury. These amounts are sometimes paid by a third party, such as an insurance company or an employees' trust. In either case, these payments are subject to social security, Medicare, and FUTA taxes. These taxes don't apply to sick pay paid more than 6 calendar months after the last calendar month in which the employee worked for the employer. The payments are always subject to federal income tax. See section 6 of Pub. 15-A for more information.

 For purposes of this publication, all references to "sick pay" mean ordinary sick pay, not "qualified sick leave wages" under the FFCRA, as amended by the COVID-related Tax Relief Act of 2020, and the ARP.

Identity protection services. The value of identity protection services provided by an employer to an employee isn't included in an employee's gross income and doesn't need to be reported on an information return (such as Form W-2) filed for an employee. This includes identity protection services provided before a data breach occurs. This exception doesn't apply to cash received instead of identity protection services or to proceeds received under an identity theft insurance policy. For more information, see Announcement 2015-22, 2015-35 I.R.B. 288, available at *IRS.gov/irb/2015-35_IRB#ANN-2015-22*; and Announcement 2016-02, 2016-3 I.R.B. 283, available at *IRS.gov/irb/2016-03_IRB#ANN-2016-02*.

6. Tips

Cash tips your employee receives from customers are generally subject to withholding. Your employee must report cash tips to you by the 10th of the month after the month the tips are received. Cash tips include tips paid by cash, check, debit card, and credit card. The report should include tips you paid over to the employee for charge customers, tips the employee received directly from customers, and tips received from other employees under any tip-sharing arrangement. Both directly and indirectly tipped employees must report tips to you. No report is required for months when tips are less than $20. Your employee reports the tips on Form 4070 or on a similar statement. The statement must be signed and dated by the employee and must include:

- The employee's name, address, and SSN;
- Your name and address;
- The month and year (or the beginning and ending dates, if the statement is for a period of less than 1 calendar month) the report covers; and
- The total of tips received during the month or period.

Both Forms 4070 and 4070-A, Employee's Daily Record of Tips, are included in Pub. 1244, Employee's Daily Record of Tips and Report to Employer.

 You're permitted to establish a system for electronic tip reporting by employees. See Regulations section 31.6053-1(d).

Collecting taxes on tips. You must collect federal income tax, employee social security tax, and employee Medicare tax on the employee's tips. The withholding rules for withholding an employee's share of Medicare tax on tips also apply to withholding the Additional Medicare Tax once wages and tips exceed $200,000 in the calendar year.

You can collect these taxes from the employee's wages (excluding tips) or from other funds they make available. See *Tips are treated as supplemental wages* in section 7 for more information. Stop collecting the employee social security tax when their wages and tips for tax year 2023 reach $160,200; collect the income and employee Medicare taxes for the whole year on all wages and tips. You're responsible for the employer social security tax on wages and tips until the wages (including tips) reach the limit. You're responsible for the employer Medicare tax for the whole year on all wages and tips. Tips are considered to be paid at the time the employee reports them to you. Deposit taxes on tips based on your deposit schedule as described in section 11. File Form 941 or Form 944 to report withholding and employment taxes on tips.

Ordering rule. If, by the 10th of the month after the month for which you received an employee's report on tips, you don't have enough employee funds available to deduct the employee tax, you no longer have to collect it. If there aren't enough funds available, withhold taxes in the following order.

1. Withhold on regular wages and other compensation.
2. Withhold social security and Medicare taxes on tips.
3. Withhold income tax on tips.

Reporting tips. Report tips and any collected and uncollected social security and Medicare taxes on Form W-2 and on Form 941, lines 5b, 5c, and, if applicable, 5c (Form 944, lines 4b, 4c, and, if applicable, 4d). Report a negative adjustment on Form 941, line 9 (Form 944, line 6), for the uncollected social security and Medicare taxes. Enter the amount of uncollected social security tax and Medicare tax in box 12 of Form W-2 with codes "A" and "B," respectively. Don't include any uncollected Additional Medicare Tax in box 12 of Form W-2. For additional information on reporting tips, see section 13 and the General Instructions for Forms W-2 and W-3.

Revenue Ruling 2012-18 provides guidance for employers regarding social security and Medicare taxes imposed on tips, including information on the reporting of the employer share of social security and Medicare taxes under section 3121(q), the difference between tips and service charges, and the section 45B credit. See Revenue Ruling 2012-18, 2012-26 I.R.B. 1032, available at *IRS.gov/irb/2012-26_IRB#RR-2012-18*.

FUTA tax on tips. If an employee reports to you in writing $20 or more of tips in a month, the tips are also subject to FUTA tax.

Allocated tips. If you operate a large food or beverage establishment, you must report allocated tips under certain circumstances. However, don't withhold income, social security, or Medicare taxes on allocated tips.

A large food or beverage establishment is one that provides food or beverages for consumption on the premises, where tipping is customary, and where there were normally more than 10 employees on a typical business day during the preceding year.

The tips may be allocated by one of three methods—hours worked, gross receipts, or good faith agreement. For information about these allocation methods, and for information about required electronic filing of Form 8027, see the Instructions for Form 8027. For more information on filing Form 8027 electronically with the IRS, see Pub. 1239.

Tip Rate Determination and Education Program. Employers may participate in the Tip Rate Determination and Education Program. The program primarily consists of two voluntary agreements developed to improve tip income reporting by helping taxpayers to understand and meet their tip reporting responsibilities. The two agreements are the Tip Rate Determination Agreement (TRDA) and the Tip Reporting Alternative Commitment (TRAC). A tip agreement, the Gaming Industry Tip Compliance Agreement (GITCA), is available for the gaming (casino) industry. For more information, see Pub. 3144.

More information. Advise your employees to see Pub. 531 or use the IRS Interactive Tax Assistant at *IRS.gov/TipIncome* for help in determining if their tip income is taxable and for information about how to report tip income.

7. Supplemental Wages

Supplemental wages are wage payments to an employee that aren't regular wages. They include, but aren't limited to, bonuses, commissions, overtime pay, payments for accumulated sick leave, severance pay, awards, prizes, back pay, reported tips, retroactive pay increases, and payments for nondeductible moving expenses. However, employers have the option to treat overtime pay and tips as regular wages instead of supplemental wages. Other payments subject to the supplemental wage rules include taxable fringe benefits and expense allowances paid under a nonaccountable plan. How you withhold on supplemental wages depends on whether the supplemental payment is identified as a separate payment from regular wages. See Regulations section 31.3402(g)-1 for additional guidance. Also see Revenue Ruling 2008-29, 2008-24 I.R.B. 1149, available at *IRS.gov/irb/2008-24_IRB#RR-2008-29*.

Withholding on supplemental wages when an employee receives more than $1 million of supplemental wages from you during the calendar year. Special rules apply to the extent supplemental wages paid to any one employee during the calendar year exceed $1 million. If a supplemental wage payment, together with other supplemental wage payments made to the employee during the calendar year, exceeds $1 million, the excess is subject to withholding at 37% (or the highest rate of income tax for the year). Withhold using the 37% rate without regard to the employee's Form W-4. In determining supplemental wages paid to the employee during the year, include payments from all businesses under common control. For more information, see Treasury Decision 9276, 2006-37 I.R.B. 423, available at *IRS.gov/irb/2006-37_IRB#TD-9276*.

Withholding on supplemental wage payments to an employee who doesn't receive $1 million of supplemental wages during the calendar year. If the supplemental wages paid to the employee during the calendar year are less than or equal to $1 million, the following rules apply in determining the amount of income tax to be withheld.

Supplemental wages combined with regular wages. If you pay supplemental wages with regular wages but don't specify the amount of each, withhold federal income tax as if the total were a single payment for a regular payroll period.

Supplemental wages identified separately from regular wages. If you pay supplemental wages separately (or combine them in a single payment and specify the amount of each), the federal income tax withholding method depends partly on whether you withhold income tax from your employee's regular wages.

1. If you withheld income tax from an employee's regular wages in the current or immediately preceding calendar year, you can use one of the following methods for the supplemental wages.

   a. Withhold a flat 22% (no other percentage allowed).

   b. If the supplemental wages are paid concurrently with regular wages, add the supplemental wages to the concurrently paid regular wages and withhold federal income tax as if the total were a single payment for a regular payroll period. If there are no concurrently paid regular wages, add the supplemental wages to, alternatively, either the regular wages paid or to be paid for the current payroll period or the regular wages paid for the preceding payroll period. Figure the income tax withholding as if the total of the regular wages and supplemental wages is a single payment. Subtract the tax already withheld or to be withheld from the regular wages. Withhold the remaining tax from the supplemental wages. If there were other payments of supplemental wages paid during the payroll period made before the current payment of supplemental wages, aggregate all the payments of supplemental wages paid during the payroll period with the regular wages paid during the payroll period, figure the tax on the total, subtract the tax already withheld from the regular wages and the previous supplemental wage payments, and withhold the remaining tax.

2. If you didn't withhold income tax from the employee's regular wages in the current or immediately preceding calendar year, use method 1b.

Regardless of the method you use to withhold income tax on supplemental wages, they're subject to social security, Medicare, and FUTA taxes.

Example 1. You pay John Peters a base salary on the 1st of each month. John's most recent Form W-4 is from 2018, and John is single, claims one withholding allowance, and didn't enter an amount for additional withholding on Form W-4. In January, John is paid $1,000. You decide to use the Wage Bracket Method of withholding. Using Worksheet 3 and the withholding tables in section 3 of Pub. 15-T, you withhold $20 from this amount. In February, John receives salary of $1,000 plus a commission of $500, which you combine with regular wages and don't separately identify. You figure the withholding based on the total of $1,500. The correct withholding from the tables is $72.

Example 2. You pay Sharon Warren a base salary on the 1st of each month. Sharon submitted a 2023 Form W-4 and checked the box for Single or Married filing separately. Sharon didn't complete Steps 2, 3, and 4 on Form W-4. Sharon's May 1 pay is $2,000. You decide to use the Wage Bracket Method of withholding. Using Worksheet 2 and the withholding tables in section 2 of Pub. 15-T, you withhold $86. On May 15, Sharon receives a bonus of $1,000. Electing to use supplemental wage withholding method 1b, you do the following.

1. Add the bonus amount to the amount of wages from the most recent base salary pay date (May 1) ($2,000 + $1,000 = $3,000).

2. Determine the amount of withholding on the combined $3,000 amount to be $202 using the wage bracket tables.

3. Subtract the amount withheld from wages on the most recent base salary pay date (May 1) from the combined withholding amount ($202 – $86 = $116).

4. Withhold $116 from the bonus payment.

Example 3. The facts are the same as in *Example 2*, except you elect to use the flat rate method of withholding on the bonus. You withhold 22% of $1,000, or $220, from Sharon's bonus payment.

Example 4. The facts are the same as in *Example 2*, except you elect to pay Sharon a second bonus of $2,000 on May 29. Using supplemental wage withholding method 1b, you do the following.

1. Add the first and second bonus amounts to the amount of wages from the most recent base salary pay date (May 1) ($2,000 + $1,000 + $2,000 = $5,000).

2. Determine the amount of withholding on the combined $5,000 amount to be $461 using the wage bracket tables.

3. Subtract the amounts withheld from wages on the most recent base salary pay date (May 1) and the amounts withheld from the first bonus payment from the combined withholding amount ($461 – $86 – $116 = $259).

4. Withhold $259 from the second bonus payment.

Tips are treated as supplemental wages. Withhold income tax on tips from wages earned by the employee or from other funds the employee makes available. Don't withhold the income tax due on tips from employee tips. If an employee receives regular wages and reports tips, figure income tax withholding as if the tips were supplemental wages. If you withheld income tax from the regular wages in the current or immediately preceding calendar year, you can withhold on the tips by method 1a or 1b discussed earlier in this section under *Supplemental wages identified separately from regular wages*. If you didn't withhold income tax from the regular wages in the current or immediately preceding calendar year, add the tips to the regular wages and withhold income tax on the total by method 1b discussed earlier. Employers also have the option to treat tips as regular wages rather than supplemental wages. Service charges aren't tips; therefore, withhold taxes on service charges as you would on regular wages.

Vacation pay. Vacation pay is subject to withholding as if it were a regular wage payment. When vacation pay is in addition to regular wages for the vacation period (for example, an annual lump-sum payment for unused vacation leave), treat it as a supplemental wage payment. If the vacation pay is for a time longer than your usual payroll period, spread it over the pay periods for which you pay it.

8. Payroll Period

Your payroll period is a period of service for which you usually pay wages. When you have a regular payroll period, withhold income tax for that time period even if your employee doesn't work the full period.

No regular payroll period. When you don't have a regular payroll period, withhold the tax as if you paid wages for a daily or miscellaneous payroll period. Figure the number of days (including Sundays and holidays) in the period covered by the wage payment. If the wages are unrelated to a specific length of time (for example, commissions paid on completion of a sale), count back the number of days from the payment period to the latest of:

- The last wage payment made during the same calendar year;
- The date employment began, if during the same calendar year; or
- January 1 of the same year.

Employee paid for period less than 1 week. When you pay an employee for a period of less than 1 week, and the employee signs a statement under penalties of perjury indicating they aren't working for any other employer during the same week for wages subject to withholding, figure withholding based on a weekly payroll period. If the employee later begins to work for another employer for wages subject to withholding, the employee must notify you within 10 days. You then figure withholding based on the daily or miscellaneous period.

9. Withholding From Employees' Wages

Federal Income Tax Withholding

Redesigned Form W-4. The IRS redesigned Form W-4 for 2020 and subsequent years. Before 2020, the value of a withholding allowance was tied to the amount of the personal exemption. Due to changes in the law, taxpayers can no longer claim personal exemptions or dependency exemptions; therefore, Form W-4 no longer asks an employee to report the number of withholding allowances that they are claiming. The revised Form W-4 is divided into five steps. Step 1 and Step 5 apply to all employees. In Step 1, employees enter personal information like their name and filing status. In Step 5, employees sign the form. Employees who complete only Step 1 and Step 5 will have their withholding figured based on their filing status's standard deduction and tax rates with no other adjustments. If applicable, in Step 2, employees increase their withholding to account for higher tax rates due to income from other jobs in their household. Under Step 2, employees either enter an additional amount to withhold per payroll period in Step 4(c) or check the box in Step 2(c) for higher withholding rate tables to apply to their wages. In Step 3, employees decrease their withholding by reporting the annual amount of any credits they will claim on their income tax return. In Step 4, employees may increase or decrease their withholding based on the annual amount of other income or deductions they will report on their income tax return and they may also request any additional federal income tax they want withheld each pay period.

An employee who submitted Form W-4 in any year before 2020 isn't required to submit a new form merely because of the redesign. Employers will continue to figure withholding based on the information from the employee's most recently submitted Form W-4. The withholding tables in Pub. 15-T allow employers to figure withholding based on a Form W-4 for 2019 or earlier, as well as the redesigned Form W-4. While you may ask your employee first paid wages before 2020 that hasn't yet submitted a redesigned Form W-4 to submit a new Form W-4 using the redesigned version of the form, you should explain to them that they're not required to do this and if they don't submit a new Form W-4, withholding will continue based on a valid Form W-4 previously submitted. All newly hired employees must use the redesigned form. Similarly, any other employees who wish to adjust their withholding must use the redesigned form.

Pub. 15-T provides an optional computational bridge to treat 2019 and earlier Forms W-4 as if they were 2020 or later Forms W-4 for purposes of figuring federal income tax withholding. This computational bridge allows you to use computational procedures and data fields for a 2020 and later Form W-4 to arrive at the equivalent withholding for an employee that would have applied using the computational procedures and data fields on a 2019 or earlier Form W-4. See *How To Treat 2019 and Earlier Forms W-4 as if They Were 2020 or Later Forms W-4* in the *Introduction* section of Pub. 15-T.

More information. For more information about the redesigned Form W-4 and regulations that provide guidance for employers concerning income tax withholding from employees' wages, see Treasury Decision 9924, 2020-44 I.R.B. 943, available at *IRS.gov/irb/2020-44_IRB#TD-9924*. For information about Form W-4, go to *IRS.gov/FormW4*. Employer instructions on how to figure employee withholding are provided in Pub. 15-T, available at *IRS.gov/Pub15T*.

Using Form W-4 to figure withholding. To know how much federal income tax to withhold from employees' wages, you should have a Form W-4 on file for each employee. Encourage your employees to file an updated Form W-4 for 2023, especially if they owed taxes or received a large refund when filing their 2022 tax return.

Ask all new employees to give you a signed Form W-4 when they start work. Make the form effective with the first wage payment. If a new employee doesn't give you a completed Form W-4 in 2023 (including an employee who previously worked for you and was rehired in 2023, and who fails to furnish a Form W-4), treat the new employee as if they had checked the box for Single or Married filing separately in Step 1(c) and made no entries in Step 2, Step 3, or Step 4 of the 2023 Form W-4. An employee who was paid wages before 2020 and who failed to furnish a Form W-4 should continue to be treated as single and claiming zero allowances on a 2019 Form W-4. If you use the optional computational bridge, described earlier under *Redesigned Form W-4*, you may treat this employee as if they had checked the box for Single or Married filing separately in Step 1(c), and made no entries in

Step 2 and Step 3, an entry of $8,600 in Step 4(a), and an entry of zero in Step 4(b) of the 2023 Form W-4.

Form in Spanish. You can provide Formulario W-4(SP) in place of Form W-4 to your Spanish-speaking employees. For more information, see Pub. 17(SP). The rules discussed in this section that apply to Form W-4 also apply to Formulario W-4(SP).

Electronic system to receive Form W-4. You may establish a system to electronically receive Forms W-4 from your employees. See Regulations section 31.3402(f)(5)-1(c) and Pub. 15-T for more information.

Effective date of Form W-4. A Form W-4 for 2022 or earlier years remains in effect for 2023 unless the employee gives you a 2023 Form W-4. When you receive a new Form W-4 from an employee, don't adjust withholding for pay periods before the effective date of the new form. If an employee gives you a Form W-4 that replaces an existing Form W-4, begin withholding no later than the start of the first payroll period ending on or after the 30th day from the date when you received the replacement Form W-4. For exceptions, see *Exemption from federal income tax withholding*, *IRS review of requested Forms W-4*, and *Invalid Forms W-4*, later in this section.

 A Form W-4 that makes a change for the next calendar year won't take effect in the current calendar year.

Successor employer. If you're a successor employer (see *Successor employer*, later in this section), secure new Forms W-4 from the transferred employees unless the "Alternative Procedure" in section 5 of Revenue Procedure 2004-53 applies. See Revenue Procedure 2004-53, 2004-34 I.R.B. 320, available at *IRS.gov/irb/2004-34_IRB#RP-2004-53*.

Completing Form W-4. The amount of any federal income tax withholding must be based on filing status, income (including income from other jobs), deductions, and credits. Your employees may not base their withholding amounts on a fixed dollar amount or percentage. However, an employee may specify a dollar amount to be withheld each pay period in addition to the amount of withholding based on filing status and other information reported on Form W-4.

Employees that are married filing jointly and have spouses that also currently work, or employees that hold more than one job at the same time, should account for their higher tax rate by completing Step 2 of their 2023 Form W-4. Employees also have the option to report on their 2023 Form W-4 other income they will receive that isn't subject to withholding and other deductions they will claim in order to increase the accuracy of their federal income tax withholding.

See Pub. 505 for more information about completing Form W-4. Along with Form W-4, you may wish to order Pub. 505 for use by your employees.

Don't accept any withholding or estimated tax payments from your employees in addition to withholding based on their Form W-4. If they require additional withholding, they should submit a new Form W-4 and, if necessary, pay estimated tax by filing Form 1040-ES or by using EFTPS to make estimated tax payments. Employees who receive tips may provide funds to their employer for withholding on tips; see *Collecting taxes on tips* in section 6.

Exemption from federal income tax withholding. Generally, an employee may claim exemption from federal income tax withholding because they had no income tax liability last year and expect none this year. See the Form W-4 instructions for more information. However, the wages are still subject to social security and Medicare taxes. See also *Invalid Forms W-4*, later in this section.

A Form W-4 claiming exemption from withholding is effective when it is given to the employer and only for that calendar year. To continue to be exempt from withholding, an employee must give you a new Form W-4 by February 15. If the employee doesn't give you a new Form W-4 by February 15, begin withholding as if they had checked the box for Single or Married filing separately in Step 1(c) and made no entries in Step 2, Step 3, or Step 4 of the 2023 Form W-4. If the employee provides a new Form W-4 claiming exemption from withholding on February 16 or later, you may apply it to future wages but don't refund any taxes withheld while the exempt status wasn't in place.

Withholding income taxes on the wages of nonresident alien employees. In general, you must withhold federal income taxes on the wages of nonresident alien employees. However, see Pub. 515 for exceptions to this general rule. Also see section 3 of Pub. 51 for guidance on H-2A visa workers.

Withholding adjustment for nonresident alien employees. Nonresident aliens may not claim the standard deduction on their tax returns; therefore, employers must add an amount to the wages of nonresident alien employees performing services within the United States in order to figure the amount of federal income tax to withhold from their wages. The amount is added to their wages solely for calculating federal income tax withholding. The amount isn't included in any box on the employee's Form W-2 and doesn't increase the income tax liability of the employee. The amount also doesn't increase the social security tax or Medicare tax liability of the employer or the employee or the FUTA tax liability of the employer. See *Withholding Adjustment for Nonresident Alien Employees* in the *Introduction* section of Pub. 15-T for the amount to add to their wages for the payroll period.

Supplemental wage payment. The adjustment for determining the amount of income tax withholding for nonresident alien employees doesn't apply to a supplemental wage payment (see section 7) if the 37% mandatory flat rate withholding applies or if the 22% optional flat rate withholding is being used to calculate income tax withholding on the supplemental wage payment.

Nonresident alien employee's Form W-4. When completing Forms W-4, nonresident aliens are required to:

- Not claim exemption from income tax withholding (even if they meet both of the conditions to claim exemption from withholding listed in the Form W-4 instructions);

- Request withholding as if they're single, regardless of their actual filing status;
- Not claim the child tax credit or credit for other dependents in Step 3 of Form W-4 (if the nonresident alien is a resident of Canada, Mexico, or South Korea, or a student from India, or a business apprentice from India, they may claim, under certain circumstances (see Pub. 519), the child tax credit or credit for other dependents); and
- Write "Nonresident Alien" or "NRA" in the space below Step 4(c) of Form W-4.

If you maintain an electronic Form W-4 system, you should provide a field for nonresident aliens to enter nonresident alien status instead of writing "Nonresident Alien" or "NRA" in the space below Step 4(c) of Form W-4. You should instruct nonresident aliens to see Notice 1392, Supplemental Form W-4 Instructions for Nonresident Aliens, before completing Form W-4.

Form 8233. If a nonresident alien employee claims a tax treaty exemption from withholding, the employee must submit Form 8233 with respect to the income exempt under the treaty, instead of Form W-4. For more information, see the Instructions for Form 8233 and *Pay for Personal Services Performed* under *Withholding on Specific Income* in Pub. 515.

IRS review of requested Forms W-4. When requested by the IRS, you must make original Forms W-4 available for inspection by an IRS employee. You may also be directed to send certain Forms W-4 to the IRS. You may receive a notice from the IRS requiring you to submit a copy of Form W-4 for one or more of your named employees. Send the requested copy or copies of Form W-4 to the IRS at the address provided and in the manner directed by the notice. The IRS may also require you to submit copies of Form W-4 to the IRS as directed by a revenue procedure or notice published in the Internal Revenue Bulletin. When we refer to Form W-4, the same rules apply to Formulario W-4(SP), its Spanish translation.

After submitting a copy of a requested Form W-4 to the IRS, continue to withhold federal income tax based on that Form W-4 if it is valid (see *Invalid Forms W-4*, later in this section). However, if the IRS later notifies you in writing that the employee isn't entitled to claim exemption from withholding or a claimed amount of deductions or credits, withhold federal income tax based on the effective date, employee's permitted filing status, and withholding instructions specified in the IRS notice (commonly referred to as a "lock-in letter").

Initial lock-in letter. The IRS uses information reported on Form W-2 to identify employees with withholding compliance problems. In some cases, if a serious under-withholding problem is found to exist for a particular employee, the IRS may issue a lock-in letter to the employer specifying the employee's permitted filing status and providing withholding instructions for the specific employee. You'll also receive a copy for the employee that identifies the permitted filing status and provides a description of the withholding instructions you're required to follow and the process by which the employee can provide additional information to the IRS for purposes of determining the appropriate withholding and/or modifying the specified filing status. You must furnish the employee copy to the employee within 10 business days of receipt if the employee is employed by you as of the date of the notice. You may follow any reasonable business practice to furnish the employee copy to the employee. Begin withholding based on the notice on the date specified in the notice.

Implementation of lock-in letter. When you receive the notice specifying the permitted filing status and providing withholding instructions, you may not withhold immediately on the basis of the notice. You must begin withholding tax on the basis of the notice for any wages paid after the date specified in the notice. The delay between your receipt of the notice and the date to begin the withholding on the basis of the notice permits the employee time to contact the IRS.

Seasonal employees and employees not currently performing services. If you receive a notice for an employee who isn't currently performing services for you, you're still required to furnish the employee copy to the employee and withhold based on the notice if any of the following apply.

- You're paying wages for the employee's prior services and the wages are subject to income tax withholding on or after the date specified in the notice.
- You reasonably expect the employee to resume services within 12 months of the date of the notice.
- The employee is on a leave of absence that doesn't exceed 12 months or the employee has a right to re-employment after the leave of absence.

Termination and rehire of employees. If you must furnish and withhold based on the notice and the employment relationship is terminated after the date of the notice, you must continue to withhold based on the notice if you continue to pay any wages subject to income tax withholding. You must also withhold based on the notice or modification notice (explained next) if the employee resumes the employment relationship with you within 12 months after the termination of the employment relationship.

Modification notice. After issuing the notice specifying the permitted filing status and providing withholding instructions, the IRS may issue a subsequent notice (modification notice) that modifies the original notice. The modification notice may change the permitted filing status and withholding instructions. You must withhold federal income tax based on the effective date specified in the modification notice.

New Form W-4 after IRS notice. After the IRS issues a notice or modification notice, if the employee provides you with a new Form W-4 claiming complete exemption from withholding or a completed Form W-4 that results in less withholding than would result under the IRS notice or modification notice, disregard the new Form

W-4. You must withhold based on the notice or modification notice unless the IRS notifies you to withhold based on the new Form W-4. If the employee wants to put a new Form W-4 into effect that results in less withholding than required, the employee must contact the IRS.

If, after you receive an IRS notice or modification notice, your employee gives you a new completed Form W-4 that results in more withholding than would result under the notice or modification notice, you must withhold tax based on the new Form W-4. Otherwise, disregard any subsequent Forms W-4 provided by the employee and withhold based on the IRS notice or modification notice.

 If, in a year before 2020, you received a lock-in letter for an employee, then for 2023 you should continue to follow the instructions in the lock-in letter. You will use the withholding methods described in Pub. 15-T for an employee with a Form W-4 from 2019 or earlier, or you may use the optional computational bridge to treat 2019 and earlier Forms W-4 as if they were 2020 or later Forms W-4 for purposes of figuring federal income tax withholding. See How To Treat 2019 and Earlier Forms W-4 as if They Were 2020 or Later Forms W-4 in the Introduction section of Pub. 15-T. You should continue following the instructions in the pre-2020 lock-in letter until you receive a letter releasing your employee from the lock-in procedures, you receive a modification notice, or your employee gives you a new Form W-4 that results in more withholding than would result under the notice.

For additional information about employer withholding compliance, see IRS.gov/WHC.

Substitute Forms W-4. You're encouraged to have your employees use the official version of Form W-4. You may use a substitute version of Form W-4 to meet your business needs. However, your substitute Form W-4 must contain language that is identical to the official Form W-4 and your form must meet all current IRS rules for substitute forms. At the time you provide your substitute form to the employee, you must provide them with all tables, instructions, and worksheets from the current Form W-4. For more information, see Pub. 15-T.

You can't accept substitute Forms W-4 developed by employees. An employee who submits an employee-developed substitute Form W-4 after October 10, 2007, will be treated as failing to furnish a Form W-4. However, continue to honor any valid employee-developed Forms W-4 you accepted before October 11, 2007.

Invalid Forms W-4. Any unauthorized change or addition to Form W-4 makes it invalid. This includes taking out any language by which the employee certifies the form is correct. A Form W-4 is also invalid if, by the date an employee gives it to you, they clearly indicate it is false. An employee who submits a false Form W-4 may be subject to a $500 penalty. You may treat a Form W-4 as invalid if the employee wrote "exempt" below Step 4(c) and checked the box in Step 2(c) or entered numbers for Steps 3 and 4.

When you get an invalid Form W-4, don't use it to figure federal income tax withholding. Tell the employee it is invalid and ask for another one. If the employee doesn't give you a valid one, and you have an earlier Form W-4 for this employee that is valid, withhold as you did before. If you don't have an earlier Form W-4 that is valid, withhold tax as if the employee had checked the box for Single or Married filing separately in Step 1(c) and made no entries in Step 2, Step 3, or Step 4 of the 2023 Form W-4. However, an employee who was paid wages in 2019 who never submitted a valid Form W-4 and submits an invalid Form W-4 in 2023 should continue to be treated as single and claiming zero allowances on a 2019 Form W-4. If you use the optional computational bridge, described earlier under Redesigned Form W-4, you may treat this employee as if they had checked the box for Single or Married filing separately in Step 1(c), and made no entries in Step 2 and Step 3, an entry of $8,600 in Step 4(a), and an entry of zero in Step 4(b) of the 2023 Form W-4.

Amounts exempt from levy on wages, salary, and other income. If you receive a Notice of Levy on Wages, Salary, and Other Income (Forms 668-W(ACS), 668-W(c)(DO), or 668-W(ICS)), you must withhold amounts as described in the instructions for these forms. Pub. 1494 has tables to figure the amount exempt from levy. If a levy issued in a prior year is still in effect and the taxpayer submits a new Statement of Exemptions and Filing Status, use the current year Pub. 1494 to figure the exempt amount.

Social Security and Medicare Taxes

The Federal Insurance Contributions Act (FICA) provides for a federal system of old-age, survivors, disability, and hospital insurance. The old-age, survivors, and disability insurance part is financed by the social security tax. The hospital insurance part is financed by the Medicare tax. Each of these taxes is reported separately.

Generally, you're required to withhold social security and Medicare taxes from your employees' wages and pay the employer share of these taxes. Certain types of wages and compensation aren't subject to social security and Medicare taxes. See section 5 and section 15 for details. Generally, employee wages are subject to social security and Medicare taxes regardless of the employee's age or whether they are receiving social security benefits. If the employee reported tips, see section 6.

Tax rates and the social security wage base limit. Social security and Medicare taxes have different rates and only the social security tax has a wage base limit. The wage base limit is the maximum wage subject to the tax for the year. Determine the amount of withholding for social security and Medicare taxes by multiplying each payment by the employee tax rate.

For 2023, the social security tax rate is 6.2% (amount withheld) each for the employer and employee (12.4% total). The social security wage base limit is $160,200. The tax rate for Medicare is 1.45% (amount withheld) each for the employee and employer (2.9% total). There is no wage base limit for Medicare tax; all covered wages are subject to Medicare tax.

Qualified sick leave wages and qualified family leave wages for leave taken after March 31, 2020, and before April 1, 2021, aren't subject to the employer share of social security tax; therefore, the tax rate on these wages is 6.2%. Qualified sick leave wages and qualified family leave wages for leave taken after March 31, 2021, and before October 1, 2021, are subject to both the employer share (6.2%) and employee share (6.2%) of social security tax (12.4% total).

Additional Medicare Tax withholding. In addition to withholding Medicare tax at 1.45%, you must withhold a 0.9% Additional Medicare Tax from wages you pay to an employee in excess of $200,000 in a calendar year. You're required to begin withholding Additional Medicare Tax in the pay period in which you pay wages in excess of $200,000 to an employee and continue to withhold it each pay period until the end of the calendar year. Additional Medicare Tax is only imposed on the employee. There is no employer share of Additional Medicare Tax. All wages that are subject to Medicare tax are subject to Additional Medicare Tax withholding if paid in excess of the $200,000 withholding threshold.

For more information on what wages are subject to Medicare tax, see section 15. For more information on Additional Medicare Tax, go to *IRS.gov/ADMTfaqs*.

Successor employer. When corporate acquisitions meet certain requirements, wages paid by the predecessor are treated as if paid by the successor for purposes of applying the social security wage base and for applying the Additional Medicare Tax withholding threshold (that is, $200,000 in a calendar year). You should determine whether or not you should file Schedule D (Form 941), Report of Discrepancies Caused by Acquisitions, Statutory Mergers, or Consolidations, by reviewing the Instructions for Schedule D (Form 941). See Regulations section 31.3121(a)(1)-1(b) for more information. Also see Revenue Procedure 2004-53, 2004-34 I.R.B. 320, available at *IRS.gov/irb/2004-34_IRB#RP-2004-53*.

Example. Early in 2023, you bought all of the assets of a plumbing business from Mr. Martin. Mr. Brown, who had been employed by Mr. Martin and received $2,000 in wages before the date of purchase, continued to work for you. The wages you paid to Mr. Brown are subject to social security taxes on the first $158,200 ($160,200 minus $2,000). Medicare tax is due on all of the wages you pay Mr. Brown during the calendar year. You should include the $2,000 Mr. Brown received while employed by Mr. Martin in determining whether Mr. Brown's wages exceed the $200,000 for Additional Medicare Tax withholding threshold.

Motion picture project employers. All wages paid by a motion picture project employer to a motion picture project worker during a calendar year are subject to a single social security tax wage base ($160,200 for 2023) and a single FUTA tax wage base ($7,000 for 2023) regardless of the worker's status as a common law employee of multiple clients of the motion picture project employer. For more information, including the definition of a motion picture project employer and motion picture project worker, see section 3512.

Withholding social security and Medicare taxes on nonresident alien employees. In general, if you pay wages to nonresident alien employees, you must withhold social security and Medicare taxes as you would for a U.S. citizen or resident alien. However, see Pub. 515 for exceptions to this general rule.

International social security agreements. The United States has social security agreements, also known as totalization agreements, with many countries that eliminate dual social security coverage and taxation. Compensation subject to social security and Medicare taxes may be exempt under one of these agreements. You can get more information and a list of agreement countries from the SSA at *SSA.gov/international*. Also see Pub. 519, U.S. Tax Guide for Aliens.

Religious exemption. An exemption from social security and Medicare taxes is available to members of a recognized religious sect opposed to insurance. This exemption is available only if both the employee and the employer are members of the sect. For more information, see Pub. 517.

Foreign persons treated as American employers. Under section 3121(z), a foreign person who meets both of the following conditions is generally treated as an American employer for purposes of paying FICA taxes on wages paid to an employee who is a U.S. citizen or resident.

1. The foreign person is a member of a domestically controlled group of entities.

2. The employee of the foreign person performs services in connection with a contract between the U.S. Government (or an instrumentality of the U.S. Government) and any member of the domestically controlled group of entities. Ownership of more than 50% constitutes control.

Part-Time Workers

Part-time workers and workers hired for short periods of time are treated the same as full-time employees for federal income tax withholding and social security, Medicare, and FUTA tax purposes.

Generally, it doesn't matter whether the part-time worker or worker hired for a short period of time has another job or has the maximum amount of social security tax withheld by another employer. See *Successor employer*, earlier, for an exception to this rule.

Income tax withholding may be figured the same way as for full-time workers or it may be figured by the part-year employment method explained in section 6 of Pub. 15-T.

10. Required Notice to Employees About the Earned Income Credit (EIC)

You must notify employees who have no federal income tax withheld that they may be able to claim a tax refund because of the EIC. Although you don't have to notify employees who claim exemption from withholding on Form W-4 about the EIC, you're encouraged to notify any employees whose wages for 2022 were less than $53,057 ($59,187 if married filing jointly) that they may be eligible to claim the credit for 2022. This is because eligible employees may get a refund of the amount of the EIC that is more than the tax they owe.

You'll meet this notification requirement if you issue the employee Form W-2 with the EIC notice on the back of Copy B, or a substitute Form W-2 with the same statement. You'll also meet the requirement by providing Notice 797, Possible Federal Tax Refund Due to the Earned Income Credit (EIC), or your own statement that contains the same wording.

If a substitute for Form W-2 is given to the employee on time but doesn't have the required statement, you must notify the employee within 1 week of the date the substitute for Form W-2 is given. If Form W-2 is required but isn't given on time, you must give the employee Notice 797 or your written statement by the date Form W-2 is required to be given. If Form W-2 isn't required, you must notify the employee by February 7, 2023.

11. Depositing Taxes

If an employer is eligible to claim a credit for qualified sick and family leave wages during 2023, the employer can reduce their deposits by the amount of their anticipated credit. Employers won't be subject to an FTD penalty for properly reducing their deposits if certain conditions are met. For more information on reducing deposits, see Notice 2020-22, 2020-17 I.R.B. 664, available at IRS.gov/irb/2020-17_IRB#NOT-2020-22; Notice 2021-24, 2021-18 I.R.B. 1122, available at IRS.gov/irb/2021-18_IRB#NOT-2021-24; and the Instructions for Form 941 or the Instructions for Form 944. For more information about the credit for qualified sick and family leave wages, go to IRS.gov/PLC.

Generally, you must deposit federal income tax withheld and both the employer and employee social security and Medicare taxes. You must use EFT to make all federal tax deposits. See *How To Deposit*, later in this section, for information on electronic deposit requirements.

Payment with return. You may make a payment with a timely filed Form 941 or Form 944 instead of depositing without incurring a penalty, if one of the following applies.

- You're a monthly schedule depositor (defined later) and make a payment in accordance with the *Accuracy of Deposits Rule*, discussed later in this section. This payment may be $2,500 or more.

- Your Form 941 total tax liability (Form 941, line 12) for either the current quarter or the prior quarter is less than $2,500, and you didn't incur a $100,000 next-day deposit obligation during the current quarter. If you aren't sure your total tax liability for the current quarter will be less than $2,500 (and your liability for the prior quarter wasn't less than $2,500), make deposits using the semiweekly or monthly rules so you won't be subject to an FTD penalty.

- Your Form 944 net tax liability for the year (Form 944, line 9) is less than $2,500.

- Your Form 944 net tax liability for the year (Form 944, line 9) is $2,500 or more and you already deposited the taxes you owed for the first, second, and third quarters of the year; your net tax for the fourth quarter is less than $2,500; and you're paying, in full, the tax you owe for the fourth quarter with a timely filed return.

Separate deposit requirements for nonpayroll (Form 945) tax liabilities. Separate deposits are required for nonpayroll and payroll income tax withholding. Don't combine deposits for Forms 941 (or Form 944) and Form 945 tax liabilities. Generally, the deposit rules for nonpayroll liabilities are the same as discussed next, except the rules apply to an annual rather than a quarterly return period. If the total amount of tax for the year reported on Form 945 is less than $2,500, you're not required to make deposits during the year. See the separate Instructions for Form 945 for more information.

When To Deposit

There are two deposit schedules—monthly and semiweekly—for determining when you deposit social security, Medicare, and withheld federal income taxes. These schedules tell you when a deposit is due after a tax liability arises. Your tax liability is based on the dates payments were made or wages were paid. For taxable noncash fringe benefits, see *When taxable fringe benefits are treated as paid* in section 5. Before the beginning of each calendar year, you must determine which of the two deposit schedules you're required to use. The deposit schedule you must use is based on the total tax liability you reported on Forms 941, line 12, or Form 944, line 9, during a lookback period, discussed next. Your deposit schedule isn't determined by how often you pay your employees or make deposits. See special rules for Forms 944 and 945 later. Also see *Application of Monthly and Semiweekly Schedules*, later in this section.

These rules don't apply to FUTA tax. See section 14 for information on depositing FUTA tax.

Lookback period. If you're a Form 941 filer, your deposit schedule for a calendar year is determined from the total taxes reported on Forms 941, line 12, in a 4-quarter lookback period. The lookback period begins July 1 and ends June 30 as shown next in Table 1. If you reported $50,000 or less of taxes for the lookback period, you're a monthly schedule depositor; if you reported more than $50,000, you're a semiweekly schedule depositor.

Table 1. Lookback Period for Calendar Year 2023

July 1, 2021, through Sept. 30, 2021	Oct. 1, 2021, through Dec. 31, 2021	Jan. 1, 2022, through Mar. 31, 2022	Apr. 1, 2022, through June 30, 2022

 The lookback period for a 2023 Form 941 filer who filed Form 944 in either 2021 or 2022 is calendar year 2021.

If you're a Form 944 filer for the current year or either of the preceding 2 years, your deposit schedule for a calendar year is determined from the total taxes reported during the second preceding calendar year (either on your Forms 941 for all 4 quarters of that year or your Form 944 for that year). The lookback period for 2023 for a Form 944 filer is calendar year 2021. If you reported $50,000 or less of taxes for the lookback period, you're a monthly schedule depositor; if you reported more than $50,000, you're a semiweekly schedule depositor.

If you're a Form 945 filer, your deposit schedule for a calendar year is determined from the total taxes reported on line 3 of your Form 945 for the second preceding calendar year. The lookback period for 2023 for a Form 945 filer is calendar year 2021.

 Your total tax liability for the lookback period is determined based on the amount of taxes you reported on Forms 941, line 12, or Form 944, line 9. Your total liability isn't reduced by the refundable portion of the credit for qualified sick and family leave wages, the refundable portion of the employee retention credit, or the refundable portion of the COBRA premium assistance credit. For more information about these credits, see the instructions for your employment tax return that were applicable during the lookback period.

Adjustments and the lookback rule. Adjustments made on Form 941-X, Form 944-X, and Form 945-X don't affect the amount of tax liability for previous periods for purposes of the lookback rule.

Example. An employer originally reported a tax liability of $45,000 for the lookback period. The employer discovered, during January 2023, that the tax reported for one of the lookback period quarters was understated by $10,000 and corrected this error by filing Form 941-X. This employer is a monthly schedule depositor for 2023 because the lookback period tax liabilities are based on the amounts originally reported, and they were $50,000 or less. The $10,000 adjustment is also not treated as part of the 2023 taxes.

Deposit period. The term "deposit period" refers to the period during which tax liabilities are accumulated for each required deposit due date. For monthly schedule depositors, the deposit period is a calendar month. The deposit periods for semiweekly schedule depositors are Wednesday through Friday and Saturday through Tuesday.

 If you're an agent with an approved Form 2678, the deposit rules apply to you based on the total employment taxes accumulated by you for your own employees and on behalf of all employers for whom you're authorized to act. For more information on an agent with an approved Form 2678, see Revenue Procedure 2013-39, 2013-52 I.R.B. 830, available at IRS.gov/irb/2013-52_IRB#RP-2013-39.

Monthly Deposit Schedule

You're a monthly schedule depositor for a calendar year if the total taxes on Forms 941, line 12, for the 4 quarters in your lookback period were $50,000 or less. Under the monthly deposit schedule, deposit employment taxes on payments made during a month by the 15th day of the following month. See also *Deposits Due on Business Days Only* and *$100,000 Next-Day Deposit Rule*, later in this section. Monthly schedule depositors shouldn't file Form 941 or Form 944 on a monthly basis.

New employers. Your tax liability for any quarter in the lookback period before you started or acquired your business is considered to be zero. Therefore, you're a monthly schedule depositor for the first calendar year of your business. However, see *$100,000 Next-Day Deposit Rule*, later in this section.

Semiweekly Deposit Schedule

You're a semiweekly schedule depositor for a calendar year if the total taxes on Forms 941, line 12, during your lookback period were more than $50,000. Under the semiweekly deposit schedule, deposit employment taxes for payments made on Wednesday, Thursday, and/or Friday by the following Wednesday. Deposit taxes for payments made on Saturday, Sunday, Monday, and/or Tuesday by the following Friday. See also *Deposits Due on Business Days Only*, later in this section.

 Semiweekly schedule depositors must complete Schedule B (Form 941), Report of Tax Liability for Semiweekly Schedule Depositors, and submit it with Form 941. If you file Form 944 or Form 945 and are a semiweekly schedule depositor, complete Form 945-A, Annual Record of Federal Tax Liability, and submit it with your return (instead of Schedule B).

Table 2. Semiweekly Deposit Schedule

IF the payday falls on a...	THEN deposit taxes by the following...
Wednesday, Thursday, and/or Friday	Wednesday.
Saturday, Sunday, Monday, and/or Tuesday	Friday.

Semiweekly deposit period spanning two quarters (Form 941 filers). If you have more than one pay date during a semiweekly period and the pay dates fall in different calendar quarters, you'll need to make **separate deposits** for the separate liabilities.

Example. If you have a pay date on Saturday, September 30, 2023 (third quarter), and another pay date on Monday, October 2, 2023 (fourth quarter), two separate deposits would be required even though the pay dates fall within the same semiweekly period. Both deposits would be due Friday, October 6, 2023.

Semiweekly deposit period spanning two return periods (Form 944 or Form 945 filers). The period covered by a return is the return period. The return period for annual Forms 944 and 945 is a calendar year. If you have more than one pay date during a semiweekly period and the pay dates fall in different return periods, you'll need to make separate deposits for the separate liabilities. For example, if a return period ends on Thursday, taxes accumulated on Wednesday and Thursday are subject to one deposit obligation, and taxes accumulated on Friday are subject to a separate obligation. Separate deposits are required because two different return periods are affected.

Summary of Steps to Determine Your Deposit Schedule

1. Identify your lookback period (see *Lookback period*, earlier in this section).
2. Add the total taxes you reported on Forms 941, line 12, during the lookback period.
3. Determine if you're a monthly or semiweekly schedule depositor:

IF the total taxes you reported in the lookback period were...	THEN you're a...
$50,000 or less	monthly schedule depositor.
more than $50,000	semiweekly schedule depositor.

Example of Monthly and Semiweekly Schedules

Rose Co. reported Form 941 taxes as follows:

2022 Lookback Period		2023 Lookback Period	
3rd Quarter 2020	$12,000	3rd Quarter 2021	$12,000
4th Quarter 2020	12,000	4th Quarter 2021	12,000
1st Quarter 2021	12,000	1st Quarter 2022	12,000
2nd Quarter 2021	12,000	2nd Quarter 2022	15,000
	$48,000		$51,000

Rose Co. is a monthly schedule depositor for 2022 because its tax liability for the 4 quarters in its lookback period (third quarter 2020 through second quarter 2021) wasn't more than $50,000. However, for 2023, Rose Co. will be a semiweekly schedule depositor because the total taxes exceeded $50,000 for the 4 quarters in its lookback period (third quarter 2021 through second quarter 2022).

Deposits Due on Business Days Only

If a deposit is required to be made on a day that isn't a business day, the deposit is considered timely if it is made by the close of the next business day. A business day is any day other than a Saturday, Sunday, or legal holiday. For example, if a deposit is required to be made on a Friday and Friday is a legal holiday, the deposit will be considered timely if it is made by the following Monday (if that Monday is a business day).

Semiweekly schedule depositors have at least 3 business days following the close of the semiweekly period to make a deposit. If any of the 3 weekdays after the end of a semiweekly period is a legal holiday, you'll have an additional day for each day that is a legal holiday to make the required deposit. For example, if a semiweekly schedule depositor accumulated taxes for payments made on Friday and the following Monday is a legal holiday, the deposit normally due on Wednesday may be made on Thursday (this allows 3 business days to make the deposit).

Legal holiday. The term "legal holiday" means any legal holiday in the District of Columbia. For purposes of the deposit rules, the term "legal holiday" doesn't include other statewide legal holidays. Legal holidays for 2023 are listed next.

- January 2—New Year's Day (observed)
- January 16—Birthday of Martin Luther King, Jr.
- February 20—Washington's Birthday
- April 17—District of Columbia Emancipation Day (observed)
- May 29—Memorial Day
- June 19—Juneteenth National Independence Day
- July 4—Independence Day
- September 4—Labor Day
- October 9—Columbus Day
- November 10—Veterans Day (observed)
- November 23—Thanksgiving Day
- December 25—Christmas Day

Application of Monthly and Semiweekly Schedules

The terms "monthly schedule depositor" and "semiweekly schedule depositor" don't refer to how often your business pays its employees or even how often you're required to make deposits. The terms identify which set of deposit rules you must follow when an employment tax liability arises. The deposit rules are based on the dates when wages are paid (cash basis), not on when tax liabilities are accrued for accounting purposes.

Monthly schedule example. Spruce Co. is a monthly schedule depositor with seasonal employees. It paid wages each Friday during May but didn't pay any wages during June. Under the monthly deposit schedule, Spruce Co. must deposit the combined tax liabilities for the May paydays by June 15. Spruce Co. doesn't have a deposit requirement for June (due by July 15) because no wages were paid and, therefore, it didn't have a tax liability for June.

Semiweekly schedule example. Green, Inc., is a semiweekly schedule depositor and pays wages once each month on the last Friday of the month. Although Green, Inc., has a semiweekly deposit schedule, it will deposit just once a month because it pays wages only once a month. The deposit, however, will be made under the semiweekly deposit schedule as follows: Green, Inc.'s tax liability for the April 28, 2023 (Friday), payday must be deposited by May 3, 2023 (Wednesday). Under the semiweekly deposit schedule, liabilities for wages paid on Wednesday through Friday must be deposited by the following Wednesday.

$100,000 Next-Day Deposit Rule

If you accumulate $100,000 or more in taxes on any day during a monthly or semiweekly deposit period (see *Deposit period*, earlier in this section), you must deposit the tax by the next business day, whether you're a monthly or semiweekly schedule depositor.

For purposes of the $100,000 rule, don't continue accumulating a tax liability after the end of a deposit period. For example, if a semiweekly schedule depositor has accumulated a liability of $95,000 on a Tuesday (of a Saturday-through-Tuesday deposit period) and accumulated a $10,000 liability on Wednesday, the $100,000 next-day deposit rule doesn't apply because the $10,000 is accumulated in the next deposit period. Thus, $95,000 must be deposited by Friday and $10,000 must be deposited by the following Wednesday.

However, once you accumulate at least $100,000 in a deposit period, stop accumulating at the end of that day and begin to accumulate anew on the next day. For example, Fir Co. is a semiweekly schedule depositor. On Monday, Fir Co. accumulates taxes of $110,000 and must deposit this amount on Tuesday, the next business day. On Tuesday, Fir Co. accumulates additional taxes of $30,000. Because the $30,000 isn't added to the previous

$110,000 and is less than $100,000, Fir Co. must deposit the $30,000 by Friday (following the semiweekly deposit schedule).

 If you're a monthly schedule depositor and accumulate a $100,000 tax liability on any day during the deposit period, you become a semiweekly schedule depositor on the next day and remain so for at least the rest of the calendar year and for the following calendar year.

Example. Elm, Inc., started its business on May 1, 2023. On Wednesday, May 3, it paid wages for the first time and accumulated a tax liability of $40,000. On Friday, May 5, Elm, Inc., paid wages and accumulated a liability of $60,000, bringing its total accumulated tax liability to $100,000. Because this was the first year of its business, the tax liability for its lookback period is considered to be zero, and it would be a monthly schedule depositor based on the lookback rules. However, since Elm, Inc., accumulated a $100,000 liability on May 5, it became a semiweekly schedule depositor on May 6. It will be a semiweekly schedule depositor for the remainder of 2023 and for 2024. Elm, Inc., is required to deposit the $100,000 by Monday, May 8, the next business day.

 The $100,000 tax liability threshold requiring a next-day deposit is determined before you consider any reduction of your liability for nonrefundable credits. For more information, see frequently asked question 17 at IRS.gov/ETD.

Accuracy of Deposits Rule

You're required to deposit 100% of your tax liability on or before the deposit due date. However, penalties won't be applied for depositing less than 100% if both of the following conditions are met.

- Any deposit shortfall doesn't exceed the greater of $100 or 2% of the amount of taxes otherwise required to be deposited.

- The deposit shortfall is paid or deposited by the shortfall makeup date as described next.

Makeup Date for Deposit Shortfall:

1. **Monthly schedule depositor.** Deposit the shortfall or pay it with your return by the due date of your return for the return period in which the shortfall occurred. You may pay the shortfall with your return even if the amount is $2,500 or more.

2. **Semiweekly schedule depositor.** Deposit by the earlier of:

    a. The first Wednesday or Friday (whichever comes first) that falls on or after the 15th day of the month following the month in which the shortfall occurred, or

    b. The due date of your return (for the return period of the tax liability).

For example, if a semiweekly schedule depositor has a deposit shortfall during May 2023, the shortfall makeup date is June 16, 2023 (Friday). However, if the shortfall occurred on the required October 4, 2023 (Wednesday), deposit due date for the September 29, 2023 (Friday), pay date, the return due date for the September 29 pay date (October 31, 2023) would come before the November 15, 2023 (Wednesday), shortfall makeup date. In this case, the shortfall must be deposited by October 31, 2023.

How To Deposit

You must deposit employment taxes, including Form 945 taxes, by EFT. See *Payment with return*, earlier in this section, for exceptions explaining when taxes may be paid with the tax return instead of being deposited.

Electronic deposit requirement. You must use EFT to make all federal tax deposits. Generally, an EFT is made using EFTPS. If you don't want to use EFTPS, you can arrange for your tax professional, financial institution, payroll service, or other trusted third party to make electronic deposits on your behalf. EFTPS is a free service provided by the Department of the Treasury. To get more information about EFTPS or to enroll in EFTPS, go to *EFTPS.gov* or call 800-555-4477. To contact EFTPS using TRS for people who are deaf, hard of hearing, or have a speech disability, dial 711 and then provide the TRS assistant the 800-555-4477 number above or 800-733-4829. Additional information about EFTPS is also available in Pub. 966.

When you receive your EIN. If you're a new employer that indicated a federal tax obligation when requesting an EIN, you'll be pre-enrolled in EFTPS. You'll receive information about Express Enrollment in your Employer Identification Number (EIN) Package and an additional mailing containing your EFTPS personal identification number (PIN) and instructions for activating your PIN. Call the toll-free number located in your "How to Activate Your Enrollment" brochure to activate your enrollment and begin making your payroll tax deposits. If you outsource any of your payroll and related tax duties to a third-party payer, such as a payroll service provider (PSP) or reporting agent, be sure to tell them about your EFTPS enrollment.

Deposit record. For your records, an EFT Trace Number will be provided with each successful payment. The number can be used as a receipt or to trace the payment.

Depositing on time. For deposits made by EFTPS to be on time, you must submit the deposit by 8 p.m. Eastern time the day before the date the deposit is due. If you use a third party to make a deposit on your behalf, they may have different cutoff times.

Same-day wire payment option. If you fail to submit a deposit transaction on EFTPS by 8 p.m. Eastern time the day before the date a deposit is due, you can still make your deposit on time by using the Federal Tax Collection Service (FTCS) to make a same-day wire payment. To use the same-day wire payment method, you'll need to make arrangements with your financial institution ahead of time. Please check with your financial institution regarding availability, deadlines, and costs. Your financial institution may charge you a fee for payments made this way. To learn more about the information you'll need to give to your financial institution to make a same-day wire payment, go to *IRS.gov/SameDayWire*.

How to claim credit for overpayments. If you deposited more than the right amount of taxes for a quarter, you can choose on Form 941 for that quarter (or on Form 944 for that year) to have the overpayment refunded or applied as a credit to your next return. Don't ask EFTPS to request a refund from the IRS for you.

Deposit Penalties

 Although the deposit penalties information provided next refers specifically to Form 941, these rules also apply to Form 945 and Form 944. The penalties won't apply if the employer qualifies for the exceptions to the deposit requirements discussed under Payment with return*, earlier in this section).*

Penalties may apply if you don't make required deposits on time or if you make deposits for less than the required amount. The penalties don't apply if any failure to make a proper and timely deposit was due to reasonable cause and not to willful neglect. If you receive a penalty notice, you can provide an explanation of why you believe reasonable cause exists.

If you timely filed your employment tax return, the IRS may also waive deposit penalties if you inadvertently failed to deposit and it was the first quarter that you were required to deposit any employment tax, or if you inadvertently failed to deposit the first time after your deposit frequency changed. You must also meet the net worth and size limitations applicable to awards of administrative and litigation costs under section 7430; for individuals, this means that your net worth can't exceed $2 million, and for businesses, your net worth can't exceed $7 million and you also can't have more than 500 employees.

The IRS may also waive the deposit penalty the first time you're required to make a deposit if you inadvertently send the payment to the IRS rather than deposit it by EFT.

For amounts not properly or timely deposited, the penalty rates are as follows.

Penalty	Charged for...
2%	Deposits made 1 to 5 days late.
5%	Deposits made 6 to 15 days late.
10%	Deposits made 16 or more days late, but before 10 days from the date of the first notice the IRS sent asking for the tax due.
10%	Amounts that should have been deposited, but instead were paid directly to the IRS, or paid with your tax return. But see *Payment with return*, earlier in this section, for exceptions.
15%	Amounts still unpaid more than 10 days after the date of the first notice the IRS sent asking for the tax due or the day on which you received notice and demand for immediate payment, whichever is earlier.

Late deposit penalty amounts are determined using calendar days, starting from the due date of the liability.

Special rule for former Form 944 filers. If you filed Form 944 for the prior year and file Forms 941 for the current year, the FTD penalty won't apply to a late deposit of employment taxes for January of the current year if the taxes are deposited in full by March 15 of the current year.

Order in which deposits are applied. Deposits are generally applied to the most recent tax liability within the quarter. If you receive an FTD penalty notice, you may designate how your deposits are to be applied in order to minimize the amount of the penalty if you do so within 90 days of the date of the notice. Follow the instructions on the penalty notice you receive. For more information on designating deposits, see Revenue Procedure 2001-58. You can find Revenue Procedure 2001-58 on page 579 of Internal Revenue Bulletin 2001-50 at *IRS.gov/pub/irs-irbs/irb01-50.pdf*.

Example. Cedar, Inc., is required to make a deposit of $1,000 on May 15 and $1,500 on June 15. It doesn't make the deposit on May 15. On June 15, Cedar, Inc., deposits $2,000. Under the deposits rule, which applies deposits to the most recent tax liability, $1,500 of the deposit is applied to the June 15 deposit and the remaining $500 is applied to the May deposit. Accordingly, $500 of the May 15 liability remains undeposited. The penalty on this underdeposit will apply as explained earlier.

Trust fund recovery penalty. If federal income, social security, or Medicare taxes that must be withheld (that is, trust fund taxes) aren't withheld or aren't deposited or paid to the U.S. Treasury, the trust fund recovery penalty may apply. The penalty is 100% of the unpaid trust fund tax. If these unpaid taxes can't be immediately collected from the employer or business, the trust fund recovery penalty may be imposed on all persons who are determined by the IRS to be responsible for collecting, accounting for, or paying over these taxes, and who acted willfully in not doing so. The trust fund recovery penalty won't apply to any amount of trust fund taxes an employer holds back in anticipation of any credits they are entitled to.

A **responsible person** can be an officer or employee of a corporation, a partner or employee of a partnership, an accountant, a volunteer director/trustee, or an employee of a sole proprietorship, or any other person or entity that is responsible for collecting, accounting for, or paying over trust fund taxes. A responsible person may also include one who signs checks for the business or otherwise has authority to cause the spending of business funds.

Willfully means voluntarily, consciously, and intentionally. A responsible person acts willfully if the person knows the required actions of collecting, accounting for, or paying over trust fund taxes aren't taking place, or recklessly disregards obvious and known risks to the government's right to receive trust fund taxes.

Separate accounting when deposits aren't made or withheld taxes aren't paid. Separate accounting may be required if you don't pay over withheld employee social security, Medicare, or income taxes; deposit required taxes; make required payments; or file tax returns. In this case, you would receive written notice from the IRS requiring you to deposit taxes into a special trust account for the U.S. Government.

 You may be charged with criminal penalties if you don't comply with the special bank deposit requirements for the special trust account for the U.S. Government.

"Averaged" FTD penalty. The IRS may assess an "averaged" FTD penalty of 2% to 10% if you're a monthly schedule depositor and didn't properly complete Form 941, line 16, when your tax liability shown on Form 941, line 12, equaled or exceeded $2,500.

The IRS may also assess an "averaged" FTD penalty of 2% to 10% if you're a semiweekly schedule depositor and your tax liability shown on Form 941, line 12, equaled or exceeded $2,500 and you:

- Completed Form 941, line 16, instead of Schedule B (Form 941);
- Failed to attach a properly completed Schedule B (Form 941); or
- Improperly completed Schedule B (Form 941) by, for example, entering tax deposits instead of tax liabilities in the numbered spaces.

The FTD penalty is figured by distributing your total tax liability shown on Form 941, line 12, equally throughout the tax period. Then we apply your deposits and payments to the averaged liabilities in the date order we received your deposits. We figure the penalty on any tax not deposited, deposited late, or not deposited in the correct amounts. Your deposits and payments may not be counted as timely because the actual dates of your tax liabilities can't be accurately determined.

You can avoid an "averaged" FTD penalty by reviewing your return before you file it. Follow these steps before submitting your Form 941.

- If you're a monthly schedule depositor, report your tax liabilities (not your deposits) in the monthly entry spaces on Form 941, line 16.
- If you're a semiweekly schedule depositor, report your tax liabilities (not your deposits) on Schedule B (Form

941) on the lines that represent the dates your employees were paid.

- Verify that your total liability shown on Form 941, line 16, or the bottom of Schedule B (Form 941) equals your tax liability shown on Form 941, line 12.

- Don't show negative amounts on Form 941, line 16, or Schedule B (Form 941).

- For prior period errors, don't adjust your tax liabilities reported on Form 941, line 16, or on Schedule B (Form 941). Instead, file an adjusted return (Form 941-X, 944-X, or 945-X) if you're also adjusting your tax liability. If you're only adjusting your deposits in response to an FTD penalty notice, see the Instructions for Schedule B (Form 941) or the Instructions for Form 945-A (for Forms 944 and 945).

 In addition to civil penalties, you may be subject to criminal prosecution (brought to trial) for willfully:

- *Evading tax;*

- *Failing to collect or truthfully account for and pay over tax;*

- *Failing to file a return, supply information, or pay any tax due;*

- *Furnishing false or fraudulent Forms W-2 to employees or failing to furnish Forms W-2;*

- *Committing fraud and providing false statements;*

- *Preparing and filing a fraudulent return; or*

- *Committing identity theft.*

12. Filing Form 941 or Form 944

Form 941. If you paid wages subject to federal income tax withholding (including withholding on sick pay and supplemental unemployment benefits) or social security and Medicare taxes, you must file Form 941 quarterly even if you have no taxes to report, unless you filed a final return, you receive an IRS notification that you're eligible to file Form 944, or the exceptions discussed later apply. Also, if you're required to file Forms 941 but believe your employment taxes for the calendar year will be $1,000 or less, and you would like to file Form 944 instead of Forms 941, you must contact the IRS during the first calendar quarter of the tax year to request to file Form 944. You must receive written notice from the IRS to file Form 944 instead of Forms 941 before you may file this form. For more information on requesting to file Form 944, including the methods and deadlines for making a request, see the Instructions for Form 944. Form 941 must be filed by the last day of the month that follows the end of the quarter. See *Calendar*, earlier.

Form 944. If you receive written notification that you qualify for the Form 944 program, you must file Form 944

instead of Form 941. You must file Form 944 even if you have no taxes to report (or you have taxes in excess of $1,000 to report) unless you filed a final return for the prior year. If you received notification to file Form 944, but prefer to file Form 941, you can request to have your filing requirement changed to Form 941 during the first calendar quarter of the tax year. For more information on requesting to file Forms 941, including the methods and deadlines for making a request, see the Instructions for Form 944. File your 2022 Form 944 by January 31, 2023. However, if you timely deposited all taxes when due, you may file by February 10, 2023.

Exceptions. The following exceptions apply to the filing requirements for Forms 941 and 944.

- **Seasonal employers who don't have to file a Form 941 for quarters when they have no tax liability because they have paid no wages.** To alert the IRS you won't have to file a return for one or more quarters during the year, check the "Seasonal employer" box on Form 941, line 18. When you fill out Form 941, be sure to check the box on the top of the form that corresponds to the quarter reported. Generally, the IRS won't inquire about unfiled returns if at least one taxable return is filed each year. However, you must check the "Seasonal employer" box on **every** Form 941 you file. Otherwise, the IRS will expect a return to be filed for each quarter.

- **Household employers reporting social security and Medicare taxes and/or withheld income tax.** If you file Form 941 or Form 944 for business employees, you may include taxes for household employees on your Form 941 or Form 944. Otherwise, report social security and Medicare taxes and income tax withholding for household employees on Schedule H (Form 1040). See Pub. 926 for more information.

- **Employers reporting wages for employees in American Samoa, Guam, the Commonwealth of the Northern Mariana Islands, the U.S. Virgin Islands, or Puerto Rico.** If your employees aren't subject to U.S. income tax withholding, use Forms 941-SS, Form 944, or Formulario 944(SP). Employers in Puerto Rico use Formularios 941-PR, Formulario 944(SP), or Form 944. If you have both employees who are subject to U.S. income tax withholding and employees who aren't subject to U.S. income tax withholding, you must file only Form 941 (or Form 944 or Formulario 944(SP)) and include all of your employees' wages on that form. For more information, see Pub. 80, Federal Tax Guide for Employers in the U.S. Virgin Islands, Guam, American Samoa, and the Commonwealth of the Northern Mariana Islands, or Pub. 179, Guía Contributiva Federal para Patronos Puertorriqueños.

- **Agricultural employers reporting social security, Medicare, and withheld income taxes.** Report these taxes on Form 943. For more information, see Pub. 51.

Employers that pay Railroad Retirement Tax Act (RRTA) taxes use Form CT-1 to report employment taxes imposed by the RRTA, and Form 941, or Form 944, to report federal income taxes withheld from their employees' wages and other compensation.

E-file. The IRS *e-file* program allows a taxpayer to electronically file Form 941 or Form 944 using a computer with an Internet connection and commercial tax preparation software. For more information, go to *IRS.gov/EmploymentEfile*, or call 866-255-0654.

Electronic filing by reporting agents. Reporting agents filing Form 940, 941, or 944 for groups of taxpayers can file them electronically. For details, see Pub. 3112, IRS *e-file* Application and Participation. For information on electronic filing of Forms 940, 941, and 944, see Revenue Procedure 2007-40, 2007-26 I.R.B. 1488, available at *IRS.gov/irb/2007-26_IRB#RP-2007-40*. For information on the different types of third-party payer arrangements, see *section 16*.

Electronic filing by CPEOs. With the exception of the first quarter for which a CPEO is certified, CPEOs are required to electronically file Form 941. Under certain circumstances, the IRS may waive the electronic filing requirement. To request a waiver, the CPEO must file a written request using the IRS Online Registration System for Professional Employer Organizations at least 45 days before the due date of the return for which the CPEO is unable to electronically file. For more information on filing a waiver request electronically, go to *IRS.gov/CPEO*.

Penalties. For each whole or part month a return isn't filed when required, there is a failure-to-file (FTF) penalty of 5% of the unpaid tax due with that return. The maximum penalty is generally 25% of the tax due. Also, for each whole or part month the tax is paid late, there is a failure-to-pay (FTP) penalty of 0.5% per month of the amount of tax. For individual filers only, the FTP penalty is reduced from 0.5% per month to 0.25% per month if an installment agreement is in effect. You must have filed your return on or before the due date of the return to qualify for the reduced penalty. The maximum amount of the FTP penalty is also 25% of the tax due. If both penalties apply in any month, the FTF penalty is reduced by the amount of the FTP penalty. The penalties won't be charged if you have reasonable cause for failing to file or pay. If you receive a penalty notice, you can provide an explanation of why you believe reasonable cause exists.

Note. In addition to any penalties, interest accrues from the due date of the tax on any unpaid balance.

If income, social security, or Medicare taxes that must be withheld aren't withheld or aren't paid, you may be personally liable for the trust fund recovery penalty. See *Trust fund recovery penalty* in section 11.

Generally, the use of a third-party payer, such as a PSP or reporting agent, doesn't relieve an employer of the responsibility to ensure tax returns are filed and all taxes are paid or deposited correctly and on time. However, see

Certified professional employer organization (CPEO), later, for an exception.

Don't file more than one Form 941 per quarter or more than one Form 944 per year. Employers with multiple locations or divisions must file only one Form 941 per quarter or one Form 944 per year. Filing more than one return may result in processing delays and may require correspondence between you and the IRS. For information on making adjustments to previously filed returns, see *section 13*.

Reminders about filing.

- Don't report more than 1 calendar quarter on a Form 941.

- If you need Form 941 or Form 944, go to *IRS.gov/Forms*. Also see *Ordering Employer Tax Forms, Instructions, and Publications*, earlier.

- Enter your name and EIN on Form 941 or Form 944. Be sure they're exactly as they appeared on earlier returns.

- See the Instructions for Form 941 or the Instructions for Form 944 for information on preparing the form.

Final return. If you go out of business, you must file a final return for the last quarter (last year for Form 944) in which wages are paid. If you continue to pay wages or other compensation for periods following termination of your business, you must file returns for those periods. See the Instructions for Form 941 or the Instructions for Form 944 for details on how to file a final return.

If you're required to file a final return, you're also required to furnish Forms W-2 to your employees and file Forms W-2 and W-3 with the SSA by the due date of your final return. Don't send an original or copy of your Form 941 or Form 944 to the SSA. See the General Instructions for Forms W-2 and W-3 for more information.

Filing late returns for previous years. Get a copy of Form 941 or Form 944 (and separate instructions) with a revision date showing the year, and, if applicable, quarter for which your delinquent return is being filed. Prior year and/or quarter Forms 941 and 944 are available, respectively, at *IRS.gov/Form941* and *IRS.gov/Form944* (select the link for all form revisions under "Other Items You May Find Useful"). Also, see *Ordering Employer Tax Forms, Instructions, and Publications*, earlier. Contact the IRS at 800-829-4933 if you have any questions about filing late returns.

Table 3. **Social Security and Medicare Tax Rates** *(for 3 Prior Years)*

Calendar Year	Wage Base Limit (each employee)	Tax Rate on Taxable Wages and Tips
2022—Social Security	$147,000	12.4%*
2022—Medicare	All Wages	2.9%
2021—Social Security	$142,800	12.4%*
2021—Medicare	All Wages	2.9%
2020—Social Security	$137,700	12.4%**
2020—Medicare	All Wages	2.9%

* Qualified sick leave wages and qualified family leave wages for leave taken after March 31, 2020, and before April 1, 2021, aren't subject to the employer share of social security tax; therefore, the tax rate on these wages is 6.2% (0.062).

** Qualified sick leave wages and qualified family leave wages aren't subject to the employer share of social security tax; therefore, the tax rate on these wages for 2020 is 6.2% (0.062).

Reconciling Forms W-2 and W-3 with Forms 941 or Form 944. When there are discrepancies between Forms 941 or Form 944 filed with the IRS and Forms W-2 and W-3 filed with the SSA, the IRS or the SSA may contact you to resolve the discrepancies.

Take the following steps to help reduce discrepancies.

1. Report bonuses as wages and as social security and Medicare wages on Forms W-2 and on Forms 941 or Form 944.

2. Report both social security and Medicare wages and taxes separately on Forms W-2 and W-3, and on Forms 941 or Form 944.

3. Report the employee share of social security taxes on Form W-2 in the box for social security tax withheld (box 4), not as social security wages.

4. Report the employee share of Medicare taxes on Form W-2 in the box for Medicare tax withheld (box 6), not as Medicare wages.

5. Make sure the social security wage amount for each employee doesn't exceed the annual social security wage base limit ($160,200 for 2023).

6. Don't report noncash wages that aren't subject to social security or Medicare taxes, as discussed earlier under *Wages not paid in money* in section 5, as social security or Medicare wages.

7. If you used an EIN on any Forms 941 or Form 944 for the year that is different from the EIN reported on Form W-3, enter the other EIN on Form W-3 in the box for "Other EIN used this year" (box h).

8. Be sure the amounts on Form W-3 are the total of amounts from Forms W-2.

9. Reconcile Form W-3 with your four quarterly Forms 941 or annual Form 944 by comparing amounts reported for the following items.

    a. Federal income tax withheld.

    b. Social security and Medicare wages.

    c. Social security and Medicare taxes. Generally, the amounts shown on Forms 941 or annual Form 944, including current year adjustments, should be approximately twice the amounts shown on Form W-3 because Form 941 and Form 944 report both the employer and employee social security and Medicare taxes while Form W-3 reports only the employee taxes.

Don't report backup withholding or withholding on nonpayroll payments, such as pensions, annuities, and gambling winnings, on Form 941 or Form 944. Withholding on nonpayroll payments is reported on Forms 1099 or W-2G and must be reported on Form 945. Only taxes and withholding reported on Form W-2 should be reported on Form 941 or Form 944.

Amounts reported on Forms W-2, W-3, and Forms 941 or Form 944 may not match for valid reasons. For example, if you withheld any Additional Medicare Tax from your employee's wages, the amount of Medicare tax that is reported on Forms 941, line 5c, column 2, or Form 944, line 4c, column 2, won't be twice the amount of the Medicare tax withheld that is reported in box 6 of Form W-3 because the Additional Medicare Tax is only imposed on the employee; there is no employer share of Additional Medicare Tax. Make sure there are valid reasons for any mismatch. Keep your reconciliation so you'll have a record of why amounts didn't match in case there are inquiries from the IRS or the SSA. See the Instructions for Schedule D (Form 941) if you need to explain any discrepancies that were caused by an acquisition, statutory merger, or consolidation.

 When reconciling Forms W-2 and W-3 to Forms 941 or Form 944, you should consider that qualified sick leave wages and qualified family leave wages for leave taken after March 31, 2020, and before April 1, 2021, aren't subject to the employer share of social security tax.

13. Reporting Adjustments to Form 941 or Form 944

Current Period Adjustments

In certain cases, amounts reported as social security and Medicare taxes on Form 941, lines 5a–5d, column 2 (Form 944, lines 4a–4d, column 2), must be adjusted to arrive at your correct tax liability (for example, excluding amounts withheld by a third-party payer or amounts you weren't required to withhold). Current period adjustments are reported on Form 941, lines 7–9, or Form 944, line 6, and include the following types of adjustments.

Fractions-of-cents adjustment. If there is a small difference between total taxes after adjustments and nonrefundable credits (Form 941, line 12; Form 944, line 9) and total deposits (Form 941, line 13a; Form 944, line 10a), i may have been caused, all or in part, by rounding to the nearest cent each time you figured payroll. This rounding occurs when you figure the amount of social security and Medicare tax to be withheld and deposited from each employee's wages. The IRS refers to rounding differences relating to employee withholding of social security and Medicare taxes as "fractions-of-cents" adjustments. If you pay your taxes with Form 941 (or Form 944) instead of making deposits because your total taxes for the quarter (year for Form 944) are less than $2,500, you may also report a fractions-of-cents adjustment.

To determine if you have a fractions-of-cents adjustment for 2023, multiply the total wages and tips for the quarter subject to:

- Social security tax reported on Form 941 or Form 944 by 6.2% (0.062),

- Medicare tax reported on Form 941 or Form 944 by 1.45% (0.0145), and

- Additional Medicare Tax reported on Form 941 or Form 944 by 0.9% (0.009).

Compare these amounts (the employee share of social security and Medicare taxes) with the total social security and Medicare taxes actually withheld from employees and shown in your payroll records for the quarter (Form 941) or the year (Form 944). If there is a small difference, the amount, positive or negative, may be a fractions-of-cents adjustment. Fractions-of-cents adjustments are reported on Form 941, line 7, or Form 944, line 6. If the actual amount withheld is less, report a negative adjustment using a minus sign (if possible; otherwise, use parentheses) in the entry space. If the actual amount is more, report a positive adjustment.

Adjustment of tax on third-party sick pay. Report both the employer and employee share of social security and Medicare taxes for sick pay on Form 941, lines 5a and 5c (Form 944, lines 4a and 4c). If the aggregate wages paid for an employee by the employer and third-party payer exceed $200,000 for the calendar year, report the Additional Medicare Tax on Form 941, line 5d (Form 944, line 4d). Show as a negative adjustment on Form 941, line 8 (Form 944, line 6), the social security and Medicare taxes withheld on sick pay by a third-party payer. See section 6 of Pub. 15-A for more information.

Adjustment of tax on tips. If, by the 10th of the month after the month you received an employee's report on tips, you don't have enough employee funds available to withhold the employee's share of social security and Medicare taxes, you no longer have to collect it. However, report the entire amount of these tips on Form 941, lines 5b and 5c (Form 944, lines 4b and 4c). If the aggregate wages and tips paid for an employee exceed $200,000 for the calendar year, report the Additional Medicare Tax on Form 941, line 5d (Form 944, line 4d). Include as a negative adjustment on Form 941, line 9 (Form 944, line 6), the total uncollected employee share of the social security and Medicare taxes.

Adjustment of tax on group-term life insurance premiums paid for former employees. The employee share of social security and Medicare taxes for premiums on group-term life insurance over $50,000 for a former employee is paid by the former employee with their tax return and isn't collected by the employer. However, include all social security and Medicare taxes for such coverage on Form 941, lines 5a and 5c (Form 944, lines 4a and 4c). If the amount paid for an employee for premiums on group-term life insurance combined with other wages exceeds $200,000 for the calendar year, report the Additional Medicare Tax on Form 941, line 5d (Form 944, line 4d). Back out the amount of the employee share of these taxes as a negative adjustment on Form 941, line 9 (Form 944, line 6). See Pub. 15-B for more information on group-term life insurance.

 For the above adjustments, prepare and retain a brief supporting statement explaining the nature and amount of each. Don't attach the statement to Form 941 or Form 944. See the General Instructions for Forms W-2 and W-3 for information on how to report the uncollected employee share of social security and Medicare taxes on tips and group-term life insurance on Form W-2.

Example. Cedar, Inc., filed Form 941 and was entitled to the following current period adjustments.

- **Fractions of cents.** Cedar, Inc., determined the amounts withheld and deposited for social security and Medicare taxes during the quarter were a net $1.44 more than the employee share of the amount figured on Form 941, lines 5a–5d, column 2 (social security and Medicare taxes). This difference was caused by adding or dropping fractions of cents when figuring social security and Medicare taxes for each wage payment. Cedar, Inc., must report a positive $1.44 fractions-of-cents adjustment on Form 941, line 7.

- **Third-party sick pay.** Cedar, Inc., included taxes of $2,000 for sick pay on Form 941, lines 5a and 5c, column 2, for social security and Medicare taxes. However, the third-party payer of the sick pay withheld and paid the employee share ($1,000) of these taxes. Cedar, Inc., is entitled to a $1,000 sick pay adjustment (negative) on Form 941, line 8.

- **Life insurance premiums.** Cedar, Inc., paid group-term life insurance premiums for policies in excess of $50,000 for former employees. The former employees must pay the employee share of the social security and Medicare taxes ($200) on the policies. However, Cedar, Inc., must include the employee share of these taxes with the social security and Medicare taxes reported on Form 941, lines 5a and 5c, column 2. Therefore, Cedar, Inc., is entitled to a negative $200 adjustment on Form 941, line 9.

No change to record of federal tax liability. Don't make any changes to your record of federal tax liability reported on Form 941, line 16, or Schedule B (Form 941) (for Form 944 filers, Form 944, line 13, or Form 945-A) for current period adjustments. The amounts reported on the record reflect the actual amounts you withheld from employees' wages for social security and Medicare taxes. Because the current period adjustments make the amounts reported on Form 941, lines 5a–5d, column 2 (Form 944, lines 4a–4d, column 2), equal the actual amounts you withheld (the amounts reported on the record), no additional changes to the record of federal tax liability are necessary for these adjustments.

Prior Period Adjustments

Forms for prior period adjustments. Use Form 941-X or Form 944-X to make a correction after you discover an error on a previously filed Form 941 or Form 944. There are also Forms 943-X, 945-X, and CT-1 X to report corrections on the corresponding returns. Use Form 843 when requesting a refund or abatement of assessed interest or penalties.

 See Revenue Ruling 2009-39, 2009-52 I.R.B. 951, for examples of how the interest-free adjustment and claim for refund rules apply in 10 different situations. You can find Revenue Ruling 2009-39 at IRS.gov/irb/2009-52_IRB#RR-2009-39.

Background. Treasury Decision 9405 changed the process for making interest-free adjustments to employment taxes reported on Form 941 and Form 944 and for filing a claim for refund of employment taxes. Treasury Decision 9405, 2008-32 I.R.B. 293, is available at IRS.gov/irb/2008-32_IRB#TD-9405. You'll use the adjustment process if you underreported employment taxes and are making a payment, or if you overreported employment taxes and will be applying the credit to the Form 941 or Form 944 period during which you file Form 941-X or Form 944-X. You'll use the claim process if you overreported employment taxes and are requesting a refund or abatement of the overreported amount. We use the terms "correct" and "corrections" to include interest-free adjustments under sections 6205 and 6413, and claims for refund and abatement under sections 6402, 6414, and 6404.

Correcting employment taxes. When you discover an error on a previously filed Form 941 or Form 944, you must:

- Correct that error using Form 941-X or Form 944-X,

- File a separate Form 941-X or Form 944-X for each Form 941 or Form 944 you're correcting, and

- File Form 941-X or Form 944-X separately. Don't file with Form 941 or Form 944.

Report current quarter adjustments for fractions of cents, third-party sick pay, tips, and group-term life insurance on Form 941 using lines 7–9, and on Form 944 using line 6. See *Current Period Adjustments*, earlier.

Report the correction of underreported and overreported amounts for the same tax period on a single Form 941-X or Form 944-X unless you're requesting a refund. If you're requesting a refund and are correcting both under-reported and overreported amounts, file one Form 941-X or Form 944-X correcting the underreported amounts only and a second Form 941-X or Form 944-X correcting the overreported amounts.

See the chart on the last page of Form 941-X or Form 944-X for help in choosing whether to use the adjustment process or the claim process. See the Instructions for Form 941-X or the Instructions for Form 944-X for details on how to make the adjustment or claim for refund or abatement.

Income tax withholding adjustments. In a current calendar year, correct prior quarter income tax withholding errors by making the correction on Form 941-X when you discover the error.

You may make an adjustment only to correct income tax withholding errors discovered during the same calendar year in which you paid the wages. This is because the employee uses the amount shown on Form W-2 or, if applicable, Form W-2c, as a credit when filing their income tax return (Form 1040, etc.).

You can't adjust amounts reported as income tax withheld in a prior calendar year unless it is to correct an administrative error or section 3509 applies. An administrative error occurs if the amount you entered on Form 941 or Form 944 isn't the amount you actually withheld. For example, if the total income tax actually withheld was incorrectly reported on Form 941 or Form 944 due to a mathematical or transposition error, this would be an administrative error. The administrative error adjustment corrects the amount reported on Form 941 or Form 944 to agree with the amount actually withheld from employees and reported on their Forms W-2.

Additional Medicare Tax withholding adjustments. Generally, the rules discussed earlier under *Income tax withholding adjustments* apply to Additional Medicare Tax withholding adjustments. That is, you may make an adjustment to correct Additional Medicare Tax withholding errors discovered during the same calendar year in which you paid wages. You can't adjust amounts reported in a prior calendar year unless it is to correct an administrative error or section 3509 applies. If you have overpaid Additional Medicare Tax, you can't file a claim for refund for the amount of the overpayment unless the amount wasn't actually withheld from the employee's wages (which would be an administrative error).

If a prior year error was a nonadministrative error, you may correct only the **wages and tips** subject to Additional Medicare Tax withholding.

Collecting underwithheld taxes from employees. If you withheld no income, social security, or Medicare taxes or less than the correct amount from an employee's wages, you can make it up from later pay to that employee. But you're the one who owes the underpayment. Reimbursement is a matter for settlement between you and the employee. Underwithheld income tax and Additional Medicare Tax must be recovered from the employee on or before the last day of the calendar year.

There are special rules for tax on tips (see section 6) and fringe benefits (see section 5).

Refunding amounts incorrectly withheld from employees. If you withheld more than the correct amount of income, social security, or Medicare taxes from wages paid, repay or reimburse the employee the excess. Any excess income tax or Additional Medicare Tax withholding must be repaid or reimbursed to the employee before the end of the calendar year in which it was withheld. Keep in your records the employee's written receipt showing the date and amount of the repayment or record of reimbursement. If you didn't repay or reimburse the employee, you must report and pay each excess amount when you file Form 941 for the quarter (or Form 944 for the year) in which you withheld too much tax.

Correcting filed Forms W-2 and W-3. When adjustments are made to correct wages and social security and Medicare taxes because of a change in the wage totals reported for a previous year, you also need to file Form W-2c and Form W-3c with the SSA. Up to 25 Forms W-2c per Form W-3c may be filed per session over the Internet, with no limit on the number of sessions. For more information, go to the SSA's Employer W-2 Filing Instructions & Information webpage at *SSA.gov/employer*.

Exceptions to interest-free corrections of employment taxes. A correction won't be eligible for interest-free treatment if:

- The failure to report relates to an issue raised in an IRS examination of a prior return, or

- The employer knowingly underreported its employment tax liability.

A correction won't be eligible for interest-free treatment after the earlier of the following.

- Receipt of an IRS notice and demand for payment after assessment.

- Receipt of an IRS notice of determination under section 7436.

Wage Repayments

If an employee repays you for wages received in error, don't offset the repayments against current year wages unless the repayments are for amounts received in error in the current year.

Repayment of current year wages. If you receive repayments for wages paid during a prior quarter in the current year, report adjustments on Form 941-X to recover income tax withholding and social security and Medicare taxes for the repaid wages.

Repayment of prior year wages. If you receive repayments for wages paid during a prior year, report an adjustment on Form 941-X or Form 944-X to recover the social security and Medicare taxes. You can't make an adjustment for income tax withholding because the wages were income to the employee for the prior year. You can't make

an adjustment for Additional Medicare Tax withholding because the employee determines liability for Additional Medicare Tax on the employee's income tax return for the prior year.

You must also file Forms W-2c and W-3c with the SSA to correct social security and Medicare wages and taxes. Don't correct wages (box 1) on Form W-2c for the amount paid in error. Give a copy of Form W-2c to the employee.

Employee reporting of repayment. The wages paid in error in the prior year remain taxable to the employee for that year. This is because the employee received and had use of those funds during that year. The employee isn't entitled to file an amended return (Form 1040-X) to recover the income tax on these wages. Instead, the employee may be entitled to a deduction or credit for the repaid wages on their income tax return for the year of repayment. However, the employee should file an amended return (Form 1040-X) to recover any Additional Medicare Tax paid on the wages paid in error in the prior year. If an employee asks about reporting their wage repayment, you may tell the employee to see *Repayments* in Pub. 525 for more information.

14. Federal Unemployment (FUTA) Tax

The Federal Unemployment Tax Act (FUTA), with state unemployment systems, provides for payments of unemployment compensation to workers who have lost their jobs. Most employers pay both a federal and a state unemployment tax. For a list of state unemployment agencies, go to the U.S. Department of Labor's website at *oui.doleta.gov/unemploy/agencies.asp*. Only the employer pays FUTA tax; it isn't withheld from the employee's wages. For more information, see the Instructions for Form 940.

 Services rendered to a federally recognized Indian tribal government (or any subdivision, subsidiary, or business wholly owned by such an Indian tribe) are exempt from FUTA tax, subject to the tribe's compliance with state law. For more information, see section 3309(d) and Pub. 4268.

Who must pay? Use the following three tests to determine whether you must pay FUTA tax. Each test applies to a different category of employee, and each is independent of the others. If a test describes your situation, you're subject to FUTA tax on the wages you pay to employees in that category during the current calendar year.

1. **General test.**
   You're subject to FUTA tax in 2023 on the wages you pay employees who aren't farmworkers or household workers if:

   a. You paid wages of $1,500 or more in any calendar quarter in 2022 or 2023, or

b. You had one or more employees for at least some part of a day in any 20 or more different weeks in 2022 or 20 or more different weeks in 2023.

2. **Household employees test.**

You're subject to FUTA tax if you paid total cash wages of $1,000 or more to household employees in any calendar quarter in 2022 or 2023. A household employee is an employee who performs household work in a private home, local college club, or local fraternity or sorority chapter.

3. **Farmworkers test.**

You're subject to FUTA tax on the wages you pay to farmworkers if:

a. You paid cash wages of $20,000 or more to farmworkers during any calendar quarter in 2022 or 2023, or

b. You employed 10 or more farmworkers during at least some part of a day (whether or not at the same time) during any 20 or more different weeks in 2022 or 20 or more different weeks in 2023.

Figuring FUTA tax. For 2023, the FUTA tax rate is 6.0%. The tax applies to the first $7,000 you pay to each employee as wages during the year. The $7,000 is the federal wage base. Your state wage base may be different.

Generally, you can take a credit against your FUTA tax for amounts you paid into state unemployment funds. The credit may be as much as 5.4% of FUTA taxable wages. If you're entitled to the maximum 5.4% credit, the FUTA tax rate after credit is 0.6%. You're entitled to the maximum credit if you paid your state unemployment taxes in full, on time, and on all the same wages as are subject to FUTA tax, and as long as the state isn't determined to be a credit reduction state. See the Instructions for Form 940 to determine the credit.

In some states, the wages subject to state unemployment tax are the same as the wages subject to FUTA tax. However, certain states exclude some types of wages from state unemployment tax, even though they're subject to FUTA tax (for example, wages paid to corporate officers, certain payments of sick pay by unions, and certain fringe benefits). In such a case, you may be required to deposit more than 0.6% FUTA tax on those wages. See the Instructions for Form 940 for further guidance.

TIP *In years when there are credit reduction states, you must include liabilities owed for credit reduction with your fourth quarter deposit. You may deposit the anticipated extra liability throughout the year, but it isn't due until the due date for the deposit for the fourth quarter, and the associated liability should be recorded as being incurred in the fourth quarter. See the Instructions for Form 940 for more information.*

Successor employer. If you acquired a business from an employer who was liable for FUTA tax, you may be able to count the wages that employer paid to the employees who continue to work for you when you figure the

$7,000 FUTA tax wage base. See the Instructions for Form 940.

Depositing FUTA tax. For deposit purposes, figure FUTA tax quarterly. Determine your FUTA tax liability by multiplying the amount of taxable wages paid during the quarter by 0.6%. Stop depositing FUTA tax on an employee's wages when taxable wages reach $7,000 for the calendar year.

If your FUTA tax liability for any calendar quarter is $500 or less, you don't have to deposit the tax. Instead, you may carry it forward and add it to the liability figured in the next quarter to see if you must make a deposit. If your FUTA tax liability for any calendar quarter is over $500 (including any FUTA tax carried forward from an earlier quarter), you must deposit the tax by EFT. See section 11 for more information on EFTs.

Household employees. You're not required to deposit FUTA taxes for household employees unless you report their wages on Form 941, 943, or 944. See Pub. 926 for more information.

When to deposit. Deposit the FUTA tax by the last day of the first month that follows the end of the quarter. If the due date for making your deposit falls on a Saturday, Sunday, or legal holiday, you may make your deposit on the next business day. See *Legal holiday*, earlier, for a list of legal holidays occurring in 2023.

If your liability for the fourth quarter (plus any undeposited amount from any earlier quarter) is over $500, deposit the entire amount by the due date of Form 940 (January 31). If it is $500 or less, you can make a deposit, pay the tax with a credit or debit card, or pay the tax with your Form 940 by January 31. If you file Form 940 electronically, you can *e-file* and use EFW to pay the balance due. For more information on paying your taxes with a credit or debit card or using EFW, go to *IRS.gov/Payments*.

Table 4. **When To Deposit FUTA Taxes**

Quarter	Ending	Due Date
Jan.–Feb.–Mar.	Mar. 31	Apr. 30
Apr.–May–June	June 30	July 31
July–Aug.–Sept.	Sept. 30	Oct. 31
Oct.–Nov.–Dec.	Dec. 31	Jan. 31

Reporting FUTA tax. Use Form 940 to report FUTA tax. File your 2022 Form 940 by January 31, 2023. However, if you deposited all FUTA tax when due, you may file on or before February 10, 2023.

Form 940 e-file. The Form 940 *e-file* program allows a taxpayer to electronically file Form 940 using a computer with an Internet connection and commercial tax preparation software. For more information, go to *IRS.gov/EmploymentEfile*, or call 866-255-0654.

Household employees. If you didn't report employment taxes for household employees on Form 941, 943, or 944, report FUTA tax for these employees on Schedule H (Form 1040). See Pub. 926 for more information. You must have an EIN to file Schedule H (Form 1040).

Electronic filing by reporting agents. Reporting agents filing Forms 940 for groups of taxpayers can file them electronically. See *Electronic filing by reporting agents* in section 12.

Electronic filing by CPEOs. CPEOs are required to electronically file Form 940. Under certain circumstances, the IRS may waive the electronic filing requirement. To request a waiver, the CPEO must file a written request using the IRS Online Registration System for Professional Employer Organizations at least 45 days before the due date of the return for which the CPEO is unable to electronically file. For more information on filing a waiver request electronically, go to *IRS.gov/CPEO*.

15. Special Rules for Various Types of Services and Payments

Section references are to the Internal Revenue Code unless otherwise noted.

Special Classes of Employment and Special Types of Payments	Treatment Under Employment Taxes		
	Income Tax Withholding	Social Security and Medicare (including Additional Medicare Tax when wages are paid in excess of $200,000)	FUTA
Aliens, nonresident.	See Pub. 515 and Pub. 519.		
Aliens, resident:			
1. Service performed in the U.S.	Same as U.S. citizen.	Same as U.S. citizen. (Exempt if any part of service as crew member of foreign vessel or aircraft is performed outside U.S.)	Same as U.S. citizen.
2. Service performed outside the U.S.	Withhold	Taxable if (1) working for an American employer, or (2) an American employer by agreement covers U.S. citizens and residents employed by its foreign affiliates.	Exempt unless on or in connection with an American vessel or aircraft and either performed under contract made in U.S., or alien is employed on such vessel or aircraft when it touches U.S. port.
Cafeteria plan benefits under section 125.	If employee chooses cash or other taxable benefit, subject to all employment taxes. If employee chooses a non-taxable benefit, the treatment is the same as if the benefit was provided outside the plan. See Pub. 15-B for more information.		
Deceased worker:			
1. Wages paid to beneficiary or estate in same calendar year as worker's death. See the General Instructions for Forms W-2 and W-3 for details.	Exempt	Taxable	Taxable
2. Wages paid to beneficiary or estate after calendar year of worker's death.	Exempt	Exempt	Exempt
Dependent care assistance programs.	Exempt to the extent it is reasonable to believe amounts are excludable from gross income under section 129.		
Disabled worker's wages paid after year in which worker became entitled to disability insurance benefits under the Social Security Act.	Withhold	Exempt if worker didn't perform any service for employer during the period for which payment is made.	Taxable
Employee business expense reimbursement:			
1. Accountable plan.			
a. Amounts not exceeding specified government rate for per diem or standard mileage.	Exempt	Exempt	Exempt
b. Amounts in excess of specified government rate for per diem or standard mileage.	Withhold	Taxable	Taxable
2. Nonaccountable plan. See section 5 for details.	Withhold	Taxable	Taxable
Family employees:			
1. Child employed by parent (or partnership in which each partner is a parent of the child).	Withhold	Exempt until age 18; age 21 for domestic service.	Exempt until age 21
2. Parent employed by child.	Withhold	Taxable if in course of the child's business. For domestic services, see section 3.	Exempt
3. Spouse employed by spouse. See section 3 for more information.	Withhold	Taxable if in course of spouse's business.	Exempt
Fishing and related activities.	See Pub. 334.		
Foreign governments and international organizations.	Exempt	Exempt	Exempt

Special Classes of Employment and Special Types of Payments	Treatment Under Employment Taxes		
	Income Tax Withholding	Social Security and Medicare (including Additional Medicare Tax when wages are paid in excess of $200,000)	FUTA
Foreign service by U.S. citizens:			
1. As U.S. Government employees.	Withhold	Same as within U.S.	Exempt
2. For foreign affiliates of American employers and other private employers.	Exempt if at time of payment (1) it is reasonable to believe employee is entitled to exclusion from income under section 911, or (2) the employer is required by law of the foreign country to withhold income tax on such payment.	Exempt unless (1) an American employer by agreement covers U.S. citizens employed by its foreign affiliates, or (2) U.S. citizen works for American employer.	Exempt unless (1) on American vessel or aircraft and work is performed under contract made in U.S. or worker is employed on vessel when it touches U.S. port, or (2) U.S. citizen works for American employer (except in a contiguous country with which the U.S. has an agreement for unemployment compensation) or in the U.S. Virgin Islands.
Fringe benefits.	Taxable on excess of fair market value of the benefit over the sum of an amount paid for it by the employee and any amount excludable by law. However, special valuation rules may apply. Benefits provided under cafeteria plans may qualify for exclusion from wages for social security, Medicare, and FUTA taxes. See Pub. 15-B for details.		
Government employment: State/local governments and political subdivisions, employees of:			
1. Salaries and wages (includes payments to most elected and appointed officials). See chapter 3 of Pub. 963.	Withhold	Generally, taxable for (1) services performed by employees who are either (a) covered under a section 218 agreement, or (b) not covered under a section 218 agreement and not a member of a public retirement system (mandatory social security and Medicare coverage); and (2) (for Medicare tax only) for services performed by employees hired or rehired after March 31, 1986, who aren't covered under a section 218 agreement or the mandatory social security provisions, unless specifically excluded by law. See Pub. 963.	Exempt
2. Election workers. Election individuals are workers who are employed to perform services for state or local governments at election booths in connection with national, state, or local elections. **Note.** File Form W-2 for payments of $600 or more even if no social security or Medicare taxes were withheld.	Exempt	Taxable if paid $2,200 or more in 2023 (lesser amount if specified by a section 218 social security agreement). See Revenue Ruling 2000-6.	Exempt
3. Emergency workers. Emergency workers who were hired on a temporary basis in response to a specific unforeseen emergency and aren't intended to become permanent employees.	Withhold	Exempt if serving on a temporary basis in case of fire, storm, snow, earthquake, flood, or similar emergency.	Exempt
U.S. federal government employees.	Withhold	Taxable for Medicare. Taxable for social security unless hired before 1984. See section 3121(b)(5).	Exempt

Special Classes of Employment and Special Types of Payments	Treatment Under Employment Taxes		
	Income Tax Withholding	Social Security and Medicare (including Additional Medicare Tax when wages are paid in excess of $200,000)	FUTA
Homeworkers (industrial, cottage industry):			
1. Common law employees.	Withhold	Taxable	Taxable
2. Statutory employees. See section 2 for details.	Exempt	Taxable if paid $100 or more in cash in a year.	Exempt
Hospital employees:			
1. Interns.	Withhold	Taxable	Exempt
2. Patients.	Withhold	Taxable (Exempt for state or local government hospitals.)	Exempt
Household employees:			
1. Domestic service in private homes.	Exempt (withhold if both employer and employee agree).	Taxable if paid $2,600 or more in cash in 2023. Exempt if performed by an individual under age 18 during any portion of the calendar year and isn't the principal occupation of the employee.	Taxable if employer paid total cash wages of $1,000 or more in any quarter in the current or preceding calendar year.
2. Domestic service in college clubs, fraternities, and sororities.	Exempt (withhold if both employer and employee agree).	Exempt if paid to regular student; also exempt if employee is paid less than $100 in a year by an income-tax-exempt employer.	Taxable if employer paid total cash wages of $1,000 or more in any quarter in the current or preceding calendar year.
Insurance for employees:			
1. Accident and health insurance premiums under a plan or system for employees and their dependents generally or for a class or classes of employees and their dependents.	Exempt (except 2% shareholder-employees of S corporations).	Exempt	Exempt
2. Group-term life insurance costs. See Pub. 15-B for details.	Exempt	Exempt, except for the cost of group-term life insurance includible in the employee's gross income. Special rules apply for former employees.	Exempt
Insurance agents or solicitors:			
1. Full-time life insurance salesperson.	Withhold only if employee under common law. See section 2.	Taxable	Taxable if (1) employee under common law, and (2) not paid solely by commissions.
2. Other salesperson of life, casualty, etc., insurance.	Withhold only if employee under common law.	Taxable only if employee under common law.	Taxable if (1) employee under common law, and (2) not paid solely by commissions.
Interest on loans with below-market interest rates (foregone interest and deemed original issue discount).	See Pub. 15-A.		
Leave-sharing plans: Amounts paid to an employee under a leave-sharing plan.	Withhold	Taxable	Taxable
Newspaper carriers and vendors: Newspaper carriers under age 18; newspaper and magazine vendors buying at fixed prices and retaining receipts from sales to customers. See Pub. 15-A for information on statutory nonemployee status.	Exempt (withhold if both employer and employee voluntarily agree).	Exempt	Exempt

Special Classes of Employment and Special Types of Payments	Treatment Under Employment Taxes		
	Income Tax Withholding	Social Security and Medicare (including Additional Medicare Tax when wages are paid in excess of $200,000)	FUTA
Noncash payments:			
1. For household work, agricultural labor, and service not in the course of the employer's trade or business.	Exempt (withhold if both employer and employee voluntarily agree).	Exempt	Exempt
2. To certain retail commission salespersons ordinarily paid solely on a cash commission basis.	Optional with employer, except to the extent employee's supplemental wages during the year exceed $1 million.	Taxable	Taxable
Nonprofit organizations.	See Pub. 15-A.		
Officers or shareholders of an S corporation: Distributions and other payments by an S corporation to a corporate officer or shareholder must be treated as wages to the extent the amounts are reasonable compensation for services to the corporation by an employee. See the Instructions for Form 1120-S.	Withhold	Taxable	Taxable
Partners: Payments to general or limited partners of a partnership. See Pub. 541 for partner reporting rules.	Exempt	Exempt	Exempt
Railroads: Payments subject to the Railroad Retirement Act. See Pub. 915 and the Instructions for Form CT-1 for more details.	Withhold	Exempt	Exempt
Religious exemptions.	See Pub. 15-A and Pub. 517.		
Retirement and pension plans:			
1. Employer contributions to a qualified plan.	Exempt	Exempt	Exempt
2. Elective employee contributions and deferrals to a plan containing a qualified cash or deferred compensation arrangement (401(k)).	Generally exempt, but see section 402(g) for limitation.	Taxable	Taxable
3. Employer contributions to individual retirement accounts under simplified employee pension (SEP) plan.	Generally exempt, but see section 402(g) for salary reduction SEP limitation.	Exempt, except for amounts contributed under a salary reduction SEP agreement.	
4. Employer contributions to section 403(b) annuities including salary reduction contributions.	Generally exempt, but see section 402(g) for limitation.	Taxable if paid through a salary reduction agreement (written or otherwise).	
5. Employee salary reduction contributions to a SIMPLE retirement account.	Exempt	Taxable	Taxable
6. Distributions from qualified retirement and pension plans and section 403(b) annuities. See Pub. 15-A for information on pensions, annuities, and employer contributions to nonqualified deferred compensation arrangements.	Withhold, but recipient may elect exemption on Form W-4P in certain cases; mandatory 20% withholding applies to an eligible rollover distribution that isn't a direct rollover; exempt for direct rollover. See Pub. 15-A.	Exempt	Exempt
7. Employer contributions to a section 457(b) plan.	Generally exempt, but see section 402(g) limitation.	Taxable	Taxable
8. Employee salary reduction contributions to a section 457(b) plan.	Generally exempt, but see section 402(g) salary reduction limitation.	Taxable	Taxable
Salespersons:			
1. Common law employees.	Withhold	Taxable	Taxable
2. Statutory employees.	Exempt	Taxable	Taxable, except for full-time life insurance sales agents.
3. Statutory nonemployees (qualified real estate agents, direct sellers, and certain companion sitters). See Pub. 15-A for details.	Exempt	Exempt	Exempt

Special Classes of Employment and Special Types of Payments	Treatment Under Employment Taxes		
	Income Tax Withholding	Social Security and Medicare (including Additional Medicare Tax when wages are paid in excess of $200,000)	FUTA
Scholarships and fellowship grants (includible in income under section 117(c)).	Withhold	Taxability depends on the nature of the employment and the status of the organization. See *Students, scholars, trainees, teachers, etc.*, below.	
Severance or dismissal pay.	Withhold	Taxable	Taxable
Service not in the course of the employer's trade or business (other than on a farm operated for profit or for household employment in private homes).	Withhold only if employee earns $50 or more in cash in a quarter and works on 24 or more different days in that quarter or in the preceding quarter.	Taxable if employee receives $100 or more in cash in a calendar year.	Taxable only if employee earns $50 or more in cash in a quarter and works on 24 or more different days in that quarter or in the preceding quarter.
Sick pay. See Pub. 15-A for more information.	Withhold	Exempt after end of 6 calendar months after the calendar month employee last worked for employer.	
Students, scholars, trainees, teachers, etc.:			
1. Student enrolled and regularly attending classes, performing services for the following.			
a. Private school, college, or university.	Withhold	Exempt	Exempt
b. Auxiliary nonprofit organization operated for and controlled by school, college, or university.	Withhold	Exempt unless services are covered by a section 218 (Social Security Act) agreement.	Exempt
c. Public school, college, or university.	Withhold	Exempt unless services are covered by a section 218 (Social Security Act) agreement.	Exempt
2. Full-time student performing service for academic credit, combining instruction with work experience as an integral part of the program.	Withhold	Taxable	Exempt unless program was established for or on behalf of an employer or group of employers.
3. Student nurse performing part-time services for nominal earnings at hospital as incidental part of training.	Withhold	Exempt	Exempt
4. Student employed by organized camps.	Withhold	Taxable	Exempt
5. Student, scholar, trainee, teacher, etc., as nonimmigrant alien under section 101(a)(15)(F), (J), (M), or (Q) of Immigration and Nationality Act (that is, aliens holding F-1, J-1, M-1, or Q-1 visas).	Withhold unless excepted by regulations.	Exempt if service is performed for purpose specified in section 101(a)(15)(F), (J), (M), or (Q) of Immigration and Nationality Act. However, these taxes may apply if the employee becomes a resident alien. See the special residency tests for exempt individuals in chapter 1 of Pub. 519.	
Supplemental unemployment compensation plan benefits.	Withhold	Exempt under certain conditions. See Pub. 15-A.	
Tips:			
1. If $20 or more in a month.	Withhold	Taxable	Taxable for all tips reported in writing to employer.
2. If less than $20 in a month. See section 6 for more information.	Exempt	Exempt	Exempt
Workers' compensation.	Exempt	Exempt	Exempt

16. Third-Party Payer Arrangements

An employer may outsource some or all of its federal employment tax withholding, reporting, and payment obligations. An employer who outsources payroll and related tax duties (that is, withholding, reporting, and paying over social security, Medicare, FUTA, and income taxes) to a third-party payer will generally remain responsible for those duties, including liability for the taxes. However, see *Certified professional employer organization (CPEO)*, later, for an exception.

If an employer outsources some or all of its payroll responsibilities, the employer should consider the following information.

- The employer remains responsible for federal tax deposits and other federal tax payments even though the employer may forward the tax amounts to the third-party payer to make the deposits and payments. If the third party fails to make the deposits and payments, the IRS may assess penalties and interest on the employer's account. As the employer, you may be liable for all taxes, penalties, and interest due. The employer may also be held personally liable for certain unpaid federal taxes.

- If the employer's account has any issues, the IRS will send correspondence to the employer at the address of record. We strongly recommend that the employer maintain its address as the address of record with the IRS. Having correspondence sent to the address of the third-party payer may significantly limit the employer's ability to be informed about tax matters involving the employer's business. Use Form 8822-B to update your business address.

- When a third party enrolls an employer in EFTPS for federal tax deposits, the employer will receive an Inquiry PIN. The employer should activate and use this Inquiry PIN to monitor its account and ensure the third party is making the required tax deposits.

The following are common third-party payers who an employer may contract with to perform payroll and related tax duties.

- Payroll service provider (PSP).
- Reporting agent.
- Agent with approved Form 2678.
- Payer designated under section 3504.
- Certified professional employer organization (CPEO).

Payroll service provider (PSP). A PSP helps administer payroll and payroll-related tax duties on behalf of the employer. A PSP may prepare paychecks for employees, prepare and file employment tax returns, prepare Form W-2, and make federal tax deposits and other federal tax payments. A PSP performs these functions using the EIN of the employer. A PSP isn't liable as either an employer or an agent of the employer for the employer's employment taxes. If an employer is using a PSP to perform its tax duties, the employer remains liable for its employment tax obligations, including liability for employment taxes.

An employer who uses a PSP should ensure the PSP is using EFTPS to make federal tax deposits on behalf of the employer so the employer can confirm that the payments are being made on its behalf.

Reporting agent. A reporting agent is a type of PSP. A reporting agent helps administer payroll and payroll-related tax duties on behalf of the employer, including authorization to electronically sign and file forms set forth on Form 8655. An employer uses Form 8655 to authorize a reporting agent to perform functions on behalf of the employer. A reporting agent performs these functions using the EIN of the employer. A reporting agent isn't liable as either an employer or an agent of the employer for the employer's employment taxes. If an employer is using a reporting agent to perform its tax duties, the employer remains liable for its employment obligations, including liability for employment taxes.

A reporting agent must use EFTPS to make federal tax deposits on behalf of an employer. The employer has access to EFTPS to confirm federal tax deposits were made on its behalf.

For more information on reporting agents, see Revenue Procedure 2012-32, 2012-34 I.R.B. 267, available at *IRS.gov/irb/2012-34_IRB#RP-2012-32*; and Pub. 1474, Technical Specifications Guide for Reporting Agent Authorization and Federal Tax Depositors.

Agent with an approved Form 2678. An agent with an approved Form 2678 helps administer payroll and related tax duties on behalf of the employer. An agent authorized under section 3504 may pay wages or compensation to some or all of the employees of an employer, prepare and file employment tax returns as set forth on Form 2678, prepare Form W-2, and make federal tax deposits and other federal tax payments. An employer uses Form 2678 to request authorization to appoint an agent to perform functions on behalf of the employer. An agent with an approved Form 2678 is authorized to perform these functions using its own EIN. The agent files a Schedule R (Form 941) or, if applicable, Schedule R (Form 943) to allocate wages, taxes, and credits claimed to the employers it represents as an agent.

If an employer is using an agent with an approved Form 2678 to perform its tax duties, the agent and the employer are jointly liable for the employment taxes and related tax duties for which the agent is authorized to perform.

Form 2678 doesn't apply to FUTA taxes reportable on Form 940 unless the employer is a home care service recipient receiving home care services through a program administered by a federal, state, or local government agency.

For more information on an agent with an approved Form 2678, see Revenue Procedure 2013-39, 2013-52 I.R.B. 830, available at *IRS.gov/irb/2013-52_IRB#RP-2013-39*.

Payer designated under section 3504. In certain circumstances, the IRS may designate a third-party payer to perform the acts of an employer. The IRS will designate a third-party payer on behalf of an employer if the third party has a service agreement with the employer. A service agreement is an agreement between the third-party payer and an employer in which the third-party payer (1) asserts it is the employer of individuals performing services for the employer; (2) pays wages to the individuals that perform services for the employer; and (3) assumes responsibility to withhold, report, and pay federal employment taxes for the wages it pays to the individuals who perform services for the employer.

A payer designated under section 3504 performs tax duties under the service agreement using its own EIN. If the IRS designates a third-party payer under section 3504, the designated payer and the employer are jointly liable for the employment taxes and related tax duties for which the third-party payer is designated.

For more information on a payer designated under section 3504, see Regulations section 31.3504-2.

Certified professional employer organization (CPEO). The Stephen Beck, Jr., Achieving a Better Life Experience Act of 2014 required the IRS to establish a voluntary certification program for professional employer organizations (PEOs). PEOs handle various payroll administration and tax reporting responsibilities for their business clients and are typically paid a fee based on payroll costs. To become and remain certified under the certification program, CPEOs must meet various requirements described in sections 3511 and 7705 and related published guidance. Certification as a CPEO may affect the employment tax liabilities of both the CPEO and its customers. A CPEO is generally treated for employment tax purposes as the employer of any individual who performs services for a customer of the CPEO and is covered by a contract described in section 7705(e)(2) between the CPEO and the customer (CPEO contract), but only for wages and other compensation paid to the individual by the CPEO. However, with respect to certain employees covered by a CPEO contract, you may also be treated as an employer of the employees and, consequently, may also be liable for federal employment taxes imposed on wages and other compensation paid by the CPEO to such employees.

CPEOs must complete Schedule R (Form 940), Schedule R (Form 941), or Schedule R (Form 943) when filing an aggregate Form 940, 941, or 943, respectively. CPEOs file Form 8973 to notify the IRS that they started or ended a service contract with a customer. To become a CPEO, the organization must apply through the IRS Online Registration System. For more information or to apply to become a CPEO, go to *IRS.gov/CPEO*. Also see Revenue Procedure 2017-14, 2017-3 I.R.B. 426, available at *IRS.gov/irb/2017-03_IRB#RP-2017-14*.

TIP *If both an employer and a section 3504 authorized agent (or CPEO or other third-party payer) paid wages to an employee during a quarter, both the employer and the section 3504 authorized agent (or CPEO or other third-party payer, if applicable) should file*

Form 941 reporting the wages each entity paid to the employee during the applicable quarter and issue Forms W-2 reporting the wages each entity paid to the employee during the year.

How To Get Tax Help

If you have questions about a tax issue; need help preparing your tax return; or want to download free publications, forms, or instructions, go to *IRS.gov* to find resources that can help you right away.

Preparing and filing your tax return. Go to *IRS.gov/EmploymentEfile* for more information on filing your employment tax returns electronically.

 Getting answers to your tax questions. On IRS.gov, you can get up-to-date information on current events and changes in tax law.

- *IRS.gov/Help*: A variety of tools to help you get answers to some of the most common tax questions.

- *IRS.gov/Forms*: Find forms, instructions, and publications. You will find details on the most recent tax changes and interactive links to help you find answers to your questions.

- You may also be able to access tax law information in your electronic filing software.

Need someone to prepare your tax return? There are various types of tax return preparers, including enrolled agents, certified public accountants (CPAs), attorneys, and many others who don't have professional credentials. If you choose to have someone prepare your tax return, choose that preparer wisely. A paid tax preparer is:

- Primarily responsible for the overall substantive accuracy of your return,

- Required to sign the return, and

- Required to include their preparer tax identification number (PTIN).

Although the tax preparer always signs the return, you're ultimately responsible for providing all the information required for the preparer to accurately prepare your return. Anyone paid to prepare tax returns for others should have a thorough understanding of tax matters. For more information on how to choose a tax preparer, go to *Tips for Choosing a Tax Preparer* on IRS.gov.

Coronavirus. Go to *IRS.gov/Coronavirus* for links to information on the impact of the coronavirus, as well as tax relief available for individuals and families, small and large businesses, and tax-exempt organizations.

Employers can register to use Business Services Online. The Social Security Administration (SSA) offers online service at *SSA.gov/employer* for fast, free, and secure online W-2 filing options to CPAs, accountants, enrolled agents, and individuals who process Form W-2 and Form W-2c.

IRS social media. Go to *IRS.gov/SocialMedia* to see the various social media tools the IRS uses to share the latest information on tax changes, scam alerts, initiatives, products, and services. At the IRS, privacy and security are our highest priority. We use these tools to share public information with you. **Don't** post your social security number (SSN) or other confidential information on social media sites. Always protect your identity when using any social networking site.

The following IRS YouTube channels provide short, informative videos on various tax-related topics in English, Spanish, and ASL.

* *Youtube.com/irsvideos*.
* *Youtube.com/irsvideosmultilingua*.
* *Youtube.com/irsvideosASL*.

Watching IRS videos. The IRS Video portal (*IRSVideos.gov*) contains video and audio presentations for individuals, small businesses, and tax professionals.

Online tax information in other languages. You can find information on *IRS.gov/MyLanguage* if English isn't your native language.

Free Over-the-Phone Interpreter (OPI) Service. The IRS is committed to serving our multilingual customers by offering OPI services. The OPI Service is a federally funded program and is available at Taxpayer Assistance Centers (TACs), other IRS offices, and every VITA/TCE return site. The OPI Service is accessible in more than 350 languages.

Accessibility Helpline available for taxpayers with disabilities. Taxpayers who need information about accessibility services can call 833-690-0598. The Accessibility Helpline can answer questions related to current and future accessibility products and services available in alternative media formats (for example, braille, large print, audio, etc.). The Accessibility Helpline doesn't have access to your IRS account. For help with tax law, refunds, or account-related issues, go to *IRS.gov/LetUsHelp*.

Disasters. Go to *Disaster Assistance and Emergency Relief for Individuals and Businesses* to review the available disaster tax relief.

Getting tax forms and publications. Go to *IRS.gov/Forms* to view, download, or print most of the forms, instructions, and publications you may need. Or, you can go to *IRS.gov/OrderForms* to place an order.

Getting tax publications and instructions in eBook format. You can also download and view popular tax publications and instructions (including Pub. 15) on mobile devices as eBooks at *IRS.gov/eBooks*.

Note. IRS eBooks have been tested using Apple's iBooks for iPad. Our eBooks haven't been tested on other dedicated eBook readers, and eBook functionality may not operate as intended.

Getting a transcript of your return. You can get a copy of your tax transcript or a copy of your return by calling 800-829-4933 or by mailing Form 4506-T (transcript request) or Form 4506 (copy of return) to the IRS.

Reporting and resolving your tax-related identity theft issues.

* Tax-related identity theft happens when someone steals your personal information to commit tax fraud. Your taxes can be affected if your EIN is used to file a fraudulent return or to claim a refund or credit.

* The IRS doesn't initiate contact with taxpayers by email, text messages (including shortened links), telephone calls, or social media channels to request or verify personal or financial information. This includes requests for personal identification numbers (PINs), passwords, or similar information for credit cards, banks, or other financial accounts.

* Go to *IRS.gov/IdentityTheft*, the IRS Identity Theft Central webpage, for information on identity theft and data security protection for taxpayers, tax professionals, and businesses. If your EIN has been lost or stolen or you suspect you're a victim of tax-related identity theft, you can learn what steps you should take.

Making a tax payment. Go to *IRS.gov/Payments* for information on how to make a payment using any of the following options.

* *Debit or Credit Card*: Choose an approved payment processor to pay online or by phone.

* *Electronic Funds Withdrawal*: Schedule a payment when filing your federal taxes using tax return preparation software or through a tax professional.

* *Electronic Federal Tax Payment System*: Best option for businesses. Enrollment is required.

* *Check or Money Order*: Mail your payment to the address listed on the notice or instructions.

* *Cash*: You may be able to pay your taxes with cash at a participating retail store.

* *Same-Day Wire*: You may be able to do same-day wire from your financial institution. Contact your financial institution for availability, cost, and time frames.

Note. The IRS uses the latest encryption technology to ensure that the electronic payments you make online, by phone, or from a mobile device using the IRS2Go app are safe and secure. Paying electronically is quick, easy, and faster than mailing in a check or money order.

What if I can't pay now? Go to *IRS.gov/Payments* for more information about your options.

* Apply for an *online payment agreement* (*IRS.gov/OPA*) to meet your tax obligation in monthly installments if you can't pay your taxes in full today. Once you complete the online process, you will receive

immediate notification of whether your agreement has been approved.

- Use the *Offer in Compromise Pre-Qualifier* to see if you can settle your tax debt for less than the full amount you owe. For more information on the Offer in Compromise program, go to *IRS.gov/OIC*.

Understanding an IRS notice or letter you've received. Go to *IRS.gov/Notices* to find additional information about responding to an IRS notice or letter.

Contacting your local IRS office. Keep in mind, many questions can be answered on IRS.gov without visiting an IRS TAC. Go to *IRS.gov/LetUsHelp* for the topics people ask about most. If you still need help, IRS TACs provide tax help when a tax issue can't be handled online or by phone. All TACs now provide service by appointment, so you'll know in advance that you can get the service you need without long wait times. Before you visit, go to *IRS.gov/TACLocator* to find the nearest TAC and to check hours, available services, and appointment options. Or, on the IRS2Go app, under the Stay Connected tab, choose the Contact Us option and click on "Local Offices."

The Taxpayer Advocate Service (TAS) Is Here To Help You

What Is TAS?

TAS is an *independent* organization within the IRS that helps taxpayers and protects taxpayer rights. Their job is to ensure that every taxpayer is treated fairly and that you know and understand your rights under the *Taxpayer Bill of Rights*.

How Can You Learn About Your Taxpayer Rights?

The Taxpayer Bill of Rights describes 10 basic rights that all taxpayers have when dealing with the IRS. Go to *TaxpayerAdvocate.IRS.gov* to help you understand what these rights mean to you and how they apply. These are *your* rights. Know them. Use them.

What Can TAS Do for You?

TAS can help you resolve problems that you can't resolve with the IRS. And their service is free. If you qualify for their assistance, you will be assigned to one advocate who will work with you throughout the process and will do everything possible to resolve your issue. TAS can help you if:

- Your problem is causing financial difficulty for you, your family, or your business;
- You face (or your business is facing) an immediate threat of adverse action; or
- You've tried repeatedly to contact the IRS but no one has responded, or the IRS hasn't responded by the date promised.

How Can You Reach TAS?

TAS has offices *in every state, the District of Columbia, and Puerto Rico*. Your local advocate's number is in your local directory and at *TaxpayerAdvocate.IRS.gov/Contact-Us*. You can also call them at 877-777-4778.

How Else Does TAS Help Taxpayers?

TAS works to resolve large-scale problems that affect many taxpayers. If you know of one of these broad issues, report it to them at *IRS.gov/SAMS*.

TAS for Tax Professionals

TAS can provide a variety of information for tax professionals, including tax law updates and guidance, TAS programs, and ways to let TAS know about systemic problems you've seen in your practice.

Index

 To help us develop a more useful index, please let us know if you have ideas for index entries. See "Comments and Suggestions" in the "Introduction" for the ways you can reach us.

A

Accuracy of deposits rule 29
Additional Medicare Tax 25, 36
Adjustments 34
Aliens, nonresident 22, 25
Allocated tips 19
Archer MSAs 16
Assistance (*See* Tax help)

B

Backup withholding 7
Business expenses, employee 15

C

Calendar 8
Certified professional employer organizations (CPEOs) 3, 46
Change of business address or responsible party 7
Correcting employment taxes 36
Correcting errors (prior period adjustments) 36
Criminal prosecution

D

Delivery services, private 8
Depositing taxes:
    Penalties 30
    Rules 26
Differential wage payments 17
Disaster tax relief 2

E

E-file 33
E-news for payroll professionals 8
Election worker 10
Electronic deposit requirement 30
Electronic Federal Tax Payment System (EFTPS) 30
Electronic filing 4, 33
Eligibility for employment 5
Employees defined 11
Employer identification number (EIN) 11
Employer responsibilities 6

F

Family employees 13
Final return 33
Foreign persons treated as American employers 25
Form 944 32
Fringe benefits 17
FUTA tax 37

G

Government employers 10

H

Health insurance plans 16
Health savings accounts (HSAs) 16
Hiring new employees 5
Household employees 32

I

Identity protection services 18
Income tax withholding 21
Information returns 5
International social security agreements 25

L

Long-term-care insurance 16
Lookback period 26

M

Meals and lodging 16
Medicaid waiver payments 3
Medical care 17
Medical savings accounts (MSAs) 16
Medicare tax 24
Mileage 16
Monthly deposit schedule 27
Motion picture project employers 25
Moving expense reimbursement 2

N

New employees 5
Noncash wages 16
Nonemployee compensation 7

O

Outsourcing payroll duties 3

P

Part-time workers 25
Payroll period 20
Payroll service provider (PSP) 45
Penalties 30, 33
Private delivery services (PDSs) 8
Publications (*See* Tax help)

Q

Qualified small business payroll tax credit for increasing research activities 2

R

Reconciling Forms W-2 and Forms 941 or Form 944 34
Recordkeeping 7
Reimbursements 15
Repayments, wages 37

S

Reporting agent 45

Seasonal employers 32
Semiweekly deposit schedule 27
Severance payments 4
Sick pay 18
Social security and Medicare taxes 24
Social security number, employee 14
Spouse 12
Standard mileage rate 16
Statutory employees 11
Statutory nonemployees 12
Successor employer 25, 38
Supplemental wages 19

T

Tax help 46
Telephone help 8
Third-party payer arrangements 45
Third-party sick pay tax adjustment 35
Tip rate determination agreement 19
Tip rate determination and education program 19
Tips 18, 20
Trust fund recovery penalty 31

U

Unemployment tax, federal 37

V

Vacation pay 20

W

Wage repayments 37
Wages defined 15
Wages not paid in money 16
Withholding:
    Backup 7
    Certificate 21
    Exemption 22
    Fringe benefits 17
    Income tax 21
    Levies 24
    Nonresident aliens 25
    Pensions and annuities 6
    Social security and Medicare taxes 24
    Tips 20

Z

Zero wage return 4